Creative Thought

CREATIVE THOUGHT

AN INVESTIGATION OF CONCEPTUAL STRUCTURES AND PROCESSES

EDITED BY
THOMAS B. WARD
STEVEN M. SMITH
JYOTSNA VAID

AMERICAN PSYCHOLOGICAL ASSOCIATION • WASHINGTON, DC

Published by
American Psychological Association
750 First Street, NE
Washington, DC 20002

Copies may be ordered from
APA Order Department
P.O. Box 92984
Washington, DC 20090-2984

In the UK and Europe, copies may be ordered from
American Psychological Association
3 Henrietta Street
Covent Garden, London
WC2E 8LU England

Typeset in Minion by University Graphics, Inc., York, PA
Printer: Edwards Brothers, Inc., Ann Arbor, MI
Cover Designer: Berg Design, Albany NY
Technical/Production Editor: Tanya Y. Alexander

Library of Congress Cataloging-in-Publication Data

Creative thought : an investigation of conceptual structures and processes / Thomas B. Ward. Steven M. Smith. Jyotsna Vaid, editors.
p. cm.
Based on APA Science Conference, Texas A&M University, May 1995.
Includes bibliographical references and index.
ISBN 1-55798-404–2 (casebinding)
1. Creative thinking—Congresses. 2. Creative ability—Congresses. I. Ward, Thomas B. II. Smith, Steven M. III. Vaid, Jyotsna. IV. APA Science Conference (1995) : Texas A&M University)
BF408.C7475 1997
153.3′5—dc21 97-892
CIP

British Library Cataloguing-in-Publication Data
A CIP record is available from the British Library

Printed in the United States of America
First edition

APA Science Volumes

Best Methods for the Analysis of Change: Recent Advances, Unanswered Questions, Future Directions

Cardiovascular Reactivity to Psychological Stress and Disease

The Challenge in Mathematics and Science Education: Psychology's Response

Changing Employment Relations: Behavioral and Social Perspectives

Cognition: Conceptual and Methodological Issues

Cognitive Bases of Musical Communication

Conceptualization and Measurement of Organism–Environment Interaction

Converging Operations in the Study of Visual Selective Attention

Creative Thought: An Investigation of Conceptual Structures and Processes

Developmental Psychoacoustics

Diversity in Work Teams: Research Paradigms for a Changing Workplace

Emotion and Culture: Empirical Studies of Mutual Influence

Emotion, Disclosure, and Health

Evolving Explanations of Development: Ecological Approaches to Organism–Environment Systems

Examining Lives in Context: Perspectives on the Ecology of Human Development

Hostility, Coping, and Health

Organ Donation and Transplantation: Psychological and Behavioral Factors

The Perception of Structure

Perspectives on Socially Shared Cognition

Psychological Testing of Hispanics

Psychology of Women's Health: Progress and Challenges in Research and Application
Researching Community Psychology: Issues of Theory and Methods
Sleep and Cognition
Sleep Onset: Normal and Abnormal Processes
Stereotype Accuracy: Toward Appreciating Group Differences
Stereotyped Movements: Brain and Behavior Relationships
Studying Lives Through Time: Personality and Development
The Suggestibility of Children's Recollections: Implications for Eyewitness Testimony
Taste, Experience, and Feeding: Development and Learning
Temperament: Individual Differences at the Interface of Biology and Behavior
Through the Looking Glass: Issues of Psychological Well-Being in Captive Nonhuman Primates

APA expects to publish volumes on the following conference topics:

Attribution Processes, Person Perception, and Social Interaction: The Legacy of Ned Jones
Children Exposed to Family Violence
Computational Modeling of Behavior Processes in Organizations
Experimental Psychopathology and Pathogenesis of Schizophrenia
Genetic, Ethological, and Evolutionary Perspectives on Human Development
Global Prospects for Education: Development, Culture, and Schooling
Intelligence on the Rise: Secular Changes in IQ and Related Measures
Maintaining and Promoting Integrity in Behavioral Science Research
Marital and Family Therapy Outcome and Process Research
Measuring Changes in Patients Following Psychological and Pharmacological Interventions
Models of Gender and Gender Differences: Then and Now
Psychology Beyond the Threshold: Conference on General and Applied Experimental Psychology and a Festschrift for William N. Dember

Psychophysiological Study of Attention
Structure and Context in Language Processing

As part of its continuing and expanding commitment to enhance the dissemination of scientific psychological knowledge, the Science Directorate of the APA established a Scientific Conferences Program. A series of volumes resulting from these conferences is produced jointly by the Science Directorate and the Office of Communications. A call for proposals is issued twice annually by the Scientific Directorate, which, collaboratively with the APA Board of Scientific Affairs, evaluates the proposals and selects several conferences for funding. This important effort has resulted in an exceptional series of meetings and scholarly volumes, each of which has contributed to the dissemination of research and dialogue in these topical areas.

The APA Science Directorate's conferences funding program has supported 45 conferences since its inception in 1988. To date, 31 volumes resulting from conferences have been published.

William C. Howell, PhD
Executive Director

Virginia E. Holt
Assistant Executive Director

Contents

Contributors

Lawrence W. Barsalou, University of Chicago
Sarah Brem, Northwestern University
Cristina Cacciari, Universita di Bologna, Italy
Michelene T. H. Chi, University of Pittsburgh
Piercarla Cicogna, Universita di Bologna, Italy
Kevin Dunbar, McGill University, Canada
Ron Ferguson, Northwestern University
Ken Forbus, Northwestern University
Christina L. Gagné, University of Illinois at Urbana-Champaign
Dedre Gentner, Northwestern University
Raymond W. Gibbs, Jr., University of California, Santa Cruz
Arthur M. Glenberg, University of Wisconsin, Madison
Sam Glucksberg, Princeton University
James A. Hampton, The City University, London
Eva Feder Kittay, State University of New York at Stony Brook
Maria Chiara Levorato, Universita di Padova, Italy
Valerie S. Makin, Columbia University
Deanna Ann Manfredi, National Analysts, Philadelphia, PA
Arthur B. Markman, Columbia University
Matthew S. McGlone, Lafayette College
Gregory L. Murphy, University of Illinois at Urbana-Champaign
David N. Perkins, Harvard Graduate School of Education
Jesse J. Prinz, University of Chicago
Annette Rümmele, University of Tubingen, Germany
Gudrun Schwarzer, University of Tubingen, Germany
Edward J. Shoben, University of Illinois at Urbana-Champaign

Dean Keith Simonton, University of California, Davis
Steven M. Smith, Texas A&M University
Paul Thagard, University of Waterloo, Canada
Jyotsna Vaid, Texas A&M University
Thomas B. Ward, Texas A&M University
Friedrich Wilkening, University of Tubingen, Germany
Edward J. Wisniewski, Northwestern University
Philip Wolff, Northwestern University
Takashi Yamauchi, Columbia University

Preface

In his classic work *The Ascent of Man* (1973), Jacob Bronowski asserted that humans are distinguished from other animals by our "imaginative gifts." His statement reflects the fact that although we share many biological properties with other organisms, our minds function differently. We think generatively, and we transform our thoughts into tangible, novel creations. Because generativity seems so central to our identity it has been the focus of formal and informal inquiry from a wide range of perspectives. Our goal in the present volume is to highlight one particularly promising perspective on human creativity. We have drawn together many of the premier contributors to the field of cognitive psychology whose research programs have great potential for helping to advance the scientific understanding of this hallmark of human thought. More specifically, we have asked researchers with special expertise in conceptual structures and processes to consider how their research can provide new insights into the nature of creative functioning.

As in most other areas of cognitive psychology, research on concepts and categories has provided a wealth of information about the more receptive aspects of cognition (e.g., how people classify category instances) but has been less systematic in assessing the more generative aspects (e.g., how people use their concepts to develop something new). Here, the contributors to this volume focus on the latter with the hope of stimulating additional work on this important topic.

The focus of this volume is at once both narrow and broad. It is narrow in the sense that virtually all areas of cognitive science are potentially relevant to creativity, yet we have included only research dealing with conceptual structures and processes. Future volumes could reasonably be devoted to issues such as implicit versus explicit memory, problem solving, the role of working memory capacity, selective attention, and so on. Indeed another recent work examined in depth the role of mental imagery in creative functioning, namely, Roskos-Ewoldsen, Intons-Peterson, and Anderson's (1993) *Imagery, Creativity, and Discovery: A Cognitive Perspective.*

However, the current approach is also broad in the sense that we have considered a wide range of structures and processes from as concrete as how children integrate information about height and width (Wilkening, Schwarzer, & Rümmele) to as abstract as how Kepler used analogy in developing his view of the universe (Gentner et al.). In between, we have focused on topics as diverse as how perceptual symbol systems may underlie mundane (and possibly extraordinary) creativity (Barsalou & Prinz), how contemporary scientists use analogical reasoning on-line (Dunbar), how people interpret conceptual combinations (Wisniewski; Shoben & Gagne) and conjunctions (Hampton), how they comprehend metaphor (Glucksberg, Manfredi, & McGlone; Gibbs), how they build new categories (Markman, Yamauchi, & Makin) and extend (Cacciari, Levorato, & Cicogna) or re-represent (Chi) old ones, how they construct mental models to create meaning from words (Glenberg), and how they extend the meanings of words to cover new situations (Murphy). We have also included more integrative commentaries on the individual presentations (Thagard, Simonton, Kittay, and Perkins).

The chapters are arranged into four sections, each closing with a commentary. Each section examines conceptual processes with plainly evident links to anecdotal reports of creativity, empirical evidence that they are associated with emergent ideas, or both. The four broad topics are conceptual combination, conceptual expansion, metaphor, and analogy. Clearly, other conceptual processes and structures could have been examined, but this volume is an important starting point in an approach to creative functioning rather than the definitive word on the issue. Our great hope is that the work reported here will inspire other researchers to more directly probe the links between conceptual functioning and creativity.

All of the chapters in the present volume grew out of presentations made at what we informally dubbed the "Creative Concepts Conference."

This shorthand title reflects the fact that our focus was primarily on research relevant to the nature and structure of conceptual representations and the processes that operate on them. The conference was sponsored by the American Psychological Association (APA) Science Directorate and the Department of Psychology, College of Liberal Arts, College of Education, and College of Architecture at Texas A&M University. In particular, we thank Virginia Holt and the staff of the Science Directorate for their help and advice throughout the entire process and Paul Wellman, Woodrow Jones, Ben Crouch, Charles Shea, and Walter Wendler of Texas A&M for their efforts and generosity. In addition, we thank Judy Nemes, Tanya Alexander, and the editorial staff at APA, and an anonymous reviewer who provided extensive comments on all chapters. The contributors also generously commented on each other's chapters. We also thank the contributors for participating in the conference, the individuals who added an extra dimension to the conference by presenting posters, and the audience for asking difficult questions and sparking stimulating discussion. We also gratefully acknowledge the assistance of Steve Balfour, Jeff Brown, Barbara Glover, Jay Schumacher, Cindy Sifonis, Debbie Tindell, and Missi Wilkenfeld, without whom the conference would have been a disorganized disaster. They gave generously of their time; we thank them one and all.

1

Conceptual Structures and Processes in Creative Thought

Thomas B. Ward, Steven M. Smith, and Jyotsna Vaid

The human mind is an enormously creative instrument. Our ability to go beyond concrete experiences to produce novel ideas is one of our most salient characteristics. Whether it be a scientist proposing a theory, an author imagining a character, a parent dreaming up an activity to entertain children, or a speaker seeking a figurative way to express a thought, humans are constantly about the business of constructing and modifying new mental representations that are relevant to some goal. Indeed, it is our capacity for this type of creative, generative thought that distinguishes us most clearly from other species. Thus, it is surprising that, with some notable exceptions, mainstream cognitive psychologists have eschewed direct, systematic attempts to understand the ways in which people generate and extrapolate on new ideas, that is, the way they function creatively.

How is it that the science of the mind has for so long ignored one of the most obvious properties of its central object of study? The answers are many and varied (e.g., see Finke, Ward, & Smith, 1992), but rather than dwell on them here, we simply try to articulate the dual case that a complete account of human cognition requires an explication of the ways in which cognition is generative and that a complete account of creativity requires an understanding of the basic cognitive processes from which it emerges.

THE COGNITIVE REVOLUTION AND THE UBIQUITY OF GENERATIVE THOUGHT

The cognitive revolution that began in psychology more than three decades ago has culminated in a rich diversity of approaches to human thought and has set the stage for achieving major breakthroughs in our scientific understanding of creative thinking. Researchers have learned a great deal about the workings of the human mind, including how people acquire an astonishing variety of simple and complex concepts (e.g., see Komatsu, 1992; Medin, 1989), how we store and retrieve a multitude of specific and general memories, how we visualize and mentally transform the world in vivid detail (e.g., see Finke, 1989; Kosslyn, 1980), and how we master the exquisitely flexible and dynamically productive skill of human language. It is now time to apply this vast amount of theoretical and empirical knowledge in earnest to the domain of creative thought.

There are both theoretical and practical reasons for cognitive psychologists to focus attention more centrally on creative thinking. From a theoretical standpoint, understanding creative capacity is integral to a complete account of human cognition for the simple reason that human thought is so essentially generative. Despite the fact that most research in the cognitive sciences has not focused on creativity, per se, one of the most consistent observations is how strikingly flexible human thought can be. A notable example of this inherent creativity is the generative nature of language whereby people produce and comprehend a near infinite variety of constructions from a modest collection of words and a handful of basic rules for combining them. Other examples of the creative nature of human cognition abound as well.

Humans are prodigious builders of cognitive structures. Out of an ongoing stream of discrete experiences we construct a vast array of concepts that bridge the gaps between otherwise separate events and give coherence to our world. When we form these new concepts, or modify or extend old ones, presumably we create new cognitive entities that did not exist prior to those activities. In addition, because these concepts serve the purposes of understanding, organizing, classifying, and communicating about the world, they also satisfy another criterion of creativity, namely, usefulness. Hence, at its core or essence, the continual growth of categorical and conceptual knowledge is in itself a creative phenomenon.

Not only do we build elaborate conceptual structures for conventional taxonomic groupings, such as animals, vehicles, and furniture, we also readily construct ad hoc categories, such as "things to take from your home in the event of a fire" on the spot as we need them (Barsalou, 1983, 1991). Even our taxonomic groupings are flexible in that our judgments about how typical a given instance is of the category in question can vary greatly with the context (Barsalou, 1987; Roth & Shoben, 1983). At one extreme one might even argue that most of our concepts are not fixed entities at all, but rather temporary structures that we construct or create in response to recent events and the current situation (e.g., see Barsalou, 1987). Nor are we stuck with single concepts, for we can easily combine two or more existing concepts to develop or express a completely new idea.

We emphasize the generativity of language and conceptualization here, not to slight the more dramatic forms of creativity, such as musical composition, artistic creation, and scientific discovery, but to highlight the fact that generative thought is not unusual. It is not limited to situations in which a creative genius crafts a new concept that will inspire future generations of innovators. Rather, it is ubiquitous, present in the most commonplace of human activities. Furthermore, it is the continual evolution of cognitive structures that underlies and makes possible more dramatic creative accomplishments. Without the basic capacity to form, modify, extend, and combine simple and complex concepts, no creativity would be possible at all.

Clearly, there are also practical reasons for wanting to achieve a thorough understanding of the cognitive processes that lead to creative outcomes. Creativity is, after all, the engine that drives human progress. When applied effectively, creative thinking can better the human condition through miraculous advances in science, medicine, and technology; enrich our lives through exquisite works of art, music, and literature; and help us solve pressing personal, corporate, and societal problems. Our ability to think creatively gives us an important tool for adapting to the world around us. However, to utilize this important human resource most productively, we must understand it more clearly, and therein lies a central task for cognitive science.

Having broached the lofty topic of understanding creativity, however, it is important to be clear on a more modest aim of the current volume. This book, like the conference from which it evolved, is primarily a collaborative effort to understand the nature of some of the basic cognitive processes and structures that underlie creative and noncreative forms of thought. *It is more about those processes and structures than about creativity in its own right.* It is only by understanding the basic underlying principles of cognitive functioning, however, that one may ultimately achieve a complete understanding of creativity.

CREATIVE COGNITION

The assumption that understanding basic cognitive principles is essential to understanding creativity undergirds the field called *creative cognition*, which is a relatively new area of investigation that attempts to characterize creativity in terms of fundamental cognitive processes acting on previously stored knowledge (Finke et al., 1992; Smith, Ward, & Finke, 1995). According to the creative cognition view, creativity in all domains, including science, technology, medicine, the arts, and day-to-day living, emerges from a relatively small set of basic mental operations.

Truth in advertising also requires that we clarify how creativity is conceptualized within the creative cognition framework. In contrast to approaches that would ascribe creativity only to a small set of geniuses who have earned a place in history by producing dramatic breakthroughs, or that would emphasize individual differences in performance on standardized measures, creative cognition focuses mainly on what might be called "normative" creativity, that is, the generative potential that is inherent in the operating characteristics of most normal human brains. To clarify this perspective, consider the Ape–Einstein test. Even if you do not think of yourself and those around you as especially creative, are you more like the most creative ape that has ever existed or are you more like Einstein? In-laws aside, the answer is obvious. There really is something special about the generativity of the human mind that sets people apart, and it is worthy of study in its own right.

The creative cognition view represents a hard-core, cognitive science approach emphasizing basic cognitive structures and processes. What is the nature of the specific processes that lead to the emergence of the novel cognitive structures that, in turn, are the basis of human creativity? What is the role of existing cognitive structures in the development of those new concepts?

The vast majority of novel mental entities that most individuals produce on a regular basis do not represent earth-shattering new developments, and some may not be useful at all. It may even be helpful to distinguish between mundane forms of creativity that characterize the day-to-day activities of virtually all ordinary humans and the more striking forms of genius that seem to occur only rarely, and only among a limited set of individuals. However, at the same time, it is also useful to consider the possibility that the mundane and the exotic represent endpoints on a continuum of human creativity. Underlying those differing manifestations of generative thought are the same sets of mental processes. The processes may be deployed to different degrees and in different combinations to cognitive structures of varying degrees of complexity, flexibility, and richness, but they are nevertheless the same processes in principle. That is, in the creative cognition view, the differences between mundane creativity and genius are quantitative rather than qualitative (see, however, Simonton, this volume, for an alternative view). Examining in detail the basic mental processes that seem to be associated with the development of novel ideas therefore can shed light on both types of outcome.

CONCEPTUAL STRUCTURES AND PROCESSES

The contributions to this volume can be thought of as exemplars of the creative cognition approach. They all focus, in one way or another, on fundamental cognitive processes and structures. However, like exemplars of other concepts, the contributions may exhibit a kind of graded structure, with some adhering more or less to our assumption about the role of basic processes in mundane and extraordinary forms of generativity. They also exhibit a range of emphasis, with some mentioning creativity in a cursory way and focusing primarily on theoretical accounts of the processes themselves, and others confronting real-world creativity more directly.

In the sections that follow we discuss several conceptual processes that are crucial to creative thought, and we attempt to integrate prior work in these areas with the efforts of the other contributors to this volume. We should note, however, that creativity is not synonymous with any one of these processes. Rather, it may be better thought of as the outcome of the operation of all of these processes in concert.

CONCEPTUAL COMBINATION

Conceptual combination has long been touted as a wellspring of creativity for writers, artists, musicians, scientists, and other innovators (see Ward, Finke, & Smith, 1995, for a multitude of examples). The common intuition among creators and observers of the creative process is that the merging of two or more concepts can result in a novel entity that is more than the simple sum of its component parts. If the novel offspring from such a merger is also in any way useful, then, by definition, conceptual combination is a process that can lead to creativity.

The generative power of conceptual combination can be seen in instances as vastly different as Shakespeare's richly evocative characterization of parting as "sweet sorrow," and recent attempts to position automobiles in a novel location in the space of possible vehicles by using contrastive combinations such as "affordable luxury." Indeed Rothenberg (1979, 1995) argued that much creativity results from simultaneously holding in mind two opposing concepts, a process he terms *Janusian thinking*, in reference to the Roman deity Janus who had two faces pointing in opposite directions. Rothenberg describes several historical instances to support this case, including Mozart's music and Kekule's dramatic insight regarding the nature of the benzene molecule.

No one has expressed this notion of emergence more eloquently than the noted fantasy writer Stephen Donaldson (1992) who observed that "Rather like a binary poison—or a magic potion—two inert elements combine to produce something of frightening potency" (p. 223). Another less colorful analogy that nevertheless captures the resulting emergent structure is that hydrogen and oxygen merge to form water, a product with properties quite different from either of the component gases that make it up.

If conceptual combination is one of the basic processes that can produce a creative outcome, then to gain a full appreciation of the nature of creativity one must develop a thorough understanding of that process, of the "nuts and bolts" of the cognitive system. What is the nature of the process whereby people combine two or more existing concepts to produce or express a new idea? What is the process by which observers comprehend those new constructions?

The intuition that conceptual combination is a potential source of creative accomplishment is surely correct. Conceptual combination is clearly a source of conceptual change and growth. In its simplest form, the mere act of forming or comprehending a novel combination is creative in the sense that a formerly nonexistent concept (a new mental entity) is brought into being. For instance, even if the concept *maroon carrot* only differs from one's existing concept of an ordinary orange carrot in the filler for the "color" slot in its schematic representation, *maroon carrot* is still a novel construction, a new concept. Beyond this most obvious source of novelty, however, is the fact that conceptual combination can bring about changes not only in the most evident slot (e.g., color as in the case above), but in other properties of the existing concept that are conceptually related to that property (e.g., see Medin & Shoben, 1988). For instance, a listener might understand that a maroon carrot could differ from an orange one, not just in color, but also in its taste, texture, concentration of certain vitamins, or popularity in College Station versus Austin, Texas. In addition, conceptual combination can lead to the emergence of new properties that were either not present or at least not particularly evident in either of the components of the combination (e.g., see Gagne & Murphy, in press;

Hampton, 1987; Murphy, 1988). So for instance, a maroon carrot might have the property of being genetically engineered, which is true neither of maroon things nor of carrots in general.

The ability to produce and comprehend novel combinations is one of the basic tools in the cognitive workshop of most human beings, and it has been the object of considerable recent research (e.g., Gagne & Shoben, in press; Gray & Smith, 1995; Hampton, 1987; Murphy, 1988; Rips, 1995; Shoben, 1993; Wisniewski & Gentner, 1991). Anecdotally, consider how nearly all observers readily understood recent combinations such as "home page," "conference call," "religious right," and playing the "race card." As these everyday examples illustrate, not all novel combinations result in dramatic change, but they generally represent at least the identification, consolidation, or articulation of a new concept, if not its outright construction. *Religious right* for instance, refers to a group of people with a well-defined set of beliefs who have begun to attempt to influence the political process in this country. Even if a listener already had the group in mind as a concept, the label might nevertheless help to consolidate the concept.

Having a label to quickly identify a concept can also invite additional exploration. What parallels exist between the activities of the religious right and those of earlier religiously influenced activists? Articulating the concept race card invites one to explore race relations in general and their specific role in the American justice system. To the extent that a new combination allows people to see concepts in a new light it is a potential source of conceptual change.

So, how do people comprehend novel combinations, and what determines the likelihood that new properties will emerge. In the present volume, Shoben and Gagne explore the idea that comprehending new constructions is a matter of finding the most plausible relation between the component concepts. They marshal evidence to support the idea that a concept's past history of relations with other concepts is a good gauge of the relations it is likely to bear to yet another concept in a novel pairing. Without denying that comprehension sometimes involves relation linking, Wisniewski examines other strategies of interpretation, including the idea that comprehending involves integrating properties from the components or hybridizing them. He also describes how the latter are not simply a matter of directly transferring properties from one component to another, but rather involve a more active set of comparison, construction, and integration processes. Hampton pursues a slightly different set of issues. Just how frequently do new properties emerge from a novel conjunction, and are there some types of combinations that are more likely than others to lead to emergent outcomes? In discussing all three of these first contributions, Thagard raises the point that an overriding principle at work might be the drive to find a coherent interpretation. Failure to find a satisfactorily coherent interpretation might trigger the additional search that could result in dramatic forms of creativity.

However, understanding conceptual combination means more than just knowing how people comprehend novel combinations of words and meanings. A particularly important aspect of conceptual combination is the kind of reasoning scientists must do regarding the multiple variables in their disciplines. How do variables combine to determine the relevant phenomena of any field of investigation? How do arousal and task complexity, for instance, combine to determine performance in cognitive tasks? Anyone who has taught statistics or experimental design knows how difficult it is for many students to understand the concept of a statistical interaction. Yet without the ability to see that variables can combine in nonadditive ways, students cannot master the known complexities of a field and scientists cannot discover new ones.

Because understanding how variables interact is fundamental to creative progress in virtually any science, understanding how people reason about combinations of variables is one of the keys to unlocking the puzzle of creative accomplishment. There is a rich history of research on developmental changes in the integration of information from different dimensions (Anderson & Cuneo, 1978; Wilkening, 1979, 1981), and in the present volume, Wilkening, Schwarzer, and Rümmele tie that work explicitly to the issue of creative accomplishment in science. They argue that, in principle, the cognitive changes that underlie developmental progress from additive to multiplicative rules in children's judgments about area are not different from those associated with historically important creative discoveries that involved a realization of interactive relationships among variables. Thus, cognitive development is a natural laboratory for understanding the nature of creative advances.

CONCEPTUAL EXPANSION

Conceptual combination is clearly a process vital to creativity, but it is certainly not the only one. People regularly construct, stretch, extend, modify, and refine single concepts to fit new situations. We use the term *conceptual expansion* to refer in general to this generative tendency in human conceptual functioning. Clearly, this process is relevant to many forms of creative activity. Architects constantly use their concepts of various types of buildings to draft new instances. Design engineers do the same with a plethora of mechanical devices. Composers craft new songs, and writers pen new instances of characters and scenes. This list could easily be extended to scientists, chefs, artists, and any other types of individuals who are in the business of producing something new.

Despite the ubiquity of conceptual expansion in human activities, surprisingly little is known about it. Clearly, when people are asked to design new objects from an existing category (e.g., coins), and they are explicitly instructed to avoid being creative or silly, they produce items that look very much like typical objects from that category (e.g., Rubin & Kontis, 1983). Somewhat surprisingly, however, they also develop highly stereotypic entities when freed from real-world constraints and when encouraged to be as imaginative as they can (Ward, 1994, 1995). For instance, when asked to draw animals that might live on another planet and told to use their wildest imagination, college students tended to produce creatures highly similar to Earth animals in that they were bilaterally symmetric and possessed ordinary appendages (e.g., legs) and sense organs (e.g., eyes). Thus, the basic tendency is for the characteristic properties of existing concepts to be projected directly onto the novel instances generated in conceptual expansion, a phenomenon Ward (1994, 1995) referred to as *structured imagination.*

Nor is the structuring of new instances by old concepts limited to college students in laboratory experiments. Innovators as diverse as science fiction writers and design engineers show the same phenomenon. For instance, even though extraterrestrials could take virtually any form, casual observation of science fiction creatures suggests that most of them resemble Earth animals to a striking degree, and more systematic content analyses of aliens from the literature verify this apparent tendency (Ward, 1994). Likewise, design engineers tend to pattern new solutions after prototypic earlier designs—a practice that can lead to nonoptimal designs (Condoor, Brock, & Burger, 1993)—and they are especially influenced by recently encountered category instances (Jansson & Smith, 1991), as are college student participants in psychology experiments (Marsh, Landau, & Hicks, 1996; Smith, Ward, & Schumacher, 1993).

The tendency for conceptual expansion to be driven by the characteristic properties of known concepts is pervasive, and it has striking real-world implications. An interesting historical case is that early railway passenger cars were patterned heavily after existing stage coaches, including outside seating for the conductors. The design raised a host of additional engineering problems (White, 1978) and even resulted in loss of life (Ward, 1995; Ward et al., 1995). No one would deny that railways revolutionized travel in the 1800s, yet this clear instance of technological creativity was nevertheless heavily structured in a nonoptimal way by the existing knowledge of the day.

We know that imagination is structured, but we know little about the developmental course of that structuring. Is children's imagination as constrained as that of adults? An early study by Karmiloff-Smith (1990) suggests that young children may be even more constrained in that they are less likely than older children to incorporate elements from other domains when they create nonexistent people or houses. However, how likely are young children to preserve exact properties of existing concepts, such as the symmetry, senses, and appendages of known Earth animals? In the present volume, Cacciari, Levorato, and Cicogna examine such structuring of imagination in children. Contrary to the fanciful view of children as natural creators who are stifled by the school system, their data clearly show young children to be as heavily constrained by prior knowledge as are adults. This developmental continuity in the existence of structured imagination is an important finding, and it raises the possibility of using tasks of imagination as vehicles for assessing developmental change in knowledge structures.

What about the formation of new categories? Again, to some extent, all category formation is generative in the sense that people are somehow able to create internal representations that bridge the gaps between otherwise discrete experiences with diverse objects in the real world. Thus, all work on category acquisition is potentially relevant. In this volume, Markman, Yamauchi, and Makin look at how people form new categories, but their research moves significantly beyond standard category learning paradigms. They show how the way people interact with exemplars influences the nature of the new categories they create (see also Ross, 1996). Markman et al. also examine how participants working together on particular tasks evolve a common category structure for the materials they must use. Beyond adding an important look at the initial evolution of categories, Markman et al.'s work is crucial because creativity is often a social process in which different individuals collaborate on some bigger task. Clearly, the way they communicate with one another about the relevant concepts will have a major impact on the way in which they judge and represent their categories and may ultimately influence how successfully creative (or creatively successful) they are. Put in present terms, how successful they are in negotiating a mutually agreed on conceptual expansion for a domain will drastically influence their chance of doing something creative as a group.

Murphy (this volume) examines a slightly different aspect of conceptual expansion, namely, polysemy. Some words have multiple meanings, and it is an open question how those meanings continue to evolve. Polysemy is particularly intriguing because, unlike the case of homonymy in which a word has two or more unrelated meanings (e.g., *bank* as a financial institution versus the side of a river), polysemy highlights meanings that are variants on a common theme (e.g., *bank* as a financial institution, the structure housing that institution, the board of directors or employees of the institution, and so on). Thus, polysemy provides a natural window on how the meanings of individual concepts are expanded.

Clearly, generating a new meaning, as an author might do, is a creative act, but simply understanding a new meaning must result in conceptual expansion as well, albeit of a more passive nature. Murphy's data are consistent with the idea that the acceptability of new meanings is heavily influenced by the existing meanings for a term. Thus, again, the evidence points to a heavy structuring of new ideas by the specific nature of the concepts that have come before.

Chi (this volume) examines an aspect of conceptual expansion having to do with change or refinement of existing concepts. She considers the possibility that creativity involves re-representing concepts from one ontological tree to another. To the extent that initial ideas about a given concept place it in the wrong ontological category, making the leap to understand the concept correctly will be difficult. Interestingly, this view fits with the observation of an apparent constraint on the nature of myths (see Kelly & Keil, 1985). When mythical transformations occur, they tend to respect ontological boundaries (e.g., changing a frog into a prince) rather than crossing those boundaries (e.g., turning a prince into a rock).

Barsalou (this volume) presents a more purely theoretical analysis regarding the type of knowledge structure that might underlie the enormous flexibility of human thought. He argues for a perceptual symbol system with meaningful links to actual perceptual experiences. Although it is bound to be controversial, it is a provocative view and a clear example of what cognitive science can offer to a rigorous understanding of the creative process. Without such precise models regarding the nature of human knowledge, real progress in understanding the creative application of that knowledge will not be possible.

In discussing the contributions to this section, Simonton raises the important question of whether observations of "mundane" forms of creativity enlighten us about more extreme forms of creativity, as exhibited by those who would be classified as geniuses. It is an open (and difficult, but crucial) question as to whether these differing forms of generative thought represent endpoints on a continuum or discrete markers on opposite sides of an unbridgeable chasm.

METAPHOR

Metaphor and other forms of figurative expression are at once evidence of creative functioning in those who produce them, and spurs to creative discovery and enlightenment those who hear or read them. The world of literature and creative writing would be barren indeed if not for metaphor. Good writers constantly exhibit creativity in their figurative descriptions of otherwise commonplace objects, events, and emotions. However, metaphor can also inspire readers to think about otherwise familiar situations in new ways. In other words, it can bring about changes in their existing cognitive representations of a given domain.

Comprehending metaphors might bring about changes in conceptual structures in at least three ways. First, it might be that when we hear a metaphor, we interpret it as a kind of categorical assertion in which the target is being identified as a member of a category of which the vehicle is a prototypic member (e.g., Glucksberg & Keysar, 1990). For instance, on hearing that "children are sponges," we might come to understand that they are members of a class of things that quickly absorb what they are exposed to. To the extent that those categories are ad hoc or newly formed, they are novel mental constructions (e.g., see Barsalou, 1983). Consequently, this would be a clear instance of a mundane form of creativity. Alternatively, comprehending a metaphor might involve aligning objects and features across the domains being compared with the consequence that the domains themselves undergo reorganization (see Kelly & Keil, 1987; Tourangeau & Sternberg, 1982). Finally, comprehending a metaphor might result in emergent properties that were salient neither in the vehicle nor the topic prior to the terms' being paired in the metaphor (Tourangeau & Rips, 1991).

Still, we have much to learn about the nature of metaphor, and as with the other conceptual phenomena examined in this volume, a complete understanding of creativity demands a complete understanding of the processes involved. In the present volume Glucksberg et al. articulate the notion of "dual reference," in which the name for the vehicle of a metaphor refers not only to the vehicle itself, but also to a superordinate attributive category that supplies the properties that are being ascribed to the topic of the metaphor. For instance, "sponges" in the above metaphor refers to sponges, per se, but also to the category of things that absorb. Glucksberg et al. examine how metaphor comprehension can result in conceptual change in two ways: expanding existing categories by adding new members and creating new categories if the needed ones do not already exist. Presumably, we could expand "absorbent things" to include children, or create that concept in the process of comprehending the metaphor. They also show how metaphor comprehension can be delayed by prior highlighting of the specific, literal meaning of the vehicle and how the restrictiveness and ambiguity of the topic and vehicle can affect comprehension.

Taking a somewhat different tack, Gibbs considers the idea that our creative, metaphoric speech, like our language in general, is constrained by the fact that we exist in a particular type of body, which results in a particular range of experiences in the world. Presumably, we have a sense of balance, symmetry, and so forth, and these bodily experiences influence the way we think and express ourselves. Gibbs, for instance, analyzes Hamlet's soliloquy, an unmistakably exquisite instance of creative writing, in terms of how it relates to the bodily experiences of symmetry and balance. Rather than sticking solely with content analyses of creative works, however, Gibbs adds another important creative cognition ingredient by reporting on laboratory experiments that examine the role of bodily based conceptual metaphors in the way people understand poetry. This embodied cognition theme also crops up in Barsalou's notion of perceptual symbol systems and Glenberg's analysis of the nature of mental models.

Kittay (this volume) rightly identifies some of the advantages and shortcomings of the theoretical positions advanced by Glucksberg et al. and Gibbs and puts them in a broader context. Although it is clear that they do not provide all of the answers, the chapters, taken together, are an important starting point on a creative cognition approach to the role of metaphor in creative functioning.

As is true of the bulk of work on metaphor, the contributions to the present volume focus primarily on the receptive side of metaphor. There is a surprising lack of information about how people produce novel metaphors. Presumably, production is guided by constraints on communication, by the potential inherent in dual reference and ad hoc category production, and by the nature of bodily experience in the world, but the empirical case is waiting to be made.

ANALOGY AND MENTAL MODELS

Analogy too has often been noted as a source of great creative advancement. A classic case from the world of science is the analogy, attributed to Lord Ernest Rutherford, between the structure of the hydrogen atom and the structure of a planetary system. An equally classic case from literature is the progression of the same themes from *Tristan and Isolde*, to *Romeo and Juliet*, to *West Side Story*. The technological equivalent is Edison's patterning of his electric light distribution system directly on the existing gas distribution system of his day. All three cases are unmistakable instances of creativity, and all involve a clear analogical mapping of some, but not all, properties from one domain to another.

Observers with a practical bent have often advised would-be innovators to use analogies of various sorts (e.g., Gordon, 1961). One suggestion for instance is to use analogies from nature. Presumably, these would be effective because, under the pressures of natural selection, biological systems have evolved enormously adaptive mechanisms for solving particular problems. The classic instance of this type of analogy is de Mestral's development of Velcro from the starting point of burrs that clung to his clothing.

However, what do we know about the fundamental processes involved in analogical reasoning and transfer? How does it work? How common is it? Are there different forms of analogy with distinctly different implications for the likelihood of achieving a creative outcome? Much recent theoretical and empirical work has gone into understanding the nature of analogical processes and how they lead to creative advances (e.g., Gentner, 1983, 1989; Holland, Holyoak, Nisbett, & Thagard, 1986; Holyoak & Thagard, 1989, 1995), but much also remains to be learned.

Contributions to the literature on analogical thought often focus either on anecdotal accounts of highly creative analogies, or on tightly controlled laboratory-based studies of less dramatic forms of analogy. Both types of research have their place, but neither alone can give a complete picture of the role of analogy in creative functioning. In the present volume we have two contributions that extend the range of inquiry about analogy.

Gentner et al. (this volume) examine the historical case of one of the world's great analogical thinkers, Johannes Kepler. They relate his activities to the principles underlying a precise characterization of the analogical reasoning process, namely, the structure mapping engine (SME; see Falkenhainer, Forbus, & Gentner, 1989). They consider in depth the processes of highlighting, projection, re-representation, and restructuring. In so doing Gentner et al. show how anecdotal accounts and precise theorizing about the exact nature of cognitive processes can complement one another. Anecdotes alone are often vague and fail to identify with precision the processes at work. At the same time, purely theoretical approaches can be precise without necessarily having much to do with the real world. When both forms of inquiry are combined, true progress is possible.

Dunbar (this volume) reports an incredibly ambitious study of online analogical reasoning in contemporary molecular biologists. In contrast to the "far analogies" of Kepler and others that populate historical accounts of creative discovery, Dunbar finds much more use of "near analogies" to highly similar biological systems. It may be the case that far analogies are rare as sources of creative advancement, or it may be that they occur primarily at the early stages of investigation rather than in highly developed disciplines such as molecular biology. In any case, without a creative cognition approach to creativity, the distinction between near and far analogies, and their respective roles in the discovery, may never have been considered.

Dunbar also identifies several other important aspects of scientific reasoning that contribute to creative discoveries. One of these is the fact that reasoning is often distributed across members of a laboratory group. Thus, as with Markman et al.'s focus on cooperative category formation, one sees again that a complete account of cognitive processes will have to include reference to how those processes are shared among members of a group or extended community.

Although people regularly reason creatively by way of analogy, other complex forms of thought, such as mental models, also play an obvious role. Mental models have a rich history in cognitive psychology. They appear to be associated with complex forms of reasoning (Gentner & Stevens, 1983; Johnson-Laird, 1983), and they can serve as a basis for various forms of discovery (e.g., Glenberg, Meyer, & Lindem, 1987). As with other conceptual structures and processes, if mental models play a role in creativity, then an understanding of creativity demands that we study the nature of mental models. Glenberg (this volume) examines the nature of the mental models people construct as they derive meaning from words. He considers and rejects the possibility that mental models are spatial in nature, and concludes that they are embodied and influenced by the very fact that, as humans, we have a certain type of body and exist in relation to certain properties of the physical world.

KNOWLEDGE: ITS NATURE AND ROLE IN CREATIVE FUNCTIONING

Creativity is not conceptual combination. Nor is it conceptual expansion, metaphor, analogy, mental model construction, or any other single process. It is an outcome of subsets of those and other processes acting in concert to expand the frontiers of knowledge and conceptualization in a given domain. Creativity may even be better thought of as the entire system by which processes operate on structures to produce outcomes that are novel but nevertheless rooted in existing knowledge.

Existing Knowledge

One theme to emerge quite clearly from prior studies and from the contributions to this volume is the overwhelmingly powerful role of prior knowledge in creative endeavors. Because novelty is one requirement for a creative idea, most approaches to creativity focus on novelty to the exclusion of the background knowledge that gives the novelty its meaning. So much of creativity, however, depends on a thinker retaining information that has proven useful in the past. Without some meaningful link to what has come before—a property Finke (1995) described as structural connectedness—novel ideas are unlikely to be of much use and therefore are unlikely to be deemed creative. In understanding the nature of creativity, then, it is just as important to focus on how old knowledge influences new ideas as it is to focus on novelty, per se (e.g., see Karmiloff-Smith, 1990; Marsh et al., 1996; Smith, 1995; Smith et al., 1993; Ward, 1994, 1995; Ward et al., 1995).

Many contributors to this volume have noted how novel constructions are constrained by existing knowledge. In discussing the computational level of why people combine concepts, for instance, Wisniewski describes how speakers and listeners assume constraints on combinations. One such constraint is that although the meanings of combinations are novel, they nevertheless share commonalities with their components, particularly the head noun in the combination. A maroon carrot is, after all, still some type of carrot, for instance. Thus, prior knowledge is essential and applied fairly directly to the comprehension process. Shoben and Gagne emphasize a different though equally powerful aspect of prior knowledge, the combinatorial history of the components. Their claim is that a person's knowledge of how a term has combined with others in the past will influence their interpretation of a novel combination involving that term. If chocolate ordinarily participates in a "made of" relation, then it is highly likely that most people will interpret "chocolate dog" as a dog made of chocolate. Wilkening et al. stress the parallels between continuity in development and the gradual, incremental nature of creative discovery in which new knowledge is built on old knowledge in small steps.

Cacciari et al. clearly show the role of prior knowledge in their studies of children's development of imaginary animals and use of idiom. As in prior research with adults (Ward, 1994), characteristic properties of known Earth animals, such as appendages and sense organs arranged into symmetric relational structures, dominated children's imagination. Similarly, Murphy demonstrates that the acceptability of a new meaning for a novel polysemous word is directly tied to previous meanings. New meanings are not unconstrained; they cannot just move freely in any direction. Chi also illustrates the role of prior knowledge in terms of the ontological tree to which a known concept has been assigned. If a concept (e.g., heat) has been assigned to the wrong ontological tree (e.g., material things) it requires a mental leap and presumably a large investment of cognitive resources to come to the right understanding that it is part of another tree (e.g., processes).

Dunbar shows how contemporary scientists use near analogies in making new breakthroughs. The simplest characterization of this phenomenon is that they are making heavy use of existing knowledge and moving only a small way beyond it (cf. Wilkening et al.). Gentner et al. argue that even instances of far analogies, such as Kepler's, represent compelling links to prior knowledge as the thinker gradually fleshes out the full range of implications of the analogy.

Structuring Forces

If existing structures and processes are essential to creativity, then one must come to understand them better to understand creativity better. Certainly, we know that communication constraints (e.g., Glucksberg et al.; Markman et al., Wisniewski), characteristic properties (Cacciari et al.), ontological category membership (Chi), prior uses (Murphy; Shoben & Gagne), and participation in multiple relations (Gentner et al.) all matter. However, there is also evidence that simply being human and existing in a particular body in a particular world matter to the nature of our cognitive representations and, hence, to our potential for creative functioning. This notion of embodied cognition manifests itself in the nature of our basic knowledge representation (Barsalou & Prinz), our mental models (Glenberg), and our metaphoric production and comprehension (Gibbs).

Emergence and Change

Even with all of the structuring by prior knowledge, there is also cognitive change. Just as a connection to what is useful from the past is necessary to creativity so is a breaking from the past. Even here, however, prior knowledge is useful as the backdrop against which to depict the change. Properties emerge from conceptual combinations that were not part of either of the components, and this may happen more often when the components are less similar (Wisniewski), less easily merged into a relational link (Shoben & Gagne), less coherent (Thagard), or more novel (Hampton). Likewise, the new concepts that emerge from metaphor comprehension are not simply a conjunction of the properties of the topic and vehicle (Glucksberg et al.). In addition, even when combinations and metaphors involve a mapping of components from one concept to another, it is not a simple mapping. The mapped properties tend to be changed or constructed along the way (Glucksberg et al., Wisniewski).

The Importance of Effort

A related theme is that useful emergence and change is not necessarily an automatic byproduct of conceptual combination or any other process. In that sense, some of the metaphors for conceptual combination (e.g., hydrogen and oxygen into water) are not as apt as they might be in that they imply an almost automatic, dramatic change. However, there is nothing magical about merely putting two terms together that will automatically lead to wonderful new emergent ideas. Real creativity might be better thought of as appearing when people engage in the cognitive labor of exploring the possible mappings between concept representations to develop original though sensible interpretations. For instance, in Hampton's (this volume) work, imaginary combinations only resulted in interesting products from some of the research participants. Others did not take the task as seriously, did not work out complete and interesting mappings, and consequently did not come up with creative ideas. In Chi's chapter it is evident that the mental leaps needed to jump from one ontological tree to another require cognitive effort. In Gentner et al.'s work it is clear that what differentiated Kepler from most other analogizers is the single-minded vigor with which he pursued the analogies he considered. Thus, we should note that one important difference between mundane and dramatic forms of creativity may simply be the intensity and thoroughness with which the individual executes the cognitive processes involved.

Production and Comprehension of New Ideas

We should also make a distinction between producing a new creative idea as a writer, composer, or scientist might and being exposed to that idea. The first is the most obvious form of creativity that has always been acknowledged. The second, however, is more subtle and less often noted. Clearly, hearing a novel combination or metaphor, a new analogy, or an unusual use of a term has the potential to provoke cognitive change in the observer. These conceptual forms invite the observer to develop novel concepts and to consider old ones in a new light, and thus they are sources for the continual evolution of cognitive structures as much as they are its products.

Clearly, an understanding of creativity demands a focus on producing as well as on comprehending. In the present volume, Wisniewski, Shoben and Gagne, Hampton, and Glucksberg et al. focus mainly on comprehension, whereas Cacciari et al., Markman et al., and Gentner et al. focus more on production. Other contributors balance between these emphases, with Murphy distinguishing between producing and understanding new polysemous meanings, Gibbs looking at the output of poets and individuals' understanding of their works, Dunbar considering that some analogies may drive discoveries whereas others are used to explain them, and both Wilkening et al. and Chi emphasizing the role of cognitive structures and processes both in making creative scientific advances as well as in understanding them in educational settings. Learning that heat is a process, for instance, may require a creative leap, just as coming to that realization to begin with did.

Conceptual Inertia

The structuring of new ideas by old knowledge can be characterized as a kind of *conceptual inertia.* This construct represents a fairly direct analogy from the world of physical laws to the world of mental laws, and is intended as a counterpoint to the construct of conceptual change as well as a context within which to interpret conceptual change: Objects resist change; an object at rest remains so, and an object in motion continues in the same direction unless impacted by some force. Conceptual inertia is the property of conceptual systems that causes them to resist change. Just as physical objects resist changes in state, ideas resist movement from their current state, and change in the direction of their movement. Thus, when people develop new ideas, those ideas tend to resemble old ones; new ideas do not move much beyond old ones without a good deal of cognitive effort being applied. Much conceptual change is slow and incremental whether in science (Dunbar; Gentner et al.; Wilkening et al.), everyday imagination (Cacciari et al.), or a wide range of other creative endeavors (Ward et al., 1995). New meanings tend to continue in the direction set by prior meanings (Murphy).

Whether conceptual inertia is more than a superficial analogy remains to be seen. One deeper prediction might be that the more massive the prior knowledge structure, the more cognitive force required to change it. This is consistent with the notion that the properties of an old structure that are most likely to influence a new idea are those that participate in a broad set of relations with other features rather than those that exist in isolation. This prediction is reminiscent of Gentner's structure mapping theory of what makes a good analogy (e.g., Gentner, 1989). A related prediction is that sudden, dramatic change might occur when enough force builds up from a series of small changes and new ideas to put a very large existing structure in motion.

Prior knowledge is neither all good nor all bad; its utility must be judged in terms of the goals of the thinker and how it contributes to or detracts from those goals. Knowledge can lead to important advances or it can inhibit and constrain. Most important, however, creative ideas are always a mix of old and new information. Thus, understanding the nature of knowledge and its application to new situations is essential to understanding creativity. The contributions to this volume, and their links to prior research on conceptual structures and processes, should be viewed as an important starting point along the path to that understanding.

REFERENCES

Anderson, N. H., & Cuneo, D. O. (1978). The height + width rule in children's judgments of quantity. *Journal of Experimental Psychology: General, 107*, 335–378.

Barsalou, L. W. (1983). Ad hoc categories. *Memory & Cognition, 11*, 211–227.

Barsalou, L. W. (1987). The instability of graded structure: Implications for the nature of concepts. In U. Neisser (Ed.), *Concepts and conceptual development: Ecological and intellectual factors in categorization* (pp. 101–140). Cambridge, England: Cambridge University Press.

Barsalou, L. W. (1991). Deriving categories to achieve goals. In G. H. Bower (Ed.), *The psychology of learning and motivation: Advances in research and theory* (Vol. 27, pp. 1–64). San Diego, CA: Academic Press.

Condoor, S. S., Brock, H. R., & Burger, C. P. (1993, June). *Innovation through early recognition of critical design parameters.* Paper presented at the meeting of the American Society for Engineering Education, Urbana, IL.

Donaldson, S. (1992). *The real story.* New York: Bantam Books.

Falkenhainer, B., Forbus, K. D., & Gentner, D. (1989). The structure-mapping engine: An algorithm and examples. *Artificial Intelligence, 41*, 1–63.

Finke, R. A. (1989). *Principles of mental imagery.* Cambridge, MA: MIT Press.

Finke, R. A. (1995). Creative realism. In S. M. Smith, T. B. Ward, & R. A. Finke (Eds.), *The creative cognition approach* (pp. 303–326). Cambridge, MA: MIT Press.

Finke, R. A., Ward, T. B., & Smith, S. M. (1992). *Creative cognition: Theory, research, and applications.* Cambridge, MA: MIT Press.

Gagne, C. L., & Murphy, G. L. (in press). The influence of discourse context on the availability of features in conceptual combination. *Discourse Processes.*

Gagne, C. L., & Shoben, E. J. (in press). The influence of thematic relations on the comprehension of nonpredicating combinations. *Journal of Experimental Psychology: Learning, Memory, and Cognition.*

Gentner, D. (1983). Structure mapping: A theoretical framework for analogy. *Cognitive Science, 7*, 155–170.

Gentner, D. (1989). The mechanisms of analogical learning. In S. Vosniadou & A. Ortony (Eds.), *Similarity and analogical reasoning* (pp. 199–241). Cambridge, England: Cambridge University Press.

Gentner, D., & Stevens, A. L. (Eds.). (1983). *Mental models.* Hillsdale, NJ: Erlbaum.

Glenberg, A. M., Meyer, M., & Lindem, K. (1987). Mental models contribute to foregrounding during text comprehension. *Journal of Memory and Language, 26*, 69–83.

Glucksberg, S., & Keysar, B. (1990). Understanding metaphorical comparisons: Beyond similarity. *Psychological Review, 97*, 3–18.

Gordon, W. (1961). *Synectics: The development of creative capacity.* New York: Harper & Row.

Gray, K. C., & Smith, E. E. (1995). The role of instance retrieval in understanding complex concepts. *Memory & Cognition, 23*, 665–674.

Hampton, J. A. (1987). Inheritance of attributes in natural concept conjunctions. *Memory & Cognition, 15*, 55–71.

Holland, J. H., Holyoak, K. J., Nisbett, R. E., & Thagard, P. R. (1986). *Induction: Processes of inference, learning, and discovery.* Cambridge, MA: MIT Press.

Holyoak, K. J., & Thagard, P. R. (1989). A computational model of analogical problem solving. In S. Vosniadou & A. Ortony (Eds.), *Similarity and analogical reasoning* (pp. 242–266). ` Cambridge, England: Cambridge University Press.

Holyoak, K. J., & Thagard, P. R. (1995). *Mental leaps.* Cambridge, MA: MIT Press.

Jansson, D. G., & Smith, S. M. (1991). Design fixation. *Design Studies, 12*, 3–11.

Johnson-Laird, P. N. (1983). *Mental models: Towards a cognitive science of language, inference, and consciousness.* Cambridge, England: Cambridge University Press.

Karmiloff-Smith, A. (1990). Constraints on representational change: Evidence from children's drawing. *Cognition, 34*, 57–83.

Kelly, M. H., & Keil, F. C. (1985). The more things change . . . : Metamorphoses and conceptual structure. *Cognitive Science, 9*, 403–416.

Kelly, M. H., & Keil, F. C. (1987). Metaphor comprehension and knowledge of semantic domains. *Metaphor and Symbolic Activity, 2*, 33–51.

Komatsu, L. K. (1992). Recent views of conceptual structure. *Psychological Bulletin, 112*, 500–526.

Kosslyn, S. M. (1980). *Image and mind.* Cambridge, MA: Harvard University Press.

Marsh, R. L., Landau, J. D., & Hicks, J. L. (1996). How examples may (and may not) constrain creativity. *Memory & Cognition, 24*, 669–680.

Medin, D. L. (1989). Concepts and conceptual structure. *American Psychologist, 44*, 1469–1481.

Medin, D. L., & Shoben, E. J. (1988). Context and structure in conceptual combination. *Cognitive Psychology, 20*, 158–190.

Murphy, G. L. (1988). Comprehending complex concepts. *Cognitive Science, 12*, 529–562.

Rips, L. J. (1995). The current status of research on concept combination. *Mind and Language, 10*, 72–104.

Ross, B. H. (1996). Category representations and the effects of interacting with instances. *Journal of Experimental Psychology: Learning, Memory, and Cognition, 22,* 1249–1265.

Roth, E. M., & Shoben, E. J. (1983). The effect of context on the structure of categories. *Cognitive Psychology, 15,* 346–378.

Rothenberg, A. (1979). *The emerging goddess.* Chicago, IL: University of Chicago Press.

Rothenberg, A. (1995). Creative cognitive processes in Kekule's discovery of the structure of the benzene molecule. *American Journal of Psychology, 108,* 419–438.

Rubin, D. C., & Kontis, T. C. (1983). A schema for common cents. *Memory & Cognition, 11,* 335–341.

Shoben, E. J. (1993). Non-predicating conceptual combinations. In G. V. Nakamura, R. Taraban, & D. L. Medin (Eds.), *Categorization by humans and machines. The psychology of learning and motivation* (Vol. 29, pp. 391–409). San Diego, CA: Academic Press.

Smith, S. M. (1995). Fixation, incubation, and insight in memory and creative thinking (pp. 135–156). In S. M. Smith, T. B. Ward, & R. A. Finke (Eds.), *The creative cognition approach.* Cambridge, MA: MIT Press.

Smith, S. M., Ward, T. B., & Finke, R. A. (Eds.). (1995). *The creative cognition approach.* Cambridge, MA: MIT Press.

Smith, S. M., Ward, T. B., & Schumacher, J. S. (1993). Constraining effects of examples in a creative generation task. *Memory & Cognition, 21,* 837–845.

Tourangeau, R., & Rips, L. (1991). Interpreting and evaluating metaphors. *Journal of Memory and Language, 30,* 452–472.

Tourangeau, R., & Sternberg, R. J. (1982). Understanding and appreciating metaphors. *Cognition, 11,* 203–244.

Ward, T. B. (1994). Structured imagination: The role of conceptual structure in exemplar generation. *Cognitive Psychology, 27,* 1–40.

Ward, T. B. (1995). What's old about new ideas? In S. M. Smith, T. B. Ward, & R. A. Finke (Eds.), *The creative cognition approach* (pp. 157–178). Cambridge, MA: MIT Press.

Ward, T. B., Finke, R. A., & Smith, S. M. (1995). *Creativity and the mind: Discovering the genius within.* New York: Plenum Press.

White, J. H. (1978). *The American railroad passenger car.* Baltimore: Johns Hopkins University Press.

Wilkening, F. (1979). Combining of stimulus dimensions in children's and adults' judgments of area: An information integration analysis. *Developmental Psychology, 15,* 25–33.

Wilkening, F. (1981). Integrating velocity, time, and distance information: A developmental study. *Cognitive Psychology,* 13, 231–247.

Wisniewski, E. J., & Gentner, D. (1991). On the combinatorial semantics of noun pairs: Minor and major adjustments to meaning. In G. B. Simpson (Ed.), *Understanding word and sentence* (pp. 241–284). Amsterdam, The Netherlands: Elsevier Science.

PART ONE

Conceptual Combination

2

Thematic Relations and the Creation of Combined Concepts

Edward J. Shoben and Christina L. Gagné

People are able to make sense of what they hear or read. This ability has been known at least since the publication of Chomsky's (1965) seminal work, in which he showed that people are able to produce and comprehend an infinite variety of sentences. People also are able to understand and produce combinations of words with which they have had no prior experience. Thus, for example, someone might describe an appliance used to heat a cottage in a forest as a *wood furnace* even though he or she may never have encountered this combination before. Moreover, this phrase will be readily interpreted as "a furnace that uses wood as fuel" by virtually any listener. This operation allows the listener to create an entirely new concept.

These noun–noun combinations are particularly interesting in that there is no set rule by which the relation between the two constituents can be determined. For example, a *flu ache* is an ache caused by flu, but a *leg ache* is a pain in the leg. Similarly, *horse hair* is hair that comes from a horse, but a *horse book* is a book about horses. In other words, conceptual combination involves finding the relation that is appropriate based on the modifier and the head noun. This relation is not necessarily the same for all combinations that have the same modifier or the same head noun. Instead, the selection of a relation takes into account both the modifier and the head noun. Thus, the creation of a new concept is not simply the application of a simple rule but a more complicated selection of one relation from among many alternatives.

These *non-predicating* combinations are often contrasted with *predicating ones*, such as a *red X*, which can be interpreted as "an X that is red." Although the shade of red that is represented by such combinations as *red apple* and *red blood* (Halff, Ortony, & Anderson, 1976) can vary, in both cases what is meant is that the noun has the characteristic of redness.

In this chapter, we first describe the two prominent approaches to the study of conceptual combination. We then review some of the data that we have collected that we regard as particularly helpful in choosing between these two approaches. Finally, we present a model of the comprehension of combined concepts and conclude by offering some speculations on how people produce combined concepts.

Some researchers (Murphy, 1988, 1990; Smith, Osherson, Rips, & Keane, 1988) have favored an approach in which the head noun is conceptualized as a schema. According to this view, the modifier selects and fills a slot in the head noun's schema. A second view is that for non-predicating combinations a number of relations can connect the noun and modifier. Some have argued (most notably Levi, 1978) that there is a finite number of relations into which these non-predicating combinations can enter. We consider each of these approaches in turn.

THE SCHEMA APPROACH

The first approach assumes that the head noun is represented by a schema that lists various dimensions along with possible filler values for each dimension (Murphy, 1988; 1990; Smith et al., 1988). Conceptual combination involves the modifier selecting an appropriate dimension in the head noun and becoming the filler value for that dimension. For example, the modifier in *red apple* selects the "color" dimension in the head noun *apple*. According to Murphy's (1988, 1990) schema modification model, the ease with which a combined concept can be understood is a function of the ease with which the proper slot is selected. If the required dimension is present in the head noun, then it will be easier to comprehend the combination than if the required dimension is absent and must be constructed on the basis of world knowledge.

World knowledge is used in two ways according to the schema modification model. First, it can be used to determine which dimension should be filled by the modifier. For example, world knowledge may prompt us to fill the "habitat" dimension in the *apartment* schema during the comprehension of *apartment dog*. Second, world knowledge allows for the alteration of dimensions that are not directly specified by the modifier. To illustrate, the color dimension in the head noun *apple* is selected in the case of *green apple*. Subsequently, world knowledge may be used to elaborate the schema so that other dimensions, such as "taste," are also changed during conceptual combination. Thus, the taste dimension would have the value "sour" for *green apple*.

THE TAXONOMIC APPROACH

The taxonomic approach assumes a taxonomy of thematic relations into which all these non-predicating combinations can be classified. There are a number of taxonomies that vary in terms of their level of formality. Downing (1977), for example, specified a number of relations that closely match those classifications proposed by Levi (1978).

Researchers who espouse a taxonomic approach tacitly assume that there are a fixed and relatively small number of relations that need be specified. Although this assumption is shared by many, it should be noted that there are those (e.g., Clark, 1983) who believe that the number of relations is virtually infinite and is largely determined by context. Although we do not intend to understate the role of context, it does seem useful to us to determine what utility a finite set of relations provides.

Our own taxonomy begins with Levi (1978). As indicated in Table 1, there are 16 relations. The first six are best conceived of as three pairs. Thus, for example, there are causals in which the modifier CAUSES the head

Table 1

Relational Categories

1.	Noun Causes modifier	9.	Noun Uses modifier
2.	Modifier Causes noun	10.	Noun Located modifier
3.	Noun Has modifier	11.	Noun About modifier
4.	Modifier Has noun	12.	Noun During modifier
5.	Noun Makes modifier	13.	Noun Used By modifier
6.	Noun Made Of modifier	14.	Modifier Located noun
7.	Noun For modifier	15.	Noun Derived From modifier
8.	Modifier Is noun	16.	Noun By modifier

noun, as in *flu-headache*, and causals in which the head noun CAUSES the modifier, as in *malarial mosquitoes.* Similarly, there are "has" relations in which the head noun HAS modifier (e.g., *picture book*) and "has" relations in which the modifier HAS head noun (e.g., *lemon peel*). This parallelism breaks down somewhat when we get to "make" relations. *Honey bee* is indeed an example of a head noun that MAKES modifier, but *plastic car* is not really plastic that makes a car but a car MADE OF plastic. From here, the classification includes FOR relations, as in *cat medicine*; IS relations, as in *servant girl*; USE relations, as in *wood stove*; and LOCATIVE relations, as in *mountain stream.*

These 10 relations are taken directly from Levi (1978). In addition to these, she also included a number of nominalizations that we have classified as an ABOUT relation, such as *tax law.* To these we have added a number of others. For example, we have added a subset of the locative relation to express time-based relations (i.e., DURING) and the relation BY (e.g., *student vote*).

The critical question, of course, is how well this taxonomy subsumes the use of non-predicating combinations. First, are there combinations of this type that are not in the taxonomy? The answer to this question is certainly affirmative. Combinations such as *party girl* are interpreted as "a girl who likes parties," and this relation is not (at present) in the taxonomy. One solution to this problem is simply to place a "modifier who likes noun" in the taxonomy; the question is whether this kind of relation is used frequently enough to warrant inclusion. Clearly, if there are 50 similar exceptions, then our idea of a finite set of relations loses much, if not all, of its viability as an account of conceptual combination. However, the question for these apparent exceptions is whether they can be placed into existing categories, whether they require new ones, or whether they are simply odd singletons, such as *finger lakes* (i.e., lakes that are shaped like fingers). In the case of *party girl*, we suspect that we will be forced to add an additional category as combinations such as *baseball boy*, *hat child*, and *clothes person* come readily to mind.

In addition, our taxonomy does not purport to account for metaphorical interpretations of otherwise nonsensical combinations. For example, a *tarantula teacher* is unlikely to be interpreted as a teacher who trains tarantulas to do tricks; rather, a *tarantula teacher* is more likely to be interpreted as someone who is ferocious and threatening. Last, this taxonomy does not include the kind of property-matching strategy discussed by Wisniewski (see chap. 3) in which a combination is interpreted as a head noun that resembles a modifier. Thus, for example, our taxonomy does not include combinations like *skunk squirrel* or *snake light* that are interpreted as "a squirrel that resembles a skunk" or "a light that resembles a snake," respectively. We do not dispute that property matches occur; however, we contend that property matches are the interpretation of last resort. Thus, for example, a *robin worm* is not a worm that resembles a robin but a worm for a robin. We also doubt that the occurrence of these property matches is very common in everyday speech and writing. None, for example, appeared in our corpus.

Even if we accept a taxonomic approach, it remains to formulate this approach into a psychological model from this approach. Although there are certainly other possibilities, we (Gagné & Shoben, 1997) have elected to make some specific assumptions and then test their implications.

First, we assume that people know about the relations and their relative frequency of use. For example, most people believe that a *chocolate X* is an X made of chocolate. Our claim is that people know that MADE OF is a relation and that it is quite common for the modifier *chocolate.* Although the MADE OF relation is the most likely relation for the combinations using the modifier *chocolate,* it is not the only possible relation. There are counterexamples such as *chocolate recipe, chocolate allergy,* or *chocolate hive.* We will discuss later how one arrives at these specific interpretations.

Although the modifier *chocolate* is readily interpreted as a MADE OF relation, the appropriate relation is not nearly so available for a combination such as *juvenile X.* This combination could be interpreted as an X who is juvenile, as in a *juvenile criminal,* or an X for a juvenile, as in a *juvenile court.* To consider one last possibility, a *juvenile X* also could be an X about juveniles, as in *juvenile law.*

Although there is no single dominant relation in this last example, one knows intuitively that the ABOUT relation is less likely than the other two. How does one know this fact about relative frequency? We consider the hypothesis that people make use of frequency information. In other words, people know not only what a word means but how it is used. For example, the use of the relation *noun* LOCATED *modifier* is very common for modifiers such as *urban* but almost unheard of for modifiers such as *juvenile.*

One possible manifestation of this stored frequency information is that, for a given modifier, each relation has a particular strength. Possible interpretations for combined concepts are based primarily on the strength of each relation for the modifier of the combined concept.

This account makes some striking predictions. First, it predicts that combinations that use infrequent (and consequently, weak) relations should be difficult to understand relative to combinations that use relatively frequent relations. Ignoring the role of the head noun for the moment and focusing on the modifier, consider the combinations *mountain stream* and *mountain range. Mountain stream* is a locative, a common relation for *mountain. Mountain range,* however, is not a locative; rather, it is a range made up of mountains.

Although most people would agree that *mountain range* is a much more frequent combination than *mountain stream,* Shoben and Medin (reported in Shoben, 1991) found that *mountain range* took appreciably longer for individuals to judge as a legitimate combination. Perhaps one reason for this delay is that the MADE OF relation is very unusual for *mountain.*

Although all of these examples involve modifiers, there is no a priori reason why the same analysis could not be done for head nouns as well. Theoretically, one could determine the relative frequency of these various relations for head nouns as easily as one could for modifiers. Whether the role of frequency is symmetric for modifiers and head nouns is one focus of the experiments we discuss later in the chapter.

Thus far, however, this account has been entirely speculative. The reader has been asked to agree to many unsupported assertions about frequency. One might reasonably ask how one might measure this frequency. We approached this problem in the following way: We took the corpus developed by Shoben and Medin (reported in Shoben, 1991) as the starting point for our count of relative frequency.

Shoben and Medin (reported in Shoben, 1991) created their corpus by selecting 10 examples of each of the 10 relations provided by Levi (1978). Subsequently, they combined all unique modifiers with all unique head nouns. This procedure resulted in a 91 × 91 matrix (after duplications were eliminated). We (Gagné & Shoben, 1997) considered all possible modifier–head noun pairs generated by this matrix and eliminated all those for which we could not obtain a nonmetaphorical, sensible reading (such as *salivary underwear*). We classified the remaining plausible combinations according to our taxonomy (as illustrated in Table 1). Through this analysis we obtained a distribution of relations for each modifier and for each head noun in our corpus.

This procedure was not intended to provide a representative sample of conceptual combinations in the language. Indeed, the relative frequency of the examples provided by Levi (1978) was likely to vary considerably. Rather, our intent was to generate as wide a variety of conceptual combinations as possible. We hoped to be at least moderately successful in using the taxonomy of relations to generate a wide range of conceptual combinations.

For example, the modifier *plastic* entered into 41 sensible combinations in our corpus. Of these, 28 used the MADE OF relation, 7 used the head ABOUT modifier relation, 2 used the head DERIVED FROM modifier relation, 1 used the modifier CAUSES head relation, 1 used the head LOCATED modifier relation, and 1 used the modifier FOR head relation. Other modifiers had distributions that were less one-sided. For example, *juvenile* could enter many different relations, none of which was dominant. This modifier was used 49 times in our corpus, in nine different thematic roles. FOR was the most common relation (19), followed by HAS (11), IS (6), ABOUT (5), and five other relations with frequencies of two or less.

Given our distribution, we were able to select combinations whose thematic relation was either very common or very rare for an individual modifier or head noun. To make such a determination, however, we had to define *rare* and *common* operationally. As our examples *juvenile* and *mountain* make clear, we could not simply define *common* in terms of some fixed percentage as the highest percentage for juvenile was 33%, and this percentage was not the lowest in our corpus. Consequently, we defined high frequency in terms of cumulative frequency. Taking an arbitrary figure of 60%, we selected the highest frequency relation. If that relation had a frequency greater than 60%, then it was the only relation that we characterized as high frequency. All other relations were considered low frequency for that word. In the case of *mountain*, for example, locative was the only high-frequency relation.

When there was no such dominant relation, we selected relations in order of frequency until that 60% criterion was reached. Thus, for example, in the case of *juvenile*, the highest frequency relation was FOR. Because the frequency of this relation was less than 60%, we also included the next most frequent relation, HAS, as high frequency. We repeated this process for all head nouns and modifiers until we reached criterion.

The result of this process was a list of high-frequency (as defined earlier) relations for each of the modifiers and each of the head nouns in our corpus. When we looked at the combinations formed by these modifiers and head nouns, we could then classify them as (a) high–high (HH), where the relation was high frequency for both modifier and head noun;

(b) high–low (HL), where the relation was high frequency for the modifier but low frequency for the head noun; (c) low–high (LH), where the relation was low frequency for the modifier but high frequency for the head noun; and (d) low–low (LL), where the relation was low frequency for both the modifier and the head noun.

The resulting distribution of combinations was anything but rectangular with respect to relation frequency. Of our 3,239 combinations, HH predominated, followed by HL and LH. Most interestingly, there were almost no LL. Moreover, those that we had classified as LL were either ambiguous in interpretation or were only marginally sensible (e.g., *vegetable bar*).

One might argue that the paucity of LL combinations resulted from the way in which we defined *high frequency*. However, even if we assume that only 30% of our modifiers and head nouns were classified as low frequency, then we would still expect, on the basis of chance, that 9% of our combinations would be LLs. Even with such conservative assumptions, we had far fewer LL combinations than chance would predict, and even those that we did find were in fact "bad" combinations: They were either ambiguous or could be construed as not having a sensible meaning.

EXPERIMENTAL FINDINGS

The primary goal of our experiments was to determine whether the frequency of the relation required for interpreting the combination made a difference in the ease with which a combined concept could be understood. More specifically, did a particular relation's frequency of use affect the comprehensibility of the combined concept?

A second goal of these experiments was to determine whether the effects of relation frequency would be symmetric. The schema model, for example, appears to focus on the head noun as the primary link in the comprehension of conceptual combinations. Although the schema model does not, without additional assumptions, predict any effect of relation frequency, it nevertheless suggests that characteristics of the head noun should have more influence than characteristics of the modifier. Thus, whatever effects we find might be more pronounced in the head noun.

Alternatively, one might focus on the fact that we read left to right in English and, therefore, temporal constraints might lead to a greater influence of the modifier because modifiers normally precede their nouns in English. Because modifiers are accessed prior to the head nouns, information associated with the modifier may have a greater influence on conceptual combination than does information associated with the head noun.

There is a third, more speculative, possibility. Many terms can be used as both modifiers and head nouns. Thus, for example, there are *cloud bursts*, *cloud banks*, and *cloud gases*, but there also are *storm clouds*, *bomb clouds*, and *gas clouds*. If relation frequency matters, then it might be difficult, if not impossible, for people to store the frequencies of the thematic relations for both the modifier and the head noun functions of each concept. Consequently, we might find an asymmetry in which there is an effect of either the modifier or the head noun but no effect of the other constituent.

Experimental Design

We (Gagné & Shoben, 1997) conducted two experiments in which the frequency of the head noun and the frequency of the modifier were varied independently. Because of the paucity of LL combinations, a completely balanced design was not possible. Thus, in two experiments we examined the comprehension time for non-predicating HH, HL, and LH combinations. We also varied whether we controlled for the individual words or for the number of thematic relations. For example, in our first experiment, the identical words were used in all three conditions. Thus, for example, *mountain* appeared in all three conditions as a modifier, and *cloud* appeared in all three conditions as a head noun. In the second experiment, we controlled the thematic relation, so that there were an equal number of each relation type in each condition (HH, HL, and LH). In both experiments, participants were timed as they decided whether a particular combination was sensible or not.

Results

The results indicated that the frequency of relation mattered, but only for the modifier. There was no effect of relation frequency for the head noun.

The response times for the first experiment were 1068, 1072, and 1152 ms for conditions HH, HL, and LH, respectively. There was a robust effect of modifier frequency such that HH combinations were a reliable 84 ms faster than their LH counterparts. There was little hint, however, of a corresponding effect for head noun relation frequency. HH pairs were a nonsignificant 4 ms faster than their HL counterparts. The same pattern of results was obtained in the second experiment in which the response times were 1138, 1156, and 1265 ms for conditions HH, HL, and LH, respectively.

In addition to this analysis of reaction times, we also examined the effect of relation frequency using a stepwise regression. This analysis permitted us to examine frequency in a more fine-grained way than the high–low dichotomy of our original design. Here we examined two variables. First, we looked at the ranked frequency of the constituent, which was a more subtle method of examining our high–low manipulation. Second, we looked at the number of dominant relations for both the head noun and the modifier.

We chose this second variable because of our intuition that modifiers with only a single dominant relation might be easier to comprehend than those with a more diverse set of common thematic relations. We included this variable for the head noun to provide a further check on our rather startling finding that there was no effect of relation frequency for head nouns.

The results of our regression analysis supported our original reaction time findings. For the modifiers, both relation frequency variables were significantly correlated with response time. For the head nouns, the corresponding correlations did not differ appreciably (or significantly) from zero. Interestingly, both the ranked frequency of the thematic relation and the number of dominant relations accounted for significant variance among the response times. The raw correlations for these two variables were of approximately equal magnitude.

The empirical findings then were threefold: First, there was an effect of relation frequency on comprehension such that higher relation frequency led to faster comprehension time. Second, this effect held only for the relation frequency of the modifier; the relation frequency of the head noun had no effect. Third, for the modifier, the number of dominant relations had an effect such that comprehension time was faster when the modifier had fewer dominant relations.

These results are not easily handled by existing models. For example, the schema modification model (Murphy, 1988) assumes that conceptual combination involves finding an appropriate slot for the head noun. For example, understanding *wood stove* involves filling the fuel "slot" for the head noun *stove.* Without additional assumptions, this account argues for the primacy of the head noun; if the slot is readily located, then comprehension should be relatively easy. That is, the HH combinations should be easier to comprehend than the HL combinations. However, this was not the case. Furthermore, our finding that the frequency of the relation for the head noun was immaterial is clearly at variance with this prediction. Moreover, the fact that relations matter at all is not predicted by the schema modification model.

THE COMPETITION AMONG RELATIONS IN NOMINALS (CARIN) MODEL

A viable alternative is that people know not only what non-predicating modifiers mean but also how they are used. Thus, for example, just as people know that fruit exemplars vary from typical ones like *apple* to atypical ones like *kumquat,* they also know that *chocolate* is usually used in a compositional sense (MADE OF) but also is used occasionally in an ABOUT relation.

Our theory is that people have a distribution of relations for modifiers. To take *mountain* as an example, the LOCATED relation (*mountain stream*) is stronger than the ABOUT relation (*mountain magazine*) or the MADE OF relation (*mountain range*). Our CARIN model assumes that all of these relations compete for the interpretation of the combined concept and that the difficulty of interpretation is a function of the relative strength of the selected relation. We assume further that the frequency of a relation (as determined by our corpus) is a reasonable index of its strength.

According to this account, ease of interpretation depends on the strength of the required relation. To return to the *mountain* example, it is easier to obtain the correct interpretation for *mountain stream* than it is for *mountain magazine* because the LOCATIVE relation is of greater strength than the ABOUT relation. In other words, it is easier to understand a highly frequent relation than it is to understand a less frequent relation.

Although frequency is the primary determinant of comprehension speed, relative strength also plays a role. Thus, for example, the presence of other high-strength thematic relations should slow the correct interpretation of conceptual combinations. For example, the frequencies (in percentages) of the three most frequent relations for the modifier *headache* are 33.3, 33.3, and 20.8, and the frequencies of the three most frequent relations for the modifier *juvenile* are 33.6, 19.8, and 14.7. Although the frequency of the most frequent relation is almost identical for both modifiers, the selection of this most common relation for *juvenile* should be easier because the frequency of the second and third most frequent relation is lower for *juvenile* than it is for headache.

Thus, the principal claim of the CARIN model is that comprehension difficulty depends both on the strength of the appropriate relation and on the strength of the alternatives. One straightforward way to formalize this claim is to establish a ratio whose numerator is an index of the strength of the correct relation and whose denominator is the sum of the strengths of the correct relation plus the strengths of three most likely alternatives. This ratio is just Luce's (1959) choice rule in which the strength of the first choice is weighed against the strength of other competing relations. We used relative frequency (expressed as a proportion) as our index of strength. For example, let us again consider the combination *mountain stream*, which uses the locative relation. In our corpus, the locative interpretation is given to 81.9% of all combinations. The three next highest are ABOUT, USES, and MADE OF with percentages of 10.1, 2.2, and 1.4, respectively. Thus, the ratio we described would be .819/(.819 + .101 + .022 + .014), or .86. In contrast, we would obtain a relatively low ratio [.101/(.101 + .819 + .022 + .014)], or .11 for *mountain magazine*, where the numerator would be .101 and the denominator would remain the same. Consequently, our model predicts that *mountain stream* should be comprehended more readily than *mountain magazine.*

For combined concepts that lack a single, dominant thematic relation, the situation changes markedly. Here, the difference between readily comprehensible, high-strength combinations and more difficult, low-strength ones is reduced. *Juvenile* provides a good example of this point. This modifier has frequencies (in percentages) of 33.6, 19.8, 14.7, and 10.3, corresponding to the relations FOR, HAS, ABOUT, and IS, respectively. Consequently, for a combination like *juvenile food* (FOR), the critical ratio would be .336/(.336 + .198 + .147 + .103), or .43. Using a less common relation like *juvenile instincts* (HAS), the ratio is .198/(.198 + .336 + .147 + .103), or .25. It is important to notice that the difference between the ratios for *juvenile food* and *juvenile instincts* is not nearly as great as the difference between the ratios corresponding to *mountain stream* and *mountain magazine.* Thus, although it should be more difficult in both cases to select a relation that is not the most frequent, it will be even more difficult when the modifier is *mountain* than when the modifier is *juvenile* because the most frequent relation is highly dominant for *mountain.*

Following other applications of Luce's choice rule (Rumelhart & Abrahamsen, 1973; Sadler & Shoben, 1993), we used an exponential decay function ($e^{-ap_{\text{relation}}}$) to compute the strength ratio for the selected relation, where p_{relation} was the proportion in our corpus of a particular relation and a was a free parameter that did not vary with p_{relation}. The strength ratio ranged from 0 to 1 and was the value obtained from the ratio:

$$\frac{e^{-ap_{\text{selected}}}}{e^{-ap_{\text{selected}}} + e^{-ap_1} + e^{-ap_2} + e^{-ap_3}}$$

We computed the strength ratios for the combinations in our experiments and correlated these values with our mean reaction times for each item. Given that each individual contributed only one data point for each item, these item means were not particularly stable. Moreover, our combinations varied not only in length but also in word frequency. Despite these data limitations, correlations between response time and the strength ratio were fairly high at .44 for one experiment and .35 for the other. For both experiments, the optimum value of *a* was about 36.

To determine how much predictability we could obtain, we also examined the contribution of word frequency and word length. Because of the counterbalancing in our first experiment (where each word was used once in each condition), we expected these variables to contribute less than they would in our other experiment. To test this notion, we performed a stepwise regression for each data set using the strength ratio, log modifier word frequency, log head noun word frequency, modifier word length, and head noun word length as predictor variables. Our expectations were confirmed. Correlations increased, and the increase caused by these word variables was less in our first experiment (in which each modifier and each head noun appeared in each condition) than in our second experiment. In the first study, inclusion of the log frequency and length of the modifier increased the multiple R to .54. The variables for the head noun did not account for significant variance. For the other study, three variables (log modifier frequency, modifier word length, and log head noun frequency) entered into the regression model along with the strength ratio, and the multiple R increased to .64. The contribution of the strength ratio measure accounted for the greatest amount of variance in the first experiment and was second only to the log frequency of the modifier in the fit to our second experiment.

Given the variability that is inevitably present when each individual provides but one data point, we regard the fits of the model as quite good. Our multiple Rs are quite comparable, for example, to those that Whaley (1978) obtained for nonword lexical decisions, even though his response times were half as long as ours. In addition, our fits are at least as good as those obtained by Holyoak's (1978) reference point model; Shoben, Cech, and Schwanenflugel's (1983) subtraction model; and Chumbley's (1986) model.

Moreover, there are reasons to suspect that the fit of the model is understated. As noted earlier, mean response times are based on single response times from each individual, and such numbers are notoriously unstable. Second, our estimates of relation strength are based not on frequencies in the real world but on frequencies in our corpus. Given the way in which our corpus was generated, it is undoubtedly the case that a more systematic sampling of combinations would have provided a more accurate estimate of relation strength.

Understanding Conceptual Combinations

The most controversial aspect of our model is the assumption that people know how modifiers are used. Although most theories do not claim such extensive knowledge about how concepts are used, such a claim is certainly not unprecedented. Such a claim, for example, is certainly consistent with the distributional assumptions made by connectionist models (e.g., Seidenberg, 1992). More specifically, there has been considerable recent work on verbs that suggests that people know not only what a concept means but how it is used (MacDonald, 1994; MacDonald, Pearlmutter, & Seidenberg, 1994; Trueswell, Tanenhaus, & Kello, 1993).

To take just one example, MacDonald et al. (1994) and MacDonald (1994) contrasted the verbs *fought* and *captured* in sentences like, "The ruthless dictator, fought/captured in the coup, was hated throughout the country." Although *captured* is often used as a reduced relative, *fought* is rarely used in this way; it is much more frequently used as a main verb. Consistent with the idea that people know this distributional information, participants in their study found reduced relatives that used *fought* much harder to understand.

Thus, there is some precedent for assuming that people can use distributional information. People know how some verbs are used; there is no reason to assume that they would not have similar distributional information at their disposal for modifiers as well.

One additional question is whether conceptual combinations are always interpreted by assigning a thematic relation to them. There are clearly counterexamples. First, some combinations are metaphors. An *ice teacher*, for instance, is unlikely to be a teacher who uses ice, but rather one who is interpersonally cold. Second, there are combinations like *skunk squirrel* (see Wisniewski, chap. 3) where the interpretation is likely to be a squirrel that has some attribute (like a white stripe) of a skunk.

We suggest, however, that these kinds of interpretations are secondary to the strategy of relation assignment. That is, people always try to assign a thematic relation to a combination; however, if they are unable to assign a relation, they seek a metaphorical or property-matching solution. This prediction could be easily tested experimentally. In any event, we suspect that these two strategies are relatively rare.

The Role of the Head Noun

Although the asymmetrically strong influence of the modifier was certainly not intuitively obvious to us, perhaps the most surprising finding was the absence of an effect of the head noun. Most accounts of which attributes are inherited by the combined concept (Hampton, 1987; Murphy, 1988; Wisniewski & Gentner, 1991) have argued for the primacy of the head noun over the modifier. As Murphy has argued, an *apartment dog* has most of the attributes of *dog* and very few of the attributes of *apartment.*

Thus, one should not interpret our results as demonstrating that there is no role for the head noun. On the contrary, there obviously is a role, as the work on attribute inheritance shows. What our results do indicate, however, is that the modifier is the component that guides the selection of the thematic relation.

Viewed in this way, the selection of the relation between the head noun and the modifier obviates the need for the distinction between predicating and non-predicating combinations. Predicating combinations are simply those that use the head noun IS modifier relation. We view this simplification as important because it eliminates the need for the processing system to decide at the outset whether the combination is predicating or otherwise.

SPECULATIONS ABOUT PRODUCTION

To this point, our chapter has focused on how people comprehend non-predicating combinations. It seems reasonable to inquire at this juncture whether we can use our CARIN model of comprehension as a starting point for an understanding of production processes.

One fact that any production account must recognize is that most of these combinations are novel. Although one can certainly argue that some of the combinations are familiar and, therefore, may have a separate lexical entry, it is certainly the case that combinations such as *plastics law*, *admiralty debate*, *fruit utensil*, and *wood furnace* are not in the lexicon of the average speaker. At the same time, it is clear that each of these combinations is readily interpretable.

But how do people produce these combinations? It appears to us that one might start with the modifier. For example, if one starts with a *plastic X*, then it is almost certainly an *X* made of plastic. One example of this kind of dominance of frequency information is that a *plastic book* is likely to be interpreted in this fashion even though a book about plastic is at least as plausible an interpretation.

Our speculation is that when people generate combinations, they generate them in a familiar way. That is, they are likely to generate combinations that use the modifier in a common thematic relation. Thus, for example, *software money* is likely to be generated when one wants to talk about funds earmarked for software and not to describe the genesis of dollars in the Bill Gates family fortune.

One could also speculate that using modifiers in uncommon ways requires a certain amount of creativity, perhaps because ready analogies are not available. Thus, according to this account, one could readily talk about a *wood lantern* because wood is often used in this "use" way. As in *wood stove* and *wood fire*, in which wood is used in a way similar to that in which it is used in *wood lantern*. On the other hand, *wood rash* should be relatively difficult to generate because examples of *wood X* that mean an *X* caused by wood are relatively rare.

In general, our suspicion is that people more commonly engage in "mundane" creativity as opposed to "extraordinary" creativity. Just as Cacciari, Levorato, and Cicogna (chap. 7) have found that the novel entities imagined by young children preserve most of the properties of standard categories, so too do most novel uses of concepts rely on standard relations. To take this argument one speculative step further, one might say that most creation of new concepts is a highly constrained application of an old and frequent relation to a new domain. Such speculation is consistent with Dunbar's (chap. 17) work on scientific reasoning that suggests that new ideas develop primarily from clear analogies to related domains.

CONCLUSION

Thematic relations matter. There are a large number of them in English, and some are clearly more common than others. However, the frequency that matters in conceptual combination is the frequency with which these relations are used with particular modifiers. Although we have considerable confidence that these conclusions are warranted for comprehension, such a claim is not much more than speculation with respect to production. Nevertheless, it would seem unlikely that thematic relations would play no role in the generation of conceptual combinations.

REFERENCES

Chomsky, N. (1965). *Aspects of a theory of syntax.* Cambridge, MA: MIT Press.

Chumbley, J. (1986). The roles of typicality, instance, dominance, and category dominance in verifying category membership. *Journal of Experimental Psychology: Learning, Memory, and Cognition, 12,* 257–267.

Clark, H. (1983). Making sense of nonce sense. In G. Flores d'Aracais & R. J. Jarvella (Eds.), *The process of language understanding.* New York: Wiley.

Downing, P. (1977). On the creation and use of English compound nouns. *Language, 53,* 810–842.

Gagné, C. L., & Shoben, E. J. (1997). Influence of thematic relations on the comprehension of modifier–noun combinations. *Journal of Experimental Psychology: Learning, Memory, and Cognition, 23,* 71–87.

Halff, H. M, Ortony, A., & Anderson, R. C. (1976). A context-sensitive representation of word meaning. *Memory and Cognition, 4,* 378–383.

Hampton, J. (1987). Inheritance of attributes in natural concept conjunctions. *Memory and Cognition, 15,* 55–71.

Holyoak, K. (1978). Comparative judgments with numerical reference points. *Cognitive Psychology, 10,* 203–243.

Levi, J. (1978). *The syntax and semantics of complex nominals.* San Diego, CA: Academic Press.

Luce, R. (1959). *Individual choice behavior.* New York: Wiley.

MacDonald, M. (1994). Probabilistic constraints and syntactic ambiguity resolution. *Language and Cognitive Processes, 9,* 157–201.

MacDonald, M., Pearlmutter, N., & Seidenberg, M. (1994). Lexical nature of syntactic ambiguity resolution. *Psychological Review, 4,* 676–703.

Murphy, G. (1988). Comprehending complex concepts. *Cognitive Science, 12,* 529–562.

Murphy, G. (1990). Noun phrase interpretation and conceptual combination. *Journal of Memory and Language, 29,* 259–288.

Rumelhart, D., & Abrahamsen, A. (1973). A model for analogical reasoning. *Cognitive Psychology, 15,* 346–378.

Sadler, D., & Shoben, E. (1993). Context effects on semantic domains as seen in analogy solutions. *Journal of Experimental Psychology: Learning, Memory, and Cognition, 19,* 128–147.

Seidenberg, M. (1992). Connectionism without tears. In S. Davis (Ed.), *Connectionism: Theory and practice* (pp. 84–122). Cambridge, England: Cambridge University Press.

Shoben, E. (1991). Predicating and nonpredicating combinations. In P. J. Schwanenflugal (Ed.), *The psychology of word meanings* (pp. 117–135). Hillsdale, NJ: Erlbaum.

Shoben, E., Cech, C., & Schwanenflugel, P. (1983). The role of subtractions and comparisons in comparative judgments involving numerical reference points. *Journal of Experimental Psychology: Human Perception and Performance, 9,* 226–241.

Smith, E., Osherson, D., Rips, L., & Keane, M. (1988). Combining prototypes: A selective modification model. *Cognitive Science, 12,* 485–527.

Trueswell, J., Tanenhaus, M., & Kello, C. (1993). Verb specific constraints in sentence processing: Separating effects of lexical preference from garden-paths. *Journal of Experimental Psychology: Learning, Memory, and Cognition, 19,* 528–553.

Whaley, C. (1978). Word–nonword classification time. *Journal of Verbal Learning and Verbal Behavior, 17,* 143–154.

Wisniewski, E., & Gentner, D. (1991). On the combinatorial semantics of noun pairs: Minor and major adjustments to meaning. In G. B. Simpson (Ed.), *Understanding word and sentence* (pp. 241–284). Amsterdam, The Netherlands: Elsevier Science.

3

Conceptual Combination: Possibilities and Esthetics

Edward J. Wisniewski

Much of language understanding involves combining concepts into new, coherent representations, as in understanding a sentence. In cognitive psychology, there has been much recent interest in one particular aspect of conceptual combination: how people interpret novel noun–noun combinations.[1] For example, one might interpret *frog bowl* as a bowl for housing pet frogs. People create novel combinations in order to specify referents of discourse contexts and to extend the vocabulary of their language (Downing, 1977; Gerrig & Murphy, 1992). Besides their role in language, the study of novel combinations can inform theories of concepts (Hampton, 1987; Markman & Wisniewski, in press; Medin & Shoben, 1988). For example, studies of conceptual combination have identified

I thank Doug Medin and Tom Ward for trenchant comments on a previous draft and Bob Dylan for providing some of the inspiration.

[1]Many combinations involve more than two nouns (e.g., FBI shoe print expert). Although researchers typically have not examined these combinations, the motivations for their use and the processes involved in understanding them are probably similar to those involved in understanding noun–noun combinations. On the other hand, multiple noun combinations introduce other ambiguities into understanding such as determining which noun modifies another. Whereas the leftmost noun typically modifies the rightmost (head) noun in a noun–noun combination, this generalization does not hold for multiple noun–noun combinations. For example, although *shoe* modifies *print* in FBI shoe print expert, *FBI* modifies *expert.*

ways that prototype theories need to be extended (Medin & Shoben, 1988) as well as differences between the conceptual structure of superordinates and basic level concepts (Markman & Wisniewski, in press).

In general, the creation of new concepts by combining existing ones is a powerful and common way of expanding knowledge. For example, a recent newspaper article used the phrase *car boat* to refer to a new kind of boat that is also a car. Such a phrase provides access to a wealth of inferences that one can reasonably draw about this novel entity that do not necessarily need to be empirically derived. There is also a sense of creativity in bringing together disparate concepts to form new concepts that people readily understand (e.g., as in the use of *boomerang flu* to refer to a flu that goes away and comes back, or *bait car* to refer to a car that is used to catch carjackers). However, in psychology, formal models of concept learning primarily acquire new concepts by applying empirical methods to many examples of a category (Wisniewski, 1995). There has been considerably less emphasis on how existing concepts are combined and modified to produce new ones.

There are at least three levels at which one can understand conceptual combination. Marr (1982) referred to these levels as the computational, algorithmic, and implementational levels. The *computational* level addresses both the goal or purpose of conceptual combination (why people combine concepts) and what results from combining concepts (the output of conceptual combination). The *algorithmic* level describes procedures for how concepts are combined to produce the output. Most psychological approaches to understanding conceptual combination have been formulated at this level (Cohen & Murphy, 1984; Heit & Barsalou, 1996; Martin & Billman, 1994; Shoben, 1993; Shoben & Gagne, this volume; Smith, Osherson, Rips, & Keane, 1988; Thagard, 1984). Finally, the *implementational* level specifies how the algorithm is realized in a physical device, such as a human brain or a digital computer. These levels are not independent and an explanation at one level can constrain that at another level. For example, an algorithmic account of conceptual combination depends on knowing what the output of that algorithm should be (an aspect of the computational level account).

In this chapter, I provide a computational level account of conceptual combination and relate this account to present algorithmic (processing) level descriptions. One conclusion is that models fall short in explaining the basic phenomena that characterize conceptual combination. Perhaps of greatest importance, concepts change when they combine, and current models do not go far enough in carrying out and representing this change. Constrained by this computational level account, I then provide an algorithmic level sketch of how concepts combine and change. This sketch does not constitute a full-fledged model, and more empirical work is needed to flesh out the details. However, I believe that my account is an advance over current views and that it captures essential ingredients that must go into a more comprehensive model. In particular, this account highlights the importance of two additional processes (comparison and construction) that have not been emphasized in the research on conceptual combination. Finally, I suggest that the interpretation of nominal metaphors also involves comparison and construction processes. However, psychological models of metaphor understanding emphasize one or the other of these processes, but not both. A central theme of this chapter is that conceptual change does not usually involve the straightforward transfer of knowledge from one concept or domain to another. Rather, knowledge in one concept guides the construction of new knowledge in another concept. In this sense, conceptual change is creative in going beyond simple addition. This view is the rule rather than the exception. A fundamental challenge to models of novel language understanding is specifying processes that use knowledge in one domain to construct knowledge in another domain.

A COMPUTATIONAL LEVEL ACCOUNT: WHY PEOPLE COMBINE CONCEPTS

Conceptual combination occurs in a communicative context and serves at least three goals. First, people create novel combinations in order to designate significantly new categories: ones that have important, enduring characteristics that distinguish them from similar categories. For example, in contrast to fish bowls and cereal bowls, a frog bowl is typically used to contain frogs and may also have an island-like glass structure in its middle for this purpose. Second, combinations are often used to convey information in a concise and efficient way. For example, *football parking* designates an area for parking one's car while attending a football game. Even though this phrase is somewhat elliptical readers generally understand what it means. Third, combinations function as anaphora in that they are used to refer back to a previous referent in a discourse context. For example, after describing a man who received the first artificial heart (Barney Clark), a speaker may use the phrase *heart man* to assert new information about this man, and listeners can determine its referent and construct its interpretation (Gerrig & Murphy, 1992). The use of anaphora helps to link information to the appropriate referent and thus establish cohesion in discourse contexts.

In achieving these goals, the speaker and listener implicitly assume certain constraints on the production and interpretation of a novel combination. First, the combination refers to a category that differs in some way from other categories named by the (rightmost) head noun: Frog bowls are different from other types of bowls. Second, the source of this difference comes from the (leftmost) modifier noun: In contrast to other bowls, frog bowls house frogs. Third, despite this difference, the referent of the combination shares important commonalities with the head noun category: Although frog bowls are different from other bowls, they are still containers and shaped like other bowls. In general, these constraints are consistent with basic goals of communication such as being informative and relevant, and avoiding ambiguity (Grice, 1975; Wilson & Sperber, 1981).

It would appear that speakers and listeners adhere to these constraints in producing and interpreting novel combinations. Imagine how bizarre a novel phrase that did not follow these constraints would sound. For example, suppose that *skunk squirrel* referred to any squirrel (violating the first constraint) or referred to a special kind of squirrel whose specialness had nothing to do with skunks (violating the second constraint), or did not refer to squirrels in any sort of way (violating the third constraint).

Why do people produce novel combinations that obey these constraints? Typically, people need to refer to changes in their environment: a newly discovered disease, a newly created product, an important change to something old. In general, people create change by modifying the familiar in small steps (leaving much constant), and they attempt to understand and refer to change by relating it to the familiar (Murphy, this volume; Ward, 1994; Weber & Dixon, 1989). Using a novel combination captures both constancy and change. For example, recently in a grocery store, *seafood sausage* was used to refer to patties of ground up seafood. In this case, people can use the concepts *seafood* and *sausage* and their interaction to infer properties of sausage that are likely to remain constant (shape, size, edibleness, method of cooking) and those that are likely to change (composition, calorie level, cooking time).

In addition to explaining why people combine concepts, a computational level account specifies the output or result of conceptual combination. Determining what people compute when they combine concepts defines the generality to be attained by a model. Furthermore, knowing what people compute constrains a model's processing assumptions. For example, a psychologically plausible model should not compute things that people do not compute (cf. Pinker & Prince's, 1988, critique of Rumelhart & McClelland's, 1986, connectionist model of learning the past tense of English verbs).

A COMPUTATIONAL LEVEL ACCOUNT: THE OUTPUT OF COMBINING CONCEPTS

One way to determine the output that results from combining concepts is to examine individuals' interpretations of novel combinations. In many studies, I have asked research participants to assume that they have heard a novel combination in a conversation and to describe its most plausible meaning (Markman & Wisniewski, in press; Wisniewski, 1996a; Wisniewski & Gentner, 1991; Wisniewski & Love, 1996; Wisniewsk & Markman, 1993). The combinations are novel in the sense that they do not occur as lexicalized entries in dictionaries and people have generally not heard or seen them before. In many cases they were created by arbitrarily or randomly pairing their constituents, which generally produces novel combinations. Although the combinations are novel, their constituents name common, familiar things including human-made artifacts, plants or their parts, substances, abstract terms, and events. In these studies, participants typically proceed through the task at their own pace, writing down meanings for 15 to 20 novel combinations. From these studies, I have collected a very large and fairly representative set of interpretations involving approximately 500 novel combinations with 10 to 20 interpretations per combination (Wisniewski, 1995).

Kinds of Combinations

Analyses of these interpretations suggest that people combine concepts in three basic ways (Wisniewski, 1996a). Two of these ways, relation linking and property interpretation, are very common among novel combinations. *Relation-linking* interpretations involve a relation between the referents of the modifier and head concepts. For example, people sometimes interpret *robin snake* as "a snake that eats robins." In *property* interpretations, people assert that one or more properties of the modifier concept apply in some way to the head concept, as in "snake with a red underbelly," for *robin snake.* A third less frequent type of interpretation is *hybridization.* These interpretations refer to a combination of the constituents (e.g., a *robin canary* is "a bird that is a cross between the two—half robin and half canary") or to a conjunction of the constituents (e.g., a *musician painter* could refer to someone who is both a musician and a painter). Note that logically, there could be other kinds of interpretations. For example, a combination could refer to a disjunction of its constituents. However, this combination type and others do not appear (at least in English).

There are important conceptual distinctions between these combination types—for example, if one pictures a robin snake, interpreted by relation linking as "a snake that eats a robin," one sees a snake eating a robin. However, in picturing a robin snake, interpreted by property construction as "a snake with a red underbelly," one sees only a snake (whose underbelly has a color similar to that of a robin). There are also important conceptual distinctions between hybrids and relation-linking and property interpretation types—for example, a *robin canary*, interpreted with a property as a "canary with a red breast" or by relation linking as a "canary that preys on robins" is a canary, but a *robin canary* that is a cross between the two is not just a canary.

In these studies, I have focused on novel combinations in contrast to familiar ones (e.g., shoe box, bookstore) because it is more difficult to infer interpretation processes from the latter. Meanings of familiar combinations have often been modified or augmented after their initial creation (Levi, 1978). For example, eggplant once referred to a small, white, egg-shaped vegetable but now typically refers to a larger, purple, oblong vegetable (Elliot, 1988). Nevertheless, it is easy to find familar examples of these combinations, and linguistic classifications of familiar combinations are generally consistent with the claim of three basic types (see Wisniewski, 1996a, in press; Wisniewski & Love, 1996, for many familiar examples of these types).

Similarity Effects

The similarity between the modifier and head concepts strongly affects the kind of interpretation that is produced. In particular, a robust finding is that combinations with highly similar constituents (e.g., *robin canary*, *magazine newspaper*) almost always yield property interpretations or hybrids. My colleagues and I have obtained this result in many studies and have never failed to replicate this finding (Markman & Wisniewski, in press; Wisniewski, 1996a; Wisniewski & Love, 1996; Wisniewski & Markman, 1993). In one study (Wisniewski, 1996a; Experiment 2), 92% of 320 interpretations of 32 highly similar combinations were interpreted using these two strategies. For example, some property interpretations included "horse that produces milk," for *cow horse* and "newspaper with glossy ads" for *magazine newspaper*.

When the constituents of a combination are not similar, people are more likely to interpret the combination by relation linking (e.g., *apartment piano* is often interpreted as "a piano found in an apartment " and *cow cabbage* is often interpreted as "cabbage eaten by cows"). Also, when people do interpret dissimilar combinations using properties, their meanings are more likely to involve emergent properties (i.e., properties not represented in either constituent, Wilkenfeld, 1995; Wisniewski, 1991a, 1991b). People can be quite creative in this regard. For example, one participant interpreted *ant canary* as "a canary with two feathers on its head which look like antennae." As another example, individuals sometimes interpret *rake pencil* as "a pencil with multiple lead points."

Referential Scope

The use of a novel combination indicates one or more new referents. In many combinations, these referents are subsets of the categories typically named by the constituents of a combination. For example, people might refer to a kind of jar that is used to hold very small books as a *book jar.* The books and jars referred to by *book jar* are subsets of the things that one would typically name with the terms *book* and *jar.* In many respects, this assumption is consistent with the goals of the computational level account. A speaker who uses the typical referent of a noun may be more likely to succeed in conveying what he or she intends the listener to understand.

Nevertheless, people are more creative and flexible in their interpretation of a noun's referent. The potential *referential scope* of a noun is broader. First, as implied by property interpretations, people construe the modifier noun as referring to a property or characteristic of the thing named by the noun rather than the thing itself. For example, a common interpretation of *skunk squirrel* is "a squirrel with black and white stripes." In this case, the referent of *skunk* is one of its properties and not the things that people call skunks. Second, people can treat a noun as referring to a representation of a thing rather than the thing itself. For example, a not infrequent interpretation of *moose pencil* is "a pencil with an eraser that looked like a moose." This interpretation refers to a representation of *moose* rather than to a moose as in "pencil stepped on by a moose." Finally, people also interpret nouns as referring to things associated with a constituent, such as something that is thematically related to the constituent. For example, people often interpret *tiger chair* as "a chair made of tiger skin."

This flexibility is not a rare phenomenon and occurs in many familiar combinations (see Wisniewski, 1996a, for examples). Furthermore, this flexibility is evident in a major theory of metaphor understanding that assumes that nouns refer both to things and to prototypical properties of those things (Glucksberg & Keysar, 1990; Glucksberg, Manfredi, & McGlone, this volume). For example, in the literal statement "my job at the jail," *jail* refers to a jail, but in the nominal methaphor "my job is a jail," it refers to properties exemplified by jails such as "confining."

Adopting this broader referential scope for a noun helps achieve the communicative goals of conceptual combination: The use of novel combinations of familiar terms efficiently captures new situations. For example, using *artist* to refer to the works of an artist allows someone to use the novel phrase *artist collector* to efficiently refer to a collector of the works of an artist (see also Nunberg, 1979). People almost always derive this meaning in the absence of any context. Without this flexibility, people might have to use a longer and perhaps more awkward sounding phrase, such as "the collector of the works of the artist." The use of these concise labels would not be possible if people could not flexibly expand the referential scope of a noun.

At the same time, this extended referential power has limits and is constrained. In general, people construe a noun's referent in only a few basic ways, and the referents are conceptually related to the noun's typical category. That is, the extended referential scope of a noun is limited to a property, representation, or thematic associate of the typical referent of the noun.

Conceptual Change

Conceptual combination is a process that involves conceptual change or rerepresentation. For example, consider *zebra clam*, interpreted as a "clam with stripes." Combining *zebra* and *clam* produces a new concept that is a modification of *clam*. What is the nature of that change? Of importance, the meaning of the new concept *zebra clam* is not "a copy of zebra's stripes," which has been added to the meaning of *clam*. Rather the stripes of a zebra clam are shorter and thinner than those of a zebra, and they run along the outside of a clam shell and not a zebra body. In a sense, a property in the modifier acts as a source of information for instantiating a new version of that property in the head concept. The new version is constructed to fit constraints specified by both the modifier and head concepts. For example, the stripes of a zebra clam might show an alternating dark and light pattern (as they do in a zebra) but they also might be shorter and thinner than those of a zebra to be consistent with the size of a clam. This example illustrates that combining concepts can go beyond the simple copying of knowledge over from one concept to another. Instead, conceptual combination is creative in that new knowledge emerges out of interactions between different representations.

Of importance, this construction process is quite common. Many novel combinations are interpreted in this manner (Wisniewski, 1996b). It is also easy to find familiar combinations that refer to entities having a property resembling but not identical to that of the modifier. For example, the shapes of *butterfly chair*, *butterfly valve*, and *butterfly clip* are variations on the shape of a butterfly. *Zebra mussel*, *zebra fish*, *zebra wood*, and *zebra finch* refer to objects with different variants of a zebra's stripes. *Accordion bag* and *accordian pleat* refer to objects with different instantiations of an accordion's folds (see Wisniewski, in press, for other examples). Presumably, when people first coined these phrases they had to determine that a property of the "object to be named" was related to one of another object. For example, in wanting to create a new name for a mussel with stripes, they had to determine that the stripes were related to those of a zebra (as opposed to those of the American flag, a barber pole, or a tiger). To see such a relation, people may have had to invoke the construction process.

Summary

An extensive analysis of the meanings of novel combinations suggests that there are three basic kinds of interpretations. The similarity between the constituents strongly affects which kind of interpretation is selected: Combinations with highly similar constituents are almost always interpreted either by property construction or by hybridization. People are also flexible in how they interpret the referent of a noun. Although people interpret a noun as referring to the object or thing typically named by that noun, the referent can also be a property, representation, or a thematic associate of the object. Of importance, combining concepts can involve property construction in which a property of the modifier is used to guide the creation of a new property in the combination. Concepts are not combined simply by adding a copy of a property of the modifier to the new combination.

ALGORITHMIC LEVEL: CURRENT MODELS OF HOW PEOPLE COMBINE CONCEPTS

There are two processing accounts of how people combine concepts, which are fairly broad in scope: the thematic relations approach and the schema approach.[2] Both accounts assume that the meaning of a combination involves a relation between the referents of the constituents. In the *thematic relations* view, nouns are combined by determining an abstract relation that holds between the nouns (Coolen, van Jaarsveld, & Schreuder, 1991; Shoben, 1993; Shoben & Gagne, this volume). These approaches assume that there are a relatively small set of such relations (perhaps one or two dozen). In evaluating this view, researchers have typically drawn on the relations that linguists have used to classify familiar combinations (e.g., Downing, 1977; Levi, 1978). For example, Levi (1978) suggested that 16 relations can be used to classify the meanings of most familiar combinations (e.g., the *for* relation, plant food; the *cause* relation, electric shock; the *make* relation, etc.).

The most developed view of the thematic relations approach is the work by Shoben (1993) and his colleagues (see Shoben & Gagne, this volume). They assume that a noun's combinatorial history influences inter-

[2]I have excluded from this discussion models that describe how people interpret hybrid combinations—those that refer to a conjunction of their constituents, such as *pet fish* (Hampton, 1987; Martin & Billman, 1994; Thagard, 1984). I have also excluded a model of how certain adjectives are combined with nouns (Smith, Osherson, Rips, & Keane, 1988). In general, it is not possible to straightforwardly extend these models to account for other kinds of combinations (see Murphy, 1988; Wisniewski & Gentner, 1991, for arguments).

pretation of a novel phrase involving that noun. That is, people use the distributional knowledge of how nouns have been previously combined to interpret a novel combination. For example, when *mountain* is used as a modifier it typically instantiates a locative relation (e.g., mountain stream, mountain resort, mountain goat) and is only rarely involved in other types of relations (e.g., mountain range). Therefore, people may interpret a novel combination such as *mountain fish* as "fish found in the mountains" by using their knowledge that *mountain* has been previously combined with other nouns in a similar manner. A second assumption is that the modifier's combinatorial history has more influence on interpretation (because it precedes the head noun). In a series of studies, Shoben and Gagne (this volume) show that the time to judge the sensibility of a novel combination is a function of the relative frequency of abstract relations associated with the modifier noun rather than with the head noun.

In the *schema approach*, a concept is viewed as a schema or frame. A schema represents the basic knowledge that people have about a place, event, or object which has been acquired from everyday interactions with these things or from other sources of knowledge such as written materials. Schemas represent this knowledge in the form of slots and fillers that refer to the dimensions of the entity, along with their typical or default values (Minsky, 1975; Rumelhart, 1980). For example, a schema for *elephant* might include the slots *color* and *habitat* and the typical fillers *gray* and *zoo*, respectively. Schema-based models link concepts by relations through a process of slot filling (Brachman, 1978; Cohen & Murphy, 1984; Murphy, 1988; Shoben, 1993). For example, according to the concept specialization model (Cohen & Murphy, 1984; Murphy, 1988), one interprets a noun–noun combination by filling a slot of the head noun with the modifier noun. According to this account, one might interpret *robin snake* by filling a slot in *snake* (e.g., the slot *eats*) with the modifier concept *robin* to produce the meaning "a snake that eats robins." As a result, the filled slot captures a relation between the objects denoted by the modifier and head concepts. To explain which slot is selected to be filled by the modifier, these models emphasize the importance of constraints on the fillers of a slot. That is, a slot specifies preconditions that must be met by a potential filler. For example, the filler of the *eats* slot of *snake* would have to be edible, whereas the filler of the *contains* slot of *box* would have to be smaller than a box. These constraints are derived from people's typical interactions with the referents of concepts.

Although the thematic relations and schema views are similar in assuming that interpretation involves linking one referent to another through a relation, there are two important differences between the approaches. First, they emphasize different levels of abstraction in characterizing the meanings of combinations. Whereas the abstract relations view postulates that a relatively small set of very general relations exhausts the ways that nouns can be combined, the schema approach does not make an analogous claim for slots. Rather, slots represent more specific relations. Second, the thematic relations view emphasizes a noun's combinatorial history in determining the interpretation of a novel combination, whereas the schema view emphasizes constraints on slots in determining meanings.

There are several reasons to believe that the schema approach better accounts for how people combine concepts. First, the use of more specific slots rather than abstract relations captures distinctions between meanings to which people are clearly sensitive. For example, in the abstract relations view, the novel combinations *paint spoon* and *blueberry spoon* would share the FOR relation between their constituents. However, the for relation fails to capture crucial differences between people's interpretations of these combinations: A paint spoon is used to stir paint (and not to eat paint), but a blueberry spoon is used to eat blueberries (and not to stir them). These distinctions seem to be part of the basic, core meaning of such novel combinations that arise from the specific knowledge captured in the constituent concepts.

The schema approach could capture these differences by assuming that the concept *spoon* represents the different functions of a spoon (*stirring* and *eating*) and the slots associated with these functions. For example, both functions would have agent, instrument, and object slots along with appropriate constraints (e.g., the filler of the object slot in *eating* must be edible). In *paint spoon*, *paint* would fill the object slot of *stirring* but not the object slot of *eating* because paint can be stirred but is not edible. In *blueberry spoon, blueberry* would fill the object slot of *eating* but not the object slot of *stirring* because blueberries are edible and cannot be stirred.

Second, the thematic relations view overly emphasizes the role of a noun's combinatorial history in determining meaning. On the one hand, there is some evidence that how a noun combines with another is influenced by how it has been previously combined (Shoben & Gagne, this volume). However, combinatorial history may be more of an effect rather than a cause. For example, most familiar combinations of the form *X box* (in which *X* stands for another noun) have the meaning "box that contains *X*" (Urdang & Abate, 1983). However, it cannot be the frequency of these past meanings per se that determines whether people will interpret a novel *X box* in the same way. Some combinations are not interpreted in this manner (e.g., *skyscraper box*). Rather, as emphasized in the schema approach, interpretation involves figuring out whether a meaning is plausible (e.g., can *X* fit into a box?). That most familiar *X boxes* have the interpretation, "box that contains *X*" more likely reflects the intuition that there are few constraints on what can be contained in a box (as most things can be enclosed). The function of a noun's combinatorial history is probably to suggest candidate meanings that previously have been useful (and thus narrow down the search space), but most of the work in interpretation is determining a plausible meaning and creating a new representation.

In summary, two general proposals have been offered to explain how people combine concepts. The schema approach appears to be a more plausible psychological model. However, the computational level account suggests that both the thematic relations and schema views do not go far enough in explaining how people combine concepts. There are three major areas where such approaches are incomplete. First, both approaches focus on processes that derive relational interpretations of combinations and have not addressed the derivation of property and hybrid interpretations. Yet, property interpretations are common for many novel combinations (Wisniewski, 1996a) and not infrequent among familiar combinations (Wisniewski & Love, 1996). As I suggest later, property and hybrid interpretations require processes that differ from those that determine relations between the modifier and head concepts. Second, current approaches assume that the referential scope of a noun is fairly narrow: It is taken to refer to the object or thing typically named by that noun. In contrast, a noun can refer to a property, representation, or thematic associate of the noun's typical referent.

Third, the models capture relatively small changes in representation that result when concepts combine. In the thematic relations approach, a new concept is created by linking one constituent to another through a relation. Being linked to another constituent is the only sense in which a constituent's representation undergoes modification. In schema approaches, a new concept is created by replacing the typical value of a slot with a new value (Cohen & Murphy, 1984; Murphy, 1988; Smith et al., 1988). One schema approach, the concept specialization model, goes further than slot value replacement by postulating an additional stage of processing that also involves conceptual change (Cohen & Murphy, 1984; Murphy, 1988). After slot value replacement, people use their world knowledge to elaborate or "fix up" this concept by adding attributes to a combination. For example, in interpreting *apartment dog* as "a dog that lives in an apartment," people may recall actual dogs that they know and use the memories to modify the combination by adding properties such as "yappy and neurotic" (Murphy, 1988; p. 540). Thus, this model's notion of conceptual change not only involves slot value replacement but also adds new attributes to the combination. However, as I have suggested, conceptual change does not generally result from adding attributes.

UPPING THE ANTE: TOWARD A COMPREHENSIVE MODEL

The task of algorithmically specifying how people combine concepts is a difficult one. In this section, I describe an approach to conceptual combination that attempts to capture a broader range of psychological phenomena. My description does not constitute a full-fledged model. However, it identifies what appear to be necessary ingredients that must go into constructing a model.

Representational Assumptions

On the basis of the phenomena that I have presented, it is clear that a model has no hope of succeeding if it uses simple representations of nouns. Much research suggests that concepts have complex representational structure (Barsalou, 1993; Barsalou & Hale, 1992; Cohen & Murphy, 1984; Gentner, 1989; Murphy, 1988; Ortony, 1979; Palmer, 1978; Wisniewski & Medin, 1994). In keeping with the strengths of the schema approach, I assume that a noun is a schema that consists of slots and fillers. Of importance, the fillers of the schema can themselves be representationally complex, also consisting of schemas with slots and fillers (cf. Ortony, 1979). As a result, processes that operate on a schema could be recursively applied to its fillers (see also Barsalou & Hale, 1992). A noun schema represents a variety of knowledge about its referent, including its typical properties (e.g., an object would have size, shape, color, parts, and so on) as well as the everyday interactions that the referent has with other entitites. I refer to these interactions as *scenarios.* In the latter case, for example, there could be a *function* slot in *soap* with the filler *cleaning.* This filler would be a scenario with the possible roles or slots of *agent, instrument,* and *recipient* and the typical fillers *person, soap,* and *solid object,* respectively. In this sense, the scenario representation of such everyday interactions is analogous to verb representations that describe actions, events, or states (cf. Fillmore, 1968; Levin, 1993; Schank, 1972). Finally, there are typically interconnections between components of a schema that capture dependencies between slots and fillers. For example, a complex property of *hammer,* such as "for pounding in nails," depends on the hammer having a handle, being grasped and lifted in a certain way, having a blunt, solid end, and so on.

At a general level, there are two basic steps in combining concepts, although these steps merge with each other and there is no clear border between them. First, people must determine what knowledge will initiate the formation of the new combination. That is, they must figure out which property of the modifier to integrate into the head noun or which relation will link the modifier and head concepts. People must then create a new representation. For example, the common interpretation of *fork spoon* as "a spoon with prongs" involves identifying the property "has prongs" of the modifier *fork* as the candidate property for guiding the construction of a new property in *fork spoon.* On the basis of participants' interpretations, the new representation typically corresponds to a spoon with prongs on the opposite end from the spoon's bowl or a spoon with short prongs emanating from the tip of the bowl (as in a spork or runcible spoon). Below, I suggest that different processes are involved in property interpretation and relation linking.

Identifying Potential Properties

Deriving a property interpretation requires finding a *difference* between the modifier and head concepts that forms the basis of the property that will be constructed in the head concept. This claim follows from a computational level goal of conceptual combination: the need to create a new category differing in some significant way from the category referred to by the head noun and whose difference is related in some way to the modifier.

The need to find a difference raises three logical questions: How do people determine this difference, why does this difference (and not some other one) form the basis for the new combination, and where in the head concept is the difference integrated? For example, to interpret *zebra horse* as "a horse with stripes," people must determine that zebras have stripes but horses do not and therefore that this difference could form the basis of the interpretation. In general, people are not sensitive to the absence of information, and thus concepts do not explicitly represent the absence of properties (e.g., see Nisbett & Ross, 1980, for evidence). People also tend to select this particular difference for the interpretation of *zebra horse* and not other possible differences (e.g., lives versus does not live in Africa). Finally, people believe that a zebra horse is one with stripes that run down the sides of the zebra horse's body and neck just as they do in a zebra. They do not, for example, think that the stripes of a zebra horse are on its tail. Thus, the difference is integrated into certain parts of the representation and not others.

Finding Differences and Integrating Them in Concepts

One can begin to address these questions by assuming that people use a comparison process to align or put into correspondence the structure of the modifier and head concepts (Wisniewski, 1996a, 1996b; Wisniewski & Gentner, 1991; Wisniewski & Markman, 1993). This assumption was inspired by some models of metaphor and analogy understanding that have emphasized the importance of comparison (Gentner, 1983, 1989; Holyoak & Thagard, 1989). By aligning the structure that is common to the head and modifier concepts, people find differences that then form the basis of an interpretation (cf. Markman & Gentner, 1993). The idea is that any pair of concepts will have both commonalities and differences. Finding commonalities leads to finding differences because commonalities are interconnected or related to differences. To illustrate, consider again *zebra horse.* Roughly speaking, one puts the representation of a horse's body into correspondence with the representation of a zebra's body because they are similarly shaped and because they have similar conceptual relations to similar components. (Similar, vertically oriented legs are connected to a similar underside of the body at similar places.) By aligning this common structure, one finds an important difference between zebras and horses (having versus not having stripes).

Besides determining differences between concepts, the comparison process suggests where a property can be integrated into the representation of the combination. For example, in placing the body and neck of *horse* into correspondence with the body and neck of *zebra* and noting a difference (having versus not having stripes), the comparison process has determined where the stripes can be incorporated into *zebra horse.* (If a zebra only had stripes on its tail, the comparison process would suggest that a zebra horse only had stripes on its tail.)

There is much evidence that people use the commonalities between mental representations to find differences. Markman and Gentner (1993) asked research participants to list commonalities and differences of word pairs. Not surprisingly, participants listed more commonalities for pairs of similar words than for pairs of dissimilar words. However, the reverse did not hold: Participants did not list more differences for dissimilar pairs than for similar pairs. Instead, they (somewhat paradoxically) listed more differences for the similar pairs, and importantly, the differences were conceptually related to the commonalities (see also Gentner & Markman,

1994; Markman & Wisniewski, in press). For example, when participants listed "has wheels" as a commonality of car and motorcycle, they also tended to list "has four wheels versus two wheels" as a difference. Of importance, there is evidence that people use a comparison process in combining concepts (Wisniewski, 1996a).

There may be a variety of ways (not necessarily mutually exclusive) in which the comparison process is instantiated (Wisniewski, 1996a, discussed the possibilities). The major point to be made is that such a process is necessary whatever the actual mechanism is that carries it out. For example, I have described the comparison process as if it aligns one mental representation with another to find a difference. However, as an alternative, a property of the modifier might be accessible prior to the comparison process. For example, a linguistic context might indicate the property of the modifier that is relevant to the novel combination (cf. Gerrig & Murphy, 1992), or a prototypical property of the modifier might be rapidly activated on reading the modifier (cf. Barsalou, 1982; Glucksberg & Keysar, 1990). In these cases, comparison is still necessary to establish where the property is to be integrated into the head concept. For example, even though "having stripes" might be highly accessible on reading *zebra*, people still must determine how it fits into *horse*. It is the correspondences between the bodies and necks of zebras and horses that suggest that the stripes run alongside the neck and body of a zebra horse. These correspondences are determined by the comparison process. Furthermore, the comparison process may also be necessary to establish that the property of the modifier is not already present in the head noun concept. For example, a salient property of zebras is their shape, yet this property would not form the basis of an interpretation of *zebra horse*, as horses have a very similar shape. The comparison process identifies this commonality and thus prevents it from being used in the interpretation.

Selecting a Difference

In general, there are multiple differences between concepts. At least several factors influence which difference is selected. One factor is the discourse setting that may suggest the relevant difference. Another factor is a property's cue and category validity. The *cue validity* of a property with respect to a category is the conditional probability that something belongs to a category given that it has the property. For example, given that something has wings, it is very probable that it is a bird (although it could be a bat or an insect). The *category validity* of a property with respect to a category is the conditional probability that something has the property given that it is in the category. For example, given that something is a bird, it is very probable that it has wings. When people derive property interpretations, they tend to select properties that are high in cue and category validity (Wisniewski, in press).

This finding makes sense given the communicative goals of the computational level account. Properties high in cue and category validity are representative of the category and distinguish it from other categories. A property with perfect cue and category validity unambiguously identifies the members of the category. Therefore, in cooperative communication, a listener is most likely to think of properties high in cue and category validity in understanding a novel combination, and speakers may construct combinations with these properties in mind.

Of course, cue and category validity cannot be the only factors that determine selection. Appealing solely to these factors predicts interpretations of combinations that people never give. For example, people would probably never literally interpret *fork tennis balls* as "tennis balls with prongs" or as "a package of four tennis balls" even though these interpretations are derived from a property of *fork* that is very high in cue and category validity (i.e., "has four prongs"). Again, the communicative goals of the computational level account constrain selection. The interpretation "tennis balls with prongs" compromises the functionality of *tennis balls* and may result in a referent that is outside the acceptable scope for *tennis balls.* On the flip side, the interpretation "package of four tennis balls" may stretch people's ability to see the connection between the "has four prongs" property of *fork* and the "package of four tennis balls" meaning of *fork tennis balls.* In this case, "has four prongs" is used to construct a new property in *fork tennis balls* that preserves so little of the "has four prongs" that it lies outside the acceptable referential scope of "has four prongs."

These constraints, coupled with the comparison process, provide the beginning of an algorithmic account of property construction. To illustrate, I return to *fork spoon* and provide a more detailed account of how it is interpreted as "a spoon with prongs" (see Wisniewski, in press, for more examples). People could begin by aligning the handle of *fork* with the handle of *spoon*, and the end of *fork* with the end of *spoon* and note an important difference: Forks have prongs on their ends but spoons have "little bowls" on their ends (of course, other variations on the comparison process are possible, as noted earlier). The comparison process identifies where in the representation of *spoon* the property "has prongs" can be incorporated (on the end of *spoon*). However, there is a conflict between mentally connecting this property to the *end* of *spoon* and staying within the referential scope of *spoon*. In particular, one cannot mentally replace *little bowl* with *prongs* or mentally add the full length prongs to the end of the little bowl because these manipulations would create fork spoons, which functionally are forks but not spoons (thus violating communicative goals of the computational level account). People can resolve this conflict by mentally attaching the prongs to the end of the little bowl and shortening them (as in a runcible spoon or a *spork*). Alternatively, they could mentally attach the prongs to the top end of the spoon. In these cases, the prongs of a fork spoon are similar but not identical to those of a fork: They are either attached to an end that is opposite to the little bowl or they are shorter and attached to the end of the little bowl. Furthermore, the attachment to the opposite end or the shortening preserves the function of a spoon while still yielding a property that resembles the one from which it originated.

Identifying Plausible Relations

In contrast to comparing the modifier and head noun representations in order to find an important difference that forms the basis of a new property, finding a relation between constituents amounts to constructing a plausible scenario involving the constituents. In this case, a plausible scenario is one in which each constituent is bound to a different role within the same scenario. For example, a plausible interpretation of *truck soap* is "soap for cleaning trucks" because *truck* can be bound to the recipient role of *cleaning* (i.e., the thing being cleaned) and *soap* to the instrument role (what is used to do the cleaning).

Clearly, a model of conceptual combination must assign and bind constituents to plausible roles in a scenario. However, analogous to property construction, the exact details of such a role assignment process are not well understood, and they remain an issue for future research. In assigning a constituent to a role, the process must determine the fit between the role and the constituent. Like the previously described schema approach (e.g., Murphy, 1988), fit is based on how well a constituent matches the preconditions of the role. If there is a sufficient match, the constituent is assigned to that role. However, examining how people combine concepts suggests that role fitting can be more interactive than suggested by the schema approach. That is, rather than finding a plausible role for a constituent, the constituent may be modified to plausibly fit a role. For example, a frequent interpretation of *robin termite* is "a termite that eats robin nests" (Wisniewski, 1996a). In this case, people construe *robin* in such a way that it plausibly fits the "what is eaten" role of the *eats* scenario (*robin nest* fits the constraints of what termites eat, whereas *robin* does not). As another example, *elephant box* is sometimes interpreted as "a very large, sturdy box for containing elephants" (Wisniewski, 1996a). In this case, a typical box is modified in such a way that *elephant* can plausibly fit the "what is contained" role of the *contains* scenario.

Plausible Properties Versus Plausible Relations

Up to this point, I have suggested that there are two different processes involved in combining concepts: a process that identifies and constructs properties and a process that links concepts by relations. One issue concerns the relationship between these processes. Do they operate concurrently or is there a preferred strategy for interpreting novel combinations? Some researchers have suggested that identifying and constructing properties is a last resort strategy—one that is used only when the constituents of a combination do not fit into a plausible scenario (Downing, 1977; Shoben & Gagne, this volume; Wisniewski & Gentner, 1991). Although more research is needed to resolve this issue, recent work calls into question the "scenario first" hypothesis. In particular, which process dominates depends on factors such as the similarity between constituents and whether a process has succeeded in the previous context (Wisniewski & Love, 1996).

THE RELATION BETWEEN CONCEPTUAL COMBINATION AND NOMINAL METAPHORS

Recently, I have argued that property interpretations of noun–noun combinations are similar to interpretations of nominal metaphor interpretations (Wisniewski, in press). Nominal metaphors are language constructions of the form *X is a Y*, in which *X* and *Y* refer to nouns. A nominal metaphor can be rephrased as a noun–noun combination by reversing the order of the nouns and dropping the form of *be* to produce the phrase *YX*. Just as the modifier of a noun–noun combination is construed as a property that is then applied to the head noun, so is the vehicle of a nominal metaphor construed as a property that is then applied to the topic. For example, *that job is a jail* can be rephrased as *that jail job*. Both constructions can be interpreted as "a job that is confining."

On the other hand, there are clear differences between noun–noun combinations and nominal metaphors. Noun–noun combinations allow for other kinds of interpretations (i.e., relation linking and hybridization). For example, people do not interpret "that job is a jail" by linking *job* and *jail* through a relation as in "that job is *at* a jail," whereas "that jail job" can be interpreted in this manner. There may be a variety of more subtle differences between these language constructions (see Wisniewski, in press, for details).

Nevertheless, given the correspondence between property interpretations of combinations and nominal metaphor interpretations, it is a short step to suggest that both phenomena involve the same processes. Previously, I argued that property interpretation involves two processes: a comparison process that aligns the modifier and head nouns to determine differences between them and a process that constructs a new property that is integrated into the head noun. In like fashion, nominal metaphors would be understood by comparing and aligning the vehicle with the topic to determine differences between them and constructing a new property that is integrated into the topic.

Of theoretical interest, current models of metaphor understanding embody one or the other process (to varying degrees) but not both (see Wisniewski, in press, for more details). In general, there have been two distinct approaches to metaphor understanding in cognitive psychology. The *comparison approach* has focused more on analogies than on metaphors but generally assumes that both are interpreted using similar processes. Thus, a metaphor is understood by first aligning or putting into correspondence representational structure of the topic with that of the vehicle through a comparison process. These models include the structure mapping engine (SME; Falkenhainer, Forbus, & Gentner, 1989; Gentner, 1983, 1989) and the analogical constraint mapping engine (ACME; Holyoak & Thagard, 1989). Alignment is potentially a computationally intractable problem (Holyoak & Thagard, 1989) so much of the emphasis in the comparison approach has been on determining the psychological factors that constrain this process (see Gentner, 1983, 1989; Holyoak & Thagard, 1989, for details). However in the comparison approach, there has been considerably less emphasis on constructing new properties in the topic on the basis of properties of the vehicle. In fact, the typical view is that knowledge transfer is a copy and addition process (Falkenhainer et al., 1989; Gentner, 1989; Holyoak & Thagard, 1989; Hummel & Holyoak, 1996).

However, my analysis of conceptual combination suggests that this copy and addition process is generally not used to understand metaphors or analogies. Furthermore, metaphors and analogies prototypically involve comparisons of conceptually different domains with different predicates applying to each domain. Therefore, metaphors generally cannot be understood by straightforward transfer of predicates from one domain to another because the predicates in one domain will often not apply in the other domain. Even when they do apply they may not apply in the same way. For example, on understanding "the atom is like the solar system," people's sense in which electrons revolve around a nucleus may be different from their sense in which planets revolve around the sun. (The frequency and size of revolutions are different in these domains.) As previously noted, people are sensitive to such differences in conceptual combination (Wisniewski, 1996b).

A second view of metaphor understanding is the interactive property attribution approach (Glucksberg & Keysar, 1990; Glucksberg et al., this volume; McGlone, 1996). The strengths and limitations of this view are the reverse of those of the comparison approach: It acknowledges the importance of construction but does not specify a role for comparison. For example, in earlier work on which this approach is based, Glucksberg, Gildea, and Bookin (1982) described how the same properties of the vehicle *butcher* are differentially instantiated in the topics *surgeon* and *pianist*:

> The statement *X is a butcher* can always be taken to mean that X is negatively evaluated, and that X is grossly and characteristically incompetent as well. The particular way that X's incompetence is instantiated will depend on who or what X might be. If X is a surgeon, the incompetence takes the form of botched operations, with bleeding, disfigurement, and death the likely consequences. If a pianist is a butcher, then the competence is not merely the forgetting of certain parts of the piano pieces or the lack in the repertoire, but that the music is plowed through insensitively, too loudly, without any hint of subtlety or beauty. (p. 95)

In these examples, the authors imply that the vehicle provides information that acts as a source for the construction of new properties in topic. Metaphors are not understood by copying over predicates and replacing arguments but rather by a construction process similar to the one I have proposed in conceptual combination.

However, the property attribution approach does not specify a role for comparison in metaphor understanding. In fact, advocates of this approach have often criticized the comparison view (Glucksberg et al., this volume; McGlone, 1996). However, a comparison process is important for two reasons. First, the comparison process uses commonalities between the topic and vehicle to find differences which will form the basis of the interpretation. Second, the comparison process finds correspondences between the topic and vehicle which indicate where new properties are to be integrated into the topic.

In summary, the interpretation of nominal metaphors may use the same processes as those involved in property interpretations of noun–noun combinations (i.e., comparison and construction). Current models of metaphor understanding have emphasized the importance of either comparison or construction, but not both. A complete model must employ both processes.

CONCLUSION

Providing a processing (algorithmic) account of how people combine concepts is a difficult task. I hope, however, that this chapter has taken some important steps toward achieving this objective. As a first step, I outlined the goals of conceptual combination and described the important phenomena that result when people combine concepts. In the latter regard, I identified three conceptually distinct kinds of combinations that cover the combinatorial space. Of importance, I highlighted the necessity of conceptual change when concepts combine. This computational level explanation is an essential prerequisite for developing a processing account. It delineates the range of output that the algorithm should produce. In addition, why people combine concepts also constrains how they combine them.

As a second step, I described several processes that operate when people combine concepts. These processes correspond to the conceptually distinct types of output that I identified in the computational level account. One process incorporates the constituents into a plausible scenario in which the constituents play different functional roles. A second process compares the constituents to find important differences between them. One or more of these differences provide the basis for modifying the head noun constituent. Of importance, I have shown why a comparison process is crucial to combining concepts in this manner. It provides a psychologically plausible way to determine differences and indicates where they should be integrated into a concept. Of crucial importance, this integration involves conceptual change of a form that goes beyond the addition of relatively unmodified knowledge to a concept. Properties are constructed in a concept rather than added to a concept. The modifier concept provides a property that acts as a source of information for the construction of a new property. The head concept provides constraints on how this property is created and instantiated. I also suggested that these comparison and property construction processes characterize how nominal metaphors are understood.

Although I have characterized the property construction process at a general level, an important problem to solve is specifying in more detail how this process operates and how it produces conceptual change. This problem is perhaps one of the most important ones to solve in language understanding.

REFERENCES

Barsalou, L. W. (1982). Context-independent and context-dependent information in concepts. *Memory & Cognition, 10*, 82–93.

Barsalou, L. W. (1993). Flexibility, structure, and linguistic vagary in concepts: Manifestations of a compositional system of perceptual symbols. In A. C. Collins, S. E. Gathercole, M. A. Conway, & P. E. M. Morris (Eds.), *Theories of memory* (pp. 29–101). Hillsdale, NJ: Erlbaum.

Barsalou, L. W., & Hale, C. R. (1992). Components of conceptual representation: From feature lists to recursive frames. In I. Van Mechelen, J. Hampton, R. Michalski, & P. Theuns (Eds.), *Categories and concepts: Theoretical views and inductive data analysis* (pp. 97–144). San Diego, CA: Academic Press.

Brachman, R. J. (1978). *A structural paradigm for representing knowledge* (BBN Report No. 3605). Cambridge, MA: Bolt, Beranck, & Newman.

Cohen, B., & Murphy, G. L. (1984). Models of concepts, *Cognitive Science, 8*, 27–58.

Coolen, R., van Jaarsveld, H. J., & Schreuder, R. (1991). The interpretation of isolated novel nominal compounds. *Memory & Cognition, 19*, 341–352.

Downing, P. (1977). On the creation and use of English compound nouns. *Language, 53*, 810–842.

Elliot, R. (1988). *The complete vegetarian cuisine.* New York: Pantheon Books.

Falkenhainer, B., Forbus, K. D., & Gentner, D. (1989). The structure mapping engine: Algorithm and examples. *Artificial Intelligence, 41*, 1–63.

Fillmore, C. J. (1968). The case for case. In E. Bach & R. T. Harms (Eds.), *Unconstraineds in linguistic theory* (pp. 1–88). New York: Holt, Rinehart & Winston.

Gentner, D. (1983). Structure-mapping: A theoretical framework for analogy. *Cognitive Science, 7*, 155–170.

Gentner, D. (1989). The mechanisms of analogical learning. In S. Vosniadou & A. Ortony (Eds.), *Similarity, analogy, and thought* (pp. 199–241). Cambridge, England: Cambridge University Press.

Gentner, D., & Markman, A. B. (1994). Structural alignment in comparison: No difference without similarity. *Psychological Science, 5*(3), 152–158.

Gerrig, R. J., & Murphy, G. L. (1992). Contextual influences on the comprehension of complex concepts. *Language and Cognitive Processes, 7*, 205–230.

Glucksberg, S., Gildea, P., & Bookin, H. B. (1982). On understanding nonliteral speech: Can people ignore metaphors? *Journal of Verbal Learning and Verbal Behavior, 21*, 85–98.

Glucksberg, S. , & Keysar, B. (1990). Understanding metaphorical comparisons. Beyond similarity. *Psychological Review, 97*, 3–18.

Grice, H. P. (1975). Logic and conversation. In P. Cole & J. L. Morgan (Eds.), *Syntax and Semantics, 3, Speech Acts.* New York: Academic Press.

Hampton, J. A. (1987). Inheritance of attributes in natural concept conjunctions. *Memory & Cognition, 15*, 55–71.

Heit, E., & Barsalou, L.W. (1996). The instantiation principle in natural categories. *Memory, 4*, 413–451.

Holyoak, K. J., & Thagard, P. (1989). Analogical mapping by constraint satisfaction. *Cognitive Science, 13*, 295–355.

Hummel, J. E., & Holyoak, K. J. (1996). LISA: A computational model of analogical inference and schema induction. In G. W. Cottrell (Ed.), *Proceedings of the Eighteenth Annual Conference of the Cognitive Science Society.* Hillsdale, NJ: Erlbaum.

Levi, J. N. (1978). *The syntax and semantics of complex nominals.* San Diego, CA: Academic Press.

Levin, B. (1993). *English verb classes and alterations: A preliminary investigation.* Chicago, IL: University of Chicago Press.

Markman, A. B., & Gentner, D. (1993). Splitting the differences: A structural alignment view of similarity. *Journal of Memory and Language, 32*, 517–535.

Markman, A. B., & Wisniewski, E. J. (in press). Similar and different: The differentiation of basic level categories. *Journal of Experimental Psychology: Learning, Memory and Cognition.*

Marr, D. (1982). *Vision.* San Francisco: W. H. Freeman.

Martin, J. D., & Billman, D. O. (1994). Acquiring and combining overlapping concepts. *Machine Learning, 16,* 121–155.

McGlone, M. S. (1996). Conceptual metaphors and figurative language interpretation: Food for thought? *Journal of Memory and Language, 35,* 544–565.

Medin, D. L., & Shoben, E. J. (1988). Context and structure in conceptual combination. *Cognitive Psychology, 20,* 158–190.

Minsky, M. (1975). A framework for representing knowledge. In P. H. Winston (Ed.), *The psychology of computer vision* (pp. 211–277). New York: McGraw-Hill.

Murphy, G. L. (1988). Comprehending complex concepts. *Cognitive Science, 12,* 529–562.

Nisbett, R. E., & Ross, L. (1980). *Human inference: Strategies and shortcomings of social judgment.* Englewood Cliffs, NJ: Prentice-Hall.

Nunberg, G. (1979). The non-uniqueness of semantic solutions. Polysemy. *Linguistics & Philosophy, 3,* 143–184.

Ortony, A. (1979). Beyond literal similarity. *Psychological Review, 86,* 161–180.

Palmer, S. E. (1978). Fundamental aspects of cognitive representation. In E. Rosch & B. B. Lloyd (Eds.), *Cognition and categorization* (pp. 259–303). Hillsdale, NJ: Erlbaum.

Pinker, S., & Prince, A. (1988). On language and connectionism: Analysis of a parallel distributed processing model of language acquisition. *Cognition, 28,* 73–193.

Rumelhart, D. E. (1980). Schemata: The building blocks of cognition. In R. J. Spiro, B. C. Bruce, & W. F. Brewer (Eds.), *Theoretical issues in reading comprehension* (pp. 33–58). Hillsdale, NJ: Erlbaum.

Rumelhart, D. E., & McClelland, J. L.(1986). On learning past tenses of English verbs. In J. L. McClelland, D. E. Rumelhart, and the PDP Research Group (Eds.), *Parallel distributed processing: Explorations in the microstructure of cognition* (Vol. 2, pp. 216–271). *Psychological and biological models.* Cambridge, MA: Bradford Books/MIT Press.

Schank, R. (1972). *Conceptual information processing.* New York: Elsevier.

Shoben, E. J. (1993). Comprehending nonpredicating conceptual combinations. In G. Nakamura, R. Taraban, & D. Medin (Eds.), *The psychology of learning and motivation* (Vol. 20, pp. 391–409). San Diego, CA: Academic Press.

Smith, E. E., Osherson, D. N., Rips, L. J., & Keane, M. (1988). Combining prototypes: A modification model. *Cognitive Science, 12*, 485–527.

Thagard, P. (1984). Conceptual combination and scientific discovery. In P. Asquith & P. Kitcher (Eds.), *PSA* (Vol. 1). East Lansing, MI: Philosophy of Science Association.

Urdang, L., & Abate, F. R. (1983). *Idioms and phrases index.* Detroit, MI: Book Tower.

Ward, T. B. (1994). Structured imagination: The role of category structure in exemplar generation. *Cognitive Psychology, 27*, 1–40.

Weber, R. J., & Dixon, S. (1989). Invention and gain analysis. *Cognitive Psychology, 21*, 283–302.

Wilkenfeld, M. J. (1995). Conceptual combination: Does similarity predict emergence? Unpublished master's thesis, Texas A&M University, College Station.

Wilson, D., & Sperber, D. (1981). On Grice's theory of conversation. In P. Werth (Ed.), *Conversation and discourse.* London: Croom Helm.

Wisniewski, E. J. (1991a, May). Modeling conceptual combination. Paper presented at the Conference on Categorization and Category Learning in Humans and Machines, Department of Psychology, Texas Tech University, Lubbock.

Wisniewski, E. J. (1991b, May). *Relations versus properties: The effects of similarity on conceptual combination.* Paper presented at the Symposium on Conceptual Combination, Annual Meeting of the Midwestern Psychological Association, Chicago, IL.

Wisniewski, E. J. (1995). Prior knowledge and functionally related features in concept learning. *Journal of Experimental Psychology: Learning, Memory, and Cognition, 21*, 449–468.

Wisniewski, E. J. (1996a). Construal and similarity in conceptual combination. *Journal of Memory and Language, 35*, 434–453.

Wisniewski, E. J. (1996b). *Property instantiation in conceptual combination.* Manuscript submitted for publication.

Wisniewski, E. J. (in press). When concepts combine. *Psychonomic Bulletin & Review.*

Wisniewski, E. J., & Gentner, D. (1991). On the combinatorial semantics of noun pairs: Minor and major adjustments to meaning. In G. B. Simpson (Ed.), *Understanding word and sentence* (pp. 241–284). Amsterdam, The Netherlands: Elsevier Science.

Wisniewski, E. J., & Love, B. (1996). *Properties versus relations in conceptual combination.* Manuscript in preparation.

Wisniewski, E. J., & Markman, A. B. (1993). The role of structural alignment in conceptual combination, *Proceedings of the Fifteenth Annual Conference of the Cognitive Science Society* (pp. 1083–1086). Boulder, CO: Erlbaum.

Wisniewski, E. J., & Medin, D. L. (1994). On the interaction of theory and data in concept learning. *Cognitive Science, 18(2)*, 221–282.

4

Emergent Attributes in Combined Concepts

James A. Hampton

The aim of this chapter is to review recent evidence on the creative processes involved when concepts are combined in conjunctions. Shoben and Gagné and Wisniewski (see chaps. 2 and 3, respectively) have written about their research into a particularly interesting form of conceptual combination, namely noun–noun and adjective–noun modification in English. Many of these combinations are *nonpredicating* in the sense that the combined concept does not refer to a category formed by the conjunction of the two constituent concept categories. For example, *school furniture* normally does not refer to the overlap of the two sets of schools and furniture. If it did, then presumably it would refer to an empty set in the normal world. These combinations are of particular interest for the study of creative cognitive processes because when faced with novel combinations out of context, one is forced to a leap of the imagination to construct a sensible interpretation. This process is used to good effect by the *Far Side* cartoonist Gary Larson. In numerous cartoons he takes an unusual conceptual combination and draws an interpretation with comic effects. For example, in one cartoon two cave men ride through the air on their "time log," and in another a most unwarlike tribe of savages is playing "jungle triangles."

In contrast, the main focus of my research (Hampton, 1986, 1987, 1988a, 1988b, 1991, 1996, in press) has been conceptual combinations that are (at least prima facie) predicating or intersective conjunctive combinations; that is, the complex concept refers (apparently) to the overlap of things that are in both constituent concept categories. Some noun–noun and adjective–noun combinations have this interpretation; for example, *pet fish* or *veterinary surgeon.* To force a more explicit conjunctive interpretation and to remove the multiple ambiguity that is possible in novel combinations, the research has used relative clause constructions. Thus, to refer to the overlap between two sets *A* and *B*, I have used the expressions, *A which are also B* and *B which are also A*. (These are logically equivalent expressions in terms of their set extensions although they are not always psychologically equivalent.)

Interest in these conjunctive concepts has focused on two aspects, one extensional and the other intensional. The extensional aspect concerns how the category membership of such concepts is related to the category membership of their two constituents (Hampton, 1988b, 1996). If the concepts are true conjunctions, then category membership in the conjunctive concept should be restricted only to those instances that are members of both constituent concept categories. The second, intensional, question concerns what attributes are seen as characterizing or defining the conjunction and how these relate to the attributes of each constituent concept (Hampton, 1987; Hampton & Dillane, 1993).

The issue of creativity enters this process with the demonstration that in spite of their apparent simplicity such combinations are not straightforwardly compositional. Across a range of experiments and materials, it appears, for example, that people are prepared to loosen the criterion for category membership when considering conjunctive classes. People frequently place in the conjunctive category items that they have excluded from one of the constituents. For example, they may judge chess to be a typical game but not a sport. However, when asked subsequently whether it is a *sport which is a game*, they often say yes. Hampton (1988b) argued that people judge membership in conjunctive concept categories on the basis of similarity to a composite prototype representation of the conjunction. Such similarity-based categorization then gives rise to nonlogical effects (Hampton, 1995). The broadening of category criteria evidenced in these studies can be seen as closely related to issues of polysemy and the flexible shift in the meaning of terms across different contexts (see Murphy, chap. 10).

On the intensional side, most of the attributes of the constituent concepts are also commonly considered to be true of the conjunction—a result termed *attribute inheritance.* Attribute inheritance is a common characteristic of knowledge representation systems in artificial intelligence (and has been developed as a basic mechanism of object-oriented computer programming languages). If a property is generally true of a class, then it also should be generally true of subsets of that class. For example, if it is true that all fish have gills, then having gills also should be true of Scottish fish, pet fish, salmon, tropical fish, or any other subset of the general class. It follows that if one forms the conjunction (set overlap) of two categories, then all the attributes that are true of each category also should be true of the conjunction.

However, attribute inheritance for common semantic categories does not always follow this axiom. As Rosch and Mervis (1975) and others (Hampton, 1979, 1981) have shown, the problem is that many of the attributes that people list as true of a category are not "universally" true of that category. When asked to describe a category such as *bird* by listing different properties, people typically generate a list such as the following:

has wings
flies
has feathers
is lightweight
has a beak
lays eggs
has two legs
migrates in winter

People do not differentiate between attributes that are true of the whole class (such as having feathers, a beak, and two legs) and those that are true of a majority of the class (such as flying, being lightweight, and migrating in winter). When one examines the pattern of attribute inheritance for such categories (Hampton, 1987), it appears that people do follow the logical rule for those attributes that they consider necessary or universally true of the class. However, other attributes (i.e., properties that are only generally true of one constituent category) may sometimes not get inherited. I call this *attribute inheritance failure*—properties that are true of a constituent but not of the conjunction. The converse of inheritance failure is the finding of *emergent attributes.* These are attributes that are never generated as true of either constituent or judged to be true of either constituent, but that nonetheless are considered to be true of the conjunction. These emergent attributes are perhaps the most interesting source of creativity in the process of concept conjunction, using "creativity" in the sense in which Barsalou (see chap. 11) uses it—of mundane processes that generate apparently novel information. It is on emergent attributes that this chapter will focus. Table 1 shows the different possible outcomes of an attribute inheritance experiment.

EMERGENT ATTRIBUTES

Why do we see emergent attributes in concept conjunctions, and what can we learn from them about the nature of semantic representations of concepts and the creative processes that use them?

Table 1

Attribute Inheritance

		A that are also B	
Category A	Category B	True	False
True	True	*Inheritance*	*Inheritance failure*
True	False	*Inheritance*	*Inheritance failure*
False	True	*Inheritance*	*Inheritance failure*
False	False	*Emergence*	*Correctly false*

NOTE: *Default rule—set union*: Any attribute that is true of *A* or true of *B* will be true of the conjunction *A which are also B*.

Emergent attributes probably arise from two different processes. The first is based on a knowledge of particular object classes in the world that happen to fall in the conjunction. For example, *pets that are also birds* are judged to *live in cages* and to *talk*, and these properties are considered false of *pets* or *birds* considered separately. The fact that pet birds talk could not be derived from any knowledge of pets or birds: It is an accidental fact about the domestication of particular bird species like parrots and myna birds. (There are probably good justifications that can be offered to explain why these birds make popular pets. The point is that one could not predict a priori that pet birds would have this property.) These extension-based emergent attributes should not be considered, therefore, the result of creative cognitive processes: They break what Lance Rips has called the *no peeking principle* (Rips, 1995). Elsewhere (Hampton, 1988b), I refer to such examples as cases of *extensional feedback*. That is, we use a conceptual combination such as *pet bird* to identify an extensional set of instances (parrots, parakeets, etc.), and then knowledge of these individuals takes over.

The second process for generating emergent properties involves construction of a possible scenario for the conjunctive category. When faced with a novel conjunction, for example, *snake that is also a pet* or *hand grenade that is also a toy*, we are required to turn to what Rips (1995) or Murphy and Medin (1985) would refer to as the "theory" of the domain in which the concepts are embedded. We need to construct a mental model of a member of the conjunctive category and to resolve some of the possible conflicts between the two concepts. If people are unfamiliar with pet birds, it is still possible that they would produce the attribute *live in cages*. They might produce this attribute by noting the inconsistency of keeping a domesticated animal that is able to fly long distances, is hard to catch, can feed itself in the wild, and is not desirous of human company. (Alternatively, they might suppose that pet birds have *clipped wings*.) Similarly, the idea of a pet snake, or even a pet skunk, brings to mind the problems that are potentially involved in a scenario in which a snake or skunk is allowed into the relatively civilized environment of one's home. Therefore, it could be inferred from consideration of such scenarios that the pet snake should have no venom gland and that the pet skunk should have no capability to stink up the house. To achieve this, either surgery (or possibly genetic engineering) might be proposed. Emergent properties then may arise as a solution to a perceived problem deriving from the combination of the two concepts.

EVIDENCE FOR EMERGENT ATTRIBUTES

It is often easier to generate examples of emergent attributes in an anecdotal fashion than to obtain hard evidence for them. I propose to review in broad terms the results of a number of studies in which emergent attributes figured as a topic of interest. Most of the studies involved attribute generation and rating tasks. Groups of participants generated attributes for two constituents and for their conjunction. Further groups then rated the full list of attributes for their applicability or appropriateness as descriptions of the two constituents and their conjunction. *Emergent attributes* are defined in these studies as those that are rated as true of neither constituent but nonetheless are rated as true of the conjunction. The final study to be reported involved asking participants to give descriptions of conjunctions of sets that do not normally overlap.

I do not discuss each study in great detail. Fuller accounts can be found elsewhere for many of the studies. My intention in this chapter is to focus on the following simple questions. What is the rate of emergent attributes in conjunctions, what kind of attributes are they, and what processes have given rise to them? We can then use this information to arrive at some idea of the level of creativity involved in the interpretation of such phrases.

Conjunctions of Semantic Categories

Table 2 shows examples of emergent properties that were found in the study reported in Hampton (1987). To recap the procedure, different groups of participants first generated attributes that they felt were true of either one or the other constituent or of the conjunction. From these listings, a final list of all attributes generated to the pair of categories was

Table 2

Examples of Emergent Attributes From Hampton (1987)

Conjunction	Emergent attribute
Vehicles that are also machines	Are large
Pets that are also birds	Are small Are kept in a cage Have claws
Birds that are also pets	Are small Are kept in a cage Are pretty
Buildings that are also dwellings	Are tall
Tools that are also weapons	Are sharp Have a blade for cutting Have a point
Sports that are also games	Have spectators
Games that are also sports	Have spectators Are done professionally for money

NOTE: From "Inheritance of Attributes in Natural Concept Conjunctions," by J. A. Hampton, 1987, *Memory & Cognition*. Copyright 1987 by the Psychonomic Society. Reprinted with permission.

drawn up, and new groups of participants made ratings of how important each attribute was for either one or the other constituent or for their conjunction. From these importance ratings, a scale of importance was created, and emergent attributes were identified as those with a rating above the midpoint of the scale for the conjunction but below the midpoint of the scale for each of the constituents (full details can be found in Hampton, 1987). Two methods of scoring were used to identify emergent attributes. A strict scoring required the attribute to be rated as unimportant for both constituents and important for both ways of ordering the conjunction (i.e., *birds that are pets* and *pets that are birds*). Under strict scoring only a total of 3 attributes out of 174 were classified as emergent. A more lenient method of scoring allowed the attribute to be important for either version of the conjunction and produced an additional 11 emergent attributes. These are shown in Table 2. (Five other conjunctions had no emergent attributes at all.)

As shown in Table 2, emergent properties are more common in categories that have a low set overlap. For example, because *most pets are not birds*, and *most birds are not pets*, this pair of categories shows more emergent properties. Where the degree of overlap is quite high (as with *machines* and *vehicles*, or *sports* and *games*), the level of emergent attributes is much lower. It is also apparent that the incidence of emergent attributes is quite low. (Of 37 attributes judged to be unimportant for both constituents, only 8% were judged important for both forms of the conjunction.)

The actual examples of emergent attributes show that most of them are of the extensional feedback kind (e.g., *pet birds that talk*). Other attributes like *are small* or *are large* need to be treated with caution because they are inherently relative to some unspecified standard. In view of the small number of emergent attributes, it must be concluded that there is relatively little evidence for creative emergence as a result of problem solving or conflict resolution in these conjunctions.

Conjunctions With a Negated Constituent

In another series of experiments (Hampton, 1989), a similar procedure was applied to conjunctions in which the constituent in the relative clause was negated. We now have conjunctions like the following examples:

Buildings which are not dwellings
Vehicles which are not machines

In a study of attribute inheritance with these categories, participants rated the proportion of each category for which an attribute was true. By using negated constituents, a test of emergent properties can be applied that should rule out those that are the result of extensional feedback. If an attribute is judged to be true of none of the head noun category (e.g., *buildings*), then it should follow that it is also true of none of any subset of the category (e.g., *buildings which are not dwellings*).

Emergent attributes were defined then as those rated as having a frequency of 0% for the head noun category *A*, but a frequency greater than zero for *A which are not B*. (We cannot define emergence here in terms of attributes that are false for the relative clause constituent because there is no logical link between the frequency of an attribute for class *B* and its frequency for the class *not B*. Whether a property is 100% or 0% true of *dwellings*, we can make no inference about its frequency for some class that is *not dwellings*.)

Across six category pairs, there were 51 attributes with median rated proportion for *A* of 0%, and of these, 24 were also considered to be 0% true of *A which are not B* (i.e., they followed the logic of the situation). Eleven violated the constraint but only slightly (median of 0%–5% for the conjunction) and thus could be the result of statistical noise. Only 6 attributes in the whole study had ratings of 10% or more for the conjunction *A which are not B* and 0% for the category *A* alone. These 6 emergent attributes are shown in Table 3.

The emergent attributes are evidence for a broadening of conceptual categories once they are modified. *Dwellings* are not seen as *for relaxation out of the home*; that is, people typically imagine that a dwelling and a home are synonymous. When asked to consider *dwellings that are not buildings*, the category of temporary dwellings (like a tent used on a camping trip) come to be included in the more general category. The same appears to work for the *vehicles* example, an extending of the category from mechanical means of transport to a broader category of any means of transport. Stretching of concepts appears to be a source of emergent attributes and a part of creative cognition, as has often been identified in the problem-solving tradition of psychology (e.g., see Boden, 1991; Johnson-Laird, 1988). It is also notable, however, that just as with the first study, relatively few truly emergent attributes were found, and those that

Table 3

Emergent Attributes for Negated Conjunctions

Conjunction	Attribute	Frequency
Dwellings that are not buildings	Are for relaxation out of the home	10%
Household appliances that are not furniture	Are for play	20%
Vehicles that are not machines	Are natural	35%
	Are self-motivating	12.5%
	Are rafts	10%
Birds that are not pets	Have a nose	52.5%

NOTE: From *Papers From the 1989 Edinburgh Round Table on the Mental Lexicon: Vol. 4. Edinburgh Working Papers in Cognitive Sciences* by J. A. Hampton, 1989, Edinburgh, Scotland: University of Edinburgh, Center for Cognitive Science. Copyright 1989 by University of Edinburgh Press. Reprinted with permission.

were depended largely on finding familiar instances rather than on creating novel solutions to the problem.

Personality Traits

When considering different studies of attribute inheritance, it is worthwhile to describe briefly a study by Hampson (1990). Hampson took pairs of personality traits that could be either congruent (*unsociable and unfriendly*) or incongruent (*thorough and haphazard*). Earlier work by Asch (1946) showed how almost any pair of traits can be imagined to co-occur in an individual. In Hampson's study, groups of participants generated behaviors that were either likely or unlikely for each trait considered alone and for the traits in conjunction. Other groups then made likelihood ratings of the behaviors for each constituent and their conjunction. The results were analyzed for attribute inheritance along the same lines as in Hampton (1987). For congruent traits, Hampson found complete attribute inheritance. If a behavior was likely for either constituent, then it was likely for the conjunction; if it was unlikely for both constituents, it was unlikely for the conjunction. This pattern occurred for 31 of the 32 attributes. For incongruent pairs of traits, however, 16 out of 25 behaviors that were likely for at least one constituent were inherited by the conjunction, whereas the other 9 were not inherited. Some interaction between the traits was thus occurring for the incongruent traits. It is interesting, that there were no emergent attributes observed in any of the trait pairs. Although participants were encouraged to imagine behaviors that would be likely for people with incongruent traits, they did not generate behaviors that were at the same time unlikely of the two constituent traits.

Although inheritance failure is not as clear an example of creative processing as is emergence, it too can be seen as evidence for a form of creativity. When two incongruent traits are combined and behaviors considered likely for one constituent are now no longer considered probable for the conjunction, this is evidence that a novel concept has been constructed out of the two constituent traits. Certain behaviors are inherited, and others are not, and this process of selectivity shows the creation of a novel personality trait.

Social Categories

A richer domain for investigating how fuzzy categories combine is the area of social categorization, involving occupational and social stereotypes. A recent project that I have been conducting with Margaret Dillane and Laura Oren involves taking inconsistent social stereotypes and forming their conjunctions. Earlier studies that followed this procedure (e.g., Hastie, Schroeder, & Weber, 1990; Kunda, Miller, & Clare, 1990) found that people are inclined to generate emergent attributes in order to explain the apparent contradiction. If asked to describe a *Harvard-educated carpenter*, respondents in the Kunda et al. (1990) study described possible reasons why a Harvard-educated person should become a carpenter (e.g., college dropout, disillusionment with the academic world, or alternatively an ambition to "design new methods and objects in carpentry").

Kunda et al. (1990) applied a relatively qualitative research method to the problem. Hastie et al. (1990) used a more quantitative approach in their second experiment. Congruent and incongruent pairs of stereotypes were constructed, such as *feminist social worker* and *Republican bank teller* (which were congruent) versus *feminist bank teller* and *Republican social worker* (which were incongruent). Individuals rated such conjunctions and their individual component concepts on a series of 15 bipolar personality dimensions, such as *ambitious–unambitious* or *warm–cold.* The results were then analyzed individually for each person to find cases where the rating on a dimension for the conjunction fell at least one scale step outside the range defined by the two component concepts. These cases were taken as evidence of emergent properties because they showed a judgment of a personality trait that was neither inherited from one of the constituent concepts nor an average of the two constituents. A high proportion of conjunctive ratings were of this kind (e.g., 23% for congruent and 33% for incongruent conjunctions). This study, therefore, confirms that social categories are a rich source of emergent properties. Hastie et al. (1990) also asked participants to think aloud while making their judgments and then analyzed the possible sources of emergent attributes into three processes. First, some people brought to mind a relevant case from memory. For example, they knew someone who was at least similar to the stereotype being constructed and thus could use that case as a basis for generalization. Second, people sometimes appealed to general rules about life. For example, any woman doing a man's job would have to have certain qualities. In this case, a more deductive inference was made by identifying the conjunction as an example of some more general category. Third, as a final strategy participants conducted a "mental simulation" of the scenario; they created mental images and elaborated on how persons would react to the incongruent situation in which they found themselves. This third strategy is probably the closest to the process of creativity, involving as it does imagination and the creation of a novel scenario.

We were interested in studying this process of resolving incongruent social stereotypes and in seeing whether it could be affected by a manipulation of the background "theory" that people applied to the task. To manipulate the background context, we asked people to adopt the point of view of a particular social group. This is a manipulation that was first introduced into the field by Barsalou and Sewell (1984) and was shown to have a marked effect on typicality ratings in taxonomic and goal-derived categories (see also Barsalou, 1987).

Our task involved people making judgments about two constituent categories that were always incongruent pairs (e.g., a *socialist* and a *stockbroker*) and then about their conjunction (e.g., a *socialist stockbroker*). In doing the task, people were asked to take one of two points of view; either that of a socialist or that of a stockbroker. The procedure involved different groups of participants who first generated possible descriptive attributes for either constituent or the conjunction from either point of view. A second set of participants then rated the appropriateness of the descriptions generated for each of the categories from each point of view.

Point of view had a large effect on the attributes considered true of the conjunction. The most common pattern, found in seven of the eight sets of materials for the first experiment, was one of *antagonism.* If taking a socialist point of view, then a socialist stockbroker was considered to be similar to any other stockbroker and to share few of the positive attributes of other socialists. Appropriateness of the attributes for the conjunction was largely predicted by appropriateness for the "other" constituent category (i.e., the one other than the adopted point of view). The same was true for those taking the stockbroker's point of view (i.e., socialist stockbrokers were little different from other socialists for this group of people). As a result, there was very little correlation between the two sets of attribute appropriateness ratings when comparing one point of view with another.

When attribute inheritance was investigated, however, there was evidence for some emergent attributes. Table 4 shows the attribute inheritance pattern for all attributes. To help with the interpretation, we divided attributes on the basis of the ratings of a new group of participants into those that were positively evaluated (i.e., good things to be) for the point of view and those that were negative. Out of 210 attributes across the four pairs of categories, only 2 were judged true of both categories. Of the remainder, 65 (all positive) were judged true of one's own point of view; of these only 11 (17%) were inherited by the conjunction. There were 80 attributes that were judged as true of the "other" category, the majority

Table 4

Inheritance Pattern for Attributes of Social Stereotype Categories

	Positively valued		Negatively valued	
Attribute	Inherited	Not inherited	Inherited	Not inherited
True of both	2	0	0	0
True of point of view	11	54	0	0
True of "other"	7	6	48	19
True of neither	4	26	18	15

(84%) of which were evaluated negatively, and 55 (69%) of which were inherited by the conjunction. The pattern of antagonistic interpretation of the conjunction, therefore, was confirmed in this analysis, with the majority of inherited attributes being negatively evaluated and considered true of the "other" category from the point of view adopted.

A total of 63 attributes were false of both constituents, of which 22 (35%) were considered true of the conjunction and therefore emergent. These attributes are shown in Table 5. Some of these were not particularly surprising and tended to be obvious attributes, such as *confused* or *inconsistent*, which describe the fact that the categories are uncommon as conjunctions.

The pair that gave most emergent attributes was the *Oxford graduate–factory worker* pair. There was evidence that the Oxford graduate point of view attributed membership of the conjunction to laziness, disaffection, or mental illness, whereas the factory worker attributed it to failure and underachievement. It might have been expected that cases like *socialist stockbroker* would engender attributes such as *is a hypocrite.* This attribute was indeed commonly rated as true of the conjunction but did not turn out to be emergent because from each point of view it also was seen as being true of the opposing constituent category.

A second experiment manipulated the gender consistency inherent in the point of view adopted. The experiment involved a further series of 8 pairs of social stereotypes, all of which were linked with gender. One of

Table 5

Emergent Attributes in Social Stereotype Categories

Category A	Category B	Point of view	Emergent attribute
Conservative	Trade unionist	Conservative	Traitor
Conservative	Trade unionist	Trade unionist	Traitor
			Confused
			Strange
Socialist	Stockbroker	Socialist	Champagne socialist
			Traitor
			Unconventional
			Unrealistic
Socialist	Stockbroker	Stockbroker	Champagne socialist
			Not a true socialist
			Unconventional
Oxford graduate	Factory worker	Oxford graduate	Disaffected
			Lazy
			Possible mental breakdown
			Something wrong with him
			Unconventional
Oxford graduate	Factory worker	Factory worker	Failure
			Something wrong with him
			Unconventional
			Underachiever
Rugby player	Man who knits	Rugby player	Confused
			Relaxed
Rugby player	Man who knits	Man who knits	—

each pair was a typically male occupation, and the other was a typically female one. For example, one of the pairs was a *car mechanic who reads romantic fiction.* Half the participants were told that this applied to a man, and half that it applied to a woman. Different groups of people generated descriptive attributes from different points of view, whereas others rated their appropriateness—again from a particular point of view. The full design involved 12 different sets of judgments, obtained from 12 different groups of participants. Taking the *car mechanic who reads romantic fiction* as an example, one group was asked to take the point of view of a male car mechanic (a gender consistent point of view) and judge the appropriateness of the attributes for describing a male car mechanic. A second group judged the same category (*male car mechanic*) but took the point of view of a male who reads romantic fiction (a gender inconsistent point of view). A third and a fourth group judged the alternative category (*a male who reads romantic fiction*) from the same two points of view, respectively. The fifth and sixth groups judged the combined category (*a male car mechanic who reads romantic fiction*) from the same two points of view again. Finally, groups 7 to 12 repeated the whole design with the same categories but with female points of view about females in place of male points of view about males. Emergent attributes were analyzed for each point of view and each gender. Examples are shown in Table 6.

Table 6

Emergent Attributes With Gender Consistent and Inconsistent Stereotypes

	Points of view			
	Male		Female	
Categories	Consistent	Inconsistent	Consistent	Inconsistent
Car mechanic who reads romantic fiction	Dissatisfied Elusive	Dissatisfied Reliable Lonely Soppy	Ambitious Broad-minded Clever	Easygoing Calm Charming Caring Intelligent
Tractor driver who is a ballet dancer	Passive Unserious	Confused Dirty Eccentric Peculiar	Bold Unconventional Enjoys herself Satisfied	Soft
Fighter pilot who is a child minder	—	Untroubled	Contradictory	Fun loving

	Points of view			
	Male		Female	
Categories	Consistent	Inconsistent	Consistent	Inconsistent
Road digger who does embroidery	Single	Unusual	Adventurous	Unstereotypical
	Multitalented		Challenger	Unusual
	Dare to be different		Just does a job	Positive
			Healthy	
	Easy			
Football hooligan who is a house husband/wife	Homosexual	Vain	Eager	Antisocial
	Changeable	Changeable	Sporty	
			Unfulfilled	
			Adventurous	
			Football supporter	
Rugby player who knits	—	Brave	—	Organized
		Funny		Well-rounded
		Eccentric		
		Strange		
		Uncaring of image		
Refuse collector who makes cakes	Confused	Miserable	Simple	Adept
	Articulate	Unsociable	Broad-minded	Clever
	Simple	Unusual	Determined	Enjoys life
		Strange	Equality	Fulfilled
				Multitalented
				Positive
				Same beneath
				Broad-minded
				Determined
				Fun loving
Boxer who is a nurse	Repressed	Dissatisfied	—	—
	Uncompetitive	Rival		
	Emotionally split			
	Strange			

The patterns in this data are complex. It appears that there are some small differences between gender consistent and gender inconsistent points of view and much larger differences between the male and female versions of the materials (participants of both sexes contributed to both halves of the design). The pattern of antagonism was found more commonly when the point of view was a gender consistent one (e.g., a male fighter pilot or a female child minder). It also was much more common for the male points of view to be antagonistic than for the female points of view. Female points of view tended to be more integrational—taking good and bad points from each constituent. Note also in Table 6 how the female points of view about females tended to involve many more positively valued emergent attributes than the equivalent male categories. A quick estimate indicates that for the men there were 19 negative attributes and only 8 positive, whereas for the women there were 34 positive attributes and only 3 negative. Male points of view appeared to take a much more negative and antagonistic view of the conjunction than did female points of view. It is interesting (but beyond the scope of this chapter) to speculate on the meaning of this result for British culture and gender stereotypes. It is apparent that male points of view are more antagonistic and that males are less able to belong to incongruent categories without being seen in a primarily negative way by those who belong in only one of the categories. These results, however, must be tempered with the important caveat that these are the opinions of people adopting points of view rather than the opinions of people actually in the social categories. It is indeed a remarkable feat of creativity that people are able to perform this task with such apparently clear and systematic results. The ability to adopt the point of view of others is surely at the heart of our empathetic understanding of each other.

IMAGINATION AND CONCEPT CONJUNCTIONS

The final study to be reported concerns imaginary objects. The original aim of this small study was to ask people to combine concepts that could not ordinarily be combined and hence to place the flexibility of their concepts under considerable strain. The procedure was to ask people to imagine apparently contradictory or impossible objects, thus forcing them to stretch and bend their concepts to meet the constraints of the task. The procedure, therefore, may bring to the fore those creative and problem-solving strategies that may normally be applied in cases of novel conceptual combination. From the point of view of the theory of concept representation, the procedure also can be understood by analogy with an atom smasher in physics (i.e., what bits fly off, and what remains at the core?). As concepts are stretched, how do they change?

The study used the nine concept pairs shown in Table 7 and the following instructions:

> Try to imagine each object and describe as fully as possible attributes which you would expect it to have and ways in which it would differ from more typical examples of the same categories. Use drawings if you wish. After each one, rate how hard it was to imagine. (Scale: 1 = *easy*, 4 = *hard*)

Table 7

Pairs of Concepts Used in the Imaginary Object Experiment, With Mean Rated Difficulty (1 = Easy, 4 = Hard)

	Difficulty	
Imaginary object	A–B	B–A
A piece of furniture that is also a kind of fruit	2.6	3.0
A vehicle that is also a kind of fish	1.8	2.6
A food that is also a kind of rock	2.7	2.5
A fruit that is also a kind of human dwelling	1.6	3.1*
A bird that is also a kind of kitchen utensil	2.2	3.4*
A food flavoring that is also a kind of tool	2.9	3.6
A computer that is also a kind of teacup	2.1	3.2*
A cooking stove that is also a kind of bicycle	2.2	2.9
A lampshade that is also a kind of book	1.9	2.4

NOTE: Asterisk indicates a significant difference ($p < .05$) between the order *A–B* and the order *B–A*.

The mean rated difficulty of each pair of concepts is also shown in Table 7. One group of 10 participants received the concepts paired in one order, and another group of 10 were given the reverse order for each pair. One person did not complete the task and was excluded from the data analysis.

Overall, one order group found the task easier than the other, and indeed there were significant differences in difficulty between the different pairs. The interaction was not significant, so that it is likely that difference of order reflected participants' differences rather than a real difference between the *A–B* and *B–A* orders. The hardest pair for both groups was *A food flavoring that is also a kind of tool.*

There are many notable features of these data. One is the degree of variability among participants in the amount of creative ingenuity shown. For the purposes of conceptual combination research, it is striking how much theory-based problem solving is required to arrive at an elaborated solution. Some people were content to go for a weak surface similarity, an analogy, or even a pun (*a skate as a fish that is a vehicle*). However, those who took on the task wholeheartedly were able to generate ingenious solutions. Figure 1 shows some of the more successful attempts. The method is particularly revealing of the process of identifying "incompatibilities" between the concepts. Table 8 lists some of the more obvious incompatibilities that were identified in participants' responses and to which they tried to provide solutions. Often the solution could go either way. Thus, when faced with the problem that fruit is perishable whereas furniture is durable, some individuals changed the fruit concept and imagined a fruit that was highly durable and took a very long time to decay. However, others changed their furniture concept and imagined that this piece of furniture would need regular replacement as it rotted away. Others solved the problem by allowing the fruit to remain on its vine in the living room and provided it with a large flower pot.

As a result of choosing between these two alternatives, it was common to find different respondents making opposing claims. One person said that the lampshade book would catch fire, whereas another claimed that it was fire resistant. One person pointed out the problem, whereas the other added an emergent property to deal with it.

A piece of furniture that is also a kind of fruit

A vehicle that is also a kind of fish

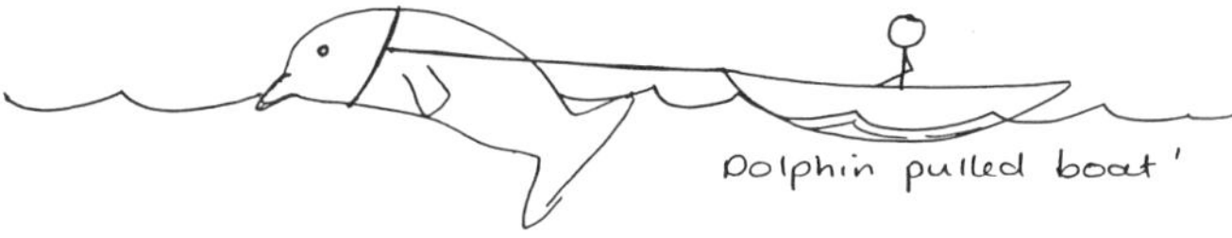

A bird that is also a kind of kitchen utensil

Figure 1

Examples of drawings produced by participants in the impossible objects task.

Another notable feature of the results was the way that the task encouraged people to discover links; that is, an alignment of parts (see Markman & Gentner, 1993). This was particularly noticeable in the imposition of unusual functions onto objects; for example, the core of a giant fruit was hollowed out into a spiral staircase, the tubes of a bicycle frame were filled with steam that could be released to do the cooking, the pedalling of the bicycle was the energy source for the stove, or the minerals in a rock provided a healthy source of nutritional supplement. The alignment of function and structure provided a creative way in which the two concepts could be "glued" together in a sensible way.

Often, analyzing the responses simply in terms of the attributes listed does not capture the way in which the two schema have been integrated

Table 8

Examples of Inconsistent or Conflicting Attributes

Conjunction: A that is B	A attributes	B attributes
A fruit that is a kind of furniture	Perishable	Durable
	Squashy	Firm
A vehicle that is a kind of fish	Controlled	Self-motivated
	For people	Under water
	Safe	Slippery
A food that is a kind of rock	Edible	Hard
	Perishable	Tasteless
		Permanent
A fruit that is a kind of human dwelling	Edible	Hungry inhabitants
	Flimsy	Provides shelter
	Moves around	Anchored to foundation
	Grows	Fixed in size
A bird that is a kind of kitchen utensil	Wild	Functional
	Delicate	Durable
	Eats food	For preparing food
	Unhygienic	For cooking
	Moves	Stable
A food flavoring that is a kind of tool	Liquid/powder	Solid
	Taste	No Taste
A computer that is a kind of teacup	Heat sensitive	Heat resistant
	Water sensitive	Water resistant
	Intelligent	Simple
A cooking stove that is a kind of bicycle	Hot	People sit on it
A lampshade that is a kind of book	Limited surface	Long story
	Transparent	Many pages
	Close to bulb	Flammable

(i.e., emergent attributes often involve relational attributes, linking parts and functions together). Table 9 shows some of these alignments in each of the category pairs.

Emergent attributes were clearly very common in this task. Attributes were classified in an informal way by the author into those that were mainly

Table 9

Alignment of Properties Between Categories in Imaginary Objects

Conjunction: A that is B	Alignable attributes
A fruit that is a kind of furniture	Tough skin could be a chair covering Soft texture
A vehicle that is a kind of fish	Moves along Needs fuel—eats other fish
A food that is a kind of rock	Contains minerals
A fruit that is a kind of human dwelling	Weatherproof exterior Hollow interior
A bird that is a kind of kitchen utensil	Sharp beak—used for opening cans Eats foods—useful to dispose of rubbish
A food flavoring that is a kind of tool	—
A computer that is a kind of teacup	Needs energy—supplied by heat of tea Has display—tea leaves show results
A cooking stove that is a kind of bicycle	Needs power—supplied by pedals
A lampshade that is a kind of book	Writing is on the shade Lamp provides light for reading

true of one or the other category and those that were mainly true only of the combination. On a rough count across all nine pairs of concepts there were approximately 220 attributes mainly true of one or the other constituent concepts and 170 that were emergent. Table 10 illustrates some of these emergent properties.

Table 10

Examples of Emergent Attributes in Imaginary Objects

Furniture—fruit	Bird—kitchen utensil
Gives out heat	Serrated beak
Needs renewing	Stiff
Regenerates itself	Holds things
Grows in a flower pot	Cannot fly
Grows slowly	Eats kitchen rubbish
	Strong jaw
Vehicle—fish	
Tame and docile	Food flavoring—tool
Wears a harness	Reacts with chemicals
Has a sealed cockpit	
Friendly	Computer—teacup
	Dispenses tea
Food—rock	Powered by heat
Swallowed whole	Tells the time
Rubbery texture	Buttons on the side of the cup
Fruit—human dwelling	Cooking stove—bicycle
Rope ladder to top	Difficult to ride
Just one room	Steam valves on the handlebars
Hollowed out	Switch off before mounting
Anchored to the ground	
Does not rot	
Transparent outer covering	

There was also evidence that people tried to find instantiations of general classes in order to help with the problem. For example, *furniture that is a fruit* was instantiated by different people in terms of an easy *chair/orange*, a *bench/banana*, or a *pouf/pumpkin*. In this way, people were selecting a basic level class for elaboration (Rosch, Mervis, Gray, Johnson, & Boyes-Braem, 1976). Basic level classes have been shown to provide easier processing in a number of tasks, and it may be that the greater facility with which people can process basic level classes is also helpful in the imaginary object task. In a similar task, Ward (1994) found that when participants were asked to create novel creatures, they tended to adopt particular basic level earth animals as templates for the generation of novelty.

Finally, it is interesting to see the extent to which the criteria for category membership get stretched when the pressure is on. For example, when instantiating to basic level classes, people would take whales and dolphins to count as fish (they need to be intelligent to serve as vehicles) or would include pumpkins, tomatoes, and even mushrooms as fruits, coral as a rock, and a calculator and an automatic teamaker as a computer.

CONCLUSION

Concept conjunctions are a source of insight into creative problem solving, particularly when the conjoined concepts are not normally seen as overlapping. In the case of conjunctions of overlapping object categories, a major source of emergent attributes derives from the identification of a familiar object class that falls within the conjunction. Experiments on combinations, such as *pet fish* or *dwellings which are not buildings*, reveal emergent attributes that are almost certainly based on knowledge of examples of such objects as parakeets, or tents.

People can be categorized in a very wide range of ways, and social stereotypes are a rich domain in which to study processes of conceptual combination. Work on personality by Hampson (1990) suggested that incongruent personality traits rarely, if ever, lead to emergent attributes although inheritance failure is quite common. Incongruent social stereotypes, however, do provide emergent features. The research reported here suggests that adoption of a particular point of view encourages an antagonistic (us vs. them) approach to conjunctions involving one's own group and a rival. However, where the point of view adopted is itself an unlikely category, then there is a less antagonistic approach. Furthermore, there are gender differences in the degree to which the antagonistic pattern is seen. We do not yet know the reasons for these results, nor exactly what it is about particular viewpoints that makes them more or less antagonistic. The fact that incongruent social categorization leads to emergent personality ascriptions, whereas incongruent personality traits do not lead to emergent behavioral ascriptions is also very interesting (assuming that it is borne out by future research). This result may be taken as indicating a preferred direction of causal attribution—from traits to behavior rather than from behavior to traits. Traits are seen as the causal agents of behaviors (and hence of social–occupational categories). They can therefore be imagined and inferred in order to explain patterns of unusual behavior. On the other hand, unusual behaviors are rarely generated in order to make sense of inconsistent patterns of trait ascriptions.

Where the conjunction of two classes is normally an empty set, then people must rely on creative processes to construct a mental model of imaginary objects that could fulfill at least some of the conjoint constraints implied by the conjunction. This process is revealing of processes that may well be occurring at a less obvious level in more mundane novel combinations. It also may be a source of interesting data about cognitive processes that characterize more creative individuals. There were systematic differences between individuals in their interest in and their ability to complete the task. The individual differences highlight the fact that the creative combination of concepts is not an automatic process but involves cognitive effort. Successful creative solutions involve an extensive exploration of the possible mappings between concept representations, together with imaginative ways of resolving the problematic incongruities that arise. There also was a degree of playfulness and humor that characterized the most well-developed solutions to the impossible objects task. Training individuals in this kind of task may prove of value in fostering their creativity and enhancing their ability to solve design problems in a novel way.

REFERENCES

Asch, S. E. (1946). Forming impressions of personality. *Journal of Abnormal and Social Psychology, 41*, 258–290.

Barsalou, L. W. (1987). The instability of graded structure: Implications for the nature of concepts. In U. Neisser (Ed.), *Concepts and conceptual development: Ecological and intellectual bases of categories* (pp. 101–140). Cambridge, England: Cambridge University Press.

Barsalou, L. W., & Sewell, D. R. (1984). *Constructing representations of categories from different points of view* (Emory Cognition, Project Report No. 2). Atlanta: Emory.

Boden, M. (1991). *The creative mind: Myths and mechanisms.* London: Abacus.

Hampson, S. E. (1990). Reconciling inconsistent information: Impressions of personality from combinations of traits. *European Journal of Personality, 4*, 157–172.

Hampton, J. A. (1979). Polymorphous concepts in semantic memory. *Journal of Verbal Learning and Verbal Behavior, 18*, 441–461.

Hampton, J. A. (1981). An investigation of the nature of abstract concepts. *Memory & Cognition, 9*, 149–156.

Hampton, J. A. (1986, November). *Conjunction, disjunction, and negation of natural concepts.* Paper presented to the 27th annual meeting of the Psychonomic Society, New Orleans, LA.

Hampton, J. A. (1987). Inheritance of attributes in natural concept conjunctions. *Memory & Cognition, 15*, 55–71.

Hampton, J. A. (1988a). Disjunction of natural concepts. *Memory & Cognition, 16*, 579–591.

Hampton, J. A. (1988b). Overextension of conjunctive concepts: Evidence for a unitary model of concept typicality and class inclusion. *Journal of Experimental Psychology: Learning, Memory, and Cognition, 14*, 12–32.

Hampton, J. A. (1989). Attribute inheritance under negation. In G. Dunbar, B. Franks, & T. Myers (Eds.), *Papers from the 1989 Edinburgh Round Table on the Mental Lexicon: Vol. 4. Edinburgh working papers in cognitive science* (pp. 51–60). Edinburgh, Scotland: University of Edinburgh, Centre for Cognitive Science.

Hampton, J. A. (1991). The combination of prototype concepts. In P. Schwanenflugel (Ed.), *The psychology of word meanings* (pp. 91–116). Hillsdale, NJ: Erlbaum.

Hampton, J. A. (1995). Similarity-based categorization: The development of prototype theory. *Psychological Belgica, 35*, 103–125.

Hampton, J. A. (1996). Conjunctions of visually based categories: Overextension and compensation. *Journal of Experimental Psychology: Learning, Memory, and Cognition, 22,* 378–396.

Hampton, J. A. (in press). Conceptual combination. In K. Lamberts & D. Shanks (Eds.), *Knowledge, Concepts, and Categories.* London: UCL Press.

Hampton, J. A., & Dillane, M. (1993, November). *Taking a point of view on attribute inheritance.* Paper presented to the 34th annual convention of the Psychonomic Society, Washington, DC.

Hastie, R., Schroeder, C., & Weber, R. (1990). Creating complex social conjunction categories from simple categories. *Bulletin of the Psychonomic Society, 28,* 242–247.

Johnson-Laird, P. N. (1988). Freedom and constraint in creativity. In R. J. Sternberg (Ed.), *The nature of creativity* (pp. 202–219). Cambridge, England: Cambridge University Press.

Kunda, Z., Miller, D. T., & Claire, T. (1990). Combining social concepts: The role of causal reasoning. *Cognitive Science, 14,* 551–577.

Markman, A. B., & Gentner, D. (1993). Structural alignment during similarity comparisons. *Cognitive Psychology, 25,* 431–467.

Murphy, G. L., & Medin, D. L. (1985). The role of theories in conceptual coherence. *Psychological Review, 92,* 289–316.

Rips, L. J. (1995). The current status of research on concept combination. *Mind and Language, 10,* 72–104.

Rosch, E., & Mervis, C. B. (1975). Family resemblances: Studies in the internal structure of categories. *Cognitive Psychology, 7,* 573–605.

Rosch, E., Mervis, C. B., Gray, W. D., Johnson, D. M., & Boyes-Braem, P. (1976). Basic objects in natural categories. *Cognitive Psychology, 8,* 382–439.

Ward, T. B. (1994). Structured imagination. The role of category structure in exemplar generation. *Cognitive Psychology, 27,* 1–40.

5

The Developmental Emergence of Multiplicative Combinations

Friedrich Wilkening, Gudrun Schwarzer, and Annette Rümmele

The history of science has shown that new insights are often gained when a previously supposed independence of factors from one another is proved incorrect. One prominent case is Einstein's theory of relativity. Whereas the laws of classical mechanics postulated by Galileo and Newton assumed that two speeds simply add up if they have the same direction, Einstein disproved this addition theorem in the framework of relativity theory. Through his discovery that the speed of light represents the limit of all speeds, the addition theorem was rendered implausible. Einstein showed that, when combining speeds, the sum of the speeds has to be multiplied with a factor containing the product of the individual speeds in proportion to the speed of light. The inclusion of this multiplicative component in the integration rule ensures that any combination of speeds will never exceed the speed of light (Fölsing, 1953).

In comparison to combinations by addition, nonadditive combinations in general and multiplicative ones in particular are held to be fundamental requirements of creative thinking. In contrast to the effects of additive combinations, which can be traced back to the original elements without loss of information, multiplicative combinations can create new properties surpassing the original components. However, such interactive relationships are usually difficult to comprehend. This is probably because, generally, people's first guess is that two or more factors operate independently from each other and function on an additive level in producing the effect. An assumption of independence is cognitively less strenuous and in many areas and situations quite, or even perfectly, correct. For example, the total duration of two successive events is, of course, the sum of the single durations (see Wilkening, Levin, & Druyan, 1987). Similarly, when the likability of a person is judged on the basis of two personality adjectives, the single words may keep their meanings independently of the context, that is, they combine according to an adding-type rule to form the overall impression—contrary to a commonly held belief that the meaning changes with context (Anderson, 1966). Hence, noninteraction rules for dimensional combination can be valid and reasonable in both the physical and social realm.

Nevertheless, as behavior becomes more complex, interaction must be taken into account more frequently, meaning that the effects of a factor cannot be judged in isolation but depend on which value is given on the other factors. It seems as if there are cognitive barriers to a spontaneous understanding of nonadditive concepts. Even after lengthy formal training in statistics and experimental design, students often have difficulty understanding and defining the concept of interaction (Keppel, 1991).

In scientific areas such as physics, the rules stating if and how the variables interact are normative, determined by a widely accepted law. Multiplicative or divisional combinations play a central role in many of these laws. However, in the social sciences, no such normative stipulations generally exist. For example, if one examines the roles intention and incurred damage play in making moral judgments, it can be meaningful and reasonable to use either adding-type or multiplying-type combinations, depending on the given context. The task here could be to judge the amount of punishment a wrongdoer should get for certain degrees of intention (accidental vs. intentional) and damage (a lot vs. a little). If the judgment is based on an additive rule, the damage done is treated independently of the intention. Graphically, this rule would show up in a pattern of parallel curves if different factorial combinations of degrees of intention and damage are judged on a linear rating scale (see Figure 1a). If however, a person thinks that the effect of intention (on the amount of punishment, for example) should increase as the incurred damage increases, a multiplying-type rule could be assumed. Graphically, this would produce a diverging fan pattern of the judgments (Figure 1b). Numerous other nonadditive combinations along with multiplication are plausible for the interaction of intention and damage (see Figure 1c). Such configural patterns of judgments generally come into being when specific levels on one dimension are considered unique for the task at hand. In the case of moral judgments, each of these rules, additive, multiplicative, and configural, could be diagnosed for individual children and adults (e.g., Hommers, 1988; Leon, 1980).

Additive and multiplicative principles have been found to operate in many other domains, and on a more preconscious level in the area of visual perception. In the perception of easily analyzable stimuli, differing

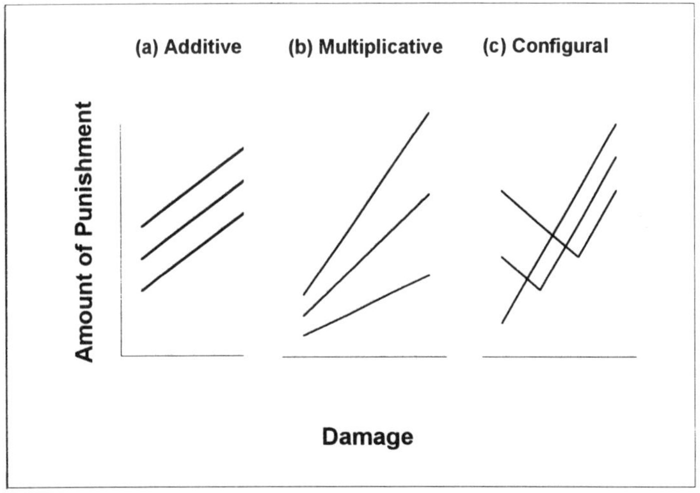

Figure 1

Data patterns for some hypothetical rules for integrating intent and damage information in moral judgments. For each panel, damage is increasing along the horizontal axis, and each separate line reflects a different level of intent.

from one another in size and brightness, for example, the dimensions seem to combine additively. On the other hand, in the perception of more complex stimuli such as colors differing in hue, saturation, and brightness, the dimensions often appear to combine nonadditively, with the data following multiplying-type rules under some circumstances (Garner, 1974; Wilkening & Lange, 1989). The dependence of the processing mode on the structure of the stimulus has also been observed in melody perception (Schwarzer, 1993). Thus, dimensional interactions also occur in perception, with the potential of giving the stimulus new, perhaps unexpected properties. On even higher levels of cognitive functioning, the mechanism of dimensional combination, described as "creative process" by Rothenberg (1979), can also be observed in the domains of music and arts. Mozart or Bach, for example, used ascending and descending scales and triads to achieve some of the most famous or creative works. Pointillist or impressionist painting also achieves stunning visual scenes that show much more than small, individual dots of paint.

Multiplicative combinations can thus be observed in various domains and on different levels of thought. If such combinations are seen as important agents for creative thinking and behavior, the crucial question is when and how they arise. Studying their emergence in the natural course of development may provide a key to an answer. On the one hand, there is ample evidence that young children in particular have difficulty with nonadditive concepts. On the other hand, we know that adults apply multiplicative rules in at least some domains. Therefore, the developmental approach may be useful for obtaining a deeper understanding of multiplicative emergence.

The normative rule prescribes a multiplicative combination not only in the combination of speeds traveling in the same direction, as in our introductory example, but also in countless other fields of physics and mathematics. Thus, the calculation of area of geometric forms; of time, speed, and distance of movements; and of trajectories of thrown balls all are based on a multiplicative integration of dimensions. Clearly an ability to reason multiplicatively is essential for productive and creative thinking in many scientific fields. The main purpose of this chapter is to explain how children arrive at a multiplicative understanding in these domains. Intuitive physics and intuitive geometry seem to be ideal fields to study this development. Here, there is no dispute as to the normative rules nature gives and, thus, for what the development should aim. From the first years of a child's life, the environment provides correct feedback in every situation, so that the rules may be acquired intuitively, at least in principle. Formal training about multiplicative rules follows in school. However, many—if not all—situations are new for children, and it is interesting to see whether and how they make use of the experiences about multiplicativity they may have had earlier when they are faced with a novel task.

RECTANGLE AREA: A PROTOTYPE FOR MULTIPLICATION

The essential property of multiplicative interaction of dimensions, particularly in comparison with additive combination, may be best illustrated using the analogy of two lines—as a metaphorical example. Two lines can be put together, one after the other, in one dimension. The effect of the second line on the total length, then, is independent of what is already given. The result of this additive combination is still a line, a unidimensional distance.

The situation is very different when the two lines are put together perpendicularly and the lengths are combined by multiplication. What results then is not just a longer line but a new entity: area. This new entity has new properties; area is something one can, for example, write on or play on. Moreover, the two lines—the dimensions of the rectangle—are now no longer independent of each other. The effect of increasing the value on one dimension (e.g., height) is greater the greater the value on the other dimension (e.g., width), which is the essence of multiplicative interaction.

How does an understanding of the multiplication principle develop? As the foregoing considerations suggest, this question may be studied most straightforwardly by examining children's and adults' judgments of rectangle area. Anderson and Cuneo (1978) and Wilkening (1978, 1979) conducted such experiments more than a decade ago. We use their work as a starting point for our discussion and try to reinterpret the data in terms of creative concepts, with multiplication as a possible building block for new conceptualizations.

A first question is, Are multiplicative rules part of people's cognitive system from birth, or do they emerge late? Two basically different views have been advocated, each at the core of a classical psychological theory: According to Piaget's theory of cognitive development, children are generally unable to combine information multiplicatively in the first years of their lives. Only when they enter the stage of concrete operations, that is, at about 7 years old, do children possess the cognitive structures that allow multiplication. The Gestalt psychologists seem to postulate the contrary: In their nativist view, *nonadditivity* (judging the whole as different from the sum of its constituents) is built into people's cognitive system from the very beginning. Nonadditive cognition in general and multiplicative combinations in particular occur automatically, effortlessly.

Studying these questions requires rigorous tests for the diagnosis of additive and various nonadditive rules. Information integration theory (Anderson, 1981, 1982) provides such a methodology. We adopted the basic principles of information integration theory in the research reported in this chapter. In each task, several levels on each of the dimensions to be combined (e.g., height and width of a rectangle) were presented in a factorial design, and the participant was asked to judge or predict the outcome (e.g., area) on a linear scale. The advantage of this approach is that the investigator does not have to postulate any rules beforehand. The child is free to choose any rule, even a rule an expert might never have thought of. Such idiosyncratic rules would show up directly in the factorial plot of the responses. The developmental emergence of various forms of nonadditivity, not just multiplication, could thus be found in a rather straightforward way, and without having suggested them to the child.

These principles were applied as follows in the developmental research. In the study by Wilkening (1979), rectangle areas were presented as chocolate bars. For each rectangle, the child was asked to imagine that the bar was broken into pieces of a defined size and that the pieces were laid side by side to form a row. The child had to judge the length of the row on a linear rating scale; this response served as an indicator of the child's judgment about the area of each chocolate bar. Width and height of the rectangles was varied in a 4 × 4 factorial design, and each child judged the series of 16 stimuli in two different random orders. This allowed assessments of the integration rule on the level of the individual child, both by analyses of variance and by an inspection of the factorial plot.

In the youngest age group (5-year-olds) the data of virtually each child followed an adding rule, height + width. This was surprising because, at that time, the adding rule did not follow from any of the leading psychological theories. In Piaget's theory of cognitive development, for instance, children of this age are said to be unable to consider more than one piece of information. Therefore, centering on one dimension, either height or width, should have been expected. In this theory, if integration occurs, it always follows the correct, normative rule prescribed by the laws of mathematics or physics. The case of a nonnormative integration rule is not provided for, neither by Piaget's traditional theory nor by virtually any of the neo-Piagetian approaches.

An adding rule for area judgment also would not follow from the more perceptual theories like the Gestalt view. Just perceiving the "whole" rectangle, ignoring or at least de-emphasizing the elementary information, height and width, would according to this view automatically lead to a multiplicative pattern of area judgments—the same pattern that would result if people first considered the dimensional values, height and width, separately from each other and then integrated them by multiplication. Such a multiplicative rule originating from "wholistic" perception would have an "as-if" status only, not implying that the integration of information occurred deliberately, on an explicit level. Obviously, the young children did not make use of the possibility of the perceptual as-if multiplication. They preferred to concentrate on the single dimensions, height and width separated one from the other, and then tried to integrate this information. In doing so, they used an incorrect rule: addition. For them, the area of a rectangle appears to be a function of its height plus its width rather than its height times its width. By a loose analogy, they are like pre-Einstein physicists assuming an additive combination of speeds.

These findings were replicated several times with slight methodological variations (e.g., Mullet & Paques, 1991; Rümmele, Kühn, & Zoeke, 1990; Wilkening, 1980), and several alternative interpretations of the data have been ruled out (Wilkening, 1983). Most important, Anderson and Cuneo (1978) found essentially the same results in a pioneering series of experiments. In their study, conducted independently from the one just reported, the rectangles were presented as pizzas, and the child had to judge on a graphic rating scale how happy a hungry boy would be to get a piece of that size. The data of 5- and 6-year-olds followed again the height + width rule. For this age, thus, the adding rule for judging rectangle area appears to be solid. The adding rule seems to be a developmental precursor of the normative multiplying rule, which had already been found for the majority of 8-year-olds and for virtually all adults (Anderson & Cuneo, 1978; Wilkening, 1978, 1979).

In the present context, the question of foremost interest is, How does a multiplicative combination emerge from an additive one? What leads to the realization of nonadditivity? Unfortunately, there are only very few studies so far that have addressed these questions directly in the domain of area judgment. From the few studies available there seems to be converging evidence that sensorimotor experience may be effective. Using an information-integration approach, Wolf (1995) found that a significant number of children as young as 5 years old shifted from an adding to a multiplying rule after having played with the stimuli they would judge (areas and volumes) for a period of 10 min. Apparently, giving the children the opportunity to manually explore the material triggered the sensorimotor knowledge they already had before the experiment—the multiplying rule more likely reflecting the wholistic as-if integration mentioned earlier than explicit knowledge about the interaction of dimensions. Interestingly, the same children were found to have fallen back on the adding rule after a week, further suggesting that the change from addition to multiplication had not occurred on the explicit level of knowledge. Data from a systematic training study by Rümmele (1993), who introduced an apparatus by which children could manually produce different rectangles to match the area of various comparison stimuli are in line with Wolf's findings. In addition, Rümmele found an interesting effect between age and the level of understanding the multiplicative rule. If at all, only the oldest children in this study (10-year-olds) showed understanding of nonadditivity on an explicit level by being able to verbalize the essential principles of multiplicativity.

HOW TO COMBINE TIME AND SPEED: DEVELOPING IMPLICIT AND EXPLICIT UNDERSTANDING

If it is true that additive rules are developmental precursors of multiplicative rules and that, already at preschool age, sensorimotor experience can enhance the transition from one form of information integration to the other, then it should be of particular interest to investigate a domain that is more naturally tied to action than is rectangle area. One of the most basic laws of classical physics, speed = distance/time, provides such a domain. A simple transformation gives the multiplicative rule distance = time × speed. Children have many opportunities to experience the interrelations of these dimensions from an early age. Can they use their experiences in new contexts, and how do they come to conceptualize the multiplicative time–speed interaction?

Data from early experiments by Wilkening (1981, 1982) may provide an answer. The design of the experiment paralleled that of the rectangle area study. Area had to be replaced by distance, and height and width had to be replaced by time and speed, respectively. To make the task suitable for children, Wilkening created the scenario of an animal fleeing from a barking dog. Speed information was presented as the (imaginary) maximum running speed of a turtle, guinea pig, and cat. Time information was presented as the (tape-recorded) barking time of a dog: 2 s, 5 s, or 8 s. For each of the nine factorial time–speed combinations, the question was how far the animal would run (e.g., how far the turtle would run in 5 s). Children judged distance by placing a picture of the animal on a linear rating scale, which was presented as a footbridge leading away from the barking dog.

Here again, the youngest children (5-year-olds) simplified the normative multiplicative rule to an adding-type rule, distance = time + speed. However, this was obtained only when time information had to be retrieved from memory and, as a separate value, had to be integrated with speed information, which may be considered as a true integration (Wilkening, 1982). If the children received the speed information, that is, one of the three animals, before the dog started barking, virtually all of them invented an intelligent psychomotor strategy: They followed the imaginary movement of the animal with their eyes, slowest for the turtle and fastest for the cat, and then gave as their distance judgment that point on the scale the imaginary movement had reached when the dog stopped barking. This strategy automatically leads to a multiplicative data pattern. This, again, may reflect an as-if integration only, not necessarily implying that those children have an explicit understanding of the exact form of the time–speed interaction. An adding-type rule resulted again in another variant of the tasks, when time had to be inferred on the basis of speed and distance information (Wilkening, 1981). Here, an eye-movement strategy could not be applied easily, and the children simplified the normative rule, time = distance/speed to a subtractive one, not realizing the dimensional interaction.

The data of the older children and adults, in contrast, followed the normative rules, multiplication or division, in any condition. Apparently, they did not need the auxiliary psychomotor strategy to produce nonadditive judgment patterns, which suggests that their knowledge about the dimensional interaction was on another, higher level. Two points deserve further mention, one concerning young children's additive and one their as-if multiplicative integration. First, even if the adding rule for time and speed is incorrect, these judgments of the 5-year-olds reveal time and speed concepts that are totally different and far more advanced than postulated in Piaget's theory (see Anderson & Wilkening, 1991, for a further discussion). Second, it is remarkable that the 5-year-olds discovered the eye-movement strategy, which may give way to a conceptual understanding of the interaction, without any explicit external help. Such discoveries, first embodied in sensorimotor processes, may be the roots for the emergence of multiplicative concepts on a higher level of understanding.

THROWING BALLS: MULTIPLICATIVE KNOWLEDGE IN PEOPLE'S ACTIONS

Implicit knowledge about multiplicative interaction does not guarantee that it gets transferred to more explicit levels of understanding. Up to adulthood, different forms of knowledge sometimes appear to coexist in the same person, the dissociation of knowledge being stronger than previously assumed. Krist, Fieberg, and Wilkening (1993) showed this concept in their study of the action–judgment relation in people's intuitive physics of a straight throw.

The basic question in the task used by Krist et al. (1993) was how fast a ball had to be at the end of a horizontal ramp (like a table) to hit a target on the floor. The optimal speed for this situation follows from a multiplying-type combination of two factors: distance of the target and height of release of the ball. To assess children's and adults' knowledge of this law, horizontal distance of the target (from 30 cm to 90 cm) and height of release (from 20 cm to 95 cm) were varied in a factorial design, with speed as the dependent variable. Two conditions were introduced: judgment and action. In the judgment condition, participants judged the speed on a graphical scale. In the action condition, participants produced the speed by actually throwing a tennis ball, that is, propelling the ball on a horizontal throwing board. Children from two age groups (5- and 10-year-olds) and adults took part in this experiment. Each child and adult participated in both the judgment and action conditions in counterbalanced order.

In the action condition, all children, even the youngest, applied the correct integration rule. Each child produced a speed pattern that almost perfectly mirrored the normative rule for the height × distance interaction. There was virtually no developmental trend. On this level, children showed the same knowledge as adults in every essential aspect. The data were quite different in the judgment condition. Here, no child from the 5-year-old group integrated distance and height so that the question of additive versus multiplicative combination rule was not relevant. In the adult group, addition was now the most frequently used rule. Only a minority of participants integrated the dimensions by a multiplying-type rule, which was as frequently applied as a unidimensional rule, with judgments based on target distance only. This centering rule was used by almost all 5-year-olds for whom a rule could be assessed at all. Some of the youngest children obviously based their speed judgments on height only instead of distance only, but all of them, interestingly, did so in the wrong direction. They seemed to believe that the ball had to be faster the higher the point of release. Even some 10-year-olds and one adult adhered to this false height heuristic, a rule that never appeared in the action condition. Most important in the present context is the finding that knowledge dissociation appeared to exist even in the majority of adults: Multiplicative rules often coexisted with additive rules, even with unidimensional centering, in the same person for basically the same content. It should be emphasized that the multiplicative rules in the action condition, mentioned earlier, were not acquired in the course of the experiment; this knowledge appeared to be there from the very beginning. This conclusion rests on several observations. Perhaps the most compelling is that the same data resulted when no feedback at all was given about the produced trajectory of the ball. Furthermore, it made no difference if the judgment or the action condition was given first. That is, extremely relevant experience in the action task appeared to be ineffective in the judgment context.

CONCLUSION

In a series of experiments, we observed multiplicative combinations in different domains and on different levels of thinking and acting. What do these data reveal about creative concepts and, in particular, about their emergence in the course of development? Nobody would doubt that Einstein's taking interactive relationships into account in his theory of relativity, thereby gaining new knowledge in physics, was a creative accomplishment. But there seems to be no qualitative difference to a child's first intuitive consideration of multiplicative combinations in somewhat simpler fields of physics or geometry. In both cases, cognition is creative in the sense that something new emerges out of the given information.

Discovering multiplicative interaction is thus nothing exceptional, restricted to geniuses like Einstein, but something that occurs quite often in the normal course of development, even without formal training. At the same time, our data have shown that there seem to be remarkable cognitive barriers to people's grasp of multiplicative combinations and to their understanding of the general principle of dimensional interaction. At least on the explicit level, thought and knowledge seem to have a strong tendency to additivity until adulthood. Additive rules often represent an initial, first-guess strategy for integrating the information (Anderson & Cuneo, 1978). These rules are probably particularly resistant to the transition to multiplicative combination because, in many cases, applying addition is reasonable. Indeed, additive rules often provide good approximations, good enough at least in the normal range for the dimensions in question. This was true for the addition of speeds (not approaching the speed of light) in Newtonian physics, and it holds also in the following example, more closely tied to everyday experience: Some airlines state as "volume" limit for normal baggage a sum of the three dimensions (height + width + depth), although multiplication would, of course, be required by the normative rule. As long as the pieces to be judged have the form of a normal suitcase, however, the addition is good enough for this task—virtually always identifying the same pieces as excess baggage that would have been identified by the correct rule of multiplication. Nevertheless, addition of dimensions is wrong for calculating volume, and it would be a mistake to accept it as a general rule.

If failing to take dimensional interactions into account should be a general tendency of cognition, especially in early phases of development, this might have interesting implications for creative concepts in fields other than intuitive physics. For example, on combining verbal concepts (e.g., Hampton, 1987; Wisniewski, 1991), children may come up with different meanings for the compound than adults will. For children, the combined concept should mirror the meanings of the individual concepts and nothing more, whereas for adults, fully new meanings could emerge not based on an additive composition of the parts. This may become an interesting question for further research (see chapters in this volume by Hampton, Shoben & Gagne, and Wisniewski).

On the more implicit levels of knowledge, particularly in sensorimotor actions, there seems to be no comparable tendency to simplify to addition. Here, we found multiplicative rules even in young children. These implicit forms of knowledge may be developmental precursors, triggering the understanding of multiplicative interaction on the more explicit levels of knowledge. However, it does not have to be taken for granted that such a transition will always occur. Our data in the intuitive physics tasks have shown a remarkable degree of knowledge dissociation even within a quite narrow domain.

Taken together, the findings suggest that there is in no way a stagelike development of the understanding of nonadditivity and of multiplicative interaction. In fact, traditional stage theorists, in their assumption of pure knowledge structures as well-defined entities and in their search for pure concepts such as multiplication, have largely misled scientific inquiry. Not only is there missing evidence for the generality of stages, but even within domains the stage view is highly implausible. In the development of multiplicative concepts, different levels of knowledge often seem to act together in the same individual. Sensorimotor knowledge, concrete and formal operations, to use Piagetian terms, can go hand in hand. The development of concepts of multiplicative interaction appears to exhibit continual expansion, ramification, and interlocking with other abilities and knowledge, as suggested by the assemblage view of cognitive development (Anderson & Wilkening, 1991).

The assemblage view of development appears to mirror the processes that led to great creative discoveries more closely than traditional stage theories do. Modern analyses of the history of extraordinary discoveries have shown that the scientists generally gained their knowledge not in one fell swoop but in small steps, often in diverse fields only finally interlocking with each other (Grassoff & May, 1995). Darwin's theory of evolution and the discovery of the double helix structure of DNA by Watson and Crick are examples of such continual knowledge development (Weisberg, 1986; see also Dunbar, this volume). Patterns of gradual change and strong links to prior knowledge have been observed in many other aspects of creative functioning: in general imagination, for example (Ward, 1994), and even in young children (see Cacciari, Levorato, & Cicogna, this volume). As to the much more basic concept of multiplicative interaction considered in this chapter, young children were shown to have the potential for a perhaps analogous continual development. Their initially implicit integration rules may be building blocks for new knowledge constellations, which then may form the foundation for new insights on a higher level. Studying such a development requires that children perform tasks that activate existing knowledge structures on the one hand and that can only be performed through new combinations of this knowledge on the other. This research strategy, designing batteries of tasks, follows directly from Anderson and Wilkening's (1991) assemblage view. Cognitive development may then become an even more fruitful field for the study of creative cognition.

REFERENCES

Anderson, N. H. (1966). Component ratings in impression formation. *Psychonomic Science, 6*, 279–280.

Anderson, N. H. (1981). *Foundations of information integration theory*. San Diego, CA: Academic Press.

Anderson, N. H. (1982). *Methods of information integration theory*. San Diego, CA: Academic Press.

Anderson, N. H., & Cuneo, D. O. (1978). The height + width rule in children's judgments of quantity. *Journal of Experimental Psychology: General, 107*, 335–378.

Anderson, N. H., & Wilkening, F. (1991). Adaptive thinking in intuitive physics. In N. H. Anderson (Ed.), *Contributions to information integration theory. Vol. 3: Developmental* (pp. 1–42). Hillsdale, NJ: Erlbaum.

Fölsing, A. (1953). *Albert Einstein: Eine biographie* [Albert Einstein: A biography]. Frankfurt: Suhrkamp.

Garner, W. R. (1974). *The processing of information and structure*. Hillsdale, NJ: Erlbaum.

Grasshoff, G., & May, M. (1995, March). *From historical case studies to systematic methods of discovery*. Paper presented at the American Association of Artificial Intelligence Spring Symposium: "Systematic Methods of Scientific Discovery," Stanford, CA.

Hampton, J. A. (1987). Inheritance of attributes in natural concept conjunctions. *Memory & Cognition, 15,* 55–71.

Hommers, W. (1988). Entschuldigung und entschädigung für einen diebstahl [Exculpation and compensation for a theft]. *Zeitschrift für Entwicklungspsychologie und Pädagogische Psychologie, 20,* 121–133.

Keppel, G. (1991). Design and analysis: A researcher's handbook. Englewood Cliffs, NJ: Prentice-Hall.

Krist, H., Fieberg, E. L., & Wilkening, F. (1993). Intuitive physics in action and judgment: The development of kowledge about projectile motion. *Journal of Experimental Psychology: Learning, Memory, and Cognition, 19,* 952–966.

Leon, M. (1980). Integration of intent and consequence information in children's moral judgments. In F. Wilkening, J. Becker, & T. Trabasso (Eds.), *Information integration by children* (pp. 71–97). Hillsdale, NJ: Erlbaum.

Mullet, E., & Paques, P. (1991). The height + width = area of a rectangle rule in five-year-olds: Effect of stimulus distribution and graduation of the response scale. *Journal of Experimental Child Psychology, 52,* 336–343.

Rothenberg, A. (1979*). The emerging goddess: The creative process in art, science and other fields.* Chicago: University Press.

Rümmele, A. (1993). *Entwicklung des flächenkonzepts: Eine trainingsstudie* [Development of the concept of area: A training study]. Münster, Germany: Waxmann.

Rümmele, A., Kühn, H., & Zoeke, B. (1990). Alters- und methodenspezifische strategien der informationsintegration [Age- and method-specific strategies for the integration of information]. *Zeitschrift für Entwicklungspsychologie und Pädagogische Psychologie, 22,* 155–165.

Schwarzer, G. (1993*). Entwicklung der melodiewahrnehmung: Analytische und holistische prozesse* [Development of melody perception: Analytical and holistic processes]. Heidelberg, Germany: Asanger.

Ward, T. B. (1994). A structured imagination: The role of category structure in exemplar generation. *Cognitive Psychology, 27,* 1–40.

Weisberg, R. W. (1986). Creativity: Genius and other myths. New York: Freeman.

Wilkening, F. (1978). Beachtung und addition zweier dimensionen: Eine alternative zu Piagets Zentrierungsannahme [Consideration and addition of two dimensions: An alternative to Piaget's centering assumption]. *Zeitschrift für Entwicklungspsychologie und Pädagogische Psychologie, 10,* 99–102.

Wilkening, F. (1979). Combining of stimulus dimensions in children's and adults' judgments of area: An information integration analysis. *Developmental Psychology, 15,* 25–33.

Wilkening, F. (1980). Development of dimensional integration in children's perceptual judgment: Experiments with area, volume, and velocity. In F. Wilkening, J. Becker & T. Trabasso (Eds.), *Information integration by children* (pp. 47–69). Hillsdale, NJ: Erlbaum.

Wilkening, F. (1981). Integrating velocity, time, and distance information: A developmental study. *Cognitive Psychology, 13,* 231–247.

Wilkening, F. (1982). Children's knowledge about time, distance, and velocity interrelations. In W. J. Friedman (Ed.), *The developmental psychology of time* (pp. 87–112). San Diego, CA: Academic Press.

Wilkening, F. (1983). Entwicklung der informationsintegration: Eine antwort auf Gigerenzers kritik [Development of information interpretation: A reply to Gigerenzer's critique]. *Zeitschrift für Entwicklungspsychologie und Pädagogische Psychologie, 15,* 207–215.

Wilkening, F., & Lange, K. (1989). When is children's perception holistic? Goals and styles in processing multidimensional stimuli. In T. Globerson & T. Zelniker (Eds.), *Cognitive style and cognitive development* (pp. 141–171). Norwood, NJ: Ablex.

Wilkening, F., Levin, I., & Druyan, S. (1987). Children's counting strategies for time quantification and integration. *Developmental Psychology, 23,* 823–831.

Wisniewski, E. J. (1991, October). *Modeling conceptual combination.* Paper presented at the conference on Categorization and Category Learning by Humans and Machines, Lubbock, TX.

Wolf, Y. (1995). Estimation of Euclidian quantity by 5- and 6-year-old children: Facilitating a multiplication rule. *Journal of Experimental Child Psychology, 59,* 49–75.

6

Coherent and Creative Conceptual Combinations

Paul Thagard

Conceptual combinations range from the utterly mundane to the sublimely creative. Mundane combinations include a myriad of adjective–noun and noun–noun juxtapositions that crop up in everyday speaking and writing, such as *blue car*, *cooked carrots*, and *radio phone*. Creative combinations include some of the most important theoretical constructions in science, such as *sound wave*, *bacterial infection*, and *natural selection*. Both mundane and creative conceptual combinations are essential to people's attempts to make sense of the world and other's utterances about it. This chapter shows how the various aspects of conceptual combination discussed by Hampton (this volume), Shoben and Gagné (this volume), and Wisniewski (this volume) can be unified by viewing them as parts of a general coherence mechanism that people use to make sense of what they see and hear.

The section on conceptual coherence uses a newly developed general characterization of coherence to describe how conceptual coherence is as-

I have benefited from conversations with Ziva Kunda and from support from the Natural Sciences and Engineering Research Council of Canada. Thanks to Tom Ward for helpful comments on an earlier draft.

sessed whenever people attempt to make sense of a particular situation using the stock of concepts that are available to them as part of their mental systems. The section "Coherence-Driven Conceptual Combination" shows how mundane conceptual combinations can be understood in terms of an extended version of such conceptual coherence, as available concepts prove adequate for dealing with a situation. "Incoherence-Driven Conceptual Combination" describes more creative kinds of conceptual combinations that arise because of failures of conceptual coherence.

CONCEPTUAL COHERENCE: STRATEGIES FOR MAKING SENSE

The notion of coherence has been widely used in philosophy, psychology, and elsewhere but usually has remained only vaguely specified. Conceptual coherence is a matter of combining a set of concepts to make sense of a situation or set of situations.[1] For example, if you are told that someone is a computational philosopher, you need to be able to use the information stored with your concepts of *computational* and *philosopher* to make sense of the person in question. But what does it mean to achieve conceptual coherence?

Kunda and Thagard (1996) have developed a theory of interpersonal impression formation based on the coherence of social concepts. Social stereotypes, such as those about *women*, *blacks*, and *lawyers*, provide often useful tools for making sense of people, but their application can be problematic when stereotypes conflict with each other or with particular traits and behaviors that apply to people. What do you make, for example, of a black woman lawyer whose hobby is racing monster trucks? Kunda and Thagard account for a dozen central phenomena of stereotype application by viewing impression formation as a kind of parallel constraint satisfaction, and they present a connectionist model that simulates the impression formation of people (IMP) in many social psychological experiments.

[1]By "conceptual coherence" I mean the problem of coming up with a coherent interpretation based on multiple concepts. This is different from the problem of conceptual coherence discussed by Murphy and Medin (1985), which concerns why a given set of objects is grouped together to form a category. Another issue not discussed in this chapter is the coherence of a whole conceptual system (Thagard, 1993).

An account of conceptual coherence can naturally be abstracted from IMP. When people are presented with an object or situation, a variety of concepts may potentially apply. The potentially applicable concepts constitute the set of elements that must either be accepted (applied to the situation) or rejected (not applied to the situation). As in IMP, the positive constraints between concepts are the associations between them based on statistical correlations or causal relations. For example, the *lawyer* concept is for most people associated with concepts such as *professional, educated,* and *intelligent.* In contrast, if you have a concept of *monster–truck–racer,* it is probably associated with the concepts *working class* and *uneducated.* Negative constraints between concepts are based either on contradictions (e.g., between *man* and *woman*) or on weaker negative correlations such as that between *lawyer* and *poor.* Thus, a conceptual coherence problem can be defined as one that requires people to apply some concepts to a situation and withhold other concepts in such a way as to maximize the overall satisfaction of the constraints determined by the positive and negative associations between the concepts.

In some situations, such as a *black woman lawyer racing monster trucks* or *colorless green ideas sleeping furiously,* conceptual coherence may fail in that the optimal coherence judgment is still not very good. The concepts available to apply to a situation do not fit together well enough to make minimal sense of that situation. Satisfying some constraints requires violating too many other constraints for the conceptual interpretation to be admissible, even if it is the best available. Such failures of intelligibility may call into question a person's whole system of concepts and even lead to conceptual revolutions (Thagard, 1992).

Conceptual coherence is an instance of coherence conceived of as maximization of constraint satisfaction. Following is a sketch of a general theory of coherence that is developed in more detail elsewhere (Thagard & Verbeurgt, 1997).

1. Elements are representations such as concepts, propositions, parts of images, goals, actions, and so on.
2. Elements can cohere (fit together) or incohere (resist fitting to-

gether). Coherence relations include explanation, deduction, facilitation, association, and so on. Incoherence relations include inconsistency, incompatibility, and negative association.

3. If two elements cohere, there is a positive constraint between them. If two elements incohere, there is a negative constraint between them.
4. Elements are to be divided into those that are accepted and those that are rejected.
5. A positive constraint between two elements can be satisfied either by accepting both of the elements or by rejecting both of the elements.
6. A negative constraint between two elements can be satisfied only by accepting one element and rejecting the other.
7. The coherence problem consists of dividing a set of elements into accepted and rejected sets in a way that satisfies the most constraints.

Many kinds of cognition, including hypothesis evaluation, concept application, analogy, and decision making, are coherence problems.

More formally, Thagard and Verbeurgt (1997) define a coherence problem as follows.[2] Let E be a finite set of elements $\{e_i\}$ and C be a set of constraints on E understood as a set $\{(e_i, e_j)\}$ of pairs of elements of E. C divides into $C+$, the positive constraints on E, and $C-$, the negative constraints on E. With each constraint is associated a number w, which is the weight (strength) of the constraint. The problem is to partition E into two sets, A and R, in a way that maximizes compliance with the following two coherence conditions:

$$\text{if } (e_i, e_j) \text{ is in } C+, \text{ then } e_i \text{ is in } A \text{ if and only if } e_j \text{ is in } A. \quad (1)$$
$$\text{if } (e_i, e_j) \text{ is in } C-, \text{ then } e_i \text{ is in } A \text{ if and only if } e_j \text{ is in } R. \quad (2)$$

Let W be the weight of the partition, that is, the sum of the weights of the satisfied constraints. The coherence problem is then to partition E into A

[2] I borrow a few paragraphs from Thagard and Verbeurgt (1997). The notion of coherence maximizing is an abstraction from connectionist ideas about maximizing goodness of fit or harmony.

and R in a way that maximizes W. Because coherence between two elements is a symmetric relation, the order of the elements in the constraints does not matter.

Maximizing coherence is a difficult computational problem: Verbeurgt has proved that it belongs to a class of problems generally considered to be computationally intractable, so that no algorithms are available that are both efficient and guaranteed correct. Nevertheless, good approximation algorithms are available. Here is how to translate a coherence problem into a problem that can be solved in a connectionist network:

1. For every element e_i of E, construct a unit u_i that is a node in a network of units U. These units are very roughly analogous to neurons in the brain.
2. For every positive constraint in $C+$ on elements e_i and e_j, construct an excitatory link between the corresponding units u_i and u_j.
3. For every negative constraint in $C-$ on elements e_i and e_j, construct an inhibitory link between the corresponding units u_i and u_j.
4. Assign each unit u_i an equal initial activation (say, .01), then update the activation of all the units in parallel. The updated activation of a unit is calculated on the basis of its current activation, the weights on links to other units, and the activation of units to which it is linked. A number of equations are available for specifying how this updating is done. Typically, activation is constrained to remain between a minimum (e.g., -1) and a maximum (e.g., 1).
5. Continue the updating of activation until all units have settled—achieved unchanging activation values. If a unit u_i has final activation above a specified threshold (e.g., 0), then the element e_i represented by u_i is deemed to be accepted. Otherwise, e_i is rejected.

One then gets a partition of elements of E into accepted and rejected sets by virtue of the network U settling in such a way that some units are activated and others rejected. Intuitively, this solution is a natural one for coherence problems. Just as we want two coherent elements to be accepted or rejected together, so two units connected by an excitatory link will be activated or deactivated together. Just as we want two incoherent elements to be such that one is accepted and the other is rejected, so two units connected by an inhibitory link will tend to suppress each other's activation, with one activated and the other deactivated. A solution that enforces the two conditions on maximizing coherence is provided by the parallel update algorithm that adjusts the activation of all units at once on the basis of their links and previous activation values.

The characterization of coherence in terms of constraint satisfaction applies equally well to work on explanatory coherence (Thagard, 1992), analogical coherence (Holyoak & Thagard, 1995), and deliberative coherence (Thagard & Millgram, 1995). As in the IMP account of stereotype application, conceptual coherence operates with a set of elements that are concepts and a set of constraints on the basis of positive and negative associations between concepts.

COHERENCE-DRIVEN CONCEPTUAL COMBINATION

The problem of conceptual combination can be viewed as a special case of conceptual coherence in which people need to make sense of how a modifier such as *computational* can apply to a head noun such as *philosopher.* The various representations discussed by researchers on conceptual combination—schemas, attributes, features, and relations—are all concepts in my terminology. As Shoben and Gagné (this volume) point out, only some combinations apply the modifier as a predicate to the head noun. A *court philosopher* is a philosopher who serves a royal court, not a philosopher who is also a court. They list a plausible set of relations that can hold between the noun and the modifier, including *cause, has, makes, made of, for, is, uses, located, derived from, about, during,* and *by.* They apply Luce's choice rule to predict, on the basis of frequency of use of relations between heads and modifiers, the relations individuals will expect to hold.

In contrast to Shoben and Gagné's abstract relations view, Wisniewski defends a schema approach in which conceptual combination consists essentially in filling a slot in the head noun with a filler suggested by the modifier. Slots represent a large number of possible features or relations, not the small number considered by the abstract relations view. Wisniewski identifies three basic kinds of combinations in English: *relation-linking* combinations that involve a relation between the referents of the modifier and head concepts, *property integration* combinations that apply one or more properties of the modifier concept to the head concept, and *hybrid* combinations that refer either to a combination of the constituents or to a conjunction of the constituents.

I now sketch a coherence-based computational model of how people select the appropriate relations and make other inferences in framing conceptual combinations. This model is intended to apply both to the selection of relations found in Shoben and Gagné's account and to the combination of schemas found in Wisniewski's account.

I conjecture that when people encounter a modifier–head combination they unconsciously proceed as follows:

1. Construct a constraint network whose elements are possible inferences to be made concerning the object denoted by the head and whose constraints are based on frequencies of association between the elements associated with the head and the modifier.
2. Use connectionist algorithms to do a parallel calculation that maximizes coherence by accepting some elements and rejecting others.
3. The result is an interpretation of the relation between the head and modifier, as well as a collection of inferences about the object denoted by the head as characterized by the modifier.
4. If the most coherent interpretation is nevertheless not very coherent, then move to other mechanisms such as analogy and explanation that produce the incoherence-driven conceptual combinations discussed in the next section.

As in the IMP model of Kunda and Thagard (1996), I assume that every concept has a network of associated concepts. The associated concepts include the kind of information required by both the abstract relations and schemas views of conceptual combination. How coherence-based conceptual combination can work is best seen by taking an example of predicating combination wherein the object denoted by the head has the property denoted by the modifier, as in *big dog.* In this case, the modifier fills a slot or adds a new slot. Here is a richer example taken from IMP's simulation of the phenomenon of subtyping, in which the inferences normally drawn from a stereotype are overruled by particular information about a person. Some people's stereotypes of blacks include the association of their being aggressive, perhaps because their stereotype of a black person is that of a poor "ghetto" inhabitant. On the other hand, the combination *well-dressed black man* suggests a different association, namely, that a black businessman is not expected to be aggressive. Figure 1 shows a constraint network that captures these different associations. To

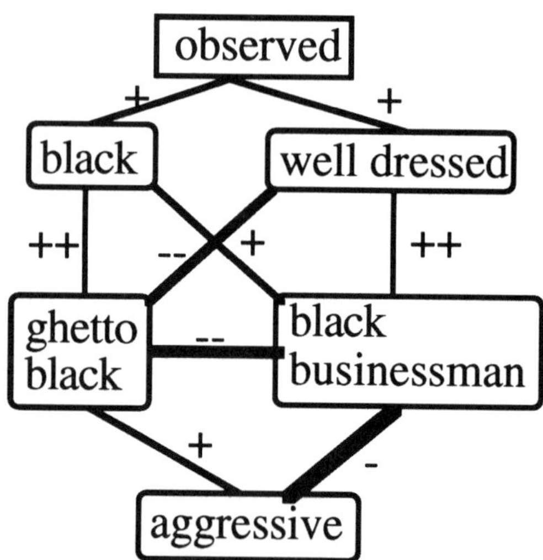

Figure 1

A constraint network for combining *well-dressed* and *black.* Thin lines with pluses indicate positive constraints. Thick lines with minuses indicate negative constraints. This network rejects *aggressive*; but, if *well-dressed* is not connected to *observed,* the network accepts *aggressive.* From "Forming Impressions From Stereotypes, Traits, and Behaviors: A Parallel-Constraint-Satisfaction Theory," by Z. Kunda and P. Thagard, 1996, *Psychological Review, 103,* p. 290. Copyright 1996 by the American Psychological Association.

perform the conceptual combination *well-dressed black man*, a person needs to come up with the most coherent interpretation (i.e., the interpretation that best satisfies the constraints). Positive constraints include the associations that poor blacks are aggressive, whereas negative constraints include the negative association that poor blacks tend not to be businessmen. IMP uses a connectionist algorithm to judge that the most coherent interpretation of *well-dressed black man* given the associations in Figure 1 involves the rejection of aggressiveness. IMP calculates how to perform the property overlap of the given concepts, but it is also capable of going beyond that overlap to introduce concepts that are associated with associates of the initial concepts. In Figure 1, *aggressive* and its negation are not directly associated with *well-dressed* or *black man* but can nevertheless emerge as part of the interpretation of the combined concepts.

Although IMP appears adequate to model many predicating conceptual combinations, it is not powerful enough to handle nonpredicating combinations such as *apartment dog*. I conjecture that such combinations will require a broader kind of constraint network in which thematic relations are used to choose the most coherent interpretation on the basis of semantic knowledge, factual knowledge, and context. How to construct such networks in detail is not obvious, but Figure 2 suggests their general structure. The oval nodes in Figure 2 represent hypotheses about what kind of relation holds between the head and modifier, including property overlap (as modeled by IMP), property application, location, and so on. Factual knowledge, semantic knowledge, and context all provide positive constraints that support different interpretations to different degrees. Because the different possible relations between the head and modifier are incompatible with each other, there are strong negative constraints between the elements representing different interpretations. Thus, nonpredicating conceptual combination can also be viewed as a coherence problem that subsumes predicating conceptual combination as a special case. If an IMP-like process achieves sufficient coherence in property overlap, this should support the property overlap node that implies for a particular case that conceptual combination is predicating. For example, the coherence of interpreting the combination *small apartment* as referring to

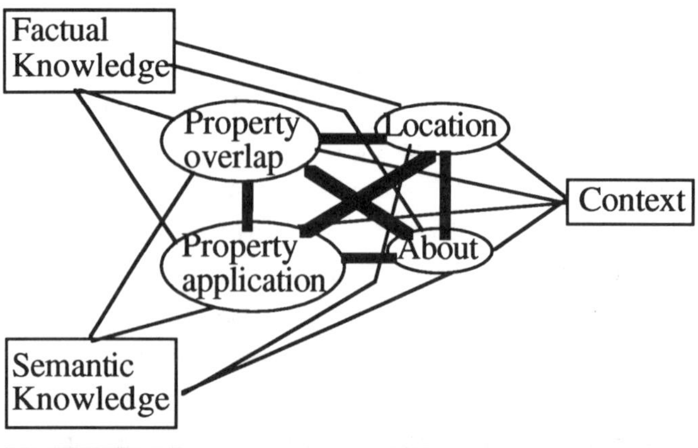

Figure 2

Constraint network for some thematic relations. The thin lines indicate positive constraints; the thick lines indicate negative constraints.

something that is both an apartment and small would support the property overlap node. Developing a full, detailed, psychologically plausible model of nonpredicating as well as predicating conceptual combination will be difficult because of the possible relevance of such a wide range of factual, semantic, and contextual knowledge.

INCOHERENCE-DRIVEN CONCEPTUAL COMBINATION

In the airport on the way to the conference at Texas A&M that inspired this book, I saw a business magazine with the cover story "How to Keep Your Employees From Becoming Web Potatoes." The combination *web potato* was new to me, and initially I could find no coherent interpretation of it. It is hard to understand how something could be both a web and a potato, so property overlap is not a reasonable interpretation. Application of thematic relations such as cause, about, location, and so on is equally problematic. Then I remembered the slang expression *couch potato*, which is used for people who watch too much television and suddenly interpreted a web potato analogously as someone who spends too much time on the World Wide Web. It helped that I could immediately think of some examples of people I know who are web potatoes.

This example illustrates how failure to find a coherent conceptual combination can lead to a more far-flung search for interpretations that evoke high-level cognitive processes such as analogy. Analogy can also be thought of as a kind of coherence process in which a constraint-satisfying correspondence is found between a source analog and a target analog (Holyoak & Thagard, 1995). Analogy is not the only possible source for new interpretations. Kunda, Miller, & Claire (1990) showed that surprising combinations such as *Harvard-educated carpenter* and *blind lawyer* generate causal reasoning in which people form new hypotheses to explain, for example, what might lead someone with a Harvard degree to become a carpenter. Hampton (this volume) shows additional examples of how conceptual combination can lead to emergent properties (i.e., properties not originally associated with either the head or the modifier concepts). This kind of emergent conceptual combination is often *abductive*, in that it involves the formation of explanatory hypotheses to explain how the modifier can apply to the head. (Abductive inference, or *abduction* as C. S. Peirce dubbed it, involves the formation and acceptance of explanatory hypotheses.) Like scientists, research participants who generate emergent properties using causal or explanatory reasoning realize they need to go beyond recognition of an initial lack of coherence in combined concepts to develop novel coherent interpretations.

Analogy and abduction are the two major sources of theoretical creativity in science (Thagard, 1988, 1992). For example, Darwin's seminal combination, *natural selection*, was both analogical and abductive: It depended on an analogy to the familiar process of artificial selection by breeders; and it involved the postulation that selection could become natural by virtue of a struggle for existence in the face of reproductive principles. Similarly, the ancient combination *sound wave* was analogical in that it depended on an analogy between sound and water, and it was abductive in that it used the wave hypothesis to explain the behavior of many sound phenomena such as echoing. Analogy and abduction are not, however, peculiar to creative scientists. In everyday life, people frequently use analogies to solve mundane problems like adapting last year's income tax preparation to do this year's tax forms, and people abductively infer explanations for why their cars fail to start or why their spouses are in a bad mood.

Thus, relatively creative conceptual combinations such as *web potato* and *natural selection* require leaps beyond the coherence-driven constraint-satisfying reconciliation of associations and thematic relations. They are incoherence-driven in that failure to find a sufficiently coherent interpretation triggers a broader search for an interpretation using analogical and explanatory mechanisms. I am not claiming that *all* creative conceptual combinations are incoherence-driven, as coherence-driven conceptual combination can produce emergent attributes such as *nonaggressive* from *well-dressed black* in Figure 1. I conjecture, however, that the most creative conceptual combinations arise from the more constructive and less associative mechanisms of abduction and analogy.

The distinction between coherence-driven and incoherence-driven combinations is analogous to the distinction between additive and multiplicative principles (Wilkening, Schwarzer, & Rümmele, this volume). Just as incoherence-driven conceptual combinations go beyond coherence-driven ones in the complexity of the new inferences they can yield, so multiplicative rules in physics and other domains make possible a richer account of phenomena than additive rules can provide.

CONCLUSION

I have tried to show how the insights about conceptual combination afforded by Hampton, Wisniewski, and Shoben and Gagné can all be embedded within a coherentist framework. Coherence viewed as constraint satisfaction enables one to see how people combine a modifier and head concept in the most common case wherein both concepts are predicated of something, but also suggests how to think of competition among competing thematic relations. When coherence fails, the potentially more creative cognitive processes of analogy and abduction are triggered. Emergent interpretations of combined concepts can contribute not only to conceptual coherence (the fit of a set of concepts with particular things) but also to analogical coherence (the fit of analogs with each other) and to explanatory coherence (the fit of hypotheses with what they explain). I have suggested that the overwhelming cognitive imperative underlying conceptual combination is to be coherent. Fortunately, when coherence fails, one sometimes can follow a more unusual cognitive imperative: Be creative.

REFERENCES

Holyoak, K. J., & Thagard, P. (1995). *Mental leaps: Analogy in creative thought.* Cambridge, MA: MIT Press/Bradford Books.

Kunda, Z., Miller, D., & Claire, T. (1990). Combining social concepts: The role of causal reasoning. *Cognitive Science, 14,* 551–577.

Kunda, Z., & Thagard, P. (1996). Forming impressions using stereotypes, traits, and behaviors: A parallel constraint satisfaction theory. *Psychological Review, 103,* 284–308.

Murphy, G., & Medin, D. (1985). The role of theories in conceptual coherence. *Psychological Review, 92,* 289–316.

Thagard, P. (1988). *Computational philosophy of science.* Cambridge, MA: MIT Press/Bradford Books.

Thagard, P. (1992). *Conceptual revolutions.* Princeton, NJ: Princeton University Press.

Thagard, P. (1993). Computational tractability and conceptual coherence: Why do computer scientists believe that P ≠ NP? *Canadian Journal of Philosophy, 23,* 349–364.

Thagard, P., & Millgram, E. (1995). Inference to the best plan: A coherence theory of decision. In A. Ram & D. B. Leake (Eds.), *Goal-driven learning* (pp. 439–454). Cambridge, MA: MIT Press.

Thagard, P., & Verbeurgt, K. (1997). *Coherence.* Unpublished manuscript, University of Waterloo, Waterloo, Ontario, Canada.

PART TWO

Conceptual Expansion

7

Imagination at Work: Conceptual and Linguistic Creativity in Children

Cristina Cacciari, Maria Chiara Levorato, and Piercarla Cicogna

This chapter examines two aspects of children's creative functioning: (a) drawing imaginary objects and (b) processing existing idioms and coining new figurative expressions. These two aspects might reveal different patterns of creative behavior and therefore tell us even more about development in creativity. In the first part of the chapter, we concentrate on whether an imaginal activity such as drawing imaginary artifacts and animals is constrained by and predictable on the basis of everyday categorization processes or whether children are able to go beyond the everyday world and imagine alternative scenarios. In the second part, we consider the extent to which children's creativity in language is bound to literality or whether children are able to master figurative language in creative ways, both in comprehension and production tasks.

IMAGINAL CREATIVITY

In a recent set of studies on the cognitive structures underlying imaginative tasks, Ward (1994, 1995) found that when adults were required to

We thank Cinzia Toschi and Chiara Astolfi for collecting part of the data we present here. We also thank the organizers and participants in the Creative Concepts Conference who provided us with a theoretically exciting conference and made us think more thoroughly and creatively about our work.

imagine and draw nonexistent creatures living on a planet, they generated creatures bilaterally symmetric, with sense organs, appendages, and so forth. That is, the creatures were "highly structured in terms of characteristic properties of common earth species, including single attributes, relations within and between species, and attribute correlations" (Ward, 1994, p. 30). On the basis of these results, Ward concluded that imaginative thinking shares most if not all of the structures, knowledge base, and processes of ordinary thinking.

Far from any romantic view of imagination, mundane imaginative productions of this sort appear to be structured and directed by knowledge of the categories and percepts that are most related to what is to be imagined: "When people use their imagination to develop new ideas, those ideas are heavily structured in predictable ways by the properties of existing categories and concepts " (Ward, 1995, p. 157). Thus, newly generated exemplars not only maintain particular properties of existing categories, but their structure is predicted on the basis of the properties of such categories as well.

What happens when the "creator" is a child? Although the imagination of children is commonly believed to be more spontaneous, more vivid, and richer in specific forms than that of adults (Brann, 1991; Cohen & MacKeith, 1991), existing evidence suggests that children start with a very rigid representation of the features characteristic of a category. Karmiloff-Smith (1990) used drawings of nonexistent houses, individuals, and animals produced by children of different ages (age range from 4 to 11) as clues to illustrate general constraints on internal representational change and flexibility. She found that children were indeed rarely flexible and highly constrained by the structure of existing categories. In particular, children younger than 8 years of age were only able to introduce changes in the size and shape of imaginary entities and to omit some essential features, but they were not able to insert elements belonging to different ontological categories (e.g., they drew, for instance, a person with only one leg, arm, and eye). Older children also used structural changes, for instance, inserting elements of the same category (e.g., a person with two heads or six arms) more than of different categories (e.g., a house with wings or eyes). Karmiloff-Smith's results suggest that children's creations, as those of adults, generally do not follow alternative paths. Existing categories bound children and adults to the same extent.

In a recent study, we investigated children's capacities to draw imaginary entities. Thirty-eight preschoolers (4 years, 4 months–5 years, 11 months) and 38 fifth graders (10 years, 2 months–11 years, 4 months; overall 33 boys and 43 girls), randomly assigned to two groups, participated in an experiment to test whether an artifact (i.e., a house) and a natural kind (i.e., an animal) might elicit different imaginary entities. Children were asked to draw either an imaginary house or an imaginary animal. Younger children were also asked to draw a "real" house and a real animal to be sure they were able to perform such tasks.

The Imaginary House

The children were asked to imagine a fantastic, nonexistent house and to draw it. To clarify possible ambiguities, the children were then requested to comment on and describe their drawings. We obtained 38 drawings (19 for each age group) of imaginary houses that were independently coded by two coders according to the nonexclusive presence of the following features: (a) anthropomorphic features, (b) characteristics or parts typically belonging to a house (e.g., roof, windows, door), and (c) the structural changes introduced with respect to a real house (Karmiloff-Smith, 1990). The imaginary houses drawn by children shared many of the parts houses typically have: They had roofs, chimneys, doors, windows, and so forth (see Table 1). However, in many cases they also lacked some features that are typical of a real house: In 37.3% of the cases for older children and in 27.8% for younger children, imaginary houses either did not have, for instance, windows, a roof, or a door, or they had plenty of them. Many younger and older children drew houses with many chimneys, doors, windows, and so forth, which might correspond to the image of a multistoried house—different, for younger children, from the typical single-storied house they produced.

A fundamental characteristic of these drawings is that the imaginary houses were "humanized" by means of animate or living features (eyes,

Table 1

Percentages of Attributes in Children's Drawings of Imaginary Houses for Two Age Groups

	% Attributes	
Attribute type	5-year-olds	11-year-olds
Basic element		
Doors	67	63
Chimney	61	42
Roof	94	94
Windows	67	52
Human feature		
Mouth	33	57
Eyes	39	63
Nose	28	52
Hair	39	10
Arms	11	57
Feet	—	31

hair, flowers) and conventional inanimate features usually associated with human beings (shoes, toys, watches) and their environment.

Interesting developmental differences emerged between the two age groups. The presence of anthropomorphic features (e.g., mouth, eyes, nose, feet, arms, and hair) in the drawings of the children of the two age groups suggests that older children tended to humanize their drawings much more than younger ones (45% vs. 25%). Interestingly, these human body features were always bilaterally symmetrical. Also nontypical features such as hats, watches, hearts, and numbers were used especially by older children. Overall, elements not belonging to the category *house* were present in all drawings of the older children but in only 55% of those of the younger children—a result that is consistent with Karmiloff-Smith's (1990) data, supporting the conclusion that older children are more able to use cross-categorial features than younger children.

As to the structural changes introduced (see Table 2), all of the older children modified the shape or dimension of elements of the house (e.g., windows with the shape of a heart, doors patterned as mouths) compared with only 55% of the younger children. A comparable difference between older and younger children was also found in Karmiloff-Smith's study. The global shape of the house was changed less by older (26%) than by younger children (50%). Position and orientation were rarely changed in either group's drawings (22% and 10%, respectively, by younger and older children), suggesting that these spatial properties played a minor role (cf. Levorato & Massironi, 1992).

The older children's drawings could be considered as more original than those produced by the younger children, especially because the older children omitted more elements that are typical of an existing house (e.g., windows, chimneys) and inserted elements belonging to other categories. It should be noted, however, that such elements corresponded most to the fairly standardized humanization procedure usually found in children's books and cartoons. Thus, the possibility exists that older children were more familiar with a conventionalized depiction style than were younger

Table 2

Percentages of Structural Changes Identified in Children's Drawings of Imaginary Houses for Two Age Groups

Type of structural change	% Structural changes	
	5-year-olds	11-year-olds
Shape and dimensions of elements	55	100
Whole shape	26	50
Absence of elements	39	52
Orientation and position changes	22	10
Cross-category insertions	55	100

children. Examples of drawings produced by children of both age groups can be seen in Figure 1.

The Imaginary Animal

Both age groups were required to draw an animal that did not exist so that we obtained 19 drawings for each age level. Each child was then asked to comment on the animal she or he had just drawn and to clarify any possible ambiguities. Afterward (within the same day), the children were asked to draw another animal belonging to the same species as the first. This was done to investigate the stability of the properties attributed to imaginary creatures. To make this instruction clear, children were told that they should imagine and draw "the cousin" of the imaginary animal they had previously drawn.

To code children's drawings, we adapted categories previously used by Ward (1994) and Karmiloff-Smith (1990). Drawings were therefore coded according to the nonexclusive presence of features of the following sort: (a) bilateral symmetry, (b) appendages, (c) sense organs, and (d) structural changes (i.e., introduced with respect to existing animals). As in Ward's study on adults, the imaginary animals the children drew, although very inventive, were nonetheless patterned mostly after and predictable from the properties of the animals children are most familiar with. Let us examine the animals the children imagined and drew (see Table 3). Most drawings were of four-pawed animals (overall 68.4%), bilaterally symmetric, especially in the older children's drawings (95% vs. 73% for younger children). They all had appendages, especially paws (100% vs. 84%, for older and younger children, respectively) and a tail. They also had sense organs, especially eyes (100% vs. 95%), a mouth (79% vs. 58%), a nose (37% vs. 68%), and ears (26% vs. 53%). Not surprisingly, the older children produced overall more detailed parts for both appendages and sense organs than did the younger children.

These results suggest that the imaginary animals the children drew reproduced the main characteristics of real animals. To analyze the extent to which these imaginary creatures were different from real animals, we examined the kinds of structural change the children introduced. The

(a) SHAPE AND/OR DIMENSIONS OF ELEMENTS CHANGED

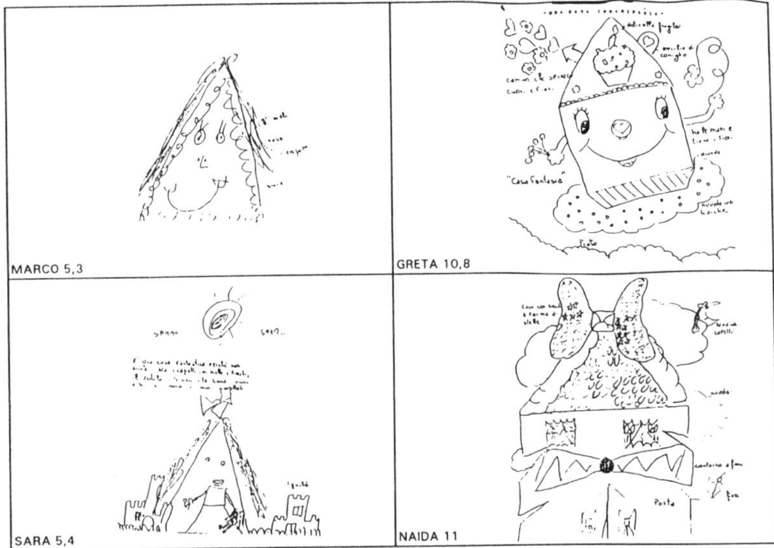

(b) WHOLE SHAPE CHANGED

Figure 1

Examples of children's drawings in which (a) the shape and/or dimensions of elements changed or (b) the whole shape changed.

Table 3

Percentages of Attributes in Children's Drawings of Two "Related" Animals for Two Age Groups

	% Attributes			
	First animal		Second animal	
Attribute type	5-year-olds	11-year-olds	5-year-olds	11-year-olds
Bilateral symmetry	73	95	95	95
Appendage				
Paws	84	100	79	100
Arms	21	37	16	42
Wings	16	26	21	21
Tail	51	68	47	58
Neck	37	68	16	58
Sense receptor				
Nose	37	68	42	68
Mouth	79	58	58	63
Ears	26	53	26	37
Eyes	95	100	95	100

NOTE: Animals were "related" in that children were asked to draw a nonexistent animal (first animal) and its "cousin" (second animal).

global shape,[1] as in the imaginary house drawings, was modified by all of the older children but by fewer of the younger children (37%). The older children also consistently modified the shape and dimensions of single elements (89% vs. 53% of the younger children). The children inserted features belonging to other animals (e.g., wings on a four-legged animal; 74% vs. 26%, respectively, for older and younger children) or used elements of different categories from those of animals (68% vs. 26%, respectively, for older and younger children). As in the drawings of nonexistent houses, the elements belonging to different categories from those of animals (e.g.,

[1]We considered the shape to be modified whenever children mixed up shapes belonging to different Earth animals; the same was applied to the changes in the shape of single elements.

hands, hats, flowers, sky) were rather conventional and corresponded to a humanization of the animals (e.g., hands, ribbons) or belonged to the environment in which pets typically live (e.g., flowers, a lawn, the sun; see Table 4).

Interestingly, younger children were more likely to use living or natural features (e.g., flowers, hands, sun, lawn, sky) instead of inanimate features. Such differences almost disappeared in older children, who used as many animate features as inanimate features (e.g., hat, lipstick, glasses, ball). The position and orientation were rarely changed, as in the imaginary house drawings (10% vs. 26%). Examples of drawings for both age groups can be seen in Figure 2). When asked to produce a second member of the same species of imaginary animals, the children drew creatures that matched the first ones in terms of bilateral symmetry of parts (such as appendages and sense organs) and also matched the ways in which these

Table 4

Percentages of Structural Changes in Children's Drawings of "Related" Imaginary Animals for Two Age Groups

	% Structural changes			
	First animal		Second animal	
Type of structural change	5-year-olds	11-year-olds	5-year-olds	11-year-olds
Shape and dimensions of elements	53	89	53	89
Whole shape	37	100	21	89
Absence of elements	42	42	37	42
Insertion of elements of a same category	26	74	10	53
Orientation and position changes	10	26	10	26
Cross-category insertions	26	68	10	63

NOTE: Animals were "related" in that children were asked to draw a nonexistent animal (first animal) and its "cousin" (second animal).

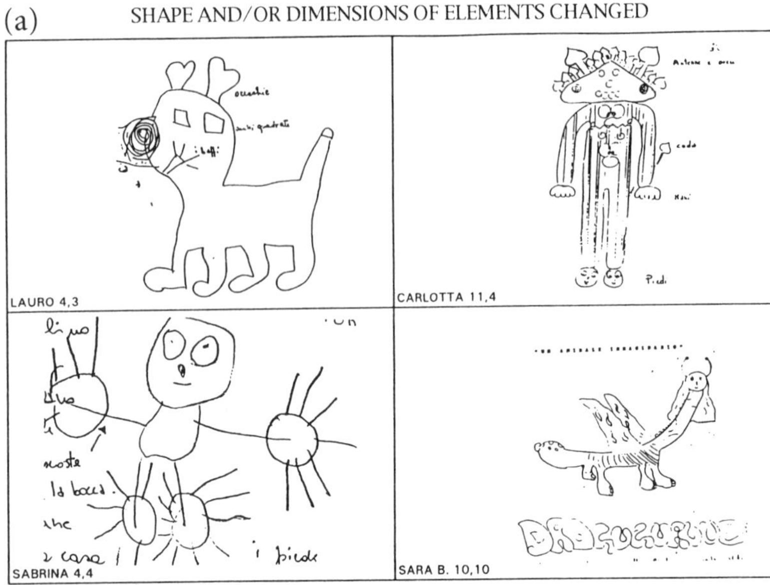

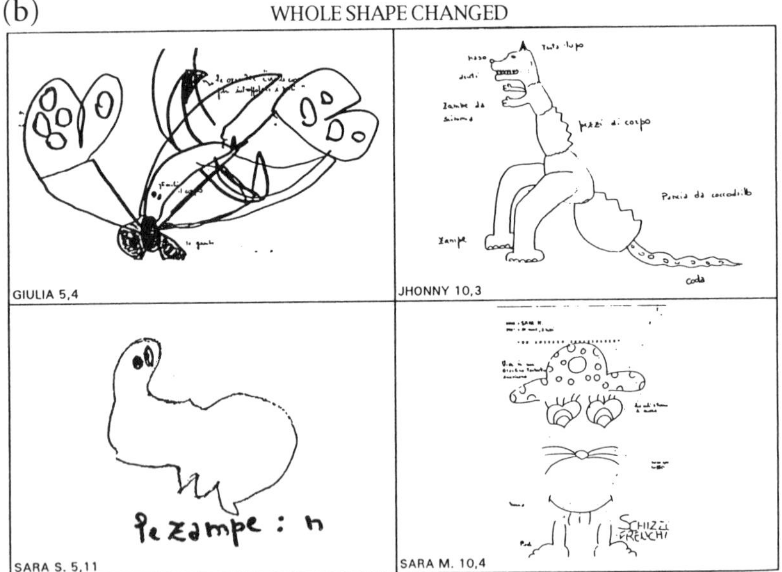

Figure 2

Examples of children's drawings in which the (a) shape and/or dimensions of elements changed, the (b) whole shape changed, the (c) position and orientation changed, or (d) cross-category insertions were made.

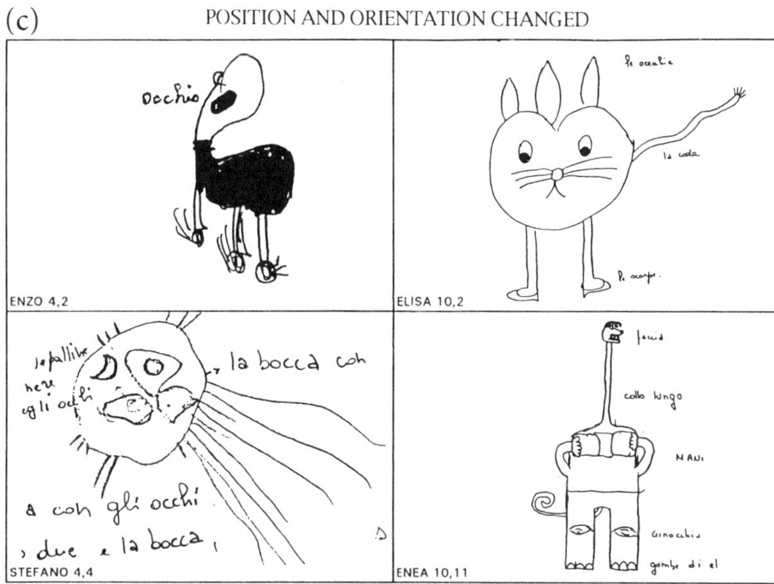

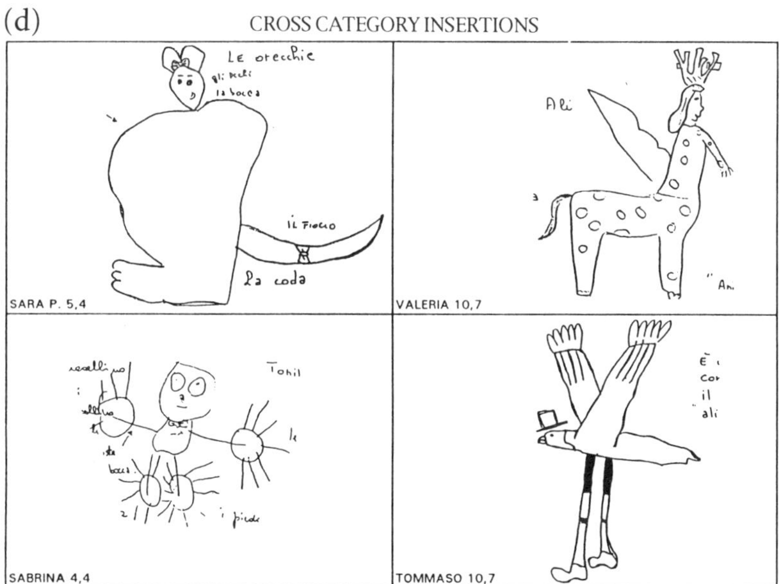

Figure 2 (cont.)

parts correlated and were aligned (Markman & Gentner, 1993). In the second drawing session, children were just as likely to develop a creature that differed in shape from an earth animal as they were in the first session.

Children changed the shape of animals in their drawings as often as they changed the elements. (Table 4 reports similar percentages for changes to the global structure and elements of the earth animals.) This confirmed, once again, the centrality of properties such as shape—as well as structurally aligned parts—in predicting category membership even when dealing with categories of nonexistent animals (Landau, Smith, & Jones, 1988; Tversky & Hemenway, 1984). Children were not influenced by existing animals in their drawings of such imaginary animal species. Both the structure and content of the mapping of the properties of Earth entities onto imagined creatures were predictable from what we know about existing animals (see Hampton, this volume).

Very few within-species variations emerged, as shown by the percentages reported in Table 3; namely, for younger children there was an increase (from 73% to 95%) in the bilateral symmetry of the objects they drew. There was also an increase (from 21% to 37% for younger children and from 89% to 100% for older children) in the changes both groups made to the global shape of Earth animals in their drawings. Interestingly, the older children changed the shape of the "cousin" (52.6%) more than the younger children (15.8%), who, in turn, changed the gender of the cousin more than the older children (36.8% vs. 21%, respectively, for younger and older children). Such changes in gender (overall 28.9%) were attributed on the basis of the comments that children wrote on the drawing. Fewer elements either belonging to the same animal category or to other categories were used by both age groups. Overall, the cousin of the imaginary animal was also inspired by the attributes and properties of real world animals.

The intraspecies consistency we obtained when the children were asked to generate a new exemplar of the imaginary animal species confirmed that not only were these creations highly structured but also that such structures are characteristic of the common animals. This suggested, once again, "important commonalities across creative and noncreative aspects of categorization" (Ward, 1994, p. 30; cf. Finke, Ward, & Smith, 1992; Perkins, 1981; Weisberg, 1988).

Whether children produced these imagined creatures by remembering specific animals (e.g., a child told the experimenter that she had in mind "my grandmother's cat") or by melding general schematic knowledge about animals and everyday environments is an issue beyond the scope of the present study.

Children used their existing conceptual structures to produce new creations with transformation procedures similar to those described by Kelly and Keil (1985) for literary metamorphoses (e.g., Ovidian ones), namely, transformations based on ontological categories such as animals, plants, and human beings, and on the animate–inanimate distinction. At first glance, such a distinction seemed to be blurred by the children when they drew houses with hair or animals with hats, but the conventionality of these features made us wonder whether they could be interpreted as genuine cases of ontological violation.

Individuals—be they adults or children—if not provided with specific environmental constraints follow a "path of least resistance" (Ward, 1994), that is, they retrieve a specific instance of a given category and pattern the new creation after it, regardless of whether they were required to imagine and draw an artifact such as a house or a natural kind such as an animal.

The results of this experiment suggest that children were at the same time graphically creative and conventional and—like adults—were unable to go beyond what was predictable for noncreative categorization processes on the basis of existing schematic knowledge. They were conventional or literal, so to speak, in their attempt to imagine nonexistent houses and animals, because to be inventive they used mainly a basic and frequent device such as humanization or they recombined attributes and properties of real entities.

Such conventionality can, of course, be due to the instruction and type of task children were asked to perform. The choice of asking children to produce an imaginary version of very common and familiar entities, such as houses or animals, might have triggered the activation of a highly structured conceptual knowledge that is more difficult to abandon, presumably, than that associated with less familiar entities. Also, in the instructions we did not specify any contextual constraint as to possible environments where such imaginary entities might live or exist. It should be noted, however, that in Ward's (1994) study on adults, the presence of a similar constraint did not change the nature of the imaginary creatures adults produced with respect to a no-constraint instruction.

If one accepts the view that new creative ideas are produced at the crossroad of old and new schemata, and not necessarily as a violation of existing concepts (Ward, 1995), then it is not contradictory to consider these drawings as creative productions although conventionally inspired. As frequently happens in advertising, the recombination of existing graphic symbols is a powerful means for image creativity (Appiano, 1991), as suggested also by those who defined *imagination* as the ability to rearrange one's perceptual experience (Olson, 1970).

In the second part of this chapter, we examine the abilities children exhibit when asked to recombine language in creative ways. Results concerning figurative language processing in children (Cacciari & Levorato, 1989, 1995a, 1995b; Levorato & Cacciari, 1992, 1995) suggest that the productive nature of language indeed allows children to recombine existing meanings in unpredictable but sensible ways.

LINGUISTIC CREATIVITY IN CHILDREN

In this section we examine results from different sources to illustrate the extent to which children are able to go beyond literality in language as it is reflected by the ability to comprehend, produce, and explain a specific type of figurative expression, namely, idiom. For many years, a consistent lack of interest in figurative language has governed the developmental literature with the predominant view that children are unable to understand figurative expressions until their teenage years (i.e., metaphors, idioms, proverbs, and so forth; Ackerman, 1982; Lodge & Leach, 1975; Nippold & Tarrant Martin, 1989; Prinz, 1983). Recent work on figurative competence acquisition has raised questions about such a view. A growing body of evidence now shows that even 7-year-old children can, for instance, understand idiomatic expressions, especially when embedded in highly informative contexts (Ackerman, 1982; Cacciari & Levorato, 1989; Gibbs, 1987, 1991; Levorato & Cacciari, 1992, 1995; Winner, 1988). Yet how are idioms acquired? The acquisition of idioms is not based on a rote learning mechanism but is instead grounded in the acquisition of a figurative competence (Levorato & Cacciari, 1995) that develops parallel to more general cognitive capacities and concerns various forms of figurative language (idioms, metaphors, proverbs, and so on). Such figurative competence consists of a coordinated set of abilities that are integrated within the more general cognitive mechanism underlying semantic competence and language comprehension (Levorato & Cacciari, 1992, 1995). Such abilities can be summarized as follows: (a) understanding the dominant, peripheral, and additional related meanings of a word and its position in a given semantic domain; (b) suspending a purely literal–referential strategy; a prerequisite not only for figurative language comprehension but also for that of most of our linguistic repertoire (e.g. polysemous words, meaning indeterminacy, and ambiguity; see Murphy, this volume); (c) being aware that language is governed by conventions according to which what is said and what is meant do not always coincide; and (d) using contextual information to construct a coherent semantic representation of a text that must also integrate the lexical and semantic information carried by the figurative expression.

According to the figurative competence model (Levorato & Cacciari, 1995), the development of figurative language understanding and production is a long-lasting process (taking place from 7 to 11 years of age) that can be schematized in terms of nonsequential phases in which the capacity to elaborate language and the levels of knowledge acquired and activated qualitatively differ. Although, as we show further on, the comprehension and production of figurative meanings are acquired with a different time course (see Table 5), they both derive from the ability to go beyond a local, piece-by-piece elaboration of a text to search for a global and coherent meaning.

To point out the ways and extent to which children are able to go beyond literality to exhibit a creative linguistic behavior, we selected some

Table 5

Development of Figurative Competence in Comprehension and Production

Phase	Comprehension	Production
1	Literal	Literal
2	Figurative	Literal
3	Idiomatic	Figurative
4	Idiomatic	Idiomatic

NOTE: From "The Effects of Different Tasks on the Comprehension and Production of Idioms in Children," by M. C. Levorato and C. Cacciari, 1995, *Journal of Experimental Child Psychology*. Copyright 1994 by Academic Press. Reprinted with permission.

of the many results from studies on the acquisition of idiomatic expressions, and particularly those concerning (a) metalinguistic judgments on the semantic motivation for idioms' meaning (Cacciari & Levorato, 1995b), (b) the production of figurative language (Cacciari & Levorato, 1989; Levorato & Cacciari, 1992, 1995), and (c) the coinage of new figurative expressions (Cacciari & Levorato, 1995a).

Making Sense of Idioms: Why Do We Break the Ice?

For years, the commonly held view was that idioms were long words with semantically empty constituents. Hence, no role whatsoever should be attributed to the meanings of the words composing the idiom, as their relation to the overall figurative meaning was either lost or purely accidental. Recent models on idiom representation have raised questions about this view as well as the comprehension models derived from it (see Cacciari & Tabossi, 1993). New experimental questions have emerged to uncover the type of knowledge that people use when asked to interpret idioms, or to form a mental image of their meaning (Cacciari, 1993; Cacciari & Glucksberg, 1990, 1995; Gibbs, 1994). Although most of this literature has focused on adults, developmental studies have been conducted as well (Cacciari & Levorato, 1995b; Gibbs, 1987, 1991). Gibbs (1987), for instance, showed that children might learn idioms differently depending on the syntactic and semantic transparency of idioms. Syntactically non-modifiable idioms such as "put on some weight" could be learned in a rote manner, whereas metaphorically transparent idioms such as "cry over spilled milk" might involve some metaphorical reasoning strategy because of a transparent relationship between the literal and the figurative meanings.

These studies suggest that not only are children able to understand idioms but they also have intuitions and metalinguistic capacities similar to, if not more ingenious than, those of adults. In a study that investigated the effect of semantic transparency on children's capacity to paraphrase, explain, and provide a semantic motivation for idioms' meanings, Cacciari and Levorato (1995b) used three types of familiar Italian idioms: (a) *Quasi-metaphorical idioms* use the same communicative strategy as good metaphors (see Glucksberg, this volume) because they "call to mind a prototypical or stereotypical instance of an entire category of people, events, situations or actions" (Glucksberg, 1993, p. 18; e.g., "to be like two drops of water" means being very similar; "to be like dogs and cats" means being enemies); (b) *transparent idioms* have a discernible relationship between the component words and the idiom's stipulated meaning (e.g., "looking for a needle in a haystack," "crying over spilled milk"); (c) *opaque idioms* are those in which no apparent relationship is perceived between literal and idiomatic meanings (e.g., "cutting the rope," which means escaping).

We hypothesized a direct relationship between level of semantic transparency and children's capacity to paraphrase, explain, and motivate an idiom's meaning. Forty-five 10-year-old children were asked to (a) paraphrase either opaque, transparent, or quasi-metaphorical idioms; (b) explain the reason motivating the idiom's meaning; (c) answer whether a 6-year-old child might understand the idiom; and (d) illustrate the ways in which a young child might come to understand it.

Not surprisingly, children found quasi-metaphorical idioms easiest to paraphrase (see Figure 3). Three of the answers given by children when asked to motivate an idiom's meaning are particularly interesting for investigating their metalinguistic capacities:

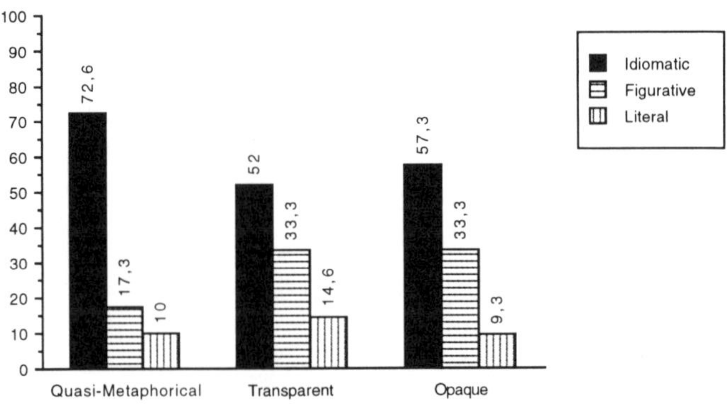

Figure 3

Percentage of idiomatic, figurative, and literal paraphrases for quasi-metaphorical, transparent, and opaque idioms.

1. *The properties of the literal referent.* Children mentioned the properties that typically characterize the person, object, or action used as referent (or vehicle) in the idiom. For instance, for "being as two drops of water" (being very similar), a child referred to the fact that drops of water are all alike; for "being like dogs and cats"(being enemies), a child noted that cats and dogs are enemies; for "being afraid of one's own shadow" (being afraid of everything), a child wrote that "a shadow is harmless."
2. *The properties of the idiomatic referent.* Children listed the characteristics that a person (or event) has when it is described by an idiom. For instance, for "looking for a needle in a haystack," a child said that "there are people that complicate things so much and want to look for something that cannot be found"; for "being like dogs and cats," a child wrote that "because two people hate each other"; for "crying over spilled milk," a child pointed to the phrase "because one cries after having done something and not before."
3. *Analogies between the literal referent and the idiomatic referent.* Children elaborated on the relationship between the action or character literally described by an idiom and its figurative meaning. For "breaking the ice," a child elaborated with the following: "The ice is

hard to be broken and the more the time passes and the more the silence gets iced" or "if something wrong happened to you, you break the ice when you overcome your regret." For "being at the seventh sky" ("being in seventh heaven"), a child gave the following elaborations: "Because one is so happy that she or he is able to make jumps as big as to reach up to the seventh sky" or "Everyone knows that the sky is wonderful, so if such a thing as a seventh sky existed, could you imagine just how wonderful it must be?"

The percentages of different types of explanations for quasi-metaphorical, transparent, and opaque idioms are shown in Figure 4. Again not surprisingly, children found quasi-metaphorical idioms easiest to explain on the basis of the properties of the literal referent (42% of the answers). Quasi-metaphorical idiom structure typifies, in fact, the figurative meaning by using highly salient "literal" examples most often very close to children's everyday lives (dogs, cats, drops of water, and so forth). This mechanism allows an easy instantiation and generalization of the meaning of this type of idiom. Their literal referents are, therefore, relevant and can be used to explain and interpret an idiom's meaning.

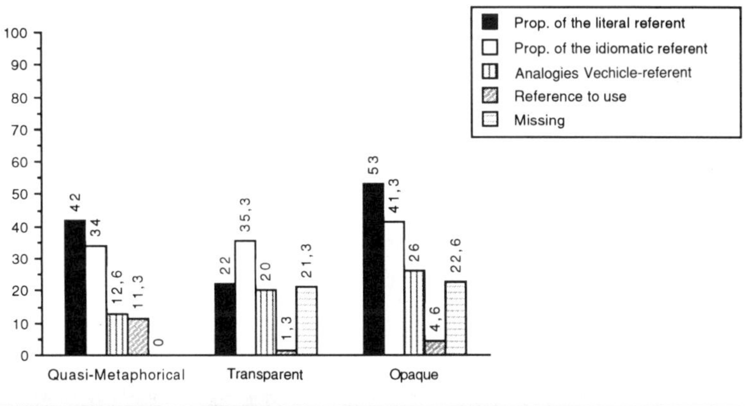

Figure 4

Percentage of different types of explanations for quasi-metaphorical, transparent, and opaque idioms.

Children mentioned the idiomatic referent, that is, the characteristics that a person or event must have to be described by an idiom, especially with transparent idioms (35.3%). Analogies were not much used (overall, 19.5%), which is not surprising because they are cognitively much more complex than the other answers. Rarely used for quasi-metaphorical idioms, analogies were, instead, used for transparent and opaque idioms (20% and 26%, respectively).

When asked to explain how a young child might understand an idiom, that is, what strategies the child might use to ultimately get to the idiomatic meaning, the children indicated several ways. Figure 5 shows the percentages of answers for the quasi-metaphoric, transparent, and opaque categories. However, we highlight here only those that account for the most interesting findings regarding children's linguistic and conceptual creativity:

1. *Observing what is literally expressed by the idiom.* For instance, for the idiom "drowning in a glass of water" ("getting lost over nothing") a child wrote that a younger child might understand the idiom's meaning by thinking that "it is impossible to drown in a glass of water be-

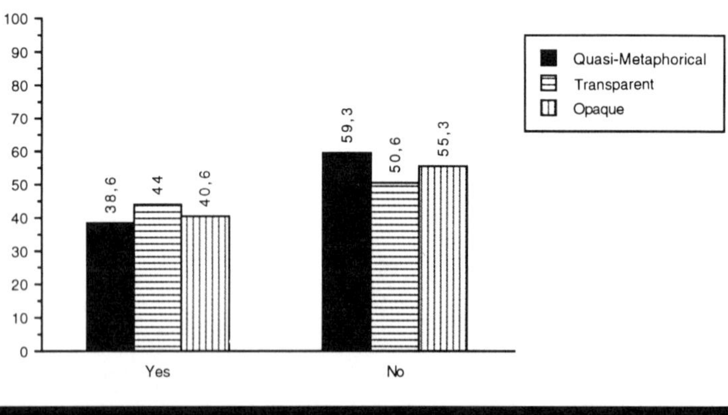

Figure 5

Percentage of different types of answers to the question, "How can a 6-year-old understand *idiom*?"

cause a glass is too small, so it means that you are worried for nothing." Another child suggested for "crying over spilled milk" that "one should spill milk and then despair." For "being afraid of one's own shadow" a child argued that a possibility was "to put him/herself in front of a lamp and watch his/her shadow." For "being as mute as a fish," the strategy to grasp the idiom's meaning was to try "looking at an aquarium and observing the big conversations of fishes!"

2. *Observing (or performing) the idiomatic referent expressed by the idiom.* For instance, for "cutting the rope"(escaping) a child wrote that "she or he should feel afraid and then escape very quickly." For "being among the clouds" (being absentminded), a child wrote, "you are in the classroom, the teacher is explaining and you are thinking of something else." Another child suggested, "make him/her remember that it happened to him/her too to be thinking about something else while someone was asking him/her something." For "costing an eye of the head" (costing a lot of money), a child suggested "watching a person that is spending a lot of money."

Again as expected, the answer that we coded as "observing the literal action" was given mostly for quasi-metaphorical idioms (49.3%). Here, in fact, the literal referent of the idiom is in itself an instance of the idiomatic meaning and exemplifies the action expressed by the idiomatic meaning. For example, "fishes" are animals that prototypically stand for silence and social distance. Cats and dogs are traditional enemies, any drop of water is by definition similar to another, and so forth. It is as if for children a careful observation of the environment (cats and dogs, two drops of water, and so forth) might allow an understanding of what idioms are about. "Observing the idiomatic referent" was chosen for both transparent idioms (32.6%) and opaque idioms (22%). The choice of the answer "observing the idiomatic action" could be ambiguous. In fact, whereas for transparent idioms it might indicate the perception of a link, if not a direct mapping, from literal to idiomatic referents, in the case of opaque idioms it might represent a "best guess" type of answer, namely, a "naive" belief that the meaning of words is self-evident.

How Can One Break the Ice?

Producing an idiom is more difficult than comprehending it, and, in fact, the capacity to produce idioms is acquired as one of the last steps in the development of figurative competence. Comprehension precedes and outpaces production, frequently by a rather large gap, but this is not an all-or-none acquisition. Both comprehension and production are, instead, preceded by a figurative, not yet idiomatic, phase. The schema reported in Table 5 (adapted from Levorato & Cacciari, 1995) summarizes the developmental phases of the comprehension and production of figurative language in children.

In a set of different studies with children of an age ranging from 7 years, 2 months old to 11 years, 4 months old (Cacciari & Levorato, 1989; Levorato & Cacciari, 1992, 1995), we presented children with short stories in which the last sentence was an idiom that described an action or mental state concerning the main character of the story. The last word of the idiom was omitted, and children were asked to complete the story with the word or words he or she considered most appropriate. For instance, in a story about a young boy who was moving to a new home and, therefore, was changing school and schoolmates, the last sentence was about his new friends at school and ended with "therefore he eventually broke" (Cacciari & Levorato, 1989). We found that children gave not only either literal or idiomatic completions but also figurative completions perfectly appropriate for expressing the mental state or action of the main character of the story. Figurative completions (39.2 % and 26.9% for third and fifth graders, respectively) were of the following sort: "the fear," "the problem," "his emotion." They were rather close in meaning to the figurative sense of the string although different from both the correct idiomatic completion ("the ice") and, of course, literal completions (e.g., "the crayon," "the book").

Figurative completions were typically produced by children who did not yet know that an idiom existed to phrase such a mental state conventionally ("break the ice"), but at the same time they perceived that language can be used figuratively. These children preferred exploiting a figurative way of expression to producing concrete, literal completions.

Third graders produced more completions in the nonliteral area (represented by figurative and idiomatic completions; 53.1%) than in the literal area (represented by literal completions 41.2%). Although this was less than fifth graders (66.9% vs. 26.2%), it was still a remarkably high percentage if one takes into account the complexity of a production task of this sort.

Evidence showing the relevance of such answers was replicated in two other studies (Levorato & Cacciari, 1992, 1995) that investigated the role of idiom familiarity and task specificity in idiom comprehension and production. Again, figurative answers were consistently used by 7- and 11-year-old children, suggesting, once more, that these answers play an interesting developmental role: They are in an intermediate phase that follows the abandonment of a literal strategy and precedes a full mastery of the idiomatic repertoire in comprehension and production (as summarized in Table 5).

New Metaphors for Common Domains

Yet, are children able to produce new figurative expressions for referring to commonly experienced actions and mental states? Slang and formulaic expressions are continuously produced and are borrowed primarily from specialized jargons or are used as signs of recognition in a group. After all, figurative language is a major source for lexical and semantic innovation. However, if few studies exist that investigate the ability of adults and children to produce literal language innovation (Clark, 1981; Clark & Hecht, 1982; Murphy, this volume), then even fewer have been conducted on the production of new figurative expressions. A general underestimation of school-age children's ability to coin new expressions may account for the fact that most studies on figurative or creative language concern comprehension instead of production. In the study we present here, children's ability to create new expressions for common actions or mental states was investigated with the aim of identifying the linguistic, conceptual, and communicative resources that children use when they create new expressions.

Linguistic creativity implies cognitive, metacognitive, and communicative abilities: When a speaker coins a new expression to signify a particular object or event, she or he has to find a reasonable balance between shared knowledge with the audience, on the one hand, and aptness and novelty on the other. In creating such expressions different abilities cooperate, for instance, taking into account that the expression has to be clear enough to allow the listener to understand the intended meaning, identifying a source domain appropriate to express it, and selecting a linguistic form consistent with the morphosyntactic rules of the language.

A list of 15 common actions or mental states (e.g., revealing a secret, telling lies, being angry, sleeping too much) was prepared. Sixty-three 11-year-old Italian children (10 years, 3 months–11 years, 5 months) volunteered to participate. For each action or mental state, children were asked to create and write down a new way of expressing it that was potentially "secret," that is, comprehensible within the group but not outside it, namely, by adults (the word *idiom* was never used). This was done to encourage the children to use figurative instead of plain literal language. The children were divided into two subgroups: Group 1 was given the list of 15 domains of reference and was asked to form a new expression with no constraint as to the syntactic form used; Group 2 was asked to form new sentences using the verb "to be" in a comparative structure ("to be like"). Children were randomly assigned to either of these two subgroups.

The answers were coded by two independent coders first as being literal or figurative. A sentence was coded as *literal* if it either paraphrased the original domain literally, or used literal examples, already existing formulaic expressions and uses, or made reference to literal consequences and causes. Conversely, an answer was coded as *figurative* whenever it used nonliteral strategies that might range from creating new metaphors to creating new neologisms and from creating new metonymies to creating new synecdoches, and so on. After a close examination of the answers, the following categories were used to classify the productions: (a) synecdoches or metonymies, (b) transparent and opaque metaphors, (c) neologisms, (d) examples, (e) common uses or formula, and (f) paraphrases. In general, conditions a through c corresponded to a figurative repertoire, and conditions d through f corresponded to a literal repertoire (see Table 6).

Table 6

Percentages of Figurative and Literal Productions by Fifth Graders According to Type of Instruction

Type of instruction	% Figurative productions				% Literal productions		
	SM	TM	OM	NEO	EX	CU	PAR
Free	6.6	18.4	14.4	0.2	20.3	18.4	16.7
Like	1.0	36.8	11.0	—	21.5	17.7	0.6
Total	3.8	27.4	12.7	0.1	20.9	18.0	8.6

NOTE: SM = Synecdoches/metonymies; TM = Transparent metaphors; OM = Opaque metaphors; NEO = Neologisms; EX = Examples; CU = Common usages and formula; PAR = Paraphrases (including consequences/causes and syntagmatic relations).

We present the percentages of figurative and literal productions with respect to children's answers in the two conditions, free creation (instruction "free") and creation in a comparative form (instruction "like") for each category (see Table 6). On the basis of the results obtained with quasi-metaphorical idioms that were easiest for children to paraphrase and explain, we expected a facilitating effect on the production of nonliteral expressions with the comparative form in the other condition.

Children might have been unable or reluctant to produce figurative expressions for several reasons. First, the task required them to propose a new way for designating actions that already had a name of their own. In addition, they may have been uncertain as to the pragmatic appropriateness of a figurative expression, as in the case of second language learners. Despite this, children created a remarkably high percentage of new figurative expressions (44.2%). It should be borne in mind that the instruction did not explicitly ask children to use a figurative means of expression. That almost half of the coinage of new expressions was figurative can, therefore, be taken as even more compelling evidence of the ability children possess to use language in creative ways. It is interesting that children were able to create expressions that were not a simple rephrasing of existing expressions or a literal paraphrase of the event or mental state. To this extent they were once again able to go beyond literality (see Figure 6). This result raises questions about the view that after a very early phase of creative linguistic behavior, school-age children enter into a "literalization" phase in which a decay in the production of figurative language occurs coinciding with an increase in their literacy (Winner, 1988).

Children produced more nonliteral expressions in the comparative instruction than in the free instruction (48.8% and 39.6%, respectively). This suggests that the operator *like* triggered a between-domains strategy more than a within-domain semantic strategy. Some examples of target domains and figurative expressions can help to reveal the semantic richness of these new expressions. Revealing a secret: "being a speaking letter," "being a musical instrument." Sleeping too much: "making the pillow sleep," "putting the glue in the pajamas," "seeing the entire sky," "breaking the sheet," "being like a stone on the ground." Working hard: "being like the water that runs," "being like a sweat producer," "being like a typewriter." Making a mistake: "opening a tap of errors." Telling lies: "opening a hole in the honesty." Being angry: "seeing the thunders," "being like a big black cloud." Betraying friends: "being like the days that change." Putting in disorder: "being like the wind."

We now focus on the linguistic form of the answers children gave. Many tropes were used (see Table 6): transparent and opaque metaphors

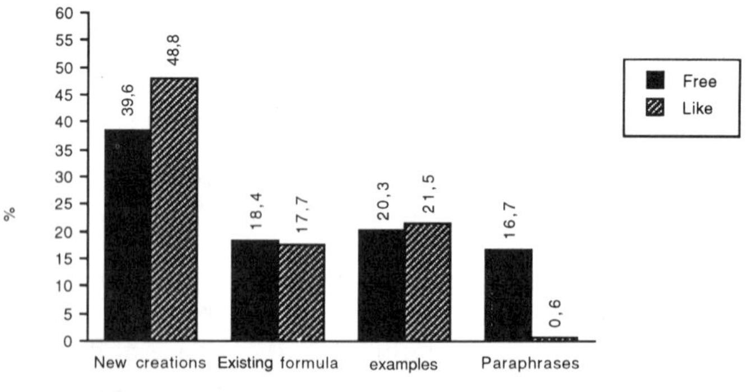

Figure 6

Expressions created by children according to the instruction type.

(27.6% and 12.7%, respectively),[2] metonymies and synecdoches (3.8%), as well as literal productions such as examples (20.9%), existing formulas or references to famous characters (Pinocchio, Alberto Tomba, Batman; 18%), and paraphrases (8.6%). Few answers (8.1%) were nonclassifiable in any of the previous categories (respectively, 4.9% in the free instruction and 11.4% in the comparative instruction category). The selection of a certain vehicle, the associations children made, and the personification they chose are not lexical accidents but reflect the beliefs children have about mental events such as making mistakes, revealing secrets, telling lies, and so forth. Therefore, the semantic domains children selected as reference points for expressing the figurative meanings can show the kinds of mapping that children considered as appropriate for figuratively "translating" a certain action or mental state. A further analysis was performed on only nonliteral expressions (that corresponded, as we said, to 44.2% of the answers) to identify the ontological categories to which their content referred. The same two raters that coded the form of the newly coined expressions also coded the frequencies with which categories such as animals, human beings, natural kinds, artifacts, and abstract concepts were used by children.

As shown in Figure 7, children used inanimate concepts (both natural and artifacts) much more than animate concepts. Also, a small percentage of psychological concepts was used (e.g., happiness, sorrow, number; 3.3%). More artifacts (e.g., objects, buildings) were used than natural inanimate kinds (e.g., thunderstorm, rock; 35.6% and 20.1%, respectively). For animate vehicles, the domain of animals (25.3%) was used more than that of human beings (15.6%). When children were asked to coin new ways for expressing human actions or states they consistently changed the semantic domain of reference.

An interesting difference emerged between the two instructions. When children were asked to form sentences using a comparative form ("to be like"), they made more reference to animals (29.1%), natural kinds

[2]A string was classified as an opaque metaphor (instead of being considered as nonsensical) whenever the figurative meaning made sense to the coders, although it required a more complex mapping from source to target domains than in the case of a transparent metaphor.

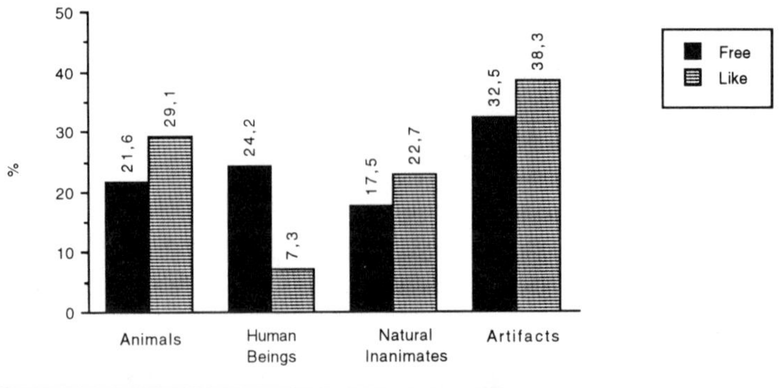

Figure 7

Categories used for creating nonliteral expressions according to the instruction type.

(22.7%), and artifacts (38.3%) than in the other instruction. The reference to human beings was the lowest (7.3%) in the comparative form that was preferred for between-domain mappings. These results suggest that artifacts that contain plenty of functional information and animals that provide typical as well as stereotypical properties are the semantic domains from which children mostly extracted their figurative repertoire. Because borrowing from other domains is one of the basic devices for constructing figurative expressions, it is not surprising that the domain of human beings was used so little.

Whereas humanization, as a graphical device, pervaded children's drawings of imaginary houses and creatures, this was not so in the production of new expressions. In creating figurative expressions, children used source domains distant from the target domains (i.e., the action or mental state for which the creation of a new expression was asked). The selected vehicles generally occupied a role or played a function in the source domain similar to that played in the target domain (as illustrated by the example of "being like a musical instrument" for "revealing a secret") where a same action, that of issuing permanent sounds, is shared by the target and the vehicle (musical instrument; Tourangeau & Sternberg, 1981).

Interestingly, whereas figurative language provides concrete referents for expressing abstract mental states, it was not infrequent for children to concretize an abstract concept (e.g., honesty) by imposing on it some concrete transformation (e.g., being holed, as in "opening a hole in honesty" for expressing "telling lies").

CONCLUSION

The main results from our studies on imagination and figurative language suggest that when children are asked to imagine and draw nonexistent artifacts (a house) or creatures (an animal) they are, at the same time, graphically creative and conceptually conventional (or literal, so to speak). In fact, they base their drawings on existing entities, projecting attributes, properties, correlations, and alignment of existent entities on nonexistent ones. Moreover, these graphical productions were predictable from what is known about the ways in which people categorize artifacts, human beings, and animals.

On the other hand, when children are asked to explain and produce figurative expressions or to create new ones, they exploit the productive nature of language and are able not only to explain the semantic structure, namely whereby certain types of idioms mean what they mean (especially when the idiom structure was exemplar based), but also to produce idioms and create new figurative expressions for concrete events and abstract mental states.

One might wonder whether the drawings produced by the children in this study (and by adults in Ward's experiments) can be considered genuine cases of mundane creativity or are more simply induction-based productions. Of course, it depends on the distinction between *creativity* and *induction* one endorses. The debate about the difference between induction and creativity has a long history in the philosophical literature. As Rodari (1973) pointed out, the distinction between perception and imagination ("faculty fingendi"), or, as Kant put it, between "reproductive imagination" and "productive imagination" (quoted in Rodari, 1973, p. 168), has been at the core of philosophical discussion about human intelligence since the 18th century. If one would like to endorse a view in which induction, unlike creativity, is based on generalization and does not add any information to an existing knowledge base (Johnson-Laird, 1993), then these drawings might be more appropriately categorized as outputs of an induction-based process.

The evidence we present on the difficulty of crossing conceptual boundaries in imaginative tasks (with the potential exception of the humanization that we discussed) and the ease in comprehending and using figurative language is not contradictory. In fact, whereas language allows individuals to recombine meanings and referents in an almost infinite number of ways (with the important limitation of the balance between novelty and comprehensibility), the ways in which one might imagine nonexistent creatures are more limited, although one might come up with numerous and composite productions. Moreover, they are more likely to be predictable from what we know about everyday categorization processes.

Is imagination structured? Of course, and in both language and conceptual recombinations. Unlike hallucinatory states where reality constraints are suspended, imagination seems to exploit the same schemata and knowledge sources that govern everyday mental life.

REFERENCES

Ackerman, B. P. (1982). On comprehending idioms: Do children get the picture? *Journal of Experimental Child Psychology, 33*, 439–454.

Appiano, A. (1991). *Pubblicità, comunicazione, immagine* [Advertising, communication, and images]. Bologna, Italy: Zanichelli.

Brann, E. T. H. (1991). *The world of the imagination. Sum and substance.* Savage, MD: Rowman & Littlefield.

Cacciari, C. (1993). The place of idioms in a literal and metaphorical world. In C. Cacciari & P. Tabossi (Eds.), *Idioms. Processing, structure and interpretation* (pp. 27–55). Hillsdale, NJ: Erlbaum.

Cacciari, C., & Glucksberg, S. (1990). Understanding idiomatic expressions: The contribution of word meanings. In G. B. Simpson (Ed.), *Understanding word and sentence* (pp. 217–240). Amsterdam: Elsevier Science.

Cacciari, C., & Glucksberg, S. (1995). Understanding idioms: Do visual images reflect figurative meanings? *European Journal of Cognitive Psychology, 7*, 283–305.

Cacciari, C., & Levorato, M. C. (1989). How children understand idioms in discourse. *Journal of Child Language, 16*, 387–405.

Cacciari, C., & Levorato, M. C. (1995a). *Creating new figurative expressions.* Manuscript in preparation.

Cacciari, C., & Levorato, M. C. (1995b). *How children make sense of idiomatic meanings.* Manuscript submitted for publication.

Cacciari, C., & Tabossi, P. (Eds.). (1993). *Idioms. Processing, structure and interpretation* (pp. 27–55). Hillsdale, NJ: Erlbaum.

Clark, E. V. (1981). Lexical innovations: How children learn to create new words. *Behavioral Development. A Series of Monographs, 2*, 29–328.

Clark, E. V., & Hecht, B. F. (1982). Learning to coin agent and instrument nouns. *Cognition, 12*, 1–24.

Cohen, D., & MacKeith, S. A. (1991). *The development of imagination.* New York: Routledge.

Finke, R. A., Ward, T. B., & Smith, S. M. (1992). *Creative cognition: Theory, research and applications.* Cambridge, MA: MIT Press.

Gibbs, W. R. (1987). Linguistic factors in children's understanding of idioms. *Journal of Child Language, 14*, 569–586.

Gibbs, W. R. (1991). Semantic analyzability in children's understanding of idioms. *Journal of Speech and Hearing Research, 34*, 613–620.

Gibbs, W. R. (1994). *The poetics of mind. Figurative thought, language and understanding.* Cambridge, England: Cambridge University Press.

Glucksberg, S. (1993). Idiom meaning and allusional content. In C. Cacciari & P. Tabossi (Eds.), *Idioms. Processing, structure and interpretation* (pp. 3–26). Hillsdale, NJ: Erlbaum.

Johnson-Laird, P. N. (1993). *Human and machine thinking.* Hillsdale, NJ: Erlbaum.

Karmiloff-Smith, A. (1990). Constraints on representational change: Evidence from children's drawings. *Cognition, 34*, 57–83.

Kelly, M. H., & Keil, F. C. (1985). The more things change . . . : Metamorphoses and conceptual structure. *Cognitive Science, 9*, 403–416.

Landau, B., Smith, L. B., & Jones, S. S. (1988). The importance of shape in early lexical development. *Cognitive Development, 3*, 299–321.

Levorato, M. C., & Cacciari, C. (1992). Children's comprehension and production of idioms: The role of context and familiarity. *Journal of Child Language, 19,* 415–433.

Levorato, M. C., & Cacciari, C. (1995). The effects of different tasks on the comprehension and production of idioms in children. *Journal of Experimental Child Psychology, 60,* 261–283.

Levorato, M. C., & Massironi, M. (1992). Dall'immagine al linguaggio. Uno studio dei processi percettivi implicati nella descrizione di figure [From image to language: A study of the perceptual processes implicated in a figure's description]. *Versus. Quaderni di Studi Semiotici, 59–60,* 141–171.

Lodge, L., & Leach, E. (1975). Children's acquisition of idioms in the English language. *Journal of Speech and Hearing Research, 18,* 521–529.

Markman, A. B., & Gentner, D. (1993). Splitting the difference: A structural alignment view of similarity. *Journal of Memory and Language, 32,* 517–535.

Nippold, M. A., & Tarrant Martin, S. (1989). Idiom interpretation in isolation versus context. A developmental study with adolescents. *Journal of Speech and Hearing Research, 32,* 58–66.

Olson, D. R. (1970). Language and thought. Aspects of a cognitive theory of semantics. *Psychological Review, 77,* 257–273.

Perkins, D. N. (1981). *The mind's best work.* Cambridge, MA: Harvard University Press.

Prinz, P. M. (1983). The development of idiomatic meaning in children. *Child Development, 51,* 1110–1119.

Rodari, G. (1973). *Grammatica della fantasia. Introduzione all'arte di inventare storie* [The grammar of imagination: An introduction to the art of inventing stories]. Torino, Italy: Einaudi.

Tourangeau, R., & Sternberg, R. J. (1981). Aptness in metaphor. *Cognitive Psychology, 13,* 27–55.

Tversky, B., & Hemenway, K. (1984). Objects, parts and categories. *Journal of Experimental Psychology: General, 113,* 169–193.

Ward, T. B. (1994). Structured imagination: The role of category structure in exemplar generation. *Cognitive Psychology, 27,* 1–40.

Ward, T. B. (1995). What's old about new ideas? In S. M. Smith, T. B. Ward, & R. A. Finke (Eds.), *The creative cognition approach* (pp. 157–178). Cambridge, MA: MIT Press.

Weisberg, R. W. (1988). Problem solving and creativity. In R. Sternberg (Ed). *The nature of creativity. Contemporary psychological perspectives* (pp. 220–238). Cambridge, England: Cambridge University Press.

Winner, E. (1988). *The point of words. Children's understanding of metaphor and irony.* Cambridge, England: Cambridge University Press.

8

The Creation of New Concepts: A Multifaceted Approach to Category Learning

Arthur B. Markman, Takashi Yamauchi,
and Valerie S. Makin

The acquisition and use of concepts are central areas of research in cognitive science, because the ability to place different items into equivalence classes underlies a wide range of cognitive abilities. Categories allow people to see discriminably different items as similar (Rosch, 1975; Smith & Medin, 1981), facilitate inductive inference of properties (Heit & Rubinstein, 1994; Osherson, Smith, Wilkie, Lopez, & Shafir, 1990), and support communication (Clark & Wilkes-Gibbs, 1986; Garrod & Anderson, 1987; Garrod & Doherty, 1994). Concepts can also be combined to form new concepts (as discussed in the chapters by Hampton, Shoben, Wilkening, and Wisniewski in this volume). Furthermore, concepts play an important role in higher level reasoning processes including analogy, metaphor, and causal induction (as discussed in the chapters by Gentner et al.; Dunbar; Gibbs; and Glucksberg, Manfredi, and McGlone in this volume).

This work is supported by National Science Foundation CAREER Award SBR-95-10924 given to Arthur B. Markman. We thank the organizers of the Creative Concepts Conference for providing us with an opportunity to discuss these ideas. In addition, we thank Tory Higgins, Bob Krauss, Trisha Lindeman, Brian Ross, and all of the participants at the conference for helpful comments and discussions.

Concept acquisition is a prime example of incremental creativity, as new information is continually added to existing representations, and information about existing concepts is used to construct representations of new items. Boden (1994) distinguished between *psychological creativity*, which consists of additions of new concepts within an individual, and *historical creativity*, which consists of the development of concepts that no person has ever had before. Ordinary concept acquisition is a process of psychological creativity in that people generally learn concepts that exist within their social network, though the addition of new information to people's network of concepts obviously requires that they go beyond the information they already possess.

In an effort to make the study of category acquisition tractable, psychologists have generally focused on how people learn to classify new items into one of a small set of categories. Furthermore, the bulk of the studies in this tradition have used some variation of a standard classification paradigm (Medin & Schaffer, 1978; Nosofsky, 1986; Nosofsky, Palmeri, & McKinley, 1994; Reed, 1972) in which an exemplar is presented to an individual, who responds with a best guess of the category to which the exemplar belongs. Generally, the individual is given feedback (though see Clapper & Bower, 1994, for an example of unsupervised category learning), and learning proceeds until he or she is able to classify the exemplars in a manner consistent with the structure specified by the experimenter. Classification has also been examined through a variety of sorting tasks in which all of the exemplars are presented at once, and individuals must sort them into groups that go together (e.g., Ahn & Medin, 1992; Lassaline & Murphy, 1996; Wattenmaker, 1995). A crucial (if implicit) assumption of this work is that the representations and processes developed by the learner in this type of experiment are sufficient to serve the varied cognitive functions for which categories are crucial.

An analysis of studies of classification suggests that many factors influence the nature of category representations, including the accessibility of memory storage (Estes, 1986; Medin & Schaffer, 1978; Ross, Perkins, & Tenpenny, 1990), the perceptual manifestation of the stimuli (Barsalou & Prinz, this volume; Glenberg, this volume Regehr & Brooks, 1993), the purposes and utilities associated with categories (Schank, Collins, & Hunter, 1986), and the background knowledge of the category learners (Keil, 1989; Medin & Wattenmaker, 1987; Murphy & Medin, 1985; Pazzani, 1991; Wattenmaker, 1995; Wisniewski & Medin, 1994). Furthermore, the processing style that people adopt affects what they learn (Elio & Anderson, 1984).

The range of factors that affects category representations suggests that what is learned about a category is a function of the information requirements of the task being carried out, as well as the current representation of that category and related categories. This task-dependent nature of learning suggests that researchers must go beyond classification tasks to explore how the use of categories affects what we learn about them. That is, we must move to a *multifaceted* view of category acquisition (see also Ross, 1996). To make this suggestion more concrete, we begin this chapter by examining three important uses of categories—classification, inference, and communication—to determine how they differ in the kinds of information required to carry out these tasks. We then present several studies that begin to address the impact of these three category uses on category creation.

CATEGORY REPRESENTATION AND CATEGORY USE

To go beyond classification, we first assume that category representations are the result of what is learned as individuals manipulate, perceive, think about, and reason with objects in the world. What people learn about an item or category in a given situation depends on how they use it. Thus, a central factor that determines what people learn is the set of information requirements for the tasks they perform with their categories. In this chapter, we focus on this aspect of concept acquisition and leave aside other factors like whether learning is failure driven (Nosofsky et al., 1994; Schank & Abelson, 1977) or whether each exposure to an exemplar affects concept representations (Medin & Schaffer, 1978). In particular, we focus on the information requirements of three representative tasks: classification, feature-inference, and communication.

Of course, it is not necessary that the primary information acquired during category learning be related to the information requirements of the task. It is certainly possible that the category learning system stores as much information as possible during acquisition with the hope that such information will be helpful later. Clearly, rich episodic traces are stored. However, integrating knowledge into our web of concepts is a computationally intensive process, and people are probably quite conservative in this aspect of categorization. In particular, they may rarely go beyond the minimum amount of effort needed to perform the current task (see also McKoon & Ratcliff, 1992). Because of this conservatism, the information requirements of the task currently being done will place crucial constraints on what information is acquired by doing that task.

The standard classification task requires the individual to learn to identify exemplars as members of one of a set of categories. In this case, the most important information is that which distinguishes exemplars of one category from exemplars of another (i.e., diagnostic information; Tversky, 1977). In some classification tasks, a single feature might be sufficient to classify nearly all of the exemplars, For example, Ahn and Medin (1992) presented people with a sorting task in which 8/10 stimuli could be classified unidimensionally. Most participants classified the stimuli in this manner and then compared the remaining items to the unidimensional classes and placed each exception in the class to which it was most similar. In other classification tasks, the diagnostic information may be whole exemplars (Medin & Schaffer, 1978), structures that take into account multiple features of objects (Wattenmaker, 1995), features and correlations between features (Medin, Altom, Edelson, & Freko, 1982), or even emergent properties that arise from the juxtaposition of category exemplars (Wisniewski & Medin, 1994).

Feature inference has different information requirements than classification. In feature inference, a person is given information about the category membership of an item and about some of the features of that item. The category task is to infer one of the missing features. For example, if you saw a dog with its back end behind a tree, you might infer the presence of a tail and the remaining two legs. This task focuses on relationships between the category label and the features of the category. In addition, this task promotes attention to relationships between features. These relationships may be statistical (e.g., birds with short wings generally have short legs), or they may reflect other relations like causal relations (e.g., birds have feathers and wings because both are adaptations suitable for flight). Unlike the classification task, information that helps distinguish between categories need not receive special attention.

Some evidence that inference involves attending to relations between concepts was provided by Lassaline and Murphy (1996) using a sorting task. People were given exemplars from two classes generated from different family resemblance structures. They were then asked to sort these exemplars. Participants tended to sort the items into classes on the basis of a single shared dimension (like the participants in the sorting task of Ahn and Medin, 1992). A second group of people was given a series of questions in which they inferred one feature of an exemplar and then were given the sorting task. These participants were more likely to sort the exemplars on the basis of the family resemblance structure, suggesting that the inference task focused participants' attention on information about relationships between features.

Some theories of classification have suggested that the category label should be treated as another feature of the category (e.g., Anderson, 1990). In this view, classification is an inference task in which people are only asked to infer the category label. Evidence that classification and feature inference are demonstrably different tasks would provide evidence against this assumption.

We now address the third use of categories, namely, communication. Communication differs from both classification and inference in that it requires simultaneous attention to both the commonalities and differences of items. Commonalities are important, because it is parsimonious to use similar labels for similar items in the world. For example, a whole range of objects in the world are labeled as *dogs*. Nonetheless, sometimes we must establish reference to unique individuals. In particular, we must distinguish like objects from each other efficiently. Thus, the differences between items that are most likely to be important are those that distinguish between similar items (which are typically different values along some corresponding aspect of the items, or *alignable differences;* A. Markman & Gentner, 1993, 1996).

Very little attention has been given to the role of communication on category formation, but there is strong reason to believe that the social context places constraints on the structure of people's category representations. For example, Freyd (1983) suggested that the polar structure of psychological dimensions results from communicative pressures. According to Freyd it is much easier to communicate a dimensional concept if the labels mark extremes than if the labels first mark arbitrary intermediate points. Furthermore, there may be constraints on the kinds of categories that a culture naturally accepts into its network of concepts (Sperber, 1985). Finally, communication permits us to learn concepts via cultural transmission so that each individual need not learn all of their concepts without assistance (Bruner, 1990; Higgins, 1992; Rogoff, 1990; Vygotsky, 1986). For example, Rogoff (1990) described ways that parents in different cultures structure new situations to facilitate chidren's acquisition of new concepts and skills. It is cultural transfer of information that has made it so difficult to study mechanisms of historical creativity (Boden, 1994), as the first person to come up with an idea had to divine it in some way, but subsequently, it could be communicated freely to other people.

Cultural transmission provides an important route to learning category structures, so that all categories need not be rooted in perceptual or bodily experience (e.g., Barsalou & Prinz, this volume; Gibbs, this volume; Glenberg, this volume, in press). This aspect of category acquisition is often neglected in the categorization literature. For example, much work in cognitive development has focused on how children come to recognize that words have meanings and that nouns often refer to objects (E. Markman, 1989; Jones & Smith, 1993; Soja, Carey, & Spelke, 1991). This work tends to focus on how a child might learn to associate linguistic sounds with internal representations of objects in the world. Although this work has generated many interesting insights into the nature of word learning, it places more emphasis on the work that the child must do to create a concept than it does on the role of the social interactions in which the category creation is embedded.

Another argument for considering the impact of communication on category acquisition explicitly is that most classification studies (particularly those in which feedback is given) involve an implicit communication between experimenter and research participant. Participants in most classification tasks do not form arbitrary and idiosyncratic sets of categories. Rather, they are asked to form the particular set of categories created by the experimenter. Thus, participants are asked to play a most difficult communication game in which information is given one exemplar at a time. However, because they are asked to provide category labels only, without having to refer both to broad classes of items and to unique exemplars, the full impact of communication on categories cannot be made apparent in studies of this kind. Finally, communication is a collaborative process (Clark, 1996; Clark & Wilkes-Gibbs, 1986; Schober & Clark, 1989), but in the typical classification study the category divisions are not established collaboratively, and the participant is given no opportunity to ask for more information to resolve a difficulty.

The discussion of information requirements is meant to set the stage for empirical investigations of the way category use affects category learning. Clearly, the particular set of information requirements offered here is oversimplified. Empirical studies have demonstrated that variations within classification tasks can yield significant differences in performance. For example, the particular information that makes up the categories has been shown to be an important determinant of the resulting category representation. Wattenmaker (1995) showed that people are more likely to sort a set of items into family resemblance groups if the categories reflect social concepts than if they reflect object concepts. Wisniewski (1995) found that the degree to which a feature is associated with a particular category following classification depends not only on the probability that the feature was paired with the category but also on the degree to which individuals expect the feature to be part of the category on the basis of their prior knowledge. Of course, if classification involves many different subcomponents, it only reinforces the importance of examining other category uses for their impact on category representation.

Our research program is starting to explore a multifaceted view of category creation. The grand design is to illuminate the way the information requirements of particular tasks affect what is learned about categories. A more modest aim is the demonstration that tasks that appear to have different information requirements have different effects on what is learned about categories. While we keep our eye on the central goal, we will be satisfied here if the more modest aim is achieved. To this end, we describe some studies that begin to address the impact of classification, inference, and communication on category learning. First, we present evidence that distinguishes between the standard classification paradigm and inference-based category learning. Then, we address the impact of communication on category acquisition.

CLASSIFICATION-BASED AND INFERENCE-BASED CATEGORY LEARNING

The central assumption of the multifaceted view is that category learning is affected by the information required to carry out a task. Because inference and classification are assumed to involve a focus on different types of information, performing these tasks should result in different category representations. To test this hypothesis, we contrasted classification-based category learning with an inference-based learning process (Yamauchi & Markman, 1995, 1996). In these studies, the stimuli were constructed using a simple family-resemblance structure with exception features like the one shown in Table 1 (Medin, Wattenmaker, & Hampson, 1987). As shown in Figure 1, the stimuli were a set of simple dimensional figures consisting of a geometric form of a given size and color placed within a frame (Medin & Schaffer, 1978).[1]

Two different acquisition procedures were contrasted. The first was the standard classification paradigm described above (as shown in Figure 2a). In the classification tasks, participants were shown one of the eight

[1]Simple dimensional stimuli were used in this study to verify the success of the methodology. We are beginning to explore these procedures with other stimulus sets.

category exemplars (A1–A4, B1–B4 from Table 1) and were asked to specify the category to which it belongs (A or B). Participants made their responses and were then given feedback. The exemplar was also shown during the feedback.

In the inference-based learning tasks (shown in Figure 2b), the participants were told the category membership of the item (e.g., Set A) and were shown the values of three of the four features of the item (e.g., its form, color, and size). The fourth feature (e.g., position) was left unspecified, and the participant was to predict the correct feature value for that category. On other trials in the inference condition, the participant inferred other features of the exemplar. After making a response, the participant was given feedback, and the entire stimulus was presented. During learning, participants in the inference task were asked to make all feature inferences except for the inferences to the "exception features" (see Table 1).[2]

Finally, some individuals participated in a mixed learning condition consisting of randomly ordered blocks of classification and inference trials. Following an initial learning phase, participants were given two transfer tasks. They classified the exemplars and the prototypes, and they did all possible feature inferences for each of the eight category examplars (including the exception features).

In the first experiment, 24 participants in each learning condition were presented with 18 blocks of 8 trials. Participants in the inference condition made more correct responses during learning (M = 93% correct) than did those in either the classification condition (M = 85% correct) or the mixed condition (M = 80% correct), suggesting that the inference condition was easiest. An interesting pattern emerged in the transfer task. For the classification of old exemplars, participants given classification learning performed better (M = 88% correct) than participants in either the inference (M = 81% correct) or mixed (M = 82% correct) condition

[2]In Table 1, the items in bold are exception features (e.g., in Category A, the exception features had value 1, but all of the other features had value 0). In the transfer task, participants made inferences for all possible inference trials, including the exception features.

Table 1

Stimulus Structure for the Comparison of Inference and Classification

Category A	Form	Color	Size	Position	Category B	Form	Color	Size	Position
A1	0	0	0	**1**	B1	1	1	1	**0**
A2	0	0	**1**	0	B2	1	1	**0**	1
A3	0	**1**	0	0	B3	1	**0**	1	1
A4	**1**	0	0	0	B4	**0**	1	1	1
Prototype	0	0	0	0	Prototype	1	1	1	1

NOTE: Exception features are shown in bold.

Figure 1

Sample stimuli from the comparison of inference-based and classification-based learning. The shaded and checked patterns that fill the shapes were shown to subjects as red and green patterns.

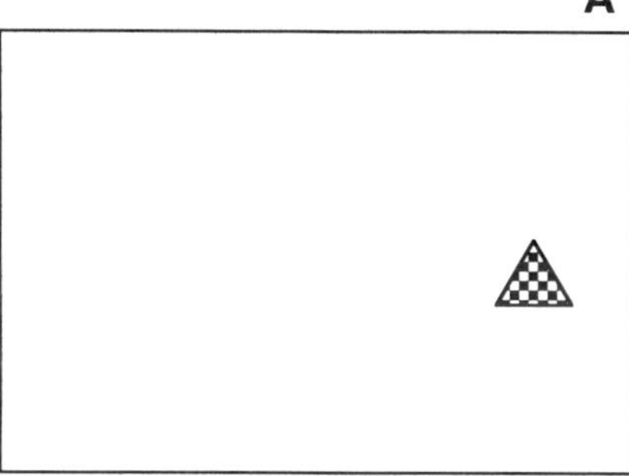

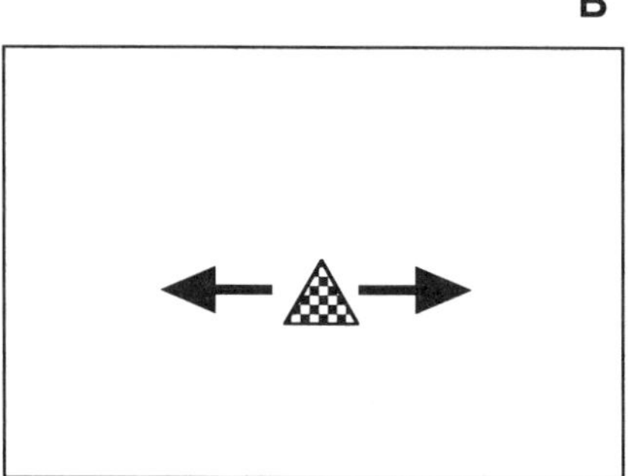

Figure 2

Examples of the classification and inference tasks.

(although the difference was not significant). The groups did not differ in their ability to classify the prototypes. In contrast, on inference transfer trials, participants in the inference-based learning group (*M* = 96%) performed better than participants in both the classification (*M* = 79%) and the mixed (*M* = 86%) groups (this difference was significant). These data suggest that transfer was appropriate to the way the categories were learned. Classification learning led to the best performance on classification transfer. Inference learning led to the best performance on inference transfer.

Inference trials for exception features present an interesting case. When individuals respond with the exception value, they are showing sensitivity to the individual exemplars. In contrast, when individuals respond with the opposite value, they are showing sensitivity to the prototype of the category. For example, referring back to Table 1, a response of 1 to the position of the form in Stimulus A1 reflects the value taken on by the exemplar, but a response of 0 reflects the value taken on by the prototype. In all three learning conditions, participants made responses that were consistent with the prototype more often than would be expected by chance, but the proportion of prototype responses was significantly higher for the inference group (*M* = 0.91) than for either the classification (*M* = 0.72) or the mixed (*M* = 0.72) group. This finding is consistent with the idea that inference-based learning focuses individuals on relationships between features within a given category.

The results for the mixed group were a bit surprising. Their performance on learning and transfer trials was worse than that of either the classification group or the inference group. However, mixed learning may simply be more difficult than either classification alone or inference alone. Thus, participants in the mixed condition may have exhibited poor transfer performance because they did not learn the items very well. To examine this possibility, the methodology of the first study was repeated, but participants continued the learning trials until they reached 90% or better accuracy across three successive blocks.

Consistent with the results of the first study, on average, the learning criterion was reached most quickly by participants in the inference condition (after an average of 9 blocks), followed by those in the classification condition (after an average of 13 blocks). The mixed condition was most difficult, requiring an average of 17 blocks to reach criterion performance. The transfer results of this study are interesting. In the classification of old exemplars, participants in the classification (M = 92%) and mixed (M = 88%) conditions performed significantly better than participants in the inference (M = 77%) condition. The groups did not differ significantly in classifying the prototypes. On old inference trials, participants in the inference (M = 94%) and mixed (M = 95%) groups performed significantly better than participants in the classification (M = 81%) group. On exception tasks, participants in all groups again gave responses that were consistent with the prototypes more often than would be expected by chance, but participants in the inference (M = 86%) condition were significantly more likely to do so than were those in the classification and mixed (M = 64% and 76%, respectively) conditions. Overall, participants' performance was best in the transfer task that matched the learning condition. Furthermore, participants in the mixed condition performed well in both transfer tasks, but only after they were given enough training trials to reach proficiency with both tasks.

It could be argued that these results simply reflect familiarity with the particular task given during learning. Participants in the inference condition were given only inference trials, not classification trials. Likewise, participants in the classification condition were given only classification trials. Thus, when these participants reached the transfer task, they may have performed more poorly on the unfamiliar task than on the familiar one. To rule out this possibility, the previous study was repeated; however, participants were first given practice on both the classification and the inference tasks with an unrelated set of stimuli. Following this practice period, participants were assigned to the inference condition or the classification condition, and they continued the learning phase until they reached the 90% criterion. The same pattern of results was obtained. Even after getting practice in both tasks, participants performed best during transfer when the learning task matched the transfer task.

Taken together, these results clearly suggest that different things are learned as a result of classification and inference, but there is a sense in which these data do not seem surprising. There is plenty of evidence for learning specific transfer (see Singley & Anderson, 1989, for a review). However, in another study, one group of participants was given the inference task until they reached the learning criterion and then was given the classification task, and continued in learning trials until they reached criterion in this task as well. A second group was shown the tasks in the reverse order. Participants who performed inference learning first needed significantly fewer blocks to learn both tasks than did participants who performed classification learning first. Furthermore, participants in this inference-first condition also had greater accuracy on the transfer trials than did participants in the classification task. The results of this last study suggest that the differences observed for the first three studies are not simply a result of learning how to carry out a particular task. Rather, these results reflect that inference and transfer lead individuals to focus on different information and that this focus affects the resulting category representations.

These studies suggest that people retain some flexibility in using categories. Participants in these studies were above chance in all of the transfer tasks regardless of the learning condition. Thus, participants were not limited solely to the task they performed during learning. Nonetheless, the data argue against the view taken by Anderson (1990) that category labels are simply one feature of an item among many and that classification is simply the inference of a single feature. Participants found inference alone to be easier than classification alone. The inference task required learning four different responses, whereas the classification task required learning only one. Furthermore, performing the inference task followed by the classification task was easier than doing the tasks in the reverse order. If both classification and inference involve the same process, it is not clear why the order in which the tasks are presented should matter. These data support the claim that inference and classification focus people on different information about the items presented during learning. The content of the resulting category representations is a function of the information requirements of these tasks.

COMMUNICATION AND CATEGORY LEARNING

Another function of categories is to enable communication. As discussed above, the information requirements of communication differ from those of classification and inference. In classification, categories must be distinguished from each other. In inference, the relationships between features within a category are paramount. In communication, a number of simultaneous constraints are involved. The category representation must be easily shared with other people who have the same category (Freyd, 1983). The category representation must be easily translated into descriptions that are efficiently transmitted. Furthermore, the commonalities and differences of related categories become important. On the one hand, efficiency would suggest that people should recognize the commonality among related categories and give similar labels to similar categories to help distinguish broader classes of related items from classes of unrelated items. On the other hand, people communicating must be able to distinguish a particular item from other similar items, necessitating the development of methods for communicating differences between related items (see Brown, 1958; Glucksberg, Krauss, & Higgins, 1975; Krauss & Fussell, 1996; and Murphy & Brownell, 1985, for discussions of these constraints).

These constraints can also be cast as a tension between identifying individual items and identifying classes of related items. Different strategies of reference are important at different times, and so our category system must support both reference to specific individuals and reference to broader classes. For example, we might want to identify the small thing behind a tree as a dog (to be contrasted with other animals), or perhaps more specifically as a poodle (to be contrasted with other dogs). This pressure to refer to items at different levels of abstraction may lead to the formation of a taxonomic hierarchy. The need to make specific references may also lead to the use of modifiers that reflect distinctions beyond the relative specificity of categories that is marked by a taxonomic hierarchy (e.g., the brown dog, or the dog that just stole my shoe). All of these forms of reference are expected to affect the way the category is represented.

The impact of communication on the creation of categories can be examined using the referential communication paradigm. Often, studies using this methodology involve asking pairs of people to jointly determine labels for a series of individual items (like pictures drawn from tangram pieces). For example, Krauss and Weinheimer (1964) and Clark and Wilkes-Gibbs (1986) found that people who establish reference to the same figure multiple times use successively shorter names for the picture across references, as the "name" for the item becomes fixed (see Krauss & Fussell, 1996, for a review of this work).

In the study we discuss here, pairs of people constructed LEGO® models collaboratively (see also Baggett & Ehrenfeucht, 1988, and Garrod & Anderson, 1987, for examples of similar tasks). LEGO models provide an interesting domain for studying the construction of categories. The LEGO system consists of connectable pieces of various shapes, sizes, and colors that can be used to construct models of objects (e.g., cars or planes). In this study, 12 pairs of people were presented with all of the pieces needed to construct two simple models (a car and a spaceship). In the first part of the experiment, the pairs named all of the pieces collaboratively. Then, one member of each pair, who was arbitrarily chosen to be the *director*, was given a set of pictorial instructions for building one of the models (half of the pairs built the car, and half built the spaceship). The pictorial instructions, which came packaged with the LEGO pieces, included diagrams that showed how to construct the model (an example is shown in Figure 3). The director's task was to communicate to the other member of the pair (the *builder*) how the model was to be constructed. The builder was not allowed to see the pictorial instructions, and the director was not permitted to manipulate the pieces. After constructing the model, each member of the pair was given one example of each piece used in the two models (52 pieces in all) and was asked to sort the pieces into groups. These sorting data were contrasted with the sorting data of another group of participants who did not build the models or communicate about the pieces.

Open-ended data collection techniques, like the analysis of conversations, yield rich data sets that must be condensed to address the questions of interest. The analyses summarized here focus on the structure of the categories built by participants as inferred from the labels they used. First,

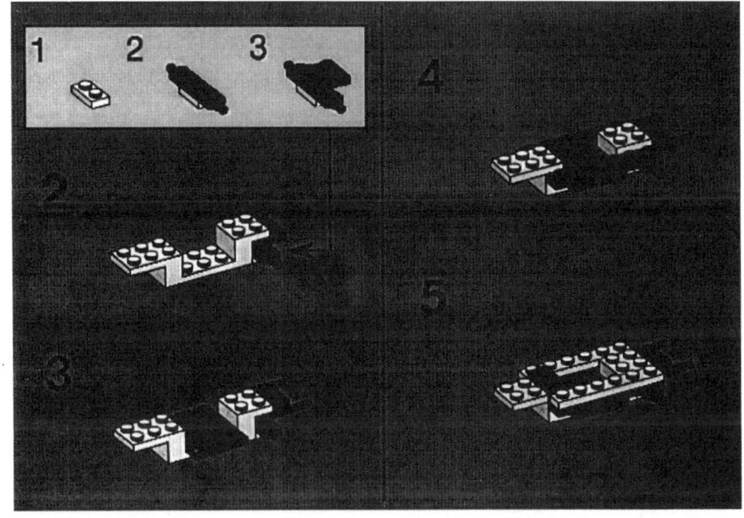

Figure 3

Sample pictorial instructions from a LEGO model. © LEGO Group, 1992. Used with permission.

we discuss the ways participants described pieces, paying particular attention to the kind of information preserved by the labels and the structure of the labels. Then, we examine the data from the sorting task and discuss parallels to what we observed in the labeling data.

The Use of Labels

The participants in this task had little difficulty establishing names for the pieces. Each dyad coordinated their conversation to allow them to settle on a set of labels. The groups differed somewhat in communicative styles. Some dyads had one member who took charge, whereas others obtained labels through a more cooperative process (see also Garrod & Doherty, 1994). All pairs settled on a naming scheme in which pieces were described by a phrase constructed around a noun (which we refer to as the *base term*) and a set of modifiers. For example, a participant might refer to a piece as a black two-prong tile with a pole. The noun *tile* is the base term in this label. There are also two-dimensional modifiers (*black* and *two-prong*), and one appendage (*with a pole*). In the following sections, we examine the base terms and the modifiers in more detail.

Base Terms

The base terms reflected the shape of the piece most frequently. For example, thin LEGO bricks were called *bars, tiles*, or *stoplights* (the latter because the studs on the top give the pieces a shape similar to that of a traffic light). Similarly, another piece with an odd shape was called a *ramp* or a *prism* by some groups. The use of shape as a basis for classification generally involved labeling pieces on the basis of a prototypical form. For example, many groups distinguished pieces that had 1 × X (e.g., 1 × 2) arrangements of studs (often called *bars* or *tiles*) from pieces that had 2 × 2 or 2 × 6 arrangements of studs, which were generally called *squares* and *rectangles*, respectively. Pieces with a 1 × X shape (e.g., 1 × 4) were all called by the same base name but were given different modifiers to denote their size. This use of shape as a dominant means of categorizing pieces is consistent with studies demonstrating children's use of shape in early word learning (e.g., Landau, Smith, & Jones, 1988).

Base terms often reflected the function of the piece as well. For example, the piece shown in Figure 4a that functioned as the hood of the car was labeled by shape (e.g., a *prism*) by 6 of the pairs and was referred to by function (e.g., a *hood*) by the remaining 6 pairs who recognized its function, or inferred its function from its shape. Furthermore, in some cases, participants shifted from a shape-based name to a function-based

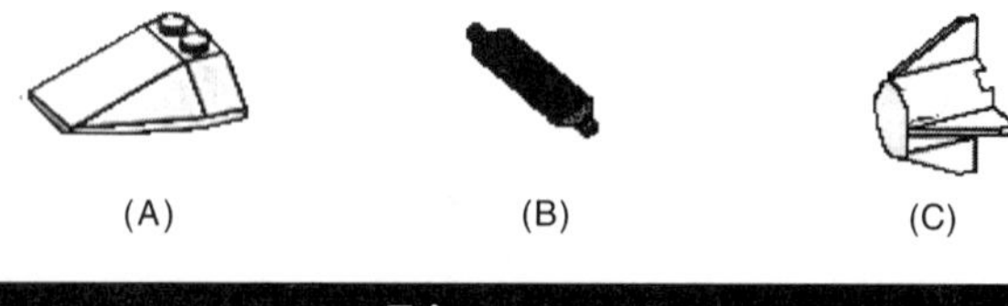

Figure 4

Three pieces referred to by subjects. (a) the hood of a car, (b) an axle, and (c) the back end of the spaceship. © LEGO Group, 1992. Used with permission.

name after discovering the function of a piece. One pair had referred to the piece in Figure 4b using the same label they used for the other 1 × X pieces. However, after putting wheels on each end of two of these pieces, one member of the pair said, "I guess we can call them *axles* now."

Finally, in many cases it was difficult to determine whether the name referred to the shape or to the function. For example, the piece shown in Figure 4c was called a *rocket* by 10 pairs. This label reflects both its shape (it looked like a rocket) and its function (it was positioned at the back of the spaceship where such a device might seem appropriate). This combination of shape and function reflects two central aspects of the building task. Shape is helpful because it provides information useful to the model builder during the visual search for a piece among the whole set of pieces. Function is useful because it suggests how the piece will be used in the model and thus the likely set of relationships it will bear to other pieces in the model (e.g., the axle will have wheels put on the end). Settling on a set of labels in which the base terms often reflect both shape and function is useful because it allows the same label to provide both kinds of information. Further research will be required to determine what individuals will do in a situation in which function and shape information cannot both be integrated into a single label. The combined use of shape and function also highlights the fact that aspects of the task in which the communicators are engaged (e.g., visual search and model building) also affect how the items are represented.

The base label clearly had a special status. This point can be seen from the use of terms like *same* and *identical*. For example, one pair had just placed two 1 × 6 red pieces on the model. The next statement by the director was, "you want to put *identical* white pieces, the white flat [on it]." Later, this director made a similar statement. After a 1 × 2 green piece was placed, the director said, "you're going to attach a red two that's *identical*." In both of these examples, the term *identical* was being used to say that the pieces were classified in the same way, even though, strictly speaking, they were not identical. Thus, the base label was assumed to carry enough information that the word *identical* was appropriate.

Modifiers

Because base terms were often applied to more than one object, they had to be modified to allow the dyad to establish reference to unique individuals. The modifiers we observed were of two distinct types: dimensional modifiers and appendages. Dimensional modifiers, like size and color, appeared before the base term in a referring statement (e.g., a *red* stoplight, or a *large* wheel). Properties used in dimensional modifiers were those for which the class of properties was relevant to all (or nearly all) of the pieces in the set (i.e., they were *alignable* properties).

Color was the most frequently used of the dimensional modifiers, with 238 instances across the 12 pairs.[3] Size was also used frequently (164 instances). Interestingly, there were two strategies for using size as a modifier. On 69 occasions, participants referred to size quantitatively by the number of studs on the piece (e.g., a *two* stoplight). On the other 95 occasions, participants referred to size qualitatively (e.g., a *small* tile). The only other dimensional modifier that was used frequently was shape, which was used 34 times to modify base terms that referred to the function of the piece.

In contrast to the dimensional modifiers, there were modifiers that referred to appendages of the items. These appendages differed from dimensional modifiers in that they appeared as prepositional phrases following the base term. For example, one group called the axle "a line *with hooks on the end*." Unlike the dimensions, the appendages were not found consistently across a set of pieces that had the same label. Thus, the prepositional phrase seemed to be marking *nonalignable* properties of the pieces that had the same label (i.e., properties that did not have correspondences across the set of contrasting items).[4]

---

[3]These frequency counts are derived from the naming task.

[4]It is possible that participants used prepositional phrases for parts, not because they were nonalignable properties but rather because this was a natural linguistic construction for dealing with parts. Although it is difficult to tease apart these possibilities, it is interesting to note that parts that were alignable across a number of different items were generally incorporated into the base label because they gave rise to a series of pieces with a distinctive shape.

Sorting Data

The general patterns derived from the labeling data were supported by the sorting data. These data were analyzed first by counting the number of times that each pair of pieces was sorted together across the 24 participants and then performing multidimensional scaling on the resulting similarity matrix. Three prominent dimensions were obtained from this analysis. The first dimension was based roughly on the shape of the pieces. At one end were the rectangular pieces, and at the other end were the irregularly shaped pieces. The second and third dimensions separated the pieces by color. The second dimension had red and green pieces on one end and gray pieces on the other. The third dimension had black pieces on one end and white pieces on the other. Assuming that the sorting data reflected participants' performance in the previous communication task to some degree, these data lend further support to the conclusion that both shape and color were central elements in the classes formed by participants.

This pattern of sorting data was different from that obtained from a separate group of participants who sorted the pieces without building any models or communicating with someone else about the pieces. The only salient dimensions to emerge from a multidimensional scaling analysis of this second set of sorting data reflected the color of the pieces. As discussed above, visual search was a key element of the building task, as the builder had to search through a set of pieces to find the particular piece that belonged in the model. This aspect of the task was incorporated into the labels, and emerged in subsequent sorting of the pieces, although it was not evident in the sorting data obtained from participants who did not build or communicate. On the basis of these data, we cannot separate the impact of building and communicating on the emergence of shape as important in participants' sorting; however, further research is being devoted to this topic.

The sorting data also allow us to address whether communicating about categories promoted consistency between the members of each pair. To this end, we determined the degree of overlap between the sorting data from each dyad. A match was counted for each pair of pieces that was sorted together by both the director and the builder. A mismatch was counted for each piece sorted together by one member of the dyad but not the other. The proportion of matches was then determined by the formula matches/(matches + mismatches).

This analysis yielded a proportion of matches of 0.34. For comparison, a random re-pairing of the matrices of the directors and builders yielded a proportion of matches of 0.23 (although the difference between these proportions was only marginally significant). These data provide preliminary evidence that the use of labels in a communicative setting has some lasting impact on the way items are classified.

Summary of Communication Study

Communication orients people toward both commonalities and differences of related items. Similar items were often given similar base terms that conveyed commonalities in shape, function, or both. Modifiers were added to the labels to distinguish between similar pieces. Participants in this study tended to incorporate information about alignable properties like size and color into dimensional modifiers. In contrast, participants made note of salient nonalignable properties, particularly parts, using prepositional phrases attached to the base noun. The sorting data suggest that the use of labels during the construction task did affect the way the pieces were later classified. Further studies are now under way to examine how an existing set of labels is extended when new pieces are presented (see the chapter by Murphy, this volume, for a discussion of constraints on extension of word meaning).

INTEGRATED CONCEPT REPRESENTATIONS

We have suggested that classification, inference, and communication differ in their information requirements, leading to differences in what is learned when these tasks are carried out. As a first pass, we have separated each of these tasks to begin to understand how they differ in the information they use and what is learned when they are performed. However, this situation is clearly not realistic.

In particular, people's experiences are not often blocked into periods of classification, followed by periods of inference, followed by periods of communication. Rather, our daily experience interleaves many different facets of category use, each of which may lead us to store away something new about our categories. It is not clear that the representations that are formed by a mixture of different types of acquisition are precisely those that would form if all types of learning were done in separate blocks. As one example of this point, the mixed learning condition in the studies of classification and inference takes only a few more blocks to learn than does classification alone, yet mixed learning leads to good transfer in both the classification and inference tasks. This finding suggests that doing inference and classification trials together during learning may lead to a different representation than develops from doing the tasks separately. Furthermore, as discussed above, performing inference learning followed by classification learning is significantly easier than performing the same two tasks in the reverse order (Yamauchi & Markman, 1996). This finding suggests that inference and classification interact in a way that may lead to different representations when the tasks are presented separately than when they are combined. In the multifaceted view, the structure of natural categories is a result of many different tasks all contributing to learning. Further research will have to examine this claim more carefully.

CATEGORIES AND CREATIVITY

We could wax eloquent about the nature of incremental creativity as demonstrated by these studies of category acquisition. It is certainly true that the acquisition of categories is a process of representation creation, in which people learn to take aspects of the world and place them in equivalence classes for the purpose of making inferences about them, communicating about them, and reasoning about them. However, category acquisition lacks the feeling of effort that seems to be central to large-scale creative acts. Historical accounts of large-scale creativity often talk about the importance of effort and of searching many possibilities for the right answer (Perkins, 1994; Schaffer, 1994). Furthermore, Dunbar's (this volume) studies of microbiologists attest to the slow and effortful way in which large-scale creative discoveries are made. Thus, although concept acquisition is creative, it may not be creative in the same way that scientific discovery and invention are creative.

Still, the study of category learning may provide insight into large-scale creative processes. Many examples of creative invention reflect the extension of existing categories to new functions (Ward, 1995). Furthermore, people who are asked to creatively extend a category they already have will often maintain many aspects of the structure of their existing categories (Cacciari, Levorato, & Cicogna, this volume; Ward, 1994). In addition, even mundane concepts can establish a foundation for great scientific advances. For example, Atran (1990) suggested that common-sense taxonomies of animals and plants laid the groundwork for subsequent scientific study. The multifaceted approach to category learning focuses on how the tasks used to learn categories affect the structure of the representations that are developed. This work is important for the study of creativity in that any understanding of how we go beyond existing categories must be based on knowledge of how categories are developed and the operations that are best used to extend them (see also Murphy, this volume).

CONCLUDING THOUGHTS

If we take seriously the idea that our categories serve multiple functions, then the representations constructed during the creation of new concepts should reflect the way we interact with our categories. Whereas some empirical studies have addressed this issue (e.g., Estes, 1994; Lassaline & Murphy, 1996), the vast majority of studies have assumed that the representations that individuals form in a simple classification task are sufficient for the set of functions that categories serve. The work presented here suggests that classification provides one avenue for learning categories but that we learn different things from different ways of interacting with a category.

The feature inference task described in the first set of studies differs from classification in the information required to perform the task successfully. Classification involves finding a small set of features that distinguish reliably between the classes. In contrast, inference requires understanding correlations (and perhaps relations) between features within a category. Consistent with the proposal that these tasks differ, research participants found it significantly more difficult to do both together than they did to do only one of the tasks. Furthermore, participants' performance in transfer tasks was better for tasks that were similar to the one they used to learn the category than for tasks that were not.

Communication differs from both classification and inference in a focus both on features common to broad classes of items and on features that distinguish similar items. This simultaneous attention to similarities and differences is like the notion of category utility proposed by Corter and Gluck (1992) to explain the advantage of the basic level of categorization in many tasks. In this vein, A. Markman and Wisniewski (in press) found that comparisons involving pairs of basic level kinds have both many commonalities and many differences, whereas comparisons involving superordinate categories have few commonalities or differences at all. Thus, natural categories do permit simultaneous attention to commonalities and (alignable) differences.

This chapter reports on developing lines of research. In future work, the distinction between inference-based learning and classification-based learning needs to be refined. It must also be determined whether inference-based learning focuses selectively on correlations between features, or whether it promotes attention to other relations between features (e.g., causal relations) as well. In communication, the factors that promote the use of related labels must be understood. Furthermore, the lasting impact of using labels to classify objects must be explored. In addition, many of our categories are learned in a social setting through extended communication. Thus, the processes mediating verbal communication may contain a powerful category learning mechanism that augments our bodily experiences as a basis of conceptual structure. Finally, other uses of categories such as their function as memory aids, their involvement in metaphor, and their use as the basis of stereotypes need to be explored to further establish the role of category use in the creation of new categories.

REFERENCES

Ahn, W. K., & Medin, D. L. (1992). A two-stage model of category construction. *Cognitive Science, 16*(1), 81–122.

Anderson, J. R. (1990). *The adaptive character of thought.* Hillsdale, NJ: Erlbaum.

Atran, S. (1990). *Cognitive foundations of natural history: Towards an anthropology of science.* Cambridge, England: Cambridge University Press.

Baggett, P., & Ehrenfeucht, A. (1988). Conceptualizing in assembly tasks. *Human Factors, 30,* 269–284.

Boden, M. A. (1994). What is creativity? In M. A. Boden (Ed.), *Dimensions of creativity* (pp. 75–117). Cambridge, MA: MIT Press.

Brown, R. (1958). How shall a thing be called? *Psychological Review, 65,* 14–21.

Bruner, J. (1990). *Acts of meaning.* Cambridge, MA: Harvard University Press.

Clapper, J. P., & Bower, G. H. (1994). Category invention in unsupervised learning. *Journal of Experimental Psychology: Learning, Memory, and Cognition, 20,* 443–460.

Clark, H. H. (1996). *Using language.* Cambridge, England: Cambridge University Press.

Clark, H. H., & Wilkes-Gibbs, D. (1986). Referring as a collaborative process. *Cognition, 22,* 1–39.

Corter, J. E., & Gluck, M. A. (1992). Explaining basic categories: Feature predictability and information. *Psychological Bulletin, 11,* 291–303.

Elio, R., & Anderson, J. R. (1984). The effects of information order and learning mode on schema abstraction. *Memory & Cognition, 12,* 20–30.

Estes, W. K. (1986). Array models for category learning. *Cognitive Psychology, 18,* 500–549.

Estes, W. K. (1994). *Classification and cognition.* Oxford, England: Oxford University Press.

Freyd, J. J. (1983). Shareability: The social psychology of epistemology. *Cognitive Science, 7,* 191–210.

Garrod, S., & Anderson, A. (1987). Saying what you mean in dialogue: A study in conceptual and semantic co-ordination. *Cognition, 27,* 181–218.

Garrod, S., & Doherty, G. (1994). Conversation, co-ordination and convention: An empirical investigation of how groups establish linguistic conventions. *Cognition, 53,* 181–215.

Glenberg, A. M. (in press). What memory is for. *Behavioral and Brain Sciences.*

Glucksberg, S., Krauss, R. M., & Higgins, E. T. (1975). The development of referential communication skills. In F. D. Horowitz (Ed.), *Review of child development research* (pp. 305–345). Chicago, IL: University of Chicago Press.

Heit, E., & Rubinstein, J. (1994). Similarity and property effects in inductive reasoning. *Journal of Experimental Psychology: Learning, Memory, and Cognition, 20,* 411–422.

Higgins, E. T. (1992). Achieving 'shared reality' in the communication game: A social action that creates meaning. *Journal of Language and Social Psychology, 11,* 107–131.

Jones, S. S., & Smith, L. B. (1993). The place of perception in children's concepts. *Cognitive Development, 8,* 113–139.

Keil, F. C. (1989). *Concepts, kinds and cognitive development.* Cambridge, MA: MIT Press.

Krauss, R. M., & Fussell, S. R. (1996). Social psychological models of interpersonal communication. In E. T. Higgins & A. Kruglanski (Eds.), *Social psychology: Handbook of basic principles* (pp. 655–701). New York: Guilford Press.

Krauss, R. M., & Weinheimer, S. (1964). Changes in the length of reference phrases as a function of social interaction: A preliminary study. *Psychonomic Science, 1,* 113–114.

Landau, B., Smith, L. B., & Jones, S. S. (1988). The importance of shape in early lexical learning. *Cognitive Development, 3,* 299–321.

Lassaline, M. E., & Murphy, G. L. (1996). Induction and category coherence. *Psychonomic Bulletin and Review, 3,* 95–99.

Markman, A. B., & Gentner, D. (1993). Splitting the differences: A structural alignment view of similarity. *Journal of Memory and Language, 32,* 517–535.

Markman, A. B., & Gentner, D. (1996). Commonalities and differences in similarity comparisons. *Memory & Cognition, 24,* 235–249.

Markman, A. B., & Wisniewski, E. J. (in press). Similar and different: The differentiation of basic level categories. *Journal of Experimental Psychology: Learning, Memory, and Cognition.*

Markman, E. M. (1989). *Categorization and naming in children.* Cambridge, MA: MIT Press.

McKoon, G., & Ratcliff, R. (1992). Inference during reading. *Psychological Review, 99,* 440–466.

Medin, D. L., Altom, M. W., Edelson, S. M., & Freko, D. (1982). Correlated symptoms and simulated medical classification. *Journal of Experimental Psychology: Learning, Memory, and Cognition, 8,* 37–50.

Medin, D. L., & Schaffer, M. M. (1978). Context theory of classification. *Psychological Review, 85,* 207–238.

Medin, D. L., & Wattenmaker, W. D., & Hampson, S. E. (1987). Family resemblance, conceptual cohesiveness and category construction. *Cognitive Psychology, 19,* 242–279.

Medin, D. L., & Wattenmaker, W. D. (1987). Category cohesiveness, theories and cognitive archeology. In U. Neisser (Ed.), Concepts and conceptual development: *Ecological and intellectual factors in categorization* (pp. 25–62), Cambridge, England: Cambridge University Press.

Murphy, G. L., & Brownell, H. H. (1985). Category differentiation in object recognition: Typicality constraints on the basic category advantage. *Journal of Experimental Psychology: Learning, Memory, and Cognition, 11,* 70–84.

Murphy, G. L., & Medin, D. L. (1985). The role of theories in conceptual coherence. *Psychological Review, 92,* 289–315.

Nosofsky, R. M. (1986). Attention, similarity and the identification–categorization relationship. *Journal of Experimental Psychology: General, 115,* 39–57.

Nosofsky, R. M., Palmeri, T. J., & McKinley, S. C. (1994). Rule-plus-exception model of classification learning. *Psychological Review, 101,* 53–97.

Osherson, D. N., Smith, E. E., Wilkie, O., Lopez, A., & Shafir, E. (1990). Category based induction. *Psychological Review, 97,* 185–200.

Pazzani, M. (1991). Learning to predict and explain: An integration of similarity based, theory-driven and explanation-based learning. *The Journal of the Learning Sciences, 1,* 153–199.

Perkins, D. N. (1994). Creativity: Beyond the Darwinian paradigm. In M. A. Boden (Ed.), *Dimensions of creativity* (pp. 119–142). Cambridge, MA: MIT Press.

Reed, S. K. (1972). Pattern recognition and categorization. *Cognitive Psychology, 3,* 382–407.

Regehr, G., & Brooks, L. R. (1993). Perceptual manifestations of an analytic structure: The priority of holistic individuation. *Journal of Experimental Psychology: General, 122,* 92–114.

Rogoff, B. (1990). *Apprenticeship in thinking: Cognitive development in social context.* Oxford, England: Oxford University Press.

Rosch, E. (1975). Cognitive representations of semantic categories. *Journal of Experimental Psychology: General, 104,* 192–233.

Ross, B. H. (1996). Category representations and the effects of interacting with instances. *Journal of Experimental Psychology: Learning, Memory, and Cognition, 22,* 1249–1265.

Ross, B. H., Perkins, S. J., & Tenpenny, P. L. (1990). Reminding-based category learning. *Cognitive Psychology, 22,* 460–492.

Schaffer, S. (1994). Making up discovery. In M. A. Boden (Ed.), *Dimensions of creativity* (13–51). Cambridge, MA: MIT Press.

Schank, R. C., & Abelson, R. (1977). *Scripts, plans, goals and understanding.* Hillsdale, NJ: Erlbaum.

Schank, R. C., Collins, G. C., & Hunter, L. E. (1986). Transcending inductive category formation in learning. *Behavioral and Brain Sciences, 9,* 639–686.

Schober, M. F., & Clark, H. H. (1989). Understanding by addressees and overhearers. *Cognitive Psychology, 21,* 211–232.

Singley, M. K., & Anderson, J. R. (1989). *The transfer of cognitive skill.* Cambridge, MA: Harvard University Press.

Smith, E. E., & Medin, D. L. (1981). *Categories and concepts.* Cambridge, MA: Harvard University Press.

Soja, N. N., Carey, S., & Spelke, E. S. (1991). Ontological categories guide young children's inductions of word meaning: Object terms and substance terms. *Cognition, 38,* 179–211.

Sperber, D. (1985). Anthropology and psychology: Towards an epidemiology of representations. *Man, 20,* 73–89.

Tversky, A. (1977). Features of similarity. *Psychological Review, 84,* 327–352.

Vygotsky, L. (1986). *Thought and language.* Cambridge, MA: MIT Press.

Ward, T. B. (1994). Structured imagination: The role of category structure in exemplar generation. *Cognitive Psychology, 27,* 1–40.

Ward, T. B. (1995). What's old about new ideas. In S. M. Smith, T. B. Ward, & R. A. Finke (Eds.), *The creative cognition approach* (pp. 157–178). Cambridge, MA: MIT Press.

Wattenmaker, W. D. (1995). Knowledge structures and linear separability: Integrating information in object and social categorization. *Cognitive Psychology, 28,* 274–328.

Wisniewski, E. J. (1995). Prior knowledge and functionally relevant features in concept learing. *Journal of Experimental Psychology: Learning, Memory, and Cognition, 21,* 449–468.

Wisniewski, E. J., & Medin, D. L. (1994). On the interaction of theory and data in concept learning. *Cognitive Science, 18,* 221–282.

Yamauchi, T., & Markman, A. B. (1995). Effects of category-learning on categorization—an analysis of inference-based and classification-based learning. In J. D. Moore & J. F. Lehman (Eds.), *Proceedings of the Seventeenth Annual Conference of the Cognitive Science Society* (pp. 786–790). Pittsburgh, PA: Erlbaum.

Yamauchi, T., & Markman, A.B. (1996). *Inference-based and classification-based learning.* Manuscript in preparation.

9

Creativity: Shifting Across Ontological Categories Flexibly

Michelene T. H. Chi

There is a general consensus that the essence of creativity is to be able to view a situation or an object from two different frames of reference, or two "unrelated matrices of thought" (Koestler, 1964). This is sometimes referred to as *restructuring*. Restructuring, thus, is often viewed as being able to see a problem in a "new way" that is fundamentally different. However, defining creativity in this way merely begs the question of what constitutes a "new way," "a different frame of reference," or "an unrelated matrix of thought?"

The goal of this chapter is to provide a specific way of characterizing what a new perspective, a new way, or a new matrix of thought might be. A new perspective is defined here as re-representing an entity or a situation from one "ontological" tree of concepts and categories to another ontological tree of concepts and categories. That is, people might store concepts and situations on associative trees that are ontologically distinct so

This research was supported in part by the A. W. Mellon Foundation and in part by Spencer Foundation Grant 199400132 while the author was a fellow at the Center for Advanced Study in the Behavioral Sciences. The opinions expressed in this chapter do not necessarily reflect the positions of the sponsoring agencies, and no official endorsement should be inferred.

that these distinct ontological trees serve as barriers that restrict our ability to understand and produce creatively. In order to have creative thoughts, we must be able to cross these ontological barriers flexibly. Thus, one definition of creativity is the flexibility with which one can think about a member of an ontological category in the context of another ontological category. I refer to this definition as "shifting across" ontological categories, as "re-representing" a concept from one ontological category to another, or merely as conceptual change. I clarify the meaning of these terms below. First, however, I present a set of terms to describe category attributes.

THE NATURE OF CATEGORY ATTRIBUTES

A category, from cognitive psychologists' point of view, is defined as a set of objects (or entities) that people believe belong together. Thus, to psychologists, a category is a conceptual structure. When people believe that a certain set of objects (or entities) belongs in the same category, they treat new instances of the category as members. This allows people to assign the same label to a new instance of the category and make inductive and deductive inferences to new category members, particularly about nonperceptible properties (Chi, Hutchinson, & Robin, 1989). Thus, there is clearly a cognitive advantage to having categories, as coding new experiences or objects as an instance of a familiar category reduces the demands of the perceptual, storage, and reasoning processes.

Psychologists, addressing the overarching question of what is the process by which people assign entities to categories (most of the psychological literature has dealt with object categories), presuppose the prior question of what constitutes a category. That is, what characteristics or attributes do class members possess that cohere them as a category? For instance, a set of objects that weigh one gram, or a set of objects that are green, does not constitute a category. What attributes, then, give a set of objects or entities the status of categoryhood? In this section, several types of attributes used to characterize categories are briefly discussed in order to clarify their definitions.

Defining Attributes

One possible characteristic of categories is whether the objects or entities satisfy a *defining* set of attributes. Nominal kind categories, such as kinship (e.g., uncle), law (e.g., felony), and geometry (e.g., triangle) have a fixed set of attributes to define them, so that for any object that satisfies all of the attributes of a category, that object must be an instance of that category. Put another way, defining attributes are necessary and sufficient to determine category membership. For example, the concept "grandmother" has the defining attributes of being female and being a parent of a parent. These two attributes are jointly sufficient to determine that any female who is a parent of a parent must be a grandmother.

Characteristic Attributes

A fixed set of defining attributes clearly cannot capture the nature of nonnominal kind categories, primarily because linguists, philosophers, and psychologists have yet to come up with a fixed unique set of attributes for most natural kind categories (McNamara & Sternberg, 1983). For example, there is no fixed set of necessary and sufficient features that can deterministically discriminate a bird from a nonbird. Most people think that birds have the properties of flying and singing. However, one would still classify a bird whose wings have been clipped as a bird. Likewise, although penguins and chickens cannot fly, they are also classified as birds. Moreover, not all instances of a category are treated equally, as would be the case if the definitional view held. Instead, some members of a given category are treated as more typical members than others. A robin, for example, is considered a more typical bird than a penguin. What this means is that people treat different members of a category differently: Typical members can be classified faster, they are rated more highly as an instance of the category for which they belong, and they are retrieved more frequently than atypical members (Smith, 1989). Thus, there is no fixed set of necessary and sufficient features to discriminate members of a category from nonmembers.

Without a unique defining set of attributes, what then determines category membership? People often tend to determine category membership on the basis of nonessential but frequent properties, such as *being sweet* for fruit (Rosch & Mervis, 1975). These nonessential but frequently occurring properties are known as *characteristic* attributes. The more characteristic attributes an instance of a category has, the more *typical* it is, according to people's ratings. Thus, category memberships are sometimes determined by the extent to which an entity embodies the most frequent characteristic features of a category.

Regardless of whether defining or characteristic attributes are used to determine category membership, how are the attributes identified? The consensus is that category membership is determined largely by physical or perceptual similarity. To some degree, category members tend to be more physically or perceptually similar to each other and dissimilar to members of another category. For example, various kinds of dogs look more similar to each other than to cats. The set of all objects weighing one gram, on the other hand, does not meet this criterion of physical similarity, thus, does not constitute a category. Perceptual similarity can refer not only to static features but also to any perceptually observable features, such as behavior (e.g., the attribute "nests in trees" for birds).

Core and Functional Attributes

Although people seem to categorize entities on the basis of perceptual attributes, these perceptual attributes are used primarily for the sake of a quick and expedient categorization of objects, as they are readily available, salient, and easy to compute. However, they are not diagnostic of concept membership. *Core* attributes are those that are usually less perceptual and more hidden; however, they are more diagnostic of category membership. For example, the core attribute of being a bird might be having bird genes (i.e., having been born of bird parents). Sometimes core attributes are referred to as the essence of a concept, or its "real nature." This real nature often refers to its genetic makeup.

Core attributes are unlike defining attributes in that they are not fixed. Whether a given gene is diagnostic of certain diseases or genes are diagnostic of being birds may change when scientists discover some other relevant core attributes (Putnam, 1975). Core attributes are also different from characteristic attributes in that core attributes are not often observable. Core attributes are moreover different from both characteristic and defining attributes in that we have only a vague idea of what the exact core attributes of any given concept are. However, we do know that they exist, and we appeal to experts to guide and tell us what they are (Malt, 1990).

Core attributes may be correlated to characteristic or perceptual attributes. For example, the concept "man" can be defined in terms of core features like adult, male, and human. However, to identify a person as a man requires characteristic attributes such as hair length, presence of a beard or mustache, and so on. These properties are related, as being a male is partly a matter of hormones, which influence physical features such as facial hair (Wattenmaker, Nakamura, & Medin, 1988).

Functional attributes are basically equivalent to core attributes. The difference is that core attributes differentiate natural kinds, whereas functional attributes differentiate artifacts. Thus, like core attributes, functional attributes also are not fixed. Instead of appealing to scientists who might discover new core attributes, we appeal in this case to the engineers of artifacts to invent new functional attributes.

Abstract, Theory-Based, or Explanation-Based Attributes

One can also propose that categories are determined by some underlying *abstract, theory-based,* or *explanation-based* attributes rather than perceptual attributes. (These terms are used more or less synonymously.) Fewer studies have focused on this type of attribute, perhaps because most entities in the world that have abstract similarity also have physical similarity. For example, consider the diet of a class of dinosaurs (such as meat-eating) as an abstract attribute. However, meat-eating dinosaurs do share several similar physical attributes, such as having sharp teeth. No research has explicitly manipulated theory-based (or abstract) attributes from perceptual (or characteristic) attributes. Exceptions do exist, especially in non-natural kind categories. Physics problems, for example, can be created that have abstract (principle-based) similarity but not physical similarity (Chi, Feltovich, & Glaser, 1981). In this case, whether a problem solver attends to the abstract or the perceptual features depends on the solver's expertise (Chi et al., 1981), or the solver's Scholastic Aptitude Test (SAT) scores (Novick, 1988).

Theory- or explanation-based attributes are generally consistent with some explanation or some prediction based on an explanation. For example, rice cakes, unbuttered popcorn, and grapefruit can form a conceptual category if one can explain their coherence. In this case, their coherence can be explained by "things to eat while on a diet" (a kind of goal-derived category; see Barsalou, 1983). Likewise, symptoms such as dizziness and earache can be conceived of as related if one can provide an explanation for them such as "symptoms that are causally related," whereas such an explanation cannot be provided for symptoms like a sore throat and skin rash (Medin, Wattenmaker, & Hampson, 1987). Thus, the coherence of these category members is not based on any perceptual similarity but, rather, on theory- or explanation-based similarity such as containing close to zero calories (Ross, 1984).

Ontological Attributes

Hierarchical Comparison of Categories

Many of the pertinent questions asked by psychologists as discussed above pertain to the nature of the set of attributes that defines a category per se rather than the relationship among categories. When the relationship among categories is invoked, most of the psychological work conceives of categories as embedded in a taxonomic or hierarchical relationship. For example, bird is a category that is subsumed under the animal supercategory, and robin is subsumed under the bird category, and so on. Thus, much of the classic work deals with the induction possibilities resulting from hierarchical relationships (see Collins & Quillian, 1969), as well as the identification of a level of categories (the basic level) at which people prefer to operate (Rosch, Mervis, Gray, Johnson, & Boyes-Braem, 1976). This basic level would, for example, correspond to the bird category as opposed to the animal category. Preference can be easily demonstrated by the fact that people prefer to identify items by their basic level names (e.g., people prefer to call a red, round fruit an "apple" rather than a "fruit" or a "McIntosh apple"); and people can determine that an object is an apple faster than they can determine that it is a fruit. Rosch et al. (1976) have several other tests of people's preferences for basic level categories. By and large, the only sense in which psychologists have discussed the overall structure of categories is in the context of hierarchies, although there are debates and discussions about the rigidity of the hierarchy and whether some lattice-like structure is also possible (Conrad, 1972)

Lateral Comparison of Categories

Assuming that individual categories are related in a hierarchical way, psychologists, by and large, have not dealt with the nature of the lateral relationship among hierarchical or taxonomic category trees. Lateral comparisons can be posed with two questions. The first is how hierarchical trees differ from each other or (put another way) how categories within *different* trees differ from each other. The second question is how lateral categories within a tree differ (i.e., how do categories on different branches of a given tree differ?).

Suppose we examine two taxonomic trees, such as material substances and processes, as depicted in Figure 1. It is of course not clear exactly how each of these taxonomic trees should be constructed. That is, exactly how should the branches or levels within each tree be constructed? Let's assume, for the sake of discussion, that the trees are organized as shown in Figure 1. How might we define how these trees differ? And how might the categories subsumed under each tree differ? For instance, how might the subcategories *event* (on the PROCESSES tree) and *natural kind* (on the material substances tree) differ (see Figure 1)? And how do categories on different branches, such as natural kind and artifact, differ within a tree? Although psychologists have not thought much about tree differences, philosophers have (see Quine, 1960, p. 275). I refer to trees of this kind (being fundamentally different) here as *ontologies* (or *ontological trees)* and their attributes as *ontological* attributes. Thus, ontologies, as defined here, refer to trees having an entire hierarchy of categories that are fundamentally different from each other. (It is not yet clear whether categories on different branches within a given tree are also ontologically distinct. Two or more categories may be considered ontologically distinct according to

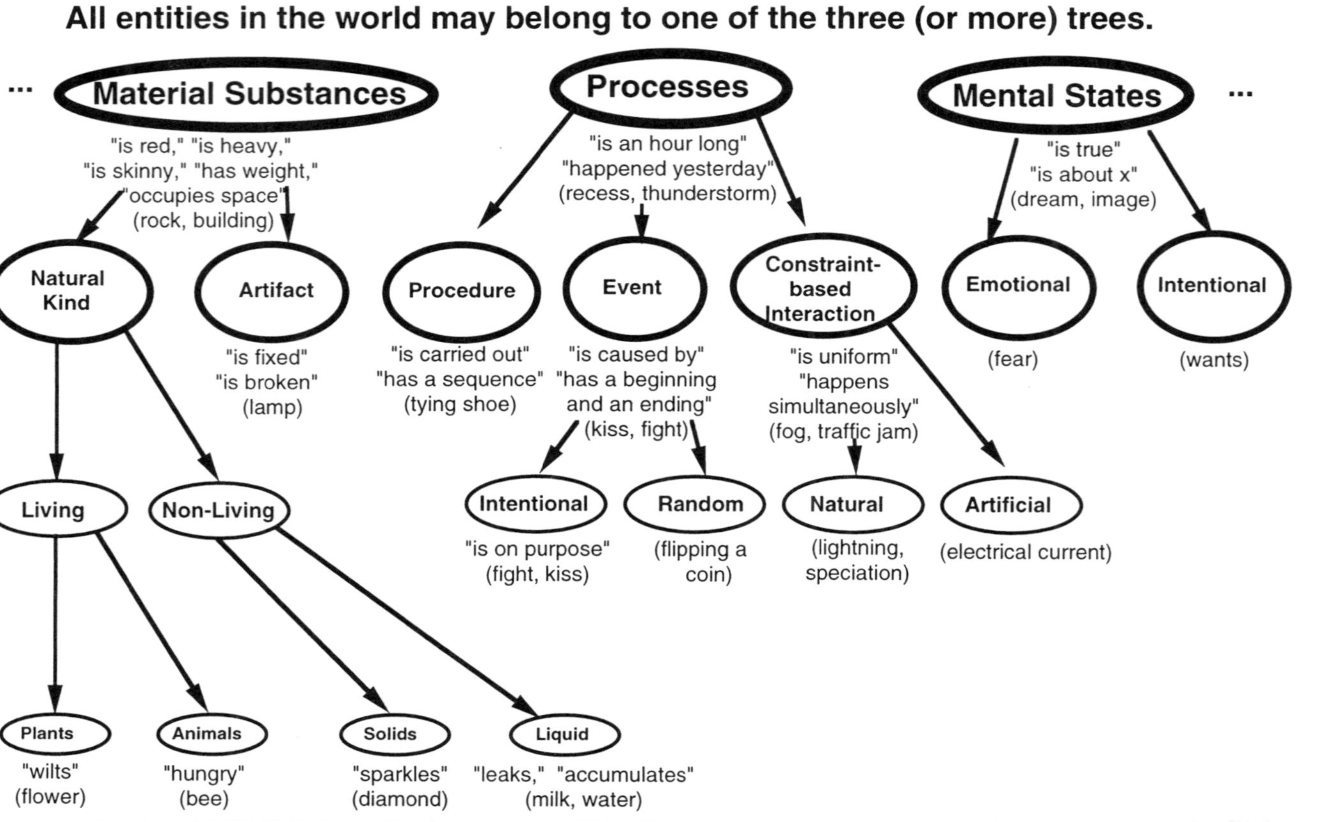

Figure 1

A plausible organization of ontological trees.

one empirical test and not according to another. More speculation about this is provided later.)

Lateral Differences Between Trees and Branches

The issue of how to define differences between trees is much more complex than the issue of determining the hierarchical relationships among categories. Hierarchical relationships can be readily defined in terms of the inheritance of generalized attributes. That is, a bird is an instance of the animal category if a bird possesses all the properties that an animal possesses, such as breathes, eats, and so forth. However, it is not as apparent how one would decide that two categories that are not on the same ontological tree are distinct. The reason this is a more complex problem is that it is much more difficult to define difference than sameness. In this context, *sameness* can be defined by an overlap or sharing of attributes; however, *difference* is more problematic because, intuitively, it does not seem to be a matter of degree. Should two entities be considered different if they share no attributes of any kind, or if they share one that is a characteristic, defining, core, or explanation-based attribute? Should they be considered different only if they share some kinds of attributes and not others?

I propose that differences in trees are dramatic (others have used the words "*radical*" and "*fundamental*") in the sense that the trees do not share any *ontological* attributes (Chi, 1992; Chi, Slotta, & de Leeuw, 1994), although they may share other types of attributes,(e.g., characteristic or explanation-based). That is, tree differences can be characterized by the nature of their ontological attributes, which are different from characteristic, defining, core, and explanation-based attributes.

The Nature of Ontological Attributes

An ontological attribute refers to a property that may or may not be possessed by a specific category member but has the potential of possessing it. For example, the class of all physical objects has the potential to possess the property of color, but not all physical objects do. Thus, a piece of glass is often transparent and colorless, but it can be made to have color. Unlike core attributes, ontological attributes are known to the average person, although he or she may not be explicitly aware of them. Although we may not be explicitly aware of ontological attributes, our implicit understanding of them can often be detected by the phrases and predicates we use to describe them. For example, to say "The baseball game lasted an hour" implies that a baseball game is a process, because only processes can have a dynamic time-dependent nature, in contrast to solid objects, which have a static nature.

Before addressing the question of how one determines an ontological attribute of a category or tree (or alternatively, the question of how one decides that a set of entities constitutes a distinct ontological tree), one may want to surmise as to the characteristics of ontological attributes. Assume that the following attributes are some of the ontological attributes of the material substances tree: block, contain, move, rest, consume, absorb, quantify, accumulate, can have color, and so on (Slotta, Chi, & Joram, 1995). (Other examples of ontological attributes or predicates are shown in quotes in Figure 1.) That is, a material substance such as a solid object like a book can block other material substances such as fluids. It can be contained, moved from one location to another (or if it is an animate object it can move of its own volition), or it can have color, and so forth.

Having asserted what some ontological attributes might be for a given tree, one can then further assert that two categories embedded in two separate trees can be said to be ontologically distinct because they do not share any ontological attributes. Philosophers have offered a way to test this by asking people to make judgments about the sensibility of sentences that use predicates from one ontological tree to modify entities on another ontological tree. For example, *an hour-long* is a predicate that may modify any member of the processes tree, but it cannot be used sensibly to modify any member of the material substances tree, such as *dog*, which is a natural kind. Thus, to say that "A dog is an hour-long" is anomalous (known as a category mistake) because even the negation of that statement ("A dog is not an hour-long") is nonsensical. On the other hand, if a member of a category is predicated by an attribute from the same tree, then at worst the statement is simply false, such as "A dog is purple." Such sensibility judgments have been used by Keil (1979) to determine the (ontological) distinctiveness of branches within the same (substances) tree, such as artifacts and natural kinds. Thus, psychologically, one can determine the distinguishability of branches by using the sensibility test. Keil (1989) also used other tests to show the distinguishability of branches within the same tree. For example, he showed that even 5-year-olds refuse to admit that there are operations that can transform a skunk to a teapot or a toy bird to a real bird.

Physical and Mental Operations to Modify an Entity or a Concept

In the physical world, entities from distinct trees (or even branches on a given tree) remain distinct despite any *physical operations* that can be performed on them. For example, a chair (an artifact) can never be made into a baby skunk (a natural kind) no matter what kind of operation (carving it up, washing it, painting it, etc.) is done to it. I argued earlier that similarly, no piecemeal *cognitive operations* (such as deleting or adding features, generalizing features, etc.) can modify a concept's characteristic, defining, or core attributes so that it changes the tree (or branch) in which the concept is embedded. To modify a concept from being embedded in one tree to another tree, one must modify its ontological attributes. However, ontological attributes are not modifiable, either physically or mentally (see Chi, 1992, for a more extended discussion).

On the other hand, it is possible to cognitively change the representation of a concept through cognitive operations if the changes do not require the concept to be re-represented across branches or trees, but rather, that the representation is merely a migration of the concept from a subordinate to a superordinate node (or vise versa), in a hierarchical manner. When multiple applications of cognitive operations such as deletion and addition of features are executed, the cumulative effect can result in a more well-defined concept, or a more generalized concept. However, all of the added or deleted features have not fundamentally changed the ontological tree in which the concept was originally embedded. This kind of change is referred to as a *belief revision*. There is abundant evidence of the gravitation of concepts from subcategories to superordinate categories, and vice versa, such as learning to differentiate and integrate concepts (Carey, 1985) and learning to integrate humans as one species of animals (see Chi, 1988, for a developmental analysis of how the concept of humans can gravitate from one part of the living things tree to another part). Thus, another way to put it is that once stored on a particular tree, a concept then inherits all of the ontological attributes of that tree. It is completely entrenched in that ontology. To change the ontological tree to which a concept belongs, one would need to modify an enormous number of attributes (in order for the concept to disinherit all of its ontological attributes).

Belief revision is a common kind of change that does not require a change in ontology. Much of learning of concepts is basically belief revision, in which one has to change a number of attributes that one knows about a concept and attach other correct attributes to it instead. For instance, suppose we originally thought that a whale is a kind of fish. There are two ways that this concept can change as we learn more about it. The first way is that we learn more about whales, such as that they breathe through a blowhole, have lungs, bear live young, and are warm-blooded. Over time, our accumulated knowledge about whales will overlap with our knowledge of mammals more than it overlaps with our knowledge of fish. Eventually, the representation of whales will be largely associated with the representation of mammals. Such migration of a concept from one branch to another branch of the same tree seems plausible, as there is a finite number of features to change.

A second way to achieve belief revision is being told directly, for example, that "a whale is a mammal and not a fish." Being told will allow us to directly link the concept whale with the category mammal rather than with the category fish. Thus, a more efficient method to change a concept's ontology might be a wholesale shift through direct instruction, which seems clearly possible for concepts on different branches of a tree (as the example of whale indicates), but would this be possible for concepts on different trees? I discuss this possibility next.

Therefore, changing features of a concept gradually in a piecemeal way (which occurs all of the time in learning and development) may be thought of as belief revision, whereas shifting a concept from one tree to another can be more aptly conceived of as conceptual change. This view of conceptual change is also shared by Thagard (1990).

CIRCUMSTANCES UNDER WHICH PEOPLE HAVE TO SHIFT ACROSS ONTOLOGICAL TREES

If one assumes that (a) concepts are loosely structured in something like a hierarchy tree; (b) trees are fundamentally distinct from one another; (c) physical entities in the world do not change ontology; and (d) ontological categories in the world correspond to the structure of people's conceptual categories, then why would one ever have to worry about shifting concepts across trees? That is, there should seldom be any need to re-represent or shift a concept from one tree to another tree, unless of course one *misrepresented* a concept in the first place. Surprisingly, however, there are many occasions when one must re-represent an entity from one tree to another. Below, I illustrate two types of occasions. For each of these occasions, the need to shift the representation has to do with the initial misrepresentation.

In Everyday Life

Is there ever an occasion in everyday life when people have to re-represent a concept so that it is stored on a different tree? This can happen on occasions when the superficially perceivable features of an entity mislead people into representing it as one kind of entity when in fact it is another kind. This can readily happen because categorization is often based on visibly perceptible features. Such is the case when whales are mistaken to be a kind of fish. However, because the perceptual features of entities we encounter in everyday life most often correlate with their underlying conceptual identity, it is seldom the case in everyday life that what we perceive misleads our identification. For example, we identify a given animal as a dog because that animal has all the characteristic features of a dog, such as a wagging tail, four legs, and so on. Thus, in everyday life, there are few occasions when we have to shift an entity from one ontological tree to another, although there are occasions when we must shift among branches of a tree, such as in the case of whales. Another more common instance of shifting across branches occurs in literature and films. The necessity of these shifts is sometimes used in literature to create a surprise or a dramatic effect. For example, in the popular children's novel *Indian in the Cupboard*, the central theme of the book is that a toy Indian comes alive. A great deal of suspense of the book is built around the discovery of this "conversion," and the main character is clearly surprised. Other examples include *Velveteen Rabbit*. Similarly, in the film *The Crying Game*, a male character is disguised as a female; the viewers are quite surprised when the disguise is removed, and they must review all of the implications of the prior scenes to determine how the character's being male may have changed them. These kinds of shifts are dramatic (thus, create a surprise reaction) precisely because they cross ontological barriers. Thus, they are much more drastic than mere mistaken identity. Misidentifying one person for another (as often occurs in mysteries) is puzzling and suspenseful, but it is not dramatic, as when one crosses ontological boundaries (such as from an artifact to a live human being, or from a female to a male).

Notice that in all of the examples cited above, either in mistaking a whale for a fish, or in mistaking a male for a female, the changes (such as from a toy Indian to a live Indian) are between branches within an ontological tree. The next context addresses a change in re-representation between trees.

Understanding a Kind of Process

As it turns out, there is an important context in which there is a pervasive need to shift concepts from one tree to another. This is the context in which we have to learn a special class of complex concepts of processes. Before describing what is unique about these concepts of processes, perhaps a distinction should be made among several kinds of such concepts.

Kinds of Process Concepts

There are at least four kinds of process concepts: events, procedures, systems, and constraint-based interactions. I have identified six features that all seem to be shared by events, procedures and systems, but none of these six features is shared by constraint-based interactions. Table 1 lists these six features, and I illustrate them in the context of an event, a baseball game.

The first feature is having identifiable or decomposable subcomponents. An event, such as a baseball game, can be decomposed into identifiable distinct segments, such as the pitcher pitching and the batter getting to first base. Second, one component (the first pitch) can be identified as the beginning and anther component can be identified as the end. Third, the subcomponents of an event occur in a sequential (unidirectional) order. For example, some distinct identifiable action or situation happens at one instance in time (such as the hitter getting to first base), and another action or situation happens later (the hitter then gets from the first base to the second base and not vice versa). Fourth, besides the initiating causal agent (such as the singing of the national anthem), there is a sequence of contingent or causal subevents within the event itself (e.g., the person on the first base does not get to run unless the batter hits the ball and did not strike out). Fifth, an event has an explicit identifiable goal (e.g., winning the game). Finally, an event typically terminates when the action or movement stops. For example, when the pitcher stops pitching, the game is over.

A system, such as the human circulatory system or a heating system, shares all of these six features of an event. In the human circulatory system, for example, there are identifiable subcomponents, such as the heart and the lung. There is a beginning and an end, such as the taking in of oxygen and the excretion of carbon dioxide. Blood that handles the delivery system flows in a sequential contingent–dependent way. The goal is to deliver oxygen to the organs and remove carbon dioxide from them. If the blood terminates its flow, then the system ceases to operate. Thus, a system has all of the six features of an event. Similarly, a procedure, such as tying one's shoes, also shares all of these six features.

In contrast, however, a constraint-based interaction (CBI) process differs from these three kinds of processes in that it does not share any of the six features. (I henceforth refer to the six features as *event-like features.*) Moreover, many concepts that embody a CBI process also operate at a level that is event-like. That is, concepts that embody a CBI process also have an observable or perceptual level that corresponds to an event, a procedure, or a system.

Take the concept of diffusion as an example. It is a process that embodies both a perceivable level that is event-like and an underlying nonobservable molecular level that is a kind of CBI process. Let us consider the perceptual level of putting a drop of red dye into a container of clear liquid. What is observed at the perceptual level is that the proportion of one kind of molecule (let's say the red dye molecule) migrates from one location to another. Once the red molecules are evenly dispersed in the clear liquid, it looks as if diffusion stops. Thus, at the perceptual level, diffusion looks like an event. Even the standard textbook definitions reinforce this notion when textbooks explain diffusion as the movement of gases and nutrients from areas of greater concentration to areas of lesser concentration.

At the molecular level, however, diffusion is really the random motion of two kinds of molecules. *Diffusion* refers to the process whereby the proportion or concentration of one kind of molecule changes over time as a function of random motion of the molecules. This process does not embody any of the six event-like characteristics (see Table 1). First, it does not have decomposable subcomponents (it is uniform). Second, nor does it have a beginning and an end (it is simultaneous), aside from an initi-

Table 1

List of Contrasting Features

Event-like features	Constraint-based interaction features
Decomposable	Uniform
A beginning and an end	Simultaneous
Sequential or unidirectional	Random or multidirectional
Contingent or causal subevents	Net effect of independent subevents
Explicit goal	Constraint-satisfaction
Terminates	Continues

ating causal agent external to the concept of diffusion (such as putting a sugar cube in a glass of water). Third, without any identifiable subcomponents, there is also no unidirectional sequential ordering (it is multidirectional; the molecules move in all directions). Fourth, neither is there a sequence of causal subevents. Diffusion is not caused by any one molecule hitting another molecule thereby causing it to move. Any one minuscule action of one molecule hitting another molecule has meaning only in the context of the rest of the molecules. That is, diffusion is the net effect of multiple independent molecules moving simultaneously. Fifth, there is no explicit goal. Diffusion is a constraint-satisfaction process. Diffusion does not occur for the purpose of reaching a state of equilibrium in which the red dye is equally distributed. Rather, diffusion occurs because the molecules simply move all of the time, and the dispersed outcome of the red molecules throughout the clear molecules is simply a probabilistic outcome. Finally, nothing terminates, although at the perceptual level diffusion may look like it terminates because there is no longer any movement (as when the red dye is equally distributed in the water). At the molecular level, the movement of the molecules continues. Nothing terminates. A better example to illustrate this last point may be the game of tug-of-war. At some point in that game, the two sides are balanced so that there is no further movement from one side to the other side. Nevertheless, the children on both sides continue to pull on the rope to keep the balance.

To sum up, a CBI process is a uniform, simultaneous, and multidirectional process rather than decomposable, sequential, and unidirectional, as are events. That is, the same action (e.g., molecular movement) occurs everywhere. Moreover, it has no explicit goal, nor does it ever terminate. Instead, it can be described as constraint satisfaction or equilibrium seeking. CBI processes of this kind occur in concepts of the physical, biological, and the social sciences, as well as in everyday life. Examples are heat transfer, electrical current, natural selection, diffusion, supply and demand, as well as children's activities such as seesawing and the game of tug-of-war, and everyday occurrences such as a flock of birds flying or a traffic jam.

Why CBI Concepts Are Hard to Learn

We have postulated that CBI concepts are uniquely different from other concepts of processes. In addition, there is considerable evidence in the science literature showing that CBI concepts are extremely hard for students to learn. One can conjecture four possible reasons why CBI concepts are particularly hard to learn: (a) They tend to be misconceived initially as either a kind of material substance or a kind of causal event when in fact they are a kind of CBI process (see Figure 1). (b) Students are unfamiliar with CBI processes. (c) Students have limitations in the flexibility with which they can transfer between the dual levels of these concepts. (d) Students are not aware that a shift in the ontological class is necessary in order to understand a CBI concept. Each is discussed below.

Misconception of Concepts

Students initially conceive of many physical science concepts as a kind of substance rather than a kind of process, or if they do think of them as a kind of process, they think of them as a kind of event rather than a CBI (Reiner, Slotta, Chi, & Resnick, in press). Take, for example, the concept of heat in mechanics. Students typically think of heat as a kind of flowing substance. Such misconceptions are revealed by the way they talk about heat, such as "shut the window to keep the heat in," as if heat is a substance that can be contained in a room. A more concrete way to capture students' misconception is to analyze the language they use in answering a question, such as which cup—a styrofoam or a ceramic one—will keep coffee hotter if both cups are sealed with airtight lids? We (Slotta et al., 1995) asked this test question of students not to see whether they could answer it correctly but to examine the nature of the reasons or justifications the students gave for their choice. For example, for one student, the prediction was that the coffee in the ceramic mug would be hotter because "the heat in the styrofoam cup is gonna escape . . . because a styrofoam cup is not totally sealed because there's, like, . . . little holes in it." On the other hand, another student predicted just the opposite, that the styrofoam mug would keep coffee hotter because "it would trap the heat better than something ceramic, because ceramic doesn't have like air bubbles in it that can absorb the heat or the coldness." However, although these two choices of outcomes are diametrically opposite, there is something similar underlying the justifications given. The similarity lies in the consistency with which justifications draw on the ontological attributes of the material substances tree. Thus, the ontological attributes of material substances may be attributes such as "can be moved," "can be contained," "block," and others (Slotta et al., 1995). These ontological attributes can be instantiated by a variety of predicates. The "move" attribute can be instantiated by predicates such as *goes, leaves, flows, escapes.* Thus, students who misconceive of heat as a kind of material substance would describe it with these kinds of predicates. This in fact is exactly what they did. With respect to the answer to the question posed above (which cup keeps the coffee hotter), students justified their explanations by appealing to the material substances attributes: "The coffee in the ceramic mug is hotter than in the styrofoam cup because the heat in the styrofoam cup is *gonna escape.*" "Escaping" applies only to material substances that can move from one location to another. Similarly, the justification given to the opposing choice was "it would *trap the heat* better than something ceramic." Again, trapping the heat means that heat is some kind of material substance that "can be contained." Thus, on the surface, these students' explanations may seem inconsistent, as if they appeal to various knowledge pieces (diSessa, 1993) to justify their views. (In fact, it is possible to get the same student to use different explanations, thus self-contradict.) However, this surface variability actually reflects an underlying commonality or coherence in the nature of their justifications. Thus, one way to capture students' misconceptions is to examine the kind of predicates they use in their justifications, and determine to which ontological class the predicates belong.

Thus far I have developed a theory that predicts how students misconceive concepts. Furthermore, a method was developed to capture the nature of these misconceptions, which reveal a principled way by which they are generated. Because these misconceptions are generated by attributes from a different ontological tree, they defy learning the correct conception, as the inappropriate ontological features have been attributed to them already.

Unfamiliarity With Constraint-Based Interaction Process Concepts

A second possible reason that CBI concepts are particularly hard to learn may be that the schema for this category of concepts does not exist in a student's repertoire, or it is not well defined. As noted earlier, a CBI concept has an alternative set of six features as listed in Table 1. In short, CBI processes possess features that are antithesis of the kind of processes students are more familiar with in their everyday encounters with events, procedures, and systems. It has been shown that when students are taught these CBI features, they can learn and understand physical science concepts significantly better (Slotta & Chi, 1996).

Lack of Correspondence Between the Dual Levels

A third possible reason for the difficulty in understanding CBI process concepts is that their surface manifestation does not correspond to their deeper mechanism. The most deceiving aspect of these CBI processes is that they have an observable level that is event-like. In diffusion, for example, there seems to be an observable unidirection to diffusion. For example, dye dropped into clear water seems to flow from one area to another area. Second, it seems to have a cause, that is, a difference in concentration. Third, diffusion seems to terminate when the dye is evenly distributed. Thus, a CBI process such as diffusion has all of the appearance of a causal event-like process. It is no wonder that CBI processes are misconceived. There lies the rub in the difficulty in learning and understanding such a concept.

The difficulty arising from the misleading surface appearance is compounded by the fact that students may not realize that two distinct sets of attributes govern the surface and the deeper mechanisms. Alternatively, it may be the case that, even if students realize this difference, it may be difficult to shift from one ontological branch (the surface appearance of causal events) to another ontological branch (the CBI process).

Lack of Awareness That a Shift Is Necessary

A fourth possible reason for the difficulty in learning CBI concepts may be that students are familiar with the CBI process category but are not aware that certain concepts belong to it (because these concepts are initially misconceived) and therefore do not realize the need to shift the ontological class in which they should represent a new concept. Thus, students fail to shift because they are not aware that such a shift is necessary. This suggests that if they are told that a shift is necessary, then they can do so readily. This is consistent with the case of changing a whale from a fish to a mammal, as well as changing a toy Indian to a real Indian. That is, we often readily acknowledge that a whale is a mammal once we are told. In both the whale and the toy Indian cases, however, the shift may occur more readily because the category to which it is shifted already exists in one's repertoire. That is, we are already familiar with the category of mammal, so being told that a given entity belongs to it supports the current interpretation. This does not, however, support the second interpretation mentioned above, namely, that it is hard to learn certain CBI concepts because we do not have CBI categorical structure in memory. At this point, however, there is no evidence to discriminate between these separate interpretations.

Thus, there are four reasons why certain physical and social science concepts are hard to learn. The nature of ontological categories plays a role in each of these reasons. First, these concepts are difficult to learn because students misconceive the correct ontological class from which these concepts belong. This conclusion is derived from analyzing the nature of ontological categories, the nature of a certain class of science and social science concepts, and the pattern of misconceptions students hold (Chi, 1992; Reiner et al., in press). Second, these concepts may be difficult to learn because students may not have the features of such a CBI ontological category in their knowledge structure. That is, categorical structure for such a class of concepts does not exist. Evidence for this interpretation is supported by a training study that attempted to teach students the features of a CBI ontological class before asking them to read about CBI process concepts. The training seemed to bolster their understanding of CBI concepts significantly (Slotta & Chi, 1996). Third, the difficulty with which these concepts are understood may be due to the difficulty students have in shifting between the causal event-like surface manifestation of these concepts and the underlying CBI concept. My student and I are currently gathering evidence to examine whether this interpretation is supported. Finally, students may not be explicitly aware of the need to shift their representation of these complex concepts from one ontological tree to another. This awareness interpretation is somewhat supported by our training study of the CBI features (Slotta & Chi, 1996), and anecdotally by evidence such as the ease with which people do shift once they are told about the true ontology of whales.

CREATIVITY

Creativity is required in understanding and in production. The framework presented in this chapter, using the learning of physical and social science concepts as a context, suggests that creativity is the ability to re-represent a concept that one has to understand from one perspective to a "fundamentally different" perspective. This "fundamentally different" perspective can be defined as a difference in ontology. The production of creative "products" can also be defined as the flexible way with which an individual crosses ontological boundaries. Major scientific discoveries seem to require the successful crossing of ontological boundaries (see Chi, 1992; Gentner, this volume).

The way creativity is defined here explains the sudden "aha" phenomenon of creativity, whereby everything all of a sudden seems to make sense. This phenomenon can be interpreted in the context of an ontological shift. This is because once a concept has been re-represented on a different ontological tree, the concept immediately inherits the attributes of that tree. This immediate inheritance can provide the "aha" phenomenon.

Are there more frequent everyday observations of creative products? Re-representing may be more common and less elusive if the ontological categories are well-known. A common occurrence is metaphors in speech. Below, examples are drawn from Lakoff (1987), in which he presented metaphors of anger as heat of a fluid in a container. Anger is an emotion, which can be thought of as occupying the ontological tree of mental states, distinct from material substances as well as processes (see Figure 1). The anger as heat metaphor can be manifested in the following type of comments:

You make my *blood boil.*
Simmer down.
I had reached the *boiling point.*
Let him *stew.*
Keep your *lid on.*

What is particularly interesting is that anger (and thereby heat) is conceptualized as a mass, a kind of material substance, because it takes the grammar of mass nouns as opposed to count nouns: Thus, one can say "How much anger has he got in him?," but not "How many angers does he have in him?" Notice that because people in general misconceive of heat as a kind of substance that can be contained, the metaphor really is analogizing anger to a substance (not a CBI process). Thus, from my previous prediction, a material substances ontology can have ontological attributes of "being contained," as in the way anger is used in "I can barely contain my rage." Moreover, the very fact that a quantifier is used confirms the fact that heat is treated as a kind of substance. Thus, it does seem that a large portion of metaphors are comparisons made between entities across ontological boundaries. The case of heat and anger crosses the boundary between the ontology of mental states and material substances. Thus, the use of metaphors, when it requires shifting across familiar ontological categories, may be a common form of creativity. It is a kind of usage that does not hamper the crossing of ontological boundaries, bolstering the interpretation that familiarity with the categories may be the secret to successful shifting. This suggests that learning complex process concepts can achieve the same ease in shifting, if individuals are taught the category features, as was done in Slotta and Chi (1996).

The goal of this chapter was to provide a definition of creativity as a shift in the way a particular concept is represented. More specifically, the most difficult and perhaps thus the most creative shifts may be those that occur across ontological trees. One can consider these to be "major" shifts. Prominent scientific discoveries tend to fall into this class of creative major shifts. Shifts that cross ontological branches may be more "minor" and occur with less resistance and more frequency, as ploys used in literature and films. Thus, although the sensibility test predicts that both shifts across branches and shifts across trees are ontological, the more stringent tests of learning and understanding of complex CBI processes, as well as the making of major scientific discoveries, predict that crossing ontological trees is more creative and occurs with less frequency.

REFERENCES

Barsalou, L.W. (1983). Ad hoc categories. *Memory & Cognition, 11*, 211–227.

Carey, S. (1985). *Conceptual change in childhood.* Cambridge, MA: MIT Press.

Chi, M. T. H. (1988). Children's lack of access and knowledge reorganization: An example from the concept of animism. In F.E. Weinert & M. Perlmutter (Eds.), *Memory development: Universal changes and individual differences* (pp. 169–194). Hillsdale, NJ: Erlbaum.

Chi, M. T .H. (1992). Conceptual change within and across ontological categories: Examples from learning and discovery in science. In R. Giere (Ed.), *Cognitive models of science: Minnesota studies in the philosophy of science* (pp. 129–186). Minneapolis, MN: University of Minnesota Press.

Chi, M. T. H., Feltovich, P., & Glaser, R. (1981). Categorization and representation of physics problems by experts and novices. *Cognitive Science, 5*, 121–152.

Chi, M. T. H., Hutchinson, J., & Robin, A. F. (1989). How inferences about novel domain-related concepts can be constrained by structured knowledge. *Merrill-Palmer Quarterly, 35*, 27–62.

Chi, M. T. H., Slotta, J. D., & de Leeuw, N. (1994). From things to processes: A theory of conceptual change for learning science concepts. *Learning and Instruction, 4*, 27–43.

Collins, A. J., & Quillian, M. R. (1969). Retrieval time from semantic memory. *Journal of Verbal Learning and Verbal Behavior, 8*, 240–247.

Conrad, C. (1972). Cognitive economy in semantic memory. *Journal of Experimental Psychology, 92,* 149–154.

diSessa, A. A. (1993). Toward an epistemology of physics. *Cognition and Instruction, 10*(2–3), 101–104.

Keil, F. (1979). *Semantic and conceptual development: An ontological perspective.* Cambridge, MA: Harvard University Press.

Keil, F. (1989). *Concepts, kinds, and cognitive development.* Cambridge, MA: MIT Press.

Koestler, A. (1964). *The act of creation.* New York: Dell.

Lakoff, G. (1987). *Women, fire, and dangerous things: What categories reveal about the mind.* Chicago: University of Chicago Press.

Malt, B. C. (1990). Features and beliefs in the mental representation of categories. *Journal of Memory and Language, 2*(9), 289–315.

McNamara, T. P., & Sternberg, R. J. (1983). Mental models of word meaning. *Journal of Verbal Learning and Verbal Behavior, 22,* 449–474.

Medin, D. L., Wattenmaker, W. D., & Hampson, S. E. (1987). Family resemblance, concept cohesiveness, and category construction. *Cognitive Psychology, 19,* 242–279.

Novick, L. R. (1988). Analogical transfer, problem similarity, and expertise. *Journal of Experimental Psychology: Learning, Memory, and Cognition, 14,* 510–520.

Putnam, H. (1975). The meaning of "meaning." In H. Putnam (Ed.), *Mind, language, and reality: Philosophical papers* (Vol. 2, pp. 215–271). Cambridge, England: Cambridge University Press.

Quine, W. O. (1960). *Word and object.* Cambridge, MA: Technology Press of the Massachusetts Institute of Technology.

Reiner, M., Slotta, J. D., Chi, M. T. H., & Resnick L. B. (in press). An underlying materialistic commitment in naive thought. *Cognition and Instruction.*

Rosch, E., & Mervis, C. B. (1975). Family resemblances: Studies in the internal structure of categories. *Cognitive Psychology, 7,* 573–605.

Rosch, E., Mervis, C. B, Gray, W. D., Johnson, D., & Boyes-Braem, P. (1976). Basic objects in natural categories. *Cognitive Psychology, 8,* 382–439.

Ross, B. H. (1984). Remindings and their effects in learning a cognitive skill. *Cognitive Psychology, 16,* 371–416.

Slotta, J. D., & Chi, M. T. H. (1996). Understanding constraint-based processes: A precursor to conceptual change in physics. In G. W. Cottrell (Ed.), *Proceedings of the Eighteenth Annual Conference of the Cognitive Science Society* (pp. 306–311). Hillsdale, NJ: Erlbaum.

Slotta, J. D., Chi, M. T. H., & Joram, E. (1995). Assessing students' misclassifications of physics concepts: An ontological basis for conceptual change. *Cognition and Instruction, 13,* 373–400.

Smith, E. E. (1989). Concepts and induction. In M. I. Posner (Ed.), *Foundations of cognitive science* (pp. 501–526). Cambridge, MA: MIT Press.

Thagard, P. (1990). Explanatory coherence. *Behavioral and Brain Sciences, 12,* 435–502.

Wattenmaker, W. D., Nakamura, G. V., & Medin, D. L. (1988). Relationships between similarity-based and explanation-based categorization. In D. Hilton (Ed.), *Contemporary science and natural explanation: Commonsense conception of causality* (pp. 205–241). New York: New York University Press.

10

Polysemy and the Creation of Novel Word Meanings

Gregory L. Murphy

Thus, an essential property of language is that it provides the means for expressing indefinitely many thoughts and for reacting appropriately in an indefinite range of new situations. (Chomsky, 1965, p. 6)

It is often said that language use is inherently creative. In addition to the more obvious creative uses, such as poetry or slang creation, linguists have told us that most of the sentences that we speak and hear are novel—to us, at least. The generative capacity of language allows us to say and understand new sentences rather than having to rely on a fixed set of messages. According to the usual "Intro to Linguistics" version of this story, however, the *means* by which we achieve this creativity is through relatively fixed representations and processes. We have a fixed lexicon, which changes only slightly over time (for adults), and a set of recursive syntactic and semantic rules that, when combined with the lexicon and each

The research reported in this chapter was supported by National Institute of Mental Health Grant MH 41704. I thank the members of the Illinois Language Processing Seminar for their helpful suggestions regarding this work and Devorah Klein, Arthur Markman, Brian Ross, and Thomas Ward for comments.

other, result in this vast profusion of sentences. (For example, it seems likely that the previous sentence has never before been written in exactly this form, and yet it does not use any novel words or syntactic constructions.)

The goal of this chapter is to question the notion of a fixed lexicon and to investigate the degree to which novel language use is due in part to a creative use of that lexicon. Although the words that we know are largely fixed, the uses to which we put them are not. Word uses can vary along a dimension of conventionality. At one end are extremely familiar, usual interpretations of words, such as using the word *dog* to refer to a four-legged barking mammal. At the other end are pure innovations, in which someone knowingly uses a word in a way that is unconventional. For example, the sentence *He wristed the ball over the net*, used in a tennis commentary (E. Clark & Clark, 1979, p. 767), takes the noun *wrist* and creates a novel verb out of it. In the middle are words that have a range of possible meanings that vary in their conventionality. To the degree that words are used in novel, unconventional ways, one can think of the word use as being creative, as I discuss below.[1]

This chapter focuses on a phenomenon in this middle range of conventionality, namely polysemy. *Polysemy* refers to the related "multiple meanings" of a word. Polysemous words should be distinguished from homonyms, which have radically different meanings that do not have any apparent relation, such as *bank* (financial institution, edge of a river), *match* (something to light fires, a game), *calf* (part of the leg, baby cow), and so on. Homonyms are not very interesting from a semantic perspective, because they generally represent a historical accident in which two

[1]Just to prove that creative language use is common, a linguistics student came into my office while I was working on this chapter to tell me about his project on the semantics of sentences like "Every man who owns a donkey beats it." (These sentences are interesting to linguists because *it* refers to a universal set—all donkeys owned by someone—rather than a single object, as one might expect.) During the course of the conversation, he used the phrases *donkey constructions*, *donkey pronouns*, and *donkey sentences* quite freely, expecting that I would understand them. However, not only were some of these phrases new to me, the word *donkey* was being used in a sense very far from its usual meaning. Instead of referring to a kind of animal, in the phrases the word referred to "sentences of the logical type exemplified by *Every man who owns a donkey beats it.* Thus, a donkey pronoun is one that has the universal reading when appearing in a sentence of that logical type. One will not find this sense of *donkey* in most dictionaries.

different lexical items have the same name. There is little or no meaningful relation between the two meanings.

In contrast, consider the uses of the word *fresh* shown in the first column of Table 1. Each time this adjective appears, it has a somewhat different interpretation: A fresh shirt is one that has been recently washed, but a fresh fish is one that has been recently caught (not rotten or frozen), and fresh paint has been recently applied to some surface. In these cases, the meanings are related (unlike the different meanings of *bank*), but they do not seem to be identical. In fact, Murphy and Andrew (1993) showed that the word *fresh* was given different synonyms and antonyms when paired with different nouns. That is, people seemed to think that the same word had a different interpretation in these different contexts. One subject's antonym responses are shown in Table 1. As can be seen, this person produced *stale* as the antonym of *fresh* when the word was presented in isolation. However, when *fresh* was used in the context of another noun, the same subject produced this response only once out of seven times. This suggests that the particular sense of *fresh* changed depending on the noun it appeared with.

THEORIES OF POLYSEMY

Polysemy is a ubiquitous part of language. In fact, it seems likely that every content word is polysemous to some extent. For example, virtually every

Table 1

One Subject's Responses in the Antonym Task

Original items: Fresh	One subject's antonyms: Stale
Fresh shirt	dirty shirt
Fresh air	polluted air
Fresh outlook	bad outlook
Fresh water	dirty water
Fresh bread	stale bread
Fresh vegetables	rotten vegetables
Fresh idea	old idea

NOTE: See Murphy and Andrew (1993).

noun referring to an object has two very related meanings: one referring to a specific example of that object and one referring to the entire class (Nunberg, 1978).

(1) a. The dog ate my hamburger.
    b. The dog is a four-legged mammal.

In (1), the same word is used to refer a single object (1a) or an entire class of objects (1b). These are two very different kinds of meanings in some sense, but they are also highly related, because the individual mentioned in 1a is a member of the class referred to in 1b. Most concrete nouns are polysemous in this way. There are also other, perhaps more interesting, forms of polysemy, as I show later.

For psycholinguists, the problem of polysemy lies in attempting to specify exactly what senses are represented in the mental lexicon and how the representations for a given word are related. The traditional view, as exemplified in most dictionaries, is to specify a separate sense for every distinguishable meaning. One standard dictionary provides 10 senses for the adjective *fresh* (some with subtypes), which can be summarized as follows: recently produced; having original strength; not known before; additional, further; inexperienced; original, spontaneous; cool and refreshing; brisk; not salt (of water); and said of a cow that has just begun to give milk. In addition to these, there are listed three noun meanings and a transitive and intransitive verb meaning. Whether the different parts of speech of the same word represent polysemy of the same lexical item (as Caramazza & Grober, 1976, suggest) or instead meanings of different lexical items is an interesting question. I focus here on the senses of a word in a given syntactic category (usually its noun uses), which is complex enough. (However, the experiments described use meaning extensions that cross syntactic category.)

In the traditional view, then, each distinguishable usage receives a different listing. As a psychological account, this view says that a given lexical item is associated to a number of different concepts or combinations of concepts. For highly polysemous words, desk dictionaries list 10 or more entries; unabridged dictionaries may list many more. However, an examination of these meanings suggests that they are not complete. For example, the sense of *fresh* meaning "not frozen" is not in my dictionary, and most entries for nouns do not make the object–class distinction shown in (1). Thus, the number of entries for a single word in the mental lexicon could be very large, larger than usually represented in a dictionary.

The alternative view is that many of these apparently distinct senses are in fact the same sense, which has different interpretations in different contexts. (I use *sense* to indicate the long-term representation of the meaning or meanings of a word and *interpretation* or *use* to indicate the meaning of a word as it is used on a specific occasion.) According to this view, *fresh* has only one sense—its core or central meaning. The other interpretations can be derived from this meaning given the context of utterance. For example, perhaps *fresh* refers to being recently made or produced, and the other uses listed in the dictionary could be derived through modification of that core meaning. If one were to say "This fish is not very fresh," it might be clear from the context that recency of manufacture is not at issue here, but that the time since the catching of the fish is the intended meaning. Alternatively, if I were to say "Those sheets aren't fresh; let me change them," a listener would understand me to mean that someone had slept in the sheets—not that the sheets had not been recently manufactured (because people change sheets on the basis of their cleanliness, not age). Thus, the exact interpretation of *fresh* in any context depends on the word it modifies and the discourse context. The listener needs to choose the interpretation that makes the most sense, given the core meaning of the word and the context.

In short, according to the alternative view, there is no need to list many senses for a given lexical item. The interpretation of that word arises through a single meaning stored in the lexicon, as further specified or modified by context. As the examples show, considerable enrichment of the core meaning may be required, presumably drawing on the participants' world knowledge (e.g., knowledge of social practices involving bed linen might be necessary to understand the use of *fresh* in *fresh sheets*). This view receives considerable elaboration and discussion below. I call the traditional view the *multiple senses* view, and the alternative the *single sense* view. It should be understood that the latter does not claim that there is always only one sense per word but rather takes the approach that the number of senses is very small.

Before attempting to evaluate these views, however, it is important to understand what is at stake. First, these two views lead to very different conceptions of both what is stored in the lexicon and how language processing works (H. Clark, 1983), as summarized in Table 2. Clearly, the lexicon in the single sense case is much simpler and smaller than in the multiple senses case. As a result, comprehension is quite different on the two views. For the multiple senses view, comprehension involves selecting the sense that is most appropriate in the sentence. That is, it involves retrieving the "recently produced" sense of *fresh* when hearing "fresh milk" but the "haven't been slept in" sense when hearing "fresh sheets." In contrast, according to the single sense view, the same sense is retrieved in the two cases (the only sense that there is for that word), but considerable work must be done in integrating this meaning with the context so that the appropriate interpretation is arrived at. Each time the word is processed, its precise interpretation must be worked out. Thus, choice of one of these alternatives has extremely important consequences for theories of processing, which have only seldom been acknowledged in writing on lexical

Table 2

Comparison of Two Primary Views of Polysemy

Category	Multiple senses view	Single sense view
Representation	Many separate entries	One unified entry
Meaning processing	Selection of correct entry	Modification and augmentation of listed meaning
Learning	Separate learning of each entry	Only one meaning is learned
Effect of context	Drives selection of sense	Actively creates intended sense
Main problems	Difficult to individuate meanings; perhaps too many senses to be learned	Stored meaning may be very abstract; some senses are too distant from "core" meaning

processing (e.g., Gerrig, 1986). One view places considerable emphasis on lexical representation, and the other primarily emphasizes elaborative processing.

A final reason for the importance of polysemy is that differences in interpretations are ubiquitous. Every time a word appears in a different sentence, a somewhat different interpretation may be derived. For example, as Anderson and Ortony (1975) pointed out, sentences like (2) and (3) emphasize different aspects of the meaning of *piano*, one focusing on musical function and the other on its weight:

(2) Fred played the piano loudly.
(3) Fred lifted the piano.

Although the meaning of *piano* does not seem to have changed, the weighting of different aspects of that meaning can change from sentence to sentence. This kind of contextual emphasis is not normally called polysemy but seems to be a less radical example of the same kind of process. The point is that contextual modification occurs not only in dramatic cases (e.g., as in *fresh*), but also in a variety of less noticeable instances, perhaps in most sentences (see Gentner & France, 1988).

Cruse (1986, p. 52) described two related cases:

(4) Arthur poured the butter into a dish.

The sense of *butter* appears to be the "normal" one here (churned product of cow's milk), but the usual expectation of solidity is overruled by the rest of the sentence.

(5) The pregnant nurse attended us.

In (5), a typical feature (that most nurses are female) is confirmed rather than overruled. These are examples of the promotion or demotion of stereotypical features, according to Cruse. One could potentially list different senses of such words (e.g., a solid and liquid sense for *butter*, a male and female sense for *nurse*), or one could list a single sense that is modified by appropriate context.

Cruse (1986) argued that cases like *butter* are not truly polysemous, but are "general" with respect to some variations. That is, *nurse* does not specify gender in its meaning, and *butter* does not specify phase (solid or liquid). Thus, in this account, there are not two meanings of *nurse*, one indicating maleness and the other femaleness—both male and female nurses are consistent with the word meaning. This solution is probably necessary, because there are many typical features that are not critical for the meanings of words, and one would not wish to suggest that there are separate senses in the lexicon for each one (e.g., nurses in an operating room, nurses in the emergency room, short nurses, thin nurses, nurses dressed in white or in blue, etc.). Thus, contextual modification of meaning must be allowed in any theory of comprehension, even for nonpolysemous words, or else every word would have innumerable lexical entries. This conclusion suggests that a certain amount of contextual modification in polysemy, as proposed by the single sense view, seems likely.

CREATIVITY

What has polysemy (or other contextual modification) got to do with creativity? In part, the answer to this question depends on one's theory of polysemy, as will be seen. On an intuitive basis, however, it seems clear that polysemy involves extending a word's use beyond its core or usual use. The word *fresh* could have had a single, well-specified meaning that does not vary with context. The fact that polysemy is so widespread suggests that there is pressure on the lexicon to extend a limited set of words to new functions rather than to invent new words for each sense. The process of extending a word to a new use is a creative one. However, the two views of polysemy place creativity in different parts of that process.

If all of the senses are prestored in the lexicon, as the multiple senses view claims, then the creativity is in a historical process. Somebody was the first person to use the word *fresh* to refer to sheets that have not been slept in. Others who initially heard and reused this sense may have exercised some degree of creativity as well. However, once the usage became conventionalized, the individual language user was no longer acting creatively. Rather, when hearing the word, or when deciding to use it, speakers selected the correct sense from the list of preexisting senses they had learned. That is, selecting the correct sense of the word would be analogous to looking in the dictionary to find the sense that seems most appropriate in the present context. In this view, then, creativity lies in the actions of a few linguistic innovators rather than in those people's everyday use of polysemous words. However, those innovators would be quite creative, because normal language use would not usually involve extending word meaning this way, and their innovation would be useful enough to enter general usage.

The single sense view attributes more creativity to speakers and listeners during their normal language processing. If only one sense is represented in the lexicon, then speakers must go through a much more productive process on-line, in which they try to stretch the stored meaning to match the present situation. For example, to explain to someone that the sheets have not yet been washed, the word *fresh* could be used, even though the entry of this word in the lexicon says nothing about washing of sheets or clothes per se. However, speakers realize that the core meaning of *fresh* could be extended to this usage, and they expect that listeners could understand this extension. Each of us would then be doing something creative whenever we used a word in a less usual way and perhaps in comprehending such novel uses. The further the interpretation is from the core meaning, the more creative our use of it would be.

It is not possible to discuss the evidence for these two views in any detail here. Suffice it to say that the views have some problems that make both of them seem somewhat unlikely. The multiple meaning view has a problem of specifying how many meanings are stored and how people identify and learn each separate meaning. When taken to an extreme, every occurrence of a word can be said to have a slightly different interpretation, and so each one would require a separate entry. That is, why wouldn't listeners faced with contexts like (2) and (3) form different senses for "heavy piano" and "loud piano"? If they wouldn't, then some account needs to be given of exactly what senses would be represented, and so far no such account has been suggested. Furthermore, the experiments I discuss herein as well as research on linguistic innovation show that individual speakers and listeners can use words in ways that cannot be represented by preexisting entries in the lexicon.

The single meaning view can explain such findings, because it assumes that much semantic processing is done through inference to a single core meaning. Thus, innovations are not in principle a problem. Furthermore, the single sense view does not need to worry about the slight variations of meaning that occur in most sentences, as it claims that only one sense is represented in the lexicon. However, this view has a problem with extremely different senses that can be found within a single word. For example, Caramazza and Grober (1976) listed 26 senses for the word *line*, ranging from abstract geometrical senses to social activities (to form a line at the movies) to a sewing usage (to line a coat). It seems unlikely that all of these senses could be quickly derived from a single core meaning. What core meaning would be consistent with all of these uses? Furthermore, it seems unlikely that very frequent uses of a word do not receive a separate representation. For example, one might expect a salesperson who frequently uses the expression "line of products" to have a separate representation for this sense of *line*, rather than to have to infer it from a basic geometric meaning every time he or she uses it.

Some linguists take a less extreme position, in which some but not all senses are thought to be listed in the lexicon (e.g., Cruse, 1986; Rice, 1992). Although this is a rather vague claim until one states which senses are represented, it is nonetheless probably correct. As a result, both forms of creativity described earlier are likely to be found. That is, for senses that are not specifically listed in the lexicon, speakers are demonstrating creativity in extending a known word to that usage. For senses that are listed in the lexicon, the original innovators who extended the word in that way (e.g., the first person to call a queue of people a line) were being creative. When a new situation arises that people want to talk about, they must develop a new means of talking about it, and extending the meaning of an already-known word is one way to do this. In such a case, speakers must go through an inferential process to decide which word to use, and listeners must decide what someone else's use of that word was intended to mean. This may not be a great leap of creativity, but a rather mundane one that is essential for everyday communication.

Until this "some but not all senses" view is specified in greater detail, we will not know how much of each kind of creativity goes on. The task for this view is to specify what senses count as different and to explain why some senses are represented whereas others are not. At this time, there is simply no theory that attempts such an explanation. However, the experiments described below do provide some relevant data.

Another form of creativity in polysemy can be found in acquisition. It has long been known that children overextend words. So, babies might call all mammals "doggie" or a variety of foods "cookie," and many liquids "juice." However, it now seems fairly clear that for much of the early acquisition period, children know the correct meaning of many words but purposely extend them in novel ways in order to communicate (E. Clark, 1983). The same child who calls sheep "doggie" may select only a dog when asked to choose one in a comprehension task. Thus, children are using their limited vocabulary in novel ways in order to refer to things. Such usage is clearly not learned from adult models, since adults do not use the words in this way (they do not call sheep "doggie"), and so a certain amount of innovation is involved. Similarly, children make up novel expressions that are not standard English in order to fill lexical gaps (E. Clark, 1993). For example, Becker (1994) found the following examples:

(6) a. You got good earsight, Dad. [hearing]
    b. Don't beater it, Mom. [mix the dough]
    c. We saw a light-man. [man who fixes lights]

It is not always clear whether the child thinks that a novel use is a legitimate word that he or she simply has not heard before or whether the use is consciously innovative. In either case, the child is creatively using the forms that are available in order to express new ideas.

Finally, at the extreme of the word uses that are clearly not prestored lie the innovations of nonce uses (H. Clark, 1983; Gerrig, 1989) that can be found throughout speech. Among these are nouns used as verbs, as in the *wristed* example; eponymous verbs and adjectives, as in "He'll do a

Richard Nixon to his opponent" or "She's very West Coast"; novel compound nouns, such as *foot race* to mean a race that is a foot long (see the chapters by Shoben and Wisniewski, as well as Murphy, 1988, 1990, 1991, for more on this topic); and even possessives, such as "That's my house," meaning "That's the house that I admire and would like to own some day." As H. Clark (1983) argued, such nonce uses cannot be explained by prestored senses because their interpretations depend so much on the context. Nonetheless, they also depend in part on the stored word meaning (e.g., *wristed* is clearly related to the meaning of the noun *wrist*), and so they also appear to count as creative extensions. Markman, Yamauchi, and Makin (this volume) find that speakers readily make up their own names for novel categories as part of a joint activity. This suggests that meaning extensions are not an unusual activity engaged in only under special task demands.

HOW SENSES ARE UNDERSTOOD

The research project that I briefly describe here investigated the processes by which novel word senses are created and understood. Thus, I do not discuss the case in which people interpret a polysemous word whose senses they are already familiar with (as in the *fresh* example and others studied by Murphy & Andrew, 1993). Instead, these experiments look at a phenomenon more explicitly related to the issue of creativity, in which a word is encountered for the first time in a novel usage.

Although much of the discussion up until now has been from the perspective of speakers, some of the same considerations apply to listeners who hear a polysemous word. The speaker wishes to talk about some situation, and he or she must choose the words that efficiently refer to it in the context. In some cases, this may require novel uses of the words. The listener is being exposed to familiar words, but some of them require novel interpretations, based on the same discourse context. Thus, although the tasks of choosing a word to speak and interpreting a spoken word are not identical, they involve many similar processes, especially in relating the lexicon to the discourse context. My experiments put subjects in the position of listeners, because this allows control of the materials, both words and contexts.

What is it that allows a word to be used in a new way? I suggest three simple hypotheses that are useful for generating predictions for the experiments. The first one says that the only constraint on extending a word use is that the context must make it clear what the intended meaning is. I call this the *comprehensibility constraint.* Thus, as long as the new meaning is understandable with a normal amount of effort, it may be created. It is possible, however, that there are other constraints on how meanings are extended, and the other hypotheses suggest further restrictions on meaning creation. The *variability constraint* proposes that the variability of the uses of a word partly determines whether it can be extended to new meanings. Some words—in fact, typically the most frequent ones—are extremely polysemous. As mentioned earlier, Caramazza and Grober (1976) listed 26 senses of the word *line*, and there is no reason to think that their list is exhaustively complete. So, perhaps people would accept a novel extension to a word like *line* more than they would to a word with fewer senses, such as *shirt.* The idea is that once a word has been identified as having multiple meanings, speakers may be more willing to extend it further.

Another constraint that I consider is the possibility that novel extensions must be built on the previously existing senses of a word. That is, it is not enough to understand what the intended meaning is—the new meaning must be related to an already-known sense. I call this the *relatedness constraint.* Consider the following examples:

(7) a. The paper fired the striking reporters.
b. The paper doesn't think that Senator Warthog is guilty.
c. The paper only prints letters from experts.

Perhaps the very first time *paper* was used to refer to a newspaper publisher (as in 7a), it was licensed by the fact that there was already a meaning of *paper* referring to the editorial staff (as in 7b), and perhaps that was partly licensed by the fact that there was already a sense referring to the editorial policy of the paper (as in 7c). The particular historical sequence

I have suggested is hypothetical; however, it seems likely that the original meaning of the word *paper* started from simpler, core meanings (sheets of the substance made from wood pulp) and then extended to senses that were farther and farther removed (newspapers, editions of newspaper, and publishers; see Sweetser, 1990, for examples from a different domain). So, like other examples of creativity, such as Ward's (1994) studies of the creation of novel animals, new word uses may have to be built on the uses that are already known.

Experiment 1

The first experiment examined the three previously discussed hypotheses of sense extension by creating new words with carefully constructed senses. To begin with, five paragraphs were created that used a novel word in slightly different ways. This diagram is a representation of the similarity of the senses of the novel words, where similar meanings are closer together:

A' A Core B B'

Every subject was exposed to the core meaning, followed by either meaning A or B (or nothing). Then they were tested on meaning A' or B', as I explain shortly. The stimuli were eight novel words supposedly used in an unfamiliar country (called "Quine"). Each word was first introduced in its core meaning, using a picture of the object, which was described in some detail. Figure 1 shows the picture of one of the stimuli, and Table 3 provides the core and extended meanings for this word, *wift.*

As this example shows, the initial core meaning of the word was as a noun naming that object. The extended uses were always verb uses (to ensure that they were extensions of the core meaning). The paragraphs were written so that they were fairly self-contained and could be mixed and matched as the experimental design required. Subjects read a series of these paragraphs and then rated the appropriateness of the final use of the novel word (either A' or B'). That use was underlined in the paragraph so that it could be easily identified. Subjects were explicitly told that every use of the word prior to the underlined one was an appropriate one.

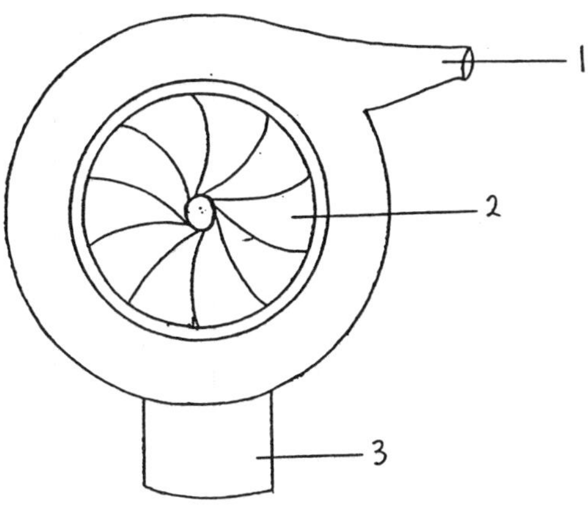

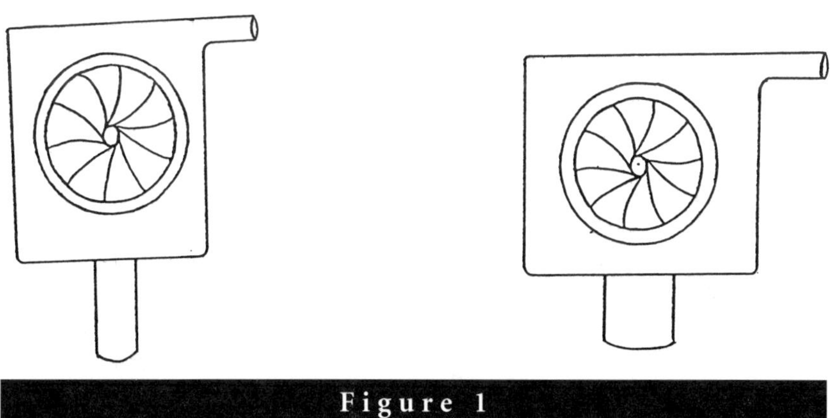

Figure 1

Picture accompanying the text shown in Table 3. Subjects had the picture available while reading and rating the test items.

There were three different conditions that varied in which paragraphs preceded the final (test) use: The final use was close to the earlier use, or distant from the earlier use, or there was no earlier use (only the core meaning). In the close conditions, subjects read the core meaning, A and A', or else the core meaning, B and B'. For example, for *wift* (see Table 3)

Table 3

Sample Materials From Experiment 1

Core meaning
When there is excess water in the soil due to excessive rain, Quinese people use a **wift** to help remove it. The pipe (3) is inserted in the ground, and the swirling blades (2) pull excess water into the pipe. The small tube (1) is an air intake valve. Thus, the wift is a kind of dehydrator for soil.
A (Context)
One time, Bill was using the wift on his garden after a very heavy rain. He was afraid that his tomatoes were going to rot after the days and days of precipitation. After he had it set up, he sat down in front of it and let the breeze it generated cool him down. He wifted himself like that for almost half an hour.
A' (Test)
Bill had a lot of yard work to do. One day he had to clean up the sidewalks, which were covered with leaves and grass clippings. To save time, Bill plugged in this tool and carried it out to the sidewalk. He used it to <u>wift</u> the leaves right off the sidewalk into the street.
B (Context)
Unfortunately, Bill wasn't very careful with this tool. One day he was working in the garden while the wift was on. He wasn't paying attention to it, and when he turned around suddenly, he stuck his elbow right into the swirling blades! He wifted his elbow quite badly, and he had to wear a bandage for a couple of weeks.
B' (Test)
One time, Bill decided to use his wift in order to make a salad. He took a cucumber and pressed it through the blades while they were whirling around. It sliced the cucumber into slivers that collected in the bottom. Then he <u>wifted</u> some lettuce and carrots. He had a really good salad.

NOTE: The numbers in parentheses refer to the labeled parts of Figure 1, which subjects could see while reading the paragraphs.

a close condition might have tested subjects on the "wift the vegetables" use after having read the "wift the elbow" use. Because the slicing of vegetables is conceptually related to the cutting of the elbow, these uses were close. In the distant conditions, subjects read the core meaning, B and A' or else the core meaning, A and B'. For example, for the *wift* item, a subject might be tested on the "wift the vegetables" use after having read the paragraph in which the wift is used as a fan. Because cooling oneself off with a wift is not very similar to cutting vegetables with a wift, these were in the distant condition. Thus, in the close conditions, the test item was similar in meaning to the meaning used in the previous paragraph, but in the distant condition, the test was rather different in meaning from the earlier extension. Finally, in the control condition, subjects read only the core paragraph and one of the test items. Note that the A' and B' meanings occurred in both close and far conditions, so the overall goodness of the meaning represented in A' or B' was not confounded with condition. In every case, the task was for subjects to judge how appropriate or normal the final use of the word was on a 1–7 scale.

The results were quite clear-cut. When the meaning was close, the appropriateness was rated fairly high (4.6). When it was distant, participants rated it significantly less appropriate (3.7), which was about the same as if there had been no prior context (3.6). (Both were significantly different from the close condition.) Although these differences were not extremely large, it should be remembered that they are comparisons of the exact same word uses in the same paragraphs—all that varies is the previous uses.

These results are evidence that an extended use of a word can allow novel uses to be perceived as more acceptable. That is, the degree to which a creative word use is perceived as appropriate depends on how related it is to other known uses. If it is "too creative," that is, too different from prior uses, readers do not think it is correct. Thus, this experiment found evidence for the relatedness constraint. How did the other constraints fare? The comprehensibility constraint does not seem to be very likely. The same uses of the word were found to be differentially acceptable depending on the prior context. Since the interpretation of the test word depended on the specific paragraph it was in, and the final paragraphs were the same in all conditions, it does not seem likely that comprehensibility of the specific test meaning varied much across conditions. Of course, subjects would be unlikely to accept an incomprehensible use of a word. However, it does not seem that any word use that can be figured out is accepted.

There was also some evidence against the variability constraint. Note that in the control condition, subjects read only one use of the word prior to the test. In the other two conditions, they read two different uses. Thus, if they were relying on the past variability of the word to decide whether it could accept a new meaning, the control condition should have been the lowest. However, this condition was instead virtually identical to the distant condition (which had two very different meanings). Acceptability of the meaning extension appeared to depend on a familiar use that was close to the tested sense; variability itself did not seem to have had an effect. Of course, this conclusion is based on a comparison of one versus two meanings, and it may be that variability has an effect when there are larger numbers of word uses (more like the 26 senses of *line* identified by Caramazza & Grober, 1976).

Experiments 2 and 3

Experiment 1 showed that a prior meaning of a word could constrain people's acceptance of a new meaning. The next two experiments looked at a rather different constraint on polysemy—not a specific known meaning but the process by which a new meaning is created. According to linguists, certain ways of extending meaning occur again and again. Does this mean that people are particularly ready to understand new meanings that are made by these familiar means? Note that this is quite different from the relatedness constraint that I explored in the last experiment. In that constraint, there had to be a specific sense that was similar to the new use. In this case, I am raising the possibility that people could be especially attuned to common processes that generate new senses. Here, using a word in an extended way would be creative in the sense of being novel, but less creative in the sense of using a familiar technique to generate the new meaning. However, a common way to be creative is to apply familiar processes to new materials, and this is an example. As Finke, Ward, and Smith (1992) pointed out, two ways to generate new ideas is through transformation of known ideas and analogical transfer from known ideas. Both of these are relevant here. For example, if you know that the word *book* can be used to refer to either an object or a text (as in 8), then you might well make a similar assumption for a word like *videodisk* (as in 9) even if you have never heard it used in the second sense.

(8) a. I put the book on the table. [physical object]
b. I see you have *Emma.* I read that book in college. [text]

(9) a. Who left the videodisk on the floor? [physical object]
b. I hated that videodisk. [text]

In short, some ways of extending word meanings are themselves conventional and can be applied to other similar meanings. Following are some common examples, as documented by Nunberg (1978), Cruse (1986) and other linguists. First is the use of the same word to refer to an object and the representation of the object. For example, (10) can refer to either an actual dog or a striking statue of a dog.

(10) Wow, look at that dog!

This sort of polysemy applies to most concrete nouns. A second form is the use of a single word to refer to an object and the substance the object is made of. In English, this is often marked by a mass–count noun distinction. For example, "I have a chicken" indicates that *chicken* is an object, but "I have some chicken" indicates that the meat of the chicken is being referred to. Thus, *chicken* is used to denote both the whole object and the substance. Similarly, in (11a), *oak* refers to a single object, whereas in (11b), it refers to the kind of wood, that is, the substance that makes up the kind of object mentioned in (11a).

(11) a. That oak is tall.
b. This table is made out of oak.

Fourth, as mentioned earlier in (1), many nouns can be used to pick out both individual objects and whole classes of objects. Fifth, many nouns also have verb meanings that mean something like "to use the object in its normal, expected way"; for example, the words *hammer*, *bicycle*, and *pencil* have verb meanings that are extensions of the basic noun meaning (see E. Clark & Clark, 1979).

In contrast to these familiar processes, there are some processes that one *could* use to generate new meanings that are not particularly common. For example, one could refer to events or objects by the locations that are associated to them, but this is not as common. That is, "I'm going to ballpark" could be an expression meaning that "I am going to play baseball," but this does not seem acceptable. The question, then, is whether people prefer to extend meanings in ways that follow the familiar transformations that have created past examples of polysemy. We can answer this question in part by considering the senses of words that have recently entered the language, such as recent inventions. Intuitively, it seems that new words corresponding to new pieces of technology have the same kinds of polysemy that similar older words have. For example, *videodisk* can be used to refer to the object, the edition of a movie, the "text" of the movie, the entire class of videodisks, and so on, just as the words *videotape, film,* and *book* can (mutatis mutandis). It seems likely that language users applied the traditional paradigms of meaning extension to this (recently) novel word, though we do not know for sure whether multiple speakers made these extensions or whether they arose from a single originator. The purpose of the present experiments was to examine this process in ordinary speakers rather than in inventors or specially selected linguistic innovators.

The second experiment also involved teaching people the names of objects using a picture. Following this description of the core meaning, there was a paragraph that used the word in an extended way. One extension of the item (the *conventional* condition) used a common form of polysemy, as derived from the linguistic literature, such as type–token, object–substance, object–representation, and so on. That is, the word would be used to refer to an individual object in the core meaning, and then might be extended to refer to a representation of the object in the extended use. The *novel* condition used nonstandard extensions, which were clear from the context, but did not follow a standard form of meaning extension. As before, subjects had to rate how appropriate they found the word in its extended meaning.

An example is shown in Table 4. The core meaning is the tool de-

Table 4

Sample Materials From Experiments 2 and 3

Core meaning

Quinese hunters use **tuks** to catch possums and other delicacies that are valued in Quine. When the animal is spotted, the hunter sneaks up on it and throws the loop (1) over the animal's head. The hunter must quickly pull the free end of the loop (4), which tightens it around the animal's neck. The tuk is held at the handle (3), and the hand guard (2) prevents the animal from scratching or biting the hand. If the hunter is strong, the animal becomes unconscious and dies very quickly, once the loop cuts off the air supply. Because so much skill is involved in using the tuk, hunters who are successful with it are very honored.

Conventional

Mary was a renowned hunter who could do incredible things with a tuk. She won a number of contests at rodeos and competitive hunting contests. Mary took up painting as a hobby to relax during the spring, when hunting was out of season. One of the first things she painted was her favorite tuk, since she figured that's what she knew best. Her friend Pat came over one day and examined her new painting. "That's a great tuk," Pat said.

Novel

Mary decided to take up tuk hunting for relaxation. Just being outdoors would be fun, she thought. But when her first hunting trips went badly, she decided she needed more help. She bought a book all about tuks, their construction, history and use. In fact, it was known as the tuk-user's bible in some circles. She kept it in her living room and read it every chance she got. One day her friend Pat came over for dinner and noticed the book on the table. "That's a great tuk," Pat said, indicating the book.

scribed in the first paragraph. In the conventional extension, a representation of a tuk is described by the word *tuk*. As described earlier, the object–representation polysemy is a well-documented form of polysemy (as in (10)). In the novel extension, a book about tuks is called a *tuk*. The story makes it clear that there is a very close connection between tuks and this particular book—it is the "tuk-user's bible." Nonetheless, this meaning extension, which does not seem very different from the object–representation extension, is not at all common in English, and so readers may not find it acceptable. That is, we do not use the word *dog* to refer both to a dog and to a book about a dog (though we do use it to refer to a statue of a dog). A paraphrase of each meaning extension is provided in Table 5.

The procedure was essentially identical to that of Experiment 1, and the results were the mean appropriateness ratings for the novel extensions and the conventional extensions. The mean rating for the conventional ex-

Table 5

Paraphrases of the Conventional and Novel Sense Extensions: Experiments 3 and 4

Wift (garden tool)
C: to use the object in the usual way
N: to use it in a nonstandard way
Tuk (hunting tool)
C: a picture of the object
N: a book about the object
Henkle (musical instrument)
C: type-token
N: place where the instrument was played
Tonklet (animal)
C: meat of the animal
N: place where the animal lived
Ruv (furniture)
C: use standardly
N: use nonstandardly
Dobma (liquor container)
C: quantity that the container can hold
N: person who makes the container
Deljid (tree)
C: wood of the tree
N: forest of that tree
Melper (weapon)
C: attack someone with the weapon
N: use weapon as a holder

NOTE: C = conventional; N = novel.

tension was 6.2, whereas the mean rating for the novel extensions was 2.9. This finding suggests that people can tell the difference between standard kinds of extensions of noun meanings and nonstandard extensions, and they like the standard ones better. In fact, the conventional extensions rated near the top of the 1–7 scale, and so they were apparently quite appropriate in an absolute sense. This suggests, then, that one constraint on creative extension of word meanings is a preference that the transformation from the known to a new meaning be a familiar one.

One possible problem with this demonstration is that the meanings themselves are different across conditions. That is, in one condition the novel meaning was something like "book about a tuk," and in the other it was "picture of a tuk." Perhaps there is something inherently more difficult or implausible about the meanings that were used in the novel extension condition. This was not a potential problem in Experiment 1, because there each meaning served in all three conditions—only the context varied. Furthermore, the contexts in Experiment 2 were different for the two meanings, and it is possible that the contexts were clearer in one case than in the other. In short, it may be that item differences irrelevant to the novelty manipulation are responsible for the results.

A third experiment addressed part of this problem by asking subjects to write down definitions of each word after they rated it. That is, subjects were told not only to decide whether the meaning was an acceptable one, but also to specify what they thought the meaning was. This allowed me to evaluate one possible explanation of the previous results, that subjects in the novel extensions never fully understood what the intended meaning was. For example, perhaps the context in Table 4 did not sufficiently indicate that Pat intends *tuk* to mean something like "book about a tuk," and so subjects down rated it. Or perhaps the meaning itself was implausible, and so subjects did not accurately recover it from the story. (Of course, such an effect itself might come about through conventionality, but my intention was that the desired meaning should be about equally clear in the two conditions.) In all other respects, the procedure was the same as that of Experiment 2.

In analyzing the results, I first examined the overall rating data to see whether they replicated those of Experiment 2. Table 6 shows that they did (in the raw ratings row): Once again, the novel meanings were considered less acceptable. A naive rater then evaluated each definition as to whether it was accurate (consistent with the intended meaning). The intended meanings were specified in advance for each sense, and the rater's task was to decide not whether subjects reiterated this meaning exactly (which would be very unlikely), but whether their definitions were consistent with the intended meaning. A 1–7 scale was used. There was a small difference in the ratings for the two conditions (see bottom row of Table 6), favoring the conventional senses. Thus, readers did seem to be more accurate with the conventional extensions, although the effect was not large. The rater found that in a few cases, subjects surprisingly gave the original definition instead of an extended meaning. Such cases were simply eliminated from analysis (and from the means shown in Table 6), as subjects clearly did not understand them. However, all but one of these cases occurred when the meaning extension was novel, suggesting that readers were particularly primed to accept extensions that followed the convention and were puzzled by different extensions.

Although there was only a small difference in the accuracy of the ratings of the two conditions, a final analysis attempted to remove this difference as an explanation of the appropriateness ratings. A subset of items

Table 6

Mean Appropriateness Ratings and Consistency of Definitions for Experiment 3

	Meaning transformation	
Category	Conventional	Novel
Raw ratings[a]	6.1	3.4
Equated accuracy	6.2	2.5
Definition consistency[b]	6.6	6.3

[a]Subjects' ratings of the appropriateness of an extended word use. [b]A judge's ratings of subjects' definitions of the extended word use.

was derived in which the ratings of the two conditions were equal, by successively eliminating the lowest-rated novel definitions. Once the definitions were equated for accuracy, the appropriateness ratings for the remaining items were reexamined. The results, shown in Table 6 (in the equated accuracy row) reveal the exact same effect of appropriateness. In fact, the effect increased somewhat. The reason for this seems to be that when subjects did not fully understand the word use, they tended to misunderstand it as being more conventional than it really was—and therefore rated it more highly. When incorrect interpretations were removed, the ratings of the remaining truly unconventional interpretations were very low. Thus, subjects' reluctance to accept the novel extensions was not due to any lack of understanding. Even when they understood them perfectly well, they did not find them appropriate uses of the word.

In short, it seems that subjects are more accepting of a novel word meaning when it is derived from a conventional meaning transformation than when it is derived from a nonstandard one. It is important to emphasize that, in every case, subjects were rating the appropriateness of a new meaning—the use of the word in a way that they had never encountered before. The comparison was between different methods of creating this new meaning. The results show that some meaning extensions are more novel than others. When the method used to extend the meaning was a nonstandard one not common in English, subjects found the use inappropriate and unrealistic. When the method was a standard one, they rated the extension as much more appropriate and as quite acceptable in an absolute sense. In some cases, extending a word to a new use may be so transparent that speakers do not realize that the meaning has subtly changed. For example, although an individual object and a class of objects are quite different things, speakers readily accept nouns as names for both of them (e.g., *dog* referring to a single pet and to the class of dogs), without noticing much difference. One might worry that it is one or two of these particularly transparent forms of polysemy that are responsible for the effect. However, the novel–conventional difference was found in all eight items in both Experiments 2 and 3. Thus, it does not seem that one or two particular forms of polysemy account for the effect.

CONCLUSIONS

What do these results mean for an understanding of linguistic creativity? Perhaps the main implication is that people are able to understand novel extensions of word meanings (within limits). They do not need to pre-store all the senses of a word. When a new sense is encountered, readers are usually able to interpret it correctly (as shown by the ratings of definitions in Experiment 3). Furthermore, they show considerable regularity in their judgments of whether the uses are appropriate. These results are significant, because the meanings tested here are known to be novel. If actual polysemous words had been used, I could not have been sure whether a given subject had or had not heard it before, and so we could not tell whether the use was pre-stored or novel. In the present experiments, all of the tested uses were novel ones, because the words themselves were novel, and the prior exposure to the word's uses was controlled.

Thus, one conclusion is that people are able to interpret novel meanings in the way that the single-sense view assumes. Of course, this in itself does not show that real words are stored with only a single sense, or even with a small number of senses. However, it does show that semantic extensions of a word are not particularly difficult or unusual to process. Thus, it seems likely that any account of polysemy should include a meaning-extension process as part of its account.

The second main implication is that the extension process has a number of constraints on it. Of course, no one would suggest that any word can be used to have any meaning, so the fact that there are *some* constraints is not in itself surprising. However, it is important to identify as specifically as possible what factors will allow speakers to extend a word in a new way, as well as factors that allow listeners to understand extensions. Experiment 1 showed that subjects were influenced by prior senses of a word in accepting a new sense. Although each paragraph was designed to clearly indicate the specific sense being tested, the acceptability of the test item was increased when a related meaning preceded it. More evidence is needed for a complete interpretation of these results, but it seems most likely that the effect is not due to the eventual comprehensibility of the final use. Rather, when there was no similar use of a word, subjects found that the test use was simply too far removed from the core meaning and so judged that speakers would not extend the word in that way.

If correct, this hypothesis suggests that words that have distant polysemous meanings must have followed a historical progression in which core meanings were extended a bit, then the extensions were extended a bit, then these extensions were extended, and so on, until a fairly distant meaning was arrived at. For example, Cruse (1986, p. 72 ff) considered the example of the word *mouth*, which applies to animals in its core meaning, but also can extend to small objects (e.g., the mouth of a bottle) or large geographical entities (the mouth of a cave or river). The distance between the core meaning and some of the extensions is very considerable, according to Cruse: "suppose one were familiar only with *mouth* used to refer to the mouth of a river, and one heard a reference to *the horse's mouth*, it is by no means certain that one's attention would be directed to the appropriate end of the horse!" (p. 73). The results of Experiment 1 suggest that very extended senses of *mouth* did not arise directly from the core meaning but were likely mediated by previous extensions that were already conventional.

Another constraint that the experiments have suggested is that conventional ways of extending word meanings are particularly favored. When novel object names were used in new ways, subjects readily accepted the new use if it followed a conventional form of meaning extension. I would argue that it is not that the preferred meaning was somehow better or clearer in and of itself. For example, there is nothing particularly clearer or simpler about the sense "picture of a tuk" (see Table 4) than "book about a tuk." However, there is a clear convention in English to extend nouns to apply to representations of the thing named by the noun, but there is no such convention in extending nouns to books about those things. Of course, there may be a reason for some extensions being preferred over others. Nunberg (1979) argued that polysemy requires a recoverable relation between the use of a word and its conventional meaning. That is, listeners must be able to identify a unique relation between the intended meaning of the word and the "usual" meaning (I am simplifying somewhat). Perhaps that relation is clearer in the conventional senses. (Note that I am not saying that the meaning is clearer but that the relation between the extended use and the known uses may be clearer.) There may be some reason that the relation between an object and a representation of it is closer than the relation between an object and a book about it. Thus, it is not certain whether the effect found in Experiments 2 and 3 was due to use of the actual convention, or whether both the effect and the convention resulted from underlying conceptual differences in the relations between senses. This is clearly an important question for future research.

The implications for creativity are consistent with other findings in the field. As noted earlier, Ward (1994) found that college students' creations of novel animals on an alien planet did include novel features or configurations, but they also followed many of the general constraints on Earth animal life. These constraints, such as symmetry, the presence of limbs and sense organs, seemed to influence most subjects' responses. Ward (1995) has found similar constraints of prior category knowledge on real-life inventions. Cacciari, Levorato, and Cicogna's (this volume) results on children's generation of idioms also showed a number of constraints on this process. Some children followed existing formulas, and the idiomatic vehicles were generally concrete rather than abstract. Similarly, Wisniewski's (this volume) studies of people's interpretations of novel noun–noun combinations revealed a number of general techniques that could account for most interpretations, such as property mapping and slot filling. Such techniques are not new ways of combining word meanings but instead are found in many existing noun–noun combinations. This is another case of a familiar process that produces novel results. Thus, the present finding that people are constrained in what they will accept (or use) as an appropriate meaning extension is consistent with other findings that existing exemplars greatly influence the production of novel entities.

Gentner's work (this volume) has a direct relevance to the present experiments in that the constraint of conventional meaning extensions is quite similar to analogical constraints that she discusses. That is, the preference for conventional means of extensions can be rephrased in terms of analogy. The core meaning of *oak* is to denote a tree, but it can be extended to refer to the wood (substance) that makes up that kind of tree. Therefore, if you learn of a new kind of tree called *hoptree* (an actual tree also called *wafer ash*), you can assume that the same word can be used to refer to the wood of this tree, even though you have never heard such a use, because it is analogous to other uses. That is, you could say "This table is made of hoptree." (The specific analogy would be oak tree is to the wood of the oak as hoptree is to the wood of the hoptree. The same relation is used in the second case to create a new meaning.) Analogical reasoning is a source of new ideas and metaphors, as argued in Gentner's chapter and by Finke et al. (1992).

It is not yet entirely clear what processes are used to generate novel meanings. For example, is a simple similarity relation to a known meaning sufficient, or is a stronger analogical relation required? Furthermore, the experiments described here do not address any differences between the generation of new meanings and the comprehension or acceptance of new meanings. It may well be that some extensions that are easy to understand and that seem appropriate are nonetheless seldom produced for some reason; they simply may not occur to most speakers.

To return to the general question with which I opened this chapter, I hope that the present discussion has shown that linguistic creativity and novelty are not simply confined to the possibility of generating more and more sentences by varying the constituent words or syntactic constructions. Even a simple sentence like "Look at that dog" could have a novel meaning if *look* or *dog* were used in a new way (e.g., to look by retrieving an encoded graphic image of a dog over a computer network). However, not all such uses are creative in an exceptional sense—they may have arisen through a similar example or by using a conventional way of extending meaning. Thus, even if I were to point out that the sentence "Therefore, further research needs to be done on the connection between polysemy and creativity" has probably never appeared in print before, I doubt whether readers will think of it as a truly creative way to end a chapter.

REFERENCES

Anderson, R. C., & Ortony, A. (1975). On putting apples into bottles—A problem of polysemy. *Cognitive Psychology, 7,* 167–180.

Becker, J. A. (1994). 'Sneak-shoes,' 'sworders' and 'nose-beards': A case study of lexical innovation. *First Language, 14,* 195–211.

Caramazza, A., & Grober, E. (1976). Polysemy and the structure of the subjective lexicon. In C. Rameh (Ed.), *Georgetown University roundtable on languages and linguistics. Semantics: Theory and application* (pp. 181–206). Washington, DC: Georgetown University Press.

Chomsky, N. (1965). *Aspects of the theory of syntax.* Cambridge, MA: MIT Press.

Clark, E. V. (1983). Meanings and concepts. In J. H. Flavell & E. M. Markman (Eds.), *Manual of child psychology, Vol. 3: Cognitive development* (pp. 787–840). New York: Wiley.

Clark, E. V. (1993). *The lexicon in acquisition.* Cambridge, England: Cambridge University Press.

Clark, E. V., & Clark, H. H. (1979). When nouns surface as verbs. *Language, 55,* 767–811.

Clark, H. H. (1983). Making sense of nonce sense. In G. B. Flores d'Arcais & R. J. Jarvella (Eds.), *The process of language understanding* (pp. 297–331). New York: Wiley.

Cruse, D. A. (1986). *Lexical semantics.* Cambridge, England: Cambridge University Press.

Finke, R. A., Ward, T. B., & Smith, S. M. (1992). *Creative cognition: Theory, research and application.* Cambridge, MA: MIT Press.

Gentner, D., & France, I. M. (1988). The verb mutability effect: Studies of the combinatorial semantics of nouns and verbs. In S. L. Small, G. W. Cottrell, & M. K. Tanenhaus (Eds.), *Lexical ambiguity resolution: Perspectives from psycholinguistics, neuropsychology, and artificial intelligence* (pp. 343–382). San Mateo, CA: Morgan Kaufman.

Gerrig, R. J. (1986). Process and products of lexical access. *Language and Cognitive Processes, 1,* 187–195.

Gerrig, R. J. (1989). The time course of sense creation. *Memory & Cognition, 17,* 194–207.

Murphy, G. L. (1988). Comprehending complex concepts. *Cognitive Science, 12,* 529–562.

Murphy, G. L. (1990). Noun phrase interpretation and conceptual combination. *Journal of Memory and Language, 29,* 259–288.

Murphy, G. L. (1991). Meaning and concepts. In P. Schwanenflugel (Ed.), *The psychology of word meanings* (pp. 11–35). Hillsdale, NJ: Erlbaum.

Murphy, G. L., & Andrew, J. M. (1993). The conceptual basis of antonymy and synonymy in adjectives. *Journal of Memory and Language, 32,* 301–319.

Nunberg, G. D. (1978). *The pragmatics of reference.* Bloomington, IN: Indiana Linguistics Club.

Nunberg, G. (1979). The non-uniqueness of semantic solutions: Polysemy. *Linguistics and Philosophy, 3,* 143–184.

Rice, S. A. (1992). Polysemy and lexical representation: The case of three English prepositions. *Proceedings of the fourteenth annual conference of the Cognitive Science Society* (pp. 89–94). Hillsdale, NJ: Erlbaum.

Sweetser, E. (1990). *From etymology to pragmatics: Metaphorical and cultural aspects of semantic structure.* Cambridge, England: Cambridge University Press.

Ward, T. B. (1994). Structured imagination: The role of category structure in exemplar generation. *Cognitive Psychology, 27,* 1–40.

Ward, T. B. (1995). What's old about new ideas? In S. M. Smith, T. B. Ward, & R. A. Finke (Eds.), *The creative cognition approach* (pp. 157–178). Cambridge, MA: MIT Press.

11

Mundane Creativity in Perceptual Symbol Systems

Lawrence W. Barsalou and Jesse J. Prinz

The study of creativity typically focuses on the exceptional, including the major accomplishments of inventors, scientists, and artists. Any casual reading of history leaves no doubt that exceptional creativity has influenced human culture. In Western culture, the exceptional accomplishments of unusually talented individuals define who we are to an enormous extent. For this reason alone, understanding exceptional creativity is essential to understanding human nature.

No less remarkable is *mundane creativity*. Whereas exceptional creativity graces a few individuals, mundane creativity graces everyone. Although exceptional acts of creativity produce dramatic changes in human culture, mundane creativity underlies the general power of natural intelligence. Like exceptional creativity, mundane creativity involves the production of novelty. All humans produce new cognitions and behaviors all the time. Because we observe such novelty day in and day out, it fails to strike us as noteworthy. Nevertheless, mundane creativity is central to what it means to be human, and explaining it is at least as important as explaining exceptional creativity. Although exceptional creativity is "flashier"

The research reported in this chapter was supported by National Science Foundation Grant SBR-9421326 to Lawrence W. Barsalou.

culturally, historically, and scientifically, mundane creativity is the workhorse that accounts for the bulk of human accomplishment and that makes exceptional creativity possible. In this chapter, we examine the nature of mundane creativity and demonstrate its central role in the human symbolic system. Our primary goal is to show that a powerful system of perceptual symbols could be responsible for this ability. In a related paper, we explore mundane creativity in perceptual symbol systems further (Prinz & Barsalou, in press).

MUNDANE CREATIVITY

Two types of mundane creativity—*productivity* and *propositional construal*—have played central roles in modern cognitive science. A third—*variable embodiment*—has received relatively little acknowledgment, for reasons that we make clear later.

Productivity

According to Chomsky's (1957) notion of linguistic creativity, all humans share a biologically based ability to produce an indefinitely large number of sentences from a finite set of syntactic rules and lexical elements (see also Kasher, 1991). Indeed, Chomsky noted that people constantly produce new sentences that they have never uttered, nor heard uttered, simply because their linguistic systems possess an inherent creative ability. For the remainder of this chapter, we refer to this type of mundane creativity as *productivity*, following standard technical usage in linguistics. Although there are many ways to construe productivity, all accounts share the property that a finite set of representations can produce an indefinitely large number of structures through combinatorial and recursive mechanisms.

Propositional Construal

A second form of mundane creativity, *propositional construal*, has also played a central role in modern cognitive science. Intuitively, a propositional construal describes some aspect of a situation in one possible manner. The process of propositional construal is creative, because the same perceived state of affairs can be construed in an indefinitely large number of ways (Goodman, 1976). Very different construals of a situation result as a function of what perceivers choose to describe and how they choose to describe it.

Propositional construals are propositional for three reasons: First, they are propositional because they capture the gist of an entity or event (Anderson & Bower, 1973; Kintsch, 1974). Rather than a linguistic sentence, a propositional construal is a representation of something that can be paraphrased linguistically in many ways (Carnap, 1956; Church, 1951; Frege, 1918/1956; Russell, 1921; Sellars, 1956; Stalnaker, 1984). Second, construals are propositional because they can be either true or false. Perceivers can construe situations correctly or incorrectly, thereby endowing the propositions that represent these construals with truth values. Third, construals are propositional because they are constructed from languages having a combinatorial syntax and semantics. As we show, such languages offer powerful systems for construing situations in many possible ways.

Thus, a propositional construal represents some aspect of an event conceptually, either correctly or incorrectly, using a combinatorial symbolic system. Because an indefinitely large number of propositions could be used to describe a given event, and because the propositions actually used can vary widely between and within individuals, propositional construal is a form of mundane creativity.[1]

Variable Embodiment

Unlike productivity and propositional construal, variable embodiment is not a form of mundane creativity that has been central to modern cognitive science (but see Goodman's, 1976, discussion of semantic properties in pictorial symbol systems). Indeed, the assumptions that underlie variable embodiment are at odds with prevailing views of the human symbolic system, as we discuss later. Thus, describing variable embodiment is

[1]To avoid confusion, it should be noted that there is a sense in which our use of *proposition* departs from common philosophical usage. Many philosophers regard propositions as Platonic objects that exist neither in the mind nor in the physical world (e.g., Church, 1951; Fodor, 1975; Frege, 1918/1956). We do not endorse this ontologically extravagant conception of propositions but regard them instead as psychological entities. This usage is not without philosophical precedent (e.g., Russell, 1921), and it has gained currency among contemporary philosophers and cognitive scientists (e.g., Pylyshyn, 1973).

difficult at this point, because it requires a perceptual symbol system, which we have yet to define. After presenting perceptual symbol systems later, we provide an account of variable embodiment and the role it plays in mundane creativity. For now, we simply describe variable embodiment as follows: If conceptual symbols reflect their embodiment in particular individuals, then continuous variability in the forms of these symbols may have semantic implications. Variable embodiment is creative, because infinite variability in the form of an embodied symbol can yield an infinite number of conceptualizations. As the same symbol is embodied in different ways, it acquires different meanings, producing another important form of mundane creativity.

MUNDANE CREATIVITY IN AMODAL SYMBOL SYSTEMS

Mundane creativity has played a central role in debates about the human symbolic system. On the one hand, the belief that perceptual representations do not exhibit mundane creativity has fueled the argument that the human symbolic system is not inherently perceptual. On the other hand, the ability of nonperceptual representations to exhibit mundane creativity has supported the argument that the human symbolic system is inherently amodal (i.e., nonperceptual). This criticism of perceptual symbol systems holds only for some accounts of them but by no means for all. Indeed, the perceptual symbol system we present here exhibits both forms of mundane creativity found in amodal symbol systems, as well as another. Before turning to perceptual symbol systems, we first define amodal symbols and illustrate how they produce mundane creativity.

Amodal Symbols

What we call *amodal symbols* have traditionally been called *propositional symbols.* We shall see later, however, that perceptual symbols can be propositional just like nonperceptual symbols. To avoid implying that perceptual symbols are not propositional, we use amodal symbols in referring to what most theorists have called propositional symbols. As we shall argue, the most distinguishing feature of traditional propositional systems is their assumption that symbols are amodal. For articulations of this assumption, see Fodor (1975), Harnad (1990), Haugeland (1985), Newell and Simon (1972), and Pylyshyn (1984).

Amodal symbols result from a process that transduces perceptual states into a nonperceptual symbolic language. According to this view, a transduction process takes perceptual states as input and produces amodal symbols as output, with the amodal symbols representing the perceptual states. These symbols are amodal because their form bears no structural resemblance to the perceptual states that produced them. For example, the amodal symbols transduced to represent the perception of a chair bear no structural resemblance to it. This lack of structural relations between amodal symbols and perceptual states is similar to the lack of structural relations between words and perceptual states. Just as the phonological and orthographic representations of the word "chair" bear no structural relations to the visual representation of a chair, neither does the amodal representation of *chair* at the conceptual level. An additional implication is that the similarity of amodal symbols to one another bears no correspondence to the similarity of perceptual states to one another. To see this, note that words for types of *furniture* have little in common phonologically (e.g., "chair," "stool," "bench"), even though perceptual states of their referents are similar. Conversely, words having similar phonological forms (e.g., "chair," "hair," "chain") have referents that produce very different perceptual states. Amodal symbols are similar to words in these ways, being unrelated structurally to the perceptual states that they represent.

Because the form of amodal symbols is uninformative about their referents, some other mechanism must allow them to establish reference. Theorists typically assume that conventional associations play this role. Through some process, conventional associations become established between amodal symbols and their referents, much like the conventional associations that develop between words and their referents. Although theorists have never specified how these associations develop, we assume that they must arise somehow in the transduction process that maps perceptual states into the amodal symbols that represent them. The relations that develop are arbitrary. If they were not, the structure of amodal symbols would be informative about their referents, and the similarity of amodal symbols to one another would be informative about the similarity of their referents to one another. As we have shown, however, amodal symbols do not exhibit these properties and are therefore related to their referents arbitrarily.

In modern cognitive science, amodal symbol systems take many forms. In philosophy and logical computation, they take the form of proof-oriented systems (e.g., Fodor, 1975; Hayes, 1985; Mitchell, Keller, & Kedar-Cabelli, 1986; Pylyshyn, 1984). In psychology, artificial intelligence, and linguistics, amodal symbol systems take the form of semantic networks, feature lists, schemata, frames, and many connectionist models. In all of these representational schemes, symbols are assumed to be amodal in form and arbitrary in reference (for reviews, see Barsalou 1992a, 1992b; Barsalou & Hale, 1993). Most important, the symbols in these schemes are not assumed to be constituted of perceptual content.

Mundane Creativity

Productivity

Amodal symbol systems exhibit a variety of fundamentally important properties, including mundane creativity. As noted earlier, theorists have often argued that productivity is central to human cognition. From Chomsky (1957) to Fodor and Pylyshyn (1988), productive mechanisms continually have been found at the heart of cognitive theory. The properties of amodal symbol systems lend themselves naturally to productive computation. Using the mechanisms of argument binding and recursion from predicate calculus, amodal symbol systems can produce infinite expressions from finite elements. Argument binding involves mapping the arguments of predicates to individuals (or to other predicates). In the predicate, *ABOVE(X,Y)*, two arguments, one for an upper region *X* and one for a lower region *Y*, can be bound to a variety of individuals across situations, as in *ABOVE(lamp, table)*, *ABOVE(bird, tree)*, and so forth. Recursion results from binding arguments to predicates, enabling infinitely deep structure. For example, the lower region of *ABOVE(X,Y)* can be instantiated with *INSIDE(M, N)*, as in *ABOVE(lamp, INSIDE(cup, box))*. Argument binding and recursion are responsible for the productive quality of many representational systems, from theories of syntax to theories of knowledge. Because a large number of individuals can be bound to arguments combinatorially, and because arguments can be bound recursively, amodal symbol systems are productive. Regardless of whether the system focuses on syntax (Chomsky, 1957) or semantics (Fodor & Pylyshyn, 1988), the same productive mechanisms play central roles. In amodal symbol systems that are less logical, slots in structures such as frames and schemata enable productivity. In all cases, these mechanisms produce an indefinite number of arbitrarily complex structures from finite elements.

Propositional Construal

Amodal symbol systems also exhibit propositional construal. Because these systems rely heavily on mechanisms derived from propositional logic and predicate calculus, they readily represent propositions. In predicate calculus, an instantiated expression construes some aspect of a situation truly or falsely. Moreover, different expressions can construe the same situation in different ways, either by describing different aspects of it or by describing the same aspect differently. For example, the propositions *ABOVE(bird, tree)* and *BESIDE(tree, lake)* could describe different aspects of the same visual scene, whereas *ABOVE(bird, tree)* and *BELOW(tree, bird)* could construe the same aspect in different ways. In amodal symbol systems that are less logical, instantiated structures, such as networks, frames, and schemata, similarly represent propositions about the world (e.g., Anderson & Bower, 1973; Barsalou, 1992a, 1992b; van Dijk & Kintsch, 1983).

Over the years, many theorists have provided compelling arguments for the importance of propositions in human cognition (see Barsalou, 1992a, for a review). In arguing against purely analogue views of mental imagery, Pylyshyn (1973, 1981) illustrated the importance of propositional construal. As he showed, a cognitive system must have a multilevel representation scheme that maps types into tokens to establish construals of an image. An undifferentiated, holistic representation, such as a picture or an analogue image, is not sufficient (but see Goodman, 1976). Instead, something along the lines of instantiated expressions, constructed from a combinatorial syntax and semantics, is necessary. Because amodal symbol systems readily formulate such expressions, they lend themselves naturally to propositional construal.

Advantages and Disadvantages of Amodal Systems

We have reviewed the advantages and disadvantages of amodal symbol systems elsewhere; thus, we do not do so here (Barsalou, 1993; Barsalou, Yeh, Luka, Olseth, Mix, & Wu, 1993). To summarize these arguments, one important advantage is the ability to implement mundane creativity. Amodal symbol systems highlight the importance of productivity and propositional construal, and they have made it clear that any adequate theory of cognition must exhibit these capabilities. Other important properties of amodal symbol systems include their ability to represent gist, to represent abstract concepts, to be expressible in formal languages, and to be implemented on computer hardware. We agree that these are highly desirable qualities, which any theory of cognition should exhibit.

Nevertheless, there are a number of problems for this view: First, we have no direct evidence that conceptual symbols in the cognitive system are amodal in form and arbitrary in reference. Second, we have no account of the transduction process that maps perceptual states into amodal symbols. Third, we have no direct evidence for any such process. Fourth, many theorists have noted problems in the reverse process of establishing reference to amodal symbols (e.g., Harnad, 1990; Searle, 1980). Fifth, this theory is so powerful that it can explain any finding post hoc, often without providing much insight into it or lending itself to an a priori prediction of the finding in the first place. For these reasons, we have come to believe that there are deep and troubling problems with amodal symbol systems that are cause for viewing them with greater skepticism than we have in the past.

PERCEPTUAL SYMBOL SYSTEMS

Perceptual Symbols

Perceptual symbols contrast with amodal symbols in origin. Whereas amodal symbols result from a transduction process that arbitrarily maps perceptual states to nonperceptual symbols, perceptual symbols result from an extraction process that selects some subset of a perceptual state and stores it as a symbol. Thus, the form of a perceptual symbol resembles the perceptual states to which it refers, and the similarity of perceptual symbols to one another is informative about the similarity of their referents. Imagine that the shape of a chair is extracted from the perception of a chair and stored in memory to function later as a symbol. The form of this symbol is related perceptually to the perceptions of subsequently perceived chairs that it might represent. Similarly, the form of this symbol is related to the form of other symbols with preceptually similar referents. For example, perceptual symbols for *chair*, *stool*, and *bench* would be more similar to each other than would be perceptual symbols for *chair*, *hair*, and *chain*. Thus, perceptual symbols bear analogical relations—not arbitrary ones—to perceptions of their referents and provide guidance about the entities and events they represent.

The idea of a perceptually based symbolic system is not new. Until the early 20th century, philosophers generally believed that perceptual representations constitute the core of human knowledge (e.g., Aristotle, 4th century BC/1961; Berkeley, 1710/1982; Locke, 1690/1959; Hume, 1739/1978; Price, 1953; Reid, 1764/1970, 1785/1969; Russell, 1919/1956). During the 20th century, philosophers raised strong objections to this view, followed more recently by cognitive scientists (e.g., Dennett, 1969; Pylyshyn, 1973; Ryle, 1949; for reviews, see Kosslyn, 1980, chap. 11; Tye, 1991). The result, until recently, has been an almost complete unwillingness to view higher cognition as perceptual, thereby allowing the default amodal view to flourish. In the last decade or so, however, cognitive scientists have begun exploring perceptual views with increasing intensity. Most notably, the cognitive linguistics movement has adopted spatial symbols extensively in their treatments of semantics (e.g., Fauconnier, 1985; Jackendoff, 1987;

Johnson, 1987; Lakoff, 1987, 1988; Lakoff & Johnson, 1980; Langacker, 1986, 1987, 1991; Sweetser, 1990; Talmy, 1983, 1988). Researchers in other areas of the cognitive sciences have also incorporated perceptual representations into the core of their theories. In the philosophy of mathematics, researchers have incorporated spatial representations explicitly into proofs, rather than using them implicitly while pretending not to (e.g., Barwise & Etchemendy, 1990, 1991; Stenning & Oberlander, 1994). In the philosophy of science, Thagard (1992) has argued that perceptual analogy has played central roles in scientific insight. In the philosophy of mind, Peacocke (1992) has argued that some thoughts contain ineliminable perceptual representations. In artificial intelligence, researchers are increasingly finding that the use of spatial representations increases computational effectiveness significantly (e.g., Glasgow, 1993). In psychology, much work can be construed as supporting the central importance of perceptual representations in general cognition, not just in mental imagery (e.g., Gernsbacher, Varner, & Faust, 1990; Glaser, 1992; Glenberg & Langston, 1992; Glenberg, Meyer, & Lindem, 1987; Johnson-Laird, 1983; Klatzky, Pelligrino, McCloskey, & Doherty, 1989; Miller & Johnson-Laird, 1976; Morrow, Greenspan, & Bower, 1987; Olseth & Barsalou, 1995; Paivio, 1986; Potter & Faulconer, 1975; Potter, Kroll, Yachzel, Carpenter, & Sherman, 1986; Potter, Valian, & Faulconer, 1977; Solomon, 1997; Wu, 1995). As a result of such findings, and also in reaction to problems with amodal symbols, psychologists are beginning to propose that the human conceptual system is inherently perceptual (e.g., Barsalou, 1993; Barsalou et al., 1993; Gibbs, 1994; Glenberg, this volume; Mandler, 1992).

Basic Assumptions

Elsewhere we have begun to develop a theory of perceptual symbol systems (Barsalou, 1993, 1997; Barsalou et al., 1993; Prinz, 1997; Prinz & Barsalou, in press). Here we summarize its basic assumptions briefly. Our goals are not to present the full theory and defend it against important concerns. Instead, we present enough of the theory to motivate an account of mundane creativity. We ask the reader to suspend judgment for the moment and to assume the core assumptions of the theory to see how mundane creativity follows. Our claim is not that this theory provides the correct account of mundane creativity. We cannot defend this claim without much further exposition. Instead, our claim is that it is possible for a theory of perceptual symbols to exhibit mundane creativity. Because it is not widely known or accepted that a perceptually based theory can produce productivity and propositional construal, we believe that it is important to demonstrate that one can. Once we establish this point, the next step will be to demonstrate that the perceptual approach provides the correct account of mundane creativity in human cognition.

Next we present the five assumptions that underlie our theory of perceptual symbols: (a) Perceptual symbols are constituted by brain states, (b) perceptual symbols are schematic, (c) perceptual symbols are multimodal, (d) perceptual symbols underlie simulation competence, and (e) simulated events frame abstract concepts. After establishing these five assumptions, we illustrate how a perceptually based system of knowledge produces mundane creativity.

Perceptual Symbols Are Constituted by Brain States

It is tempting and natural to think of perceptual symbols as mental images and conscious experiences that are like physical pictures. However, we do not define them this way. Instead, we define perceptual symbols as being constituted by brain states. We assume that high-level neurons (and sets of neurons) in perceptual systems capture information about perceived entities and events at a relatively qualitative and functional level. In perceiving an object, neurons in the visual system that represent edges, vertices, geons, textures, and spatial relations become active to represent it. Similarly, in perceiving an event, neurons that represent entities, movements, spatial positions, and temporal positions become active. Thus, a perceptual symbol that represents an event or entity is constituted by a configuration of neurons that becomes active during its processing.

Although we ground perceptual symbols in neuronal representations, we assume that they may have conscious counterparts on occasion, although not necessarily. These conscious counterparts, too, have a neuronal basis, but these neuronal representations differ from those that represent the functional information defining the perceptual symbol. This distinction between conscious and functional brain states follows from both neuropsychological and behavioral evidence. Neurophysiologically, there are different sites in the brain for the functional information in perception and its conscious representation (Damasio, 1994; Kosslyn, 1994). The phenomenon of blind sight, in which a neurologically impaired individual can process a visual stimulus without a conscious experience of it, provides one sort of neuropsychological evidence. Behaviorally, it is well-known that people often process information without being conscious of it. The phenomenon of preconscious processing, in which information is obtained from an unexperienced stimulus, provides one sort of behavioral evidence.

Perceptual Symbols Are Schematic

The idea that perceptual symbols are schematic has a long history, beginning with British Empiricists, such as Locke, and continuing to the current time with cognitive linguists (see also Mandler, 1992). On this view, a perceptual symbol does not contain an entire perceptual state but only a very small subset of the perceptual state in which it originated. These symbols become established through a symbol formation process that relies on two basic cognitive mechanisms: selective attention and memory transfer.

In the first step of this process, selective attention focuses on some aspect of a perceptual state, filtering out other aspects to a large extent. In perceiving an array of objects, a perceiver might focus attention on the shape of one object, filter out most of the object's other properties, and filter out the nonfocal objects as well. It is nearly axiomatic in the cognitive literature that people attend selectively to information in this manner (Shiffrin, 1988). For example, Garner's (1974, 1978) classic work on separable dimensions indicates that people can focus on some information in perception and filter out other information to a large extent (see also Melara & Marks, 1990).

In the second step of this process, a storage mechanism transfers selected information to long-term memory. It is nearly axiomatic in the cognitive literature that where selective attention goes, long-term storage follows. Nonattended information may be stored to some extent, but clearly the most storage occurs for attended information. Such a conclusion follows from work on encoding specificity (e.g., Tulving & Thomson, 1973), transfer appropriate processing (e.g., Morris, Bransford, & Franks, 1977), and much additional memory research. In all of this work, the information selected during learning determines which retrieval cues will be effective, indicating that selection determined storage.

The result of this symbol formation process is that a large population of perceptual fragments becomes stored in long-term memory, each being a small subset of a perceptual state. Because we define perceptual states as neuronal representations, it follows that the subsets of information extracted by selective attention are neuronal representations as well. As we show shortly, these perceptual fragments function later as symbols, establishing reference to perceived entities and entering into symbol manipulation to produce productivity and propositional construal.

Because perceptual symbols are extracted from perception, their form bears a strong resemblance to the perceptual states that produced them. Furthermore, the similarity between different perceptual symbols corresponds to the similarity between their referents. Thus, perceptual symbols are not at all like the arbitrary amodal symbols that constitute amodal symbol systems.

Perceptual Symbols Are Multimodal

The symbol formation process just described can operate on any modality of perception. Not only does it operate on vision, but it operates on any of the other four sensory modalities as well, extracting perceptual fragments that later function symbolically. This symbol formation process also operates on proprioception and introspection, extracting perceived aspects of these experiences that constitute perceptual symbols. Because perceptual symbols can be drawn from all aspects of experience, it should be clear that we are not using *perceptual* in its standard sense. Rather than referring only to perception on the modalities, *perceptual* here refers to information extracted from any perceived aspect of experience. Although consciousness may be necessary to extract these symbols initially, it may fall away as they become familiar.

Perceptual symbols drawn from introspection are especially important to this theory. We assume that the human cognitive system is biologically endowed to carry out various introspective tasks, such as representing entities in their absence and performing various information-processing operations on them. For example, people retrieve and compare representations, add information to them, delete information, and so forth. Furthermore, the human cognitive system is biologically endowed to represent and process various emotional and affective states, such as joy, anger, and irritation. We assume that the symbol formation process can focus attention on various aspects of these introspective states and store them away for later symbolic function. As we shall see later, such symbols are central to our accounts of abstract concepts.

Perceptual Symbols Underlie Simulation Competence

Perceptual symbols do not function as isolated "snapshots" of perceptual experience. Instead, they become organized into symbol systems that enable the simulation of entities and events in their absence. In perceiving a car, for example, perceptual symbols extracted from the front, sides, and rear, as well as from the passenger area, the engine, and the trunk, become organized spatially with respect to an object-centered reference frame. This enables the cognitive system to simulate perceiving the car in its absence. As the perceiver imagines moving around and inside the car, or as the car is imagined to turn, its physical features come into view in the appropriate spatial order. Similarly, the perceptual symbols extracted from an event are organized temporally to enable later simulations of its subevents correctly. In perceiving someone start a car, for example, the perceptual symbols extracted at each point become organized into a temporal sequence, later enabling a correct simulation.

Thus, the primary purpose of extracting perceptual symbols is to support simulation competence. Symbols are extracted and organized to provide the cognitive system with the ability to simulate, at some adequate level of competence, entities and events in their absence. The construct of simulation competence leads to a somewhat surprising definition of concepts: Having a concept is having the ability to simulate its referents competently in their absence.

We hasten to add several important qualifications to this account. First, we do not assume that simulation competence is ever complete. Instead, it is always partial and sketchy. Because the symbol formation process is schematic, tremendous amounts of information are omitted from the perceptual symbols that underlie simulation competence. Second, we do not assume that simulation competence is always accurate. Instead, it can contain errors, as when a perceptual symbol is stored incorrectly in a spatial or temporal configuration, or retrieved incorrectly from it. Third, inherent biases may underlie the construction of a simulation competence. In idealization, biases toward good form may "clean up" input that is messy or incomplete. For example, a slightly crooked and partially occluded line may be represented as straight and complete. Work on naive physics offers similar examples of such biases (McCloskey, 1983). Fourth, simulation competence is not simply a collection of "sense impressions." Instead, innate biases select, interpret, and organize perceptual symbols during the construction of simulation competence. In a Kantian sense, innate conceptualizations of space, time, causality, objects, and events guide the extraction, interpretation, and organization of perceptual information.

Simulated Events Frame Abstract Concepts

An important challenge for perceptually based accounts of cognition is to represent abstract concepts such as *truth*, *negation*, and *disjunction*. We do not present our approach to representing them yet, because it relies on propositional construal, which we address later. Here we simply note the basic assumptions that we have found necessary.

Most important, abstract concepts typically cannot be represented with a single snapshot of perception. Instead, the simulation of events typically frames them (Fillmore, 1985; Langacker, 1986). Abstract concepts do not refer to these events themselves but to parts of them. Nevertheless, the entire event is necessary to give the part its meaning. As we show later, the core sense of *truth* is framed by a basic event sequence that involves comparing an expectation to a perception. However, *truth* is not the event sequence but is a quality of the expectation in it. We have also found that perceptual symbols for introspective events are central to accounts of abstract concepts. Typically, these concepts include perceived aspects of internal representations, cognitive operations, and emotional states. We return to abstract concepts later in the section on propositional construal.

MUNDANE CREATIVITY IN PERCEPTUAL SYMBOL SYSTEMS

Now that we have established the basic properties of perceptual symbol systems, we demonstrate their ability to produce mundane creativity. Perceptual symbols support productivity and propositional construal in much the same way as do amodal symbol systems. In addition, perceptual symbols exhibit variable embodiment, a consequence of not being amodal.

Productivity

Perceptual symbols lend themselves naturally and elegantly to the productive construction of complex representations. From a finite set of perceptual symbols, an indefinitely large number of more complex representations can be constructed using combinatorial and recursive mechanisms. Corballis (1991) described a similar type of generativity as arising in the left hemisphere of the brain (see also Tippett, 1992). The schematic nature of perceptual symbols contributes to their productive nature: Whereas the formation of a perceptual symbol results from a schematic reduction in the content of a perceptual state, the productive formation of a complex perceptual representation results from adding information back to a perceptual symbol systematically (other forms of productivity are possible as well, as discussed later). Because perceptual symbols are schematic, they have the potential to be embellished. Because embellishment can be combinatorial and recursive, it is productive.

Figure 1 illustrates this process. Figure 1a depicts a small set of perceptual symbols, including five objects (*table, chair, lamp, box, cup*) and four spatial relations (*ABOVE, LEFT, BETWEEN, INSIDE*). None of the depictions is a complete account of its respective concept, which we assume is represented instead by a complex system of simulation competence. A given depiction is one projection of the simulation competence for which it stands metonymically. Nor do these depictions imply that conscious picturelike images constitute perceptual symbols, which we assume instead are neuronal representations. Thus, the limited depictions of perceptual symbols in this and later figures simply serve to illustrate their key

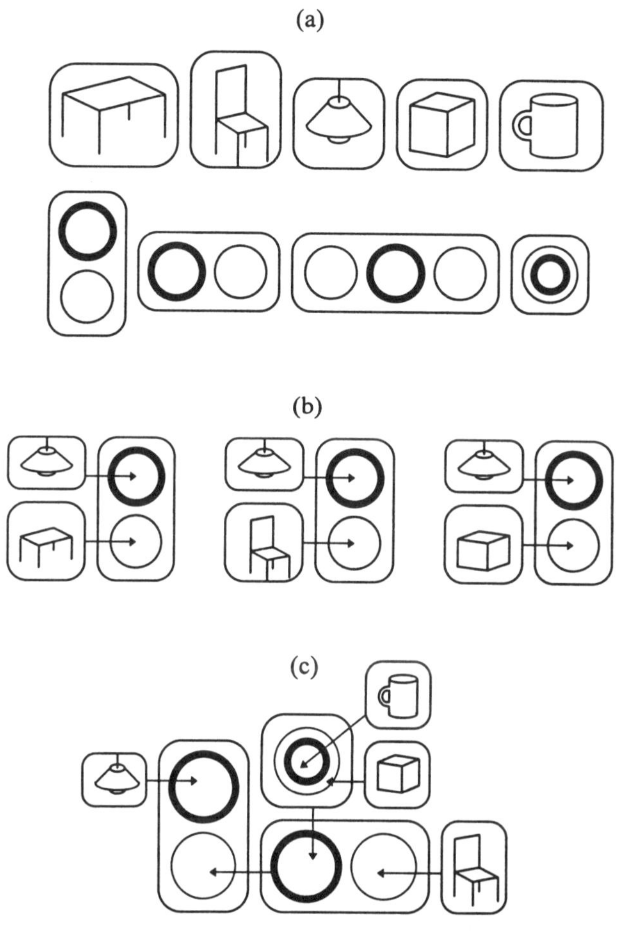

Figure 1

Illustration of how perceptual symbols produce productivity. (a) Perceptual symbols for objects and spatial relations. (b) Combinatorial use of perceptual symbols. (c) Recursive use of perceptual symbols.

properties, not to represent their full structure. Also, in the perceptual symbols for spatial relations, the emphasized regions mark the current location of selective attention (e.g., the thicker upper region for *ABOVE*). Following Talmy (1983) and Langacker (1986), we assume that the operation of selective attention on perceptual symbols carries conceptual information.

Figure 1b illustrates the combinatorial nature of perceptual symbols. As the three instantiated *ABOVE* relations demonstrate, simulating different objects in *ABOVE*'s two schematic regions can potentially produce an indefinitely large number of complex perceptual representations, such as *ABOVE(lamp, table)*, *ABOVE(lamp, chair)*, and *ABOVE(lamp, box)*. Because all pairs of known objects could be simulated in *ABOVE*, not to mention pairs of past, future, and imagined objects, the perceptual symbol for *ABOVE* is productive in a combinatorial sense.

ABOVE's combinatorial potential results from its schematic nature. When the perceptual symbol for *ABOVE* was formed, much irrelevant information was not transferred to memory, including the particular instantiations of its upper and lower regions. Thus, its representation in memory contains no instantiations of these regions, giving them the character of uninstantiated arguments in a predicate. Later, constructive perceptual processes in imagination can add other perceptual symbols to these regions, such as those for *lamp* and *table*, much in the spirit of binding values to a predicate's arguments. Thus, the schematic nature of perceptual symbols underlies and enables their productivity.

Figure 1c illustrates the recursive potential of perceptual symbols. As this complex representation illustrates, the perceptual process that embellishes schematic regions in a perceptual symbol can embed perceptual symbols within perceptual symbols indefinitely. Thus, perceptual symbols for complex configurations like *ABOVE(lamp, LEFT(INSIDE(cup, box), chair))* become possible. Because indefinitely large numbers of embedded relations can instantiate *ABOVE*'s upper region in principle, the perceptual symbol for *ABOVE* is productive in a recursive sense. Again, the schematic nature of perceptual symbols makes this possible. Because regions of perceptual symbols become "blank" through the schematization process, they can later be filled recursively.

Thus, perceptual symbols are highly productive. Because they are schematic, other perceptual symbols can be added to them combinatorially and recursively to produce an indefinitely large number of hierarchical perceptual simulations. Importantly, these embellishments of schematic regions are not limited to those experienced perceptually. Instead, the process is creative in the sense that perceptual representations never perceived can be readily constructed. For example, imagining *ABOVE* relations one has never seen is trivial, including *ABOVE(horse, barn)*, *ABOVE(lamp, horse)*, and so forth.

It is also important to note that these productive processes can apply to any perceptual symbol. Because any perceptual symbol, by definition, results from a reduction in information, the types of information eliminated can later be added back systematically. Thus, perceptual symbols of all types are potentially productive, including those for objects, external events, and introspective events.

Productivity is not limited to filling in schematic regions. Productivity can also result from replacements, transformations, and deletions of existing structure in a perceptual symbol. Imagine that a perceptual symbol for *door* includes a standard round knob. To represent different doors, the perceptual symbol for the standard knob could be replaced with a perceptual symbol for a drawer handle, it could be transformed to a smaller or larger size, or it could be deleted altogether. These sorts of operations appear widely available for processing perceptual symbols, extending their productivity further.

The combination of perceptual symbols is a constructive process that differs in important ways from classical models of symbol combination (see also Prinz & Barsalou, in press). Unlike formal semantics, the combination of two perceptual symbols often produces emergent features not salient for either in isolation. For example, Wu (1995) has shown that combining *half* with *watermelon* produces emergent properties for *watermelon* not typically observed for *watermelon* alone. Because cutting a watermelon in half exposes its inside, individuals describe the inner parts of a *half watermelon* at much higher rates than for *watermelon* alone. This finding, and others in Wu's work, strongly implicates perceptual representations in the noncompositional effects that occur frequently for conceptual combination. Langacker's (1987) notion of accommodation provides another example of how combining perceptual symbols produces emergent features.

Combining the perceptual symbol for *run* with the perceptual symbol for *human, deer,* or *robin* produces perceptual features of running not salient for each agent in isolation. As these examples illustrate, the emergence of features during the combination of perceptual symbols violates the strict compositionality associated with classical semantics. Nevertheless, the combination of perceptual symbols exhibits the fundamentally important sense of compositionality: Perceptual symbols can be combined productively to form more complex representations that are coherent and interpretable.

Finally, complex perceptual representations are not holistic, because they contain simpler perceptual symbols as parts. Thus, complex representations are richly structured, containing components, relations between components, and nested substructures of components and relations. A complex perceptual representation never becomes a holistic representation that loses this structure, because the components and relations that constitute it remain linked to the established perceptual symbols in memory that spawned them during productive computation. In other words, the tokens of perceptual symbols in a complex representation retain their individual identities, with the original perceptual symbols providing construals of them. This is one of the many possible forms of propositional construal possible with perceptual symbols, a topic we address next at greater length.

Propositional Construal

Perceptual symbols readily support propositional construal. The perceptual symbols that underlie concepts can selectively describe different aspects of a perceived situation, and they can construe a single aspect in multiple manners. The mapping of a perceptual symbol into some aspect of a perceived situation constitutes a construal of the situation that represents its gist and has a truth value. Essential to this ability is the use of multiple perceptual representations that map into each other, similar to Fauconnier's (1985) treatment of mental spaces.

Type–Token Construal

As we just saw for productivity, established perceptual symbols in memory can become bound to aspects of a complex perceptual representation during productive computation. Established perceptual symbols underlie such bindings in many other contexts as well. In construing a perceived situation, for example, established perceptual symbols become mapped to entities, events, and relations in it. Because an established perceptual symbol resides in a simulation competence, it belongs to the representation of a concept. Thus, mapping an established perceptual symbol into a perceived entity construes the entity as an instance of the concept, or in alternative terms, as a token of the type.

These type–token relations constitute propositional construals for two reasons: First, establishing different type–token relations in a situation produces different construals of it. As is illustrated in the upper left portion of Figure 2, the situation might be construed on one occasion as containing a lamp (Figure 2a). On a different occasion, however, it might be construed as containing a table (Figure 2b). The same situation is con-

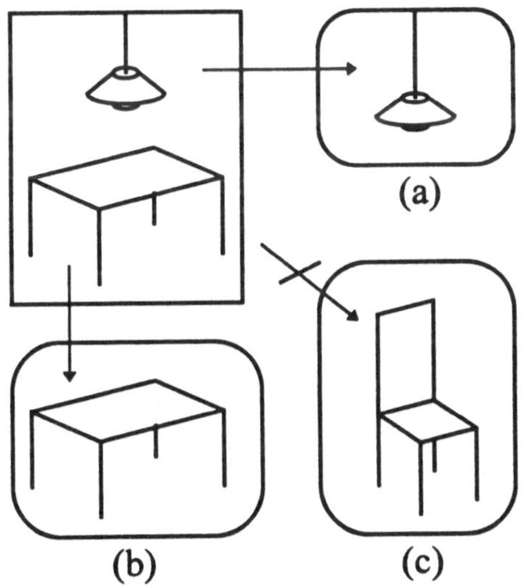

Figure 2

Illustration of how perceptual symbols produce propositional construal. (a) Mapping a perceptual symbol for *lamp* into a perceived lamp grounds the proposition that the situation contains a lamp. (b) Mapping a perceptual symbol for *table* into a perceived table grounds a different proposition that the situation contains a table. (c) Failure to map a perceptual symbol for *chair* into the situation grounds the false proposition that the situation contains a chair.

strued differently on these two occasions, because different aspects of the same situation are bound to different perceptual symbols. As Figure 2c illustrates, these construals exhibit truth values. Because a perceptual symbol for *chair* cannot be mapped into anything perceived in the situation, it is a false construal. In contrast, the construals in Figures 2a and 2b are true, because perceptual symbols for *lamp* and *table* can be mapped into perceived aspects of the situation. In this manner, attempting to map perceptual symbols to aspects of a situation produces propositional construals of it, some true and some false.

Once a successful mapping is established from a perceptual symbol to an aspect of a situation, the simulation competence that underlies the perceptual symbol provides a wealth of inferential information about the aspect. If a perceived entity is construed as a *dog*, the simulation competence for *dog* licenses possible inferences about it. If the dog is sitting still, it could be simulated as barking, wagging its tail, leaping, and so forth. Thus, establishing a type–token relation can result in a powerful construal of the token that goes considerably beyond what is perceived literally.

The second sense of propositional construal—a different construal of the same aspect—also emerges naturally from the binding of perceptual symbols to tokens. As Figure 3 illustrates, one construal of the perceived situation on the left is that the lamp is above the table. As Figure 3 further illustrates, however, another construal is that the table is below the lamp. By applying the perceptual symbol for either *ABOVE* or *BELOW* to the same aspects of the situation, two different construals result. Again, such construals have truth values, with the ability to establish them successfully determining truth. Both construals in Figure 3 are true, because *ABOVE* and *BELOW* can each be bound successfully to the situation. The same perceptual information is represented, but attention is focused on it differently.

Like productivity, the schematization of perceptual symbols underlies propositional construal. Recall that the schematization of a perceptual symbol results from eliminating most aspects of a perceptual state while maintaining a small subset. If the same information is dropped from two different perceptual symbols, it can be added back to both during their

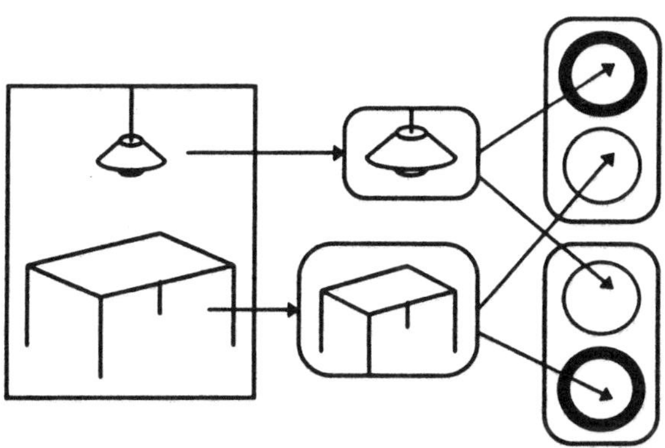

Figure 3

Further illustration of how perceptual symbols produce propositional construal. Different perceptual symbols for *above* and *below* interpret the same aspects of the situation in two different manners. Also, the embedding of perceptual symbols for *lamp* and *table* in the perceptual symbols for *above* and *below* illustrate how productivity in perceptual symbols produces hierarchical propositions.

subsequent processing. Because the same information is added back to two different perceptual symbols, it is construed differently in each. Thus, the upper regions of both *ABOVE* and *BELOW* can become bound to the lamp in Figure 3, because objects in general have been eliminated from the upper region of each during their acquisition.

Abstract Concepts

As described earlier, abstract concepts are framed against simulated event sequences that often include propositional construal. Now that we have introduced *propositional construal*, we can present our approach to representing abstract concepts. Unlike cognitive linguists (e.g., Lakoff & Johnson, 1980), we do not represent abstract concepts indirectly through metaphor but represent them directly with respect to the events that frame them (Barsalou et al., 1993).

We use the abstract concept of *truth* to illustrate our approach. Note that *truth* is a polysemous concept with many meanings and that we only attempt to represent one of these, namely, the psychological (not logical) understanding of what it means for a proposition to be true. We assume that the following event sequence frames this sense of truth: (a) An agent simulates a nonpresent situation. (b) The agent enters the situation and compares the simulation to it. (c) The agent discovers that the simulation matches the situation. For example, an agent might simulate a situation as containing a lamp above a table (Figure 4a), enter the situation (Figure 4b), and determine that the simulation matches the perceived situation (Figure 4c). On establishing the match, the agent might say, "It's true that there is a lamp above a table." We propose that the event sequence in Figure 4 grounds the meaning of "true" in this sentence. "True" does not refer to the sequence in its entirety but to a quality of the simulation that it frames, namely, that the simulation matches the perceived situation. As

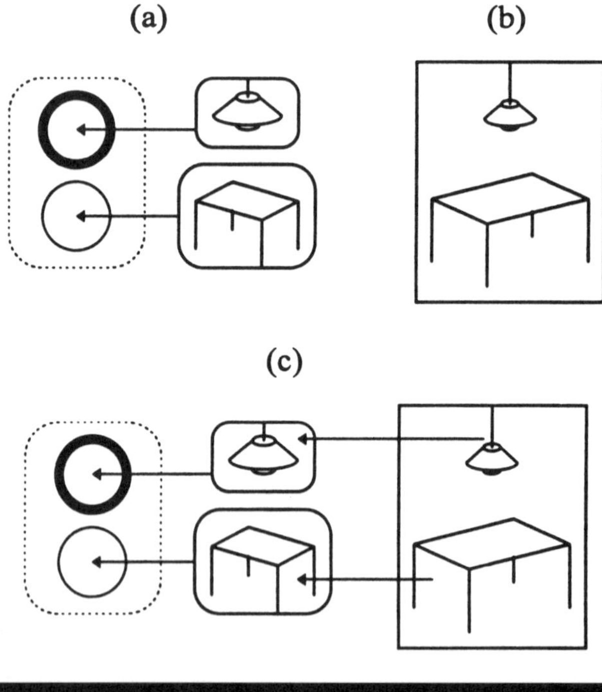

Figure 4

An account of one sense of *truth* using perceptual symbols. (a) Productive construction of a propositional construal. (b) A perceived situation. (c) Successful mapping of the construal into the situation results in attributing the quality of *truth* to the construal.

this example illustrates, an event sequence frames the concept of *truth*; this sequence includes introspective states and operations (e.g., comparison), and it includes propositional construal (i.e., the simulation construes the perceived situation).

The abstract concept of *disjunction* similarly involves these three mechanisms. Consider Figure 5, which represents a core sense of disjunction. Again, an event sequence frames the concept. In the first subevent, an agent perceives a room that contains a chair, lamp, and table (Figure 5a). Subsequently, the agent tries to recall the room (Figure 5b), remembers the chair and table, but cannot remember what was between them. Using reconstructive memory (Figure 5c), the agent alternatively simulates two possible entities that could have instantiated this region, namely, a lamp and a coat rack. While performing this alternating simulation, the agent might say, "There could have been a lamp or a coat rack between

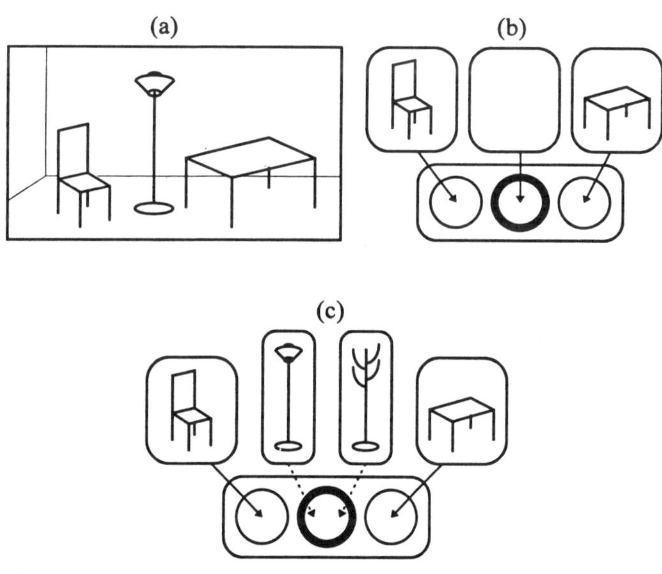

Figure 5

An account of one sense of *disjunction* using perceptual symbols. (a) A perceived situation. (b) A later attempt to recall the situation, failing to remember the middle entity. (c) Disjunctive simulation of two reconstructed entities in the middle region.

the chair and table." We propose that the meaning of "or" in this sentence is grounded in the event sequence. "Or" does not refer to the sequence in its entirety but to the alternating instantiations of its middle region. Again, an event sequence frames the abstract concept, and it includes introspective states (alternating insertion) and propositional construal (of the remembered situation).

Ad Hoc Categories

In achieving goals, people often construe entities functionally to enable goal achievement (Barsalou, 1983, 1985). According to one account of this process (Barsalou, 1991), an agent first retrieves an event frame for achieving a goal, with the frame containing schematic slots for roles such as agents, objects, instruments, locations, times, and so forth. To implement the frame successfully, these slots must be bound to entities in the environment, while satisfying constraints and optimizing ideals. To perform this instantiation process, the planner searches through a world model for possible specializations of each slot, which together constitute an ad hoc category. For example, the possible instantiations for the *location* slot of the *vacation* frame constitute the ad hoc category of *places to go on vacation.* Other ad hoc categories associated with other slots in the *vacation* frame include *times to vacation, things to pack in a suitcase, transportation to the airport,* and so forth.

Through propositional construal, perceptual symbol systems can construe an entity as belonging to multiple ad hoc categories. Figure 6a illustrates a simple room that contains a chair, a door, and a ceiling lamp. Figure 6b represents, in a highly schematic manner, a perceptual simulation of the event sequence, *prop a door open with a physical object.* Each frame in this series represents one subevent of the sequence. Because the slot, *heavy object used to prop a door open,* is a schematic region in the subevent, it can be instantiated with the perceptual symbol for an appropriate entity, such as the chair in the room. In Figure 6b, we assume that the perceptual symbol for *chair* has been inserted into the key schematic region of this simulation, such that a chair is simulated as propping the door open. On other occasions, a table may serve this function, or a floor lamp.

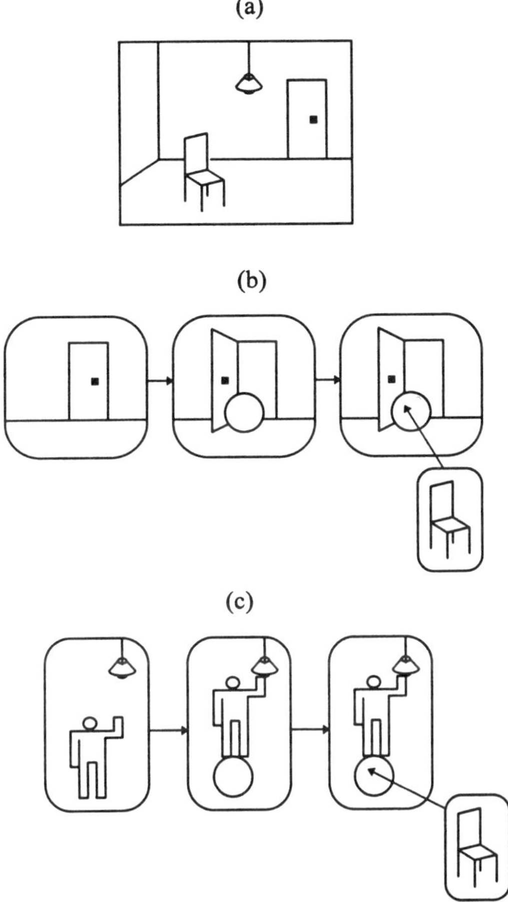

Figure 6

Illustration of how perceptual symbols ground two different ad hoc categorizations of the same entity. (a) A perceived situation. (b) Simulating the opening of a door, representing something to hold it open schematically, and instantiating the schematic region with the chair from the situation. (c) Simulating the changing of a light bulb, representing something to stand on schematically, and instantiating the schematic region with the chair from the situation.

Figure 6c alternatively construes the chair as *something to stand on to change a light bulb*. Here, the agent simulates changing the light bulb in the ceiling lamp of Figure 6a. Because multiple objects have served this goal in the past, this region of the simulated event sequence is schematic, indicating that it can be instantiated in multiple manners. On previous occasions, ladders and stools may have instantiated this region. In this particular case, however, the chair instantiates it.

As these examples illustrate, the same entity can be construed in a wide variety of ad hoc manners. By simulating perceptual symbols for the entity in schematic regions of different event sequences, it acquires different construals. Thus, a chair can be construed as *something to prop a door open with* or as *something to stand on to change a light bulb*, depending on the perceptual simulation in which it is embedded. Because most entities can be embedded in many such simulations, they can be construed in many possible ways. Most important, embedding perceptual representations of objects within perceptual simulations of events underlies such construal. This analysis leads to a perceptually based definition of ad hoc categories: An ad hoc category is a set of entities that disjunctively instantiates the same schematic region of a perceptually simulated event sequence.

Variable Embodiment

According to the functionalist perspective in modern cognitive science, the symbolic system that underlies human intelligence can be disembodied. Once we characterize the computational properties of this system successfully, we can implement it on computers and a potentially wide variety of other physical systems as well. Furthermore, the same basic symbolic system operates in all humans, independent of their biological idiosyncrasies. In general, functionalism implies that the computational system underlying human intelligence can be understood independently of the human body. Similar to characterizing computer software independently of the particular hardware that implements it, the human symbolic system can be characterized independently of the biological system in which it is embodied (for proposals of this view, see Putnam, 1960; Fodor, 1975; and Pylyshyn, 1984; for critiques, see Churchland, 1986, and Edelman, 1992).

The discrete referential nature of amodal symbols lies at the heart of modern functionalism. To see this, consider the relations in Figure 7a between different forms of the word "chair" and its referent, the picture of a chair at the top of Figure 7b. As Figure 7a illustrates, the word "chair" can be doubled in size, it can be rotated 30° counterclockwise, and it can be cut in half. In each case, however, the transformation implies nothing different about the pictured chair in Figure 7b. Doubling the size of the word "chair" does not mean that the actual chair is twice as large. Rotating "chair" 30° does not imply that the chair is rotated 30°. Cutting "chair" in half does imply that the chair is cut in half. These examples illustrate that words refer discretely. Because words bear no structural relations to their referents, structural changes in them mean nothing for structural properties in their referents. As long as the conventional link between a word and its referent remains intact, the word refers to the referent in exactly the same way, independently of transformations on the symbol.

Because amodal symbols refer in essentially the same manner as words, they refer discretely as well. It is this discrete property of amodal symbols that makes functionalism possible: Regardless of how a particu-

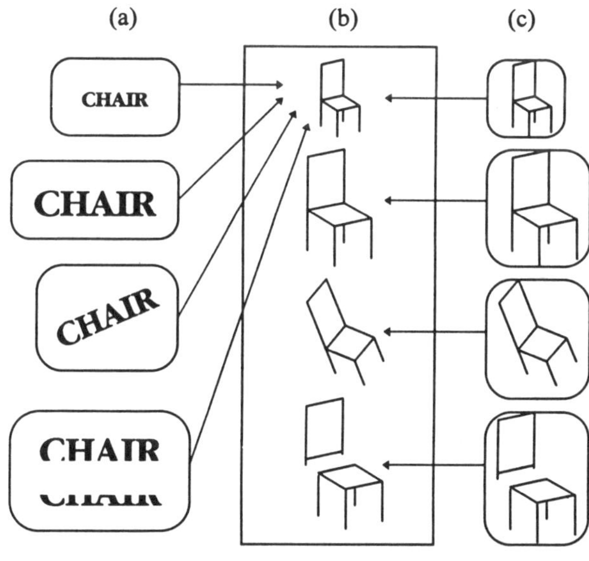

Figure 7

Illustration of variable embodiment. (a) Examples of how transformations on words and amodal symbols do not imply different meanings. (b) Possible meanings of the symbols in Panels a and c. (c) Examples of how transformations on perceptual symbols imply different meanings (i.e., variable embodiment).

lar amodal symbol is realized physically, it can still serve the same computational function. As long as the symbol plays the same functional role in a computational system, it can be implemented in humans or computers, and it can take idiosyncratic forms in different individuals. Physical variability in the form of the symbol is irrelevant, as long as it maintains the same conventional links to the world, as well as the same syntactic relations to other amodal symbols.

Perceptual symbols behave much differently. In direct contrast to amodal symbols, variability in the form of perceptual symbols has semantic implications (cf. Goodman, 1976). As Figure 7c illustrates, the perceptual symbol for *chair* can be doubled in size, it can be rotated 30°, and it can be cut in half. In each case, the transformation implies a change in the referent (Figure 7b). Doubling the size of the perceptual symbol for *chair* implies that the chair doubles in size, holding factors like depth constant. Rotating the perceptual symbol for *chair* 30° implies that the chair is rotated 30°. Cutting the perceptual symbol for *chair* in half implies that the chair is cut in half. These examples illustrate that perceptual symbols refer continuously. Because they bear structural relations to their referents, structural changes in the symbols imply structural changes in their referents, at least under many conditions.

It is the continuously referring nature of perceptual symbols that makes their embodiment critical: Differences in how a perceptual symbol is realized physically can change how it functions computationally. Implementing a perceptual symbol in a human body may produce different computational behavior than implementing it in a computer. Indeed, implementing human symbols in computers may be impossible, to the extent that computers do not share crucial physical properties with humans (e.g., Glenberg, this volume; Johnson, 1987; Lakoff, 1987). Similarly, the same perceptual symbol implemented in different human individuals may function differently, because of idiosyncrasies in individuals' perceptual systems.

Variable Embodiment as Mundane Creativity

We propose that the variable embodiment of perceptual symbols plays important adaptive functions in human cognition, constituting a third type of mundane creativity. We can think of at least two useful functions that variable embodiment might play in natural intelligence: First, variable embodiment allows individuals to adapt the perceptual symbols in their particular symbolic systems to their specific environments. Imagine that different individuals consume the same species of plants and animals as food, but consume somewhat different varieties, because they live in different locales. Through repetitive encounters with their respective foods, these different individuals develop somewhat different perceptual symbols to represent them. Because perceptual symbols naturally exhibit variable embodiment, variations in their referents become represented as variations in embodied symbols. The result is the development of somewhat different symbolic systems, each tuned optimally to its typical referents.

Variable embodiment plays a second useful function as well: Variable embodiment ensures that different individuals can match their perceptual symbols optimally to their perceptions. For example, it is well documented that individuals from the same culture differ in the detailed psychophysical structure of their color categories (Shevell & He, 1995; Smith, Pokorny, & Starr, 1976). As individuals establish perceptual symbols for colors, these symbols exhibit the peculiarities of their respective color systems. Thus, if one individual represents color categories in a somewhat idiosyncratic manner, his or her perceptual symbols will reflect this structure, such that they will be optimally tuned to match subsequent perceptions of color. In using color to perform categorization, for example, optimal accuracy will occur, because the perceived colors of referents will match the stored colors in perceptual symbols.

Because humans vary in all phenotypic traits to some extent, there is good reason to assume that they vary in all the perceptual discriminations that could be extracted into perceptual symbols, not just color. If so, then variable embodiment allows the human symbolic system to adapt itself naturally to variability in perceptual systems. In contrast, such adaptability is not in the spirit of the functionalist view. Because this view rests on amodal symbols that bear no structural relations to their referents, it neither anticipates nor naturally handles individual variability in perceptual systems.

Variable Embodiment and Concept Variability

Variable embodiment provides an explanation of between-individual and within-individual variability in human concepts (Barsalou, 1987, 1989, 1993). When different individuals' concepts of the same category are measured on a given occasion, there are usually substantial differences. Similarly, when one individual's concepts of a category are measured on different occasions, there are again robust differences. Variable embodiment offers one account of conceptual variability: Different individuals represent the same concept differently, because their perceptual symbols developed in somewhat different perceptual systems and have become tuned to somewhat different environments. A given individual represents the same concept differently over time, because his or her perceptual symbols have adapted themselves to the changing environment. In these manners, conceptual variability may reflect the adaptive functions that variable embodiment attempts to optimize.

Symbolic Commonality

We have illustrated how variable embodiment allows for substantial inter- and intra-individual variability. This variability must be complimented by commonality, which raises the question of how different individuals establish common ground in the perceptual symbols they form. There are a number of answers to this question from the perceptual perspective. The first involves the internal commonalities delivered by evolution. For all of the differences among individuals, there are many more similarities. Because human biology endows all people with roughly the same perceptual system, this guarantees a high degree of similarity in the perceptual symbols they construct. Although variable embodiment may tune these systems in important ways, the amount of tuning may be relatively small compared with the amount of shared structure.

A second source of commonality appeals to external factors. Not only do people share similar cognitive mechanisms, they also populate similar physical and social environments. Despite the large variance in climate and terrain, all regions of the planet follow the same physical laws. Moreover, all humans are exposed to similar kinds of things: conspecifics, animals, plants, water, inanimate objects, and so forth. These environmental commonalities result in a common base of perceptual experiences. Similarities in culture also ensure cognitive commonalities. Shared languages, customs, and values are made possible by cognitive commonalities, but they also reinforce and proliferate such commonalities. A culture can direct the attention of its members toward certain objects. Once an individual's attention has been directed to those objects, it is more than likely that he or she will form perceptual symbols for them. Thus, the commonalities in the symbols people construct are as much a product of culture as they are a prerequisite.

A third source of commonality is a direct consequence of how perceptual symbols are formed. Earlier, we noted that perceptual symbols are schematic. As a result, they may omit the details that distinguish one member of a category from another, and they may produce representations that are qualitative, not metric. This bias has two assets: The first is the frequently cited point that qualitative representations allow an individual to identify objects that differ in detail as members of the same category (e.g., Biederman, 1987). The second asset, much less noted, is that qualitative representations enable uniformity across individuals. If two people live in different parts of the world that have no species of bird in common, they might still form similar bird concepts, because many species of birds can be categorized using the same qualitative perceptual symbols. In this way, the schematic character of variably embodied symbols promotes inter-individual commonality.

CONCLUSION

Our primary agenda in this chapter was to demonstrate that it is possible to construct perceptual symbol systems that exhibit the desirable properties of amodal symbol systems while avoiding their problems. Thus, the perceptual symbol system that we propose exhibits productivity, propositional construal, and the ability to represent abstract concepts. In addition, it accounts naturally for symbol formation and symbol grounding, while suggesting a third type of mundane creativity, variable embodiment.

We are the first to admit that we need a strong empirical case for this view, although we believe that significant evidence already exists. Our goal, however, has not been to defend perceptual symbol systems empirically. Instead, our primary purpose has been to demonstrate that, theoretically, perceptual symbol systems can produce mundane creativity. If we can convince cognitive scientists that perceptual symbol systems are serious contenders theoretically, we have achieved our goal.

Before closing, we return to our earlier distinction between mundane and exceptional creativity. On the one hand, these two types of creativity could reflect fundamentally different cognitive mechanisms. On the other, both could reflect the same mechanisms, with exceptional creativity reflecting a greater use of them. Our deep appreciation of mundane creativity biases us toward the latter alternative, which is the one we explore here. If exceptional creativity involves a greater use of the mechanisms that underlie mundane creativity, how might this greater use be realized? At least three aspects of perceptual symbols may be relevant: higher numbers, greater subtlety, and more generality.

Having higher numbers of perceptual symbols than average may be associated with exceptional creativity. As a person extracts more perceptual symbols from perception, the productive ability to combine them grows exponentially. For example, if each perceptual symbol can be combined with every other, then the number of possible combinations grows with 2^n. Obviously, not all combinations are possible. Nevertheless the space of possible combinations grows dramatically as new perceptual symbols become available. The more perceptual symbols people know, the more likely they are to create novel combinations that lead to exceptionally creative acts. Of course, many combinations are not useful (Ward, Finke, & Smith, 1995), but if the proportion of creative combinations is a constant, then the number of creative combinations grows with the number of perceptual symbols.

The subtlety of perceptual symbols constitutes a second factor that could enable mundane creativity to produce exceptional products. Imagine that biology, culture, and language induce most humans to extract similar sets of perceptual symbols. As a result, the perceptual symbols that enter into most combinations are familiar, although these combinations may be mundanely creative to the extent that they involve "reshuffling" familiar symbols in novel ways. In contrast, when someone perceives subtle structure in perception and introspection that most people do not, the perceptual symbols extracted to represent it could subsequently produce combinations that contain unusual perceptual symbols. To the extent that a person extracts many nonsalient symbols from experience, the creative acts that reflect them may be viewed as increasingly exceptional.

The context independence of perceptual symbols constitutes a third factor that could enable mundane creativity to produce exceptional products. Imagine that most perceptual symbols are highly domain specific. Once a perceptual symbol has been extracted, its subsequent referents in the world may constitute a relatively narrow class of individuals, namely, those in the domain from which the symbol developed. In contrast, imagine that a person establishes perceptual symbols that can be mapped much more broadly into referents across domains. The ability to extend a perceptual symbol more broadly than average could be construed as a form of exceptional creativity. In a scientific sense, it could also imply a "deeper" understanding of the world. Rather than understanding each domain locally in terms of its own symbols, different domains are understood in terms of common symbols.

The more we explore perceptual symbol systems, the more impressed we are with their powers. Creativity is no exception. From the mundane to the exceptional, there is a story that can be told with perceptual symbols.

REFERENCES

Anderson, J. R., & Bower, G. H. (1973). *Human associative memory.* Washington, DC: Winston.

Aristotle. (1961). *De anima, books II and III* (D. W. Hamlyn, Trans.). Oxford, England: Oxford University Press. (Original work published 4th century B.C.)

Barsalou, L. W. (1983). Ad hoc categories. *Memory & Cognition, 11,* 211–227.

Barsalou, L. W. (1985). Ideals, central tendency, and frequency of instantiation as determinants of graded structure in categories. *Journal of Experimental Psychology: Learning, Memory, and Cognition, 11,* 629–654.

Barsalou, L. W. (1987). The instability of graded structure in concepts. In U. Neisser (Ed.), *Concepts and conceptual development: Ecological and intellectual factors in categorization* (pp. 101–140). Cambridge, England: Cambridge University Press.

Barsalou, L. W. (1989). Intra-concept similarity and its implications for inter-concept similarity. In S. Vosniadou & A. Ortony (Eds.), *Similarity and analogical reasoning* (pp. 76–121). Cambridge, England: Cambridge University Press.

Barsalou, L. W. (1991). Deriving categories to achieve goals. In G. H. Bower (Ed.), *The psychology of learning and motivation: Advances in research and theory* (Vol. 27, pp. 1–64). San Diego, CA: Academic Press.

Barsalou, L. W. (1992a). *Cognitive psychology: An overview for cognitive scientists.* Hillsdale, NJ: Erlbaum.

Barsalou, L. W. (1992b). Frames, concepts, and conceptual fields. In E. Kittay & A. Lehrer (Eds.), *Frames, fields, and contrasts: New essays in semantic and lexical organization* (pp. 21–74). Hillsdale, NJ: Erlbaum.

Barsalou, L. W. (1993). Flexibility, structure, and linguistic vagary in concepts: Manifestations of a compositional system of perceptual symbols. In A. C. Collins, S. E. Gathercole, & M. A. Conway (Eds.), *Theories of memories* (pp. 29–101). London: Erlbaum.

Barsalou, L. W. (1997). *Perceptual symbol systems.* Manuscript submitted for publication.

Barsalou, L. W., & Hale, C. R. (1993). Components of conceptual representation: From feature lists to recursive frames. In I. Van Mechelen, J. Hampton, R. Michalski, & P. Theuns (Eds.), *Categories and concepts: Theoretical views and inductive data analysis* (pp. 97–144). San Diego, CA: Academic Press.

Barsalou, L. W., Yeh, W., Luka, B. J., Olseth, K. L., Mix, K. S., & Wu, L. (1993). Concepts and meaning. In K. Beals, G. Cooke, D. Kathman, K. E. McCullough, S. Kita, & D. Testen (Eds.), *Chicago Linguistics Society 29: Papers from the parasession on conceptual representations* (pp. 23–61). University of Chicago: Chicago Linguistics Society.

Barwise, J., & Etchemendy, J. (1990). Information, infons, and inference. In R. Cooper, K. Mukai, & J. Perry (Eds.), *Situation theory and its applications* (pp. 33–78). Chicago: University of Chicago Press.

Barwise, J., & Etchemendy, J. (1991). Visual information and valid reasoning. In. W. Zimmerman & S. Cunningham (Eds.), *Visualization in mathematics* (pp. 9–24). Washington, DC: Mathematical Association of America.

Berkeley, G. (1982). *A treatise concerning the principles of human knowledge.* Indianapolis, IN: Hackett. (Original work published 1710)

Biederman, I. (1987). Recognition-by-components: A theory of human image understanding. *Psychological Review, 94,* 115–147.

Carnap, R. (1956). *Meaning and necessity.* Chicago: University of Chicago Press.

Chomsky, N. (1957). *Syntactic structures.* The Hague, the Netherlands: Mouton.

Church, A. (1951). The need for abstract entities in semantic analysis. *American Acadamy of Arts and Sciences Proceedings, 80,* 100–112.

Churchland, P. S. (1986). *Neurophilosophy: Toward a unified science of the mind/brain.* Cambridge, MA: MIT Press.

Corballis, M. C. (1991). *The lopsided ape: Evolution of the generative mind.* New York: Oxford University Press.

Damasio, A. R. (1994). *Descartes' error: Emotion, reason, and the human brain.* New York: Brosset/Putnam.

Dennett, D. C. (1969). *Content and consciousness.* London: Routledge & Kegan Paul.

Edelman, G. M. (1992). *Bright air, brilliant fire: On the matter of the mind.* New York: Basic Books.

Fauconnier, G. (1985). *Mental spaces.* Cambridge, MA: MIT Press.

Fillmore, C. J. (1985). Frames and the semantics of understanding. *Quaderni di Semantica, 6,* 222–255.

Fodor, J. A. (1975). *The language of thought.* Cambridge, MA: Harvard University Press.

Fodor, J. A., & Pylyshyn, Z. W. (1988). Connectionism and cognitive architecture: A critical analysis. *Cognition, 28,* 3–71.

Frege, G. (1956). The thought: A logical inquiry. *Mind, 65,* 289–311. (Original work published 1918)

Garner, W. R. (1974). *The processing of information and structure.* New York: Wiley.

Garner, W. R. (1978). Aspects of a stimulus: Features, dimensions, and configurations. In E. Rosch & B. B. Lloyd (Eds.), *Cognition and categorization.* Hillsdale, NJ: Erlbaum.

Gernsbacher, M. A., Varner, K. R., & Faust, M. E. (1990). Investigating differences in general comprehension skill. *Journal of Experimental Psychology: Learning, Memory, and Cognition, 16,* 430–445.

Gibbs, R. W., Jr. (1994). *Poetics of mind.* Cambridge, England: Cambridge University Press.

Glaser, W. R. (1992). Picture naming. *Cognition, 42,* 61–106.

Glasgow, J. I. (1993). The imagery debate revisited: A computational perspective. *Computational Intelligence, 9,* 309–333.

Glenberg, A. M., & Langston, W. E. (1992). Comprehension of illustrated text: Pictures help to build mental models. *Journal of Memory and Language, 31,* 129–151.

Glenberg, A. M., Meyer, M., & Lindem, K. (1987). Mental models contribute to foregrounding during text comprehension. *Journal of Memory and Language, 26,* 69–83.

Goodman, N. (1976). *Languages of art.* Indianapolis, IN: Hackett.

Harnad, S. (1990). The symbol grounding problem. *Physica D, 42,* 335–346.

Haugeland, J. (1985). *Artificial intelligence: The very idea of it.* Cambridge, MA: MIT Press.

Hayes, P. J. (1985). Naive physics I: Ontology for liquids. In J. R. Hobbs & R. C. Moore (Eds.), *Formal theories of the common sense world* (pp. 71–107). Norwood, NJ: Ablex.

Hume, D. (1978). *A treatise on human nature* (2nd ed.). Oxford, England: Oxford University Press. (Original work published 1739)

Jackendoff, R. (1987). On beyond zebra: The relation of linguistic and visual information. *Cognition, 26,* 89–114.

Johnson, M. (1987). *The body in the mind: The bodily basis of reason and imagination.* Chicago: University of Chicago Press.

Johnson-Laird, P. N. (1983). *Mental models.* Cambridge, MA: Harvard University Press.

Kasher, A. (1991). Pragmatics and Chomsky's research program. In A. Kasher (Ed.), *The Chomskyan turn* (pp. 122–149). Oxford, England: Blackwell.

Kintsch, W. (1974). *The representation of meaning in memory.* Hillsdale, NJ: Erlbaum.

Klatzky, R. L., Pelligrino, J. W., McCloskey, B. P., & Doherty, S. (1989). The role of motor representations in semantic sensibility judgments. *Journal of Memory and Language, 28,* 56–77.

Kosslyn, S. M. (1980). *Image and mind.* Cambridge, MA: Harvard University Press.

Kosslyn, S. M. (1994). *Image and brain.* Cambridge, MA: MIT Press/Bradford Books.

Lakoff, G. (1987). *Women, fire, and dangerous things: What categories reveal about the mind.* Chicago: University of Chicago Press.

Lakoff, G. (1988). Cognitive semantics. In U. Eco, M. Santambrogio, & P. Violi (Eds.),

Meaning and mental representations (pp. 119–154). Bloomington, IN: Indiana University Press.

Lakoff, G., & Johnson, M. (1980). *Metaphors we live by.* Chicago: University of Chicago Press.

Langacker, R. W. (1986). An introduction to cognitive grammar. *Cognitive Science, 10,* 1–40.

Langacker, R. W. (1987). *Foundations of cognitive grammar: Vol. 1. Theoretical prerequisites.* Stanford, CA: Stanford University Press.

Langacker, R. W. (1991). *Foundations of cognitive grammar, Volume II: Descriptive application.* Stanford, CA: Stanford University Press.

Locke, J. (1959). *An essay concerning human understanding* (1st ed., Vols. 1 and 2). New York: Dover. (Original work published 1690)

Mandler, J. M. (1992). How to build a baby: II. Conceptual primitives. *Psychological Review, 99,* 587–604.

McCloskey, M. (1983). Naive theories of motion. In D. Gentner & A. Stevens (Eds.), *Mental models* (pp. 299–324). Hillsdale, NJ: Erlbaum.

Melara, R. D., & Marks, L. E. (1990). Dimensional interactions in language processing: Investigating directions and levels of crosstalk. *Journal of Experimental Psychology: Learning, Memory, and Cognition, 16,* 539–554.

Miller, G. A., & Johnson-Laird, P. N. (1976). *Language and perception.* Cambridge, MA: Harvard University Press.

Mitchell, T. M., Keller, R. M., & Kedar-Cabelli, S. T. (1986). Explanation-based generalization: A unifying view. *Machine Learning, 1,* 47–80.

Morris, C. D., Bransford, J. D., & Franks, J. J. (1977). Levels of processing versus test-appropriate strategies. *Journal of Verbal Learning and Verbal Behavior, 16,* 519–533.

Morrow, D. G., Greenspan, S. L., & Bower, G. H. (1987). Accessibility and situation models in narrative comprehension. *Journal of Memory and Language, 26,* 165–187.

Newell, A., & Simon, H. A. (1972). *Human problem solving.* Englewood Cliffs, NJ: Prentice-Hall.

Olseth, K. L., & Barsalou, L. W. (1995). The spontaneous use of perceptual representations during conceptual processing. *Proceedings of the Seventeenth Annual Meeting of the Cognitive Science Society* (pp. 310–315). Hillsdale, NJ: Erlbaum.

Paivio, A. (1986). *Mental representations: A dual coding approach.* New York: Oxford University Press.

Peacocke, C. (1992). *A study of concepts.* Cambridge, MA: MIT Press.

Potter, M. C., & Faulconer, B. A. (1975). Time to understand pictures and words. *Nature, 253,* 437–438.

Potter, M. C., Kroll, J. F., Yachzel, B., Carpenter, E., & Sherman, J. (1986). Pictures in sentences: Understanding without words. *Journal of Experimental Psychology: General, 115,* 281–294.

Potter, M. C., Valian, V. V., & Faulconer, B. A. (1977). Representation of a sentence and its pragmatic implications: Verbal, imagistic, or abstract? *Journal of Verbal Learning and Verbal Behavior, 16,* 1–12.

Price, H. H. (1953). *Thinking and experience.* London: Hutchinson's Universal Library.

Prinz, J. J. (1997). *Perceptual cognition.* Doctoral dissertation in progress. University of Chicago.

Prinz, J. J., & Barsalou, L. W. (in press). Acquisition and productivity in perceptual symbol systems: An account of mundane creativity. In T. H. Dartnall (Ed.), *Creativity, computation, and cognition.* Cambridge, MA: MIT/AAAI Press.

Putnam, H. (1960). Minds and machines. In S. Hook (Ed.), *Dimensions of mind* (pp. 138–164). New York: Collier Books.

Pylyshyn, Z. W. (1973). What the mind's eye tells the mind's brain: A critique of mental imagery. *Psychological Bulletin, 80,* 1–24.

Pylyshyn, Z. W. (1981). The imagery debate: Analogue media versus tacit knowledge. *Psychological Review, 88,* 16–45.

Pylyshyn, Z. W. (1984). *Computation and cognition.* Cambridge, MA: MIT Press.

Reid, T. (1969). *Essays on the intellectual powers of man.* Cambridge, MA: MIT Press. (Original work published 1785)

Reid, T. (1970). *An inquiry into the human mind on the principles of common sense.* Chicago: University of Chicago Press. (Original work published 1764)

Russell, B. (1921). *The analysis of mind.* New York: Macmillan.

Russell, B. (1956). *Logic and knowledge.* London: Routledge. (Original work published 1919)

Ryle, G. (1949). *The concept of mind.* New York: Harper Collins.

Searle, J. R. (1980). Minds, brains, and programs. *Behavioral and Brain Sciences, 3,* 417–424.

Sellars, W. (1956). Empiricism and the philosophy of mind. In H. Feigl & M. Scriven

(Eds.), *Minnesota studies in the philosophy of science* (Vol. 1, pp. 293–305). Minneapolis, MN: University of Minnesota Press.

Shevell, S. K., & He, J. C. (1995). Interocular difference in Rayleigh matches of color normals. In B. Dunn (Ed.), *Colour vision deficiencies XII* (pp. 185–191). Dordrecht, the Netherlands: Kluwer Academic Press.

Shiffrin, R. M. (1988). Attention. In R. C. Atkinson, R. J. Herrnstein, G. Lindzey, & R. D. Luce (Eds.), *Stevens' handbook of experimental psychology: Learning and cognition* (Vol. 2, pp. 739–811). New York: Wiley.

Smith, V. C., Pokorny, J., & Starr, S. J. (1976). Variability of color mixture data—1. Interobserver variability in the unit coordinates. *Vision Research, 16*, 1087–1094.

Solomon, K. L. (1997). *The spontaneous use of perceptual representations during conceptual processing.* Unpublished doctoral dissertation, University of Chicago.

Stalnaker, R. (1984). *Inquiry.* Cambridge, MA: MIT Press.

Stenning, K., & Oberlander, J. (1994). Spatial inclusion and set membership: A case study of analogy at work. In K. J. Holyoak & J. A. Barnden (Eds.), *Analogical connections. Advances in connectionist and neural computation theory* (Vol. 2, pp. 446–486). Norwood, NJ: Ablex.

Sweetser, E. (1990). *From etymology to pragmatics: Metaphorical and cultural aspects of semantics.* Cambridge, England: Cambridge University Press.

Talmy, L. (1983). How language structures space. In H. Pick & L. Acredelo (Eds.), *Spatial orientation: Theory, research, and application* (pp. 225–282). New York: Plenum Press.

Talmy, L. (1988). Force dynamics in language and cognition. *Cognitive Science, 12*, 49–100.

Thagard, P. (1992). *Conceptual revolutions.* Princeton, NJ: Princeton University Press.

Tippett, L. J. (1992). The generation of visual images: A review of neuropsychological research and theory. *Psychological Bulletin, 112*, 415–432.

Tulving, E., & Thomson, D. M. (1973). Encoding specificity and retrieval processes in episodic memory. *Psychological Review, 80*, 352–373.

Tye, M. (1991). *The imagery debate.* Cambridge, MA: MIT Press.

van Dijk, T. A., & Kintsch, W. (1983). *Strategies of discourse comprehension.* San Diego, CA: Academic Press.

Ward, T. B., Finke, R. A., & Smith, S. M. (1995). *Creativity and the mind: Discovering the genius within.* New York: Plenum Press.

Wu, L. L. (1995). *Perceptual representation in conceptual combination.* Unpublished doctoral dissertation, University of Chicago.

12

Creativity in Personality, Developmental, and Social Psychology: Any Links With Cognitive Psychology?

Dean Keith Simonton

In commenting on the previous chapters in this section, I should like to begin with a disclaimer: Perhaps alone among the contributors to this book, I am not a cognitive psychologist by training. Although I hold a doctorate in social psychology, my specialty area is not even social cognition. Instead, if I had to label myself, I would say that I am a *personality, developmental*, and *social psychologist* who studies the phenomenon of exceptional creativity. By *exceptional* I mean really exceptional: The primary people in my investigations are creators who left a lasting imprint on the history of human civilization (Simonton, 1984, 1994). This means that I have a rather distinct perspective on what cognitive psychology can reveal about the creative process. What might be considered a relatively minor issue from the cognitive point of view can loom large from my outlook—and the reverse may often hold as well. Nonetheless, I also believe that psychology should represent a unified discipline that ultimately attains an integrated understanding of the phenomena under its charge. Therefore, what the cognitive psychologist has to say about creativity should not conflict with the findings of personality, developmental, and social psychologists. Moreover, all psychologists, no matter what the subdiscipline, should be willing to consider discoveries in other subdisciplines that might provide clues to the solution of certain key problems. Maybe the answer to some irksome question has already been suggested by a departmental colleague just a couple of doors down the hall. It is for this reason that I have taken great interest in the chapters in this section.

THE STUDY OF CREATIVITY

Cognitive psychologists who study creativity are fascinated with the mental processes and operations that produce creative ideas. Personality, developmental, and social psychologists, in contrast, tend to examine creativity from wider or more inclusive perspectives. The personality psychologist wishes to know how individual differences in cognitive style, dispositional traits, and motivation may be associated with creativity, whether defined as performance on a "creativity test" or measured in terms of the output of creative products. The developmental psychologist is interested in how creative potential emerges in childhood and adolescence as well as in how that creative potential is manifested in adulthood. The social psychologist, finally, is fascinated with the relationship between individual creativity and the larger social milieu, including the political and cultural environment. It is from these three distinct orientations that I direct my examination of these chapters.

Polysemy and Novel Word Meanings

Murphy's chapter addresses a fascinating question: How do words acquire novel meanings? What are the constraints on the extension of old meanings to new meanings? After examining many ways that word meanings are extended, Murphy discusses some of the constraints that are imposed on the process—the constraints of comprehensibility, variability, and relatedness. He then goes a step further and actually conducts a series of experiments that try to tease out exactly how these constraints operate in the production of polysemy. These experiments are as instructive as they are entertaining, and, in fact, *wift* and *tuk* have now entered my permanent vocabulary (albeit it is consistently flagged by my spell checker). One of the main conclusions is that expansions of polysemy entail an incremental process. New meanings build on old meanings, but the extension must be close rather than remote. If the semantic distance is too great, or certain other linguistic biases are violated, then an extended meaning will appear stretched, if it is even comprehensible at all. In other words, even the intelligible overextensions may look ugly or aesthetically unpleasant.

These conclusions are remarkably similar to the findings of empirical aesthetics. Creative artists must generate original ideas, yet that originality cannot go too far from some implicit or explicit baseline, such as a certain aesthetic style or tradition. As a consequence, the success of a work of art is often a curvilinear, inverted-U function of its originality (Berlyne, 1971). An illustration may be found in my own studies of 15,618 themes in the repertoire of classical music (e.g., Simonton, 1980a, 1987). I first used a computer to gauge each theme's *melodic originality*, which essentially measures how improbable is a sequence of notes given the diatonic scale of the Western musical tradition. I then assessed the aesthetic impact of the works in which these themes were found, using such information as performance frequencies and number of recordings. The relationship between these two variables is best described by an inverted-backwards-J curve. Evidently, the pieces that most dominate the classical repertoire are those that offer a medium level of predictability. Such themes pretty much follow the structure of the scales that define diatonic music but add enough surprises, such as chromatic notes and unusual intervals, to manifest the necessary novelty. It is interesting that the melodies that are least liked are those that depart most from the tonal conventions. These are like the incomprehensible or unpalatable extensions of meaning studied by Murphy.

Notice that a problem arises in this process of finding the level of originality that is just right. When the artists of one generation produce new works that satisfy the "happy medium," the baseline will likely shift for the next generation. The audience will become habituated to the previous novelty, and thus the new arrivals on the artistic scene will have to seek farther out for the requisite optimal level of originality. In classical music, for example, there has been a general tendency for melodic originality to increase over time (Simonton, 1980a, 1980b). Compare the modal music of the Renaissance to the chromaticism of Chopin and Wagner, and from there proceed to the atonal and serial music of Schoenberg and after. In fact, this process is so general that Martindale (1990) used it as the basis for his theory of stylistic evolution. Significantly, most of the empirical studies that he has conducted to test his theory have focused on literature. Using computerized content analytical methods, Martindale has shown how literary language within a given style tends to become increasingly more bizarre. The metaphors become more remote, for example, and semantic incongruities become more frequent. Although Martindale does not specifically address the problem, one would certainly expect that the literary lexicon would become ever more polysemous as a given style progresses and degenerates. This hypothesis is certainly well worth testing.

This brings me to my last comment on Murphy's chapter. If one is speaking of literary creativity in the English language, one certainly must mention William Shakespeare. Because the characters and plots of his plays have become so much a part of American culture, his contribution to the basic language used by all English-speaking peoples may be underappreciated. In particular, Shakespeare was a master of coining new words. A partial list of the words that appeared in Shakespeare's plays for the first time include *accessible, amazement, anchovy, assassination, baseless, birthplace, bloodstained, circumstantial, coldhearted, courtship, critical, day's work, dewdrop, distrustful, domineering, droplet, employment, epileptic, equivocal, exposure, eyeball, fashionable, foregone, hostile, inaudible, invitation, invulnerable, lament, leapfrog, love letter, majestic, monumental, ode, pageantry, paternal, pious, priceless, puppy dog, on purpose, quarrelsome, reclusive, reliance, retirement, roadway, savagery, shooting star, successful, tardiness, tranquil, transcendence, unmitigated, useless, vulnerable, watchdog,* and *zany* (see Macrone, 1990). Because many of these novelties probably involved extending old meanings new directions through various grammatical manipulations, one might say that Shakespeare was a master of polysemy—a creative genius at it perhaps. If so, this leads to several questions from the perspectives of personality, developmental, and social psychology.

1. Did Shakespeare possess some special combination of personality traits that made him especially talented in the generation of linguistic novelties? Empirical research suggests an affirmative answer. For instance, creative genius is associated with high scores on the Psychoticism dimension of the Eysenck Personality Inventory (Eysenck, 1995). High psychoticism itself is linked with a distinctive cognitive style that includes divergent thinking, associative remoteness and richness, and certain quirks of information processing (e.g., negative priming and latent inhibition). Can one speculate that these cognitive characteristics might help account for the ability to proliferate novel meanings?
2. Did Shakespeare's capacity for conceiving literature innovations change over the course of his career? Did the constraints on the generation of such variations increase or decrease over time? There exists a large body of empirical studies on longitudinal changes in style and content in the output of creative individuals (Simonton, 1994), including work on literary creators (Martindale, 1990) and even Shakespeare himself (Derks, 1994; Simonton, 1986). This work demonstrates the existence of definite agewise trends. For example, Shakespeare's own tendency to produce semantic incongruities is a curvilinear inverted-U function of age (Derks, 1994). How is this related to other life-span developmental changes, such as the trends in intelligence and divergent thinking (Simonton, 1996)?
3. Did the larger sociocultural, political, and economic milieu play some role in encouraging or supporting the creation of linguistic novelties? English language, culture, religion, society, and politics under Queen Elizabeth and King James was extremely dynamic and innovative during the period that Shakespeare was writing his plays and poems. This was the age of the Spanish Armada, the English colonization of the Americas, the Gunpowder Plot, Gilbert's monumental work on magnetism, and Harvey's revolutionary work on the circulation of the blood, the King James Bible, and so on. There already exists empirical evidence that various attributes of the zeit-

geist can affect content and style in creative products, including in literary creations (e.g., Martindale, 1975; Simonton, 1983, 1986). Hence, is it not possible that certain periods favor the production of polysemy and other linguistic innovations? If so, how do these circumstances affect what is occurring on the cognitive level?

Many more points could be raised here, but this should suffice to give an idea of the larger context in which Murphy's fascinating work might be embedded.

Conceptual and Linguistic Creativity in Children

From a developmental perspective, the studies reported by Cacciari, Levorato, and Cicogna are inherently interesting. Besides age comparisons within their investigations, the authors also make comparisons with results from similar studies using adults. Yet a developmental psychologist would also be interested in the role of individual differences in the expression of artistic or linguistic creativity. For example, there is a large and growing literature on precocious children and child prodigies in the arts (e.g., Golomb, 1995). To what extent are these exceptional talents bound by the same conventions as the more average children studied here? A personality psychologist would take this question a step farther. Creative children and adults exhibit a distinctive profile in personality traits that might dispose them to venture even more bizarre creations than are normally found in studies like these (Eysenck, 1995; Getzels & Jackson, 1962; Wallach & Kogan, 1965). For instance, they tend to be nonconformists, even anti-conformists, who spontaneously generate thoughts that are unusual, even a bit crazy. In fact, creativity is associated with high scores on the clinical scales of the Minnesota Multiphasic Personality Inventory (Barron, 1969; MacKinnon, 1978).

A social psychologist would ask a different set of questions. For example, how does social context affect the way children express visual or verbal originality? Teresa Amabile (1983) has devoted a research program to showing that creative output can be dramatically influenced by a host of factors, such as supervision, evaluation, and reward (see also Hennessey

& Amabile, 1988). Depending on the mix, these environmental effects may either enhance or decrease the amount of imagination displayed. Certainly similar phenomena would be observed here. These findings have important methodological implications as well: Because creativity is susceptible to the social context, the instructions given research participants can exert significant effects on the amount of imagination displayed.

Category Learning, Transfer, and Communication

The interesting experiments of Markman, Yamauchi, and Makin may seem far removed from the studies of creative genius that preoccupy my own research program. Nonetheless, I identified at least points of contact between the two vastly different perspectives. First, I was stimulated by Markham et al.'s studies of the role of communication in category learning. Much of creativity occurs in a social environment, the interplay between individual creators stimulating the emergence of ideas that might not arise by more solitary means (Csikszentmihalyi & Sawyer, 1995; Dunbar, 1995; Kantorovich, 1993). In addition, the exchange of information and ideas helps define the nature of new ideas. One does not have to be a staunch social constructionist to realize that such ideas are about as much a product of social exchange as they are a reflection of some underlying reality. Hence, these investigations amount to miniature forays into the social psychology of creativity.

Second, I was intrigued by Markman et al.'s inquiries into how the type of learning influences performance on transfer tasks. They showed that transfer was indeed contingent on the mode of learning, in this instance classification versus inference learning. These results remind me of recent inquiries regarding expertise acquisition (Ericsson & Charness, 1994; Ericsson, Krampe, & Tesch-Römer, 1993). One of the debates in this area is whether the most creative contributors to a particular field are simply the biggest experts. Some argue that creative geniuses are merely those individuals who know more than their less distinguished colleagues. The problem with this view is that those who make the most historic breakthroughs in a field seldom fit the pattern of typical expertise acquisition (Rostan, 1994). Indeed, the innovators will often know less, not more (Simonton, 1988). Einstein, for example, was by no means the most knowledgeable theoretical physicist of the 20th century, and he would often display a profound ignorance and naiveté about certain aspects of his field. In contrast, a large number of his contemporaries went to more prestigious schools, got far better grades, and studied under all the best masters, only to find themselves unable to offer the world a single innovative idea. Conceivably, part of the contrast between creators and experts concerns the manner in which the knowledge was acquired, which then determines how well it can be transferred to new problems. This problem of expertise acquisition is of profound interest to any developmental psychology of creativity.

Ontology and Scientific Revolutions

The work by Chi and her colleagues is quite provocative. It is certainly of immense practical value to realize that concepts tend to fall into distinct ontological categories and that these categories may differ for novice and expert in a manner that offers a stumbling block to the acquisition of expertise in the sciences. One obvious question is the extent to which these ontological categories are themselves innate or acquired: Do these represent Kantian categories that define the way the human mind is wired for information processing, or are these categories cultural products that can undergo transformations over time? Yet from my perspective a more fascinating issue is whether these findings can help researchers appreciate the nature of scientific revolutions. Very often new scientific ideas are rejected because they are said to defy "common sense." To what extent is this rejection predicated on the difficulty of changing the ontological status of a given scientific concept? It would be instructive, for example, to conduct a historiometric study of scientific revolutions that gauged directly the amount of resistance that a new idea encountered in the larger community, both scientific and lay (cf. Diamond, 1980; Donovan, Laudan, & Laudan, 1988; Hull, Tessner, & Diamond, 1978). Will it happen that those ideas that are the most difficult to acquire according to Chi's studies are also those that faced the most difficult, uphill battle to acceptance? Moreover, even after the new theory is "established," will it find itself most consistently challenged owing to the continued difficulty it encounters in recruiting new adherents from the next generation? In short, it may very well be that the processes that Chi has identified happening within a single human mind have consequences that determine the course of scientific history.

Perceptual Symbol Systems

Barsalou and Prinz's chapter is theoretical rather than empirical in nature. Nonetheless, I found the chapter most provocative. After all, it deals with a phenomenon that must lie at the very root of the creative process. This conclusion is based on the introspective reports of eminent creators themselves, who often report the kind of vague imagery (and even imageless thought) that support perceptual symbol systems (e.g., Ghiselin, 1952). This is even true in domains where one might first think that abstract logic would reign supreme, such as theoretical physics and pure mathematics (Hadamard, 1945; Roe, 1952; Root-Bernstein, 1989). Moreover, this diffuse imagery may even underlie the origination of extremely abstract ideas. The French mathematician Jacques Hadamard (1945) provided a concrete illustration when he described how he visualizes a mathematical proof. The specific example is the demonstration that there exists a prime number greater than 11 as part of a more general proof that the series of prime numbers is infinite. Corresponding to each logical statement is Hadamard's imagery, which I present in Table 1.

Significantly, the mental processing in the second column usually occurs before the formulation that appears in the first column. The former represents the initial "hunch" or "insight," whereas the latter is simply a formal translation that has greater rigor and that can be effectively communicated to the mathematical community. Hence, even in rather abstract domains of creativity, "combinatory play" with vague images can provide the basis for invention.

Throughout their chapter Barsalou and Prinz touch on issues that have direct linkages to phenomena in the creativity literature. For example, at one point they discuss the phenomenon of "multiple construals." In creativity research there is frequent discussion of the creative individual's capacity for viewing the same stimuli in multiple ways. Indeed, this cogni-

Table 1

Example of Hadamard's Use of Mental Imagery to Manipulate Abstract Mathematics

Steps in the proof	My mental pictures
I consider all primes from 2 to 11, say 2, 3, 5, 7, 11.	I see a confused mass.
I form their product $2 \times 3 \times 5 \times 7 \times 11 = N$.	*N* being a rather large number, I imagine a point rather remote from the confused mass.
I increase that product by 1, say *N* plus 1.	I see a second point a little beyond the first.
That number, if not a prime, must admit of a prime divisor, which is the required number.	I see a place somewhere between the confused mass and the first point.

NOTE: Table was constructed from Discussion text of Hadamard (1945, pp. 76–77).

tive ability provides the underpinning of some assessment devices, such as the "unusual uses" test (Guilford, 1967). In this test, the individual must conceive as many ways as possible of using some everyday object (toothpick, paperclip, brick, etc.). Those who score high on this task are able to perceive the multiple representations of the function and qualities of any given stimulus.

At the close of Barsalou and Prinz's chapter the connections become even more obvious. That is because they make a bold effort to describe the "relations between mundane and exceptional creativity." They speculate that "at least three aspects of perceptual symbols may be relevant: higher number, greater subtlety, and more generality." Let me expound a bit on each.

First, Barsalou and Prinz suggest that "having higher numbers of perceptual symbols than average may be associated with exceptional creativity." They then elaborate with the observation that the number of potential combinations of the symbolic material would increase exponentially with the number of symbols available. This very same claim was made in my own theoretical work on creativity, especially in my "chance–configuration" theory of creative genius (Simonton, 1988). One special asset of this proposition is that it enables one to explain an otherwise quite puzzling feature of exceptional creativity, namely the extreme skewness of the productivity distribution (Simonton, 1984). Unlike most psychological and behavioral attributes, which tend to be roughly described by normal distributions, the cross-sectional variation of creative output—whether per unit of time or over the entire life span—tends to fit a lognormal distribution. This means that a small percentage of the creators in any given domain tend to account for a lion's share of the total output. Typically, the top 10% who are most prolific account for about half of all contributions! Yet it is very easy to stretch a normal distribution into a lognormal distribution under the assumption of a combinatory model (Simonton, 1988). One only needs to suppose that the number of perceptual symbols fed into the combinatory process is normally distributed across individuals active within a domain. The number of possible combinations would then exhibit a lognormal distribution as a necessary consequence. Of course, as Barsalou and Prinz point out, not all of these combinations would be useful or even novel. Nonetheless, the number of truly creative combinations would probably be an approximately constant fraction of the total number of combinations produced. The lognormal distribution would still result.

Second, Barsalou and Prinz conjecture that perceptual symbols can vary in subtlety and that this variation may account for the ability to produce exceptional creative products. Although I find his use of the term *subtlety* itself somewhat subtle, I think I can say that his notion has counterparts in the creativity literature (Eysenck, 1995; Simonton, 1988, 1994). Highly creative individuals tend to possess domain-relevant concepts that are extremely rich and idiosyncratic. One way that this attribute is manifested is in the intricate network of associations that interconnect their ideas. Moreover, these associations are often quite remote in nature, and sometimes highly personal, even autistic. In any case, this associative subtlety allows the creator to combine ideas in even more unusual ways, just as is argued in Barsalou and Prinz's chapter.

Third, Barsalou and Prinz theorize that the context independence of perceptual symbols should also enable a person to display exceptional creativity. That is, not all such symbols need be highly domain specific, many cutting across two or more domains. This conjecture seems to fit what is known about the cognitive style of notable creators (Eysenck, 1995; Simonton, 1994). For example, highly creative individuals tend to exhibit extreme "category width," extending their concepts into domains that others might not deem relevant. Indeed, creative individuals tend to display an "overinclusiveness" of thought that verges on the psychopathological. They may jump from one idea to another using the loosest criteria of relevance. William James (1880) put it nicely in an essay now over a century old:

> Instead of thoughts of concrete things patiently following one another in a beaten track of habitual suggestion, we have the most abrupt cross-cuts and transitions from one idea to another, the most rarefied abstractions and discriminations, the most unheard of combination of elements, the subtlest associations of analogy; in a word, we seem suddenly introduced into a seething cauldron of ideas, where everything is fizzling and bobbling about in a state of bewildering activity, where partnerships can be joined or loosened in an instant, treadmill routine is unknown, and the unexpected seems only law. (p. 456)

In sum, Barsalou and Prinz's discussion of perceptual symbols, although initially motivated by a need to confront theories of amodal thought, can also provide a cognitive framework for treating several crucial characteristics of exceptional creators—even creative geniuses.

CONCLUDING REMARKS

I close my commentary by discussing an issue raised in several chapters in this volume. The question is the relation between mundane and exceptional creativity. This is clearly a rather critical matter. The world at large is mostly interested in the kind of creativity that produces culturally valued products. In contrast, cognitive psychologists are prone to focus more on everyday varieties of creativity. If exceptional creativity is simply a more pronounced or more exaggerated form of everyday creativity, as many have argued (e.g., Weisberg, 1992), then this difference is of small importance. However, if there is something qualitatively distinct about exceptional creativity, then the strategy of starting the inquiries "from below" may be ill-advised. So what justification is there for presuming some quantitative continuity between everyday and truly unusual instances of the phenomenon?

On the one hand, it would seem possible to order creative acts in a fairly continuous sequence from commonplace to rare forms. Take language production as a case in point. Consider the zero point here as the exact imitation of a sentence just heard. Slightly above that, perhaps, would be a verbatim repetition with a deliberate change in inflection that changes the meaning (e.g., converting a declarative into an interrogative sentence). Next would come a paraphrase of the sentence, and so forth. One would thus move progressively up the ladder of incremental creativity until one obtains the monumental utterances of a William Shakespeare. Presumably, each progressive step would not require any fundamentally different cognitive processes, but rather the processes used in previous steps would be applied with greater force or intensity.

On the other hand, it seems unlikely that there would exist no "quantum jumps" somewhere along this quantitative dimension. At some point new cognitive processes may kick in that did not participate earlier in the sequence. Or, mechanisms lower down may combine in novel ways, yielding certain emergent properties. Return again to the language example, but conceive it in a different fashion. Can one establish a continuous series connecting the call systems of primates with the linguistic output of an adult human being? It does not seem likely. The discontinuity is very obvious, and even attempts to provide apes with language training have not appreciably closed that gap. Whatever the cognitive processes may be that permit humans to generate syntactically and semantically complex sentences, the anthropoids lack them, or at least cannot organize those processes to the same end. Researchers who wanted to advance scientific understanding of human language use could not have advanced very far if they had confined their studies solely to apes or monkeys.

It is possible that the line connecting mundane and exceptional creativity exhibits the same dramatic discontinuity. Perhaps the jump occurs between the kind of creativity that permits the adaptation to the problems of everyday life and the kind of creativity that produces concrete products. Or maybe the jump appears higher up in the series, between those who have the expertise to generate products and those who have whatever else is necessary to create products that actually have an impact on their field or on the world. Perhaps there exist multiple gaps. At this point no one knows, but the only way to ever find out is to study the phenomenon of creativity at both ends. Those who investigate mundane creativity must have counterparts whose inquiries concentrate on exceptional creativity. If everything goes right, the two sets of researchers will eventually identify where the smooth meet the abrupt portions of the supposed line linking everyday creativity with creative genius.

REFERENCES

Amabile, T. M. (1983). *The social psychology of creativity.* New York: Springer-Verlag.

Barron, F. X. (1969). *Creative person and creative process.* New York: Holt, Rinehart & Winston.

Berlyne, D. (1971). *Aesthetics and psychobiology.* New York: Appleton-Century-Crofts.

Csikszentmihalyi, M., & Sawyer, K. (1995). Creative insight: The social dimension of a solitary moment. In R. J. Sternberg & J. E. Davidson (Eds.), *The nature of insight* (pp. 329–364). Cambridge, MA: MIT.

Derks, P. L. (1994). Clockwork Shakespeare: The Bard meets the Regressive Imagery Dictionary. *Empirical Studies of the Arts, 12,* 131–139.

Diamond, A. M., Jr. (1980). Age and the acceptance of cliometrics. *Journal of Economic History, 40,* 838–841.

Donovan, A., Laudan, L., & Laudan, R. (Eds.). (1988). *Scrutinizing science: Empirical studies of scientific change.* Dordrecht, The Netherlands: Kluwer.

Dunbar, K. (1995). How scientists really reason: Scientific reasoning in real-world laboratories. In R. J. Sternberg & J. E. Davidson (Eds.), *The nature of insight* (pp. 365–396). Cambridge, MA: MIT.

Ericsson, K. A., & Charness, N. (1994). Expert performance: Its structure and acquisition. *American Psychologist, 49*, 725–747.

Ericsson, K. A., Krampe, R. T., & Tesch-Römer, C. (1993). The role of deliberate practice in the acquisition of expert performance. *Psychological Review, 100*, 363–406.

Eysenck, H. J. (1995). *Genius: The natural history of creativity.* Cambridge, England: Cambridge University Press.

Getzels, J., & Jackson, P. W. (1962). *Creativity and intelligence: Explorations with gifted students.* New York: Wiley.

Ghiselin, B. (Ed.). (1952). *The creative process: A symposium.* Berkeley: University of California Press.

Golomb, C. (Ed.). (1995). *The development of artistically gifted children: Selected case studies.* Hillsdale, NJ: Erlbaum.

Guilford, J. P. (1967). *The nature of human intelligence.* New York: McGraw-Hill.

Hadamard, J. (1945). *The psychology of invention in the mathematical field.* Princeton, NJ: Princeton University Press.

Hennessey, B. A., & Amabile, T. M. (1988). The conditions of creativity. In R. J. Sternberg (Ed.), *The nature of creativity: Contemporary psychological perspectives* (pp. 11–38). Cambridge, England: Cambridge University Press.

Hull, D. L., Tessner, P. D., & Diamond, A. M. (1978). Planck's principle: Do younger scientists accept new scientific ideas with greater alacrity than older scientists? *Science, 202*, 717–723.

James, W. (1880). Great men, great thoughts, and the environment. *Atlantic Monthly, 46*, 441–459.

Kantorovich, A., (1993). *Scientific discovery: Logic and tinkering.* Albany, NY: State University of New York Press.

MacKinnon, D. W. (1978). *In search of human effectiveness.* Buffalo, NJ: Creative Education Foundation.

Macrone, M. (1990). *Brush up your Shakespeare!.* New York: Harper & Row.

Martindale, C. (1975). *Romantic progression: The psychology of literary history.* Washington, DC: Hemisphere.

Martindale, C. (1990). *The clockwork muse: The predictability of artistic styles.* New York: Basic Books.

Roe, A. (1952). *The making of a scientist.* New York: Dodd, Mead.

Root-Bernstein, R. S. (1989). *Discovering.* Cambridge, MA: Harvard University Press.

Rostan, S. M. (1994). Problem finding, problem solving, and cognitive controls: An empirical investigation of critically acclaimed productivity. *Creativity Research Journal, 7*, 97–110.

Simonton, D. K. (1980a). Thematic fame and melodic originality in classical music: A multivariate computer-content analysis. *Journal of Personality, 48*, 206–219.

Simonton, D. K. (1980b). Thematic fame, melodic originality, and musical zeitgeist: A biographical and transhistorical content analysis. *Journal of Personality and Social Psychology, 38*, 972–983.

Simonton, D. K. (1983). Dramatic greatness and content: A quantitative study of eighty-one Athenian and Shakespearean plays. *Empirical Studies of the Arts, 1*, 109–123.

Simonton, D. K. (1984). *Genius, creativity, and leadership: Historiometric inquiries.* Cambridge, MA: Harvard University Press.

Simonton, D. K. (1986). Popularity, content, and context in 37 Shakespeare plays. *Poetics, 15*, 493–510.

Simonton, D. K. (1987). Musical aesthetics and creativity in Beethoven: A computer analysis of 105 compositions. *Empirical Studies of the Arts, 5*, 87–104.

Simonton, D. K. (1988). *Scientific genius: A psychology of science.* Cambridge, England: Cambridge University Press.

Simonton, D. K. (1994). *Greatness: Who makes history and why?* New York: Guilford Press.

Simonton, D. K. (1996). Creativity. In J. E. Birren (Ed.), *Encyclopedia of Gerontology* (pp. 341–351). San Diego, CA: Academic Press.

Wallach, M. A., & Kogan, N. (1965). *Modes of thinking in young children.* New York: Holt, Rinehart & Winston.

Weisberg, R. W. (1992). *Creativity: Beyond the myth of genius.* New York: Freeman.

PART THREE

Metaphor

13

Metaphor Comprehension: How Metaphors Create New Categories

Sam Glucksberg, Deanna Ann Manfredi, and Matthew S. McGlone

Everyday conversation is littered with metaphorical language, as this sentence self-consciously illustrates. And, as this previous sentence also illustrates, figurative expressions apparently violate categories. After all, a conversation cannot literally be littered with anything, let alone with a type of language, and only animate beings can be self-conscious, certainly not sentences! Yet such sentences seem to pose no problems for people when either reading or engaging in everyday conversation.

THE PROBLEM AND A PARADOX

In this chapter we focus on one genre of figurative expressions, nominal metaphors. The focus is on nominal metaphors precisely because they are an everyday example of creative cognition in action. Although they appear to be category violations, at the same time they are used either to ex-

We are grateful for the financial support provided by Public Health Service Grant #HD25826 awarded to Princeton University and Sam Glucksberg, principal investigator. The research reported here was performed as part of a doctoral dissertation submitted to Princeton University by Deanna Ann Manfredi. We thank Philip Johnson-Laird, Dale Miller, and Steven Greene for their comments on a draft of the manuscript.

tend established categories or, if no relevant categories exist, to create new ones. Nominal metaphors are statements of the form *X* is a *Y*, where *X* is the metaphor topic and *Y* the metaphor vehicle, and where *X* is not usually considered a member of the category *Y*. Consider the following assertions, each of which involves an apparent category violation:[1]

1a. His car was a lemon.
1b. My job is a jail.
1c. My surgeon was a butcher.
1d. My butcher is a real surgeon!
1e. New York may well be the next Orange County.
1f. Our love has become a filing cabinet.

From a literalist linguistic perspective, each of these assertions is false because each commits a category error: The metaphor topic is not the same kind of thing as the metaphor vehicle. Cars cannot be citrus fruits, jobs cannot be buildings, surgeons and butchers are mutually exclusive occupations, New York cannot become a county in California, and an interpersonal relationship cannot become an item of office furniture.

If these categorical assertions are false, then how can people accept them as true? One way to make each of these statements true is to treat them not as categorical assertions, but instead as implicit comparisons. My surgeon is not really a butcher, but she or he can be like a butcher. At first glance, this makes sense, but a moment's reflection reveals that our comprehension problem is in no way solved. Exactly how could my surgeon be like a butcher, and exactly how could my car be like a lemon? Both surgeons and butchers are occupations, and both cars and lemons are nonanimate, but neither of these interpretations makes any sense. Whether an assertion is in categorical or in comparison form, a listener or reader must infer the intended ground of the metaphor; that is, one must infer what

[1]Metaphors can of course be true (e.g., "Newport will never be an Orange County"). Such assertions are not category violations, but avoiding such violations is hardly sufficient to ensure an apt expression. Newport will never be an infinite number of things, but only a small set of such things would be considered interesting or relevant. The issue of relevance is addressed later in the chapter.

a speaker (or writer) intends to say about the metaphor topic by characterizing it as, or comparing it with, the metaphor vehicle.

One clue to this puzzle may lie in what we have termed the *paradox of unlike things compared.* According to the *Random House Dictionary* (1967), metaphors involve two unlike things compared, (i.e., two things that are not of the same kind). Thus, jobs and jails, surgeons and butchers, and love and filing cabinets are each pairs of concepts that ordinarily belong to different superordinate categories. Literal comparisons, in contrast, involve two like things compared, as in

2a. Copper is like tin.
2b. Coffee is like tea.
2c. Limes are like lemons.

In each of these cases, the two terms of the comparison do belong to the same taxonomic categories (viz., metals, beverages, and citrus fruits, respectively).

Because of this difference, literal and metaphorical comparisons behave differently in a paradoxical but important way. Metaphors involve two unlike things compared, yet they can be paraphrased as categorical assertions and still retain their original meaning. Thus, one can either say "my job is a jail" or "my job is like a jail" and mean pretty much the same thing. Literal comparisons involve two like things compared, but they cannot be paraphrased as category assertions and still make sense, for example,

3a. Copper is tin.
3b. Coffee is tea.
3c. Limes are lemons.

Thus, the paradox: Two unlike things compared can be paraphrased as a categorical assertion, whereas two like things compared cannot. This paradox may hold the key to a fundamental difference between literal and metaphoric comparisons. We argue that metaphors are not understood as comparisons, but rather as property attributions that either extend old categories or create new ones (see Kittay, 1982, for a similar view).

Consider, first, how metaphors behave as categorical assertions. When a metaphor uses a conventional vehicle, that metaphor may add a new member to an existing category, as in

4a. Libraries are gold mines.
4b. Inventions can be gold mines.

In each of these assertions, the term *gold mines* is used to refer to a general category of things that are valuable in some way. In 4a, libraries are classified as gold mines, and the general concept of valuable things is instantiated as a valuable resource of books and reference materials. In 4b, that same general concept is instantiated in a different way, either as rich in monetary rewards or as productive and valuable. In both cases, a general category is instantiated so as to be relevant and diagnostic about the metaphor topic.[2]

When a term is used as a metaphor vehicle for the first time, as in novel metaphor, then a new category is created. Consider the following:

5a. New York could be the next Orange County.
5b. So, John Demjanjuk is not a Demjanjuk after all!
5c. Our love has become a filing cabinet.

What are the newly created categories in each of these assertions? In 5a, *Orange County* is used to refer to a kind of governmental entity that is bankrupted by fiscal mismanagement. Orange County, California, has come to exemplify such entities, and its name has become synonymous with any locality that finds itself in similar straits. In 5b, one finds an analogous use of a proper name. John Demjanjuk is the name of a man who stood trial in Israel on charges that he had been a sadistic Nazi prison guard at the Treblinka death camp in Poland during World War II. While the trial was going on "the name 'Demjanjuk' [had] become a noun in Israel, a word to identify an ordinary person capable of committing un-

[2]Abstract "generic" concepts are discussed and elaborated by Fauconnier and Turner (1994), who view such abstraction as a general cognitive process for constructing inferences and interpretations of the sort exemplified in metaphor comprehension.

speakable acts" (Shinoff, 1987). An Israeli spectator attending the trial and an American news reporter had the following conversation:

Israeli: "If he is a Demjanjuk, then he should be condemned to death."

Reporter: "But he is Demjanjuk, his name is John Demjanjuk."

Israeli: "I know his name is Demjanjuk, but I don't know if he is *a* Demjanjuk." (Shinoff, 1987, p. A8, emphasis added)

As it turned out, John Demjanjuk was found not guilty. He himself now no longer belonged to the category of "ordinary people capable of committing unspeakable acts," although he had given his name to that category.

For both 5a and 5b, knowledge of the literal referents of the metaphor vehicles *Orange County* and *John Demjanjuk* is a sufficient condition for understanding these metaphors. If one knows about the literal referent, Orange County, then 5a is immediately comprehensible, even if Orange County were to be used as a metaphor vehicle for the very first time. Similarly, if a reader knows about the literal referent, John Demjanjuk, then that metaphor is also immediately comprehensible.

For most people, the assertion about a love becoming a filing cabinet (5c) is not immediately understood. Why are novel metaphorical assertions such as 5a and 5b immediately understood by people who know the literal referents of the metaphor vehicles, whereas a novel assertion such as 5c is not, even though everyone knows the literal referent of filing cabinets? This question really raises two issues, one about discourse-naming strategies, the other about the processes involved in creating new categories. The first issue concerns the principles that govern how new categories are referred to; that is, how do we decide what word or words to use to talk about a newly created category? The second issue is how are such new categories created in the first place? We take these issues up in turn.

NAMING NEW CATEGORIES: DUAL REFERENCE

According to our paradox of unlike things compared, a literal comparison assertion such as "limes are like lemons" cannot be paraphrased as the categorical assertion "limes are lemons." However, all comparisons, including literal ones, can always be expressed as categorical assertions because all comparisons entail a category assignment. Consider how people usually describe similarities. How are limes and lemons alike? To this question, most people would reply that they are both citrus fruits. A likely reply to the question "how are *X* and *Y* alike?" is a category assignment, usually the closest superordinate that encompasses the two concepts, as in the following:[3]

6a. How are lemons and grapes alike? both fruits.
6b. lemons and lamb chops? both foods.
6c. lemons and insects? both organic.
6d. lemons and newspapers?

The answer to 6d is not obvious because there is no readily available category that sensibly includes both items. In keeping with this notion, the most difficult item in the Wechsler Adult Intelligence Scale's Similarities subscale (Wechsler, 1958) is how a fly and a tree are alike. The answer is that they are both alive or both organic—categories that are rather far removed from either exemplar.

If literal comparisons can be expressed in terms of joint category memberships, then metaphorical expressions should also be expressible in the same fashion. And indeed they are, as seen in the paradox of unlike things compared. However, the name of the metaphorical category also happens to be the name of one of the members of the comparison, the metaphor vehicle. As Roger Brown noted some time ago, "metaphor differs from other superordinate–subordinate relations in that the superordinate *is not given a name of its own.* Instead, the name of one subordinate [i.e., the vehicle] is extended to the other" (Brown, 1958, p. 140, emphasis added). What kind of categories are involved in such relations?

In expressions such as "my job is a jail," the concept my job is assigned

[3]The Wechsler Adult Intelligence Scale (Wechsler, 1958) includes a Similarities subscale. According to the scoring manual, the answer to a question such as "how are *X* and *Y* alike?" is the name of the category to which they belong (e.g., for banana and apple, the respondent should say that they are both fruits).

to a category that is referred to as a jail. In such assertions, the term jail has two referents. One of these referents is the literal jail (i.e., a building used to confine prisoners). The other referent is the metaphoric jail, the category that the literal concept jail exemplifies (i.e., things or situations that are involuntary, unpleasant, confining, punishing, unrewarding, oppressive, etc.). When such a category is used to characterize a metaphor topic, it functions as an *attributive category* in that it provides properties to be attributed to the metaphor topic. The category of jail in its broadest sense is such an attributive category (Glucksberg & Keysar, 1990). With extensive use, a metaphor's meaning can become conventional. When this happens, heretofore non-lexicalized categories, such as disastrous military interventions, can become lexicalized, as in the expression "Cambodia had become Vietnam's Vietnam." In this example, the dual reference function of the term *Vietnam* is explicit. It occurs twice, and its referent on the first occasion is different from its referent on the second occasion. The first mention of Vietnam refers to the country itself; the second refers to the category of disastrous military interventions that the Vietnam war has come to epitomize. Because the experience of the United States in Vietnam has become a metaphor for disastrous political and military policies, Vietnam provides a name for such policies in general. More recently, Somalia became a similar metaphor, and Bosnia has now become one as well.

Dual reference is thus a general strategy wherein the name of a prototypical category instance is used as the name for the category itself. This strategy is not unique to metaphor; it is a ubiquitous strategy for naming superordinate categories that have no names of their own. When a superordinate category is not lexicalized, then the name of a prototypical exemplar can be used as the name for that category. The use of particular brand names to refer to their generic categories provides a common example. Among the many instances of such dual reference are Kleenex for paper tissues, Xerox for copying machines, Jeep for off-road four-wheel-drive vehicles, Band-Aids for small adhesive bandages, Jello for gelatin desserts, and Q-tips for cotton swabs.[4] In classifier languages, in

[4]I thank David Albritton for calling my attention to some of these examples.

which superordinate categories are generally not lexicalized, the dual reference strategy is used routinely: prototypical exemplar names are used to refer to their superordinate categories. For example, in Hopi (a native American language spoken in the Southwest of the United States), the name for cottonwood is used to refer to the category of trees in general (Trager, 1936–1939). Yet another example of dual reference can be found in idioms in which a prototypical instance of a general category is used to refer to that category. Consider the idiom "to look for a needle in a haystack." This idiom can be used to refer simultaneously to the literal action of searching for an actual needle in an actual haystack, and to the general category of searching for a minuscule target that is hidden in a vast search space, whether that target is a physical object, such as a quark in a distant galaxy, or an abstract entity, such as an optimal move in a complex theorem-proving algorithm.

As with metaphors, expressions that use dual reference can be framed either as comparison statements or as class-inclusion statements. Thus, one can say either "my job is a jail" or "my job is like a jail"; "the Suzuki Samurai is a jeep" or "the Suzuki Samurai is like a jeep"; "Looking for the gene that controls a specific metabolic function is or is like looking for a needle in a haystack." As these examples suggest, one criterial test for dual reference is the ability to paraphrase a class membership assertion as a comparison statement, and vice versa. Because metaphors can be paraphrased in this way, metaphor vehicles are clearly used to make dual reference—to the literal category instance and to the attributive category that it exemplifies (Glucksberg & Keysar, 1990, 1993).

An Empirical Implication

According to the dual reference hypothesis, a metaphor vehicle such as *shackle* in the expression "a responsibility is a shackle" can be used to refer to the concrete, physical device that is made of metal, often has chains, can be locked around someone's arms and legs, and so forth, and it can also be use to refer to the abstract, general category of constraining entities. We refer to such abstract, general concepts as attributive categories. Such categories are used to attribute properties to topics of interest.

The intended referent of a metaphor vehicle is, therefore, to the attributive category, not to the specific concrete instance from which the category takes its name. The term *shackle* in the responsibilities metaphor refers directly to the abstract, general category of constraining entities, and only indirectly to the concrete physical object that is made of metal and is fastened on someone's arms and legs. One implication of this claim is that if the literal concrete referent of a metaphor vehicle is foregrounded, then its more abstract, general meaning—the relevant attributive category—should be less accessible for use in metaphor comprehension. Thus, if a metaphor vehicle such as *shackle* were to appear in a context that foregrounded its literal meaning, then its metaphorical meaning should be relatively less accessible.

One way to test this idea is to use a technique devised by Wolff and Gentner (1992), who developed a priming paradigm to investigate the information provided by metaphor topics and vehicles. Their reasoning was straightforward: If metaphor topics and vehicles each provide useful information for metaphor comprehension, then providing either the topic or vehicle in advance of the metaphor itself should facilitate comprehension. Metaphor topics and vehicles were each used as primes in a timed metaphor comprehension task. Participants read target metaphors that were preceded either by a blank screen or by the topic term or the vehicle term. Both topics and vehicles facilitated processing as measured by reading time. For example, people understood a metaphor such as "a responsibility is a shackle" more quickly when they were first given either the topic (responsibility) or the vehicle (shackle) in advance of the metaphor itself, compared with the baseline condition in which they saw neither word in advance.

This priming paradigm provides a way to test the idea that metaphor vehicles that are set in literal contexts do not provide useful information for understanding a metaphor using that vehicle. It would not be useful because the vehicle term would initially be understood only at its concrete level of meaning. Its more abstract, metaphorical meaning would not be generated until the metaphor itself becomes available. Therefore, seeing a metaphor vehicle in advance under such circumstances would not facilitate subsequent metaphor processing. Metaphor topics, on the other hand, are understood at just one level of abstraction: The metaphor topic term refers only to the specific concept that it names. Thus, setting a metaphor topic in an irrelevant literal context should have no particular deleterious effect on the informative value of that topic.

Manfredi (1994) tested this hypothesis by using both topics and vehicles as primes for the same kinds of metaphors that were used by Wolff and Gentner. The primes, however, were not just single words, such as *responsibility* or *shackle*, but instead could be sentences that were irrelevant to the grounds of their target metaphors. Irrelevant sentences attribute a property to the topic or the vehicle that is not related to the target metaphor (but need not conflict with it).

For example, the topic-priming sentence "a responsibility can be shared" is not relevant to the responsibility–shackle metaphor but should still facilitate metaphor comprehension. Recall that in Wolff and Gentner's experiment, a metaphor topic alone, presented in advance of a metaphor, facilitated comprehension. A metaphor topic in an unrelated sentence context should still facilitate metaphor comprehension because its meaning, or sense, is unaffected by that context. In the previous responsibilities example, the referent of the term *responsibilities* does not change from the *shackle* context to the *shared* context. In both cases, the word *responsibilities* refers to the same class of situations or states (viz., being accountable or obligated to one or more persons for something). Furthermore, that class of states or situations remains at the same level of abstraction in the two contexts.

Metaphor vehicles, on the other hand, may not retain their same meanings from one context to another because, as we claim, a metaphor vehicle has dual reference: to the literal concrete concept and to the category that it exemplifies. A priming sentence such as "a shackle can be rusty" specifies the literal concrete referent of the word *shackle*. If understanding the metaphor "responsibility is a shackle" requires understanding that the referent of the word *shackle* is the more general attributive category of entities and situations that confine, then the "rusty" context in which the word *shackle* appears should not facilitate metaphor comprehension. There is no particular reason that it should interfere either; but by referring only to the literal referent *shackles* it should not provide any useful advance information for metaphor processing. Note that there is nothing misleading about the "rusty" sentence, nor is it inconsistent with the metaphorical meaning of responsibilities being constraining like shackles. It is simply irrelevant to that meaning.

In Manfredi's (1994) experiments, college students were instructed to read metaphorical sentences such as "responsibility is a shackle" and to press a response key as soon as they understood the sentence. The time between target sentence onset and key press served as the measure of reading time, which in turn was taken as a measure of comprehension time. Manfredi used a number of different test conditions in her series of experiments, but only five need concern us here. One of the five was a control condition, in which a row of asterisks appeared on a computer screen, followed by a target sentence. This condition provided a baseline measure of comprehension time. The other four conditions used four different priming stimuli: topic alone, vehicle alone, irrelevant topic sentence, and irrelevant vehicle sentence. For the target metaphor "responsibility is a shackle," the four different primes were *responsibility*, *shackle*, *a responsibility can be shared*, and *a shackle can be rusty*.

Our predictions were straightforward: Both topic alone and vehicle alone should facilitate comprehension. Topics in irrelevant sentence contexts should also facilitate comprehension because the referent of the topic word should be unaffected by those contexts. However, vehicles in irrelevant sentence contexts refer at the concrete–literal level of abstraction, and so should not facilitate comprehension because their intended referents are at a different level of abstraction—the attributive category level.

Our results were as expected. Clear priming effects were obtained for topics and vehicles alone as well as for topics in irrelevant contexts. Mean baseline comprehension time (no prime condition) was 2,600 ms. Mean comprehension times for topic, vehicle, and unrelated topic sentence conditions were 2,298, 2,356, and 2,345 ms, respectively, indicating priming effects of about 270 ms overall. In contrast, no priming was observed for vehicles in irrelevant sentence contexts, where the mean comprehension time was slightly longer than baseline (2,617 ms). Apparently, seeing a vehicle term in a sentence that refers to the literal meaning of that vehicle provides no useful information for processing its metaphoric meaning. This finding is consistent with the notion of dual reference: Metaphor vehicles can be understood at two levels of abstraction, the literal concrete and attributive category levels. The attributive category level is the one that is relevant to metaphor comprehension.

Creating New Categories: How Topics and Vehicles Interact

The Given–New Convention and Topic and Vehicle Roles

In the kinds of metaphors we have been focusing on, the vehicle (predicate) term provides candidate properties for the topic (subject) term. The question remains, how are candidate properties generated and selected? Consider the assertion "our love has become a filing cabinet." What must people know about the concepts love and filing cabinets in order to understand what a speaker might intend by the assertion "our love has become a filing cabinet"? From a communicative viewpoint, people must be able to infer the potentially relevant properties of both the metaphor topic (e.g., our love) and metaphor vehicle (e.g., filing cabinet). Because topic and vehicle play different roles in metaphor, the kinds of properties that would be relevant for each will also differ. Metaphor topics are the given information in metaphorical assertions, whereas metaphor vehicles are the source of new information. Put most simply, the vehicle is used to characterize or describe the topic. Some property or set of properties of the metaphor vehicle is to be attributed to the metaphor topic.

For any given metaphor topic, certain attributes will be potentially relevant, whereas others will not. For the topic of love, for example, such attributes as duration (ephemeral vs. eternal and endless), level of emotional arousal (cold vs. fiery and passionate), and level of commitment (flighty vs. dedicated) could be relevant (among many others). Other attributes, such as financial cost, size, or shape would be either irrelevant or nonapplicable to the topic of love. To be relevant, a characterization on any particular attribute must be diagnostic in the sense of discriminating the particular metaphor topic from its cohort of plausible alternatives. Hence, a passionate love is importantly different from a cold love, whereas a love that began on a Monday need not be importantly different (if at all) from one that began on a Wednesday. Relevance for metaphor topics, then, might best be described at the level of dimensions of attribution rather than at the level of specific properties. Thus, a metaphor topic provides potentially relevant dimensions for attribution, but not their specific values. We refer to properties as values on dimensions of attribution. For a topic such as surgeons, for example, level of skill would be a relevant dimension. A low value on this dimension would be a negative property of surgeons, a high value would be a positive property.

According to this view, metaphor topics provide dimensions of attribution to be assigned values. Metaphor topics vary in terms of the number of dimensions that can be relevant. Some metaphor topics have relatively few relevant dimensions of attribution, and so place a high level of constraint on potential attributions. The topic "some plastic surgeons," for example, might be expected to be described in terms of such dimensions as area of specialization, skill, and cost, but not in terms of such irrelevant dimensions as height, knowledge of Greek antiquity, or musical ability. In contrast, other metaphor topics, such as "his life," provide very few constraints on potential attributions. There are far more things that one can say about a topic such as "his life" than one can say about a topic such as "some plastic surgeons." Metaphor topics can thus vary in terms of the level of constraint that they place on interpretation. High-constraining topics have relatively few dimensions of attribution; low-constraining topics have relatively many.

Metaphor vehicles play a different role. They are used to refer to the attributive categories that provide candidate properties to be attributed to a metaphor topic. Just as metaphor topics can vary in terms of their numbers of relevant dimensions, metaphor vehicles can vary with respect to the range and kinds of values that they can specify on those dimensions. Some metaphor vehicles are unambiguous in the sense that they uniquely exemplify an attributive category that can specify relevant values. Metaphor vehicles such as butcher or jail are relatively unambiguous in this way. Butcher exemplifies the category of people who are (a) incompetent in a particularly bungling and sloppy way or (b) bloody and violent; *jail* exemplifies situations that are unpleasant and confining. Other metaphor vehicles are relatively ambiguous because they do not uniquely exemplify an attributive category. Metaphor vehicles such as *garden* or *filing cabinet* are ambiguous in this way: Neither *garden* nor *filing cabinet* are prototypes of a distinct attributive category. Without a reasonably constraining topic, the candidate properties they provide cannot be uniquely identified. With such ambiguous vehicles, a metaphor topic is needed to provide the dimensions of property attribution (i.e., attribute dimensions whose values can be specified).

Even with unambiguous vehicles, metaphor topics play an important role. The metaphor vehicle butcher, for example, can be used to attribute the general property of bungling to a metaphor topic, but different topics would require different instantiations of bungling. Surgeons who are butchers cut human tissue inexpertly and so do harm instead of healing. On the other hand, a pianist who butchers a Chopin nocturne causes aesthetic rather than physical anguish. Furthermore, for a metaphor to be sensible, vehicles, whatever their level of ambiguity, always require a relevant topic. The metaphor vehicle butcher, for example, is so conventional and unambiguous that its meaning of a bungling person is listed in contemporary dictionaries as the second or third entry after *meat cutter*, yet it still requires a relevant topic to produce a sensible metaphor. Thus, an unskilled cabinetmaker can be said to butcher his or her jobs and so can be referred to as a butcher (as in "You're not having that butcher do your dining room table!"). Filing clerks, on the other hand, are not usually thought to require any appreciable level of skill or finesse to accomplish their tasks, and so to say that "my filing clerk is a butcher" would not be apt. Characterizing a filing clerk as a butcher is somewhat anomalous because level of skill is not a relevant dimension of attribution for filing clerks.

To understand a metaphor thus requires two kinds of knowledge. First, one must know enough about the topic to appreciate which kinds of characterizations would be interesting and meaningful in a particular discourse context and which would not (i.e., one must know the relevant attributes of the topic). To understand the surgeons–butchers assertion, for example, one must know that level of skill is an important attribute of surgeons. It is important because it specifies one relevant dimension of variation within the category of surgeons: Surgeons who are skillful are preferable to those who are not (to say the least!). Second, one must know enough about the metaphor vehicle to know what kinds of things it can epitomize, that is, what attributive category it might represent. Given this kind of knowledge base, metaphors with ambiguous vehicles can be readily understood when the metaphor topic has relevant dimensions of attribution and is reasonably constraining. Similarly, metaphors with relatively unconstraining topics can be readily understood when the metaphor vehicle is relevant and reasonably unambiguous. In this sense, metaphor topics and vehicles are used interactively to generate interpretations.[5]

One implication of this interaction view is that metaphor topics and vehicles contribute different kinds of information to guide comprehension. Manfredi (1994) tested this implication using the priming paradigm designed by Wolff and Gentner (1992). Wolff and Gentner reasoned that if metaphor topics and vehicles each provide useful information for metaphor comprehension, then providing either the topic or vehicle in advance of the metaphor itself should facilitate comprehension.

Metaphor topics and metaphor vehicles were each used as primes in a timed metaphor comprehension task. Both metaphor topics and vehicles facilitated processing as measured by comprehension time. Wolff and Gentner interpreted this finding as supporting a property-matching model of metaphor comprehension. According to such models, properties of a metaphor topic (e.g., responsibility) and of a metaphor vehicle (e.g., shackles) are first extracted nonselectively and then exhaustively checked against each other. Once matching properties are identified, those that are relevant and informative can then be selected as the grounds for the comparison. Once either a metaphor topic or a metaphor vehicle is provided

[5]The interaction view we propose is essentially an instantiation of Max Black's (1962, 1979) interaction theory of metaphor.

in advance of the metaphor itself, the comprehension process can begin with the hypothesized first stage: the exhaustive extraction of properties that is required before matching can begin.

Our property attribution view provides an alternative interpretation. Recall that topics can vary from having relatively few to relatively many dimensions for attribution. In this view, high-constraining topics have few such dimensions and so can provide useful information for metaphor comprehension. Low-constraining topics have many such dimensions, and so would provide very little useful information when presented in isolation. Accordingly, high-constraining topics should be highly effective as primes for metaphor processing, whereas low-constraining topics should be less so. In Wolff and Gentner's exhaustive property extraction–matching interpretation, any kind of metaphor topic should facilitate comprehension because speeding up the property extraction process can always provide a head start for the second stage of property matching.

Analogously, metaphor vehicles can vary from relatively unambiguous to relatively ambiguous. Unambiguous vehicles, presented in isolation, should provide useful information for subsequent metaphor processing, but ambiguous vehicles should not. Again, Wolff and Gentner's interpretation suggests that providing any kind of metaphor vehicle in advance, regardless of level of ambiguity, should facilitate processing because property extraction can begin sooner and so provide a head start for the subsequent property-matching stage.

Because Wolff and Gentner did not select metaphor topics and vehicles on the bases of constraint and ambiguity levels, respectively, their results cannot discriminate between their property-matching view and our interactive property attribution view. We thus designed an experiment to test the interactive property attribution view by assessing whether level of topic constraint and level of vehicle ambiguity provide differential information for metaphor comprehension. Our predictions were that highly constraining topics should be effective as primes for metaphor comprehension, whereas low-constraining topics should be either less effective or not effective at all. Analogously, unambiguous vehicles should be effective as primes for metaphor comprehension; ambiguous vehicles should be either less effective or not effective at all.

Target metaphors were presented with no advance information, or with one of four types of primes: high- or low-constraining topic, or unambiguous or ambiguous vehicle. A high-constraining topic is one that can plausibly be described in relatively few ways; a low-constraining topic is one that can be described in relatively many ways. For this experiment Manfredi first prepared a list of candidate topic terms: 15 potentially high constraining and 15 potentially low constraining. An independent group of college student participants was given a questionnaire with the 30 candidate items. These participants were asked to list for each item as many relevant things that they could think of to say about that item. If people can think of very few things to say about a topic, then one should be able to predict what might be said about that topic. If people can think of very many things to say about a topic, then one should be less able to predict what might be said about that topic.

Items that received an average of less than four questions were considered high constraining; those that received more than four questions were considered low constraining. An example of a high-constraining topic is plastic surgeon. One participant listed the following for this topic: cost of operation, quality of work, experience, and ethical questions. An example of a low-constraining topic is school. This same participant listed eight things about school: level, public–private, location, cost, quality of teaching, quality of students, extracurricular activities, and transportation to and from. The 12 highest- and lowest-rated items were selected for inclusion in the experiment proper. Examples of low-constraining topics are life, vacation, school, and crime; examples of high-constraining topics are beggar, smile, plastic surgeon, and memory.

Metaphor vehicles were generated and selected in an analogous way. An unambiguous vehicle is one about which there is high agreement about the properties it can attribute to a topic. An ambiguous vehicle is one about which people tend to disagree. Forty candidate vehicles, 20 potentially unambiguous and 20 potentially ambiguous, were presented in questionnaire form to an independent sample of participants. The items appeared in the form *X* is a *Y*, where *Y* was the concept to be rated (e.g., "*X* is a *prison*"). Participants were instructed to provide the one thing that would be (metaphorically) true of *X* given the information that *X* is a *Y* (e.g., "*X* is a prison"). For the item *X* is a life, participants offered such attributes as lotto winner, happiness, worth saving, long, easy existence, fun, and has rights. No two participants provided the same attribute for this obviously ambiguous metaphor vehicle. In contrast, there was high agreement for the concept gold mine. Over 70% of the participants listed *valuable* as a property for gold mine. The 12 items that elicited the highest agreement were selected as unambiguous vehicles; the 12 that elicited the lowest agreement were selected as ambiguous vehicles. Examples of ambiguous vehicles are garden, journey life, and filing cabinet; examples of unambiguous vehicles are prison, crutch, and weapon.

The two types of metaphor topics and two types of metaphor vehicles were then used to generate four kinds of metaphors for the experiment proper. For each of the high-constraining and low-constraining topics, a vehicle was chosen that, in the experimenters' judgment, was relatively unambiguous and produced a sensible metaphor. Similarly, for each of the unambiguous and ambiguous vehicles, a topic was chosen that, again in our judgment, was moderately constraining and also produced a sensible metaphor. The intent was to generate a set of four kinds of metaphors that would be equally comprehensible: metaphors with high- and with low-constraining topics, and metaphors with unambiguous and with ambiguous vehicles. Examples of high- and low-constraining topic metaphors, respectively, are beggars are parasites and a vacation is medicine. Examples of unambiguous- and ambiguous-vehicle metaphors, respectively, are some jobs are prisons and love is a journey. The four types of metaphors were, in fact, equally comprehensible as measured by reading times, ranging from 2,261 ms for the high-constraining topic metaphors to 2,321 ms for the low-constraining topic metaphors. This difference, of course, was not reliable.

Because our interest in this study was to evaluate the effects of topic priming as a function of topic type and vehicle priming as a function of vehicle type, the experimental items, when primed, were primed only by their relevant prime types. That is, high-constraining and low-constraining topic metaphors were presented either with a topic prime or with no prime at all (baseline condition), and unambiguous and ambiguous vehicle metaphors were presented either with a vehicle prime or with no prime at all (baseline condition). As in the experiment reported earlier, a trial presentation consisted of a row of asterisks presented for 500 ms, a priming string (e.g., Some jobs are ******) presented for 2 s (on no-prime trials, a row of asterisks), and then the target sentence (e.g., "Some jobs are prisons"), which remained on the screen until a key press. The participants' task was to read each item and then to press the response key as soon as they understood that item. Response timing was initiated when the target metaphor appeared on the screen and stopped when the response key was pressed. Reading time was then used as the measure of comprehension time.

Priming effects were assessed using mean difference scores between baseline (unprimed) and primed conditions for each metaphor type. As predicted, priming a metaphor with a topic term or a vehicle term facilitated comprehension only if the topic was high constraining or the vehicle was unambiguous. High-constraining topics were effective as primes, but low-constraining topics were not. Mean comprehension times for these two metaphor types were 1,445 ms and 2,143 ms, respectively, yielding priming effects of 816 ms and 178 ms, respectively. This latter difference (178 ms) did not approach statistical reliability. Analogously, unambiguous vehicles were effective as primes, but ambiguous vehicles were not. Mean comprehension times for these two metaphor types were 1,292 ms and 2,330 ms, respectively, yielding priming effects of 992 ms and −28 ms, respectively.

These findings are consistent with the claims that (a) level of constraint is an important characteristic of metaphor topics, and (b) ambiguity is an important characteristic of metaphor vehicles. They are inconsistent with simple property-matching models of metaphor comprehension. Recall that according to such models, metaphor comprehension begins with an exhaustive extraction of properties of both the topic and vehicle. After topic and vehicle properties have been extracted, they are then matched against one another. Because matching cannot begin until topic and vehicle properties have been extracted, advance information of the identity of any kind of metaphor topic or metaphor vehicle should be useful. It should be useful because regardless of the nature of the topic or vehicle, its properties can begin to be extracted as soon as it is identified. The sooner this process is completed, the sooner will the subsequent nondirectional matching be accomplished. Thus, with this interpretation of property-matching models, advance knowledge of low-constraining topics or of ambiguous vehicles should facilitate comprehension. The complete absence of such facilitation found by Manfredi casts serious doubt on such models.

Creating New Categories

How are new categories created by metaphors? We may not be able to answer this question in a complete or definitive way, but we are certain about how new categories are not created. They are not created by simply matching properties of one concept with those of another and using some subset of the properties in common. This kind of simple compositional mechanism seems as untenable for nominal metaphors as it is for the concepts that result from adjective–noun or noun–noun combinations. In adjective–noun combinations, for example, emergent properties often appear, as for the concept of blind lawyer. When asked to list the properties of this concept, "courageous" is a typical response. Yet this property is rarely if ever listed as a property of either blind people or of lawyers (Hampton, this volume; Kunda, Miller, & Claire, 1990). More detailed discussions of such conceptual combinations can be found in the chapters in this volume by Hampton, Shoben, and Wisniewski (see also Springer & Murphy, 1992). Each of these authors brings to bear a different set of issues and theoretical viewpoints, but all share the conclusion that a simple compositional model cannot capture the relevant phenomena. Conceptual combinations cannot be predicted from the properties of the individual concepts that enter into a combination.

Analogously, metaphor interpretations cannot be predicted from the properties of the topic and vehicle concepts individually. Indeed, for the case where an addressee is relatively unfamiliar with the topic of a metaphor, there may be no preexisting properties in common with the vehicle. If such statements were rare, they would not pose a serious problem for compositional models of metaphor interpretation. However, such cases are the rule rather than the exception. In many situations, an addressee may be familiar only with the general properties of a topic. For example, consider "Deanna's job is like a prison." If an addressee is not familiar with the particular job in question, then only the general properties of jobs are available. The properties that differentiate a particular job from others, such as high versus low pay, interesting versus boring tasks, and so forth, are not available. Yet these are precisely the kinds of properties that informative assertions are used to convey. In ordinary discourse, people rarely communicate definitional properties, as in "jobs are paid activities." Presumably, people within a speech community presuppose common knowledge and common ground about the core properties of concepts. Instead, informative assertions convey new information, such as the confining or unpleasant nature of a specific job, in contrast to other jobs that may not be. Informative metaphoric assertions thus do not, in general, involve a search for matching properties between a topic and a vehicle.[6] If an addressee's mental representation of a topic and vehicle of such an assertion included the properties that they have in common, then the assertion would not be informative!

Informative comparisons in general, and metaphors and similes in particular, must therefore involve property attribution rather than property matching. For literal comparisons, properties of a predicate that are informative about and relevant to a subject are attributed to that subject. For metaphors and similes, properties of the vehicle are attributed to the topic. This observation is consistent with Glucksberg and Keysar's (1990) portrayal of metaphoric statements as class membership assertions. According to this view, Deanna's job can be described as being like a prison

[6]Gentner and her colleagues (Gentner, this volume; Medin, Goldstone, & Gentner, 1993) have proposed elaborations of comparison models to deal with the issue of property attribution. An adequate discussion of these proposals is beyond the scope of this chapter.

because it is a prison, in the sense that it belongs to a category of unpleasant, confining situations that prisons exemplify. This category provides the properties that are attributed to the job in question.

Beyond the mechanisms of property attribution, an adequate model of metaphor must also include the discourse strategy of dual reference. As we noted earlier, an important characteristic of metaphorical comparison statements is that they can be paraphrased as class membership assertions without appreciably affecting their conveyed meaning. Property-matching models of metaphor comprehension implicitly rely on the ability of metaphors to be paraphrased as comparison statements, but these models do not address the issue of why metaphoric comparisons can be paraphrased as class membership statements, whereas literal comparisons cannot.

The dual reference hypothesis provides a principled account for this difference. In literal comparisons, the predicate term refers to only one level of abstraction. Thus, in the literal comparison "copper is like tin," the predicate *tin* refers only to that particular metal, not to the more abstract categories of metal in general. In the metaphorical comparison "my job is like a prison," the predicate *prison* can be used to refer to the category of confining entities and situations in general. Hence, one can say "my job is a prison."

How general is the concept of dual reference for metaphor? There is another class of conversational metaphors, predicative metaphor, in which verbs are used in much the same way that nouns are used in the nominal form (Miller, 1979). In expressions such as "he grabbed his bike and flew home," the verb *flew* is used metaphorically. Just as nouns in nominal metaphors can be used to make dual reference, so can verbs in predicative metaphors. The verb *flew* in the previous example can refer both to the literal act of traveling through the air and to the broader category of traveling very fast, which flying exemplifies. The broader claim is that verbs can be used to make dual reference just as nouns can. Recall that nouns can be used to make dual reference whenever a superordinate category has not been lexicalized (has no name of its own) and a category exemplar is available that is prototypical of that category. Thus, a specific product name such as Xerox can be used to name the category of copying machines that the Xerox brand exemplifies. Furthermore, the word *xerox* can also be used as a verb to refer to the act of making copies. In Britain, the brand name Hoover is used to refer to the category of vacuum cleaners that this particular brand has come to exemplify, and the word *hoover* is also used as a verb to refer to the action of vacuuming (e.g., one can say "I'll do the hoovering this week if you'll xerox that report for me").

These examples suggest that verbs are used metaphorically in the same way that nouns are used metaphorically, to make dual reference. Of course, when people use predicative metaphors, no explicit property attribution is involved, and so this aspect of our model is not relevant to predicative metaphors. However, the communicative strategy of using a single word to refer simultaneously at two levels of abstraction does seem to be operative in predicative metaphors. Thus, the dual reference aspect of our model of metaphor comprehension may be extended to the case of predicative metaphor. Empirical tests of this extension would be an important issue for future research.

REFERENCES

Black, M. (1962). *Models and metaphors.* Ithaca, NY: Cornell University Press.

Black, M. (1979). More about metaphor. In A. Ortony (Ed.), *Metaphor and thought* (pp. 19–43). Cambridge, England: Cambridge University Press.

Brown, R. (1958). *Words and things.* New York: Free Press.

Fauconnier, G., & Turner, M. (1994). *Conceptual projection and middle spaces* (Report No. 9401). La Jolla, CA: University of California, San Diego, Department of Cognitive Science.

Glucksberg, S., & Keysar, B. (1990). Understanding metaphoric comparisons: Beyond similarity. *Psychological Review, 97,* 3–18.

Glucksberg, S., & Keysar, B. (1993). How metaphors work. In A. Ortony (Ed.), *Metaphor and thought* (2nd ed. pp. 401–424). London: Oxford University Press.

Kittay, E. F. (1982). The creation of similarity: A discussion of metaphor in light of Tversky's theory of similarity. *Philosophy of Science Association, 1,* 394–405.

Kunda, Z., Miller, D. T., & Claire, T. (1990). Combining social concepts: The role of causal reasoning. *Cognitive Science, 14,* 551–577.

Manfredi, D. A. (1994). *Metaphor comprehension: A search for matching features or property attribution?* Unpublished doctoral dissertation, Princeton, NJ.

Medin, D. L., Goldstone, R. L., & Gentner, D. (1993). Respects for similarity. *Psychological Review, 100*, 254–278.

Miller, G. A. (1979). Images and models; Similes and metaphors. In A. Ortony (Ed.), *Metaphor and thought* (pp. 202–250). Cambridge, England: Cambridge University Press.

Random House Dictionary of the English Language. (1967). New York: Random House.

Shinoff, P. (1987, June 14). Demjanjuk war-crimes tribunal strikes deep fear among Jews. *San Francisco Examiner*, p. A8.

Springer, K., & Murphy, G. L. (1992). Feature availability in conceptual combination. *Psychological Science, 3*, 111–117.

Trager, G. L. (1936–1939). "Cottonwood-Tree," a south-western linguistic trait. *International Journal of American Linguistics, 9*, 117–118.

Wechsler, D. (1958). *The measurement and appraisal of adult intelligence (4th ed.).* Baltimore: Williams & Wilkins.

Wolff, P., & Gentner, D. (1992). The time course of metaphor comprehension. *Proceedings of the Fourteenth Annual conference of the Cognitive Science Society* (pp. 504–509). Hillsdale, NJ: LEA.

14

How Language Reflects the Embodied Nature of Creative Cognition

Raymond W. Gibbs, Jr.

An important way to understand human creativity is to closely examine creative works produced by individuals with exceptional talent. Consider William Shakespeare, arguably one of the greatest authors in the English-speaking world, as one example of a creative artist. Consider Shakespeare's creative genius in the opening lines from Hamlet's famous soliloquy in Act III of *Hamlet.*

To be, or not to be, that is the question:
Whether 'tis nobler in the mind to suffer
The slings and arrows of outrageous fortune,
Or to take arms against a sea of troubles
And by opposing end them. To die: to sleep-
No more; and by a sleep to say we end,
the heart-ache and the thousand natural shocks
That flesh is heir to: 'tis a consummation
Devoutly to be wish'd. To die: to sleep-
To sleep? perchance to dream. Ay, there's the rub;
For in that sleep of death what dreams may come,
When we have shuffled off to this mortal coil,
Must give us pause.

Shakespeare (1940) has brilliantly captured Hamlet's dilemma using poetic language that is rare to find among ordinary speakers. This marvelous speech still sings to most people even after hearing or reading it many times over many years. What is it about Shakespeare's poetic vision that touches people, enabling them to establish contact between Shakespeare's unique description of Hamlet's existential crisis and their own ordinary human experiences? Hamlet expresses in this famous soliloquy his suffering from an unbreakable symmetry, a stasis (see Turner, 1991). The soliloquy begins with a bare opposition "to be, or not to be," which one understands metaphorically as symmetrically opposed forces. This defines a stasis of action and decision. The question is repeated and refined. The first "to die: to sleep" introduces one force, the argument for one side of Hamlet's dilemma. The second "to die: to sleep," occupying the same point in the line where its predecessor occurred, introduces the argument for the opposing side. Hamlet is stuck in one of life's many equations and in trying to balance between different sets of opposing forces—he has become paralyzed at a point of painful equilibrium.

Writers such as Shakespeare are praised for their creative genius to think and express themselves in vivid poetic, often metaphorical, language. But what motivates Shakespeare's choice of words in describing Hamlet's crisis? And how do ordinary readers make sense of Shakespeare's tremendous creative achievement in *Hamlet*? Reading Hamlet's soliloquy, one quickly recognizes that Shakespeare intended to draw a comparison between the problem of making choices in life and the idea of being physically balanced. This metaphorical understanding of Hamlet's dilemma in terms of being physically balanced is closely related to people's experiences of feeling physically balanced in the real world. The embodied experience of feeling balanced, both within ourself and between our bodies and the external world, helps us understand Hamlet's plight, and provides part of the foundation for why Shakespeare writes about Hamlet as he did.

Hamlet's famous soliloquy illustrates how a significant part of our ability to think creatively about concepts, especially abstract ones such as those having to do with life's major decisions, is partly motivated by our bodily experiences in the real world. Thinking creatively is motivated by aspects of bodily experience in the sense that there is some tacit connection between human embodiment and how we think about different concepts and express ourselves with language in talking about, and understanding, important ideas. Systematic patterns, or experiential gestalts called *image schemas*, arise from recurring bodily experiences, such as that having to do with feeling balanced, and these patterns can be metaphorically projected to help structure abstract concepts, such as those having to do with making choices in life. Creative artists like Shakespeare elaborate on these bodily based metaphorical concepts in new, creative ways through their use of language (or art or music). The fact that we, as ordinary readers and observers, have similar metaphorical understandings of many abstract concepts—ones that arise from our own embodied experiences—allows us to make sense of creative works such as that seen in the language used in *Hamlet.* Not all aspects of creativity are rooted in, and can be predicted by, bodily experience, but an important part of how we think, reason, and use language in creative ways about human experience is motivated by our embodied experience.

The traditional view in Western intellectual history is that the mind and body are separable. In contemporary psychology the mind is viewed as disembodied. This is one reason it seems easier to study the mind as a kind of computer than it is to study how people think, reason, and imagine in everyday, embodied experience (Anderson, 1990; Massaro, 1989). Following this dominant paradigm, most scholarly work on human creativity focuses on how the mind can break away from constraining patterns of thought to facilitate divergent thinking (Baer, 1993; Runco, 1991). The body, far from being the source of many creative ideas, is recognized more as a limiting force both in how people think and act creatively and how students of the mind think about creative cognition. Yet several psychologists (Barsalou, this volume; Gibbs & Colston, 1995; Glenberg, this volume; Mandler, 1992; Varela, Thompson, & Rosch, 1991), anthropologists (Csordas, 1994), linguists (Lakoff, 1987; Lakoff & Turner, 1989; Sweetser, 1990; Turner, 1991), and philosophers (Johnson, 1987, 1993; Leder, 1990; Merleau-Ponty, 1962) have challenged traditional dualist views of mind and body and begun to explore the embodied nature of human experience. My aim in this chapter is to illustrate through example and empirical evidence how an analysis of both everyday and creative language reflects significant aspects of the embodied nature of many creative concepts.

IMAGE SCHEMAS IN LINGUISTIC MEANING

Much of the empirical work on how bodily experience underlies significant portions of how people make sense of both ordinary and creative uses of language is connected to recent studies in cognitive linguistics (Johnson, 1987, 1993; Lakoff, 1987; Lakoff & Johnson, 1980; Langacker, 1987; Talmy, 1988). One of the important claims of cognitive semantics is that much of our knowledge is not static (propositional and sentential) but is grounded in and structured by various patterns of our perceptual interactions, bodily actions, and manipulations of objects. These patterns are experiential gestalts (image schemas) that emerge throughout sensorimotor activity as we manipulate objects, orient ourselves spatially and temporally, and direct our perceptual focus for various purposes.

Image schemas can generally be defined as dynamic analog representations of spatial relations and movements in space. Although image schemas are derived from perceptual and motor processes, they are not themselves sensorimotor processes. Instead, image schemas are "primary means by which we construct or constitute order and are not mere passive receptacles into which experience is poured" (Johnson, 1987, p. 30). Image schemas exist across all perceptual modalities, which is necessary for there to be any sensorimotor coordination in our experience. As such, image schemas are at once visual, auditory, kinesthetic, and tactile.

Consider one image schema, the balance schema, to examine how its internal structure is projected onto a new domain, through use of metaphor, to motivate creative concepts. The idea of balance is something that is learned "with our bodies and not by grasping a set of rules" (Johnson, 1987, p. 74). Balancing is such a pervasive part of peoples' bodily experience that they are seldom aware of its presence in everyday life. People come to know the meaning of balance through the closely related experiences of bodily equilibrium or loss of equilibrium. For example, a baby stands, wobbles, and drops to the floor. It tries again and again, as it learns how to maintain a balanced erect posture. A young boy struggles to stay up on a two-wheeled bicycle as he learns to keep his balance while riding down the street. Each of us has experienced occasions when we have too much acid in our stomaches, when our hands get cold, our heads feel too hot, our bladders feel distended, our sinuses become swollen, and our mouths feel dry. In these and numerous other ways we learn the meanings of lack of balance or equilibrium. We respond to imbalance and disequilbrium by warming our hands, giving moisture to our mouths, draining our bladders, and so forth until we feel balanced once again. Our balance image schema emerges, then, through our experiences of maintaining our bodily systems and functions in states of equilibrium. We refer to these recurring bodily experiences as image schemas to emphasize means of structuring particular experiences schematically so that we can give order and connectedness to our perceptions and conceptions (Johnson, 1987).

A single image schema can be instantiated in many different domains because the internal structure of a single schema can be metaphorically understood. Our balance image schema, to continue with this example, is metaphorically elaborated in a large number of abstract domains of experience (e.g., psychological states such as Hamlet's, legal relationships, formal systems). In the cases of bodily and visual balance, there seems to be one basic scheme consisting of a point or axis around which forces and weights must be distributed so that they counteract or balance off one another. Our experience of bodily balance and the perception of balance is connected to our understanding of balanced personalities, balanced views, balanced systems, balanced equilibrium, the balance of power, the balance of justice, and so on. In each of these examples, the mental or the abstract concept of balance is understood and experienced in terms of our physical understanding of balance. It is not accidental that a large number of unrelated concepts (for the systematic, psychological, moral, legal, and mathematical domains) all just happen to make use of the same word *balance* and related terms (Johnson, 1991). We use the same word for all of these domains because they are structurally related by the same sort of underlying image schemas, and are metaphorically elaborated from them.

In the earlier example, Hamlet expresses his personal dilemma in part through appeal to the idea of bodily balance in which two symmetrically opposing forces (e.g., "To be or not to be; To die: to sleep") define a stasis of action that is psychologically paralyzing. My argument, again, is that what partly motivated Shakespeare to describe Hamlet's situation in the way he did rests with his tacit understanding of being psychologically balanced, an abstract concept that arises from one's recurring bodily experiences of feeling balanced (or unbalanced) in the everyday world. Readers of Shakespeare find great beauty and new insights in Hamlet's experience partly through the way Shakespeare elaborates on the common metaphorical projection of balanced bodily experience onto concepts of personality and life choices. Yet our understanding of Shakespeare's play *Hamlet*, the fact that we aesthetically respond to it in the way that we do, is partly due to our own ability to recognize that Shakespeare provides concrete instantiations for the common idea of life's decisions being like the embodied experience of feeling balanced.

Consider another image schema to examine how it is linked to people's ability to think creatively about abstract concepts. The source–path–goal schema first develops as we learn to focus our eyes and track forms as they move throughout our visual field. From such experiences, a recurring pattern becomes manifest in tracking a trajector from point A to another point B. Later on, as we move our bodies in the real world, ranging from experiences of reaching for objects to moving our entire bodies from one location to another, more varied source–path–goal experiences become salient. Although source–path–goal experiences may vary considerably (e.g., many objects, shapes, and types of paths traveled), the emergent image-schematic structure of source–path–goal can be metaphorically projected onto more abstract domains of understanding and reasoning (Johnson, 1987). This metaphorical mapping preserves the structural characteristics or the cognitive topology of the source domain (Lakoff, 1990). Thus, the source–path–goal schema gives rise to conceptual metaphors such as *purposes are destinations* that preserve the main structural characteristics of the source domain (i.e., source–path–goal). English is replete with systematic expressions that illustrate this underlying metaphorical conceptualization. For instance, students set out to get their PhDs, but along the way they get sidetracked or led astray and are diverted from their original goal. They try to get back on the right path and to keep the end in view as they move along. Eventually they may reach their goal (Johnson, 1991). It is not simply an arbitrary fact of English that people talk about their lives and careers in terms of sources, paths, and goals; rather, we metaphorically conceptualize our experiences through very basic, bodily experiences that are abstracted to form higher level metaphoric thought. This way of talking about experience shows how the *purposes are destinations* metaphor, resulting from a very basic image-schematic structure, is constitutive of our understanding of intentional action.

Some of the most creative instantiations of the source–path–goal schema are seen in great works of poetry. Consider an excerpt from a poem by the Chilean poet Pablo Neruda (1972) titled *Ode and Burgeonings.*

My wild girl, we have had
to regain time
and march backward, in the distance
of our lives, kiss after kiss,
gathering from one place what we gave
without joy, discovering in another
the secret road
that gradually brought your feet
closer to mine.

This is one of Neruda's great love poems. Speaking of love seems to stretch the limits of language—one reason why we appreciate the works of poets who find expression for such experiences. The above lines illustrate unique, poetic, instantiations of how we metaphorically conceptualize our love experiences partly in terms of journeys motivated by the source–path–goal image schema. The poet talks about going "backward, in the distance" (i.e., the path) of his love relationship with the "wild girl," stopping at those places that "we gave without joy" to find "the secret road" that brought true unity and happiness. Although these phrases appear creative, they are related in metaphorical ways to the expressions people often use to talk about love and love relationships. For instance, consider the following list of conventional expressions: *Look how far we've come, It's been a long, bumpy road, We're at a crossroads, We may have to go our separate ways, Our marriage is on the rocks,* and *We're spinning our wheels.*

These (and other) conventional expressions cluster together under one of the basic metaphorical systems of understanding: *love is a journey* (Lakoff & Johnson, 1980). This conceptual metaphor involves a tight mapping according to which entities in the domain of love (e.g., the lovers, their common goals, the love relationship, etc.) correspond systematically to entities in the domain of a journey (e.g., the traveler, the vehicle, destinations, etc.). Various inferences or entailments arise when we think of love as a journey. Among these are the inferences that the person in love is a traveler, the goal of ultimate love is a destination, the means for achieving love are routes, the difficulties one experiences in love are obstacles to travel, and the progress in a love relationship is the distance traveled. Again, it is not an arbitrary matter to speak of love relationships as being at crossroads, on the rocks, or having been on a long, bumpy road. Instead, we understand that each of these expressions is appropriate to use in talking about love relationships precisely because our common metaphorical transformation that love is conceptualized as being like a physical journey and our understanding of journeys is closely linked to the source–path–goal image schema.

This discussion of the source–path–goal schema shows that there are direct connections among recurring bodily experiences, metaphorically understood abstract concepts, and both conventional and creative language that refer to these abstract concepts. As was the case for Shakespeare's presentation of Hamlet's soliloquy, and our interpretation of it, Neruda's creative achievement in his love poem, and our ability to make sense of his writing, is very much linked to our basic embodied experiences.

The balance and source–path–goal image schemas are just two of the more than two dozen different image schemas and several image schema transformations that cognitive linguists claim appear regularly in people's everyday thinking, reasoning, and imagination (Gibbs & Colston, 1995; Johnson, 1987; Lakoff, 1987). Among some of the other notable image-schematic structures are container, path, cycle, attraction, center–periphery, and link. The cognitive linguistic studies on image schemas, and how they relate to abstract, metaphorically structured concepts, are primarily based on systematic analyses of individual linguistic expressions, such as those shown with the different conventional expressions for source–path–goal. Although this method of analyzing systematic patterns of linguistic expressions provides important empirical evidence, it suffers from the problem of lack of falsifiability as to the significance of image schemas in motivating the creative use and understanding of language. Cognitive psychologists are sometimes skeptical about theoretical notions from linguistics and philosophy that are primarily based on an individual analyst's intuitions about linguistic structure and behavior (see Gibbs, 1992; Sandra & Rice, 1995, for a discussion of this issue from psychological and linguistic perspectives). One of the main reasons for conducting experiments with large groups of people is to minimize the uncertainty in making inferences about thought and behavior in whole populations of people. The next section examines recent experimental studies that do provide potentially falsifiable evidence about the importance of embodied image schemas in how people think of and talk about abstract and, in many instances, creative concepts.

EMPIRICAL STUDIES ON EMBODIED MEANING

Over the past five years, I have conducted several different research projects that look at the influence of embodied experience on people's use and understanding of linguistic meaning. These projects, ranging from studies on understanding poetry to experiments on polysemy, use a variety of research methodologies. However, the primary strategy used has been to independently assess people's intuitions about their embodied experiences and then use this information to partly predict individuals' linguistic behavior.

Poetic Metaphors

One series of studies examined the hypothesis that readers make sense of poetry, find poetry especially apt and meaningful, because they infer various underlying bodily-based conceptual metaphors that motivate the ideas to which poetry refers. We (Gibbs & Nascimento, 1996) first analyzed people's conceptual metaphors for the concept of love by having them write about their definition of love and describe their first love experience. We analyzed the participants' protocols for different examples of linguistic expressions that were motivated by metaphorical concepts of love. For example, the expression "There is one impossible thing: to love and be apart" was classified as reflecting *love is a unity*; "Love is a gift given to people to share" was seen as an instance of *love is a valuable resource*; and "His vulnerability drew me in" illustrates *love is a natural force.* Among the most frequent conceptual metaphors in the participants' definitions of love were *love is a unity, a natural force, a substance, a physical bond, heat,* and *a journey.* Some of these conceptual metaphors, such as love is a unity, love is a natural force, and love is physical closeness, were used in conventional expressions by more than half of all of the participants in the experiment.

The presence of this fairly limited number of conceptual metaphors in participants' discourse illustrates the dominance of metaphor in people's thinking about their concept of love and their individual love experiences. People do not think about and talk about what love is in a vast number of ways but are fairly limited by several conceptual metaphors that have currency in their culture. Many of these conceptual metaphors have clear bodily connections. For instance, *love is a unity, a natural force, heat,* and *a journey* have image-schematic source domains based on recurring bodily experiences, such as containment, source–path–goal, enablement, and contiguity. Thus, one student described her first love experience as "My body was filled with a current of energy. Sparks filled my pores when I thought of him or things we'd done together," clearly referring to the *love is heat* metaphor—a mapping that is motivated by people's embodied experience of feeling heat while being in love. Similarly, the expression of another student that I was filled with tenderness "refers to the image schemas of containment, another pervasive embodied experience. Of course, speakers in different cultures will value some aspects of image-schematic experience more than others and consequently use different metaphorical language to talk about love and other important human experiences (cf. Alverson, 1995).

In the next several studies (Gibbs & Nascimento, 1996), we gathered examples of love poetry that reflected similar conceptual metaphors to those identified as implicit in college students' definitions of love and in their descriptions of their first love experiences. In a second study, we found that participants were very accurate in choosing conceptual metaphors (e.g., *love is a journey*) that motivated the poetic fragments they had just read. A third experiment indicated that participants were quite good at picking the conventional expressions (e.g., *We're at a crossroads*) that were motivated by the same conceptual metaphors (e.g., *love is a journey*) underlying the poems. The data from these studies are consistent with the hypothesis that readers partially understand poetry by recovering the conceptual metaphors that motivate what authors creatively express in their poems.

A final study examined participants' verbal statements about what they understood while reading 10 poems in a line-by-line manner. An analysis of the participants' talking-out-loud protocols showed that 78% of all statements referred to the entailments of the underlying conceptual metaphors that partly motivated the meanings of the poems participants had read. For example, when participants read the fragment from Neruda's poem *Ode and Burgeonings*, they referred to entailments of the *love is a journey* metaphor such as the path (e.g., "They learned a better path to happiness. They had to retrace their steps to find true love. They found a special road that they could travel together on in the same direction."), the goals (e.g., "The future of their love lay ahead of them. They had to catch up."), and the impediments to travel (e.g., "They managed to get over the rough places, rediscovering what was missed."). It seemed clear that readers were partially making sense of what the poems meant through their everyday metaphorical understanding of love.

In general, the data from these poetry studies demonstrate, at the very least, that people's conscious, reflective interpretations of poetry are strongly constrained by their ordinary metaphorical concepts, knowledge that is partly motivated by recurring bodily experiences (e.g., source–path–goal, containment). Readers do not necessarily create novel metaphorical mappings to understand novel, poetic language. Moreover, the vast majority of novel metaphors in poetry and literature reflect fixed patterns of metaphorical mappings between dissimilar source and target domains. The source domains most frequently used in the metaphorical mappings have bodily based image-schematic structures. Although it is often assumed that poets are especially creative in expressing new metaphorical mappings, poets are primarily making use of the same set of bodily based conceptual metaphors by which people understand everyday experience. In most cases, the true creativity in great works of poetry is found in the way poets use unconventional language to elaborate on particular, and often unexplored aspects of, entailments of familiar conceptual metaphors.

Idioms

Another of our research projects on the embodied nature of language focuses on how people use and understand idiomatic phrases (Gibbs, 1992). The traditional view of idiomaticity assumes that expressions, such as *blow your stack, flip your lid, hit the ceiling*, are "giant lexical items" whose meanings result from "dead" metaphors. However, recent work in cognitive linguistics (Lakoff, 1987) and psycholinguistics (Gibbs, 1994, 1995) suggests that idioms are not simple, dead metaphors but actually retain a good deal of their metaphoricity because they are motivated by metaphorical mappings between dissimilar source and target domains. For example, the figurative meanings of *blow your stack, flip your lid*, and *hit the ceiling* are specifically motivated by two independently existing elements in our conceptual system: *mind is a container* and *anger is heat in a pressurized container*. These two conceptual metaphors are actually two of the limited number of ways that people in Western cultures conceive of anger. Our understanding of anger (the target domain) as heated fluid in a container (the source domain) gives rise to a number of interesting entailments. For example, when the intensity of anger increases, the fluid rises (e.g., "His pent-up anger welled up inside of him"). We also know that intense heat produces steam and creates pressure on the container (e.g., "Bill is getting hot under the collar" and "Jim's just blowing off steam"). Intense anger produces pressure on the container (e.g., "He was bursting with anger"). Finally, when the pressure of the container becomes too high, the container explodes (e.g., "She blew up at me"). Each of these metaphorical entailments is a direct result of the conceptual mapping of anger onto heated fluid in a container.

Central to our understanding of the conceptual metaphor *anger is heated fluid in a container* is the embodied experience of containment. We have strong kinesthetic experiences of bodily containment ranging from situations in which our bodies are in and out of containers (e.g., bathtubs, beds, rooms, and houses) to experiences of our bodies as containers in which substances enter and exit. A big part of bodily containment is the experience of our bodies being filled with liquids, including stomach fluids, blood, and sweat, that get excreted through the skin. Under stress, we experience the feeling of our bodily fluid becoming heated.

Another set of psycholinguistic studies examined how people's intuitions of the bodily experience of containment, and several other image schemas, which serve as the source domains for several important conceptual metaphors, underlie people's use and understanding of idioms. These studies were designed to show that the specific entailments of idioms reflect the source-to-target domain mappings of their underlying conceptual metaphors (Gibbs, 1992). Most important, these metaphorical mappings preserve the cognitive topology of these embodied, image-schematic source domains.

Participants in these studies were first questioned about their understanding of events corresponding to particular bodily experiences that were viewed as motivating specific source domains in conceptual metaphors (e.g., the experience of one's body as a container filled with fluid). For instance, participants were asked to imagine the embodied experience of a sealed container filled with fluid, and then they were asked something about causation (e.g., what would cause the container to explode?), intentionality (e.g., does the container explode on purpose or does it explode through no volition of its own ?), and manner (e.g., does the explosion of the container occur in a gentle or a violent manner?).

Overall, the participants were remarkably consistent in their responses to the questions. To give one example, people responded that the cause of a sealed container exploding its contents is the internal pressure caused by the increase in the heat of the fluid inside the container. They also reported that this explosion is unintentional because containers and fluid have no intentional agency, and that the explosion occurs in a violent manner.

More interesting, though, is that people's intuitions about various source domains map onto their conceptualizations of different target domains in very predictable ways. For instance, several experiments showed that people find idioms to be more appropriate and easier to understand when they are seen in discourse contexts that are consistent with the various entailments of these phrases. Thus, research participants found it easy to process the idiomatic phrase *blow your stack* when it was read in a context that accurately described the cause of the person's anger as being due to internal pressure, where the expression of anger was unintentional and violent (all entailments that are consistent with the entailments of the source-to-target domain mappings of heated fluid in a container onto anger). However, readers took significantly longer to read *blow your stack* when any of these entailments were contradicted in the preceding story context.

These findings provide additional evidence that people's metaphorical concepts underlie their understanding of what idioms mean in written texts. Moreover, they provide significant evidence that people's intuitions about their embodied experiences can predict something about their use and understanding of idioms—expressions that are partly motivated by bodily based conceptual metaphors. Not surprisingly, many of the image schemas that underlie people's understandings of idioms are elaborated on in creative ways by poets. Consider the beginning of the poem by Adrienne Rich titled *The Phenomonelogy of Anger* (Rich, 1984).

Fantasies of murder: not enough:
to kill is to cut off from pain
but the killer goes on hurting
Not enough. When I dream of meeting
the enemy, this is my dream:
white acetylene
ripples from my body
effortlessly released
perfectly trained
on the true enemy
raking his body down to the thread
of existence
burning away his lie
leaving him in a new
world; a changed
man.

Rich's poem specifies the heated fluid representing anger as acetylene that she can focus as a weapon on the object of her emotion. Her verse is beautifully poetic, yet makes use of the same figurative modes of thought that motivate common idioms such as *blow your stack, flip your lid,* or *hit the ceiling,* as well as conventional expressions about anger such as "His pent-up anger welled up inside him." Rich's poem has great intuitive appeal precisely because she refers to, and elaborates on, a common, bodily based metaphorical view of anger. Once again, there appear to be significant links between embodied experience, image schemas, conceptual metaphors, and people's understanding of many conventional and creative linguistic expressions.

Polysemy

Perhaps (Gibbs, Beitel, Harrington, & Sanders, 1994) our most detailed set of studies on the bodily basis for linguistic meaning investigated people's intuitions about the meanings of polysemous words. Consider the word *stand* in the following sentences: "Please stand at attention"; "He wouldn't stand for such treatment"; "The clock stands on the mantle"; "The law still stands"; "He stands six foot, five"; "The part stands for the whole"; and "She had a one-night stand with a stranger." These sentences represent just a few of the many senses of *stand* that are common in everyday speech and writing. Some of these senses refer to the physical act of standing (e.g., "Please stand at attention," "The clock stands on the mantle," "He stands six foot, five"), whereas others have nonphysical, perhaps figurative, interpretations (e.g., "We stood accused of the crime," "The part stands for the whole," "He wouldn't stand for such treatment"). What are the principles that relate the different physical and figurative senses of *stand* in the examples noted above?

Some linguists in recent years have argued that the lexical organization of polysemous words is not a repository of random, idiosyncratic information but is structured by general cognitive principles that are systematic and recurrent throughout the lexicon (Brugman & Lakoff, 1988). Many of these principles arise from our phenomenological, embodied experience. One possibility is that bodily experience partly motivates people's intuitions as to why different senses of *stand* have the meanings they do. We (Gibbs et al., 1994) attempted to experimentally show that the different senses of the polysemous word *stand* are partly motivated by different image schemas that arise from people's bodily experience of standing. In a series of experiments, we showed that the meanings of the polysemous word *stand* are not arbitrary for native speakers but are motivated by people's recurring bodily experiences in the real world.

These studies attempted to assess people's intuitions of their own bodily experiences of standing to determine how their intuitions might predict people's understandings of the complex meanings of the word *stand*. A first experiment sought to determine which image schemas best reflect people's recurring bodily experiences of standing. A group of participants were guided through a brief set of bodily exercises to get them to consciously think about their own physical experience of standing. For instance, participants were asked to stand up, move around, bend over, crouch, and stretch out on their tiptoes. Having people actually engage in these behaviors facilitates participants' intuitive understandings of how their experience of standing relates to many different possible image schemas. After this standing exercise, participants then read brief descriptions of 12 image schemas that might possibly have some relationship to the experience of standing (e.g., verticality, balance, resistance, enablement, center–periphery, linkage). Finally, the participants rated the degree of relatedness of each image schema to their own embodied experience of standing. The results of this first study showed that 5 image schemas are primary to people's bodily experiences of standing (i.e., balance, verticality, center–periphery, resistance, and linkage).

A second experiment investigated people's judgments of similarity for different senses of *stand.* The participants sorted 32 different senses of *stand* into five groups on the basis of their similarity of meaning. An analysis of these groups revealed that participants did not sort physical senses of *stand* separately from nonphysical or figurative senses. For example, the physical idea of standing in "to stand at attention" was often grouped with the metaphorical senses of *stand* in "let the issue stand" and "to stand the test of time."

The third experiment in this series examined the relationship between the five image schemas for the physical experience of standing and the various senses of *stand* studied in the second study. Once again, participants were first asked to stand up and focus on different aspects of their bodily experience of standing. As they did this, the participants were presented with verbal descriptions of the five image schemas—balance, verticality, center–periphery, resistance, and linkage. Afterward, the participants were given a list of 32 senses of *stand* and asked to rate the degree of relatedness between each sense and the five image schemas.

The rating data from this third study allowed us (Gibbs et al., 1994) to construct an image schema profile for each of the 32 uses of *stand.* Several interesting similarities emerged in the image schema profiles for some of the 32 senses of *stand.* For example, "it stands to reason" and "as the matter now stands" both have the same image schema profile (in their rank–order of importance) of linkage–balance–center/periphery–resistance–verticality. The expressions "don't stand for such treatment" and "to stand against great odds" are both characterized by the image schema profile resistance–center/periphery–linkage–balance–verticality.

The primary goal of this study, however, was to assess whether the senses of *stand* viewed as being similar in meaning in the second experiment were reliably predictable from the image schema profiles obtained in this study. Statistical analyses showed that knowing the image schema profiles for different senses of *stand* allowed us to predict 79% of all the groupings of *stand* in the second study. These data provide very strong support for the hypothesis that people's understandings of the meanings of *stand* are partly motivated by image schemas that arise from their bodily experiences of standing. A fourth study showed that participants' sortings of *stand* in different groups cannot be explained simply in terms of their understanding of the contexts in which these words appeared. Thus, participants did not sort phrases such as "don't stand for such treatment" and "to stand against great odds" because these phrases refer to the same types of situations. Instead, it appears that people's similarity judgments are best attributed to their tacit understanding of how different patterns of image schemas motivate different uses of the polysemous word *stand.*

This psycholinguistic research has demonstrated that people make sense of different uses of *stand* because of their tacit understanding of several image schemas that arise partly from the ordinary bodily experience of standing. These image schemas—the most important of which are balance, verticality, center–periphery, resistance, and linkage—not only produce the grounding for many physical senses of *stand* (e.g., "he stands six foot, nine," "stand in the way," and "stand at attention") but also underlie people's understanding of complex, metaphorical uses (e.g., "the part stands for the whole," "as the matter now stands," and "the engine can't stand the constant wear"). People perceive different senses of *stand* as similar in meaning partly on the basis of the underlying image schema profile for each use of the word in context.

The results of these different research projects should not be interpreted as indicating that people automatically access some specific pattern of image schemas each time they encounter a particular use of a word, conventional expression, or creative utterance. My aim in these projects was to demonstrate that people tacitly recognize some connection between different schematic bodily experiences and various aspects of linguistic meaning, including meanings that are highly abstract, and metaphorical, or both. Psychologists often contend that cognitive linguistic research suffers from circular reasoning in that it starts with an analysis of language to infer something about the mind and body that in turn motivates different aspects of linguistic structure and behavior. However, independently assessing bodily experience of standing beforehand allows researchers to make specific predictions about people's understanding of different uses of words and expressions. Making specific experimental predictions, which can be falsified, about people's linguistic behavior is an essential ingredient for psychologists if they are to accept the psychological reality of any hypothetical construct such as image schemas.

I hasten to add that understanding how image schemas develop and get metaphorically projected to help structure abstract concepts requires detailed studies from developmental psychologists (see Gibbs & Colston, 1995; Mandler, 1992, for reviews of such work). The work I have described in this section looks at only the influence of image-schematic structures in their mature state, once they have already been used in abstract reasoning and creativity. Psychologists and others face a difficult challenge in devising experimental paradigms to better study how pervasive embodied experiences give rise to abstract concepts and creative acts. In this regard, psychologists must be open to ideas from cognitive semanticists (linguists and philosophers) who have proposed several detailed accounts of image-schematic thought and understanding (e.g., Johnson, 1987; Turner, 1991).

CONCLUSION: THE BODY IN CREATIVE CONCEPTS

People's understanding of many aspects of linguistic meaning, both conventional and creative, is strongly based in many instances on their recognition of common metaphoric concepts that are rooted in everyday bodily experience. This view of creative concepts emphasizes more of the similarities between what creative artists and ordinary people know than does the work in most areas of creative psychology. Metaphor serves as one of the pillars of the creative mind, but as each of us, artists and common folk alike, act creatively, we must recognize the constraints that our common bodily experiences and the resulting abstractive metaphoric concepts place on our creative imagination. Creativity is not merely the results of unconstrained, imaginative thinking, because the empirical evidence described in this chapter suggests a picture of bodily based metaphoric imagination as a systematic and orderly part of human cognitive processes. Although image schemas do not underlie all aspects of meaning and cognition, they are a crucial, undervalued dimension of meaning that has not been sufficiently explored by psychologists interested in creativity and cognition.

My discussion on how language reflects the embodied nature of creative concepts follows several important tenets of the creative cognition approach (Finke, Ward, & Smith, 1992; Smith, Ward, & Finke, 1995). By focusing on the cognitive processes and structures that underlie both ordinary and creative cognition, my work on embodied cognition is consistent with the claim that no single process can be identified as the single mechanism for creative cognition. Instead, my work, and that of scholars in cognitive linguistics, has attempted to show how special combinations and patterns of the same cognitive processes seen in everyday thought and language have a motivating role in explaining creativity and people's ordinary understanding of creative acts. The work described in this chapter specifically extends the creative cognition approach to include embodied meaning that underlies many aspects of ordinary and creative conceptual thought. Thus, Ward (1995) argued that "structured imagination refers to the fact that when people use their imagination to develop their ideas, those ideas are heavily structured in predictable ways by properties of existing categories and concepts" (p. 157). I believe that the linguistic and psychological work on embodied meaning suggests that many imaginative, creative ideas are derived from existing, familiar, image-schematic experiences.

The present work is consistent with the claim that examining cognition in creative contexts enables researchers to learn more and raise new questions about fundamental cognitive processes. Thus, studying how creative artists talk about abstract concepts in embodied, metaphorical ways provides additional evidence on the embodied nature of categorization processes in general.

Finally, by exploring creative cognition as an embodied experience, the research described here emphasizes the important ecological nature of creative concepts in that it makes contact with structures that naturally exist in the real world (i.e., the human body and people's perceptions of it) rather than simply focusing on the creative products of the disembodied human mind.

None of what is described here on image schemas and creativity implies that the study of creativity or creative concepts must be related to underlying, recurring patterns of bodily experience. All creativity does not reduce to human embodiment. However, it is clear that much of the motivation for why people think about concepts in the ways they do, including many creative forms, is grounded in both the mind and the body. Putting the body back into our understanding of certain concepts both provides cognitive scientists with a view of what constrains creativity and gives us the foundation for thinking creatively about our experiences in the world.

REFERENCES

Alverson, H. (1995). *Semantics and experience.* Baltimore: Johns Hopkins University Press.

Anderson, J. (1990). *Cognitive psychology and its implications.* New York: Freeman.

Baer, J. (1993). *Creativity and divergent thinking: A task-specific approach.* Hillsdale, NJ: Erlbaum.

Brugman, C., & Lakoff, G. (1988). Cognitive topology and lexical networks. In S. Small, G. Cotrell, & M. Tannenhaus (Eds.), *Lexical ambiguity resolution* (pp. 477–508). Palo Alto, CA: Morgan Kaufman.

Csordas, T. (Ed.). (1994). *Embodiment and experience: The existential ground of culture and self.* Cambridge, England: Cambridge University Press.

Finke, R., Ward, T., & Smith, S. (1992). *Creative cognition: Theory, research, and applications.* Cambridge, MA: MIT Press.

Gibbs, R. (1992). What do idioms really mean? *Journal of Memory and Language, 31*, 385–406.

Gibbs, R. (1994). *The poetics of mind: Figurative thought, language, and understanding.* Cambridge, England: Cambridge University Press.

Gibbs, R. (1995). Idiomaticity and human cognition. In M. Everaert, E-J. van der Linden, A. Schenk, & R. Schreuder (Eds.), *Idioms: Structural and psychological perspectives* (pp. 97–116). Hillsdale, NJ: Erlbaum.

Gibbs, R., Beitel, D., Harrington, M., & Sanders, P. (1994). Taking a stand on the meanings of "stand": Bodily experience as motivation for polysemy. *Journal of Semantics, 11*, 231–251.

Gibbs, R., & Colston, H. (1995). The cognitive psychological reality of image schemas and their transformations. *Cognitive Linguistics, 6*, 347–378.

Gibbs, R., & Nascimento, S. (1996). How we talk when we talk about love: Metaphorical concepts and understanding love poetry. In R. Kreuz & M. MacNulty (Eds.), *Empirical and aesthetic approaches to literature* (pp. 291–308). Norwood, NJ: Ablex.

Johnson, M. (1987). *The body in the mind.* Chicago: University of Chicago Press.

Johnson, M. (1991). Knowing through the body. *Philosophical Psychology, 4*, 3–20.

Johnson, M. (1993). *Moral imagination.* Chicago: University of Chicago Press.

Lakoff, G. (1987). *Women, fire, and dangerous things: What categories reveal about the mind.* Chicago: University of Chicago Press.

Lakoff, G. (1990). The invariance hypothesis: Is abstract reason based on image-schemas? *Cognitive Linguistics, 1*, 39–74.

Lakoff, G., & Johnson, M. (1980). *Metaphors we live by.* Chicago: University of Chicago Press.

Lakoff, G., & Turner, M. (1989). *More than cool reason: A field guide to poetic metaphor.* Chicago: University of Chicago Press.

Langacker, R. (1987). *Foundations of cognitive grammar.* Stanford: Stanford University Press.

Leder, D. (1990). *The absent body.* Chicago: University of Chicago Press.

Mandler, J. (1992). How to build a baby. *Psychological Review, 99*, 587–604.

Massaro, D. (1989). *Experimental psychology: An information processing approach.* San Diego, CA: Harcourt Brace Jovanovich.

Merleau-Ponty, M. (1962). *Phenomenology of perception.* Evanston, IL: Northwestern University Press.

Neruda, P. (1972). *The captain's verses.* New York: New Directions.

Rich, A. (1984). *The fact of a doorframe: Poems selected and new, 1950–1984.* New York: Norton.

Runco, M. (1991). *Divergent thinking.* Norwood, NJ: Ablex.

Sandra, D., & Rice, S. (1995). Network analyses of prepositional meaning: Mirroring whose mind—the linguist's or the language user's? *Cognitive Linguistics, 6,* 89–130.

Shakespeare, W. (1940). *Hamlet.* New York: Ginn.

Smith, S., Ward, T., & Finke, R. (Eds.). (1995). *The creative cognition approach.* Cambridge, MA: MIT Press.

Sweetser, E. (1990). *From etymology to pragmatics: Metaphorical and cultural aspects of semantic structure.* Cambridge, England: Cambridge University Press.

Talmy, L. (1988). Force dynamics in language and cognition. *Cognitive Science, 12,* 49–100.

Turner, M. (1991). *Reading minds: The study of English in the age of cognitive science.* Princeton, NJ: Princeton University Press.

Varela, F., Thompson, E., & Rosch, E. (1991). *The embodied mind: Cognitive science and human experience.* Cambridge, MA: MIT Press.

Ward, T. (1995). What's old about new ideas? In. S. Smith, T. Ward, & R. Finke (Eds.), *The creative cognition approach* (pp. 151–178). Cambridge, MA: MIT Press.

15

Of "Men" and Metaphors: Shakespeare, Embodiment, and Filing Cabinets

Eva Feder Kittay

531. We speak of understanding a sentence in the sense in which it can be replaced by another which says the same; but also in the sense in which it cannot be replaced by any other.

532. Then has "understanding" two different meanings here?—I would rather say that these kinds of use of "understanding" make up its meaning, make up my concept of understanding.

(Wittgenstein, ***Philosophical Investigations***)

Murderer: We are men, my liege.
Macbeth: Ay, in the catalogue ye go for men;
As hounds, and greyhound, mongrels, spaniel curs,
Shoughs, water-rugs, and demi-wolves are clept
All by the name of dogs; the valu'd file
Distinguishes the swift, the slow the subtle,
The house-keeper, the hunter, every one
According to the gift which bounteous nature
Hath in him clos'd; whereby he does receive

Particular addition, from the bill
That writes them all alike: and so of men.
Now, if you have a situation in the file,
And not I' the worst rank of manhood, say it;

(Shakespeare, ***Macbeth, Act III, Scene i***)

When Wittgenstein speaks of *understanding* a sentence both in the sense that a sentence can replace another and in the sense that it cannot, he directs us to the importance of articulation in language and thought. By *articulation,* I mean the deployment of categories and conceptual schemes to mark distinctions and relations among our experiences, to sort out those experiences and to see the world as "jointed." To articulate our experience is to attempt to "cut the world at its joints," or to construct categories in a fashion that facilitates our goals and projects. The underlying conceptual structure of literal–conventional language[1] reflects the way convention and current knowledge (the two are not always synchronized) individuates objects and categories and presents the world as jointed.

To understand a sentence in Wittgenstein's first sense—in the sense in which it can be replaced by another sentence—is to view language as describing states of affairs through the use of labels, which are arbitrarily attached to concepts and are replaceable by another set of labels. Such a conception of language and its relation to thought is necessary if one wants to explain the intertranslatability of the following sentences, for example: "Je vais à Paris," "Ich gehe nach Paris," "I go to Paris," and "I am going to Paris." If expressions were never interchangeable, either intra- or interlinguistically, communication would be seriously hampered. People's continual ability to produce novel sentences creates a superfluity of creativity, against which the translatability of sentences is a bulwark, without which communication would otherwise be unstable.

[1]See Kittay (1987, pp. 50–55) for a discussion of the need to speak of literal–conventional language, rather than just literal language in speaking of everyday language that we do not think of as figurative.

Understanding a sentence in Wittgenstein's second sense, that is, in the sense in which a sentence cannot be replaced by another, is a function of the way linguistic novelty and creativity both spur and reflect novelty and creativity in thought. Figurative language, poetic language, and most especially metaphor are our springboard to thoughts not captured in conventional and literal articulations. When we are creative, we either exploit conventional conceptualizations but push them in new directions, or we attempt to break out of their constraints by finding alternative organizations of our concepts. In the first case, we look at implications of the present conceptualization that will lead us to new knowledge or insight. In the second case, we create new categories, and new relations among those concepts and categories that we normally accept.

Researchers have noticed how difficult it is to get people to think in radically different terms. Ward (1994) found that when he asked students to draw creatures from another galaxy, they retained properties of humans: bilateral symmetry, sense organs, appendages, and so forth. Cacciari, Levorato, and Cicogna (this volume) confirmed that even children—who are presumed to be more creative than adults and whose categorical boundaries are assumed to be more fluid—did not exhibit more creativity in this respect.[2] These researchers point out that failure to get results that depart radically from the established knowledge base is consistent with that current in recent creativity literature that stresses the similarity of creative and noncreative forms of cognition (Cacciari et al., this volume).

Gluckberg, Manfredi, and McGlone (this volume) and Gibbs (this volume) propose creative linguistic and conceptual strategies that depend on the same forms of cognition on which people rely to communicate in ordinary everyday language. For the most part, these forms of cognition depend on the first aspect of Wittgenstein's sense of understanding, the paraphrasability of sentences. Most of what people communicate in everyday language could be said in different words. However, the studies of both Gluckberg et al. and Gibbs are about metaphor. If a metaphor has cognitive importance, that is, if it contributes to genuine creativity in thought

[2]They did manifest more creativity when language, rather than drawings, was the medium used. See Cacciari et al. (this volume).

and language, it is not a mere linguistic frill. In that case, understanding the metaphorical sentence will necessitate understanding how no other words will express exactly what the metaphorical expression conveys.

The question then is how these two aspects of understanding are connected and if, by examining the first use of language, one can come to understand the creativity in the second. Metaphors may be a useful link, for although metaphor is more than a linguistic embellishment, not all metaphorical sentences are instances of creative language incapable of literal paraphrase. Consider Glucksberg et al.'s examples:

1a. His car was a lemon.
1b. My job is a jail.
1c. My surgeon was a butcher.
1d. My butcher is a real surgeon!
1e. New York may well become the next Orange County.
1f. Our love has become a filing cabinet.

All examples except 1e and 1f are fairly common and transparent metaphors. All but 1f is easily paraphrased (assuming that one knows something about the fiscal disaster that Orange County, California, experienced). And if 1f is hard to paraphrase, it is also hard to understand. The first example is more a cliché than a metaphor. One hardly need to know much about lemons to know that it could be paraphrased as "His car is constantly breaking down." But even such banal metaphors lose something in translation. Example 1a also expresses the thought that he who owns the vehicle has soured on it: that its owner would want to get rid of it, just as one would like to get rid of a sour taste in one's mouth. On the other hand, the sentence "His car is constantly breaking down" does not carry the same implications. The owner of a car that frequently breaks down might relish fixing cars. Example 1a is a metaphor, not entirely paraphrasable, but also not particularly creative. It is the ability to use words in this ordinary, but metaphorical way that both Gluckberg et al. and Gibbs see as the nub of a certain form of creative use of language.

Whereas Glucksberg et al. draws our attention to ordinary metaphors such as Examples 1a–1d, Gibbs adjures us to look at the creative use of language in the works of exceptional talents such as Shakespeare. Creative artists such as Shakespeare, claims Gibbs, draw on "image schemas," which arise as a result of recurrent and shared bodily experience (Gibbs, this volume, p. 353). Their creativity derives from their ability to elaborate on common metaphorical projections based on such bodily image schemas. People's ability to make sense of these creative uses of language depends on their shared bodily experience, by which they also engage in metaphorical projections. Gibbs maintains the following:

> The fact that we, as ordinary readers and observers, have similar metaphorical understandings of many abstract concepts—ones that arise from our own embodied experience—allows us to make sense of creative works such as that seen in the language used in *Hamlet* (Gibbs, this volume, p. 353).

Using another example, Gibbs (this volume) claims that Neruda's metaphors for love in *Ode and Burgeonings*, although very poetic and inventive, conform to a metaphorical conceptualization, *Love is a journey*, which is common in our language. *Love is a journey*, is, in turn, a metaphor based on the image schema source–path–goal. Neruda's haunting images are only the more glorious cousins of a plain Jane metaphor such as "I'll go wherever love leads me." The most poetically creative metaphors, claims Gibbs, can be traced to mundane, common metaphorical projections of bodily based conceptions that we store as image schemas.

Glucksberg et al. trace the creative processes not to common bodily based image schemas but to a process of category formation that puts exemplars at the center of concept formation. Heeding Gibbs's request to look to Shakespeare to understand creativity in language, let's consider the question Macbeth poses to the men he hires to murder Banquo. Echoing the question with which Lady Macbeth had earlier confronted him, Macbeth asks "Are ye men?" Understood literally, it is odd to face an identifiable fellow human creature and ask, "Are you a man?" As the dialogue makes clear, the question is not about routine naming. Hounds, greyhounds, mongrels, spaniel curs, shoughs, water-rugs, and demi-wolves are all called "dog," says Macbeth, but this common name does nothing to distinguish among the dogs. "Dog" in this sense is a "bill that writes them all alike." Macbeth asks the murderers if they are "men enough" to do the deed. With that question he hopes to tie their commitment to the deed to any pride they may have in their manliness.

Macbeth's is a question about *exemplification,* about that "particular addition" that distinguishes each member of a category from the others, that ranks members, and that gives to a few the privileged appellation. And so Shakespeare instantiates a "best-example" model of the exemplar theory of concepts (Smith & Medin, 1981, p. 147). The question for theories of concept formation based on exemplars is "How does one subset or instance of a category come to define in people's mind a category in which the other subsets or instances vary?" (Smith & Medin, 1981, p. 147). For Shakespeare, the best example is not the typical but the most distinguished as it approaches an ideal (even if the distinction Macbeth seeks is the capacity to be brutal in the pursuit of an ambition).

That categories are sometimes identifiable through exemplars provides insight into how metaphors can be a case of category formation or class inclusion and how, as a "limiting case of category formation" (Kittay, 1982), metaphors participate in an activity that pervades cognition (Glucksberg & Keysar, 1990). At the same time, viewing metaphors as a case of category formation also allows one to understand how metaphors not only register preexisting similarities but also create similarities.[3] The theory of metaphor as a class-inclusion statement does for Glucksberg et al. what the theory of metaphor as an extension of image schemas does for Gibbs: connect the more innovative and creative use of language captured in the poetic metaphor (or the scientific analogy based on metaphor) to more ordinary and mundane forms of cognition. In this way, both succeed in presenting theories that allow one to see how the creative use of language and thought (which is metaphor at its best) emerges out of, and yet is distinguishable from, the ordinary use of language. The task that re-

[3]The canonical statement that metaphors are based on preexisting similarities but are the source of new similarity judgments is Max Black's (1954): "It would be more illuminating in some of these cases to say that the metaphor creates the similarity rather than records a similarity antecedently existing" (p. 37).

mains for us in this chapter is to evaluate these theories in terms of their capacity to account for the creative contribution of metaphor to language and thought.

"MEN" AND FILING CABINETS: METAPHOR AS CREATIVE CATEGORIZATION

The Paradox of Unlike Things

Metaphorical statements using the verb *to be*, understood literally, are either false or meaningless. Literally speaking, cars are not lemons, nor can love be or become a filing cabinet. Some of these infelicities can be described as category mistakes, that is, predications or assertions that cannot logically be made of the subject in question (Ryle, 1949). Jobs are activities; jails, in contrast, are institutions or entities. Filing cabinets are inanimate entities, whereas love may be a relationship, an emotion, or a person. One can neither literally predicate "is (a) love" of filing cabinets nor "being a filing cabinet" of love. Some of the examples of Glucksberg et al. are neither semantic nor logical anomalies but are pragmatically or empirically odd. Hypothetically, an individual can be both a butcher and a surgeon (in some historical times the same person may well have been both). However, today chances are no one would hold both positions. New York and Orange County are both American municipalities, but because they are different municipalities, it is false to say that New York is or could become Orange County.

As these nominal metaphors are false or meaningless as identifications (understood literally), how do we make sense of them as metaphors? The suggestion is that we understand them as classifications. "His car is a lemon" is a metaphorical classification in which *lemon* names a category that subsumes *his car*, just as "A dog is an animal" is a literal classification in which *dog* is subsumed under the classification *animal*. Glucksberg et al. point out that one can transform Statements 1a–1f into statements using the comparative form, but that one cannot do so with literal comparative statements. One can say "His car is a lemon" or "His car is *like* a lemon." The *like* changes little. In contrast, Glucksberg et al. offer the following examples of literal comparisons:

2a. Copper is like tin.
2b. Coffee is like tea.
2c. Limes are like lemons.

*3a. Copper is tin.
*3b. Coffee is tea.
*3c. Limes are lemons.

Because it appears paradoxical that things that are so unalike as lemons and cars can more easily be identified using the copula than things so similar as lemons and limes, Glucksberg et al. speak of "the paradox of unlike things compared."

The interchangeability of "is" and "is like" that we find in the case of metaphorical but not in the case of literal statements is a useful criterion for assessing whether a comparison is meant metaphorically or literally. It has a paradoxical air, but it is not really a paradox. From a logical perspective, if x is literally identical to y, then x is also like y, namely x is like y in all respects. From a pragmatic perspective, if we mean to say that x is y, then we do not say x is like y. In literal speech, we differentiate *is* and *is like*, using the latter to make comparisons that fall short of identity.

Still Glucksberg et al. are right to say that metaphorical identifications are not identifications at all. Furthermore, the comparative form *is like* is not a literal comparison either; instead, the *like* is itself metaphorical (Kittay, 1995). The *like* is metaphorical because the comparison is not only between two "unlike" things, but also because the things are unlike in a particular way, and once we recognize this, we can explain away the paradox. In the case of literal comparisons, the objects compared share a conceptual space within an established and conventionalized conceptual scheme. Within that space they are differentiated. In the case of metaphorical comparisons, the objects compared do not share a settled conceptual space, and it is in this regard that they are unalike. They are unlike in that they occupy positions in two distinct conceptual domains—or at least in two domains (or semantic fields) that are being differentiated for the purposes of the discussion at hand. Within each domain, however, they occupy the same role. That is what makes it possible to drop the *like* and assert a metaphorical identity. However, in asserting the metaphorical identity, a classificatory statement is implied, for what is being identified cannot truly be identified.

The earlier discussion of category violations and metaphor indicated that when we have a category violation, the terms of the predication do not sit within a conceptual space shared by the subject of the predication. For example, *lemon* and *car* share no immediate superordinate categories; they sit in different conceptual fields. However, within a conceptual space of cars, the car identified is "in the worst rank" of cars (with respect to reliability), and among fruit, lemons are in the worst rank of fruits (with respect to sweetness and pleasantness of taste). Their identity is established relative to their place in their usual conceptual domain. In the process, the vehicle, *lemon* comes to stand for the newly created category, which also becomes a newly shared conceptual space for the car and the fruit.

Metaphorical sentences such as Examples 1c–1e require a somewhat different analysis because pragmatic, rather than semantic or logical, violations are at stake. *Butcher* and *surgeon* are found in different domains because of empirical considerations. *New York* and *Orange County* may be said to share a conceptual space, because they share a superordinate term, American counties. The metaphor depends, however, not on their commonality as local municipalities but on the distinctive feature of Orange County as a municipality that has gone bankrupt—a circumstance we expect of individuals or corporations, but not governments.

This analysis of metaphorical Sentences 1c–1e sheds new light on the anomalous examples 3a–3c. Through contextual clues, the entities compared can be understood to belong to two distinct conceptual domains, even though they are usually classified as belonging to the same domain. For example, although coffee and tea are similar in that they are both caffeinated beverages often served hot and sometimes served iced, in confirmed tea-drinking nations, there is all the difference between tea and coffee. So much so that, if we are in a tea-drinking country such as Ireland, we can say of coffee-loving Swedes

4a. Coffee is the tea of Swedes.

Likewise, in spite of the closeness of lemons and limes in the category of citrus fruit, we can say

4b. Limes are the lemons of South American Cuisine.

In these sentences, two distinct semantic fields are invoked through which the otherwise similar things are distinguished, as being in different domains for the purposes of the discussion at hand. However, the identification and the comparison are figurative in that they do not take place within the classificatory scheme that governs the literal and conventional understanding of these terms. A figurative classification-*cum*-identification is made across the distinct semantic fields.

In saying that "limes are the lemons of South America" or that "coffee is the tea of the Swedes," we are creating both a new distinction and a new set of similarities between the entities compared. The new distinction is in terms of conceptual domains: Tea and coffee are not classified by virtue of their properties as beverages, but as drinks with certain distinctive roles within different cultures. Tea in this context is an Irish sort of thing, whereas coffee is a Swedish sort of thing. In any culture in which tea predominates, coffee is not a replaceable beverage even if it too contains caffeine and is a hot liquid. In comparing the two, I privilege tea as the drink that is the exemplar of a beverage with which one wakes up in the morning, refreshes one's self in late afternoon, and finishes one's meals at all times of day. As a tea drinker, I can understand the analogous role that coffee plays in another culture, however. So in constructing my metaphor, I do two things at once: (a) I locate an analogous role for coffee and tea in two distinguishable domains, and so create an identity across domains; and (b) I privilege one, the one that is within the domain that functions as the perspective from which I regard the practice of the other, and so create a new category—one in which tea and coffee coexist, but on different terms than those that make statement 3b anomalous.

Dual Reference

When the metaphoric vehicle is used as both an exemplar and as a (ad hoc) name for a category, Glucksberg et al. call this linguistic move "dual reference." Such dual reference is characteristic of metaphor, but not of literal identification statements. A similar idea was expressed by Samuel Johnson (later cited and adopted by I. A. Richards, 1936,) that in metaphor, there are "two ideas in one." Paul Henle (1965, p.178) spoke of metaphor as characterized by a "double sort of semantic relation." Henle spoke of the vehicle as an icon in the Peirceian sense (Peirce, 1931, p. 247ff). What he meant is, I believe, very close to the idea that the vehicle forms an ad hoc category by being an exemplar of that very category. In my own work, I consider it criterial that a metaphor have a double semantic content (Kittay, 1987). In my view, a metaphor is a complex sign in which the sense of the vehicle becomes the mode of expression for the topic.

What Glucksberg et al. mean when they speak of dual reference is, I believe, a useful refinement of the view that metaphorically used terms carry a double semantic content. They spell out how the dual reference serves to metaphorically redescribe the topic. The vehicle term carries its usual meaning, or rather one of its usual meanings—that meaning that places it in a category that is delimited by the topic in a specific way: "A metaphor topic provides potentially relevant dimensions for attribution, but not their specific values" (Glucksberg et al., this volume, p. 339). But at the same time, the vehicle also serves as the name of an ad hoc category by which the topic is newly classified, so the metaphor vehicles "are used to refer to the attributive categories that provide candidate properties to be attributed to a metaphor topic" (Glucksberg et al., this volume, p. 339). Topics, then, provide conditions constraining which properties of the vehicle will be considered as properties to be metaphorically attributed to the topic. Those are the properties that can be specific values of an attributive category pertinent to the topic. So in the case of the topic "surgeon" we know that surgeons are more or less skilled; on the other hand, we may not know just how skilled or unskilled a particular surgeon is. A vehicle that belongs to some attributive category, say skill, in which it exemplifies a property, say incompetence or sloppy performance, would have this property singled out as relevant.

An Argument Against Feature Matching

Glucksberg et al. claim that results of experiments confirming that a metaphor's topic and vehicle are mutually constraining at once argue against a feature-matching approach to metaphorical interpretation. A feature-matching approach, however, has the virtue of being easily modeled computationally. Glucksberg et al. have not yet provided us with a computational model for their work. I suggest that a computational model conducive to Glucksberg et al.'s approach is a mutual constraint model (e.g., Steinhart, 1995; Thagard, Holyoak, Nelson, & Gochfeld, 1990). I believe such a model can capture the interactivity that Glucksberg et al. underscore.

The feature-matching approach to metaphor has its own set of constraints that are lost when the approach is divorced from the relational account of which it is a part. In a relational account of metaphor, a metaphorical term is always part of a system or theory. In Gentner's (1982) account terms belong to theories that delimit the sense in which people are to understand them. The system (or theory) to which the topic belongs will normally serve to constrain which of the features (of both topic and vehicle) will be matched. Nonetheless, a mutual constraint model may have processing advantages (Steinhart, 1995).

THE VIEW OF METAPHORS AS *AD HOC* CATEGORIES AND A RELATIONAL THEORY OF METAPHOR

If I have correctly characterized the position of Glucksberg et al., then their view is compatible with the relational models of metaphoric transference.[4] To say that those properties (understood as values of dimensions of attri-

[4]By relational models I mean those that claim that metaphoric transfers involve a transfer of relational structures across domains. The work of Max Black (1954) and Nelson Goodman (1968), Dedre Gentner and her associates (e.g., Gentner, 1983, and Gentner, this volume), my own work and that of my collaborator Eric Steinhart (Steinhart & Kittay, 1994), and even some of the work of the cognitive semanticists, including Gibbs, could be characterized as using a relational model of metaphoric meaning. In the discussion, I will argue that Glucksberg et al.'s views are compatible with my own.

bution) contributed by the vehicle to the topic are constrained by potentially relevant dimensions for attribution designated by the topic can be made compatible with the idea that metaphors are transfers of relations across semantic fields. One simply needs to say that the dimensions of attribution are the contrasts and affinities that partially define a term and that locate a term within a conceptual domain. When a term is metaphorically assigned a property, its relation to other terms in its field is specified by reference to the relation of the topic's place in its field. So, for example, if I want to describe the skill level of a surgeon who has seriously bungled an operation, I may want to place him off the scale of the normal value of skill needed by a surgeon. To extend the value of the dimension of that attribution, I look to another field of activity in which cutting flesh takes place but in which the degree of precision in cutting needed by the surgeon is irrelevant—that is, to butchering. I import a set of values to the original field that extends it and allows me to fully characterize my incompetent surgeon.[5] When a field is so extended, a plethora of other locutions becomes available to a speaker. In this instance, I can also say

5a. The surgeon butchered his patient.
5b. The surgeon hacked away at his patient.
5c. This surgeon was better suited for a house of carnage than the operating room.
5d. These awful scars were inflicted by a butcher, not a doctor.

and so forth.

If we can characterize what happens in terms of attributes, properties, and the category membership of individual terms, why should we burden ourselves with the more cumbersome notion of semantic fields, relationships between terms, and conceptual domains? Consider Sentences 5a–5d. They illustrate how metaphors are easily extended, both in terms of the

[5]Descriptions of metaphoric processing such as this one are characterized as a temporal process, and these have run into objections (Gibbs, 1994) from those claiming that time studies indicate that most metaphoric processing occurs as quickly as the processing of literal language. The timed studies also indicate that mappings that are not usual or conventional take more time to process, particularly when an extensive context is not provided (Gibbs, 1994, p. 100). Conventional metaphors and novel mappings may indeed involve different *actual* processing strategies. At the same time, their logical and conceptual properties may be the same and describable in the two-step manner in which both Glucksberg et al. and I tend to speak.

implications that are a consequence of a particular nominal metaphor and in terms of using the various grammatical resources of a semantic field. If a surgeon is a butcher, then what this surgeon does is not "operate on," but "butcher" his patients; the place he works is no longer an operating room but a "house of carnage"; he no longer "makes incisions," he "hacks away at his subject," and so forth. Glucksberg et al. advance our understanding of how, through the double semantic move, ad hoc categories are provided when using metaphor. However, their concentration on particular terms and isolated categories does not explain this sort of productivity of metaphors. The semantic field approach and the approach used by Gibbs both give us a way to think about this form of productivity. The creativity of metaphor lies both in its productivity and in its ability to generate new categories. Metaphor allows us to push the boundaries of language by expanding the expressive possibilities of language and of thought and by offering different ways of arranging concepts, and of drawing new relations between categories.

There is another related difficulty with the dual reference model. As Glucksberg et al. point out, the dual reference of using an exemplar as a category name occurs when we speak of tissues as Kleenex, a copy as a Xerox, and so forth. Although the similarity is instructive, it is also important to note how the cases are different. If we did not know that Xerox, although used generically, is a brand name, nothing we communicate by its use would be lost. However, if we only know that *butcher* can refer to someone who bungles a job, we lose the metaphoricity of sentences such as 1c–1d, nor would we extend the metaphor in the ways suggested in Sentences 5a–5d. This difference, I suggest, is a difference between run-of-the-mill polysemy and metaphor. Because we know what a butcher is, what he does, where he does it, and how this job fits into a set of other activities and professions, we can understand the sentence as a metaphor and deploy the larger semantic field to which the term belongs. We extend the range and possible perceptions of surgery, reorder the field and its activities in light of the juxtaposition of butchery and surgery.

The conflation of a brand name with the category to which the object with the brand name belongs is, on the other hand, fairly conceptually uninteresting because the use of an exemplar as a category name does nothing to disrupt the conceptual organization to which the relevant categories belong. When the Xerox Corporation manufactured their copiers, they flooded the market with a machine that may or may not have been the first photocopying instrument of its kind, but "Xerox" became the name of a category whose introduction into the language was matched by an introduction of a new thing into people's lives: the photocopier. When I call my surgeon a butcher, or a paintbrush a pump (Schön, 1979), or love a filing cabinet, the category that is formed thereby describes not a new thing, but a new *view* of things.

Creation of a New Category

New categories are created, then, in one of two ways: Either an invention or discovery not already covered by our classificatory scheme will necessitate the introduction of a new concept (e.g., the carburetor, the HIV virus, the computer, etc.), or a new category may arise that depends on no new inventions, no additions to what already is, but resorts to what already exists. The latter can take place either when an existing category is extended to include instances that substantially alter the category (e.g., harassment extended to include unwanted sexual encounters) or when a category is newly introduced without a new objective corollary being introduced (e.g., the Freudian unconscious, which reconfigures the relations between conscious and nonconscious mental states). Metaphorically created categories are of the latter sort. Categorical statements are implicitly similarity statements, as all members of a category are so classified because of some salient similarity. Yet if metaphors do not report an antecedent similarity, but instead create the similarity, they do so by dislodging some items from familiar classifications and regrouping them with items that normally belong to different, even disjoint categories. So dislodging and regrouping items or subclassifications not only creates a new category, but also disrupts normal classifications.

Let us take a nonmetaphorical example to begin with. Consider the idea of "marital rape." This notion is an extension of the notion of rape, which has as its paradigm coerced sex by someone (usually a stranger) with whom the rape victim has never consented to have sexual relations. Because marriage is a situation in which both partners have already consented to have sexual relations, it is, at first, unclear how a husband can "rape" a wife. By understanding that consensual sex means consent to each sexual encounter, we revise the notion of rape, and the notion of marriage, so that we can speak of rape within marriage. This is a nonmetaphorical extension (even creation) of meaning because, once reconceived, the new categories are stable. Marriage means many things besides unrestrained sexual access to a partner, and sexual encounters are individuated occurrences. One comes to understand that consent on one occasion does not mean consent on any occasion. The meaning of marriage might shift, but the shift is stable.

Contrast this with a metaphoric classification. A group of researchers were attempting to create a paintbrush using synthetic bristles. They were unsuccessful in creating one that would apply paint as evenly as natural bristles until one researcher remarked, "a paintbrush is a pump." The researcher realized that "when a paintbrush is pressed against a surface, paint is forced through the *spaces between bristles* onto the surface" (Schön, 1979, p. 257) as if the liquid were being pumped. Natural bristles formed smooth curves through which the liquid flows; in contrast, the synthetic bristles bend at an angle. The insight that "a paintbrush is a pump" enabled the team to devise a synthetic brush that would curve when pressed to a surface and so allow for the smooth pumping action characteristic of natural bristles.

This is a fine example of the creative turn of mind that metaphoric thinking and metaphoric classification permits. Yet in spite of the productivity of this metaphor, we do not revise our usual classificatory scheme: We do not henceforth speak of paintbrushes and pumps as if they were one sort of thing. For the purposes of solving the problem at hand, the properties associated with pumps were tested on paintbrushes. However, once the relevant properties had been isolated, pumps remained pumps and paintbrushes remained paintbrushes.

Why are new metaphorical categories unstable? Why do they so often resist incorporation into an established classifactory scheme? Because one categorical grouping does not exist apart from other categories. To classify is to presume a scheme of classification. *X* is a *Y*, and not a *Z*; *X* is a subclass of *M* and a superordinate of *N*; *X* can be predicated of *A*, but not of *B*. New classifications, reclassifications, and extensions of categories impact in more or less profound ways on other classifications. What does the world have to be like for rape within marriage to be possible, and what does the world have to be like for a paintbrush to be a pump? What has to change in the way in which we think about the world for marital rape to be included among our concepts, and what has to change if we were to think of paintbrushes as a subset of pumps? To think of metaphoric statements as implicit categorical statements is, I think, correct and persuasive. However, by itself, it is not a theory of creativity by means of metaphor. Such a theory needs to take into consideration the interconnections among categories, the implications and presuppositions in categorical classifications that form the webs of belief that are challenged or freshly constructed in the formation of novel metaphors and the enlivening of dead or conventional ones. As Gibbs points out in this volume, fresh, creative metaphors can as well be formed from conventional metaphors that already have a hold in our thinking (Gibbs, 1994).

In the case of the metaphor "My love is a filing cabinet" I, for one, am still trying to interpret it. In a timed study I would still not have pushed the button as quickly as I would when confronted with literal sentences such as "My love is a journal editor" or "My love is lasting" or metaphorical ones such as "My love is a rose" or "My love is the sun." This is doubtless because filing cabinets are highly constrained topics, which is also to say both that the values of the dimensions of the attributes of love are not well specified by any of the properties of filing cabinets and that filing cabinets have a very well-defined, specific place in our conceptual scheme. Gibbs would say that "My love is a filing cabinet" is such a difficult metaphor to interpret because it does not adhere to one of the five conceptual metaphors by which we conceptualize love[6]: Love is a journey, love is a force, love is a unity, and so forth. However, it is still a metaphor, and when I do interpret it I will not have simply created a category that is an abstraction from file cabinets. Instead, I might use "filing cabinet" as a trope for a love in which one lover feels overanalyzed or locked away or as a way of speaking of the sad remains of a love that was once vibrant and warm, as in the following poem which I chanced upon:

The Filing Cabinet

Now we file them,
Love's memories,
In manila folders, A to Z,
Place them in steel gray
Hanging files.

Once warm and enfolding
As an old stuffed chair,
Our love then
Embraced us.

Now patterned not by our rhythms,
But dissected and desiccated,
Fractured fragments lie
Wrapped in metal drawers
And locked away.

—Anonymous

[6]Some concepts, such as love, seem to be expressible only through metaphor. What *is* love literally speaking? Some elements of the concept are fixed: It is between an individual and at least one other, and the other needn't be another individual. It is an emotion of high intensity or a disposition to act in certain ways. It creates bonds and obligations and expectations, and so forth. It is, however, a concept with much left out. Note how intentional states such as love are often characterized metaphorically. In considering why certain concepts are so often metaphorically described, I believe that one must consider how available the phenomenon in question is for public inspection. I believe that the metaphors that remain in our language and substitute for literal conceptualizations are used for concepts that are not available for public inspection and are given metaphoric characterizations that translate the experiences they give rise to into publicly available ones.

In any case, there will be a number of related concepts and categories that will be brought into the explication of that improbable but interpretable metaphor—concepts and categories that will permit the extension of the metaphor as well. When the metaphor is interpreted, our usual conceptual scheme will be disrupted, but the interconnection of concepts, the extent to which concepts depend in part on one another for their meanings—"provides a sort of inertia against which the nonstandard interpretations must work."[7] This means that the disruption of concepts is usually temporary, not permanent.[8]

METAPHORS AS EMBODIED CONCEPTS

The position of Gibbs emphasizes just such interrelations between concepts, relations that underlie systematic connections between metaphors. Although the work of some scholars (e.g., myself and Gentner et al., this volume) have emphasized the systematicity and relationality of metaphors that are novel, the work of Lakoff and Johnson (1980) and of those, such as Gibbs, who have followed their forays into cognitive semantics, have stressed the systematicity of the conventional metaphors that "litter" our everyday language.

These cognitive semanticists have taken the idea of systematicity still further. First, they claim that the interrelations between metaphors reveal

[7]I am indebted to Thomas Ward for this way of putting the point.

[8]The qualification "usually" is of great importance. Of course, some metaphors have the power to permanently alter our conceptual schemes. These metaphors eventually lose their vivacity as metaphors as they become incorporated into our conceptual schemes. Nietzsche called them *effaced metaphors* (Nietzsche, 1979). Metaphors that fall short of the power to transform our linguistic organization may still have the power to change the way we govern our affairs. Thomas Ward offered some examples that play off the metaphor "love is a filing cabinet." He suggests that "in thinking about love as a filing cabinet, isn't it possible to come away with, for example, the idea that relationships provide the comfortably confining structures that can help us to order and organize and make sense of our lives? Might a person who previously avoided commitments be moved to establish one as a result? Might another who previously viewed loving relationships as positive opportunities for growth begin to see them as uncomfortably confining repositories and start to avoid commitments?" The answer to all of these queries is "certainly." However, that is still not the same as saying that the meaning of *filing cabinet* now is standardly connected to the idea of love—that, for example, someone who fails to know of such a connection is seriously deficient in their knowledge or understanding of *filing cabinet* or *love* in the same way one would say that their understanding was defective if they failed to grasp the connection between filing cabinets and offices or love and romance.

a deeper conceptual structure that is itself metaphorical, so that metaphor is not a matter of linguistic but of conceptual structure. Second, they claim that this conceptual structure is grounded in our bodies, through the use of embodied schemas, which are then projected onto other domains. The process, they claim, results in metaphors that are easily interpretable because they rely on a shared set of recurrent, bodily patterned experiences. Gibbs, in his chapter in this volume, builds on these two theses and adds a third, relevant to the question of creativity: that the creativity of poetic metaphors is more often an extension and a variant of conventional conceptual metaphors based on image schemas than it is a new mapping across domains not already metaphorically mapped by embodied conventional metaphors.

There are merits to each of these proposals, but there are also problems. Many of the difficulties have to do with a lack of clarity about what is being proposed. Others have to do with a zealousness in cognitive semantics that allows its practitioners to overlook some important counters to their arguments. Because this chapter cannot be an exploration of all of the theses of cognitive semanticists, but only of the views put forward by Gibbs in this volume, I limit my remarks to the following: (a) Embodiment is the ground of metaphor, (b) the metaphors putatively based on image schemas dominate poetic metaphor, and (c) the notion of a conceptual metaphor is well defined.

First, however, I want to applaud the idea that creative concepts are not simply the "products of the disembodied mind" but derive from structures that already exist in the world, "that is, the human body and our perceptions of it" (Gibbs, this volume). Gibbs decries the separation of body and mind, and even more the priority of mind over body.[9] I am in full agreement. We are first and foremost embodied creatures, for whom experience is always grounded in our physicality, even as imaginatively we

[9]The duality of mind and body, a doctrine generally attributed to Descartes, is now largely out of favor with philosophers. The monism that is favored is some variety of materialism, for example, the naturalism of Daniel Dennett or the neurophysiological reductionism championed by Patricia and Paul Churchland, or a supervenience where the mental properties are said to supervene on the physical ones. However, even as mind is "reduced" to the physical, cognition itself remains almost entirely couched in mental, and not in physical, terms.

soar beyond its confines. Cognitive semantics, I believe, is right to point to the myriad ways in which our bodily structures, and our most basic physical relations to the world, give rise to relational structures that shape other interactions.

Embodiment as the Ground of Metaphor

Even as we endorse such claims, we have to take care not to reinstate the mind–body separation. We do this when we take sheer physicality as foundational. The difficulty with the claim that embodiment is the ground of all (or most) metaphors is that the body, at least as it is experienced by humans, is always already animated by mind and the products of mind, that is, culture (see Russell, 1992).

Consider Gibbs's example: *stand.* In particular, consider the expression "stand for" to mean "hold fast to a particular position." "I *stand for* the right of women to choose whether or not to bring a pregnancy to term." It is difficult to see how our bodily experience of standing would give rise to such a usage if the linguistic use were not mediated by a cultural practice in which individuals, in a seated assemblage, are asked to stand to evince their support or opposition to a point or policy. The physical experience of standing (or sitting) could not guide our understanding if the social practice were that one sits down (from, let's say, a standing position) when one wants to be counted for or against a point. One could argue that the cultural practice of standing to endorse or object to a point is itself a feature of the way in which the physical gesture of standing facilitates resistance or the exertion of effort. That could well be the case. However, without a cultural practice that specifies and gives social content to physical gesture, the gesture remains too indeterminate to carry meaning.

Similarly, consider the expression "stand down." The expression has come to mean "a cessation of normal activity," as in "After the last instance of sexual harassment aboard a Navy ship, the Navy decided to have a *stand down* throughout the force, and spend an entire week doing nothing else but exploring appropriate sexual conduct toward women in the Navy." Again, I suggest that nothing in our bodily experience of erect posture gives us a way to understand such a usage. We are most likely to learn that *a stand down* means a halt, or cessation, in the way in which we learn any lexicalized expression. However, if we know that in courtroom practice, when a witness asks to stand down from the witness chair, she asks to cease giving testimony, then we can connect the meaning of the phrase to a physical movement, but one already endowed with a socially given meaning. It is this meaning that is projected in a new domain.

Gibbs himself carefully and appropriately hedges his language, and thereby avoids a reductionist position. Of his experiments with *stand*, for example, he says, "These data provide very strong support for the hypothesis that people's understanding of *stand* is *partly* motivated by image schemas that arise from bodily experiences of standing" (Gibbs, this volume, p. 368, emphasis added). However, the emphasis on image schemas can mislead us into accepting a new foundationalism, this one based on some naturalized conception of the body's relation to the world, one which itself presupposes the very division of mind and body that cognitive semanticists say they want to challenge.

Metaphors Based on Image Schemas Dominate Poetic Metaphor

The notion that embodiment is the ground of all or even most metaphors suggests that we locate metaphors based on image schemas and that these dominate poetic metaphor. This view is problematic for two reasons. First, we can have metaphors that are very much based on our embodiment but that do not deploy the image schemas that Gibbs and other cognitive semanticists speak of. For example, consider the metaphor I heard one audience member say to his friend at the conclusion of a Martha Graham dance concert: "Now you are no longer a Martha Graham virgin." It's hard to know to what sort of image schema we ought to attribute our understanding of this metaphor—although it is both very easy to understand and it is surely grounded in bodily experience. It is by virtue of our cultural understanding of the loss of virginity as the entry into a world of previously unknown pleasure rather than, say, the loss of virginity as enduring a painful experience, or being no longer fit for a sanctified marriage, that both speaker and audience understand the metaphor in the same way.

Second, identifying a metaphor as based on a particular image schema can misdirect us as to the actual nature of the metaphor. It seems to me that this is what happens in the interpretation Gibbs offers of the famous Hamlet soliloquy. Gibbs suggests that the soliloquy incorporates the schema balance—that in the balanced measures of "To be or not to be" we see Hamlet's plight and that our shared bodily experience, captured in the schema *balance*, allows us to empathize with the quandary of the Danish prince. However, Gibbs, I think, is misled in his effort to locate the image schema in which to ground this linguistic figuration. Not balance, but stasis, is expressed in the soliloquy. It is the stasis of Buridan's ass, not the common experience of balance, that Hamlet expresses.

Of course, here too, the concept of stasis is itself a physical notion. However, a state of equilibrium can be expressive either of a harmony (attributable to a desirable balance) or of an agitation and disharmony (attributable to the pull—or repulsion—of opposing forces). Such diverse understandings of a physical state indicate once again that metaphors (and figurative language more generally) are grounded not so much in an embodiment that is universally understood as in an embodiment that can take on myriad interpretations—interpretations that depend on cultural, psychological, and situational variables. The image schema is far too abstract and too general to give us real insight into a specific metaphor or figuration.

Conceptual Metaphors

Do these image schemas, when "metaphorically projected" to another domain, yield what Gibbs and other cognitive semanticists call conceptual metaphors? Gibbs gives us an example of the image schema source–path–goal, which, when projected onto the domain of love, becomes the "conceptual metaphor" *love is a journey* and when projected to the domain of purposes and intentions becomes *purposes are destinations.* The notion is attractive for many reasons. It allows us to understand interconnections among metaphors in a comprehensive way, and because conceptual metaphors are so general, they unify the many specific metaphors—both banal and creative—that are found in our language. These interconnections and unities help explain the swiftness and ease with which we understand metaphors. These are indeed important reasons for appealing to the idea of a conceptual metaphor.

Then again, I am not entirely sure what a conceptual metaphor is and how it differs from any other sort of metaphor. As the many theories of concept formation indicate, there is not one universally accepted understanding of concepts. What may be universally accepted is that we think with concepts and articulate our experiences using concepts. As such, concepts are neither metaphorical nor literal. They are the principles we use in grouping things together—however we theorize that process. We do not, however, communicate with concepts. Concepts, whether they are universals or mental entities or functions and dispositions (Heath, 1967; Smith & Medin, 1981), require an expressive medium, usually language, to be communicated or expressed. When we use concepts in a particular way, metaphors are produced in the expressive medium (Steinhart & Kittay, 1994). We can speak of concepts that are natural kinds, that are ad hoc, that are socially constructed, and so forth, but a literal–metaphorical distinction among concepts seems to me to be ill defined. Because the notion of a conceptual metaphor does offer us a way of speaking about connections among metaphors, we need to ask if we can find an alternative understanding that will provide equally satisfactory insights.

What even the dubious poem *The Filing Cabinet* suggests is that almost any metaphor, no matter how removed from any identifiable image schemas, can serve to organize an entire set of thoughts about the topic of the metaphor. If, as I and other semantic field theorists maintain, all terms are lodged in at least one semantic field, and if metaphors project relations governing one field (those of the vehicle) onto another field (those of the topic), then all metaphors are extendable in ways that conceptual metaphors are. Furthermore, the interconnections between individual metaphors as well as extended metaphors (e.g. the interconnection between purposes as destinies and love as a journey) can also be understood as not being the function of conceptual metaphors. These interconnections are attributable to the underlying conceptual structures and processes that allow us to project one domain onto another and to the connections among concepts and conceptual domains. For example, we can look at both purposes and love in terms of journeys, destinies, movement, and alteration because both purposes and love lend themselves to agentive action, and to change and development. These are features love and purposes share with many, if not most, intentional states. We do not need image schemes or conceptual metaphors to explain why we can conceive of both purposes and love in a similar fashion.

Conceptual metaphors are supposed to be embodied concepts, resting on universally available image schemas, and so not only do the conceptual metaphors *love is a journey* and *purposes are destinations* share the schema source–path–goal, but also this schema grounds them both in a shared bodily experience. However, agency and change are also grounded in the body, but they are grounded in bodies already inhabited by minds, emotions, and enculturated beliefs. The unities and commonalities exhibited by intentional states allow us to quickly move between fields, utilizing the analogical processes responsible for metaphors.

I locate the creative contribution of metaphor not in a conceptual scheme that is metaphorically structured (in part, because I am not sure what that means) but in the analogical leaps across domains that characterize thought as surely as thought is characterized by any inference processes (viz., induction and deduction). It is the choice of fields to bring together and in the direction in which to carry out the analogies that are the mark of genius of which Aristotle (Aristotle, *Poetics*, 1954) spoke when he wrote

> But the greatest thing, by far, is to be a master of metaphor. It is the one thing that cannot be learnt from others; and it is also a sign of genius since a good metaphor implies an intuitive perception of similarity of dissimilars. Through resemblance, metaphor makes things clearer.

What cannot be learned from others is when the analogical leap across domains needs to be made, when such a projection from one domain onto another will be fruitful. In studies of the work in molecular biology laboratories, Kevin Dunbar (this volume) found that the most creative and productive ones showed a high frequency in the generation of analogies and the sustained collaborative elaboration of analogies.

Gibbs may be correct in saying that the "vast majority of novel metaphors in poetry and literature reflect fixed patterns of metaphorical mappings between dissimilar source and target domains. The source domains most frequently used in the metaphorical mappings have bodily based image schematic structures" (Gibbs, this volume, p. 362). However, this is an empirical claim that would require, first, an exhaustive study of novel metaphors in literature; second, an explicit delineation of novel versus standard or conventional metaphors; and third, a clear way of showing that a novel metaphor is, in fact, only a variation of a fixed pattern of metaphorical mappings. As far as I know, none of this work has yet been done. As of now, this is a speculation that easily can influence the choice of poems and metaphors to analyze. Without more well-founded empirical evidence, I would rather say that sometimes novel metaphors play off conventional ones by extending them in new directions; and sometimes novel metaphors involve new mappings, as for instance between paintbrushes and pumps, or love and filing cabinets. The latter, incidentally, are more difficult to interpret and take people longer to understand (Gibbs, 1994, p. 104).

By championing this more open thesis, we allow for the interesting conceptual findings available to those who generate many analogies and stimulate *many* metaphorical mappings. We can also incorporate the view that the creation of metaphor is at once the creation of ad hoc categories, for if most all creative metaphors only elaborate fixed metaphorical mappings, the creation of new categories is strongly constrained by the domains most commonly matched. The more restrictive view, I believe, does not do justice to the sort of stretching and warping of our conceptual schemes that metaphor engenders, a happy "de-forming" of fixed modes of thought that allow us to think new thoughts, devise new articulations, and find new concepts by which to understand our world.

Although creativity in language, just as creativity in thought, is always connected to the less creative forms of language and cognition, our theory must still make adequate room for that extra something, that leap of genius, which is not reducible to the commonplace.

REFERENCES

Aristotle. (1954). *Poetics* (I. Bywater Trans.). New York: Routledge.

Black, M. (1954). Metaphor. *Proceedings of the Aristotelian Society, 55.*

Gentner, D. (1982). Are scientific analogies metaphors? In D. S. Miall (Ed.), *Metaphor: Problems and perspectives* (pp. 106–112). New York: Humanities Press.

Gentner, D. (1983). Structure-mapping: A theoretical framework for analogy. *Cognitive Science, 7,* 155–170.

Gibbs, R. W., Jr. (1994). *The poetics of mind: Figurative thought, language and understanding.* Cambridge, England: Cambridge University Press.

Glucksberg, S., & Keysar, B. (1990). Understanding metaphorical comparisons: Beyond similarity. *Psychological Review, 97,* 3–18.

Goodman, N. (1968). *Languages of art.* Indianapolis, IN: Bobbs-Merrill.

Heath, P. L. (1967). Concept. In P. Edwards (Ed.), *Encyclopedia of Philosophy* (Vol. 2, pp. 177–180). New York: Macmillan/Free Press.

Henle, P. (1965). Metaphor. In P. Henle (Ed.), *Language, thought and culture* (pp. 173–195). Ann Arbor, MI: Ann Arbor Paperbacks.

Kittay, E. F. (1982). The creation of similarity: A discussion of metaphor in light of Tversky's theory of similarity. In P. D. Asquith & T. Nickles (Eds.), Proceedings of the 1982 Biennial Meeting of the *Philosophy of Science Association,* (pp. 394–405). East Lansing, MI: Philosophy of Science Association.

Kittay, E. F. (1987). *Metaphor: Its cognitive force and linguistic structure.* Oxford, England: Oxford University Press.

Kittay, E. F. (1995). Metaphor as rearranging the furniture of the mind: A reply to Donald Davidson's "What metaphors mean." In Z. Radman (Ed.), *From a metaphorical point of view: A multidisciplinary approach to the cognitive content of metaphor* (pp. 73–116). Berlin: Walter de Gruyter.

Lakoff, G., & Johnson, M. (1980). *Metaphors we live by.* Chicago: University of Chicago Press.

Nietzsche, F. (1979). On truth and lying in the moral sense. In D. Breazeale (Ed. and Trans.), *Philosophy and truth: Selections from Nietzsche's notebooks of the early 1870's* (pp. 79–97). Atlantic Highlands, NJ: Humanities Press.

Peirce, C. S. (1931). *Collected papers* (C. Hartshorne & P. Weiss, Trans., Vol. 2). Cambridge, MA: Harvard University Press.

Richards, I. A. (1936). *The philosophy of rhetoric.* Oxford, England: Oxford University Press.

Russell, J. (1992). *On following Heidegger: Metaphor and poetic leadership.* Unpublished doctoral dissertation, State University of New York at Stony Brook.

Ryle, G. (1949). *The concept of mind.* New York: Barnes & Noble.

Schön, D. A. (1979). Generative metaphor: A perspective on problem setting in social policy. In A. Ortony (Ed.), *Metaphor and thought* (pp. 254–284). Cambridge, England: Cambridge University Press.

Smith, E. E., & Medin, D. L. (1981). *Categories and concepts.* Cambridge, MA: Harvard University Press.

Steinhart, E. (1995). *A formal semantic theory of metaphor.* Unpublished doctoral dissertation, State University of New York at Stony Brook.

Steinhart, E., & Kittay, E. F. (1994). Generating metaphors from networks: A formal interpretation of the semantic field theory of metaphor. In J. Hintikka (Ed.), *Aspects of metaphor* (pp. 41–95). Dordrecht, The Netherlands: Kluwer Academic Publishing.

Thagard, P., Holyoak, K., Nelson, G., & Gochfeld, D. (1990). Analogue retrieval by constraint satisfaction. *Artificial Intelligence, 46,* 256–310.

Ward, T. B. (1994). Structured imagination: The role of category structure in exemplar generation. *Cognitive Psychology, 27,* 1–40.

16

Analogy and Creativity in the Works of Johannes Kepler

Dedre Gentner, Sarah Brem, Ron Ferguson, Philip Wolff, Arthur B. Markman, and Ken Forbus

Analogy seems to have a share in all discoveries, but in some it has the lion's share.

(Polya, 1954, p. 17)

"The roads by which men arrive at their insights into celestial matters seem to me almost as worthy of wonder as those matters in themselves."

—Johannes Kepler

Analogy is often linked with creative thought (Finke, 1990, 1995; Finke, Ward & Smith, 1992; Gentner, 1982; Hesse, 1966; Holyoak & Thagard, 1995; Koestler, 1963; Perkins, 1994; Ward, Finke, & Smith, 1995). Boden (1994b) stated that "a psychological theory of creativity needs to explain how analogical thinking works" (p. 76). Our goal in this chapter is to illuminate the processes by which analogy promotes creativity and

This work was supported by National Science Foundation Grant BNS-87-20301 and Office of Naval Research Grant N00014-92-J-1098. Ron Ferguson received support from a Northwestern University Cognitive Science Fellowship.

conceptual change. We lay out four mechanisms by which analogy can act to create changes in knowledge, and consider the sorts of changes they promote.

We draw on the works of Johannes Kepler (1571–1630) to illustrate our points. Kepler is a particularly apt subject for studying analogy in discovery. He was a highly creative thinker, whose work spans and contributes to a period of immense change in scientific theory. He was also a prolific and intense analogizer. His writings teem with analogies, ranging from playful to serious, and from local comparisons to large extended analogies that evolved over decades and that were central in his discoveries.

We examine Kepler's use of analogies as revealed in his major works and his journals. Before doing so, however, we first address two important points. First, we want to be clear that in analyzing and simulating Kepler's analogies we are not claiming to be capturing anything like the whole of his thought processes. We are merely trying to be as explicit as we can, with the understanding that much is left to be explained. Second, we use Kepler's writings to infer his thought processes. To what extent is this justified? In particular, can we assume that his extended analogies were actually used in his thought processes, as opposed to being merely rhetorical devices? There are some grounds for optimism on this point, for Kepler's writings are unusually rich in descriptions of his thought processes. Many of Kepler's commentators have noted the exceptional—at times even excessive—candor and detail of his scientific writing. Holton (1973), in noting that Kepler has been relatively neglected among the great early scientists, stated

> [Modern scientists are] . . . taught to hide behind a rigorous structure the actual steps of discovery—those guesses, errors, and occasional strokes of good luck without which creative scientific work does not usually occur. But Kepler's embarrassing candor and intense emotional involvement force him to give us a detailed account of his tortuous process. . . . He gives us lengthy accounts of his failures, though sometimes they are tinged with ill-concealed pride in the difficulty of his task. With rich imagination he frequently finds

> analogies from every phase of life, exalted or commonplace. He is apt to interrupt his scientific thoughts, either with exhortations to the reader to follow a little longer through the almost unreadable account, or with trivial side issues and textual quibbling, or with personal anecdotes or delighted exclamations about some new geometrical relation, a numerological or musical analogy. (pp. 69–70)

Kepler's inclusiveness stemmed in part from his possibly overoptimistic rather naive belief that readers would wish to follow "the roads by which men arrive at their insights into celestial matters." In the introduction to the *Astronomia Nova* (Kepler, 1609/1992) he states this agenda:

> Here it is a question not only of leading the reader to an understanding of the subject matter in the easiest way, but also, chiefly, of the arguments, meanderings, or even chance occurrences by which I the author first came upon that understanding. Thus, in telling of Christopher Columbus, Magellan, and of the Portuguese, we do not simply ignore the errors by which the first opened up America, the second, the China Sea, and the last, the coast of Africa; rather, we would not wish them omitted, which would indeed be to deprive ourselves of an enormous pleasure in reading. (p. 78)

Kepler (1609/1992) was explicit in his intention to share the difficulties of discovery: "I therefore display these occasions [errors and meanderings] scrupulously, with, no doubt, some attendant difficulty for the reader. Nevertheless, that victory is sweeter that was born in danger, and the sun emerges from the clouds with redoubled splendour" (p. 95). Accordingly, Kepler frequently included long, tedious sections of calculations made in pursuit of false assumptions, informing the reader afterward that the line of reasoning had been wrong from the start. In the midst of one such section he wrote, "If this wearisome method has filled you with loathing, it should more properly fill you with compassion for me, as I have gone through it at least seventy times" (p. 256). This is not to say that Kepler's writings are pure diaries; his commentators note that some filtering and organizing took place. But his fascination with the cognitive process of discovery led him to preserve much of the trail. A striking case occurred in 1621 when he published a second edition of his first book, the *Mysterium Cosmographicum* (Kepler, 1596/1981). Kepler's ideas had changed radically in the 25 intervening years, yet he chose not to rewrite but to leave the original text intact, adding notes that specified how and why his ideas had changed. He commented on why he preserved the errors in the original: "I enjoy recognizing them, because they tell me by what meanders, and by feeling along what walls through the darkness of ignorance, I have reached the shining gateway of truth" (Kepler, 1596/1981, p. 215).

Finally, Kepler includes a running commentary on his reactions. He makes the kinds of remarks that modern scientists cull from their papers: for example,

> If I had embarked upon this path a little more thoughtfully, I might have immediately arrived at the truth of the matter. But since I was blind from desire [to explain the deviation from a circular orbit] I did not pay attention to each and every part . . . and thus entered into new labyrinths, from which we will have to extract ourselves. (Kepler, 1609/1992, pp. 455–456)

or, from the same work, "Consider, thoughtful reader, and you will be transfixed by the force of the argument . . ." and again,

> And we, good reader, will not indulge in this splendid triumph for more than one small day . . . restrained as we are by the rumours of a new rebellion, lest the fabric of our achievement perish with excessive rejoicing. (p. 290)

The open spontaneity of Kepler's writing offers encouragement for the belief that his writings were at least partly reflective of this thinking.

TRACING KEPLER'S ANALOGIES

Kepler was a prolific analogizer. Not only in his books but also in his journals and letters, he used analogies constantly. In some cases the analogies seem simply playful. In other cases, analogizing is integral to his theorizing. This is consistent with research showing that analogies to prior knowledge can foster insight into new material (Bassok, 1990; Bassok & Holyoak,

1989; Catrambone & Holyoak, 1989; Clement, 1988; Dunbar, 1995; Forbus, Gentner, & Law, 1995; Gentner, 1982; Gentner & Gentner, 1983; Gentner, Rattermann, & Forbus, 1993; Gick & Holyoak, 1980, 1983; Holyoak, Junn, & Billman, 1984; Keane, 1988; Novick & Holyoak, 1991; Novick & Tversky, 1987; Ross, 1987; Spellman & Holyoak, 1993; Thagard, 1992).

Kepler returned to certain analogies repeatedly across different works, extending and analyzing them further on successive bouts. In this chapter, our goal is to characterize the mechanisms by which these analogies led to creative change in knowledge. We first briefly summarize the course of discovery that led him to his new account of celestial mechanics, including his use of extended analogies. We then trace Kepler's analogical processes, using structure-mapping theory to trace his inferences and analogical extensions. We show that with reasonable representational assumptions we can simulate some, though not all, of his mapping processes in a plausible manner.

KEPLER'S CELESTIAL PHYSICS

Johannes Kepler (1571–1630) is today best known for his three laws of planetary motion.[1] His far more important contributions in changing people's conception of the solar system are difficult to appreciate—ironically, in part because of his very success. The conceptual structure that existed prior to Kepler's work is now almost impossible to call forth. When Kepler began his work, the dominant view was that the heavenly bodies revolved around the Earth, supported by crystalline spheres, traveling at uniform speed in orbits made up of perfect circles. This Greek system, perfected by Ptolemy, had been in force for over 16 centuries with only minor changes.

Medieval cosmology differed from modern cosmology not only in its beliefs but also in the character of its explanations. The goal of theory was

[1]The present discussion was compiled from a variety of sources: Barker (1991, 1993); Baumgardt (1952); Butterfield, 1957; Gingerich (1993); Hanson (1958); Holton (1973); Koestler (1963); Koyré (1973); Kuhn (1957); Layzer (1984); Mason (1962); Stephenson (1994); Toulmin & Goodfield (1961); and Vickers (1984). Some of this material also appears in Gentner, Brem, Ferguson, Wolff, Levidow, Markman, and Forbus (1997) in a discussion of Kepler's conceptual change.

not to provide causal mechanisms but to reveal mathematical regularity and predictability. Here Kepler's path diverged from that of his predecessors. As Toulmin and Goodfied (1961, p. 198) put it, "The lifelong, self-appointed mission of Johann Kepler . . . was to reveal the new, inner coherence of the Sun-centered planetary system. His central aim was to produce a 'celestial physics,' a system of astronomy of a new kind, in which the forces responsible for the phenomena were brought to light." Holton (1973, p. 71) notes, "Kepler's genius lies in his early search for a physics of the solar system. He is the first to look for a universal physical law based on terrestrial mechanics to comprehend the whole universe in its quantitative details."[2] Kepler laid out his agenda as follows:

> I am much occupied with the investigation of the physical causes. My aim in this is to show that the celestial machine is to be likened not to a divine organism but rather to a clockwork . . . , insofar as nearly all the manifold movements are carried out by means of a single, quite simple magnetic force, . . . Moreover, I show how this physical conception is to be presented through calculation and geometry. (Kepler, in a 1605 letter to von Hohenburg, cited in Holton, 1973, p. 72)

To understand the magnitude of the conceptual change involved, an account of the prior state of belief is necessary. Western cosmology in the 16th century, continuing the tradition laid down by Plato and Aristotle and culminating in Ptolemy's system of the 2nd century AD, was roughly as follows:

1. The earth is at the center of the universe and is itself unmoving.
2. The earth is surrounded by physically real crystalline spheres, containing the heavenly bodies, which revolve around the Earth.
3. The Heavenly bodies move in perfect circles at uniform velocity.

---

[2]There were others, including Gilbert, in the set of early searchers, but Kepler was the first who sought to apply terrestrial physics to the universe.

(Epicycles and eccentrically positioned circles were admitted into the system to account for the observed motions.)

4. Celestial phenomena must be explained in different terms from earthly phenomena. Heavenly bodies and their spheres are made of different matter altogether. They are composed not of the four terrestrial elements—Earth, air, fire and water—but instead of a fifth element (the *quintessence)*, crystalline aether (pure, unalterable, transparent, and weightless). The farther from Earth, the purer the sphere.
5. All motion requires a mover. The outermost sphere, containing the fixed stars, is moved by an "unmoved mover," the *primum mobile.* Each sphere imparts motion to the next one in; in the Aristotelian universe, there is no empty space.
6. Celestial bodies have souls. In particular, each planet is controlled by its own spirit, which mediates its motion. (The heavenly bodies were known not to move in synchrony.)

This Aristotelian–Ptolemaic system was integrated with Catholic theology in the early 13th century by Albertus Magnus (1206–1280) and Thomas Aquinas (1225–1274). Angelic spirits were assigned to the celestial spheres in order of rank. The outermost sphere, that of the *primum mobile*, belonged to the Seraphim; next inward, the Cherubim controlled the sphere of the fixed stars; then came Thrones, Dominations, Virtues, Powers, Principalities, Archangels, and finally Angels, who controlled the sphere of the moon. The resulting conceptual scheme, dominant until the 16th century, was one of extreme intricacy, and cohesion.

Thirteen centuries after Ptolemy's model, Nicolaus Copernicus (1473–1543) published (in 1543, the year of his death) *De Revolutionibus Orbium Celestium*, proposing the idea that the Earth and other planets moved rather than the sun.[3] Copernicus argued for his system on the grounds of mathematical elegance and sufficiency, noting that the Ptolemaic system, with its vast numbers of eccentrics and epicyles, had departed

[3]Copernicus's theory was only partly heliocentric. For mathematical reasons, he placed the center of the solar system at the center of the Earth's orbit, rather than at the sun itself.

in spirit from the ancient principle of perfect circularity and regularity of movement.[4] However, Copernicus's system was not widely accepted. Even among the learned who saw the problems with the Ptolemaic system, the geocentric intuition was too strong to set aside. A more popular proposal was Tycho Brahe's system in which the five planets revolved around the sun, with the sun itself and its satellites revolving around a stationary Earth.

Kepler began as Lecturer in Mathematics at Graz in 1591, at the age of 20. He was already a confirmed Copernican, having studied the Copernican system at Tubingen with Maestlin. In his first book, *Mysterium Cosmographicum,* in 1596, he defended the Copernican view and presented his own heliocentric proposal. *Mysterium Cosmographicum* attracted the interest of Tycho Brahe (1546–1601), and in 1600 Kepler became an assistant in Tycho's observatory. When Tycho died in 1601, Kepler was appointed his successor as Imperial Mathematician of the court in Prague.

Kepler had acquired from Tycho the largest and most accurate store of astronomical observations available. He had also acquired the task of determining the orbit of Mars, a task that proved far more difficult and ultimately more revealing than Kepler had foreseen. Kepler spent the next several years trying to construct a consistent heliocentric model of the solar system based on an early version of his *equal area in equal times* assumption and on the virtually universal, self-evident principle that the orbits of the planets were (or were composed of) perfect circles. However, the fact that his calculations for Mars's orbit differed from Tycho's observations (by a mere 8° of arc) forced him to reject years of hard work and, ultimately, the ancient assumption of circularity. It is hard today to grasp how difficult it was to cast off the idea of circular orbits. Kepler in the preface to *Astronomia Nova* (Kepler, 1609/1992) commented on the "incredible" labor required to establish the existence of the solar force, largely due to his mistaken assumption of circular motion: "Because I had bound

[4]In fact, although Copernicus was able to divest his theory of the "major epicycles" that accounted for the planets' apparent retrograde motions, and of the notion of the *equant* (an imaginary point from which the calculated orbit would appear more uniform), he was forced to maintain a complex set of eccentrics and minor epicycles (Mason, 1962).

them [the planets, "the movers"] to the millstones (as it were) of circularity, under the spell of common opinion. Restrained by such fetters, the movers could not do their work" (p. 67).[5] For a seeker of mathematical regularity like Kepler, to despoil the harmony of the spheres by abandoning circular motion was a hard course to take. Far from experiencing an iconoclastic glee in overturning past beliefs, he seems to have been utterly downcast: "I have cleared the Augean stables of astronomy of cycles and spirals, and left behind me only a single cartful of dung"(cited in Koestler, 1963, p.129). After trying fruitlessly to model the planetary path with an ovoid, he at last accepted the ellipse as the shape of the orbit.[6] This led to a more precise statement of the second law of planetary motion, that a line between the sun and any planet sweeps out equal areas in equal intervals of time, and to the first law, that the planetary orbits are ellipses with the sun at one focus.[7] With this new model Kepler could replace Copernicus's (at least) 34 circles with just six ellipses.[8]

Kepler published this new view in 1609 as the *Astronomia Nova: A New Astronomy Based on Causation, or Celestial Physics.* It records his discoveries and his quest to derive the orbit of the planets—in particular, Mars, the most resistant to calculation—from causal principles.[9] This causal explanation based on mechanical forces moved him out of the kind of astronomy practiced at the time and essentially into astronomical physics. "Ye physicists, prick your ears, for now we are going to invade your

[5]Galileo (1564–1642), Kepler's brilliant contemporary and a fellow Copernican, never abandoned the belief that the planets moved in perfect circles at uniform velocity, despite receiving Kepler's evidence for elliptical orbits.

[6]After abandoning the circle, Kepler at first used the ellipse merely as a mathematical approximation to the ovoid, or egg, which had the advantage of possessing only one focus. He resisted the ellipse as a solution for physical reasons: If the sun was the unique cause of planetary motion, then there should be one unique place for it, not an arbitrary selection from between two foci as with an ellipse (Hanson, 1958, pp. 78–83).

[7]The Second Law appears in rough form in the *Mysterium Cosmographicum* (1596) and appears explicitly in Book III of the *Astronomia nova,* before the First Law in Book IV. It was in fact crucial to his derivation of the First and Third laws. The Third Law appears in the *Harmonice Mundi* in 1619.

[8]However, Kepler's system was not accepted by his contemporaries. Even those few who were willing to consider Kepler's and Copernicus's heliocentric views (including Kepler's old mentor, Maestlin) rejected his notion of a celestial physics governed by the same causal law as earthly phenomena.

[9]Hanson (1958), echoing Peirce, called Kepler's discovery of the orbit of Mars "the greatest piece of retroductive reasoning ever performed" (p. 85).

territory"(cited in Koestler, 1969, p. 325). Kepler's causal explanation of planetary motion and his three laws were a major step toward the modern conception of the solar system. According to Gingerich (1993),

> Kepler's most consequential achievement was the mechanizing and perfecting of the world system. By the *mechanization* of the solar system, I mean his insistence on "a new astronomy based on causes, or the celestial physics," as he tells us in the title of his great book. By the *perfection* of the planetary system, I mean the fantastic improvement of nearly two orders of magnitude in the prediction of planetary positions. (p. 333)[10]

How did Kepler arrive at these discoveries? We now return to the beginning, to the *Mysterium Cosmographicum* (1596), to trace the process. Kepler had Copernicus's treatise to build on. In addition, two astronomical events had helped to prepare the ground for new conceptions of the heavens. The first was a nova (or supernova) in 1572 . This new fixed star was evidence against the Aristotelian doctrine of the unchanging and incorruptible firmament. The second was a comet in 1577 (and others not long after), whose path ran through the planetary spheres. Kepler seems to have considered this fairly conclusive evidence against the view that each planet was attached to its own crystalline sphere. He continued to ponder an alternative model, that of the Stoics, who held that the heavenly bodies were intelligent and capable of self-direction (see Barker, 1991). Throughout Kepler's writings he debated whether planetary motion required an explanation in terms of intelligent mindfulness or whether it could be ascribed to a purely physical force.

THE SUN AS PRIME MOVER: THE LIGHT/ANIMA MOTRIX ANALOGY

Kepler possessed a neo-Platonist's love of mathematical regularity, but he combined it with a commitment to explanation in terms of physical causation and an equally strong commitment to empirical test. In the pref-

[10]Gingerich notes that it was the success of these predictions (the Rudophine Tables) that kept Kepler's theory alive during the two centuries after its publication.

ace to *Mysterium*, the 25-year-old Kepler stated his purpose as thus: "There were three things of which I persistently sought the reasons why they were such and not otherwise: the number, size and motion of the circles" (Kepler, 1596/1981, p. 63).

Kepler's solution to the first two questions was a system of inscribed solids that predicted the distances of the planets from the sun. This, rather quixotic model, shown in Figure 1 clearly shows Kepler's passion for mathematic regularities. The extreme particularity of this initial model is strik-

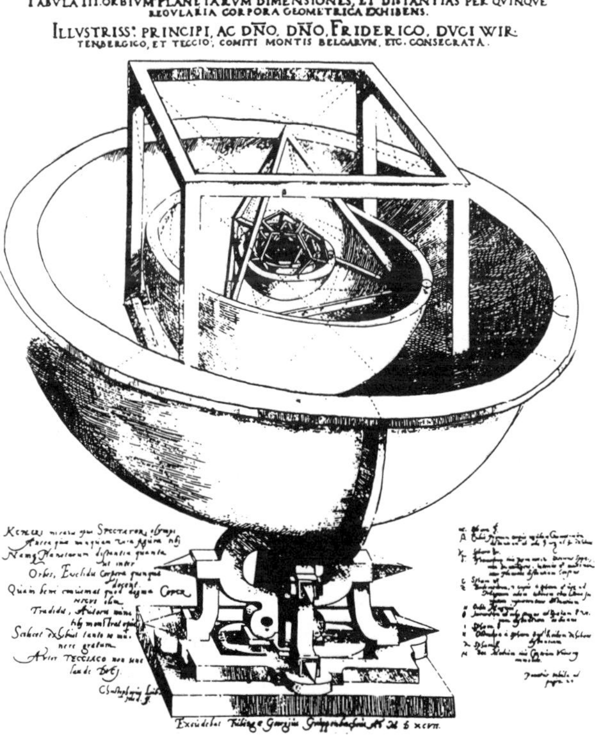

Johannes Kepler, *Mysterium cosmographicum*. Copper engraving from the first edition (Tübingen, 1596).

Figure 1

Kepler's model of the solar system from *Mysterium Cosmographicum*, showing inscribed solids. From *Mysterium Cosmographicum*, by J. Kepler (A. M. Duncan, Trans., 1981), New York: Abaris Books. Copyright 1981 by Abaris. Reprinted with permission.

ing: The distance of a given planet from the sun could only be calculated by knowing the orbit of the next innermost planet.

The work is interesting in at least two more respects. The first is Kepler's reworking of the Copernican theory to be more consistently heliocentric. Rejecting the Copernican placement of the center of the solar system as at the center of the Earth's orbit, Kepler proposed a mathematically small but physically significant change: that the center of the solar system was the sun itself. As Aiton (1976) pointed out, Kepler's causal interpretation of Copernicus's theory led to a reaxiomitization of astronomy. Kepler also posed an important question. He noticed that the periods of the outer planets were longer, relative to those of the inner planets, than could be predicted simply from the greater distances they had to travel. That is, the planets farther away from the sun moved slower than those closer to the sun. Were the "moving souls" simply weaker in the faraway planets? Kepler reasoned thus:

> One of two conclusions must be reached: either the moving souls [*motricis animae*] are weaker the further[sic] they are from the Sun; or, there is a single moving soul [*motricem animam*[11]] in the center of all the spheres, that is, in the Sun, and it impels each body more strongly in proportion to how near it is. (Kepler, 1596/1981, p. 199)

Kepler went on to apply this hypothesis to the paths of the individual planets. If motion is caused by a single *anima motrix* in the sun that weakens with distance, this would explain why each individual planet should move slower when farther from the sun. (The arguments for this claim, of course, required recasting the observational pattern from the Ptolemaic pattern into a heliocentric system.) To reason further, he used an analogy with light (see Figure 2):

> Let us suppose, then, as is highly probable, that motion is dispensed by the Sun in the same proportion as light. Now the ratio in which light spreading out from a center is weakened is stated by the opti-

[11]Kepler's annotation in 1621 states, "If for the word "soul" [*Anima*] you substitute the word "force" [*Vim*], you have the very same principle on which the Celestial Physics is established" (*Mysterium Cosmographicum*, p. 201).

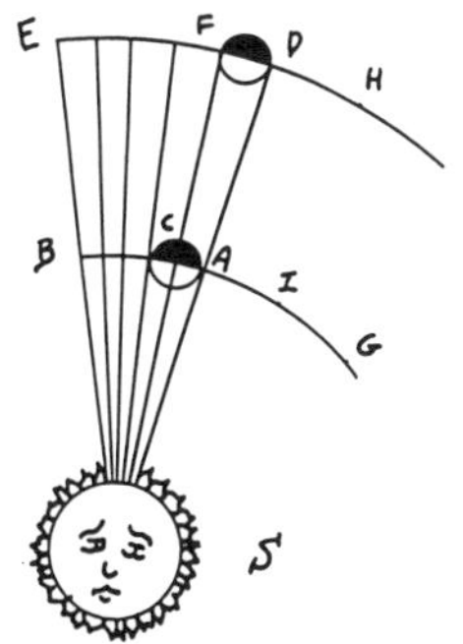

Figure 2

Kepler's depiction of the sun's light radiating outward.

> cians. For the amount of light in a small circle is the same as the amount of light or of the solar rays in the great one. Hence, as it is more concentrated in the small circle, and more thinly spread in the great one, the measure of this thinning out must be sought in the actual ratio of the circles, both for light and for the moving power [*motrice virtute*]. (Kepler, 1596/1981, p. 201)

Pushing the Analogy

Kepler returned repeatedly to the analogy between light and the motive power. In *Mysterium* (1596), the analogy functioned as a kind of existence proof that the effects of a central source could be assumed to weaken in an orderly way with distance. Kepler's many subsequent uses of this analogy served to extend and refine his notion of the anima motrix. He devoted multiple chapters of his greatest work, *Astronomia Nova* (1609), to its explanation and returned to it again in *Epitome of Copernican Astronomy* (1620). Kepler also delved further into the base domain of this analogy: the behavior of light. He published a treatise on astronomical optics (*Astronomiae Pars Optica*, 1604) and another in 1610 (*Dioptrice*). With this considerable knowledge of the behavior of light, Kepler had a base domain that was systematic and well understood and therefore ideally suited to provide inferential resources for the target (Bassok & Holyoak, 1989;

Bowdle & Gentner, 1996; Clement & Gentner, 1988; Gentner & Bowdle, 1994; Gentner & Gentner, 1983).

In *Astronomia Nova* Kepler developed this analogy much further. Early on, he challenged his motive power with the thorny question of action at a distance:

> For it was said above that this motive power is extended throughout the space of the world, in some places more concentrated and in others more spread out . . . This implies that it is poured out throughout the whole world, and yet does not exist anywhere but where there is something movable. (Kepler1609/1992, p. 382)

He answers this challenge by invoking the light analogy.

> But lest I appear to philosophize with excessive insolence, I shall propose to the reader the clearly authentic example of light, since it also makes its nest in the sun, thence to break forth into the whole world as a companion to this motive power. Who, I ask, will say that light is something material? Nevertheless, it carries out its operations with respect to place, suffers alteration, is reflected and refracted, and assumes quantities so as to be dense or rare, and to be capable of being taken as a surface wherever it falls upon something illuminable. Now just as it is said in optics, that light does not exist in the intermediate space between the source and the illuminable, this is equally true of the motive power. (Kepler, 1609/1992, p. 383)

Kepler also uses the light analogy to establish a conservation argument that the *vis motrix* is diminished with distance not through being lost but through being spread out (see Figure 3). Note his use of two further potential analogues here (odors and heat), which differ with respect to the key conservation point and serve to sharpen the parallel between light and the vis motrix.

> Since there is just as much power in a larger and more distant circle as there is in a smaller and closer one, nothing of this power is lost in traveling from its source, nothing is scattered between the source and the movable body. The emission, then, in the same man-

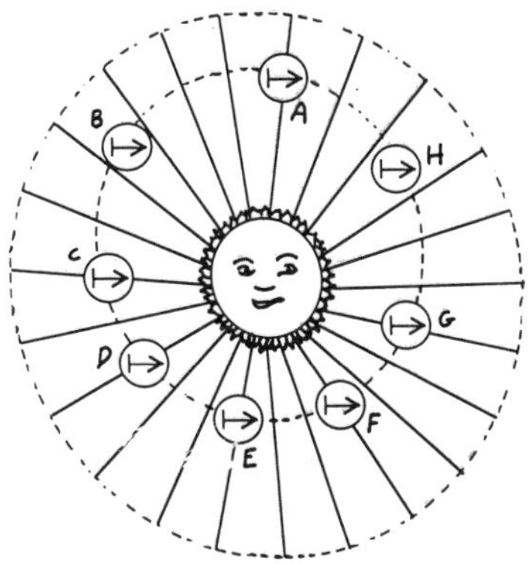

Figure 3

Kepler's depiction of the sun's motive power spreading.

> ner as light, is immaterial, unlike odours, which are accompanied by a diminution of substance, and unlike heat from a hot furnace, or anything similar which fills the intervening space. (Kepler 1609/1992, p. 381)

Modeling Analogy

To trace Kepler's analogy processes we use structure-mapping theory (Gentner, 1983, 1989) and its computational counterpart the structure-mapping engine (SME; Falkenhainer, Forbus, & Gentner, 1989). However, many of the same assumptions are shared by related models (e.g., Halford, 1993; Holyoak & Thagard, 1989; Keane, 1988). The basic idea is that analogy involves a process of alignment and projection. Assertions in a base (or source) domain are placed into correspondence with assertions in a target domain, and further assertions true of the base domain are then inferred to be potentially true of the target. Structure-mapping assumes that domain knowledge is in the form of symbolic structural descriptions that include objects, relations between objects, and higher-order relations among whole propositions. On this view, the analogical process is one of structural alignment between two mental representations to find the maximal (i.e., largest and deepest) structurally consistent match between them.

A structurally consistent match is one that satisfies the constraints of *parallel connectivity* and *one-to-one mapping* (Falkenhainer et al., 1989; Gentner, 1983, 1989; Gentner & Markman, 1993, 1994, 1997; Markman & Gentner, 1993a, 1993b, 1996; Medin, Goldstone, & Gentner, 1993). Parallel connectivity holds that if two predicates are matched, then their arguments must also match. For example, if the predicate HEAVIER(*a*,*b*) matches the predicate HEAVIER(*x*,*y*), then *a* must match *x* and *b* must match *y*. One-to-one mapping requires that each element in one representation correspond to at most one element in the other representation.

To explain why some analogies are better than others (even when factual correctness is held constant), structure-mapping uses the principle of *systematicity*—a preference for mappings that are highly interconnected and contain deep chains of higher-order relations (Forbus & Gentner, 1989; Forbus et al., 1995; Gentner, 1983, 1989; Gentner et al., 1993). Thus, the probability that an individual match will be included in the final interpretation of a comparison is higher if it is connected by higher-order relations to other systems of predicates (Bowdle & Gentner, 1996; Clement & Gentner, 1991; Gentner & Bowdle, 1994). We focus here on two predictions that derive from this framework. First, the correspondences mandated by a comparison are governed not only by local similarity but also by the degree to which the elements play the same roles in the common higher-order structure (e.g., Clement & Gentner, 1991; Gentner, 1988; Gentner & Clement, 1988; Spellman & Holyoak, 1993). Relational commonalities thus tend to outweigh object commonalities in determining the interpretation of a comparison. Second, because comparison promotes a structural alignment, differences relevant to the common structure are also highlighted by a comparison (Gentner & Markman, 1994; Markman & Gentner, 1993a, 1993b, 1996). Thus, paradoxically, comparisons can illuminate differences as well as commonalities.

SME simulates this comparison process (Falkenhainer, Forbus, & Gentner, 1986, 1989; Forbus, Ferguson, & Gentner, 1994). To capture the necessary structural distinctions we use an *n*th-order type predicate calculus. *Entities* stand for the objects or reified concepts in the domain (e.g., planet, orbit). *Attributes* are unary predicates used primarily to describe independent descriptive properties of objects (e.g., HEAVY(planet), which translates roughly as "The planet is heavy."). *Functions*[12] are used primarily to state dimensional properties (e.g., BRIGHTNESS(object), which translates as "the brightness of the object"). *Relations* are multiplace predicates that represent links between two or more entities, attributes, functions, or relations (e.g., REACH(anima, planet)—"The anima reaches the planet."). Relations must match identically in SME (or undergo re-representation, as discussed later), reflecting the principle that comparison is implicitly directed toward finding structural commonality. For example, REACH(light, object) could match REACH(anima, planet) but could not match DESTROY(anima, planet); that is, light reaching an object could match the anima reaching a planet, but not the anima destroying a planet. However, SME allows correspondences between nonidentical entities and dimensions (represented as functions) if they are embedded in like relational structures. Thus, the speed of a planet could be matched with the brightness of an object, provided both were governed by like relations. This is in accord with the principle that lower order information need not match identically.

This ability to match nonidentical functions is what permits cross-dimensional mappings, in everyday language ("a bright remark," "a dull book," "a lowdown scoundrel") as well as in science (see Gentner, Rattermann, Markman, & Kotovsky, 1995; Kotovsky & Gentner, in press). On the other hand, the principle of partial relational identity is equally crucial, for it captures the fact that not just any similarity constitutes an analogy. To cite an obvious example, "The sun attracts the planets" and "The nucleus attracts the electrons" are analogous, but "The sun attracts the planets" and "The sun is yellower than the moon" are not, because the second pair lacks a relational match.

It is crucial to note that the relational identity principle is not about words per se, nor does it require a total match of relational content: rather, there must be a nontrivial match of subrelations. In the analogy "The sun

[12]Functions, unlike attributes and relations, do not take truth values, but rather map objects onto other objects or values. For brevity we sometimes use the term *functor* to refer to all three categories: relations, attributes, and functions.

propels the planets as a lamp illuminates its objects;" the relations *propels* and *illuminates* are not identical, but the match is a good one nonetheless because these relations readily decompose to reveal a partial match of subrelations (over nonidentical functions, as is allowed): "The sun *increases the speed* of the planets as a light source *increases the brightness* of its recipient object." Thus, the principle of relational identity does not mean that the relations must *initially* match. Rather, it means that—through processes of abstraction or other forms of re-representation—relational identities are found as part of the analogical alignment process.

To represent beliefs about physical domains, we use qualitative process (QP) theory as a representation language (Forbus, 1984, 1990; Forbus & Gentner, 1986). (See Forbus, 1984, for a full description of the QP language and its model-building capabilities.) QP theory provides a representation language for expressing causal acccounts using qualitative mathematical relationships. For example, the statement QPROP+(*a*,*b*) expresses a positive qualitative relationship between the quantities *a* and *b*: that *a* is a monotonic positive function of (at least) *b*. QPROP-(*a*,*b*) expresses a negative qualitative relationship. The idea is to capture the psychological state of knowing the direction of change between two variables without needing to specify the exact nature of the function.

Relations can hold between expressions as well as entities. Higher-order relations between relations, such as causality, allow the construction of large representational structures: for example, the causal system for light reaching an object and the object's thereby being illuminated.

It is the presence of structurally interconnected representations that is the key to implementing structure-mapping. Given two representations in working memory, SME operates in a local-to-global manner to find one or a few structurally consistent matches. In the first stage, SME proposes matches between all identical predicates at any level (attribute, relation, higher-order relation, etc.) in the two representations. At this stage, there may be many mutually inconsistent matches. In the next stage, these local correspondences are coalesced into large mappings, called *kernels*, by enforcing structural consistency (one-to-one mapping and parallel connectivity).

SME then gathers these structurally consistent clusters into one or two global interpretations. At this point, it projects candidate inferences into the target. It does this by projecting into the target representation any predicates that currently belong to the common structure in the base but that are not yet present in the target. These predicates function as possible new inferences imported from the base representation to the target representation. These inferences may contain new entities (skolems) that correspond to entities that initially existed only in the base. Because candidate inferences depend solely on the structure of the match, other processes are needed to evaluate their validity (see later discussion). The mappings are given a structural evaluation, reflecting the size and depth of the matching system.

SME has many useful properties for modeling conceptual change. First, the final interpretation preserves large-scale connected structure. Second, the global interpretation does not need to be explicit at the outset. The assertions that will constitute the final point of the analogy need not be present initially in the target and need not have been extracted as a separable "goal structure" or "problem-solution structure" in the base before the comparison processes begin. SME begins blindly, using only local matches, and the final global interpretation emerges through the pull toward connectivity and systematicity in the later stages of the process. Third, SME makes spontaneous inferences from its comparison process, unlike many other models of analogy (cf. Holyoak, Novick, & Melz, 1994). Finally, this model of the analogy process allows us to delineate four specific subprocesses that can change conceptual structure: highlighting, projection, re-representation, and restructuring (Gentner & Wolff, 1996; see Figure 4).

THE FOUR ANALOGICAL PROCESSES OF CONCEPTUAL CHANGE

Highlighting

SME's first result is a matching system of predicates between the base and target. This models the psychological assumption that the process of alignment causes the matching aspects of the domains to become more salient (Elio & Anderson, 1981, 1984; Gentner & Wolff, 1996; Gick & Holyoak, 1980, 1983; Markman & Gentner, 1993a, 1993b; Medin et al., 1993; Miller, 1979; Ortony, 1979). This process of highlighting is important because hu-

Analogy as Structural Mapping
Alignment and Transfer

Ways an analogical (metaphoric) mapping can change the representation of the topic (target)

Selecting/Highlighting (Matching/Alignment)

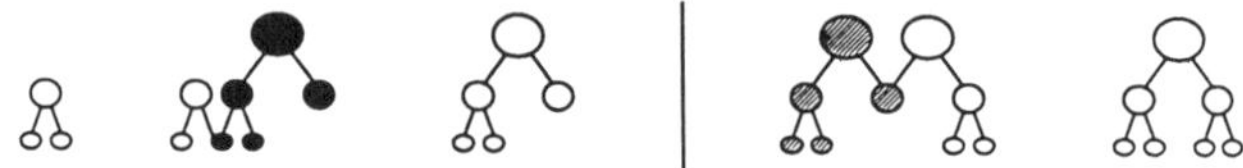

Candidate Inferences (Transfer)

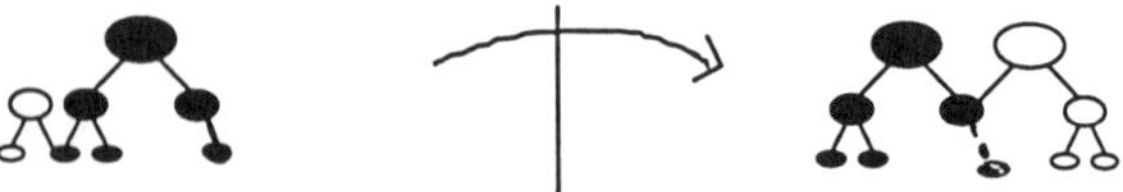

Re-representation (Provisional Alteration to Improve Match)

Figure 4

Ways analogy can create change.

man representations, we suggest, are typically large, rich, and thickly interwoven nets of concepts. In particular, early representations tend to be conservative, in the sense that they retain many specific details of the context of learning; that is, they are particularistic and contextually embedded (e.g., Brown, Collins, & Duguid, 1989; Forbus & Gentner, 1986; Medin & Ross, 1989). Highlighting can create a focus on a manageable subset of relevant information. Moreover, the relational identity constraint, combined with re-representation processes, means that the *output* of an analogy may reveal hitherto unnoticed relational commonalities. There is considerable psychological evidence that comparison can reveal nonobvious features (Gentner & Clement, 1988; Markman & Gentner, 1993a; Medin et al., 1993; Ortony, Vondruska, Foss, & Jones, 1985; Tourangeau & Rips, 1991) and that highlighting of common information can influence category formation (Elio & Anderson, 1981, 1984; Medin & Ross, 1989; Ross, 1984, 1989; Skorstad, Gentner, & Medin, 1988).

Projection of Candidate Inferences

As described earlier, SME projects candidate inferences from the base to the target domain. These projected inferences, if accepted, add to the knowledge in the target domain. However, not all inferences made by SME will be correct. Post-mapping processes, such as the application of semantic and pragmatic constraints, are necessary to ensure the correctness of the inferences (Falkenhainer, 1990; Kass, 1994; Kolodner, 1993; Novick & Holyoak, 1991).

Re-representation

In re-representation, the representation of either or both domains is changed to improve the match. Typically, this involves a kind of tinkering in order that two initially mismatching predicates can be adjusted to match. For example, suppose an analogy matches well but for a mismatch between BRIGHTER-THAN(*x,y*) and FASTER-THAN(*a,b*) (as in Kepler's analogy between light and the vis motrix). These relations can be re-represented as GREATER-THAN(BRIGHTNESS(*x*), BRIGHTNESS(*y*)) and GREATER-THAN(SPEED(*a*), SPEED(*b*)) to allow comparison. This involves a kind of decomposition or titration that separates the GREATER-THAN magnitude relation (which is common to both) from the specific dimension of increase (which is distinctive). Studies of the development of children's comparison abilities support the psychological validity of re-representation in learning: Children are better able to match cross-dimensional analogies when they have been induced to re-represent the two situations to permit noticing the common magnitude increase (Gentner & Rattermann, 1991; Gentner et al., 1995; Kotovsky & Gentner, in press). We return later to SME's implementation of re-representation.

Restructuring

Restructuring is the process of large-scale rearrangement of elements of the target domain to form a new coherent explanation. This rearrangement can take the form of adding or deleting causal links in the target domain as well as of altering specific concepts. It should perhaps be considered separately from the other three processes, or possibly as arising from a combination of the other three. For example, when little is known about a target domain, a mapping from the base can provide causal linkages that significantly alter the connectivity in the target. However, in the current account, there must be some minimal alignment as a basis for inference; even if no initial relational match exists, there must be at least a partial object mapping (which could be suggested by local similarities or pragmatically stipulated; Forbus & Oblinger, 1990; Holyoak & Thagard, 1989; Winston, 1980). We conjecture that substantial restructuring during a single mapping is comparatively rare, because normally the candidate inferences projected from the base domain will be at least compatible with the existing target structure. Furthermore, as Nersessian (1992, p. 24) pointed out, massive restructuring from a single base can be dangerous: She noted that Faraday's modeling of magnetic fields by analogy with the concrete lines of iron filings created by magnets led to an overly concrete, partly erroneous model of the fields. In general, we suspect that most restructuring occurs as a result of multiple analogies iteratively applied as well as other processes.

With these tools in hand, we now return to Johannes Kepler. To trace his analogical process, we represented parts of Kepler's expressed knowledge about light and the motive power. We applied SME to these representations to simulate the process of analogical reasoning that Kepler might have used in rethinking his conceptual model of the solar system.

Our representation of Kepler's knowledge of the nature of light is shown in Figure 5.[13] Specifically, we ascribe to Kepler five beliefs: (a) A source produces light that travels instantaneously and undetectably through space until it reaches an object, at which point the light is detectable. (b) The greater the concentration of light, the brighter the object. (c) As light spreads from a source into a greater volume of space, its concentration decreases, causing the total amount of light (the product of the volume and the concentration) to remain constant. (d) Thus, the concentration of light decreases as the object's distance from the source increases. (e) Therefore, the brightness of an object decreases with distance from a source.

Kepler's initial knowledge of the motive power was of course considerably less rich than his knowledge about light. His struggle to characterize this influence is a fascinating aspect of his conceptual evolution. Early on, he called it the *anima motrix* (motive spirit), drawing on the accepted notion of intelligences governing celestial bodies. However, he was uneasy with this and strove to find a more mechanical characterization. The analogy with light, and another with magnetism (discussed later), helped him strip the sentience from the interaction between the sun and the planets. He eventually adopted the terms vis motrix or *virtus motrix* (motive force or motive power). In our representation of this knowledge (Figure 6) we use vis motrix, reflecting Kepler's shift to a less animate and more mechanical terminology.

THE VIS MOTRIX ANALOGY AND THE PROCESS OF CONCEPTUAL CHANGE

Highlighting

When given the representations of Kepler's knowledge of light and of the sun's motive force, SME produces the interpretation shown in Figure 7a. This interpretation highlights commonalities (e.g., the similarity that in both cases the emanation makes itself known when it strikes a planet and, respectively, illuminates or moves the planet).

[13]These representations are of course not intended to be exhaustive representations of Kepler's knowledge, but of the subset necessary to make our points about analogy and conceptual change. We will not attempt here a full explanation of how Kepler selected (mostly) relevant information from the larger knowledge of light. Although this is clearly important, it is beyond the scope of this paper.

```
5a:
(PRODUCE Source light)

(CAUSE (TRAVEL light Source object space)
       (REACH light object))

(INSTANTANEOUS (TRAVEL light Source object space))

(WHILE (AND (TRAVEL light Source object space)
            (NOT (REACH light object)))
       (NOT (DETECTABLE light)))

(WHILE (AND (TRAVEL light Source object space)
            (REACH light object))
       (DETECTABLE light))

5b:
(CAUSE (REACH light object)
       (PROMOTE (BRIGHTNESS object)))

(QPROP+ (BRIGHTNESS object)
        (CONCENTRATION light object))

5c:
(CAUSE (AND (QPROP+ (VOLUME light)
                    (DISTANCE Source object))
            (QPROP- (CONCENTRATION light object)
                    (DISTANCE object Source)))
   (CONSTANT (* (VOLUME light) (CONCENTRATION light object))))

5d:
(QPROP- (CONCENTRATION light object)
        (DISTANCE object Source))

5e:
(IMPLIES (AND (QPROP- (CONCENTRATION light object)
                      (DISTANCE object Source))
              (QPROP+ (BRIGHTNESS object)
                      (CONCENTRATION light object)))
         (QPROP- (BRIGHTNESS object)
                 (DISTANCE object Source)))
```

Figure 5

Representation of the light domain, the base in the light–vis motrix analogy.

6a:

(CAUSE (REACH vis-motrix planet)
(PROMOTE (SPEED planet)))

Note: This structure matches part of the structure shown in Figure 5b for light.

6b:

(QPROP- (SPEED planet)
(DISTANCE planet Sun))

Note: This structure matches part of the structure shown in Figure 5e for light.

Figure 6

Representation of the vis motrix, the target in the light–vis motrix analogy.

Projection

As we noted earlier, highlighting influences conceptual change in two ways: (a) by identifying relevant aspects of the two domains and thereby permitting abstraction and (b) by providing the alignable structure over which two other processes of conceptual change—*projection* and *re-representation*—can operate. This is crucial, for by constraining the candidate inferences to be those connected to the aligned structure we can model an inferential process that is generative without overshooting into "wanton inferencing."[14] The vis motrix–light analogy leads to several candidate inferences. Figure 4b shows SME's inferences, which seem reasonably like those Kepler appears to have made. First, SME infers that the vis motrix travels from the sun to the planet through space. Second, it infers that the product of volume and concentration of the vis motrix is a constant. Third, SME explains that because the concentration of the vis motrix decreases with distance and the concentration of the vis motrix governs the speed of the planet, the speed of the planet will decrease with distance from the sun. Finally, SME infers that the vis motrix will be detectable only after it reaches the planet, and not on its way. That is,

[14]Eric Diettrich (personal communication, February 1994)

7a:

```
(CAUSE (REACH light object)              (CAUSE (REACH vis-motrix planet)
    (PROMOTE (BRIGHTNESS object)))           (PROMOTE (SPEED planet)))

(QPROP- (BRIGHTNESS object)              (QPROP- (SPEED planet)
        (DISTANCE object Sun))                   (DISTANCE planet Sun))
```

7b:

```
(CAUSE (TRAVEL vis-motrix Sun planet (:SKOLEM space))
       (REACH vis-motrix planet))

(CAUSE (AND (QPROP+ (VOLUME (:SKOLEM space))
                    (DISTANCE Sun planet))
            (QPROP- (CONCENTRATION vis-motrix planet)
                    (DISTANCE planet Sun)))
       (CONSTANT (* (VOLUME (:SKOLEM space))
                    (CONCENTRATION vis-motrix planet))))

(IMPLIES (AND (QPROP- (CONCENTRATION vis-motrix planet)
                      (DISTANCE planet Sun))
              (QPROP+ (SPEED planet)
                      (CONCENTRATION vis-motrix planet)))
         (QPROP- (SPEED planet) (DISTANCE planet Sun)))

(WHILE (AND (TRAVEL vis-motrix Sun planet (:SKOLEM space))
            (NOT (REACH vis-motrix planet)))
       (NOT (DETECTABLE vis-motrix)))

(WHILE (AND (TRAVEL vis-motrix Sun planet (:SKOLEM space))
            (REACH vis-motrix planet))
       (DETECTABLE vis-motrix))
```

Figure 7

Structure-mapping engine (SME) interpretation of the light–vis motrix analogy. Panel a: Interpretation (the maximal structurally consistent common structure) identified. Panel b: Candidate inferences produced for the light–vis motrix analogy. Note that the projected entity "SKOLEM space" can be filled by "space" if the vis motrix is assumed to travel through space.

```
(WHILE (AND (TRAVEL vis-motrix sun planet space)
            (NOT (REACH vis-motrix planet))
       (NOT (DETECTABLE vis-motrix))
(WHILE (AND (TRAVEL vis-motrix sun planet space)
            (REACH vis-motrix planet)
       (DETECTABLE vis-motrix)
```

Together the third and final inferences explain the phenomenon of action at a distance. These inferences can be seen in Figure 7b.

Re-representation

Earlier we suggested that the process of alignment can lead to reconstruing parts of one or both representations in such a way as to improve the alignment. Such a process may have operated on a large scale to contribute to Kepler's gradual shift toward thinking of the motive power as a physical phenomenon rather than an animistic one. However, a more locally contained example can be found shortly after the passage quoted above in the *Astronomia Nova*. Kepler here notes a discrepancy—an important alignable difference—and tries to resolve it.

> Moreover, although light itself does indeed flow forth in no time, while this power creates motion in time, nonetheless the way in which both do so is the same, if you consider them correctly. Light manifests those things which are proper to it instantaneously, but requires time to effect those which are associated with matter. It illuminates a surface in a moment, because here matter need not undergo any alteration, for all illumination takes place according to surfaces, or at least as if a property of surfaces and not as a property of corporeality as such. On the other hand, light bleaches colours in time, since here it acts upon matter *qua* matter, making it hot and expelling the contrary cold which is embedded in the body's matter and is not on its surface. In precisely the same manner, this moving power perpetually and without any interval of time is present from the sun wherever there is a suitable movable body, for it receives nothing from the movable body to cause it to be there.

On the other hand, it causes motion in time, since the movable body is material. (Kepler 1609/1992, p. 383).

Kepler believed (according to the conventional wisdom of the time) that light moved instantaneously from the sun to light up the planets:

INSTANTANEOUS (AFFECT (**light, sun, planet, space**))

However, he believed that the vis motrix required time to affect the motion of the planets. At a rough level, then, Kepler faced a mismatch between the candidate inference from light (a) and his existing knowledge (b) about the planetary motion:

(a)INSTANTANEOUS (AFFECT (vis-motrix, sun, planet, space))
(b)TIME-OCCURRING (AFFECT (vis-motrix, sun, planet, space))

Kepler admits the problem but suggests a re-representation: "Although light itself does indeed flow forth in no time, while this power creates motion in time, nonetheless the way in which both do so is the same, if you consider them correctly" (Kepler, 1609/1992, p. 383). His solution is to be more precise about the notion of AFFECT (**influence, planet**). For such an effect to occur, he reasoned, influence must travel to the planet and influence must interact with the planet somehow. Kepler suggested that travel is instantaneous for both kinds of influences (the vis motrix and light). However, whereas light need only interact with the surfaces of bodies to illuminate them (which, according to Kepler, can be done instantaneously), the vis motrix must interact with the body of the planet itself in order to cause motion, and this requires time. Thus, Kepler gains a partial identity by decomposing and re-representing a previously problematic correspondence. Now the first part of the candidate inference can be accepted, and only the second part must be rejected.

INSTANTANEOUS (TRAVEL (light, sun, planet, space))
INSTANTANEOUS (PROMOTE (BRIGHTNESS (planet))

INSTANTANEOUS (TRAVEL (vis-motrix, sun, planet, space))
TIME-OCCURRING (PROMOTE (SPEED (planet))

Alignable Differences

Given a structural alignment, connected differences become salient. Kepler (1609/1992) used these differences to deal with the question of whether the sun's light and the motive power might not in fact be the same thing (a reasonable question, given the force of the analogy). He answered that they cannot be the same, because light can be impeded by an opaque blocker (e.g., during an eclipse), yet the motive power is not thereby impeded (otherwise motion would stop during an eclipse).

> The analogy between light and motive power is not to be disturbed by rashly confusing their properties. Light is impeded by the opaque, but is not impeded by a body . . . Power acts upon the body without respect to its opacity. Therefore, since it is not correlated with the opaque, it is likewise not impeded by the opaque . . . On this account I would nearly separate light from moving power. (pp. 392–393)

A more important alignable difference concerns the degree of decrease with distance. By the time of *Astronomia Nova*, Kepler was clear about the fact that the concentration of light diminishes as the *inverse square* of distance from its source. He therefore held himself responsible for either mapping this fact into the target, or explaining why it should not be mapped. As it happens, he still required a simple inverse law for the vis motrix, because in his model the vis motrix directly caused the planetary motion.[15]

[15]Kepler's dynamics was Aristotelian: He believed that velocity was caused by (and proportional to) the motive force, (as opposed to the Newtonian view that forces cause *changes* in velocity). He held the belief of his time, that the planets would cease to move if not pushed around the sun. Thus, he conceived the motive force as acting directly to impart counter-clockwise speed to the planets (rather than imparting inward acceleration, as in Newton's system). As Koestler (1963, p. 326) noted, Kepler had made the insightful move of decomposing planetary motion into separate components, but had reversed the roles of gravity and planetary inertia. Kepler thought that the planets' *forward* motion was caused by the sun and that their *inward–outward* motion was caused by magnetism specific to each planet. In the Newtonian system, the planets' *inward* motion is caused by the sun, and their *forward* motion is caused by their own inertia.

As usual, he tackled this discrepancy head on and produced, in *Astronomia Nova*, a long mathematical argument that, because the vis motrix can cause motion only in planes perpendicular to the sun's axis of rotation, the proper analogue to the vis motrix is light spreading out, not in a sphere around the sun, but only in a plane. Thus, he justified the alignable difference that the concentration of vis motrix should decrease as a simple inverse of distance, even though the concentration of light decreases with inverse-square distance.

Restructuring

From what we have said so far, it appears that the vis motrix analogy may have contributed to Kepler's restructuring of his model of the solar system. It provided him with a structure from which to argue for a single causal "soul" in the sun, rather than moving souls in each of the planets, and it contributed to the gradual mechanization of this soul to a power or force. The analogy may also have contributed to firming the shift from crystalline spheres containing the planets to paths continually negotiated between the sun and the planets. We return to this issue in the Discussion section.

COMPLETING THE CAUSAL ACCOUNT: THE FERRYMAN AND MAGNETISM ANALOGIES

The light–vis motrix analogy provided Kepler with the crucial inference of action at a distance. By assuming that the sun rotated around its axis (a hypothesis he confirmed by noting that sunspots move) he could account for the planetary revolutions: The planets were pushed along by a kind of circular river of force whirling around the sun, weakening with distance. However, this model still was not complete, for it did not explain how a constant force from the sun could account for the librations in the planetary orbits—that is, for the fact that the planets move inward and outward from the sun in the course of a revolution. Kepler sought a mechanism whereby the planets could somehow interact with a constant push from the sun in such a way as to capture this variation. One example was a ferryman steering his ship in a constant current. Here the ship corresponds to the planet and the sun provides the circular river pushing the ship around (see Figure 8).[16]

> Particularly happy and better accommodated to our inquiry are the phenomena exhibited by the propulsion of boats. Imagine a cable or rope hanging high up across a river, suspended from both banks, and a pulley running along the rope, holding, by another rope, a skiff floating in the river. If the ferryman in the skiff, otherwise at rest, fastens his rudder or oar in the right manner, the skiff, carried crosswise by the simple force of the downward-moving river, is transported from one bank to the other, as the pulley runs along the cable above. On broader rivers they make the skiffs go in circles, send them hither and thither, and play a thousand tricks, without

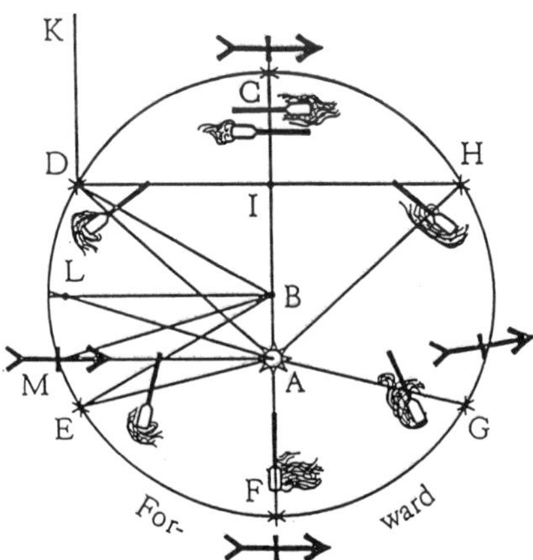

Figure 8

Kepler's analogy for the librations of the planets: The planet as ferryman in his skiff navigating in the sun's circular river; the planet as magnet interacting with the sun's magnetism.

[16]As mentioned elsewhere, in Kepler's pre-Newtonian physics the sun was required to push the planets around in their orbits, not merely to attract them.

touching the bottom or the banks, but by the use of the oar alone, directing the unified and most simple flow of the river to their own ends.

In very much the same manner, the power moving out into the world through the *species* is a kind of rapid torrent, which sweeps along all the planets, as well as, perhaps, the entire aethereal air, from west to east. It is not itself suited to attracting bodies to the sun or driving them further [sic] from it, which would be an infinitely troublesome task. It is therefore necessary that the planets themselves, rather like the skiff, have their own motive powers, as if they had riders [*vectores*] or ferrymen, by whose forethought they accomplish not only the approach to the sun and recession from the sun, but also (and this should be called the second argument) the declinations of latitudes; and as if from one bank to the other, travel across this river (which itself only follows the course of the ecliptic) from north to south and back. (Kepler, 1609/1992, p. 405)

The Magnetism Analogy

Although Kepler returned to the ferryman analogy from time to time, this analogy was unsatisfying, in part perhaps because it seemed to require too much insight from the planets. How would they know when to shift the rudder? In keeping with a lifelong quest to explain seemingly intelligent planetary behavior in terms of a mechanical interaction, Kepler sought to explain the planet's behavior purely physically. He wanted the ship without the ferryman.

Kepler's longest and most determined effort in this direction was the use of an analogy between the vis motrix and magnetism, an analogy Kepler developed over a long period. Kepler had first mentioned the magnetism analogy in the *Mysterium* (1596) as one more instance of action at a distance that might make his sun–planet force more plausible. By the time of the *Astronomia Nova* (1609) Kepler had become familiar with the work of William Gilbert (*De Magnete*, 1600/1938). In addition to setting forth the properties and behaviors of magnets, Gilbert had conjectured that the Earth might function as a giant magnet. Kepler extended this analogy to the sun and planets. Not only was magnetism another example of action at a distance, it also had the potential to explain the variations in distance. By modeling the planets and the sun as magnets, Kepler thought he could explain the inward and outward movements of the planets in terms of attractions and repulsions resulting from which poles were proximate.

In the *Epitome of Copernican Astronomy* (1621/1969), Kepler presented a long discussion of magnetism and its analogy to the planetary system. He began with a simple version of the magnetism analogy, likening the Earth to iron filings and the sun to a lodestone (magnet). This analogy, mentioned only briefly, establishes a second example of action at a distance, in that a lodestone affects the behavior of iron filings without ever making contact with the filings. In addition, like the light–vis motrix analogy, it suggests that action at a distance produces a qualitatively negative relationship between the influence of one object over another and distance. Gilbert had established this relationship between distance and magnetic influence in *De Magnete*. However, it does not explain why the planets would move closer and farther away from the sun, as iron filings would be uniformly attracted to a lodestone. Indeed, according to the iron filings analogy, the planets should be dragged into the sun.

In the second analogy, Kepler conceived of the planet as a magnet (or lodestone). This adds some new inferential power to the magnetism analogy. Kepler could now use the attractive and repulsive forces between the different poles of a pair of magnets to explain the coming together and separating of the celestial bodies. Thus, the planet would move closer to the sun when its attractive pole was turned toward the sun, and farther from the sun when the repelling pole was turned toward the sun (see Figure 9a). Given this varying distance from the sun, the planet's varying speed could also be inferred (as Kepler had already established that the planets move faster when closer to the sun—by the light–vis motrix analogy, and his second law).

Kepler was unsure whether the lodestone–vis motrix correspondences were merely analogical or actually represented an identity. He struggled with this issue throughout the *Astronomia Nova*. Early in the treatise, he wrote the following:

> The example of the magnet I have hit upon is a very pretty one, and entirely suited to the subject; indeed, it is little short of being the very truth. So why should I speak of the magnet as if it were an example? For, by the demonstration of the Englishman William Gilbert, the earth itself is a big magnet, and it is said by the same author, a defender of Copernicus,[17] to rotate once a day, just as I conjecture about the sun. And because of that rotation, and because it has magnetic fibres intersecting the line of its motion at right angles, those fibres lie in various circles about the poles of the earth parallel to its motion. I am therefore absolutely within my rights to state that the moon is carried along by the rotation of the earth and the motion of its magnetic power, only thirty times slower. (Kepler 1609/1992, chap. 34, pp. 390–391)

Later, he voiced the concern that there are significant differences between the vis motrix and magnetism, and that they therefore cannot be equated:

> I will be satisfied if this magnetic example demonstrates the general possibility of the proposed mechanism. Concerning its details, however, I have my doubts. For when the earth is in question, it is certain that its axis, whose constant and parallel direction brings about the year's seasons at the cardinal points, is not well suited to bringing about this reciprocation or this aphelion . . . And if this axis is unsuitable, it seems that there is none suitable in the earth's entire body, since there is no part of it which rests in one position while the whole body of the globe revolves in a ceaseless daily whirl about that axis. (Kepler, 1609/1992, p. 560)

Yet despite these concerns, Kepler continued to use the phrase "magnetic force" or "magnetic *species*" to describe the vis motrix throughout the text. One reason that he did so may be that the only alternative he could think of to a magnetic force was a mind in the planet, one that would somehow perceive the planet's distance from the sun (perhaps by registering the sun's

[17]Kepler was incorrect here. Although Gilbert believed that the Earth rotated on its axis, he retained a Tychonic model in which the sun and its satellite planets revolve around the Earth.

apparent diameter) and move accordingly. Kepler's desire to reduce or replace this intelligence with a mechanical force is a recurring theme in his analogies.

ADDITIONAL ASPECTS OF CREATIVE ANALOGY

We have mentioned highlighting, candidate inferences, re-representation, and restructuring as mechanisms of analogical learning. In addition, we believe at least three additional mechanisms are needed to capture creative analogy processing. First, a mechanism is needed to mediate between multiple analogies such as the magnetism analogy, the light analogy, and the ship analogy. One computational approach might be found in Burstein's (1986) CARL, which combined different analogies to build a representation of how a variable works. Spiro, Feltovich, Coulson, and Anderson (1989) have also traced the way in which multiple analogies interact (not always peacefully) in learning complex domains.

A second mechanism needed is incremental analogizing. As new information about a domain is learned or brought in, the learner must be able to extend the original mapping. It has been shown that individuals are sensitive to a recent mapping and will more quickly extend that mapping than create a new one (Boronat & Gentner, 1996; Gentner & Boronat, 1992; Gibbs & O'Brien, 1990; Keane, 1990). Keane and Brayshaw's (1988) simulation was the first to capture the finding that people's initial mappings influence the subsequent correspondences they can readily draw. We have adapted Keane and Brayshaw's technique to create an incremental version of SME, called Incremental Structure-mapping Engine (ISME), which can extend an analogy after the initial mapping. It draws further information from its long-term knowledge about the base and target to add to the working memory descriptions. It then re-maps the analogy, building on the results of the initial mapping and thus enriching the overall analogical mapping (Forbus et al., 1994). ISME can model the process of extended analogizing in problem solving. Could it partially explain creative extension processes like Kepler's? We address this question in the Discussion section.

A third mechanism—or combination of mechanisms—is one that can test the projected inferences of the mapping and make re-representations when needed. The notion of re-representation in analogical reasoning has recently been a focus of attention in analogy and case-based reasoning research (Kass, 1994; Keane, 1988; Kolodner, 1993; Novick & Holyoak, 1991). Falkenhainer's (1990) PHINEAS system has an adaptation step as part of an analogical discovery process. It constructs physical theories by analogy with previously understood examples, by iterating through what Falkenhainer called a *map/analyze cycle.* In this cycle, PHINEAS starts with a qualitative description of a physical system's behavior and a set of domain theories. If it does not have an applicable theory to explain the new behavior, it uses analogy to find an explanation. PHINEAS has an index of previously explained examples, arranged using an abstraction hierarchy of observed behaviors. PHINEAS selects and evaluates potentially analogous examples from this hierarchy and then uses SME to generate a set of correspondences between the novel behavior and the understood example. The explanation for the new behavior is then projected from the explanation of the old behavior. PHINEAS then tests this new explanation to make sure that it is coherent with its rules about physical domains. When there is conflict, PHINEAS can re-represent some predicates. It then simulates the operation of the new theory to see if the newly mapped structure in the target can produce the observed behavior.

DISCUSSION

Kepler used analogies both widely and deeply in his quest for an understanding of planetary motion. We have traced some of these analogies and modeled the processes using SME. We suggest that these analogies were instrumental to Kepler's conceptual change. Let us begin by justifying some key assumptions.

Did Kepler Use Analogy in Thinking?

The frequent use of analogies in Kepler's texts is no guarantee that these analogies drove his conceptual change. He could have used analogy solely as a rhetorical device. Although there is no way to decide this issue definitively, there are reasons to believe that at least some of Kepler's analogies were instrumental in his thought processes. First, as discussed earlier, the open and inclusive character of Kepler's writing, and his apparent insistence on taking the reader through his tortuous course of discovery, suggest that the extended analogies he provided were actually used in his thought processes. Second, and more directly, Kepler's major analogies were pursued with almost fanatical intensity across and within his major works. There are numerous detailed diagrams of base and target, and long passages that spell out the commonalities, the inferences, and the incremental extensions, as well as alignable differences between base and target and Kepler's assessment of their import. Furthermore, for both his major analogies, he delved energetically into the base domain: reading Gilbert's *De Magnete* in the case of magnetism and writing his own treatise, *Astronomiae Pars Optica*, in the case of light. Kepler's long discussions about the status of the magnetism–vis motrix comparison—whether it was purely an analogy or might instead in fact be the causal means by which the sun influenced the planets—are another indication of the seriousness with which Kepler took his analogies.

A third indication that Kepler might have used analogies in thinking is the sheer fecundity of his analogizing, which suggests that analogy was a natural mode of thought for him. In pursuit of a causal model of the planetary system, Kepler analogized sun and planet to sailors in a current, magnets, a balance beam, and light, to name only some of the more prominent analogies (see Figure 9). For example, in the *Epitome* (Kepler, 1621/1969) he compared his celestial physics—in which planetary paths arise out of interacting forces—with the fixed-firmament theories of the ancients:

> Here we entrust the planet to the river, with an oblique rudder, by the help of which the planet, while floating down, may cross from one bank to the opposite. But the ancient astronomy built a solid bridge—the solid spheres—above this river,—the latitude of the zodiac—and transports the lifeless planet along the bridge as if in a chariot. But if the whole contrivance is examined carefully, it appears that this

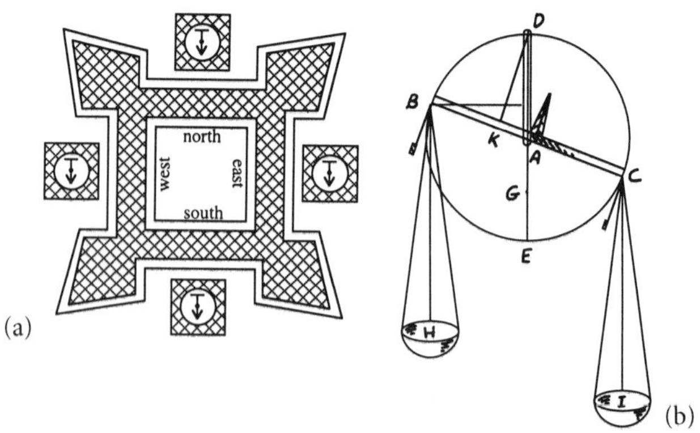

Figure 9

Examples of Kepler's multiple analogies for planetary motion: (a) magnet and (b) balance scale.

> bridge has no props by which it is supported, nor does it rest upon the earth, which they believed to be the foundation of the heavens. (pp. 182–183)

Analogies were used for matters personal as well as public. For example, Kepler complained of the astrological forecasts he often had to cast: "A mind accustomed to mathematical deduction, when confronted with the faulty foundations [of astrology] resists a long, long time, like an obstinate mule, until compelled by beating and curses to put its foot into that dirty puddle" (Kepler, 1606, in *De Stella Nova in Pede Serpentarii*, quoted in Koestler, 1963).

In another engaging passage, Kepler (1609/1992) introduced the *Astronomia Nova* to his royal patron with a long, elegant analogy treating his solution to Mars's orbit as a kind of capture of war:

> I am now at last exhibiting for the view of the public a most Noble Captive, who has been taken for a long time now through a difficult and strenuous war waged by me under the auspices of Your Majesty . . . It is he who is the most potent conqueror of human inventions, who, ridiculing all the sallies of the Astronomers, escaping their devices, and striking down the hostile throngs, kept safe

> the secret of his empire, well guarded throughout all ages past, and performed his rounds in perfect freedom with no restraints: hence, the chief complaint registered by that Priest of Nature's Mysteries and most distinguished of the Latins, C. Pliny, that "Mars is the untrackable star" . . . In this place chief praise is to be given to the diligence of Tycho Brahe, the commander-in-chief in this war, who . . . explored the habits of this enemy of ours nearly every night for twenty years, observed every aspect of the campaign, detected every stratagem, and left them fully described in books as he was dying . . . I, instructed by those books as I succeeded Brahe in this charge, first of all ceased to fear [the enemy] whom I had to some extent come to know, and then, having diligently noted the moments of time at which he was accustomed to arrive at his former positions, as if going to bed, I directed the Brahean machines thither, equipped with precise sights, as if aiming at a particular target, and besieged each position with my enquiry. (pp. 30–35)

Clearly, Kepler liked to play with analogies. But there is a fourth reason to assume that he used analogies in his thinking, namely, that he explicitly stated that he did so. For example, Vickers (1984) discussed how in the Optics (1904) Kepler treated the conic sections by analogy with light through a lens and justified this unorthodox treatment thus:

> But for us the terms in Geometry should serve the analogy (for I especially love analogies, my most faithful masters, acquainted with all the secrets of nature) and one should make great use of them in geometry, where—despite the incongruous terminology—they bring the solution of an infinity of cases lying between the extreme and the mean, and where they clearly present to our eyes the whole essence of the question. (pp. 149–150)

A more specific reference to analogy in Kepler's creative thinking occurs in his own writings about how he originally arrived at the anima motrix idea. In his 1621 annotations to *Mysterium Cosmographicum*, Kepler commented explicitly on the role of analogy in his knowledge revision process. In the original version, in 1596, he had argued that there was "a single moving soul [*motricem anima*] in the center of all the spheres, that is, in the Sun, and it impels each body more strongly in proportion to how near it is" (Kepler, 1596/1981, p. 199). In 1621, he wrote the following:

> If for the word "soul" [*Anima*] you substitute the word "force" [*Vim*], you have the very same principle on which the Celestial Physics is established . . . For once I believed that the cause which moves the planets was precisely a soul. . . . But when I pondered that this moving cause grows weaker with distance, and that the Sun's light also grows thinner with distance from the Sun, from that I concluded, that this force is something corporeal, that is, an emanation which a body emits, but an immaterial one. (Kepler, 1621/1969, p. 201)

What Did Kepler Mean by *Analogy*?

A fifth indication that Kepler took analogy seriously as a tool for thought is that he devoted some energy to discussing its proper use in thinking. He lived in a curious time with respect to the use of analogy and metaphor in discovery. The alchemists', the dominant approach to scientific phenomena, was still a major force in medieval Europe during Kepler's life. The alchemists were remarkable, from the current point of view, both in their zeal for using metaphors and analogies to explain natural phenomena and in their manner of using them. From the viewpoint of current scientific practice, their use of analogy was unrestrained, bordering on the irrational (see Gentner & Jeziorski, 1993, for a comparison of alchemical analogizing with current scientific practice). Kepler, who rarely engaged in collegial tussling, was sharply critical of this sort of analogizing. In the *Harmonice Mundi* (1619) he attempted to distinguish the proper use of analogy from the methods of alchemists, hermeticists, and others of that ilk: "I have shown that Ptolemy luxuriates in using comparisons in a poetical or rhetorical way, since the things that he compares are not real things in the heavens" (cited in Vickers, 1984, p. 153). In a letter to a colleague in 1608, Kepler attempted to make explicit the qualities that make for useful analogizing:

> I too play with symbols, and have planned a little work, Geometric Cabala, which is about the Ideas of natural things in geometry; but I play in such a way that I do not forget that I am playing. *For nothing is proved by symbols . . . unless by sure reasons it can be demonstrated that they are not merely symbolic but are descriptions of the ways in which the two things are connected and of the causes of this connexion.* (cited in Vickers, 1984, p. 155)

Kepler believed, then, that analogy is heuristic, not deductive. His second (italicized) statement sounds remarkably like a modern cognitive view: He seems to be suggesting, as we do in this chapter, that the two domains should contain the same system of relationships and causal structures (although he might also have meant that there should be causal connections between the two domains analogized). For our purposes, the key point is that he explicitly concerned himself with the proper use of analogy in thinking.

Analogy and Creativity

One indication of creativity is the magnitude of the change in ideas. Kepler's ideas changed radically over the course of his life. Many of these changes had multiple contributors, including Bruno, Copernicus, Tycho, Gilbert, Galileo, and others. However, much of the change occurred as a result of Kepler's own creative thought processes.

1. Formerly, the paths of the planets were composed of perfect circles and the planets moved at uniform velocity. Over the course of his work, Kepler shifted to the belief that the planets move in ellipses with the sun at one focus, faster when closer to the sun and slower when farther. This was a far more radical change than most of us can today

appreciate: "Before Kepler, circular motion was to the concept of a planet as 'tangibility' is to our concept of 'physical object' " (Hanson, 1958, p. 4).

2. Formerly, the planets' orbits were conceived of either as crystalline spheres containing the planets or as eternal paths, composed of circles, traveled by planetary intelligences. Kepler came to see them as paths continually negotiated between the sun and the planets. As Toulmin and Goodfield (1961) noted, "One cannot find before Kepler any clear recognition that the heavenly motions called for an explanation in terms of a *continuously* acting physical force" (p. 201, emphasis in original).
3. Formerly, celestial phenomena were considered completely separate from earthly physics. Kepler freely extended terrestrial knowledge to astronomical phenomena. He applied analogies from the domains of light, magnetism, balance scales, sailing, and the optics of lenses, among many others.
4. Formerly, the planetary system was governed by mathematical regularities. Kepler changed it to one governed by physical causality *and* a resulting mathematical regularity. As noted by Gingerich (1993),

> Copernicus gave the world a revolutionary helio*static* system, but Kepler made it into a heliocentric system. In Kepler's universe, the Sun has a fundamental physically motivated centrality that is essentially lacking in *De revolutionibus.* We have grown so accustomed to calling this the Copernican system that we usually forget than many of its attributes could better be called the Keplerian system. (p. 333)

5. Early in Kepler's work, he proposed the anima motrix as the "spirit" in the sun that could move the planets. Later, he called it the vis motrix or virtus motrix. This change could be considered an ontological change, an instance of what Thagard (1992) calls "branch jumping." It could also be analyzed as differentiation (Smith, Carey, & Wiser, 1985), analogous to the notion of "degree of heat," which differentiated into heat and temperature (Wiser & Carey, 1983).

However, in Kepler's case the split is somewhat more dramatic: An early animate–mechanistic notion differentiated or specialized into a purely mechanical notion.[18] This change marked a shift toward a mechanization of planetary forces.

One other change is harder to sum up. Early in Kepler's work, the planets (in the Stoic account—the leading account after the crystalline spheres had been punctured by Tycho's comet)—were intelligences (Barker, 1991). Kepler struggled with the notion of a planetary intelligence throughout his career. Kepler had to find a way of thinking about the planets that could predict their individual behaviors, while assigning to them the minimal possible number of animate or entient properties. Lacking any established notion of force, Kepler had to develop these ideas by gradually stripping away from the notion of "intelligence" more and more of its normal properties. For example, he asked himself whether he could explain the fact that planets go faster when nearest the sun by granting them only the ability to perceive the sun's diameter.

How should we characterize the magnitude of these changes? Theories of knowledge change distinguish degrees of alteration in the existing structure (e.g., Carey, 1985; Thagard, 1992). *Belief revision* is a change in facts believed. *Theory change* is a change in the global knowledge structure. *Conceptual change*, in some sense the most drastic, is a change in the fundamental *concepts* that compose the belief structure. Conceptual change thus requires at least locally nonalignable or incommensurable beliefs (Carey, 1985). Of the changes just mentioned, we suggest that most if not all of them would qualify as theory change, and that Statements 2 and 5 have a good claim to be full-fledged changes of concepts.

Our results indicating that Kepler used analogies in his creative thinking accord with other work on the history of science. The journals of such great contributors to the scientific enterprise as Boyle, Carnot, Darwin,

[18]The prevalence of these combined animate–mechanistic notions in the historical record is worth considering in the context of theories of cognitive development. They suggest that distinctions between domains—and even the theory of what constitutes a domain—are culturally defined rather than innately present.

Faraday, and Maxwell contain many examples of generative uses of analogy (Darden, 1992; Gentner, 1982; Gentner & Jeziorski, 1993; Nersessian, 1985, 1986, 1992; Nersessian & Resnick, 1989; Ranney & Thagard, 1988; Thagard, 1992; Tweney, 1983; Wiser, 1986; Wiser & Carey, 1983). Modern creative scientists such as Robert Oppenheimer (1956) and Sheldon Glashow (1980) have commented explicitly on the usefulness of analogy in their work. Finally, direct field observations of molecular biologists at work (Dunbar, 1995) and case studies in the history of psychology (Gentner & Grudin, 1985; Gigerenzer, 1994) demonstrate that analogy is frequently used in the everyday practice of science.

Kepler Compared With Current Scientists

It is useful to compare Kepler's use of analogy with that observed by Kevin Dunbar (1995, this volume) in his observations of microbiology laboratories. Dunbar suggests three factors that make for a productive laboratory: frequent use of analogy, attention to inconsistency, and heterogeneity of the research group. Dunbar's working question is, of course, quite different from ours; there need be no necessary connection between what makes for a creative laboratory and what makes for a creative individual. Nonetheless there are some striking commonalities. Dunbar's detailed analyses show that the highly productive microbiology laboratories are those that use analogies in quantity and take them seriously. In the successful lab groups, analogies are extended and "pushed" in group discussions. This is the most direct evidence to date that the process of working through an analogy contributes to scientists' on-line creative thinking, and it lends force to Kepler's introspection that analogy furthered—and perhaps even engendered—his theories. Another possible parallel stems from Dunbar's observation that the heterogeneity of the laboratory group contributes to creativity. Dunbar speculates that this is true in part because group heterogeneity increases the range of different analogues that can be brought to bear. The idea that a stock of different analogues is conducive to creative thought accords with our conclusions concerning Kepler. (However, we suggest that such multiplicity is helpful only if the individual analogies are dealt with energetically.) The mode of thought in which one slides and blends freely across different analogues is rarely as successful in scientific analogy as it is in expressive metaphor. This is because it typically undermines structural consistency and hence the inferential usefulness of an analogy (Gentner, 1982; Gentner & Jeziorski, 1993; Markman, 1996). Kepler seems to have profited considerably from working through the magnet and light analogues for the sun's motive power and from exploring parallels between them.

There are also commonalities not directly related to analogy. Attention to inconsistencies is another factor Dunbar singles out in his analysis of creative laboratories. Kepler worried about inconsistencies and was driven by them to keep pushing old analogies and in some cases to reject them. However, we suggest that these two factors play different roles. Attention to inconsistencies is a *motivator* of conceptual change, whereas analogy is a *process* by which conceptual change occurs.

There are also some interesting (alignable) differences between the patterns Dunbar observed and Kepler's recorded patterns. First, by far the majority of the analogies Dunbar observed are close literal similarities (what he calls *local analogies*), typically involving the same kind of organism or species, similar diseases or genetic materials, and so forth. Kepler did in fact use close analogues on many occasions. When he first noticed the key pattern that speed diminished as distance from the sun increased, he immediately applied this between-planet pattern within planets to suggest that each planet moves fastest when it is closest to the sun. This led to the first statement of the equal-areas law. As another example, his calculation of Mars's orbit depended on the reverse analogy of imagining how the Earth's orbit would appear from Mars. Again, he tested his reasoning about the sun and planets by applying that same reasoning to the Earth and its satellite moon, which he regarded as closely analogous to the sun and its satellite planets.

However, in contrast to the microbiologists, Kepler also used many distant analogies. We believe this stems in part from the different historical stages of the disciplines. Kepler was forming the new science of astrophysics, more or less in the absence of a usable physics. Given this underdeveloped state of affairs, distant analogies were in many cases his only option. There was no literal similarity to be had. In contrast, in the microbiology laboratories that Dunbar studied, the historical moment is one of a fairly well agreed-on (but not yet fully explored) framework in which there are many close analogues (similar cases) that are likely to be extremely fruitful. That is, we suspect that close analogies and far analogies may be useful at different stages in the history of a field. Local analogies are useful for filling in a framework, whereas distant analogies are used for developing a new framework.

Finally, another marked difference turns on another aspect of Dunbar's third claim: that creative labs have social interaction patterns that bring together heterogeneous knowledge. Clearly, this cannot apply literally to Kepler, who worked alone. (Though his correspondence shows steady efforts to find collegial interactions, his contemporaries on the whole found his work too radical, or too mystifying, to accept.) Should we then think of Kepler as a kind of one-man equivalent of Dunbar's heterogeneous groups, who produced a large variety of analogies and therefore a good pool of possible solutions?

This brings us to the final question. Is it possible to say exactly wherein Kepler's analogizing differed from the way in which ordinary people do analogy? The short answer, of course, would be that he was a creative genius and most people are not. But let us attempt to be more specific. One obvious partition within analogical processing is that between (a) the *retrieval* processes by which potential analogues are accessed from memory and (b) the *mapping* processes that go on after both analogues are present. There is substantial evidence for a disassociation between those two (Gentner, 1989; Gentner, Rattermann, & Forbus, 1993). Similarity-based retrieval to a probe (Process a) is considerably less discerning and structure-sensitive than is comparison of two present items (Process b). Similarity-based access to long-term memory typically produces mundane literal similarity matches or even matches that are surface-similar but not structurally similar (Gentner, Rattermann, & Forbus, 1993; Gick & Holyoak, 1980; Holyoak & Koh, 1987; Keane, 1988; Reeves & Weisberg, 1994; Ross, 1989). Yet once both analogues are present, people typically show a high degree of sensitivity to structure and can fluently carry out abstract mappings (Clement & Gentner, 1991; Gentner, Rattermann, & Forbus, 1993; Holyoak & Koh, 1987). For example, when given analogies to use in solving problems, people are typically fairly selective about choosing analogies that have genuine structural overlap with the target problem (Bassok & Holyoak, 1989; Holyoak & Koh, 1987; Novick & Holyoak, 1991; Novick & Tversky, 1987; Ross, 1987; Ross, Ryan, & Tenpenny, 1989). We have simulated subjects' retrieval patterns with the MAC/FAC simulation (Many Are Called but Few Are Chosen), in which a first stage retrieval process carries out a wide, computationally cheap and structurally insensitive search for candidate retrievals and a later stage (the FAC stage, essentially SME) performs a structural alignment over these candidate analogues (Forbus, Gentner, & Law, 1995). This system does a good job of capturing the phenomena: Retrievals based on surface similarity or on overall similarity are common, and retrievals based on purely relational similarity—the purely analogical retrievals that strike us as clever and creative—also occur, but rarely.

Thus we might be tempted to conclude that Kepler differs most radically from others in his fertile access to various prior analogues (Process a). It is certainly plausible that what most distinguishes highly creative thinkers is a high rate of spontaneous analogical retrievals. But another possibility worth considering is that it may be the mapping process (Process b) that most differentiates highly creative individuals. There are two reasons for this speculation. First, the more energetic the mapping process, the more each analogy is likely to reveal its full potential set of inferences. Second, and less obvious, we conjecture that intense mapping may promote fertile access. For if access to prior material depends on a common encoding (Forbus, Gentner, & Law, 1995), then the highlighting, inferencing, and re-representing carried out in the course of pushing analogies may benefit subsequent memory access, as such activities tend to increase the scope of common internal representations (Gentner, Rattermann, Markman, & Kotovsky, 1995). This account is consonant with Seifert, Meyer, Davidson, Patalano, & Yaniv's (1995) prepared-mind perspective on creativity, and also with Gruber's (1995) discussion of Poincaré. Thus, we suggest that a major reason for Kepler's high rate of analogical remindings is the intensity of the alignment processes he carried out on his analogies once he had them in working memory.

A further contributor to analogical fecundity might be heterogeneity of interests within an individual. Kepler's published works, besides his great works on celestial physics, included papers on optics, the nature of comets, the birthdate of Jesus, and a new method of measuring wine casks (in which he developed a method of infinitesmals that took a step toward calculus). Such diversity within an individual might be analogous to the heterogeneity of background Dunbar noted in his successful laboratory groups.

Creativity and Structure

It is a common intuition that creativity is the opposite of rigidity, that it is characterized by fluid concepts and shifting relationships and unclassifiable processes. In contrast, we have suggested that at least some kinds of creativity are better described as structure-sensitive processes operating over articulated representations. For example, SME, a system that thrives on structured representations, behaves in what might be considered to be a creative manner when it notices cross-dimensional structural matches, projects candidate inferences, infers skolomized entities, and (for ISME) incrementally extends its mapping. We suggest that analogy is an engine of creativity in part *because* it provides a fair degree of structure while inviting some alteration.

Interestingly, in a creative drawing task, Ward (1994) noted similar self-generated structure-preserving strategies. He showed that when individuals are asked to create new instances of a category, their drawings tend to rely closely either on exemplars they have just seen (Smith, Ward, & Schumacher, 1993) or on self-generated category standards (Cacciari, Levorato, & Cicogna, this volume; Ward, 1994). This is true even when individuals are explicitly told to create items that are very different. Ward et al. (1995) stressed the heavy reliance on prior structures in the creative process.

Totally fixed structure can lead to rigidity, but total fluidity is equally inimical to creative change because in such a condition no state can be interestingly distinguished from any other. To close with an analogy, the difference between two quartz crystals is interesting, but the difference between two configurations of molecules in a glass of water is not. We suggest that creativity is more like crystal building than it is like fluids shifting: It is only when the structures are intricate enough to be distinguishable that we care when a change has occurred. On this analogy, creativity is best seen when there is a large enough structure to permit significant change. The example of Kepler is more consonant with the notion of creativity as structural change than it is with creativity as fluidity. There are probably many paths to creativity. Kepler's writings reveal that analogy is one of them.

REFERENCES

Aiton, E. J. (1976). Johannes Kepler in the light of recent research. *Historical Science, 14*, 77–100.

Barker, P. (1991). Stoic contribution to early modern science. In M. J. Osler (Ed.), *Atoms, pneuma, and tranquility: Epicurean and stoic themes in European thought.* Cambridge, England: Cambridge University Press.

Barker, P. (1993). The optical theory of comets from Apian to Kepler. *Physis: Rivista Internzionale di Storia Della Scienza, 30*(1), 1–25.

Bassok, M. (1990). Transfer of domain-specific problem-solving procedures. *Journal of Experimental Psychology: Learning, Memory, and Cognition, 16*, 522–533.

Bassok, M., & Holyoak, K. J. (1989). Interdomain transfer between isomorphic topics in algebra and physics. *Journal of Experimental Psychology: Learning, Memory, and Cognition, 15*, 153–166.

Baumgardt, C. (1952). *Johannes Kepler: Life and letters.* London: Victor Gollancz.

Boden, M. A. (Ed.). (1994a). *Dimensions of creativity.* Cambridge, MA: MIT Press.

Boden, M. A. (1994b). What is creativity? In M. A. Boden (Ed.), *Dimensions of creativity* (pp. 75–117). Cambridge, MA: MIT Press.

Boronat, C., & Gentner, D. (1996). *Metaphors are (sometimes) processed as generative domain mappings.* Manuscript in preparation.

Bowdle, B. F., & Gentner, D. (1996). *Informativity and asymmetry in comparisons.* Manuscript submitted for publication.

Brown, J. S., Collins, A., & Duguid, P. (1989). Situated cognition and the culture of learning. *Educational Researcher, 18*, 32–42.

Burstein, M. H. (1986). Concept formation by incremental analogical reasoning and debugging. In R. S. Michalski, J. G. Carbonell, & T. M. Mitchell (Eds.), *Machine learning: An artificial intelligence approach* (Vol. 2, pp. 351–370). Los Altos, CA: Kaufmann.

Butterfield, H. (1957). *The origins of modern science 1300–1800.* New York: Free Press.

Carey, S. (1985). *Conceptual change in childhood.* Cambridge, MA: MIT Press.

Catrambone, R., & Holyoak, K. J. (1989). Overcoming contextual limitations on problem-solving transfer. *Journal of Experimental Psychology: Learning, Memory, and Cognition, 15,* 1147–1156.

Clement, C. A., & Gentner, D. (1988). Systematicity as a selection constraint in analogical mapping. *Proceedings of the Tenth Annual Conference of the Cognitive Science Society* (pp. 412–418). Hillsdale, NJ: Erlbaum.

Clement, C. A., & Gentner, D. (1991). Systematicity as a selection constraint in analogical mapping. *Cognitive Science, 15,* 89–132.

Clement, J. (1988). Observed methods for generating analogies in scientific problem solving. *Cognitive Science, 12,* 563–586.

Darden, L. (1992). Strategies for anomaly resolution. In R. N. Giere (Ed.), *Cognitive models of science.* Minneapolis: University of Minnesota Press.

Dunbar, K. (1995). How scientists really reason: Scientific reasoning in real-world laboratories. In R. J. Sternberg & J. E. Davidson (Eds.), *The nature of insight* (pp. 365–396). Cambridge, MA: MIT Press.

Elio, R., & Anderson, J. R. (1981). The effect of category generalizations and instance similarity on schema abstraction. *Journal of Experimental Psychology: Human Learning and Memory, 7,* 397–417.

Elio, R., & Anderson, J. R. (1984). The effects of information order and learning mode on schema abstraction. *Memory & Cognition, 12,* 20–30.

Falkenhainer, B. (1990). A unified approach to explanation and theory formation. In J. Shrager & P. Langley (Eds.), *Computational models of scientific discovery and theory formation* (pp. 157–196). San Mateo, CA: Morgan Kaufmann.

Falkenhainer, B., Forbus, K. D., & Gentner, D. (1986). The structure-mapping engine. *Proceedings of the Fifth National Conference on Artificial Intelligence* (pp. 272–277). Philadelphia, PA: Morgan Kaufmann.

Falkenhainer, B., Forbus, K. D., & Gentner, D. (1989). The structure-mapping engine: An algorithm and examples. *Artificial Intelligence,* 41, 1–63.

Finke, R. A. (1990). Creative imagery: Discoveries and inventions in visualization. Hillsdale, NJ: Erlbaum.

Finke, R. A. (1995). Creative insight and preinventive forms. In R. J. Sternberg & J. E. Davidson (Eds.), *The nature of insight* (pp. 255–280). Cambridge, MA: MIT Press.

Finke, R. A., Ward, T. B., & Smith, S. M. (1992). *Creative cognition: Theory, reserach, and applications.* Cambridge, MA: MIT Press.

Forbus, K. D. (1984). Qualitative process theory. *Journal of Artificial Intelligence, 24,* 85–168.

Forbus, K. D. (1990). Qualitative physics: Past, present, and future. In D. S. Weld & J. de Kleer (Eds.), *Readings in qualitative reasoning about physical systems* (pp. 11–39). San Mateo, CA: Morgan Kaufmann.

Forbus, K., Ferguson, R., & Gentner, D. (1994). Incremental structure-mapping. In A. Ram & K. Eislet (Eds.), *Proceedings of the Sixteenth Annual Conference of the Cognitive Science Society* (pp. 313–318). Hillsdale, NJ: Erlbaum.

Forbus, K. D., & Gentner, D. (1986). Learning physical domains: Toward a theoretical framework. In R. S. Michalski, J. G. Carbonell, & T. M. Mitchell (Eds.), *Machine learning: An artificial intelligence approach* (pp. 311–348). Los Altos, CA: Morgan Kaufmann.

Forbus, K. D., & Gentner, D. (1989). Structural evaluation of analogies: What counts? *Proceedings of the Eleventh Annual Conference of the Cognitive Science Society* (pp. 314–348). Hillsdale, NJ: Erlbaum.

Forbus, K. D., Gentner, D., & Law, K. (1995). MAC/FAC: A model of similarity-based retrieval. *Cognitive Science, 19,* 141–205.

Forbus, K. D., & Oblinger, D. (1990). Making SME greedy and pragmatic. *Proceedings of the Twelfth Annual Conference of the Cognitive Science Society* (pp. 61–68). Hillsdale, NJ: Erlbaum.

Gentner, D. (1982). Are scientific analogies metaphors? In D. S. Miall (Ed.), *Metaphor: Problems and perspectives* (pp. 106–132). Brighton, England: Harvester Press.

Gentner, D. (1983). Structure-mapping: A theoretical framework for analogy. *Cognitive Science, 7,* 155–170.

Gentner, D. (1989). The mechanisms of analogical learning. In S. Vosniadou & A. Ortony (Eds.), *Similarity and analogical reasoning* (pp. 199–241). Cambridge, England: Cambridge University Press.

Gentner, D., & Boronat, C. B. (1992). *Metaphors are (sometimes) processed as generative domain mappings.* Unpublished manuscript.

Gentner, D., & Bowdle, B. (1994). The coherence imbalance hypothesis: A functional approach to asymmetry in comparison. In A. Ram & K. Eislet (Eds.), *Proceed-*

ings of the Sixteenth Annual Conference of the Cognitive Science Society (pp. 351–356). Hillsdale, NJ: Erlbaum.

Gentner, D., Brem, S., Ferguson, R., Wolff, P., Levidow, B. B., Markman, A. B., & Forbus, K. (1997). Analogical reasoning and conceptual change: A case study of Johannes Kepler [Special issue]. *Journal of the Learning Sciences, 6,* 3–39.

Gentner, D., & Clement, C. (1988). Evidence for relational selectivity in the interpretation of analogy and metaphor. In G. H. Bower (Ed.), *The psychology of learning and motivation: Advances in research and theory* (pp. 307–358). San Diego, CA: Academic Press.

Gentner, D., & Gentner, D. R. (1983). Flowing waters or teeming crowds: Mental models of electricity. In D. Gentner & A. Stevens (Eds.), *Mental models* (pp. 99–129). Hillsdale, NJ: Erlbaum.

Gentner, D., & Grudin, J. (1985). The evolution of mental metaphors in psychology: A 90-year retrospective. *American Psychologist, 40,* 181–192.

Gentner, D., & Jeziorski, M. (1993). The shift from metaphor to analogy in Western science. In A. Ortony (Ed.), *Metaphor and thought* (pp. 447–480). Cambridge, England: Cambridge University Press.

Gentner, D., & Markman, A. B. (1993). Analogy—Watershed or Waterloo? Structural alignment and the development of connectionist models of cognition. In S. J. Hanson, J. D. Cowan, & C. L. Giles (Eds.), *Advances in neural information processing systems, Vol. 5* (pp. 855–862). San Mateo, CA: Morgan Kauffman.

Gentner, D., & Markman, A. B. (1994). Structural alignment in comparison: No difference without similarity. *Psychological Science, 5,* 152–158.

Gentner, D., & Markman, A. B. (1997). Structure-mapping in analogy and similarity. *American Psychologist, 52,* 45–56.

Gentner, D., & Rattermann, M. J. (1991). Language and the career of similarity. In S. A. Gelman & J. P. Byrnes (Eds.), *Perspectives on language and thought: Interrelations in development* (pp. 225–277). Cambridge, England: Cambridge University Press.

Gentner, D., Rattermann, M. J., & Forbus, K. D. (1993). The roles of similarity in transfer: Separating retrievability from inferential soundness. *Cognitive Psychology, 25,* 524–575.

Gentner, D., Rattermann, M. J., Markman, A. B., & Kotovsky, L. (1995). Two forces in the development of relational similarity. In T. J. Simon & G. S. Halford (Eds.), *Developing cognitive competence: New approaches to process modeling* (pp. 263–313). Hillsdale, NJ: Erlbaum.

Gentner, D., & Wolff, P. (1996). *The primacy of alignment in the comprehension of metaphor.* Manuscript in preparation.

Gibbs, R. W., Jr., & O'Brien, J. E. (1990). Idioms and mental imagery: The metaphorical motivation for idiomatic meaning. *Cognition, 36,* 35–68.

Gick, M. L., & Holyoak, K. J. (1980). Analogical problem solving. *Cognitive Psychology, 12,* 306–355.

Gick, M. L., & Holyoak, K. J. (1983). Schema induction and analogical transfer. *Cognitive Psychology, 15,* 1–38.

Gigerenzer, G. (1994). Where do new ideas come from? In M. A. Boden (Ed.), *Dimensions of Creativity* (pp. 53–74). Cambridge, MA: MIT Press.

Gilbert, W. (1938). *On the loadstone* (sic) *and magnetic bodies, and on the great magnet the earth: A new physiology, demonstrated with many arguments and experiments* (P. Fleury Mottelay, Trans.) Ann Arbor, MI: Edwards Brothers. (Original work published 1600)

Gingerich, O. (1993). *The eye of heaven.* New York: The American Institute of Physics.

Glashow, S. L. (1980). Towards a unified theory: Threads in a tapestry. Nobel prize lecture, December 1979. *Science, 210,* 1319–1323.

Gruber, H. E. (1995). Insight and affect in the history of science. In R. J. Sternberg & J. E. Davidson (Eds.), *The nature of insight* (pp. 397–432). Cambridge, MA: MIT Press.

Halford, G. S. (1993). *Children's understanding: The development of mental models.* Hillsdale, NJ: Erlbaum.

Hanson, N. R. (1958). *Patterns of discovery: An inquiry into the conceptual foundations of science.* Cambridge, England: Cambridge University Press.

Hesse, M. B. (1966). *Models and analogies in science.* Notre Dame, IN: University of Notre Dame Press.

Holton, G. (1973). *Thematic origins of scientific thought.* Cambridge, MA: Harvard University Press.

Holyoak, K. J., Junn, E. N., & Billman, D. O. (1984). Development of analogical problem-solving skill. *Child Development, 55,* 2042–2055.

Holyoak, K. J., & Koh, K. (1987). Surface and structural similarity in analogical transfer. *Memory & Cognition, 15,* 332–340.

Holyoak, K. J., Novick, L. R., & Melz, E. R. (1994). Component processes in analogical transfer: Mapping, pattern completion, and adaptation. In K. J. Holyoak & J. A. Barnden (Eds.), *Advances in connectionist and neural computation theory: Vol. 2. Analogical connections* (pp. 113–180). Norwood, NJ: Ablex.

Holyoak, K. J., & Thagard, P. R. (1989). Analogical mapping by constraint satisfaction. *Cognitive Science, 13*, 295–355.

Holyoak, K. J., & Thagard, P. R. (1995). *Mental leaps.* Cambridge, MA: MIT Press.

Kass, A. (1994). Tweaker: Adapting old explanations to new situations. In R. Schank, A. Kass, & C. K. Riesbeck (Eds.), *Inside case-based explanation* (pp. 263–295). Hillsdale, NJ: Erlbaum.

Keane, M. T. (1988). Analogical mechanisms. *Artificial Intelligence Review, 2*, 229–250.

Keane, M. T. G. (1990). Incremental analogizing: Theory and model. In K. J. Gilhooly, M. T. G. Kenae, R. H. Logie, & G. Erdos (Eds.), *Lines of thinking* (Vol. 1). Chichester, England: Wiley.

Keane, M. T., & Brayshaw, M. (1988). The incremental analogical machine: A computational model of analogy. In D. Sleeman (Ed.), *Third European working session on machine learning* (pp. 53–62). San Mateo, CA: Kaufman.

Kepler, J. (1969). *Epitome of Copernican astronomy* (C. G. Wallis, Trans.). New York: Kraus. (Original work published 1621)

Kepler, J. (1981). *Mysterium cosmographicum I, II* (A. M. Duncan, Trans.). (2nd ed.). New York: Abaris Books. (Original work published 1596, annotated 1621)

Kepler, J. (1992). *Astronomia nova [New astronomy]* (W. Donahue, Trans.). Cambridge, England: Cambridge University Press. (Original work published 1609)

Koestler, A. (1963). *The sleepwalkers.* New York: Grosset & Dunlap, The Universal Library.

Koestler, A. (1969). *The act of creation.* New York: Macmillan.

Kolodner, J. L. (1993). *Case-based reasoning.* San Mateo, CA: Morgan Kaufmann.

Kotovsky, L., & Gentner, D. (in press). Comparison and categorization in the development of relational similarity. *Child Development.*

Koyré, A. (1973). *The astronomical revolution; Copernicus, Kepler, Borelli* (R. E. W. Maddison, Trans.). Ithaca, NY: Cornell University Press. (Original work published 1892)

Kuhn, T. S. (1957). *The Copernican revolution: Planetary astronomy in the development of Western thought.* Cambridge, MA: Harvard University Press.

Layzer, D. (1984). *Constructing the universe.* New York: Scientific American.

Markman, A. B. (1996). *Constraints on analogical inference.* Manuscript in preparation.

Markman, A. B., & Gentner, D. (1993a). Splitting the differences: A structural alignment view of similarity. *Journal of Memory and Language, 32*, 517–535.

Markman, A. B., & Gentner, D. (1993b). Structural alignment during similarity comparisons. *Cognitive Psychology, 25*, 431–467.

Markman, A. B., & Gentner, D. (1996). Commonalities and differences in similarity comparisons. *Memory & Cognition, 24*, 235–249.

Mason, S. F. (1962). *A history of the sciences.* New York: Macmillan.

Medin, D. L., Goldstone, R. L., & Gentner, D. (1993). Respects for similarity. *Psychological Review, 100*, 254–278.

Medin, D. L., & Ross, B. H. (1989). The specific character of abstract thought: Categorization, problem-solving, and induction. In R. J. Sternberg (Ed.), *Advances in the psychology of human intelligence* (Vol. 5, pp. 189–223). Hillsdale, NJ: Erlbaum.

Miller, G. A. (1979). Images and models, similes and metaphors. In A. Ortony (Ed.), *Metaphor and thought* (pp. 202–250). Cambridge, England: Cambridge University Press.

Nersessian, N. J. (1992). How do scientists think? Capturing the dynamics of conceptual change in science. In R. N. Giere & H. Feigl (Eds.), *Minnesota studies in the philosophy of science* (pp. 3–44). Minneapolis: University of Minnesota Press.

Nersessian, N. J., & Resnick, L. B. (1989). Comparing historical and intuitive explanations of motion: Does naive physics have a structure? *Proceedings of the Eleventh Annual Conference of the Cognitive Science Society* (pp. 412–420). Hillsdale, NJ: Erlbaum.

Novick, L. R., & Holyoak, K. J. (1991). Mathematical problem solving by analogy. *Journal of Experimental Psychology: Learning, Memory, & Cognition, 17*, 398–415.

Novick, L. R., & Tversky, B. (1987). Cognitive constraints on ordering operations: The case of geometric analogies. *Journal of Experimental Psychology: General, 116*, 50–67.

Oppenheimer, R. (1956). Analogy in science. *American Psychologist, 11*, 127–135.

Ortony, A. (1979). Beyond literal similarity. *Psychological Review, 86*, 161–180.

Ortony, A., Vondruska, R. J., Foss, M. A., & Jones, L. E. (1985). Salience, similes, and the asymmetry of similarity. *Journal of Memory and Language, 24*, 569–594.

Perkins, D. N. (1994). Creativity: Beyond the Darwinian paradigm. In M. A. Boden (Ed.), *Dimensions of creativity* (pp. 119–142). Cambridge, MA: MIT Press.

Polya, G. (1954). *Mathematics and plausible reasoning: Induction and analogy in mathematics* (Vol. 1). Princeton, NJ: Princeton University Press.

Ranney, M., & Thagard, P. (1988). Explanatory coherence and belief revision in naive physics. *Proceedings of the Tenth Annual Conference of the Cognitive Science Society* (pp. 426–432). Hillsdale, NJ: Erlbaum.

Reeves, L. M., & Weisberg, R. W. (1994). The role of content and abstract information in analogical transfer. *Psychological Bulletin, 115*, 381–400.

Ross, B. H. (1984). Remindings and their effects in learning a cognitive skill. *Cognitive Psychology, 16*, 371–416.

Ross, B. H. (1987). This is like that: The use of earlier problems and the separation of similarity effects. *Journal of Experimental Psychology: Learning, Memory, and Cognition, 13*, 629–639.

Ross, B. H. (1989). Distinguishing types of superficial similarities: Different effects on the access and use of earlier examples. *Journal of Experimental Psychology: Learning, Memory, and Cognition, 15*, 456–468.

Ross, B. H., Ryan, W. J., & Tenpenny, P. L. (1989). The access of relevant information for solving problems. *Memory & Cognition, 17*, 639–651.

Seifert, C. M., Meyer, D. E., Davidson, N., Patalano, A. L., & Yaniv, I. (1995). Demystification of cognitive insight: Opportunistic assimilation and the prepared-mind perspective. In R. J. Sternberg & J. E. Davidson (Eds.), *The nature of insight* (pp. 65–124). Cambridge, MA: MIT Press.

Skorstad, J., Gentner, D., & Medin, D. (1988). Abstraction processes during concept learning: A structural view. *Proceedings of the Tenth Annual Conference of the Cognitive Science Society* (pp. 419–425). Hillsdale, NJ: Erlbaum.

Smith, C., Carey, S., & Wiser, M. (1985). On differentiation: A case study of the development of the concepts of size, weight, and density. *Cognition, 21*, 177–237.

Smith, S. M., Ward, T. B., & Schumacher, J. S. (1993). Constraining effects of examples on a creative generation task. *Memory & Cognition, 21*, 837–845.

Spellman, B. A., & Holyoak, K. J. (1993). An inhibitory mechanism for goal-directed analogical mapping. *Proceedings of the Fifteenth Annual Conference of the Cognitive Science Society* (pp. 947–952). Hillsdale, NJ: Erlbaum.

Spiro, R. J., Feltovich, P. J., Coulson, R. L., & Anderson, D. K. (1989). Multiple analogies for complex concepts: Antidotes for analogy-induced misconception in advanced knowledge acquisition. In S. Vosniadou & A. Ortony (Eds.), *Similarity and analogical reasoning* (pp. 498–531). Cambridge, England: Cambridge University Press.

Stephenson, B. (1994). *Kepler's physical astronomy.* Princeton, NJ: Princeton University Press.

Thagard, P. (1989). Explanatory coherence. *Behavioral and Brain Sciences, 12*, 435–502.

Thagard, P. (1992). *Conceptual revolutions.* Princeton, NJ: Princeton University Press.

Toulmin, S., & Goodfield, J. (1961). *The fabric of the heavens.* New York: Harper.

Tourangeau, R., & Rips, L. (1991). Interpreting and evaluating metaphors. *Journal of Memory and Language, 30*, 452–472.

Tweney, R. D. (1983, June). *Cognitive psychology and the analysis of science: Michael Faraday and the uses of experiment.* Paper presented at the 9th Annual Meeting of the Society for Philosophy and Psychology, Wellesley College, Wellesley, MA.

Vickers, B. (1984). Analogy versus identity: The rejection of occult symbolism, 1580–1680. In B. Vickers (Ed.), *Occult and scientific mentalities in the Renaissance* (pp. 95–163). Cambridge, England: Cambridge University Press.

Ward, T. B. (1994). Structured imagination: The role of category structure in exemplar generation. *Cognitive Psychology, 27*, 1–40.

Ward, T. B., Finke, R. A., & Smith, S. M. (1995). Creativity and the mind: Discovering the genius within. New York: Plenum Press.

Winston, P. H. (1980). Learning and reasoning by analogy. *Communications of the ACM, 23*, 689–703.

Wiser, M. (1986). *Learning about heat and temperature: A content-based historically inspired approach to a novice–expert shift.* Paper presented at the National Science Foundation Conference on the Psychology of Physics Problem Solving: Theory and Practice, New York.

Wiser, M., & Carey, S. (1983). When heat and temperature were one. In D. Gentner & A. L. Stevens (Eds.), *Mental models* (pp. 267–297). Hillsdale, NJ: Erlbaum.

17

How Scientists Think: On-Line Creativity and Conceptual Change in Science

Kevin Dunbar

This chapter reports an investigation of "On-line Creativity." I present a new account of the cognitive and social mechanisms underlying complex thinking of creative scientists as they work on significant problems in contemporary science. I lay out an innovative methodology that I have developed for investigating creative and complex thinking in a real-world context. Using this method, I have discovered that there are a number of strategies that are used in contemporary science that increase scientists' likelihood of making discoveries. The findings reported in this chapter provide new insights into complex scientific thinking and will dispel many of the myths surrounding the generation of new concepts and scientific discoveries.

This research was made possible by a grant from the Spencer Foundation. The research was also supported by Grant OGP0037356 from the National Sciences and Engineering Council of Canada and a leave of absence given by the Department of Psychology at McGill University. I thank Laura Ann Petitto for her extensive comments on a draft of the manuscript. I also thank Tom Ward, Keith Holyoak, and Maude A. St. Laurent for their comments on a draft of this chapter. Finally, I thank all of the scientists who opened up their laboratories and their minds for this research.

IN VIVO COGNITION: A NEW WAY OF INVESTIGATING COGNITION

There is an extensive background in cognitive research on thinking, reasoning, and problem solving processes that form the foundation for creative cognition (see Dunbar, in press; Holyoak, 1995, for recent reviews). However, to a large extent, research on reasoning has demonstrated that participants in psychology experiments make vast numbers of thinking and reasoning errors even in the most simple problems. How is creative thought even possible if people make so many reasoning errors? One problem with research on reasoning is that the concepts and stimuli that the research participants are asked to use are often arbitrary and involve no background knowledge (cf. Dunbar, 1995; Klahr & Dunbar, 1988). I have proposed that one way of determining which reasoning errors are specific and which are general is to investigate cognition in the cognitive laboratory and the real world (Dunbar, 1995). Psychologists should conduct both in vitro and in vivo research to understand thinking. *In vitro* research is the standard psychological experiment where individuals are brought into the laboratory and controlled experiments are conducted. As can be seen from the research reported in this volume, this approach yields many insights into the psychological mechanisms underlying complex thinking. The use of an *in vivo* methodology in which on-line thinking and reasoning are investigated in a real-world context yields fundamental insights into the basic cognitive mechanisms underlying complex cognition and creativity. The results of in vivo cognitive research can then be used as a basis for further in vitro work in which controlled experiments are conducted. In this chapter, I outline some of the results of my ongoing in vivo research on creative scientific thinking. I relate this research to more common in vitro research to show that the in vivo method generates new basic models of cognitive processes and opens up avenues for new in vitro research.

On-Line Scientific Thinking

Scientific thinking is an ideal domain in which to develop theories of creative cognition and complex thinking (see Klahr, 1994, for a recent review of this literature). First, scientists are constantly adding to knowledge and, less frequently, developing new concepts and theories. Second, scientists already have a rich background of knowledge in their domain that they use as a foundation for their thought. Third, much creativity occurs in groups rather than individuals alone. Contemporary science, which includes psychology, entails an experimental context that involves a group. No longer is the lone scientist under the lightbulb the norm for science. Rather, groups containing members with different levels of experience and different scientific backgrounds form the basis of contemporary science. Little is known about the way in which groups reason. Thus, scientific groups are a very important source of creative thinking and reasoning. In sum, by investigating science as it is practiced it is possible to address key questions about the nature of thinking and creativity, uncover fundamental processes that underlie complex thinking, and suggest strategies for enhancing creative thought.

Method

The research program that I have developed centers on understanding the cognitive and social mechanisms involved in current day science. I have selected molecular biology as a scientific domain to investigate because this domain is of central importance to contemporary science. Many of the brightest and most creative minds in science are attracted to this field, and molecular biology receives a very significant proportion of funding in science and medicine. Furthermore, the field of molecular biology is undergoing an immense period of scientific discovery and breakthrough, making it an ideal domain in which to investigate creative thinking.

Having identified molecular biology as a scientific domain I then sought to identify leading laboratories in the United States that I could investigate. My goal was to investigate the thinking and reasoning strategies that leading scientists use while conducting their research. After consulting with a number of scientists, including one Nobel Prize winner, and extensively reviewing the literature, I identified six world-renowned scientists at a major U.S. university. All scientists were internationally known for conducting innovative research that frequently stretched the boundaries of their field. Each scientist was concerned with discovering new biological mechanisms that give fundamental insights into biology. Having identified the six laboratories, I then contacted the scientists and asked them to participate in my research. All six agreed to participate in the study. I then interviewed the scientists to determine what their current research projects were, what the scientists in their labs were doing, and what their plans for the coming year were. Following this consultation I then selected four laboratories as being most suitable for investigation.

The goal of this research was to identify the points in time at which innovative scientific thinking occurs, capture this thinking on audio- and videotape, and then analyze the processes involved in the scientists' thinking and reasoning. To this end I spent a year in the four selected molecular biology laboratories. I spent the first four months becoming familiar with the scientists in the laboratory, staying in the labs during the day, attending lab meetings, interviewing the scientists in the lab, and reading grant proposals and drafts of papers. I discovered that the laboratory meeting is one of the central places in which new ideas and concepts are generated. Each laboratory had a weekly meeting that all of the members of the lab attended. The senior scientist, who manages the lab, is present as well as the postdoctoral fellows, graduate students, and technicians. In the lab meetings, a scientist presents his or her latest research, which is conducted with the senior scientist. Members of the lab ask questions about the research and propose new experiments, hypotheses, and interpretations, often forcing the presenting scientist to reconceptualize his or her ideas. Totally new concepts are generated and modified by members of the laboratory at some of the meetings. Often the senior scientist plays a crucial role in the development of new ideas and concepts. The scientists' reasoning at lab meetings is often spontaneous, and the on-line interactions concern some of the most creative moments in science. The finding that lab meetings are a central source of creative thinking and reasoning is also important because the reasoning that occurs at these meetings occurs through presentations and spontaneous interactions in which the scientists develop their ideas. Because the scientists talk out loud during the meetings there is an external record of thinking and reasoning. Using this method it is possible to directly monitor thinking and reasoning rather than uncover reasoning through post hoc interviews, questionnaires, or think-aloud protocols. The scientists externalize much of their thinking through interactions with other scientists in the lab. Thus, by recording laboratory meetings it is possible to gain access to on-line thinking and reasoning without influencing the way the scientists think.

Following my initial data collection phase, I evaluated the best method of collecting data on scientific thinking. I found that the laboratory meetings provide a much more accurate picture of the conceptual life of a laboratory than interviews, lab books, or papers. In fact, I found that the scientists were often unable to remember the steps in the development of a particular concept. The laboratory meetings provided a far more veridical and complete record of the evolution of ideas than other sources of information. Thus, I selected the laboratory meetings as the core source of data and the interviews and papers as supplemental sources of information. Thus, the particular method that I used to collect data revolved around the discovery that the laboratory meetings are central to the conceptual life of a laboratory.

I constructed a before–during–after design for uncovering the effects of laboratory meetings on the scientists' theories and methods: Before a lab meeting I interviewed the scientists to find out what their hypotheses were, what they thought the data meant, and what they were going to do next. I then audio or videotaped the scientists during the lab meeting. After the meeting I interviewed the scientists to determine whether the lab meeting affected their knowledge. I also interviewed the senior scientists about their conceptualization of the research project. This was a cyclical process in which I observed the scientists present work a number of times. By the end of the year, I had collected data on 19 scientific research projects. In addition to recording laboratory meetings I conducted interviews with members of the laboratory, was given copies of grant proposals and drafts of papers, and attended lectures by the senior scientists and many impromptu meetings. Thus, I collected data on all aspects of scientific research with the laboratory meeting as the central focus.

The Laboratories

Data on 21 scientists in the four laboratories were collected, as well as data from the 4 senior scientists. My current analyses focus on the 4 senior scientists and 19 scientists in the laboratories. Twelve of the scientists were postdoctoral fellows, 5 were graduate students, and 2 were research technicians. The four laboratories that were studied were either developmental biology labs or just worked with pathogens (disease-causing viruses and bacteria). Furthermore, the senior scientists varied in terms of experience. Two were full professors, 1 was an associate professor, 1 one was an assistant professor. By varying the types of subdomains that the scientists work in and their level of experience, it is possible to determine whether these factors influence their research.

All the scientists allowed me free access to their laboratories, to interview anyone in the laboratory, to attend any meeting, to read and keep copies of their grant proposals (including the pink sheets), to attend their talks and lectures, and to read drafts of their papers. Thus, I was given full access to the day-to-day activities of the laboratories. In addition, the scientists frequently asked me to attend impromptu meetings and discussions, and they often called when they felt that interesting events were occurring in the lab.

I selected research projects for study on the basis of whether the project had just started or was about to begin. In addition, I consulted extensively with the senior scientists in choosing the research projects to investigate. Once I had selected the projects, I then met with the senior scientists, postdocs, graduate students, and technicians that were involved in the research. All members of the four laboratories agreed to cooperate.

Laboratory A. Laboratory A was run by a senior scientist who has over 300 publications and numerous awards. This laboratory has had many discoveries that have appeared on the front page of the *New York Times, Science, Nature, Cell,* and so forth. His laboratory consisted of 22 postdoctoral fellows, 5 graduate students, and 4 technicians. I selected four research projects to follow. Two of the four research projects were successful and led to scientific discoveries. Importantly, neither I nor the scientists involved realized that a discovery was about to be made when I started following their research. It was only after a few months of following the research projects that the discoveries were made. Thus, I had collected data before, during, and after a discovery had been made. One of the researchers discovered a new gene that controls cell differentiation, and another had discovered how certain cells proliferate into certain regions of the body. Importantly, the latter discovery actually occurred during a laboratory meeting at which I was present and was tape-recording; that is, I have the moment of discovery on tape. This project forms the basis of the research discussed in the section titled "Anatomy of a Conceptual Change." Of the two remaining projects, one was unsuccessful and the other had not progressed significantly within the data collection period.

Laboratory B. Laboratory B was run by a scientist who has made many important discoveries in molecular biology. He has numerous publications and has trained many now eminent scientists. His current research program involved determining a general model of how certain genes control traits in a novel type of bacterium. His laboratory had 3 postdocs, 5 graduate students, and 1 technician. I have analyzed two of the research projects that were conducted in his laboratory. One of the research projects has resulted in two publications; however, the scientists were unable to reach their goal of discovering the function of a component of a gene. The other project made minimal progress.

Laboratory C. Laboratory C was run by an associate professor who has made a number of important discoveries on how DNA and RNA are coded in two different types of parasites. The lab consisted of 4 postdocs, 2 graduate students, and 1 lab technician. I followed research projects conducted by the 4 postdocs. All the research projects resulted in significant breakthroughs that have been published in the major scientific journals such as *Science.*

Laboratory D. Laboratory D was run by an assistant professor who is already famous for his work on viral mechanisms and his creative approach to uncovering gene function. The laboratory consisted of 4 postdocs, 6 graduate students, and 2 lab technicians. His current research program is centered on discovering the mechanism by which certain genes in the HIV virus allow the virus to infiltrate into the host organism. He has evolved a research program that has employed a number of novel and ingenious techniques to discover how this works. These research projects are now leading to a new model of an important component of HIV activity that has wide-ranging theoretical and practical implications for molecular biology. The director of Laboratory D also invented a new genetic technique. I was present for the implementation and development of this technique. This technique has been widely referenced and reviewed in many major scientific journals.

Data Analysis

Transcription. Transcriptions and coding were done by two independent transcribers with backgrounds in molecular biology.

Coding. All coding was conducted by coding the transcriptions into a computerized database. Multiple coders were used, and reliability checks were conducted by independent coders. In this section, I provide a very general overview of the coding techniques used. I provide a more detailed account of coding in the method discussions of other sections of this chapter. The basic unit of analysis is the statement or utterance. A statement is essentially equivalent to a clause or sentence. Statements were chosen as the basic unit of analysis as they contain a verb phrase, which in turn contains the core mental operation (proposition or idea) that the presenter is employing at the time. Thus, we treat statements at meetings in the same way that statements are treated in standard protocol analyses (cf. Ericsson & Simon, 1993). I used the corpora of statements made to build a representation of scientists' mental operations. Using techniques borrowed from protocol analyses, statements can be aggregated by episodes, solution steps, and processes. One can switch between different levels of analyses, depending on the questions that one is asking of the data. The MacSHAPA coding and database software system was used to code the data (Sanderson et al., 1994).

Summary of Results

The research reported in this chapter provides a snapshot of my current analyses and interpretation of the cognitive processes involved in creativity in science. I now address three main sources of creative cognition. First, I present an analysis of the role of analogy. Second, I outline my analyses of scientists' treatment of unexpected findings. Third, I discuss some of the findings on distributed reasoning. Finally, I present a case study of a conceptual change that involved all three of the aforementioned strategies.

ANALOGY

Analogy has been regarded as a very important psychological process involved in creative cognition and has been the focus of intense investigation over the past 15 years, culminating in a number of detailed models of the cognitive processes involved in analogical reasoning (e.g., Forbus, Gentner, & Law, 1995; Holyoak & Thagard, 1989, 1994).[1] Accounts of analogy distinguish between two components of an analogy: the target and the base. The *target* is the concept or problem that the scientist is attempting to solve or explain. The *base* is another piece of knowledge that the scientist uses to understand the target, or explain the target to others. When the scientist makes an analogy he or she maps features of the base onto features of the target. By mapping the features of the base onto the target new features of the target may be discovered, or the features of the target can be rearranged so that a new concept is invented, or the scientist can highlight a specific feature of the target for other people. To illustrate this discussion of analogy I borrow an analogy that Rutherford (Rhodes, 1986) ostensibly used in his research. When Rutherford was attempting to understand the structure of the atom he made an analogy to the solar system. In this case, the target was the atom and the base was the solar system. Rutherford ostensibly mapped the idea that the planets revolve around the sun onto the atom, and he argued that the electrons revolve around the nucleus. Thus, a number of historians have argued that by drawing an analogy to the solar system, Rutherford was able to propose a new account of the structure of the atom. By mapping the feature

[1]Many cognitive accounts of analogy start with a reference to analogy in science and have noted that the types of distant analogies alluded to in the literature on the history of science are rarely used by participants in psychology experiments.

of the planets revolving around the sun, Rutherford was able to align his data with those predicted by a solar analogy. According to this view, the analogy resulted in a major restructuring of his knowledge, and a scientific discovery was made.[2]

The Rutherford example highlights two key assumptions that researchers in the creativity literature have made about the role of analogy in science. The view of analogy in the creativity literature has been that when a scientist makes an analogy (a) the source is usually from a very different domain,[3] and (b) the role of analogy is to restructure the scientist's knowledge in a gestaltlike manner (e.g., Boden, 1993; Koestler, 1964). One of the questions I want to ask here is whether this is a valid picture of the role of analogy in science. The question can be divided into a number of more detailed questions: Do scientists use analogies at all? If they do, are they the distant analogies that have been talked about in the historical creativity literature? Do less distant analogies play any role in science, as the emprical psychological work suggests (see Forbus et al., 1995; Holyoak & Thagard, 1994)? Does analogy work alone, or does it work in conjunction with other mental operations? Is analogy involved in scientific discoveries and conceptual change in science?

Method

I investigated the use of analogy at 16 meetings (4 meetings for each of the 4 labs). All analogies were coded by two independent coders. Any time a scientist referred to another base of knowledge to either (a) explain a concept or (b) use that other base of knowledge to modify the concept, it was coded as an analogy. Three representative analogies follow:

1a. *Within organism: An HIV to HIV analogy.* "Um. In the case of HIV it's 5 bases away, umm. So, um to study RT (reaction time) using a

[2]There is some controversy about whether the solar system analogy played a causal role in Rutherford's discovery of the structure of the atom. Whatever the real case may be, my point is that researchers have used such examples to emphasize the critical revolutionary role that this particular type of distant analogy plays in scientific discovery and conceptual change.

[3]Most cognitive accounts of analogy have made no assumptions about how distant the source and the target are in science. In fact, Holyoak and Thagard (1994) have made a list of the most important analogies in science over the past 2,000 years and have found very few distant analogies. However, when researchers do allude to analogy in science they tend to give examples wherein the source and the target are distant.

substrate that more closely mimics the in vivo situation is difficult. Because um, number one, you will need to anneal six surface strands together. Number two, it is really doubtful that since there is only a five base pair here, where they hold this complicated structure together."

1b. *Other organism: An Ebola virus to Herpes virus analogy.* "The problem with Ebola is that it is AT rich. So you can't really do some analysis, analysis of homology with the, uh, genome because of this very AT rich, uh, richness. That would not be the case for herpes and could give a better answer for some of the putative homology."

1c. *Nonbiological or distant: Monkeys to PCR (polymerase chain reaction) analogy.* "You know, just because you can see 10 molecules that still isn't working in my book. A monkey will eventually type Shakespeare, given the opportunity. PCR is not unlike that. You do it a billion times and you probably will find one thing that happened to be right."

Note that instances where a scientist stated that *X* was like *Y* were not coded as analogies. That is, statements of similarity that neither gave explanations nor resulted in the mapping of features from the base to the target were not coded as analogies. Once the analogies were found, they were coded along a number of dimensions. The coding dimensions are specified in the section dealing with that dimension.

Results

Frequency of Analogy Use

There were 99 analogies used during the 16 meetings ($M = 6.1$ analogies per meeting). The range of analogy use was 2 to 14 analogies per meeting. All four labs used analogies. There were a total of 25, 30, 31, 13 analogies, respectively, for Labs A, B, C, and D. Thus, analogies were frequently used at laboratory meetings.

Range of Analogy Use

The range over which the analogies were used was coded. Range is an index of how far apart the base and target were for each analogy. Analogies were coded as being *within organism*, *other organism*, or *nonbiological.* *Within-organism* analogies are those wherein the base and the target are from within the same organism. In the previous within-organism example (1a), the scientist has drawn an analogy between the way the HIV virus works in an in vivo context and how an in vitro HIV could be made by mapping from the in vivo HIV onto the in vitro HIV construct. *Other-organism* analogies are those in which the base and the target are from two different organisms, as in Example 1b (analogy between the Ebola virus and the Herpes virus). In this analogy, the scientist points out the differences between Ebola and Herpes to show why Ebola is a better organism to research a particular question. *Nonbiological* or *distant* analogies are those in which the base is taken from a nonbiological domain. In Example 1c (Nonbiological or distant: Monkeys to PCR analogy), the scientist highlights the fact that a finding could be due to chance by drawing an analogy between a monkey typing Shakespeare and the polymerase chain reaction, generating a chance result. Note that this type of distant analogy has received the most attention in the literature.

Almost all of the 99 analogies were either within organism (40) or other organism (57). There were only 2 nonbiological analogies. Thus, the bulk of analogical reasoning happened when the base and targets were from the domain of biology. This result is very important. Most accounts of analogy in science focus on distant analogies, yet only 2 of the 99 analogies used by the scientists were of this type.

Goals and Analogy Use

Categories of goals were formulated by searching for goals in the database rather than imposing them on the data a priori. From this emerged four dominant goals: formulate a hypothesis, design an experiment, provide an explanation, and fix an experiment (when an experiment went awry the scientists often drew analogies to procedures used in other experiments and proposed replacing one step in the faulty experiment with a step from an analogically similar experiment). Almost half (45) of the analogies occurred when the goal was to provide an explanation. Usually, the explanations were of methodological issues. There were 21 analogies for design an experiment, 10 for fix an experiment, and 23 for formulate a hypothesis.

Next, I discuss the relation between goals and range. Table 1 reports the number of analogies for each combination of goal and range. The table shows a number of interesting relations between a scientist's goals and the range over which the analogy is drawn. First, it can be seen that the two nonbiological analogies were used to make explanations; they were not used to formulate hypotheses. Although there were only two nonbiological analogies in the 16 meetings coded, there were two other nonbiological analogies in the database. All four of these nonbiological or distant analogies were used to explain a concept to members of the laboratory. Thus, nonbiological or distant analogies are rare and generally used for explanations rather than to generate new hypotheses and concepts.

I now turn to a discussion of the within-organism and other-organism analogies and goals. There was little difference in range between designing and fixing experiments. Scientists were equally likely to draw an analogy from the same organism or a different organism when designing or fixing an experiment. The major interaction of goals with range was in hypothesis generation. The scientists tended to use analogies to other organisms when formulating a new hypothesis. For example, a scientist might in attempting to determine the function of a gene in one organism (e.g., a gene in malaria) draw an analogy to a gene in another organism

Table 1

Scientists' Goals for Within-Organism, Other-Organism, and Nonbiological Analogies

Type of goal	Within organism	Other organism	Nonbiological
Hypothesis	3	20	0
Design experiment	9	12	0
Fix experiment	5	5	0
Explain	23	20	2

(e.g., a similar gene in clams). If the scientist knows what the gene does in one organism (e.g., in clams), she or he can then map the functions of that gene over to the organism that they are working on (e.g., the similar gene in malaria). Thus, rather than the source of hypotheses being analogies made to nonbiological or distant domains, when formulating hypotheses the scientists make analogies to other organisms.

How do Scientists Generate Their Analogies?

How do scientists retrieve the sources for between- and within-organism analogies? One possibility is that the scientists recall specific experiments conducted in their labs or journal articles they have read. If we break down the range of the analogies by whether the scientists were recalling specific cases when they were making analogies (such as specific experiments that were conducted in the past, references to particular research articles, or experiments conducted by researchers in the field), we can see that 31 of the 40 within-organism analogies recalled a specific case. In contrast, only 6 of the 57 other-organism analogies recalled a specific case. Thus, when scientists make analogies to the same organism, they tend to recall a specific case. However, when scientists make analogies to a different organism, they do not recall specific cases. In addition, 22 of the 31 within-organism analogies recalled cases of previous experiments conducted in the lab. Thus, when the researchers made analogies to the same organism, the bulk of the analogies were to previous experiments conducted in that lab.

How did the scientists use analogies to other organisms without recalling a specific case? Psychological research has shown that individuals have great difficulty going outside their current problem to make an analogy (e.g., Gick & Holyoak, 1983), yet the scientists were able to transcend this problem. How? An analysis of analogies to other organisms revealed that the scientists had two main ways of circumventing this analog retrieval problem. First, molecular biologists have a tool available to them that gives them another way of retrieving base analogs: homology. Second, the scientists had an abstract knowledge of the biological mechanisms that exist in other organisms. Scientists can use their knowledge of biological mechanisms to search memory for organisms that use a particular biological mechanism.

I discuss each of the ways of retrieving base analogs in turn. Scientists use homology to determine the molecular structure of a gene by sequencing each base pair in the gene. The scientists then type the sequence of their gene into a computer and search a database of genes for a gene that has a similar coding. If the scientist finds a gene or genes with a similar sequence (i.e., a homologous gene), and the function of that gene is known, the scientist can infer that the gene may have the same function in their organism. That is, the scientist maps the function of the homologous gene onto the gene being investigated. Thus, homology allows the scientist to both retrieve analogs and propose new hypotheses about gene function. Not only does the homology allow the scientist to infer new hypotheses concerning the biological function of the gene, but the scientist can also use the methodologies that the previous researchers used when conducting their research. Importantly, the same homology can provide new hypotheses and new methods that the scientist can use in his or her research. The scientists in my study generated 31 of the 57 other-organism analogies by using homology. Thus, homology allowed them to generate other potential base analogs. As can be seen from Table 2, the scientists used homology to infer biological mechanisms and the methods that they should use in their experiments.

I now turn to analogies to other organisms that were not based on homology. The scientists were more likely to use biological mechanisms

Table 2

Types of Knowledge Retrieved by Analogies on the Basis of Homology and Nonhomology for Other-Organism Analogies

Type of knowledge	Homology	Nonhomology
Biological mechanism	10	16
Experimental method	17	7
Problems with methods	4	3

as a retrieval cue. For instance, the scientists might think that "E.coli performs a particular function by splicing the protein at the AT site; perhaps our organism splices the protein in the same way." The scientists' knowledge of biological mechanisms is often tied to particular organisms, and these organisms become part of the analogy.

Summary and Discussion of Analogy Results

Analogy was frequently used in all of the laboratories. Most of the analogies that were observed in the current study were biological. Only 2 of the 99 analogies were nonbiological or distant. These findings shed new light on the role of analogy in science. Most historical accounts of analogy in science have tended to focus on very distant analogies; yet, the results of these investigations suggest that distant analogies are not an important component of contemporary science. There are a number of reasons for the differences between these findings and those discussed in the literature on the history of science or the creativity literature. First, many of the distant analogies that scientists have mentioned in the history of science may not have had a role in the making of a discovery. In fact, a number of historical analysts have argued that the Rutherford solar system analogy, and the snake analogy mentioned by Kekulé in his discovery of the structure of the benzene ring had no role in the respective discoveries (Rhodes, 1986; Wotiz & Rudofsky, 1984).[4] The data presented here suggest that it may be the case that scientists use distant analogies to explain a new concept to an audience rather than that distant analogies have a causal role in making a discovery. I am currently monitoring the scientists' publications to see if more distant analogies seep into their accounts of their findings.[5] Second, the types of analogies that the scientists use in on-line reasoning are easy to forget. In fact, in postlab meeting interviews

---

[4]I thank Bill Brewer for bringing this article on Kekulé's discovery of the benzene ring to my attention.

[5]Some researchers have suggested that perhaps the evidence of distant analogies is an index of the maturation, or lack thereof, of the development of a field (with presumably a higher incidence of distant analogies occurring at the beginning of a field). However, there is nothing in my data that supports this view. Note that the scientists in my study were pioneering totally new concepts, in an uncharted conceptual space. In this view one would expect to see many distant analogies relative to the other types, which was not the case.

the scientists rarely remembered the analogies that were generated during the meeting. Thus, analogies are often used as a scaffolding that the scientists use in the construction of new theories and methodologies. Once the new concepts and methods have been advanced the analogy can be discarded. Many of these analogies will not make their way into the notebooks of the scientists, and thus the historical record will not show that the within-organism or other-organism analogies had a role in the discovery of a new concept or invention of a new method.[6]

More than one analogy may be involved in a particular discovery, and one particular analogy may not be responsible for a particular conceptual change, but a group of quite different analogies may be causally involved in making a breakthrough. Again, because no one analogy made a major restructure of knowledge, the scientists may not have recalled a particular within-organism or other-organism analogy as being a factor in the discovery. However, when all of the analogies that are involved in making a discovery are examined, only analogies of very specific types will be seen to have played a major role in scientific reasoning and discovery. Moreover, as is shown later, analogy is not the only mechanism that comprises conceptual change. In the next three sections I show that other key cognitive mechanisms produce conceptual change. Thus, analogy, while important, is but one of a complex of mechanisms that produce conceptual change. At the close of this chapter, I explain what this complex of mechanisms is and show how together they contribute to scientific discovery and conceptual change.

UNEXPECTED FINDINGS AND CONFIRMATION BIAS

There is a large literature in psychology and philosophy of science on what happens when scientists get unexpected results from their experiments. In the psychological literature researchers have investigated this in terms of

[6]My in vitro investigations of analogical reasoning also reveal that research participants have little awareness of, or memory for, the mental steps involved in making a discovery, even directly after having made a major conceptual shift (Dunbar & Schunn, 1990; Schunn & Dunbar, 1996).

confirmation biases; individuals tend to seek evidence that is consistent with their hypothesis and ignore evidence that is not. Researchers have repeatedly found evidence that research participants engage in this type of behavior and have argued that scientists have similar reasoning biases (cf. Klayman & Ha, 1987; Tweney, Doherty, & Mynatt, 1982). However, before one accepts the generality of the results of these types of experiments it is important to note some of the large differences between the tasks that research participants perform and what scientists do. Most important, there is no actual scientific knowledge involved in the psychological tasks; the to-be-discovered concepts are arbitrary, and the links between hypothesis, experiment, and data are straightforward. For example, the 2–4–6 task is one that has been widely used (Wason, 1960). In this task, the experimenter asks an individual to determine the rule underlying a sequence of numbers. The individual is given a triad of numbers, such as the numbers 2, 4, 6, and is told that this number triad is an example of the rule. The individual is then told that she or he can generate other triads and that the experimenter will determine whether the triad is an example of the rule. Finally, the individual is told that when certain she should state the rule. Many research participants tend to generate triads that are consistent with their hypotheses; they attempt to confirm their hypotheses.[7] On the basis of experiments such as these, researchers have argued that this confirmation bias is a general phenomenon that both lay people and scientists must avoid if they are to reason correctly.

Although the confirmation bias view of science has received much empirical support, another related phenomenon is the issue of unexpected findings. A number of researchers have argued that a useful strategy in science is to focus on unexpected findings. According to this view, scientists work with a heuristic such as "if the finding is unexpected, then set a goal of discovering the causes of the unexpected finding" (cf. Dunbar, 1993, 1996; Kulkarni & Simon, 1988). This view of reasoning is quite different from that implied by the confirmation bias viewpoint. According to this viewpoint,

[7]The common rule that research participants must discover is "numbers of increasing magnitude." Research participants generally propose the rule "even numbers increasing by 2" and only generate triads consistent with this rule.

when unexpected findings are inconsistent, scientists should focus on the finding rather than ignore it. Thus, there are two conceptions of what scientists may do. Of course, it may be the case that under certain circumstances the scientists may focus on unexpected findings, and under other circumstances they may ignore the findings and behave like the participants in psychology experiments (cf. Tweney, 1989). The goal of the following analyses was to investigate these questions in a real scientific environment.

Method

My graduate student Lisa Baker and I decided to investigate the role of unexpected findings by analyzing the scientists' reactions to unexpected findings at four laboratory meetings in Lab A (see also Baker & Dunbar, 1996). We chose Lab A because scientists there had obtained many expected and unexpected findings and thus provided much data to investigate these issues. We had two independent coders code every unexpected finding in each of the four lab meetings. All findings in which the scientist had previously predicted a different result, or expressed surprise at the obtained result, were coded as *unexpected.* All findings that were consistent with the predictions were coded as *expected.* A third category of findings consisted of those that occurred in exploratory experiments. Here the scientist did not have any predictions one way or the other and conducted the experiment to see what would happen. The results of these types of experiments were coded as *exploratory.*

Results

Our first step was to determine how common expected, unexpected, and exploratory findings were? In four meetings there were six experiments reported with 70 conditions. There were 22 expected, 18 unexpected, and 30 exploratory findings. Clearly, unexpected findings are common. We coded all expected and unexpected findings on the basis of whether the scientists tried to explain away their results or whether they built theories with the findings. To do this, we coded the number of reasoning blocks the scientists engaged in following both expected and unexpected findings. A reasoning block was a group of statements that involved reasoning about a particular finding. One finding can generate many different reasoning blocks. The number of reasoning blocks generated by expected and unexpected findings can be used as an index of how much attention scientists give to these types of findings. There was more reasoning for unexpected (179 reasoning blocks) than expected (42) findings. Furthermore, when confronted with unexpected findings, scientists were much more likely to engage in theory building than to attempt to explain the results away. Thus, 161 reasoning blocks were concerned with theory building, and 18 reasoning blocks were concerned with attributing the result to some sort of error. Thus, scientists do pay attention to unexpected findings.

The previous analyses applied purely to whether the scientist who conducted and presented the research was likely to attend to an unexpected finding. We next investigated whether the group also attended to unexpected findings. We calculated the number of reasoning blocks that anyone other than the presenter devoted to unexpected and expected findings. Again, we found much more reasoning by the group when faced with unexpected compared with expected findings. As a measure of group attention to unexpected findings we also counted the number of interactions for expected and unexpected findings. We found 23 interactions for expected findings and 176 interactions for unexpected findings. These results indicate that the group also pays attention to unexpected findings and uses the findings to propose new hypotheses and experiments.

Another question that can be asked about the scientists' use of unexpected findings is whether there was any difference between the scientists' treatment of unexpected findings that were consistent with their hypothesis and those that were inconsistent with their hypothesis. An unexpected finding that is consistent with a scientist's hypothesis can occur, for example, when the scientist expects a certain type of result to occur, but the size of the effect is much greater than expected. In this type of situation, the result is consistent with the hypothesis but the size of the effect is unexpected. An unexpected inconsistent finding is one in which a qualitatively different type of outcome occurs. We coded the 18 unexpected findings along these dimensions and found that 8 unexpected findings were consistent with scientists' expectations and that 10 unexpected findings were inconsistent with their expectations. We then coded the findings that resulted in the proposal of new hypotheses. We found that 4 of the 8 consistent findings resulted in new hypotheses and 8 of 10 inconsistent findings resulted in new hypotheses. These results indicate that the scientists attended to the unexpected findings even when the findings were inconsistent with their hypothesis.

We recently have been conducting new analyses of scientists' reactions to unexpected findings to determine whether the time at which an unexpected finding occurs affects whether an unexpected finding is attended to. We found that there are two dimensions of an unexpected finding that determine whether the unexpected finding is attended to. The first is whether the unexpected finding is unexpected relative to a core hypothesis in the field or to an auxiliary hypothesis that the scientist has proposed to get the experiment to work. Another dimension is how early or late in the research project the unexpected finding occurs. We found that when the unexpected finding occurs early and is not a core hypothesis, the scientists will not devote much attention to it. However, if the unexpected finding occurs early and is unexpected relative to the central assumptions of the field, the scientists will focus on the finding. When the unexpected finding occurs late in the research project the scientists will attend to it regardless of whether it is a core or an auxiliary hypothesis. Note that the situation in which the scientists ignore unexpected findings is very similar to that of individuals in psychology experiments: The individuals are early in the experiment, and the hypotheses are not core assumptions. Thus, it is only under very restricted circumstances that one finds a similarity between the results of psychology experiments on confirmation bias.

Our analyses of unexpected findings indicate that scientists do attend to unexpected and inconsistent findings. Why do the scientists attend to unexpected and often inconsistent findings? One reason is that in real science unexpected findings are frequent. The fact that unexpected findings are frequent may have a major effect on the scientists' ability to deal with these types of findings. It may be the case that the longer a scientist is in the field, the more unexpected findings the scientist has encountered and the more likely it is that the scientist has developed strategies or heuristics for dealing with them. Thus, the way a scientist deals with unexpected findings depends on the specific strategies he or she has developed to attempt to reconcile them.[8] Participants in psychology experiments are unlikely to have developed strategies for dealing with unexpected findings and may prefer to focus on their current goal, ignoring unexpected results (as in Dunbar, 1993). As they encounter more and more evidence that is inconsistent, they are eventually forced to attend to unexpected findings.

DISTRIBUTED REASONING

Most cognitive research on scientific reasoning focuses on individuals reasoning about a problem. However, much of modern science is conducted by groups of scientists rather than individuals. Furthermore, much of the cognitive work has demonstrated that individuals make many different types of reasoning errors. In this section, I investigate whether reasoning in groups can circumvent certain individual reasoning errors. In particular I explore the issue of distributed reasoning in science. *Distributed reasoning* happens when different members of a group reason about topics such as a hypothesis, experiment, methodology, or interpretation of a result while adding new elements to the topic under discussion. The question that I will ask is whether distributed reasoning of this sort helps circumvent problems that individual participants display in standard experiments.

One of the major tasks for both individuals in psychology experiments and scientists confronted with new data is to determine what types of inductions to make from new data. There are infinitely many inductions that can be made from a set of data, and this is a potential place where differ-

[8]Lovett and Anderson (in press) have shown that history of success plays a role in determining what strategy research participants use to solve a problem. They have shown that research participants use both their history of success and the current problem-solving context to determine the type of problem-solving strategy to use. I argue that scientists use a similar set of heuristics. Whether they will use unexpected findings or not will depend on both the history of success and current context.

ent members of the group can make different inductions from the same data. To examine this, I explored the role that the group played in the types of inductions that a scientist in an HIV lab made during his talk. At this talk the scientist presented five sets of findings and made 11 inductions about the mechanisms that the HIV virus uses. The members of the lab often disagreed with the inductions that the scientist made and modified his inductions. The other members of the lab limited (3), expanded (1), replaced (2), or discarded (1) a total of 7 of the 11 inductions.

This pattern of challenging inductions was ubiquitous across all labs and provides important information about the role of distributed reasoning. Individuals have great difficulty generating alternative inductions from data and also have great difficulty limiting and expanding inductions. Distributed reasoning helps circumvent these difficulties. When distributed reasoning occurs, the group quickly focuses on the reasoning that has occurred, and the other members of the laboratory generate different representations. These new representations make it possible for them to propose alternative inductions, deductions, and causal explanations. Thus, distributed reasoning provides new premises and models that an individual may not be able to generate when reasoning alone.

Another issue relevant to distributed reasoning is the number of people involved in the reasoning. In the previously mentioned HIV lab I investigated the number of inductions and deductions that were shared. That is, how many inductions and deductions occur in which one premise is provided by one person, and another premise is provided by another person. We found that 30% of inductions and deductions were shared by more than one individual. We also found that 12% of all inductions and deductions had more than two participants. Furthermore, inductions of one individual sometimes formed the basis of a deduction for other individuals.

Distributed reasoning consists of scientists performing cognitive operations on information (e.g., induction) and then passing the results of the operation on to other scientists in the group. The other scientists then use the results of the first operation as the input to further cognitive operations. Together, the results of these cognitive operations are then used to build new cognitive representations: scientific theories and new experiments. How and when the information is passed between individuals depends on the goals of the individuals and the group, as well as the knowledge bases that the scientists have at their disposal. The generation of different representations during distributed reasoning helps scientists circumvent one of the major reasoning difficulties that individuals have: that of generating alternative hypotheses, explanations, theories, and experiments.

The results of these analyses of distributed reasoning are different from the results of brainstorming experiments and creativity in group experiments. Many studies have shown that when a group of people is asked to generate novel concepts, the group performs no better than individuals. However, in the research reported in this chapter it can be seen that groups of scientists do generate new concepts and that distributed reasoning is an important factor. The difference in findings is twofold. First, in psychology experiments the participants are not part of a group sharing common knowledge and values. Usually, individuals in psychology experiments are randomly thrown together for the purpose of the experiment. Second, the types of problems given to the participants are often arbitrary and require little background knowledge. In the science labs investigated in this chapter, the scientists had overlapping backgrounds and shared goals about the research. Furthermore, the members of the lab had slightly different types of knowledge that they could bring to bear on the problem. Taken together, these results suggest that entirely new experiments on group reasoning need to be conducted using real groups' reasoning about real problems, with significant background knowledge and diversity of knowledge. The prediction is that in this type of situation groups of individuals perform more creatively than individuals.

ANATOMY OF A CONCEPTUAL CHANGE

The account of the cognitive processes underlying scientific creativity offered so far is static. I have demonstrated that analogy is an important part of current day science, that scientists reason about unexpected findings, and that distributed reasoning is a potentially important concept in science. I now turn to the issue of how all three aspects of scientific reasoning form a complex of mechanisms that work together to produce a conceptual change in a group of scientists at a meeting.

Many recent analyses of theory change in the history of science have focused on the notion of conceptual change (e.g., Carey, 1992; Nersessian, 1992; Thagard, 1992). *Conceptual change* has been defined as changes in scientific theories that occur when new concepts are proposed and old concepts must be radically changed or replaced to accommodate the new concepts. One example of this type of conceptual change noted in the literature is the 16th-century shift from a unitary concept of heat and temperature to two new concepts: one involving heat and one involving temperature (Wiser & Carey, 1983). It is conceptual change of this type that I now discuss.

Here I provide a dynamic account of a conceptual change that occurred in Lab A and use this example to show how in this situation different forms of reasoning worked together to produce entirely new concepts. To preserve the anonymity of this lab, I have been obliged to change the names of the diseases and the specific mechanisms involved in the diseases. Alas, I have also had to render intentionally vague specific aspects of the scientists' discussion that factored critically in the conceptual change. Nonetheless, I have tried hard to leave intact the essence of the complex of mechanisms that contributed to these scientists' conceptual change.

Let me begin with some background on the discovery. A postdoctoral fellow had recently come to a world-famous immunology lab. He had decided to investigate the way that B-cells cause a particular autoimmune disease. He had been conducting experiments in collaboration with another postdoc in another lab. Their work began with an analogy. Twenty years before, a researcher had noticed that an autoimmune disease in rabbits called CVX was very similar to a human autoimmune disease. Since then, the CVX diseases in rabbits has been used as a model for the human disease LOA. The postdocs investigated the disease in yet another organism (hamsters) because the postdoc's lab used hamsters and had facilities that could be used to investigate the mechanisms underlying the CVX disease that few other laboratories had. Overall, the motivation for his research was based on analogies between the human LOA disease, the rabbit CVX disease, and the hamster CVX disease.

One May afternoon the postdoc gave a talk about his latest experiments. He began with analogies between the human LOA disease and the CVX disease in rabbits, noting where the similarities and differences between the two diseases arose. He then moved to analogies between the CVX disease in rabbits and in hamsters. The first set of experiments resulted in a small amount of discussion and suggestions for future experiments. Then the postdoc started to discuss some experiments in which the results were very unusual. The postdoc had conducted a straightforward experiment. He had two conditions: one that caused colmenia disease in the joints and the other that caused the CVX disease in the heart. Both the heart and the joints are immune-privileged sites that do not normally allow B-cells in. In fact, the only types of B-cells that have been found in the heart are CVX B-cells, and the only B-cells that have been found in the joints are the colmenia B-cells. The postdocs expected that the B-cells that cause the disease in the heart would go to the heart and the B-cells that cause the disease in the joints would go to the joints. Instead, they found both types of B-cells in the heart and in the joints. This was an unexpected finding. The postdoc reached the part of his presentation wherein he discussed these results. He was surprised and excited by what he found. The result was unusual. It was at this point that the conceptual change began to unfold.

The director of the lab was intrigued. He asked the postdoc how it happened. The postdoc said he did not know. The director then made the question more specific. He asked the postdoc what properties were common to the colmenia and CVX B-cells that allowed them entry into the heart. The postdoc made an analogy to some other experiments that another postdoc in the lab had conducted and induced that the CVX and colmenia cells were both methylated. The director and other postdocs in the lab then made a series of inductions and deductions that led to a causal explanation for the unexpected finding. The reasoning was distributed over the members of the lab. However, the explanations they offered did not account for some other aspects of the findings, and another round of distributed reasoning occurred. This distributed reasoning resulted in a conceptual change: They proposed two new biological mechanisms to replace the unitary concept they had all assumed up to that point. Previously, it had been assumed that CVX cells only go to the heart and that colmenia cells only go to the joint; that is, B-cells have organ-specific attractions. The assumption was that once these cells got into the organ, they started the disease in that organ. Thus, there was one mechanism that caused both the entry into the organ and the initiation of the disease. The members' distributed reasoning led them to the conclusion that entry into the organ and the initiation of the disease were caused by two different mechanisms. They then had to propose what these mechanisms could be. They proposed two mechanisms that could together account for the CVX B-cells' causing the disease. One postdoc drew an analogy back to the human disease and mapped the mechanisms that had been proposed for the CVX disease onto the human disease. They modified their new model to fit the analogy to the human disease and thus ended up proposing a new model that not only explained the mechanisms underlying the three diseases but also had major ramifications for whole classes of autoimmune diseases.

By proposing two new mechanisms the scientists had to also change a number of other concepts in their knowledge of autoimmune diseases. It was at this point that everyone in the lab realized that a conceptual change had occurred, and they all shouted in excitement. This was followed by some further analogies in which other postdocs suggested other experiments. Finally, a postdoc made an analogy to the methods that other researchers have used and the methods that the postdoc had used, explaining why their rival's lab had not made the discovery they had just made.

This account of a conceptual change reveals some important characteristics of the mechanisms underlying conceptual change. First, there was no one reasoning mechanism underlying the conceptual change. Analogy, induction, deduction, causal reasoning, and distributed reasoning were all involved. Second, analogy was a significant component of the conceptual change, but all of the analogies that were used were either to the same organism or to other organisms: Conceptual change can and does occur without distant analogies. Third, the scientists had little memory for any of the on-line analogies used at the meeting. I asked the postdoc who conducted the research how the "discovery" was made. I asked this question one week later, a month later, three months later, and nine months later. On none of these occasions did he recall the spontaneous analogies used, or that distributed reasoning was involved. Thus, much of the on-line cognitive processes that went into the conceptual change would have disappeared without a record if I had not taped the original meeting.

CONCLUSION: CREATIVE COGNITION IS A TINKERER

The investigation of the cognitive mechanisms involved in on-line scientific thinking and reasoning reveal a number of important mechanisms underlying creative cognition. The main idea is that no single cognitive process is responsible for creative thought. I have found that scientists use a variety of cognitive mechanisms to produce any single new concept or theory. Creative ideas and novel concepts arise through a series of small changes produced by a variety of different cognitive mechanisms. It may be the case that reasoning and conceptual change are related in much the same way that a series of minor mutations produce major changes in organisms during evolution. In conceptual change, small mutations in concepts occur due to analogy and other reasoning mechanisms. Overall, a series of small changes will produce major changes in a concept. Conceptual change, like evolutionary change, is the result of tinkering. From a psychological point of view this account of conceptual change explains why it is so hard to discover the underpinnings of creativity. The many incremental steps that are involved in creative cognition are often lost and forgotten, and the act of creation becomes a mythical entity in which the final step in the creative process is often seen as the cause of the new concept. This leads to the proposal of entities such as distant analogies and insight as more important in creativity than they really are.

A further question is whether the cognitive processes underlying creative conceptual change are different from the processes underlying simple changes in concepts. I would argue that they are not. Exactly the same types of cognitive processes that are involved in the more mundane aspects of conducting science were involved in the moments of true conceptual change outlined previously. The question then arises as to what has made these scientists so productive and what has launched them to the forefront of their fields? The answer lies in their choice of research topics. Each of the scientists has developed research programs around difficult topics for which there were few simple answers or an abundance of ready-made techniques available. To conduct their research the scientists had to invent new techniques and engage in research that was risky. Thus, the factor that unifies the creative scientists in this sample is their ability to take risks. Each of the scientists conducted both high- and low-risk experiments in their laboratories. Although taking risks does not in itself lead to success, risk taking in combination with the use of the various reasoning strategies discussed in this chapter provide the context in which discoveries can be made.

The view of creativity offered here is quite different from that offered in the creativity literature. Authors such as Boden (1993) have proposed that the main way that analogy is involved in creative discoveries in science is by having major restructuring of concepts. Here, I have argued that analogy is involved in a very different way. Many very specific analogies are made that in conjunction with other reasoning mechanisms produce both modifications in existing concepts and entirely new concepts. The reason for the difference between my conclusions and that of others in the creativity literature is the differences in methodologies used. By looking at on-line reasoning rather than scientists' patchy reconstructions of a scientific discovery or breakthrough, it is possible to discover the specific cognitive mechanisms underlying creative thought. As I have argued elsewhere in this chapter, much of the cognition involved in creative thought works as a form of scaffolding. Once a new concept is generated the cognitive scaffolding is thrown away and scientists cannot reconstruct the cognitive steps that went into the discovery. Because of this, scientists, like historians, reconstruct their creative moments, often from their lab books. Unfortunately, many of the key cognitive steps made in a discovery do not end up in the lab books. Thus, many of these reconstructions are based on partial information, and, as a result, myths surrounding the creative process develop.

An important question about the research presented in this chapter is whether the findings are generalizable to other domains. There are numerous reasons to expect that these findings are indeed generalizable. First, I have observed similar types of reasoning strategies in biology laboratories at other universities (Dunbar, Patel, Baker, & Dama, 1995). Second, we have observed similar reasoning in clinical situations wherein medical doctors reason about patients (Dunbar et al., 1995; Patel, Dunbar, & Kaufman, 1995). I am now starting to investigate whether the same types of reasoning strategies occur in a business context.

Molecular biologists have some special tools that other scientists and nonscientists do not have, such as the use of the structure of DNA to search for homologies in a database. These scientists have the advantage of a way of representing their data that makes it possible to quickly and efficiently search for analogs. By representing their knowledge in a standardized fashion and searching for structural patterns that are similar to the one they are interested in, the scientists solve the problem of how to retrieve relevant analogies. Thus, homology makes finding base analogs easier. Ultimately, using homology gives the scientists another route to access base analogs. Once the scientists retrieve these base analogs, they use the same cognitive processes for constructing analogies as they do when they search their own memories for base analogs. Can scientists in other domains retrieve analogs in a similar fashion? The answer depends on the way the knowledge in a field is codified. If knowledge is coded in a structural manner, then it should be possible for the scientists to search for analogs with a similar structure and generate new analogies. It will be interesting to see whether the new databases that have arisen in virtually all fields will allow scientists to encode structural information, thereby allowing the scientists in a field to retrieve source analogs. This would ease one step in drawing analogies and could serve as a useful aid to scientists in all fields.

Overall, the research reported in this chapter demonstrates that it is possible to investigate complex creative cognition in real-world contexts. This in vivo research makes it possible to discover fundamental mechanisms of creative cognition and how multiple cognitive processes work together to produce conceptual change. Furthermore, this in vivo approach both makes it possible to discover what aspects of in vitro research are generalizable and suggests new types of experiments that can be conducted in the cognitive laboratory.

REFERENCES

Baker, L., & Dunbar, K. (1996). *How scientists use unexpected findings.* Manuscript in preparation.

Boden, M. (1993). *The creative mind: Myths and mechanisms.* New York: Basic Books.

Carey, S. (1992). The origin and evolution of everyday concepts. In R. N. Giere (Ed.), *Minnesota studies in the philosophy of science. Vol XV: Cognitive models of science* (pp. 89–128). Minneapolis: University of Minnesota Press.

Dunbar, K. (1993). Concept discovery in a scientific domain. *Cognitive Science, 17,* 397–434.

Dunbar, K. (1995). How scientists really reason: Scientific reasoning in real-world laboratories. In R. J. Sternberg & J. Davidson (Eds.), *Mechanisms of insight* (pp. 365–395). Cambridge, MA: MIT Press.

Dunbar, K. (1996). *Online analogical reasoning in scientific laboratories.* Manuscript submitted for publication.

Dunbar, K. (in press). Problem solving. In W. Bechtel & G. Graham (Eds.), *A companion to cognitive science.* Cambridge, MA: Blackwell.

Dunbar, K., Patel, V., Baker, L., & Dama, M. (1995, November). *Group reasoning strategies in knowledge rich domains.* Paper presented at the 36th annual meeting of the Psychonomic Society, Los Angeles, CA.

Dunbar, K., & Schunn, C. D. (1990). The temporal nature of scientific discovery: The roles of priming and analogy. *Proceedings of the 12th Annual Meeting of the Cognitive Science Society* (pp. 90–100). Hillsdale, NJ: Erlbaum.

Ericsson, K. A., & Simon H. A. (1993). *Protocol analysis: Verbal reports as data* (rev. ed.). Cambridge, MA: MIT Press.

Forbus, K., Gentner, D., & Law, K. (1995). MAC/FAC: A model of similarity-based retrieval. *Cognitive Science, 14,* 144–206.

Gick, M. L., & Holyoak, K. J. (1983). Schema induction and analogical transfer. *Cognitive Psychology, 14,* 1–38.

Holyoak, K. J. (1995). Problem solving. In E. Smith & D. Osherson (Eds.), An invitation to cognitive science (2nd ed., pp. 267–296). Cambridge, MA: MIT Press.

Holyoak, K. J., & Thagard, P. (1989). Analogical mapping by constraint satisfaction. *Cognitive Science, 13,* 295–355.

Holyoak, K. J., & Thagard, P. (1994). *Mental leaps.* Cambridge, MA: MIT Press.

Klahr, D. (1994). Searching for cognition in cognitive models of science. *Psycoloquy, 5,* 68.

Klahr, D., & Dunbar, K. (1988). Dual space search during scientific reasoning. *Cognitive Science, 12,* 1–48.

Klayman, J., & Ha, Y. (1987). Confirmation, disconfirmation, and information in hypothesis testing. *Psychological Review, 94,* 211–228.

Koestler, A. (1964). *The act of creation.* London: Macmillian.

Kulkarni, D., & Simon, H. A. (1988). The processes of scientific discovery: The strategy of experimentation. *Cognitive Science, 12,* 139–176.

Lovett, M. C., & Anderson, J. R. (in press). History of success. *Cognitive Psychology.*

Nersessian, N. (1992). How do scientists think? Capturing the dynamics of conceptual change in science. In R. N. Giere (Ed.), *Minnesota studies in the philosophy of science. Vol. XV: Cognitive models of science* (pp. 3–44). Minneapolis: University of Minnesota Press.

Patel, V., Dunbar, K., & Kaufman, D. (1995, November). *Distributed reasoning in medical and scientific contexts.* Annual Meeting of the Psychonomic Society, Los Angeles, CA.

Rhodes, R. (1986). *The making of the atomic bomb.* New York: Simon & Schuster.

Sanderson, P. M., Scott, J. J. P., Johnston, T., Mainzer, J., Watanabe, L. M., & James, J. M. (1994). MacSHAPA and the enterprise of exploratory sequential data analysis (ESDA). *International Journal of Human Computer Studies, 41,* 633–681.

Schunn, C. D., & Dunbar, K. (1996). Priming and awareness in complex reasoning. *Memory & Cognition, 24,* 271–284.

Thagard, P. (1992). *Conceptual revolutions.* Cambridge, MA: MIT Press.

Tweney, R. D. (1989). Five questions for computationalists. In J. Shrager & P. Langley (Eds.), *Computational models of scientific discovery and theory formation* (pp. 471–484). San Mateo, CA: Morgan Kaufmann.

Tweney, R. D., Doherty, M. E., & Mynatt, C. R. (Eds.). (1982). *On scientific thinking.* New York: Columbia University Press.

Wason, P. C. (1960). On the failure to eliminate hypotheses in a conceptual task. *Quarterly Journal of Experimental Psychology, 12*, 129–140.

Wiser, M., & Carey, S. (1983). When heat and temperature were on. In D. Gentner & A. L. Stevens (Eds.), *Mental models* (pp. 267–297). Hillsdale, NJ: LEA.

Wotiz, J. H., & Rudofsky, S. (1984, August). Kekulé's dreams: Fact or fiction? *Chemistry in Britain*, pp. 720–723.

18

Mental Models, Space, and Embodied Cognition

Arthur M. Glenberg

Language comprehension is a creative act; there is little that is transparent between words and meaning. Instead, meaning is the result of a creative, constructive process. I begin this chapter by justifying this claim. Then I take two swipes at figuring out how meanings are created from words. Both of these swipes are based on the notion of mental models as cognitive constructions that underlie comprehension. The first swipe treats mental models as constructions in an analog of Euclidean space. This sort of mental model provides a type of inference engine for some creative acts involved in language comprehension. Unfortunately, the data from several experiments demonstrate that this conception of mental models is incorrect. The second swipe considers mental models to be embodied. On an embodied account of meaning, understanding is in terms of the bodily, physical actions available to animals living in a three-dimensional world. This account is similar to ideas offered by Barsalou (this volume) and Gibbs (this volume).

LANGUAGE COMPREHENSION AS A CREATIVE ACT

The constructivist approach to language (Bransford, Barclay, & Franks, 1972; Gernsbacher, 1990; Graesser, Singer, & Trabasso, 1994) is that comprehension is much more than encoding individual words, much more than encoding words and their grammatical relations. Instead, at the heart of language comprehension are inferences that go well beyond the words. There are examples of this sort of creative act at just about every level of analysis from phoneme and letter perception to word meaning to understanding the meaning of a whole discourse. Consider briefly just a few of these levels.

All languages use pronouns such as *he, she,* and *it,* and a critical component of understanding is appreciating the people, objects, and events to which the pronouns refer. One might think that this is a relatively easy task because the pronoun itself provides some clues, such as gender and number. Often however, those clues are insufficient to unambiguously assign a referent to pronoun. For example, consider the following snippet of text:

> Janice asked Mary for a loan, but she refused.

It is clear to all competent readers of English who it is that did the refusing (i.e., the anaphor of the pronoun *she*), but that understanding cannot be based on number and gender. Instead one has to use one's knowledge of situations involving asking (particularly asking for loans) to figure out who is refusing whom. This sort of ambiguity is not an isolated or unusual instance; it is commonplace.

Ambiguity of meaning is not peculiar to pronouns; just about any word or phrase can be used in a variety of senses. For example, there is formal work on understanding of metaphorical language such as "My job is a jail" (Glucksberg & Keysar, 1990) or "Love is a journey" (Lakoff & Johnson, 1980). Understanding these phrases requires a nonliteral interpretation of the words. Whereas researchers have yet to reach a thorough understanding of how people understand metaphorical language, several factors are clear. First, metaphor is not infrequent. Instead people (i.e., ordinary language users) use metaphor all of the time. Second, language comprehenders do not find metaphor difficult to understand. In fact, metaphorical language appears to be understood as easily (sometimes more easily) as the equivalent nonmetaphorical language. Interestingly, nonliteral interpretation is not restricted to metaphor. Virtually any word can be made to take on multitudes of meanings depending on the context. "Look at the horse" will mean very different things when uttered in a museum in front of a picture, at the racetrack, and at the gym.

Furthermore, language comprehension is not simply based on the meanings of words or phrases. For example, learning from language often requires inferences that are tantamount to generating new (at least for the reader or listener) knowledge. Consider the following sentence adopted from Noordman, Vonk, and Kempff (1992):

> Chlorine compounds make good propellants because they react with almost no other substances.

In understanding such a sentence one learns not only that chlorine compounds make good propellants, not only that they react with few substances, but also that one of the characteristics of a good propellant is that it does not react with the substance that it propels. This knowledge is simply not "in" the language; it is added creatively.

As another example, consider the following paragraph about subatomic particles.

> Three particles, A, B, and C, are distinguished only by their energy. The A-particle is in the lowest energy state, the B-particle is in the next higher energy state, and the C-particle is in the next higher energy state. Because the C-particle is so energetic, it is unstable and quickly decays by losing a photon. When this happens, the C-particle drops into the next lower energy state.

On reading such text, an individual may make several inferences that are tantamount to learning well beyond any information "in" the text. One inference would be that the C-particle is now in the same energy state as the B-particle. Furthermore, given that the particles are distinguished solely by their energies, one might infer that the C-particle has now become a B-particle. How do we do that?

MENTAL MODELS OF LANGUAGE COMPREHENSION

When people apprehend the meaning of text, what do they do? A currently popular account is to propose that several levels of representation are constructed. One level consists of words or wordlike representations. Another level is a mental model or situational representation. The key intuition behind a mental model is that it is a representation of what the language is about, rather than a representation of the language itself. To make the distinction a bit clearer, consider the following:

> Art is taller than Carl, and Doug is taller than Carl.

A representation of the text would (presumably) have strong connections between the elements about which explicit statements are made: a connection between Art and Carl and a connection between Doug and Carl. Mental models are not about elements in the text, however, but about the situation the text describes. Thus, a mental model might represent three people and their differences in height. In fact, the mental model might also represent the possibility that Art and Doug are about the same height.

Because mental models are about the world, rather than about the text, they are just what is needed for language to fulfill its purpose of communicating about the world. Thus, language is able to instruct people about situations not immediately perceptible (e.g., descriptions of foreign lands), and we can get a sense of those situations because mental models are, in some sense, a substitute for perception. Similarly, language can be used to direct behavior toward real objects (e.g., to follow a recipe or to assemble a toy) because the cognitive representation based on the language is about those real objects, not just about the text (see Tannenhaus, Spivey-

Knowlton, Eberhard, & Sedivy, 1995, for a particularly compelling demonstration of the integration of language and objects).

The trick used in much of the mental models research has been to separate the structure of the text from the structure of the situation, or layout, described in the text. Then, to the extent that one can demonstrate that cognitive representations track the structure of the layout rather than the structure of the text, one has evidence for the creation of mental models. Often this separation is accomplished by describing a spatial layout, because the two- or three-dimensional structure of the layout can be quite different from the linear structure of the text used to describe the layout. For example, in Glenberg, Meyer, and Lindem (1987), individuals read one of two alternative versions of critical texts. In one version (Example a), a target object (sweatshirt) is described as physically associated with a main actor (John), and then the main actor is described as changing location. In the second version (Example b), the target object and the actor are described as physically dissociated.

> (a) John was preparing for a marathon in August. After doing a few warm-up exercises he put on his sweatshirt and went jogging. He jogged halfway around the lake without too much difficulty.
> (b) John was preparing for a marathon in August. After doing a few warm-up exercises he took off his sweatshirt and went jogging. He jogged halfway around the lake without too much difficulty.

Although the target is never mentioned again in the text, in the actual situation being described (and hence in the putative mental model), the target object moves with the main actor. Thus, to the extent that the main actor is an easily accessible concept, the target object should be easily accessible. In contrast, when the target and the actor are dissociated, although the actor remains accessible, the target object may not be. Glenberg et al. (1987) demonstrated just this sort of differential accessibility: After reading the text, "sweatshirt" was more accessible in Example a than in Example b. This finding indicates that the cognitive representation tracked the situation, not (just) the text.

This same sort of trick can be played with nonspatial dimensions of experience, such as time. In Glenberg and Langston (1992), the texts described the temporal ordering of steps in a procedure. When individuals were given diagrams to help them appreciate the ordering, the data indicated that readers constructed mental models reflecting the ordering of the steps (when performing the procedure) rather than the order in which the steps were described in the text.

In both of these studies, spatial information seems important. In Glenberg et al. (1987) the texts described movements in space to associate or dissociate the object and the actor. In Glenberg and Langston (1992), spatial information took the form of diagrams. Other investigators (e.g., Mani & Johnson-Laird, 1982; Morrow, Bower, & Greenspan, 1989; O'Brien & Albrecht, 1992) have also traded on spatial relations to ensure that the structure of the situation differs from the structure of the text (but see Fernandez & Saiz, 1989, for an interesting counterexample). This reliance on spatial-like situations leads one to wonder whether the focus on space is simply a convenient technique for investigating mental models or whether mental models are inherently spatial.

FIRST SWIPE: A EUCLIDEAN SPACE MENTAL MODEL

Virtually all theories of mental models propose that the models are about situations in the world, not about texts. Other than that, however, there is little agreement as to characteristics of mental models and little specificity. Glenberg and Langston (1992) and Glenberg, Kruley, and Langston (1994) proposed a Euclidean space version of mental models that preserves the aboutness character, provides a way of accounting for the sort of creative inferences people can make, and that makes several unique predictions. (Euclidean models are also consistent with the work of Johnson-Laird, 1983, p. 422; Denis, Gonçlaves, & Memmi, 1995; and Rinck & Bower, 1995.) The Glenberg et al. (1994) theory is based explicitly on the notion of a mental model having the properties of a three-dimensional, Euclidean space. Such a model could be used to structure a representation of the environment as perceived, and it could be used to construct a representation from language describing objects and their layouts. Glenberg et al. also demonstrated how such a mental model could be used to underlie the understanding of nonspatial texts.

According to the Euclidean space model, mental models are constructed using the limited-capacity, visual–spatial sketch pad of working memory (Baddeley, 1986). When the text is about nonspatial dimensions, readers choose which nonspatial dimensions to map onto spatial dimensions. Thus, in a text about the ordering of steps in a procedure, a reader might choose to assign "time" to the up–down dimension, or in reading a text about the energy levels of subatomic particles, "amount of energy" may be assigned to the left–right dimension. Choice of assignment may depend on previous experience with the domain or may reflect the use of spatial metaphors such as "more is up" (Lakoff, 1987; Langston, 1994). In addition to mapping between text-relevant dimensions and spatial dimensions in working memory, readers insert into the model cognitive elements representing components of the discourse, such as objects (e.g., a sweatshirt), people (e.g., main actors), and more abstract ideas. Understanding the flow of a discourse is tantamount to operating on the three-dimensional model according to the "instructions" given by the discourse. Breaks in coherence arise when, for example, the text refers to objects using devices such as pronouns that assume easy accessibility of a concept, and the corresponding concept is not represented in the model; or, confusion occurs when the text asserts a relation contrary to the (spatial) relations found in the model.

The Euclidean space model can also serve as a constrained inference generator to produce new knowledge. Glenberg and Langston (1992) proposed a process that they called *noticing*. Noticing occurs when attention is focused on a particular element in the model because it has just been inserted into the model space or because the text has directed a change in the model involving that element (e.g., Particle C loses energy). Then, other elements in the model that are near to the focused element are noticed and the relation between the two elements (e.g., that Particle C is now at the same energy level as Particle B) is encoded into long-term memory.

Thus, noticing serves to derive new information consistent with the model of the situation.

Several constraints save the process of noticing from the standard criticism that artificial inference generation is unbounded, whereas human inferences are very bounded. First, noticing only works along text-relevant dimensions that are assigned to a working memory dimension. Second, noticing only works among cognitive elements that are resident in the capacity-limited working memory. Third, noticing only works when a particular element is attended. Thus, it is not surprising that people do not notice all possible relations and that what they do notice is biased by their own interests and experiences: Those special interests determine which text-relevant dimensions are assigned to working memory dimensions. Glenberg et al. (1994) used a computer simulation of the Euclidean space model to demonstrate that it is consistent with many of the findings in the mental models literature.

Several examples of real-life creative discoveries can be labeled as *noticing*, but it is not clear that the label is being used in the same way as in the Euclidean model. For example, the discovery of penicillin has been described as a serendipitous noticing that some molds inhibited bacterial growth. However, this sort of noticing may well require a sophisticated mechanism, such as analogical mapping (see Gentner, this volume), rather than simple noticing by spatial contiguity in a Euclidean model.

The key to the Euclidean space model is noticing. Without it, the model is subject to several criticisms. Without noticing, there is little to recommend the model as a source of new, creative knowledge, the sort of knowledge that seems to come with language understanding. Also, without noticing, it is not clear what the model buys in terms of representation. That is, the model, like a picture, would need to be inspected by some other processes (a homunculus) to reveal information. This sort of inspection only pushes the problem of comprehension back to another level. Glenberg and Langston (1992) discussed some data consistent with the operation of noticing, but their experiments did not provide a direct test of noticing.

DIRECT TESTS OF THE NOTICING HYPOTHESIS

To test the noticing hypothesis, we (Langston, Kramer, & Glenberg, in press) made the following assumption: When a cognitive element in the model is noticed by virtue of being spatially close to an attended element, the noticed element will be more accessible than it would be otherwise. We then manipulated descriptions of layouts so that a particular element should be noticed (and relatively accessible), or not noticed (and relatively inaccessible). For example, consider the following Examples a and b. Example a describes the spatial relation between the TDK tape and the BASF tape.

> (a) Will was arranging the cassette tapes on his desk in order of quality. He put down the Kmart tape first. He put the TDK tape in front of the Kmart tape because it is of higher quality. He put the BASF tape just behind the TDK tape.
> (b) Will was arranging the cassette tapes on his desk in order of quality. He put down the Kmart tape first. He put the TDK tape in front of the Kmart tape because it is of higher quality. He put the BASF tape just in front of the TDK tape.

The text does not explicitly mention the relation between the Kmart brand tape and the BASF tape. Nonetheless, in the putative spatial mental model, these two tapes are near one another and should engender noticing. That is, placing an element corresponding to the BASF tape into the model (and thus focusing attention on that element) should lead to noticing and enhanced accessibility of the element corresponding to the Kmart tape. Contrast this with the situation for Example b. The text is identical except for the assertion that the BASF tape is "in front" of the TDK tape rather than "just behind" the TDK tape. Importantly, in the spatial mental model corresponding to this text, the BASF tape is not near to the Kmart tape. Thus, noticing of the Kmart tape is less likely in Example b than in Example a, and it is predicted that the Kmart tape will be less accessible in Example b than in Example a.

Langston et al. (in press) tested this prediction in a series of seven experiments. Across the experiments, accessibility was measured using speeded item recognition (see Glenberg et al., 1987, for a demonstration that this dependent measure is sensitive to the structure of a mental model) and time to read a sentence referring to the to-be-noticed item (see Rinck & Bower, 1995, for a demonstration that reading time is sensitive to structure of a mental model). The experiments also manipulated the modality of presentation of the texts (auditory or visual), the number of items described in the text (3–6), the number of dimensions in the layout of the items (1–2), and whether the verbal description was accompanied by a picture of part of the layout.

The results of these experiments can be summarized succinctly: There was no consistent evidence for noticing. What is one to make of these results? Of course, there is the possibility that the experiments were poorly done or did not effectively tap noticing. Given the use of multiple dependent measures, multiple layouts, and very high statistical power (when the data are collapsed across experiments), we think that these objections do not stand up to inspection. Do these data mean that people are not sensitive to spatial information conveyed by text? Surely this conclusion goes too far. Evidence from many other experiments (as a small sample consider, in addition to studies reviewed before, Denis & Cocude, 1992; Franklin & Tversky, 1990; McNamara, 1986) show sensitivity to spatial information. Instead, we think that these data are consistent with two related conclusions. First, when spatial relations are not explicitly stated (or portrayed in a picture), they are unlikely to be automatically noticed (in a cognitive model). Second, given that noticing seems to be the main benefit of forming a mental model in a Euclidean space, and given that there is no noticing, there is little reason to posit that mental models are Euclidean.

Data from several other studies converge on similar conclusions. For example, Rinck and Bower (1995; see also, Rinck, Hähnel, Bower, & Glowalla, in press) used a procedure in which individuals first memorize the layout of rooms in a building. Next, they read text describing the actions of a protagonist in the building. A basic finding is that time to read a sentence referring to a room recently visited by the protagonist is a monotonic function of the distance between the protagonist and the room. This finding appears consistent with the Euclidean space model, but note that the tested rooms are explicitly mentioned in the text. Importantly, the time to read a sentence referring to a room not recently visited (but familiar because of the memorization of the layout), did not show a monotonic distance effect. Much like the data testing the noticing hypothesis, if the relations are not made explicit, they are not noticed.

What seems to be wrong about the Euclidean model is that it assumes an unstructured representation of space, a representation in which only Euclidean distance matters. In contrast, Franklin and Tversky's (1990) work on the "spatial framework" shows that efficiency of retrieving information about spatial layouts depends on the axis queried. Readers are fastest retrieving information about the up–down axis, next regarding front–back, and slowest for left–right. This should not happen if all that matters is Euclidean distance. McNamara's (1986; McNamara, Hardy, & Hirtle, 1989) work on spatial representation shows effects of regions. That is, people seem to represent metric information within regions (e.g., a neighborhood on a map), but not between regions. This region effect implies that the representation of space is hierarchically structured, not Euclidean. Talmy's (1983) analysis of spatial prepositions, and Hayward and Tarr's (1995) empirical work supporting the analysis, indicate that language and perception deal with highly structured conceptions of space.

In summary, three facts are well supported. First, mental models, that is, representations of what a discourse is about, seem to underlie language comprehension. Second, mental models are sensitive to spatial layout. Third, the structure of a mental model is not Euclidean. Where do we go from here?

SECOND SWIPE: EMBODIMENT

The important function of language is to convey meaning. Thus, an analysis of language ought to include an analysis of what meaning is and how it is brought about. In what follows I sketch the traditional approach to meaning and outline what is wrong with it. I then try to show how ideas of embodiment can correct some of the problems with the traditional approach and what a mental model might be like from an embodied point of view. Finally, I briefly discuss how an embodied mental model can contribute to creative cognition.

Standard Approaches to Meaning

Modern cognitive psychology has not done well by meaning. Researchers have adopted approaches based on Aristotelian categories and propositional analyses of formal languages. Unfortunately, (a) neither the categories in the head nor the categories in the world are Aristotelian, and (b) natural language is not a formal language. Consequently, as I show, our accounts of meaning are meaningless.

Meaning to a cognitive psychologist is a notion about semantic memory and the structure of categories. That is, objects and events take on meaning when people assign them to categories that have meaning. So, what are these categories and how do they take on meaning? Two standard approaches to categories are the feature list approach (Smith, Shoben, & Rips, 1974) and the propositional structure approach (Collins & Loftus, 1975). Consider the feature list approach first. The basic idea is that words and objects take on meaning by belonging to categories (e.g., chair, animal, blonde), and belonging to a category requires having the right defining features. Thus, a chair may have as defining features a seat, a back, legs, and so forth. Although perfectly sensible on the surface, there are many logical and empirical problems with this approach to meaning (see Barsalou, 1993). First, one needs more than a list of features to make a category. Importantly, the features must have the right relations to one another. For example, it is not enough for a chair to have legs, but the legs must be below the seat and support the seat. Second, human categories do not seem to have an Aristotelian structure based on defining features. Instead, many of our categories have a more extended structure that Lakoff (1987) termed *radial.* That is, the category has some central members, and other members are related to the central members not by sharing features but by metaphorical extension. As one example, Lakoff considers the category *mother.* In Western cultures there is the prototypical birth mother that bears a child and nurtures it. However, there are many other types of mothers, including a biological mother who provides genetic materials but does not bear the child or nurture it, a surrogate mother who bears the child but does not provide genetic material, adoptive mothers, and so forth. Furthermore, one can speak of the mother of invention, and the mother of all wars, and can understand a father or a teacher to be mother.

A third problem with the feature list approach is that categories in the world do not seem to have an Aristotelian structure. For example, not even experts in biology agree as to proper criteria for classification (see Lakoff, 1987, for examples). Thus, by the standard account, it does not seem possible for us to know that a zebra is a zebra if neither the categories in the world nor the categories in our head have defining features.

Fourth, and most critically, cognitive psychologists have not succeeded in identifying or even clearly speculating about the nature of those defining features. Most theories suppose that they are abstract, amodal, arbitrary elements that take on their meaning by being embedded in a web of relations. This approach has serious logical and empirical problems. The logical problems include the symbol grounding problem (e.g., Harnad, 1990; Searle, 1980) that meaning cannot arise solely from syntactic relations between arbitrary symbols. Imagine, for example, the insurmountable difficulty of learning the meaning of the words in a new language if all that one had was a dictionary written in that language. Complex relations among meaningless symbols (the words in the new language) will not lead to meaning. The empirical problem is that human performance in category tasks is very much influenced by context and modality (Barsalou, 1993; Hintzman, 1986; Jacoby & Dallas, 1981).

The propositional structure approach fares a little better. Propositions do appear to give structure to categorical knowledge. Thus, propositions would seem to account for the fact that our knowledge about chairs includes the fact that the legs support the seat. Nonetheless, the propositional approach runs afoul of the other criticisms. In particular, the elements that make up propositions are supposed to be arbitrary and have no intrinsic meaning so that they can be manipulated by syntactic rules. This brings us back to the symbol grounding problem: Simply asserting relations between arbitrary symbols will never give rise to meaning. Furthermore, there is no account of how a cognitive system could have developed (individually or as a species) meaningless elements, nor is there any clear account for how meaning can eventually be introduced into a system of meaningless symbols.

How did we get ourselves into this mess? The problem stems from trying to develop psychological theories of meaning on the basis of philosophers' analyses of formal languages. Because natural language is messy, most philosophical accounts of meaning have been constructed within a formal language, such as predicate calculus. The symbols in a formal language are intended to be meaningless so that they can be operated on by formal syntactic procedures. These symbols and sentences are given meaning by mapping them onto elements in a formal model of the world. Not only is that mapping formidable (and perhaps impossible in principle, see Putnam, 1981), but also it requires the sorts of Aristotelian categories that do not appear to exist in the real world.

Note that the philosopher's problem is very different from the psychologist's problem. The philosopher is dealing with a formal language the elements of which are designed to be meaningless, whereas the psychologist is dealing with a natural language with elements that are designed to convey meaning. The philosopher is attempting to discover the "universal" meaning of formal sentences, that is, what a given set of relations among elements will mean for all times and all places. In natural languages, however, the meaning of a sentence depends critically on its context as well as on the experiences of the individual hearing the sentence. The psychologist needs to discover how a natural language sentence can have a particular meaning for a particular individual.

To reiterate: A central function of natural language is to convey meaning, and so researchers should be focusing on how language does that. Unfortunately, the standard theories of meaning are not up to the task.

Embodied Meaning

In response to this problem, cognitive scientists have been developing alternative accounts of meaning and language based on the idea of embodiment. An embodied account of meaning suggests that meaning is not independent of human functioning and that a sentence cannot have a universal meaning separate from the people doing the comprehending. Instead, embodied meaning is intrinsically embedded in human functioning. Rather than abstract meaningless elements, basic elements of embodied meaning reflect human capabilities, goals, emotions, and perception. For example, Lakoff (1987) based his system of meaning on gestalt perception, formation of basic categories, and a general ability to imagine. Gibbs (this volume) demonstrates how comprehension of idiomatic language is based on naive understanding of how the body works. Mandler (1992) analyzed what infants are capable of learning and responding to and suggested how these capabilities can be used to construct elements of meaning. Barsalou (1993, this volume) supposes that elements of meaning are perceptual symbols abstracted from experience. Because these perceptual symbols are compositional, they can be combined in a rule-like manner with other perceptual symbols to represent complex and novel thoughts.

All of these accounts attempt to solve two problems. First, they attempt to ground the elements of meaning in human experience to give the elements meaning. Second, they attempt to demonstrate how the elements can be combined to account for people's structural (i.e., relational) knowledge. The approaches of Barsalou, Lakoff, and Mandler are similar in that they are based on discrete units of meaning. In contrast, the account that I develop attempts to solve these problems of meaning using a system that is continuous and analogical.

Begin by considering not language, but objects and events. What makes a chair meaningful, or for that matter, a car, a river, a greeting, or a kiss? All of these objects and events can be accommodated to the same type of meaning, namely, the types of actions they sanction. Thus, the meaning of a chair is the sort of human, bodily action that it affords. This is not a universal meaning because the meaning does not exist independent of humans. Also, the meaning is for a particular human being by virtue of that particular human being's bodily capabilities. What is a chair for you may not be a chair for a small child, and vice versa. A perfectly good chair for a small child may be too small for an adult, and hence for the adult it is a toy chair. Similarly, what is a fordable stream for an experienced hiker may be a formidable torrent for a novice.

Importantly, the action-based meaning of an object depends on context and past experience. Thus, in the context of changing a lightbulb, a chair can be a ladder, and in the context of surviving a disaster, a chair can be a source of fuel. These changes in meaning are clearly related to experience. Without experience with Maier's pendulum problem, most people would not conceive of a pair of pliers as a pendulum weight. Nonetheless, what makes experience with Maier's problem meaningful are the actions the experience sanctions, that is, how the experience changes the actions available to us in dealing with pliers.

Meanings of components of situations smoothly combine, and I call this combination "mesh." For example, actions that define a cup's function (e.g., that the handle can be grasped) must be meshed with constraints on action produced by the cup's location on a high shelf (e.g., that the arm will have to be stretched above the head in order to grasp the handle) and constraints on action produced by the body's capabilities (the shelf is too high to reach, I will have to use a chair). This combination of meaning by meshing patterns of action is a type of compositional meaning. That is, the meaning of the cup combines with that of the shelf, and the fact that the shelf is high. The composition is continuous rather than discrete. Thus, each small change in characteristics of the shape of the cup's handle, the height of the shelf, and the length of my arms are meshed into slightly different possibilities, slightly different meanings.

A developmental story can be offered for this sort of meaning. It seems unlikely that an infant could develop categories of interaction from scratch. Instead, I propose that cognitive and perceptual systems have evolved to encode the world by the sorts of bodily interactions available to members of a particular species. Thus, a human infant is born with the capability to represent objects in terms of whether they can be grasped, sucked, or perhaps offer support. In contrast, whereas a newborn cat may be the human infant's peer in determining suckability, because the kitten does not have a hand, the kitten will have no conception of graspability. Note that by this proposal, initial encoding does not require direct manipulation of objects: Humans are born with a rudimentary ability to conceptualize the sorts of interactions beings of our sort are capable of performing. This proposal is consistent with research demonstrating the remarkable cognitive capabilities of infants and newborns. For example, Kaye and Bower (1994) have demonstrated that infants as young as a few hours old are sensitive to the visual appearance of the pacifier on which they are sucking (but which they have never seen). The feat is not incomprehensible if one attributes to the newborn the ability to encode objects in terms of the actions they support. Thus, the proprioceptive information from the mouth, lips, and tongue specify a suckable object of a particular shape, and the visual information specifies the same object.

Clearly when people perceive the world they see qualities such as color, in addition to those that determine interaction. Nonetheless, predominant aspects of experience such as shape, texture, and distance seem to be related to action. Importantly, the way people structure basic categories seems to be controlled by shape, and in particular, shapes corresponding to parts of objects (Tversky & Hemenway, 1984). Because parts determine object function and how people can interact with objects, categorization by partonomy is in accord with the proposal that action underlies meaning. Also, research by Freyd (e.g., Freyd & Pantzer, 1995) on dynamic representations is broadly consistent with an action-based account of meaning.

Not all meaning, however, is given directly by physical shape and capability for human interaction. Some meanings are learned and depend on an individual's experiences in the world. This is particularly true of socially determined meanings such as ownership (whose cup is whose in the coffee room) and relationship (whose spouse is whose at a party). Thus, a theory of meaning must account for how particular experiences combine with information from the environment in determining meaning. Note, however, that socially determined meaning can also be thought of in terms of action. The shape and texture of the cup determine which actions are possible, whereas ownership of the cup determines which actions are permissible.

How is it that one person sees a cup, whereas I see my cup? How is it that a hiker sees a random arrangement of trees in the forest, and the guide, by virtue of his or her experience, sees a trail? Certainly the guide is seeing the same trees in the same forest, but what differs is his or her way of structuring the components of the scene in terms of possible action. Thus, the guide can see how turning sideways here (to fit between two trees) and bending there (to go under a branch) can lead to a connected, continuous set of actions that enable travel from here to there. The guide's ability to conceptualize the continuous actions as humanly possible is what makes the layout a path (for the guide).

For both the cup and the path, we combine current stimulation with memory for previous interactions to form a new conceptualization of the actions possible in the current situation. There is an important constraint on this combination: The current stimulation takes precedence. I refer to this as clamping the environment (Glenberg, in press). That is, conceptualizing the world in terms of possible actions (i.e., cognition) is tightly clamped to or controlled by current environmental stimulation. Clamping is necessary to prevent hallucination. Thus, when faced with a stream transformed into a raging torrent by a flash flood, all of our memories of previous crossings of the stream should not (and given clamping, cannot) result in an action-based conceptualization in which crossing is a possibility. Clamping notwithstanding, combination of current stimulation and past experience can often be combined seamlessly because they occur in the same medium, the medium of human bodily action. Thus, my current understanding of the cup (something that I can grasp, heft, and use as a container) meshes perfectly with my memories of undertaking those actions with that cup. Similarly, the guide can mesh current stimulation and memory of past encounters with the path because they both are encoded as patterns of action.

Now consider the slightly different case of the guide considering whether a newly encountered stream is fordable. Current stimulation (e.g., the arrangement of rocks near the edge of the stream, the guide's position relative to the rocks, and components of the guide's own body, such as leg length) produces a conceptualization of the situation in terms of the actions possible for the guide, such as stepping onto the first rock. In a familiar situation, the guide's memory might also be the source of further possible actions, such as the possibility of stepping onto successive rocks. In a newly encountered situation, however, how is the guide to know that further action will be possible following the initial step? Two options are available. The first option is for the guide to take the first step in order to get his or her body into a new position to determine whether the second step is possible. In this case, it is only when the guide is in the middle of the stream that she or he recognizes that the rocks do not provide a continuous path (not the hallmark of a very successful guide).

The second option requires control over conceptualization, essentially through imagination. Consider what it would mean for the guide to imagine whether she or he can ford the stream dryshod. Previously, I mentioned that conceptualization (i.e., the actions afforded by current stimulation) must be controlled primarily by the environment to avoid hallucination. Imagination, however, is a type of controlled hallucination that involves two components. The first is a conscious effort of will to suppress the environment's control over conceptualization. It is important that this suppression be conscious to avoid taking inappropriate action. Normally, our conceptualization of the environment is in terms of actions that can be taken. Once we allow imagination to take over, however, actions specified by the imagined situation may not be safe (e.g., crossing the raging torrent). It is only our conscious awareness that the conceptualization is not controlled by the current environment that prevents dangerous or embarrassing action.

The second component of imagination is mesh. The guide must manipulate his or her conceptualization of the environment (the actions possible in that environment) in a way that meshes with constraints on the actions available to his or her body. Thus, the guide can mesh the distances between the rocks with the length of his or her leg to consider the possibility of stepping from rock to rock.

It seems likely that the more constraints that must be provided from memory, the less surety that the imagined meshed actions will be successful. Before taking a first step, we need only to mesh constraints from the environment with those of our bodies. In imagining the second step, however, we must mesh constraints from our bodies with the imagined environment (the environment after the first step is made), and that environment is different from current stimulation. Because the imagined environment is unlikely to fully encode all constraints (e.g., the slipperiness of the rocks, the effect of a strong breeze), validity of the predictions will be decreased.

At first glance this proposal for embodied meaning would seem to be limited to concrete objects, and thus the proposal would appear to be unable to account for our understanding of abstract concepts. In contrast, an example of how people can understand abstract relations using simple embodied components is provided by Talmy's (1988) compelling analysis of cause. Talmy noted that cause can be conceptualized in terms of simple forces such as pushing. Furthermore, causal situations seem to involve an agonist that is either attempting to change or attempting to avoid change, an antagonist acting against the agonist (e.g., by pushing), and a difference in force applied by the agonist and antagonist. Talmy noted that people use verbs of causation when the antagonist overcomes the agonist. Thus, a sentence such as "The boy caused the rock to slide" can be understood as an agonist (the rock) wishing to remain still, being overcome by the stronger force of the antagonist (the boy) acting against it. A similar conception of cause can be used to understand a sentence about a more abstract situation, such as "The falling bond market caused the dollar to slide."

Importantly, the components of pushing, resisting a push, and overcoming a push are common sorts of bodily experiences. Thus, these experiences may well underlie people's understanding of abstract concepts. Talmy's analysis raises again the main question of how language conveys meaning, and we now have most of the tools needed to deal with this question. In brief, language, like imagination, works by meshing conceptualizations.

The meaning of a sentence is the actions that it sanctions. Thus, a sentence that asserts a relation between two objects is meaningful to us when we appreciate how that assertion constrains interacting with the objects. It is inappropriate, however, to think of each sentence as contributing independently to the meaning of the whole. Consider again, a physical situation. The meaning of a Coke bottle depends not just on the bottle, but also on the situation in which it is embedded. The bottle might be a source of libation in a desert, an obstacle in a road, or a weapon in a fight. This sort of meaning is infinitely varied, but not arbitrary. The meaning is not arbitrary because the shape of the bottle (and other physical properties) constrain how we can interact with it. The meaning of the bottle is infinitely varied because the situations in which actions involving the bottle can mesh are themselves infinitely varied.

The same is true of sentences in a natural language. The meaning of a particular sentence is not given solely by the sentence, but nor is the meaning of the sentence arbitrary. Instead, the meaning of the sentence is given by how constraints on action given by the sentence mesh with the action patterns induced by language (or events) occurring before the sentence in question is uttered. Thus, the meaning of a sentence about a bottle (e.g., "She used the bottle") will depend on how the action-based interpretation of the sentence meshes with the action-based interpretation of the context.

These ideas suggest a way of thinking about coherence in language. What makes a string of sentences hang together rather than remain a random collection? One suggestion is that the sentences must share referents in order to link together. However, strings of coreferential sentences can appear bizarre as in the following:

> Coffee is made from beans. Beans are produced by plants. Plants grow in the soil. Soil contains micro-organisms . . .

Instead, consider the following criteria for local coherence. Sentences cohere to the extent that the action-based coding of each sentence meshes with the action-based coding of the situation. That is, we get a sense that the sentences cohere when they mutually modify each other's meaning, and this mutual modification is in the medium of potential actions.

This approach allows us to understand three subtypes of local coherence as arising from the same mechanism. These subtypes deal with language primarily directed toward the current environment (e.g., instructions on how to assemble a toy), language completely removed from the current environment (e.g, a humorous description of someone assembling a toy), and comprehension of the current environment itself. When language is being used to comment on current stimulation, it directs us to envision previously unnoticed relations and their support of possible action (e.g., "Use the stove bolt to attach Handle A to Slot B."). Much as a Gestalt psychologist would have it, the language helps us to restructure the perceptual field. Unlike the gestalt suggestion that restructuring is toward simplicity, here the restructuring is in terms of what actions are humanly possible. The sentences do not cohere by virtue of their linguistic form alone. If an individual does not know what a stove bolt is (or how to use it), or if he or she cannot find Slot B, or if Handle A appears to be too large to fit into the slot, then the sentences cannot mesh, the individual will not understand, and the sentences will appear incoherent.

A similar analysis applies when language is used to describe situations that have no counterpart in the immediate present. Sentences will cohere to the extent that there is a mutual modification of the action-based representations of the sentences and the action-based representation of the situation described so far.

Finally, the analysis of coherence holds for comprehension of real objects in real environments. People's understanding of the environment is a function of the extent to which they can conceptualize the mutual patterns of action. If an individual is flung into a strange, surreal environment filled with implements he or she does not know how to use, the experience is one of incoherence, because he or she cannot conceive of how the objects fit together.

To play out the metaphor, in all of these situations, coherence is like following a path. What makes the path a path (for us) is that the stepping stones can be envisioned as supporting continuity of action, although that may require twisting our bodies sideways and ducking under low branches. Similarly, sentences become a text when they allow us to traverse the text by deriving a connected, continuous set of actions from here (in the text) to there. Just as it is a creative leap of the imagination to see the stones as connected, it is a creative leap to see the sentences as coherent. Both leaps are possible because we are able to mesh meanings within the medium of bodily action.

Given this embodied account of meaning, what is a mental model? It is simply an embodied conceptualization. Because action requires particulars of shape and layout, mental models (embodied conceptualizations) are sensitive to objects and their layouts. However, these mental models are not unstructured Euclidean spaces. Instead they are structured by the actions we are capable of performing.

REPRISE: CREATIVITY IN AN EMBODIED COGNITIVE SYSTEM

It may well be that meaning is embodied, but that creativity has nothing to do with embodied meaning. For example, as humans become more facile with formal logic, we may develop the ability to think by manipulating abstract propositions. Perhaps those individuals who are most creative are those who have best learned to think propositionally. Perhaps, but there are good reasons to doubt such an account. For example, people reason far better in a meaningful context than when the context is stripped away, leaving something close propositions. An embodied account of creativity begins at the right starting point. It deals with meaning; it is contextualized; it is the stuff of imagination. Furthermore, it comes with natural constraints that may help us understand why some instances of creative cognition seem so astounding, others ordinary, and others bizarre or childish.

The embodied account of cognition provides two perspectives on creative thought. First, much of ordinary conceptualization is creative. Meaningful interpretation of the environment (and language) is imposed, that is, created. The interpretation is meaningful (to us) because it is in terms of how we can act. The interpretation is creative in that it must take into account the particulars of the environment, our bodies, and our experiences.

In addition to this "ordinary" form of creative thinking, some creative thought requires suppression of stimulation to manipulate conceptualization. Recall that clamping forces conceptualization to be consistent with current stimulation, and thus there may not be much room for creative reconsideration of the possibilities for action. Thus, suppression of clamping may be just what is required to be creative. This view helps to explain why creative thought requires relative quiet: Suppressing the environment is effortful, and the amount of effort is determined by the attention-getting qualities of the environment. A quiet, nondistracting environment facilitates creative thought by reducing the effort needed to suppress the environment's control over conceptualization.

Once we have managed to suppress the environment's control over conceptualization, a type of tradeoff will determine whether our thoughts are viewed as childish daydreaming or creative. The tradeoff is between suppression and maintenance of important constraints on action. Suppressing all constraints on action leads to childlike or dreamlike thoughts, such as contemplating the possibility of flying or moving back through time. Because many physical constraints cannot be overcome in reality, these thoughts have little practical import. Alternatively, one can suppress constraints on action that are a matter of convention, rather than physics. Thus, one can imagine new types of society by eliminating, for example, constraints of ownership. Also, suppression of some features of the environment may allow a new mesh between a conventional conceptual framework and new patterns of action. For example, a designer may be struggling to devise a keyboard that can be used with the hands and forearms in a straight line rather than bent at the wrists. The layout of the standard keyboard, with a linear arrangement of keys, will not mesh with this new pattern of action. Suppressing the linear structure of the keyboard, the designer may imagine an angled keyboard that eliminates the need to bend the wrists.

This tradeoff is a balancing act. Creativity demands a conceptualization (pattern of possible actions) that maintains the necessary physical and conventional constraints on action while using mesh to drive the conceptual system into a new action pattern. The trick is that the environment provides the most reliable constraints on action (we do not bump into tables or fall off cliffs), and yet the environment is just what needs to be suppressed to manipulate the conceptualization creatively.

The balancing act between suppression and constraints suggests why sketches, visual imagery, and language can play a role in creative thinking (see Cheng & Simon, 1995, for a different account of the benefits of diagrams). By the simple expediency of not including to-be-ignored constraints in a sketch, the sketch can help us maintain particular constraints (e.g., that Slot B must accept Handle A) while ignoring others. Similarly, a competent language user has learned to use words and sentences to drive the conceptual system. Thus, verbal rehearsal may be a mechanism to maintain particular constraints on action while meshing the conceptualization with new patterns of action. In this way, we talk ourselves into states that can be interesting, exciting, and sometimes creative.

REFERENCES

Baddeley, A. D. (1986). *Working memory.* Oxford, England: Oxford University Press.

Barsalou, L. W. (1993). Flexibility, structure, and linguistic vagary in concepts: Manifestations of a compositional system of perceptual symbols. In A. C. Collins, S. E. Gathercole, & M. A. Conway (Eds.), *Theories of memories* (pp. 29–101). London: Erlbaum.

Bransford, J. D., Barclay, J. R., & Franks, J. J. (1972). Sentence memory: A constructive versus interpretive approach. *Cognitive Psychology, 3,* 193–209.

Cheng, P. C-H., & Simon, H. A. (1995). Scientific discovery and creative reasoning with diagrams. In S. M. Smith, T. B. Ward, & R. A. Finke (Eds.), *The creative cognition approach* (pp. 205–228). Cambridge, MA: MIT Press.

Collins, A. M., & Loftus, E. F. (1975). A spreading-activation theory of semantic memory. *Psychological Review, 82,* 407–428.

Denis, M., & Cocude, M. (1992). Structural properties of visual images constructed from poorly or well-structured verbal descriptions. *Memory & Cognition, 20,* 497–506.

Denis, M., Gonçlaves, M-R., & Memmi, D. (1995). Mental scanning of visual images generated from verbal descriptions: Towards a model of image accuracy. *Neuropsychologia, 33,* 1511–1530.

Fernandez, A., & Saiz, C. (1989, July). *Foregrounding of trait information during text comprehension.* Paper presented at the First European Congress of Psychology, Amsterdam, The Netherlands.

Franklin, N., & Tversky, B. (1990). Searching imagined environments. *Journal of Experimental Psychology: General, 119,* 63–76.

Freyd, J. J., & Pantzer, T. M. (1995). Static patterns moving in the mind. In S. M. Smith, T. B. Ward, & R. A. Finke (Eds.), *The creative cognition approach* (pp. 179–204). Cambridge, MA: MIT Press.

Gernsbacher, M. A. (1990). *Language comprehension as structure building.* Hillsdale, NJ: Erlbaum.

Glenberg, A. M. (in press). What memory is for. *Behavioral and Brain Sciences.*

Glenberg, A. M., Kruley, P., & Langston, W. E. (1994). Analogical processes in comprehension: Simulation of a mental model. In M. A. Gernsbacher (Ed.), *Handbook of psycholinguistics* (pp. 609–640). San Diego, CA: Academic Press.

Glenberg, A. M., & Langston, W. E. (1992). Comprehension of illustrated text: Pictures help to build mental models. *Journal of Memory and Language, 31,* 129–131.

Glenberg, A. M., Meyer, M., & Lindem, K. (1987). Mental models contribute to foregrounding during text comprehension. *Journal of Memory and Language, 26,* 69–83.

Glucksberg, S., & Keysar, B. (1990). Understanding metaphorical comparisons: Beyond similarity. *Psychological Review, 97,* 3–18.

Graesser, A. C., Singer, M., & Trabasso, T. (1994). Constructing inferences during narrative text comprehension. *Psychological Review, 101,* 371–396.

Harnad, S. (1990). The symbol grounding problem. *Physica D, 42,* 335–346.

Hayward, W. G., & Tarr, M. J. (1995). Spatial language and spatial representation. *Cognition, 55,* 39–84.

Hintzman, D. L. (1986). "Schema abstraction" in a multiple-trace memory model. *Psychological Review, 93,* 411–428.

Jacoby, L. L., & Dallas, M. (1981). On the relationship between autobiographical memory and perceptual learning. *Journal of Experimental Psychology: General, 110,* 306–340.

Johnson-Laird, P. N. (1983). *Mental models.* Cambridge, MA: Harvard University Press.

Kaye, K. L., & Bower, T. G. R. (1994). Learning and intermodal transfer of information in newborns. *Psychological Science, 5,* 286–288.

Lakoff, G. (1987). *Women, fire, and dangerous things: What categories reveal about the mind.* Chicago: University of Chicago Press.

Lakoff, G., & Johnson, M. (1980). *Metaphors we live by.* Chicago: University of Chicago Press.

Langston, W. E. (1994). *The use of spatial metaphors when thinking about nonspatial domains.* Ann Arbor, MI: UMI Dissertation Services.

Langston, W., Kramer, D. C., & Glenberg, A. M. (in press). The representation of space in mental models derived from text. *Memory & Cognition.*

Mandler, J. M. (1992). How to build a baby: II. Conceptual primitives. *Psychological Review, 99,* 587–604.

Mani, K., & Johnson-Laird, P. N. (1982). The mental representation of spatial descriptions. *Memory & Cognition, 10,* 181–187.

McNamara, T. P. (1986). Mental representation of spatial relations. *Cognitive Psychology, 18,* 87–121.

McNamara, T. P., Hardy, J. K., & Hirtle, S. C. (1989). Subjective hierarchies in spatial memory. *Journal of Experimental Psychology: Learning, Memory, and Cognition, 15,* 211–227.

Morrow, D. G., Bower, G. H., & Greenspan, S. L. (1989). Updating situation models during narrative comprehension. *Journal of Verbal Learning and Verbal Behavior, 28,* 292–312.

Noordman, L. G. M., Vonk, W., & Kempff, H. J. (1992). Causal inferences during the reading of expository texts. *Journal of Memory and Language, 31,* 573–590.

O'Brien, E. J., & Albrecht, J. E. (1992). Comprehension strategies in the development of a mental model. *Journal of Experimental Psychology: Learning, Memory, and Cognition, 18,* 777–784.

Putnam, H. (1981). *Reason, truth, and history.* Cambridge, England: Cambridge University Press.

Rinck, M., & Bower, G. H. (1995). Anaphora resolution and the focus of attention in situation models. *Journal of Memory and Language, 34,* 110–131.

Rinck, M., Hähnel, A., Bower, G., & Glowalla, U. (in press). *The metrics of spatial situation models. Journal of Experimental Psychology: Learning, Memory, and Cognition.*

Searle, J. R. (1980). Minds, brains and programs. *Behavioral and Brain Sciences, 3,* 417–424.

Smith, E. E., Shoben, E. J., & Rips, L. J. (1974). Structure and process in semantic memory: A featural model for semantic decision. *Psychological Review, 81*, 214–241.

Talmy, L. (1983). How language structures space. In H. Pick & L. Acredolo (Eds.), *Spatial orientation: Theory, research, and application* (pp. 225–282). New York: Plenum Press.

Talmy, L. (1988). Force dynamics in language and cognition. *Cognitive Science, 12*, 49–100.

Tannenhaus, M. K., Spivey-Knowlton, M. J., Eberhard, K. M., & Sedivy, J. C. (1995). Integration of visual and linguistic information in spoken language comprehension. *Science, 268*, 1632–1634.

Tversky, B., & Hemenway, K. (1984). Objects, parts, and categories. *Journal of Experimental Psychology: General, 113*, 169–197.

19

Creativity's Camel: The Role of Analogy in Invention

David N. Perkins

Polonius: *My Lord, the queen would speak with you, and presently.*
Hamlet: *Do you see yonder cloud that's almost in shape of a camel?*
Polonius: *By the mass, and 'tis like a camel, indeed.*
Hamlet: *Methinks it is like a weasel.*
Polonius: *It is backed like a weasel.*
Hamlet: *Or like a whale?*
Polonius: *Very like a whale.*

Hamlet, Act III, Scene ii

How creativity happens puzzles laypersons and scholars alike, but one way or another it does. Boundaries get transcended, conventions subverted, stereotypes perverted, templates turned topsy-turvy, and new and innovative theories, symphonies, sonnets, and devices come into be-

This article responds to chapters 16 through 18 of this volume. Some of the ideas discussed here were developed with support from the MacArthur Foundation and the Spencer Foundation, with the caveat that neither organization necessarily subscribes to them. I am most grateful for their support.

ing. Although it all can seem quite magical, scholars of creativity have committed themselves to coherent causal accounts of the work of creation.

A favorite mechanism in such accounts is analogical thinking. By nature a boundary breaker, analogy offers a plausible way by which thinking can escape from familiar ruts. Analogy or something close to it has been held to play a key role in the building of scientific theories (e.g., the Rutherford model of the atom; cf. Gentner, Brem, Ferguson, Wolff, Levidow, Markman, and Forgus, this volume), invention of devices and processes (e.g., Gutenberg's invention of moveable type; Koestler, 1964; see also Weber & Perkins, 1992), humor (Koestler, 1964; Minsky, 1983), and more. Analogy is the focus of two of the three chapters leading up to this commentary, those by Dunbar and by Gentner et al. The chapter by Arthur Glenberg, although not about analogy directly, addresses the nature of mental models, analogy arguably being one important kind of mental model. With all of this attention to analogy in the service of creativity, it is tempting to add an analogy about analogy itself. Inspired by Hamlet's camels in the clouds, one could say that analogy is creativity's camel, the creature that carries people's cognitive capacities across the desert of unworkable possibilities from the familiar to true innovation.

Yet the quote from *Hamlet* suggests that some problems need attention before granting analogy the title of creativity's camel, or at least one of creativity's several important camels. In this vignette, Hamlet pokes fun at Polonius, leading him by his cognitive nose to recognize one and then another and then another pattern in the amorphous clouds overhead. Hamlet and Shakespeare remind us how easy it is to project patterns on chaos. Such cognitive play is creative in a small way but not in a big way. It recommends what I call the first Polonius problem: What is the difference between mundane and exceptional creativity?

The way Hamlet teases Polonius also suggests a second puzzle. Altogether too much can be seen in the clouds, without any real insight attached. Similarly, in any situation that invites creativity a promiscuous search for analogies might yield a combinatorial explosion of quirky connections with only rarely a meaningful link, thus the second Polonius problem: How can analogy avoid a combinatorial explosion of meaningless whimsy and contribute to exceptional creativity?

Finally, Hamlet's menagerie in the clouds reminds us that humans are not the sole source of invention if one interprets invention broadly. Nature invents, producing such oddly diverse creatures as camels, weasels, and whales. But if analogy is creativity's camel, how do mindless generative processes like Darwinian evolution get along without it? Or do they get along without it? The third Polonius problem: Does analogy figure in exceptional creativity outside of individual human creativity?

In the sections that follow, I offer solutions to the three Polonius problems, drawing on as well as commenting on the three previous chapters and folding in some ideas of my own.

WHAT IS THE DIFFERENCE BETWEEN MUNDANE AND EXCEPTIONAL CREATIVITY?

A fundamental precept of contemporary cognitive science holds that cognition almost always functions creatively. In Jerome Bruner's classic phrase, people "go beyond the information given" (Bruner, 1973). Hamlet easily finds vague semblances of creatures in the clouds, and Polonius even more gets lured by Hamlet into affirming these fancies. In navigating the everyday world, people routinely extrapolate and interpolate to complete partly occluded objects and interpret events. Arthur Glenberg, in his chapter "Mental Models, Space, and Embodied Cognition" offers examples from ordinary speech. Sentences like "Janice asked Mary for a loan, but she refused" leave no doubt as to the proper antecedent for *she.* Metaphors like "My job is a jail" prove transparent, even though they would puzzle most computer programs designed to interpret language.

Unquestionably creative in a sense, but also commonplace, such generative aspects of cognition demonstrate what might be called *mundane creativity.* They are part and parcel of everyday cognitive functioning, achievements that almost everyone routinely accomplishes. Although they certainly call for explanation, they also raise a question of contrast, the first Polonius problem: How do these mundane manifestations of creativity contrast with the creativity of Shakespeare, Einstein, or Beethoven?

One view of the matter comes from a framework I have developed over the past several years—the theory of *creative systems* (Perkins, 1992, 1994, 1995). The theory focuses on how adaptive novelty comes about, whether produced by an individual human creator, groups, computer programs (cf. Boden, 1991), biological evolution (cf. Dawkins, 1976, 1987), or other systems that yield adaptive novelty from time to time. The basic approach treats the production of adaptive novelty as the consequence of search through a space of possibilities—possible symphonies, inventions, or theories in the case of human creators, or possible biological forms in the case of Darwinian evolution. The approach derives from the work of investigators who have modeled problem solving as search in a problem space (Langley, Simon, Bradshaw, & Zytkow, 1987; Newell, 1990; Newell & Simon, 1972). However, the aim is not to propose computer simulation models of problem solving or invention but to highlight certain broad qualitative features of creative search (cf. Perkins, 1981).

The "topography" of a possibility space can make solutions relatively accessible or very hard to find. In an easy possibility space, an iterative hill-climbing process that follows symptoms of promise can home in on a solution relatively rapidly. However, in a less friendly space, iterative hill-climbing processes can get trapped by local maxima or lose their way in regions that lack a clear gradient. Synthesizing such considerations, creative systems theory proposes that four difficulties characterize possibility spaces that pose creative challenges.

1. *The wilderness problem.* Suitable solutions occur sparsely scattered in a large space of inadequate solutions. Imagine a poet searching for the right adjective for a certain spot in a poem: Many words might provide a prosaic fit, but few would offer just the right sound and connotations to energize the phrase. Or think of Thomas Edison screening hundreds of possibilities in a "drag hunt" as he called it to find a good filament for a lightbulb or for other purposes (cf. Carlson & Gorman, 1992).

2. *The plateau problem.* In large regions, there is no clear gradient of promise. The poet cannot tell reliably from one marginally suitable word whether another lies in the same neighborhood. A near miss for an adequate lightbulb filament does not necessarily point to a better related substance. The possibility space is full of flat, directionless plateaus.
3. *The canyon problem.* Search proceeds within limiting and often unrecognized boundaries, with suitable resolutions in another part of the possibility space altogether. Perhaps the poet needs to abandon the search for the perfect adjective and re-frame the entire phrase. Perhaps tempting as one class of substances is for a filament, other classes entirely need to be considered.
4. *The oasis problem.* It is hard to abandon the neighborhood of a promising partial solution even when the partial solution resists refinement. The poet finds an adjective with a small measure of zip and tries to make it work by adding other words or tries to convince himself or herself that it is good enough. A certain substance almost provides a functional filament. After endless hours of trying different sizes and shapes, it is difficult to let the invested effort go and move on. In artificial intelligence terms, this is the problem of *local maxima.*

To package these characteristics in a wholistic metaphor, one can speak of *Klondike spaces* as possibility spaces that show the wilderness, plateau, canyon, and oasis problems. The image is one of searching for gold in the Klondike, a substance sparsely distributed (the wilderness problem), with only occasional gradients pointing to lodes (the plateau problem), with deposits often over the mountain rather than in the valley where you are looking (the canyon problem), and with the constant temptation to work over a low yield area rather than seek a richer deposit (the oasis problem). *Homing spaces* contrast with Klondike spaces. Homing spaces are possibility spaces with a clear gradient of promise that an iterative search process can track to a solution. Of course, extreme Klondike and extreme Homing spaces mark ends of a continuum, with most search spaces somewhere in between.

Of course, the possibility space of a problem is not entirely determined by the logic of the problem. It also reflects the construal of the problem-solving agent, the way the agent encodes the problem. For example, expertise often allows a problem-solving agent to encode a problem in a Homing space that a novice agent would encode in a Klondike space. What is routine problem solving for experts can be creative problem solving for novices. Also, sometimes searches in a Klondike space come to resolution when the problem-solving agent finds a new representation as part of the search process that reveals a hitherto masked Homing gradient (Perkins, 1994).

Creative systems theory offers an answer to the first Polonius problem. Exceptional creativity reflects search in Klondike spaces or near-Klondike spaces. For instance, genuinely novel and effective theories or inventions prove hard to find because of the wilderness, plateau, canyon, and oasis problems in the search spaces involved.

In contrast, mundane creativity requires only routine problem solving. Yes, the person (or other cognitive agent) must go beyond the information given; but the problem solving occurs in a Homing space or something close to a Homing space. This virtually guarantees that solutions are achieved quickly and reliably. For example, semblances of animals are easily found in clouds because the standards for what counts as a solution are low. A very rough match will do, so there are many solutions and not much of a wilderness problem. A phrase like "My job is a jail" may require something of a Klondike search to come up with, but understanding the phrase calls only for mundane creativity. Because the source (jail) and the target (job) of the analogy are directly given, the hearer need only construct the mapping between them. There is only one obvious option that proves readily elaborated: easy hill climbing, with no disorienting plateaus or deceptive canyons or oases to divert the process.

The answer to the first Polonius problem offered by creative systems theory has an interesting twist. One might expect the answer to foreground contrasts in the psychological processes that serve mundane versus exceptional creativity; but creative systems theory emphasizes contrasts in the topography of the possibility spaces involved. What makes a product exceptionally creative is its "lostness" in a Klondike wilderness replete with plateaus, canyons, and oases. Although this has implications for the kinds of processes that best navigate Klondike spaces, topographical challenges and not psychological processes define creativity.

HOW CAN ANALOGY AVOID A COMBINATORIAL EXPLOSION OF MEANINGLESS WHIMSY AND CONTRIBUTE TO EXCEPTIONAL CREATIVITY?

The challenge of combinatorial explosions is central to heuristic search. The game of chess provides the classic example. Chess-playing computer programs must look ahead to anticipate patterns of loss or gain of pieces and, ultimately, checkmate. However, the number of possibilities to examine increases exponentially with each further move considered and quickly outstrips the capacity of any conceivable computer, never mind contemporary machines. Accordingly, chess-playing programs adopt heuristics to prune the search tree vigorously, eliminating branches that show little promise or marked loss even though in principle they might lead to reversals of fortune that would make them worthwhile.

Hamlet's teasing of Polonius points to the possibility of a monstrous combinatorial explosion in the use of analogy. At least in chess the players operate within the possibility space of chess moves and strategies. However, when analogy enters, the boundaries seem to crumble. Rough matches at the camel-in-the-clouds level are all over the place. Which ones will really pay off? How to keep such a process under control and yielding fruit becomes a vexed problem. Fortunately, each of the preceding three articles offers some insight.

Kevin Dunbar's studies of research in molecular biology laboratories tracked the moment-to-moment evolution of ideas as investigators in these laboratories worked and talked with one another. In support of creativity's camel, Dunbar reports extensive use of analogies in the evolution of theories, experiments, and explanations. However, his classification of kinds of analogies reassures us about the second Polonius problem. Sorted into three categories—within-organism, across-organisms, and nonbiological—the analogies hardly touched the third category at all. When nonbiological analogies occurred, they always figured in explanation, not in theory generation. In other words, the analogies were relatively conservative, reflecting tight fits between the problem at hand and the investigators' rich knowledge of the same and related organisms.

If this risks being too conservative, another camel of creativity helped keep the scientists out of theoretical ruts: attention to unexpected findings. Although research on laypeople suggests that "confirmation bias" dominates human reasoning, Dunbar found that scientists in the laboratories he studied paid assiduous attention to findings that ran counter to expectations. Efforts to explain such findings often led to important new hypotheses. Dunbar notes that unexpected findings proved not rare but common. To ignore them would be truly disastrous and any competent person in a scientific setting would have learned to take them seriously and use them to fuel progress. Dunbar points out that participants in typical psychology experiments that have demonstrated strong confirmation bias are at the front end of the learning curve; they have not had time to recognize and learn to cope with and capitalize on the phenomenon.

Dunbar also documents how the discourse among investigators serves to edit analogies and other elements of discourse like theories, discarding weak ideas, repairing weaknesses, and combining different analogies and other ideas to advance a theory further. This is an example of what Dunbar calls distributed reasoning and what has been called distributed cognition or distributed intelligence (Salomon, 1993). A single analogy becomes one element in a complex constructive process. Indeed, Dunbar finds that the analogies that figured along the way are typically forgotten by the participants. In summary, the use of near rather than far analogies as elements in a complex web of reasoning sustained across multiple minds makes the entire process suitably conservative and quells the combinatorial explosion.

Dedre Gentner and her colleagues focus on a historical case, Johannes Kepler's development of his theory of the orbital motions of the planets. They underscore how radical Kepler's concept was, how much of a departure from the norms of the day. Not only did Kepler maintain the

Copernican concept of an orbiting Earth but also he argued for elliptical rather than circular orbits, the sun as the central agent guiding planets in those orbits, and causal agencies of a physical nature in contrast with the earlier idea that the planets possessed a kind of intelligence with which they tracked their paths.

Kepler arrived at these ideas partly through a rich and persistent use of analogies. He used a startling array of analogies for one or another purpose (e.g., the sun and planets as magnets and the way ferry boats on ropes can use their rudders to tap the force of the current). Particularly central to Kepler's thinking was an analogy between light and what he termed the *vis motrix*, a power radiating from the sun that Kepler thought pushed the planets along their paths. The vis motrix was not light itself, Kepler recognized, because eclipses, which blocked light, did not send Earth spinning off in an unexpected direction; however, the vis motrix behaved like light, its influence lessening with distance from the sun as the vis motrix became spread out over a larger region of space.

Kepler's fondness for analogies might seem to lead straight into a combinatorial explosion. However, Gentner et al. point out that Kepler was a sharp critic of the promiscuous analogizing common to the alchemical theorizing of the day. Fruitful analogies must past tests. Gentner et al. clarify the nature of those tests by applying to Kepler's discoveries their structure mapping engine, a computer model of analogical thinking. The structure mapping engine seeks matches between a base domain (e.g., light and illumination of objects) and a target domain (e.g., the posited vis motrix and the response of the planets) that preserve structural relations between the domains, even though single entities and simple properties may be mapped onto quite different entities and properties. Such constraints eliminate superficial analogies (camels in clouds) and set up conditions for an analogy building understanding, for instance, by highlighting (matched aspects of the two domains become more salient), projection (candidate inferences are carried over from the base to the target domain), or re-representation (the representation of either or both domains is altered to improve the match).

Dunbar and Gentner et al. seem to disagree on the role of *near* (within domains) versus *far* (across domains) analogies. Dunbar's findings suggest that far analogies are rare. Dunbar proposes that they may not figure as importantly in scientific discovery as has often been held. Gentner et al. suggest in reply that this may vary with the maturity of the field. They point out that Kepler had little to work with but far analogies, lacking a real physics on which to found his reasoning. In contrast, the scientists Dunbar investigated were working within richly developed paradigms. The moral may simply be that *close* analogies serve best when available, but sometimes they are not. It is also conceivable that when paradigm change is at stake, close analogies may tend to preserve the status quo, as they inherently draw on the established paradigm. Far analogies may stand a better chance of transforming the paradigm. After all, the paradigm from which Kepler escaped was itself replete with its own analogies.

Arthur Glenberg does not address analogical thinking directly. His view is broader. He treats the role of mental models in mundane and exceptional creativity. As noted earlier, Glenberg focuses first and foremost on mundane creativity, as in the interpretation of speech and text. He argues that Euclidean mental models that represent objects embedded in time and space mediate people's understanding. However, he offers evidence that pure Euclidean models will not do. People's mental models must be seen as saturated with affordances, patterns of plausible action for the self as an agent. These "embodied" models provide a better account of how people make sense of speech in particular and the world in general.

Although Glenberg says little about analogy, the connection is easily made. An analogy can be seen as a kind of mental model that involves a map from a base to a target domain. Glenberg's stance that mental models are embodied, potential action oriented, makes sense as well. A good structure mapping from base to target (to use Gentner et al.'s terms) establishes not just surface relations but also deeper relations that allow mapping across processes and potential actions. For an example from Kepler, the action of light radiating out corresponds to the action of the vis motrix radiating out.

Glenberg offers a provocative broad-stroke view of exceptional creativity on the basis of his notion of embodied models. He argues that immediate stimulation "clamps" people's mental models. Through imagination one can release these clamps selectively and explore possibilities contrary to immediate stimulation, possibilities that extrapolate beyond it or even violate it. Glenberg views such explorations as "controlled hallucination," controlled because, if all goes well, they do not delude us about reality but present us with options for reconceiving or redirecting it. Again it is easy to bring analogy into the picture. By nature, analogy is a clamp releaser. When a structure mapping relates a base to a target domain, this foregrounds deep structural homologies at the expense of the clamps of surface features in either domain. As to the problem of promiscuous connection making, Glenberg makes the general point that effective creativity requires a balancing act between the suppression and maintenance of constraints. The mechanisms incorporated in Gentner et al.'s structure mapping engine offer an account of what that balancing act should look like in the case of analogy.

In summary, the offerings of Dunbar, Gentner et al., and Glenberg provide considerable insight about the second Polonius problem. Collectively, they disclose how analogy can function generatively while not getting out of hand. Conservative practices and distributed reasoning within a paradigm (Dunbar), constraints that promote mapping of deep structures (Gentner et al.), and the right balance of clamped and unclamped constraints (Glenberg) favor search processes that work with a manageable number of good-bet analogies.

A look back at the theory of creative systems also helps clarify the contribution of analogy. As noted earlier, the free use of analogy threatens to exacerbate the wilderness problem by creating a huge wilderness of possible analogies, most of them not illuminating. However, constraints such as those just discussed reduce the options in play, trimming the wilderness. The plateau problem concerns lack of clear signs for a fruitful direction of search. Here, a good analogy can help by highlighting features of the target domain otherwise not salient and projecting onto the target domain clues about direction from the base domain, highlighting and projecting being two of the ways mentioned by Gentner et al. by which analogy delivers on its promise.

As to the canyon problem (search bounded away from solutions), analogy inherently has the power to step across canyons by relating one domain to another. Finally, the oasis problem (search lingering in the neighborhood of promising solutions that will not quite work) also gets an assist from a good analogy, which abruptly transports thinking well away from the oasis into a new realm altogether.

All this encourages the image of analogy as creativity's camel, or one of them; however, this particular camel is no panacea of course. Although analogies can be helpful, they can also be entrapping. For instance, an analogy that half works can create a canyon hard to get out of, an oasis hard to leave behind. For example, Spiro, Feltovich, Coulson, and Anderson (1989) have documented the limitations of simple analogies in medical reasoning and urged the importance of multiple analogies that, played off against one another, can support better reasoning. Misconceptions in science and mathematics appear to trace back in part to overextended analogies, for example, the notion that because multiplication distributes over addition so must other operations, like taking square roots (Perkins & Simmons, 1988). To ride the camel once more, creativity's camel has a bad temper and sometimes bites, but often carries the load nonetheless.

DOES ANALOGY FIGURE IN EXCEPTIONAL CREATIVITY OUTSIDE OF INDIVIDUAL HUMAN CREATIVITY?

Recall that creative systems theory aims to explain the emergence of adaptive novelty in cases besides the individual human creator. Through Darwinian or neo-Darwinian processes of natural selection, adaptive novelty emerges in the biological world (Dawkins, 1976, 1987; Gould, 1989). Language and customs evolve in societies, perhaps in a quasi-Darwinian way (Dawkins, 1976). Certain artificial intelligence programs create after a fashion (Boden, 1991).

In these and other contexts, the work of creation gets done one way or another. It is natural to ask whether creativity's camel has a contribution to make. At first thought, the answer might seem to be "no" for most of them. Artificial intelligence aside, the other examples mentioned are conspicuous for their mindlessness. The biological world has no designer to direct the evolution of organisms, hence Richard Dawkins' metaphor "the blind watchmaker" (Dawkins, 1987). Whereas human minds make up society, they do not usually function mindfully as minds in the evolution of customs and languages. Yet the use of analogy as explored so far seems to be an emphatically mindful exercise, full of intense cogitation.

With this point granted, what might be called analogs of analogy appear remarkably often in the work of creative systems. In the biological world, one of the most common cases appears to be convergent evolution. Insects, birds, and bats display homologies in their flying apparatus even though their evolutionary ancestry is quite different. Likewise, fish and seals show common features of fin structure and body streamlining.

Of course, analogy has no causal role in such homologies. They arise not because of any map from base to target domain but simply because the physical world constrains the ecological opportunities for organisms. Flying and swimming, to occur at all and with reasonable energy efficiency, have to respect physical realities. Accordingly, such analogies might be called circumstantial. They simply reflect the common circumstances of very different organisms and evolutionary paths.

Analogy comes closer to playing a causal role in another common biological phenomenon, mimicry. A well-known example is the viceroy moth, whose markings mimic those of the monarch butterfly. Monarch butterflies have evolved to taste bad to birds, certainly a survival trait. The viceroy gets a free ride on the monarch's adaptation by mimicking its appearance.

Whereas in circumstantial analogy, the one and the other case bear a resemblance because of external factors, in the viceroy's case of what one might call *connotative analogy*, the analogy is indeed the very point. Of course, this still contrasts with the full-scale analogies considered before, in which the analogy is not the aim of the process but rather the engine of the process, a means along the way to discovery.

Still another analogy-like process operates when preexisting structures adapt to new roles, preserving homologies between the original and new versions. A classic example would be the adaptation of forelimbs into wings in both birds and bats. This process might be called *recruitment analogy*, because old structures are recruited and modified to new ends. It comes closer to analogy as discussed earlier because the metamorphic processes involved amount to a kind of structure mapping. However, the target arises as the product of the process, rather than both base and target existing beforehand.

A final analogy-like process occurs in the biological world when a basic structural scheme differentiates into diverse adaptations. Arthropod segmentation is a core example (Gould, 1989). Arthropods are made of segmented body units. Some segments have differentiated into mouth parts, some into leg units, some into tail units, but all share a basic scheme and thereby bear analogy to one another. Therefore, this process might be called *schematic analogy*. It could also be seen as a complicated case of recruitment analogy, wherein early structures differentiate out in multiple directions to yield diverse, elaborately adapted structures.

These various analogical phenomena are not at all limited to the biological world. For instance, they can be found in the development of languages as well. Circumstantial analogy occurs when selection pressures in language use favor brevity of frequently used terms or foster common contractions, for example. Connotative analogy occurs when terms piggyback on the connotations of earlier terms for part of their cachet, as in automobile brand names like Thunderbird or Jaguar or names for medicines like Bufferin and Anacin that remind us of aspirin.

According to Lakoff and Johnson's *Metaphors We Live By* (1980), what amounts to recruitment analogy is a wholesale enterprise in natural language, where terms with concrete physical referents get recruited to serve more abstract functions, as in phrases like "taking a stand" or "exploring ideas" or "advancing your agenda." Creative systems theory itself plays this game with its geographically based metaphors of the wilderness, plateau, canyon, and oasis problems. As to schematic analogy, this also appears over and over in language as phrases of a particular form diversify to fill distinct semantic roles, as in railway station, fire station, sentry station, ranger station, and space station.

It should be said again that none of these are full-scale cases of analogy as treated earlier, with a previously existing base and target, a map made between them, and the map mined for illumination, yielding a new theory or product. At least in the biological world, it is hard to see how such a full-fledged case of invention by analogy could arise. Nonetheless, several more limited forms of analogy plainly figure in the production of adaptive novelty in the biological world and in other creative systems. This in turn issues an invitation to look back at human invention solo or in teams, where these quasi-analogies certainly figure alongside full analogies in doing the work of invention. Besides creativity's full-scale camel, there are some dromedaries that merit attention.

REFERENCES

Boden, M. (1991). *The creative mind: Myths and mechanisms.* New York: Basic Books.

Bruner, J. (1973). Going beyond the information given. In J. Anglin (Ed.), *Beyond the information given* (pp. 218–238). New York: Norton.

Carlson, W. B., & Gorman, M. (1992). A cognitive framework to understand technological creativity: Bell, Edison, and the telephone. In R. J. Weber & D. N. Perkins (Eds.), *Inventive minds: Creativity in technology* (pp. 48–79). New York: Oxford University Press.

Dawkins, R. (1976). *The selfish gene.* New York: Oxford University Press.

Dawkins, R. (1987). *The blind watchmaker: Why the evidence of evolution reveals a universe without design.* New York: Norton.

Gould, S. J. (1989). *Wonderful life: The Burgess Shale and the nature of history.* New York: W. W. Norton.

Koestler, A. (1964). *The act of creation.* New York: Dell.

Lakoff, G., & Johnson, M. (1980). *Metaphors we live by.* Chicago: University of Chicago Press.

Langley, P., Simon, H. A., Bradshaw, G. L., & Zytkow, J. M. (1987). *Scientific discovery: Computational explorations of the creative processes.* Cambridge, MA: MIT Press.

Minsky, M. (1983). Jokes and the logic of the cognitive unconscious. In R. Groner, M. Groner, & W. F. Bischof (Eds.), *Methods of heuristics* (pp. 171–194). Hillsdale, NJ: Erlbaum.

Newell, A. (1990). *Theories of cognition.* Cambridge, MA: Harvard University Press.

Newell, A., & Simon, H. (1972). *Human problem solving.* Englewood Cliffs, NJ: Prentice-Hall.

Perkins, D. N. (1981). *The mind's best work.* Cambridge, MA: Harvard University Press.

Perkins, D. N. (1992). The topography of invention. In R. J. Weber & D. N. Perkins (Eds.), *Inventive minds: Creativity in technology* (pp. 238–250). New York: Oxford University Press.

Perkins, D. N. (1994). Creativity: Beyond the Darwinian paradigm. In M. Boden (Ed.), *Dimensions of creativity* (pp. 119–142). Cambridge, MA: MIT Press.

Perkins, D. N. (1995). Insight in minds and genes. In R. J. Sternberg & J. E. Davidson (Eds.), *The nature of insight* (pp. 495–533). Cambridge, MA: MIT Press.

Perkins, D. N., & Simmons, R. (1988). Patterns of misunderstanding: An integrative model of misconceptions in science, mathematics, and programming. *Review of Educational Research, 58*(3), 303–326.

Salomon, G. (Ed.). (1993). *Distributed cognitions.* New York: Cambridge University Press.

Spiro, R. J., Feltovich, P. J., Coulson, R. L., & Anderson, D. R. (1989). Multiple analogies for complex concepts: Antidotes for analogy-induced misconception in advanced knowledge acquisition. In S. Vosniadou & A. Ortony (Eds.), *Similarity and analogical reasoning* (pp. 498–531). New York: Cambridge University Press.

Weber, R. J., & Perkins, D. N. (1992). *Inventive minds: Creativity in technology.* New York: Oxford University Press.

Author Index

Numbers in italics refer to listings in the reference sections.

Subject Index

About the Editors

Thomas B. Ward, PhD, is professor of psychology at Texas A&M University. His research focuses on the nature of concepts, including how they are acquired, structured, and used in creative and noncreative endeavors. Dr. Ward has also conducted basic and applied studies concerned with increasing the innovative potential of new ideas. He is one of the founding members of the Creative Cognition Research Group, has served on the editorial board of *Child Development*, and currently serves as associate editor of *Memory & Cognition.*

Steven M. Smith, PhD, is associate professor of psychology at Texas A&M University. He has conducted research on memory blocks and creative thinking blocks since 1979, when he received his doctoral degree from the University of Wisconsin. Dr. Smith has published three books on creative cognition, including *The Creative Cognition Approach*, and he is on the editorial board of the *Journal of Creative Behavior.* Dr. Smith has also investigated conformity and incubation effects in thinking.

Jyotsna Vaid, PhD, is associate professor of psychology at Texas A&M University. The focus of her research is cognitive and neuropsychological aspects of language functioning in bilinguals. Dr. Vaid has published numerous journal articles and a book, *Language Processing in Bilinguals* (1986), in this area. Her research has also explored language and number processing, and the cognitive processing of humor.